W9-ANF-105

For Reference

Not to be taken

from this library

# SOMETHING ABOUT THE AUTHOR®

Something about
the Author *was named
an "Outstanding
Reference Source,"
the highest honor given
by the American
Library Association
Reference and Adult
Services Division.*

ISSN 0276-816X

# something about the author®

**Facts and Pictures about Authors
and Illustrators of Books for Young People**

# volume 135

GALE®

JAN    2003

809
som
V. 135

THOMSON
™
GALE

Detroit • New York • San Diego • San Francisco • Cleveland • New Haven, Conn. • Waterville, Maine • London • Munich

**THOMSON**

**GALE**

**Something about the Author, Volume 135**

**Project Editor**
Scot Peacock

**Editorial**
Katy Balcer, Sara Constantakis, Anna Marie Dahn, Alana Joli Foster, Arlene M. Johnson, Michelle Kazensky, Julie Keppen, Joshua Kondek, Lisa Kumar, Thomas McMahon, Jenai A. Mynatt, Judith L. Pyko, Mary Ruby, Susan Strickland, Anita Sundaresan, Maikue Vang, Tracey Watson, Denay L. Wilding, Thomas Wiloch, Emiene Shija Wright

**Research**
Michelle Campbell, Nicodemus Ford, Sarah Genik, Barbara McNeil, Tamara C. Nott, Gary J. Oudersluys, Tracie A. Richardson, Cheryl L. Warnock

**Permissions**
Debra Freitas, Shalice Shah-Caldwell

**Imaging and Multimedia**
Dean Dauphinais, Robert Duncan, Leitha Etheridge-Sims, Mary K. Grimes, Lezlie Light, Michael Logusz, Dan Newell, David G. Oblender, Christine O'Bryan, Kelly A. Quin, Luke Rademacher

**Manufacturing**
Stacy L. Melson

© 2003 by Gale. Gale is an imprint of The Gale Group, Inc., a division of Thomson Learning, Inc.

Gale and Design™ and Thomson Learning™ are trademarks used herein under license.

*For more information, contact*
The Gale Group, Inc.
27500 Drake Rd.
Farmington Hills, MI 48331-3535
Or you can visit our internet site at
http://www.gale.com

**ALL RIGHTS RESERVED**
No part of this work covered by the copyright herein may be reproduced or used in any form or by any means—graphic, electronic, or mechanical, including photocopying, recording, taping, Web distribution, or information storage retrieval systems—without the written permission of the publisher.

This publication is a creative work fully protected by all applicable copyright laws, as well as by misappropriation, trade secret, unfair competition, and other applicable laws. The authors and editors of this work have added value to the underlying factual material herein through one or more of the following: unique and original selection, coordination, expression, arrangement, and classification of the information.

For permission to use material from the product, submit your request via the Web at http://www.gale-edit.com/permissions, or you may download our Permissions Request form and submit your request by fax or mail to:

*Permissions Department*
The Gale Group, Inc.
27500 Drake Rd.
Farmington Hills, MI 48331-3535
Permissions Hotline:
248-699-8006 or 800-877-4253, etc. 8006
Fax 248-699-8074 or 800-762-4058

Since this page cannot legibly accommodate all copyright notices, the acknowledgments constitute an extension of the copyright notice.

While every effort has been made to secure permission to reprint material and to ensure the reliability of the information presented in this publication, the Gale Group neither guarantees the accuracy of the data contained herein nor assumes any responsibility for errors, omissions or discrepancies. Gale accepts no payment for listing; and inclusion in the publication of any organization, agency, institution, publication, service, or individual does not imply endorsement of the editors or publisher. Errors brought to the attention of the publisher and verified to the satisfaction of the publisher will be corrected in future editions.

**LIBRARY OF CONGRESS CATALOG CARD NUMBER 72-27107**

ISBN 0-7876-5207-5
ISSN 0276-816X

Printed in the United States of America
10 9 8 7 6 5 4 3 2 1

# Contents

# Authors in Forthcoming Volumes

Below are some of the authors and illustrators that will be featured in upcoming volumes of *SATA*. These include new entries on the swiftly rising stars of the field, as well as completely revised and updated entries (indicated with *) on some of the most notable and best-loved creators of books for children.

**Lois McMaster Bujold:** Bujold is widely known in the field of science fiction for her witty, believable tales of Miles Vorkosigan, the protagonist of a series that is over a dozen books and growing. Bujold is considered a master at character development and the nuances of human interaction—qualities not always found in modern science fiction. Bujold has written many other critically acclaimed science fiction works as well; she has received the Nebula Award three times and the Hugo Award four times. In 2002 Bujold published *Diplomatic Immunity.*

**\*Brock Cole:** A philosophy professor turned painter, illustrator, and writer, Cole has created picture books acclaimed for their expressiveness as well as depth of detail. He has also written three young adult novels which have won numerous awards for their realistic portrayal of contemporary issues; *The Facts Speak for Themselves* was a National Book Award nominee in 1997. Cole published the self-illustrated *Larky Mavis* in 2001.

**\*Sneed B. Collard III:** Collard is an award-winning author of nonfiction works for children and young adults. A conservationist at heart, Collar has written about subjects as varied as bird beaks, fireflies, and the Great Barrier Reef. His 2000 work *The Forest in the Clouds* was a Teacher's Choice selection by the International Reading Association and was named an Outstanding Trade Science Book for Children by the Children's Book Council/National Science Teachers Association.

**\*Debbie Dadey:** Dadey has written scores of popular and compelling easy-reader novels for primary-grade and middle-grade readers which blend tongue-in-cheek horror with fast-paced storytelling skills. Working with Marcia Thornton Jones on such popular series as the "Adventures of the Bailey School Kids" and "Barkley's School for Dogs," Dadey has attracted legions of young readers to a jaunty world of gremlins, wizards, pirates, and aliens. Dadey's solo efforts have also produced the "Marty" series and the "Bobby" series for younger readers. Other of Dadey's solo books, such as *Cherokee Sister* and *Whistler's Hollow,* are for somewhat older readers and of a more serious nature.

**\*Dan Gutman:** Gutman is a prolific author who writes sports-related fiction and nonfiction for children. Although he started his writing career by penning nonfiction titles such as *World Series Classics* and *The Way Baseball Works,* he has captured a younger audience with his humorous middle-grade novels. Among Gutman's most popular books for younger readers are the installments in his time-travel "Baseball Card Adventure" series as well as *The Green Monster from Left Field* and *The Million-Dollar Shot.* In 2002 he published *Shoeless Joe and Me.*

**\*Russell Hoban:** In his nearly eighty books for children and adults, including novels, picture books, and poetry collections, Hoban manages to turn death and rejection into allegories of everyday life, peppered with a wry sort of sad humor and aphoristic patches that make him immensely quotable. As a children's author, he is best known for his tales about loveable Frances and for his moving adventure quest *The Mouse and His Child.* Hoban published *Jim's Lion* in 2001.

**Patrick Jones:** Jones is a library consultant whose specialization in the needs of young adult readers had made him something of an expert in the field. In addition to lecturing and publishing articles in a number of journals devoted to the concerns of librarians, Jones has authored several books designed to aid colleagues in developing young adults' interest in reading. Among his works are *What's So Scary about R. L. Stine?* and *Do It Right!: Best Practices in Customer Service to Young Adults in Schools and Public Libraries.*

**\*Geraldine McCaughrean:** McCaughrean has written novels for young adults and stories for young children; she has translated and adapted tales, myths, and legends from various cultures, and she has written adult fiction and textbooks. Whatever her subject, however, the author brings a flair for intricate prose and exciting storytelling to her writing. McCaughrean's first novel, *A Little Lower Than the Angels,* was published to great acclaim, winning the Whitbread Award. She published a young adult novel, *The Kite Rider,* in 2002.

**\*Sally Farrell Odgers:** Odgers is an Australian writer who lives in Latrobe, the rural town in Tasmania where she was born and raised. Her works range from children's picture books to adult romance novels, from stories of farm life to tales of science fiction. Her quest fantasy, *Candle Iron,* won the Aurealis Award for Best Long Fiction in 2001.

**\*Ellen Raskin:** Raskin's career in children's literature spanned almost two decades and encompassed eighteen of her own self-illustrated picture books and young adult novels, as well as almost thirty titles she illustrated for other authors. Her career was bookended by her first self-illustrated title, *Nothing Ever Happens on My Block* and her last book, the Newbery Award-winning *The Westing Game.* Humor, ingenuity, verbal and visual play, and a constant desire to make readers "see" the world as it really is were the hallmarks of her work both for young children and for older readers.

**Shelley Tanaka:** Canadian author Tanaka began her career penning picture books and nonfiction works for children, but she is perhaps best known for her "I Was There" series, which draws readers into events from history. Featuring such intriguing titles as *Discovering the Iceman: What Was It Like to Find a 5,300-Year-Old Mummy?,* the series mixes fact and fiction in a way that engages even the most history-adverse reader. In these works, Tanaka frames each event from history within a fictional narrative, then provides a factual backdrop and photographs and other illustrations to ground her story.

**Uzo Unobagha:** Unobagha is a native of Nigeria who immigrated to the United States and became a naturalized citizen in 2000. Her debut work *Off to the Sweet Shores of Africa and Other Talking Drum Rhymes* received a Notable Book citation from the American Library Association.

# Introduction

*Something about the Author* (*SATA*) is an ongoing reference series that examines the lives and works of authors and illustrators of books for children. *SATA* includes not only well-known writers and artists but also less prominent individuals whose works are just coming to be recognized. This series is often the only readily available information source on emerging authors and illustrators. You'll find *SATA* informative and entertaining, whether you are a student, a librarian, an English teacher, a parent, or simply an adult who enjoys children's literature.

## What's Inside SATA

*SATA* provides detailed information about authors and illustrators who span the full time range of children's literature, from early figures like John Newbery and L. Frank Baum to contemporary figures like Judy Blume and Richard Peck. Authors in the series represent primarily English-speaking countries, particularly the United States, Canada, and the United Kingdom. Also included, however, are authors from around the world whose works are available in English translation. The writings represented in *SATA* include those created intentionally for children and young adults as well as those written for a general audience and known to interest younger readers. These writings cover the entire spectrum of children's literature, including picture books, humor, folk and fairy tales, animal stories, mystery and adventure, science fiction and fantasy, historical fiction, poetry and nonsense verse, drama, biography, and nonfiction.

Obituaries are also included in *SATA* and are intended not only as death notices but also as concise overviews of people's lives and work. Additionally, each edition features newly revised and updated entries for a selection of *SATA* listees who remain of interest to today's readers and who have been active enough to require extensive revisions of their earlier biographies.

## Autobiography Feature

Beginning with Volume 103, *SATA* features two or more specially commissioned autobiographical essays in each volume. These unique essays, averaging about ten thousand words in length and illustrated with an abundance of personal photos, present an entertaining and informative first-person perspective on the lives and careers of prominent authors and illustrators profiled in *SATA*.

## Two Convenient Indexes

In response to suggestions from librarians, *SATA* indexes no longer appear in every volume but are included in alternate (odd-numbered) volumes of the series, beginning with Volume 57.

*SATA* continues to include two indexes that cumulate with each alternate volume: the Illustrations Index, arranged by the name of the illustrator, gives the number of the volume and page where the illustrator's work appears in the current volume as well as all preceding volumes in the series; the Author Index gives the number of the volume in which a person's biographical sketch, autobiographical essay, or obituary appears in the current volume as well as all preceding volumes in the series.

These indexes also include references to authors and illustrators who appear in Gale's *Yesterday's Authors of Books for Children, Children's Literature Review,* and *Something about the Author Autobiography Series.*

## Easy-to-Use Entry Format

Whether you're already familiar with the *SATA* series or just getting acquainted, you will want to be aware of the kind of information that an entry provides. In every *SATA* entry the editors attempt to give as complete a picture of the person's life and work as possible. A typical entry in *SATA* includes the following clearly labeled information sections:

- *PERSONAL:* date and place of birth and death, parents' names and occupations, name of spouse, date of marriage, names of children, educational institutions attended, degrees received, religious and political affiliations, hobbies and other interests.

- *ADDRESSES:* complete home, office, electronic mail, and agent addresses, whenever available.

- *CAREER:* name of employer, position, and dates for each career post; art exhibitions; military service; memberships and offices held in professional and civic organizations.

- *AWARDS, HONORS:* literary and professional awards received.

- *WRITINGS:* title-by-title chronological bibliography of books written and/or illustrated, listed by genre when known; lists of other notable publications, such as plays, screenplays, and periodical contributions.

- *ADAPTATIONS:* a list of films, television programs, plays, CD-ROMs, recordings, and other media presentations that have been adapted from the author's work.

- *WORK IN PROGRESS:* description of projects in progress.

- *SIDELIGHTS:* a biographical portrait of the author or illustrator's development, either directly from the biographee—and often written specifically for the *SATA* entry—or gathered from diaries, letters, interviews, or other published sources.

- *BIOGRAPHICAL AND CRITICAL SOURCES:* cites sources quoted in "Sidelights" along with references for further reading.

- *EXTENSIVE ILLUSTRATIONS:* photographs, movie stills, book illustrations, and other interesting visual materials supplement the text.

## How a SATA Entry Is Compiled

A *SATA* entry progresses through a series of steps. If the biographee is living, the *SATA* editors try to secure information directly from him or her through a questionnaire. From the information that the biographee supplies, the editors prepare an entry, filling in any essential missing details with research and/or telephone interviews. If possible, the author or illustrator is sent a copy of the entry to check for accuracy and completeness.

If the biographee is deceased or cannot be reached by questionnaire, the *SATA* editors examine a wide variety of published sources to gather information for an entry. Biographical and bibliographic sources are consulted, as are book reviews, feature articles, published interviews, and material sometimes obtained from the biographee's family, publishers, agent, or other associates.

Entries that have not been verified by the biographees or their representatives are marked with an asterisk (*).

## Contact the Editor

We encourage our readers to examine the entire *SATA* series. Please write and tell us if we can make *SATA* even more helpful to you. Give your comments and suggestions to the editor:

*BY MAIL:*   Editor, *Something about the Author,* The Gale Group, 27500 Drake Rd., Farmington Hills, MI 48331-3535.

*BY TELEPHONE:*   (800) 877-GALE

*BY FAX:*   (248) 699-8054

# *Something about the Author* Product Advisory Board

The editors of *Something about the Author* are dedicated to maintaining a high standard of excellence by publishing comprehensive, accurate, and highly readable entries on a wide array of writers for children and young adults. In addition to the quality of the content, the editors take pride in the graphic design of the series, which is intended to be orderly yet inviting, allowing readers to utilize the pages of *SATA* easily and with efficiency. Despite the longevity of the *SATA* print series, and the success of its format, we are mindful that the vitality of a literary reference product is dependent on its ability to serve its users over time. As literature, and attitudes about literature, constantly evolve, so do the reference needs of students, teachers, scholars, journalists, researchers, and book club members. To be certain that we continue to keep pace with the expectations of our customers, the editors of *SATA* listen carefully to their comments regarding the value, utility, and quality of the series. Librarians, who have firsthand knowledge of the needs of library users, are a valuable resource for us. The *Something about the Author* Product Advisory Board, made up of school, public, and academic librarians, is a forum to promote focused feedback about *SATA* on a regular basis. The nine-member advisory board includes the following individuals, whom the editors wish to thank for sharing their expertise:

- **Eva M. Davis,** Teen Services Librarian, Plymouth District Library, Plymouth, Michigan

- **Joan B. Eisenberg,** Lower School Librarian, Milton Academy, Milton, Massachusetts

- **Francisca Goldsmith,** Teen Services Librarian, Berkeley Public Library, Berkeley, California

- **Harriet Hagenbruch,** Curriculum Materials Center/Education Librarian, Axinn Library, Hofstra University, Hempstead, New York

- **Monica F. Irlbacher,** Young Adult Librarian, Middletown Thrall Library, Middletown, New York

- **Robyn Lupa,** Head of Children's Services, Jefferson County Public Library, Lakewood, Colorado

- **Eric Norton,** Head of Children's Services, McMillan Memorial Library, Wisconsin Rapids, Wisconsin

- **Victor L. Schill,** Assistant Branch Librarian/Children's Librarian, Harris County Public Library/Fairbanks Branch, Houston, Texas

- **Caryn Sipos,** Community Librarian, Three Creeks Community Library, Vancouver, Washington

# *Acknowledgments*

Grateful acknowledgment is made to the following publishers, authors, and artists whose works appear in this volume.

**ALEXANDER, LLOYD (CHUDLEY).** Cover of *The Black Cauldron*, by Lloyd Alexander. Yearling, 1965. Copyright © 1965 by Lloyd Alexander. Reproduced by permission of Random House Children's Books, a division of Random House, Inc./ Cover of *The Book of Three*, by Lloyd Alexander. Yearling, 1990. Reproduced by permission of Random House Children's Books, a division of Random House, Inc./ From a cover of *The Illyrian Adventure,* by Lloyd Alexander. Copyright © 1986 by Lloyd Alexander. Jacket illustration by Stephen Marchesi. Reproduced by permission of Stephen Marchesi./ Alexander, Lloyd, photograph. AP/Wide World Photos. Reproduced by permission.

**APPERLEY, DAWN.** Apperley, Dawn, photograph. Reproduced by permission.

**BARTOLETTI, SUSAN CAMPBELL.** Illustration by David Christiana from *The Christmas Promise*, by Susan Bartoletti. Published by the Blue Sky Press, an imprint of Scholastic Inc. Illustration copyright © 2001 by David Christiana. Reproduced by permission./ Shannon, David, illustrator. From a cover of *No Man's Land: A Young Soldier's Story,* by Susan Campbell Bartoletti. Published by the Blue Sky Press, an imprint of Scholastic Inc. Illustration copyright © 1999 by David Shannon. Reproduced by permission./ Bartoletti, Susan Campbell, photograph © by Stephanie Klein-Davis. Reproduced by permission.

**BENDICK, JEANNE.** Bendick, Jeanne, illustrator. From a cover of *Archimedes and the Door of Science,* by Jeanne Bendick. Bethlem Books, 1995. Reproduced by permission.

**BERENSTAIN, JAN(ICE).** Berenstain, Jan, and Stan Berenstain, illustrators. From an illustration in their *The Berenstain Bears and the Truth.* Random House, 1983. Copyright © 1983 by Berenstains, Inc. All rights reserved. Reproduced by permission of Random House Children's Books, a division of Random House, Inc./ Berenstain, Jan, and Stan Berenstain, illustrators. From an illustration in their *The Berenstain Bears' New Baby.* Random House, 1974. Copyright © 1974 by Stanley Berenstain and Janice Berenstain. Reproduced by permission of Random House Children's Books, a division of Random House, Inc./ Berenstain, Stan and Jan, photograph by Jack Rosen. Reproduced by permission of Random House, Inc.

**BERENSTAIN, STAN(LEY).** Berenstain, Jan, and Stan Berenstain, illustrators. From an illustration in their *The Berenstain Bears Learn about Strangers.* Random House, 1985. Copyright © 1985 by Berenstains, Inc. All rights reserved. Reproduced by permission of Random House, Inc./ Berenstain, Stan and Jan, illustrators. From an illustration in their *The Berenstain Bears on the Moon.* Beginner Books, 1985. Copyright © 1985 by Berenstains, Inc. Reproduced by permission of Random House Children's Books, a Division of Random House, Inc.

**BOWERMASTER, JON.** Wiltsie, Gordon, photographer. From a photograph in *Over the Top of the World,* by Will Steger and Jon Bowermaster. Scholastic Press, a division of Scholastic Inc., 1997. Photograph © Gordon Wiltsie/International Arctic Project. Reproduced by permission.

**BUZZEO, TONI.** Buzzeo, Toni, photograph. Reproduced by permission.

**CARTER, ANNE LAUREL.** Carter, Anne Laurel, photograph. Reproduced by permission.

**COTTLE, JOAN.** Cottle, Joan, photograph. Reproduced by permission.

**CULLINAN, BERNICE E(LLINGER).** Massaro, Kathy, illustrator. From a cover of *Easy Poetry Lessons That Dazzle and Delight,* by David L. Harrison and Bernice E. Cullinan. Scholastic, 1999. Reproduced by permission./ Cullinan, Bernice E., photograph. Reproduced by permission./ Colin, Paul, illustrator. From a cover of *Read to Me*, by Bernice E. Cullinan. Scholastic, 2000. Cover illustration copyright © 2000 by Scholastic Inc. Reproduced by permission.

**EDWARDS, HAZEL (EILEEN).** Niland, Deborah, illustrator. From an illustration in *My Hippopotamus Is on Our Caravan Roof Getting Sunburnt,* by Hazel Edwards. Hodder Headline Australia, 1989. Illustration copyright © 1989 by Deborah Niland. Reproduced by permission.

**FARNSWORTH, BILL.** Farnsworth, Bill, illustrator. From an illustration in *A Humble Life: Plain Poems,* by Linda Oatman High. Eerdmans Books for Young Readers, 2001. Illustration copyright © 2001 by Bill Farnsworth. Reproduced by permission.

**FOREMAN, MICHAEL.** Foreman, Michael, illustrator. From an illustration in *Arthur: High King of Britain,* by Michael Morpurgo. Harcourt Brace & Company, 1995. Illustrations copyright © 1994 by Michael Foreman. Reproduced in the United Kingdom by permission of Pavillion Books, in the rest of the world by permission of Harcourt, Inc./ Foreman, Michael, illustrator. From an illustration in *Peter Pan and Wendy,* by J. M. Barrie. C. N. Potter, 1988. Illustrations © 1988 by Michael Foreman. Reproduced in the U.S. by permission of Clarkson Potter/Publishers, a division of Random House, Inc., in the rest of the world by permission of Pavillion Books Ltd./ Foreman, Michael, illustrator. From an illustration in his *War Boy: A Country Childhood.* Arcade Publishing, 1990. © 1989 by Michael Foreman. Reproduced by permission of Pavillion Books./ Foreman, Michael, photograph. Mark Gerson. Reproduced by permission.

**FRADIN, DENNIS BRINDELL.** From a cover of his *Arizona.* Childrens Press, 1993. Reproduced by permission./ From an illustration in *Samuel Adams: The Father of American Independence,* by Dennis Brindell Fradin. Clarion Books, 1998. Courtesy of the Library of Congress./ Fradin, Dennis Brindell, photograph by Judith Bloom Fradin. Reproduced by permission.

**GARLAND, SARAH.** From an illustration in her *Doing the Garden.* The Bodley Head, 1992. Copyright © 1992 by Sarah Garland. Reproduced by permission of The Random House Group Limited./ Garland, Sarah. From an illustration in her *Ellie's Breakfast.* The Bodley Head, 1997. Copyright © 1997 by Sarah Garland. Reproduced by permission of The Random House Group Limited.

**GUEST, JACQUELINE.** Domm, Jeff, illustrator. From a cover of *Lightning Rider,* by Jacqueline Guest. James Lorimer & Co., 2000. Reproduced by permission.

**HAAS, (KATHERINE) JESSIE.** Haas, Jessie, wearing wide-brimmed hat, photograph. © June T. Campbell. Reproduced by permission./ Haas, Jessie, standing next to her horse, Josey, photograph. © June T. Campbell. Reproduced by permission./ Haas, Jessie, standing next to her horse, River Echo Atherton, photograph. © June T. Campbell. Reproduced by permission./ All other photographs reproduced by permission of the author.

**HARLAN, JUDITH.** Palen, Debbie, illustrator. From an illustration in *Girl Talk,* by Judith Harlan. Walker and Company, 1997. Illustration copyright © 1997 by Debbie Palen. Reproduced by permission.

**HEINE, HELME.** Heine, Helme, illustrator. From an illustration in his *Friends Go Adventuring.* Aladdin Paperbacks, 1998. Copyright © 1994 by Diogenes Verlag AG, Zurich. English translation copyright © 1995 by Margaret K. McElderry Books, New York. Reproduced by permission./ Heine, Helme, illustrator. From an illustration in his *The Pearl.* Aladdin Books, 1988. Text and illustration copyright 9c) 1984 by Gertraud Midde.hauve Verlag GmbH & Co., KG, Koln. English translation copyright © 1985 by J.M. Dent & Sons Ltd. Reproduced by permission of Margaret K. McElderry Books, an imprint of Simon & Schuster Children's Publishing Division.

**HERRIOT, JAMES.** Holmes, Lesley, illustrator. From an illustration in *James Herriot's Animal Stories,* by James Herriot. St. Martin's Press, 1997. Illustations © 1997 by Lesley Holmes. Reproduced by permission of the author./ Herriot, James, photograph. AP/Wide World Photos. Reproduced by permission.

**HOLABIRD, KATHARINE.** Craig, Helen, illustrator. From an illustration in *Angelina's Baby Sister,* by Katharine Holabird. Pleasant Company, 1987. Illustration copyright © 1987 by Helen Craig. Reproduced by permission./ Craig, Helen, illustrator. From an illustration in *Angelina and Alice,* by Katharine Holabird. Pleasant Company, 1987. Illustration copyright © 1987 by Helen Craig. Reproduced by permission.

**HUTCHINS, HAZEL J.** Ohi, Ruth, illustrator. From an illustration in *Yancy and Bear,* by Hazel J. Hutchins. Annick Press Ltd., 1996. Illustration copyright © 1996 by Ruth Ohi. Reproduced by permission.

**JONAS, ANN.** Illustration from *Round Trip,* by Ann Jonas. Scholastic, 1983. Reproduced by permission of the author./ Jonas, Ann, photograph by Donald Crews. Reproduced by permission of Ann Jonas.

**KING-SMITH, DICK.** Chesak, Lina, illustrator. From an illustration in *Charlie Muffin's Miracle Mouse,* by Dick King-Smith. Crown Publishers, 1999. Illustrations © 1999 by Lina Chesak. Reproduced by permission of Random House Children's Books, a division of Random House, Inc./ Barton, Jill, illustrator. From an illustration in *Lady Lollipop,* by Dick King-Smith. Walker Books, 2000. Illustrations © 2000 by Jill Barton. Text © 2000 Dick King-Smith. Reproduced by permission of Walker Books Ltd./ Kronheimer, Ann, illustrator. From an illustration in *Mysterious Miss Slade,* by Dick King-Smith. Knopf, 2000. Illustrations © 1999 by Ann Kronheimer. Reproduced by permission./ Yeo, Brad, illustrator. From a cover of *Spider Sparrow,* by Dick King-Smith. Yearling, 2000. Copyright © 1998 by Fox Busters Ltd. Illustrations © 1998 by Peter Bailey. Jacket illustration © 2000 by Andrew Davidson. Reproduced by permission of Dell Publishing, a division of Random House, Inc.

**KROLL, STEVEN.** All photographs reproduced by permission of the author.

**LAWRENCE, IAIN.** Whelan, Patrick, illustrator. From a jacket of *The Buccaneers,* by Lain Lawrence. Delacorte Press, 2001. Reproduced by permission of Random House Children's Books, a division of Random House, Inc./ McAfee, Steve, illustrator. From a jacket of *Lord of the Nutcracker Men,* by Lain Lawrence. Delacorte Press, 2001. Reproduced by permission of Random House Children's Books, a division of Random House, Inc.

**MAYER, MERCER.** Mayer, Mercer, illustrator. From an illustration in his *Little Critter's Joke Book.* Golden Books, 1993. © 1993 Mercer Mayer. Reproduced by permission Golden Books, an imprint of Random House Children's Books, a division of Random House, Inc./ Mayer, Mercer, photograph. Reproduced by permission of Golden Books, an imprint of Random House Children's Books, a division of Random House, Inc.

**MCCLUNG, ROBERT M(ARSHALL).** Hines, Bob and Robert M. McClung, illustrators. From an illustration in *Last of the Wild,* by Robert McClung. The Shoe String Press, Inc., 1997. © 1997 Robert M. McClung. All rights reserved. Reproduced by permission./ Hines, Bob, illustrator. From an illustration in *Lost Wild America: The Story of Our Extinct and Vanishing Wildlife,* by Robert M. McClung. Linnet Books, 1993. © 1969, 1993 Robert M. McClung. Reproduced by permission.

**MILELLI, PASCAL.** Milelli, Pascal, illustrator. From an illustration in *Rainbow Bay,* by Stephen Eaton Hume. Raincoast Books, 1997. Illustration copyright © 1997 by Pascal Milelli. Reproduced by permission.

**NAIDOO, BEVERLEY.** Naidoo, Beverley, photograph by David Mallett Reproduced by permission of Beverley Naidoo and David Mallett.

**ORLEV, URI.** Titherington, Jeanne, illustrator. From a cover of *The Island on Bird Street,* by Uri Orlev, translated by Hillel Halkin. Houghton Mifflin, 1984. Reproduced by permission./ Doney, Todd, illustrator. From a jacket of *The Lady with the Hat,* by Uri Orlev. Translated by Hillel Halkin. Houghton Mifflin Company, 1995. Jacket art © 1995 by Todd Doney. Reproduced by permission of Houghton Mifflin Company./ Doney, Todd, illustrator. From a jacket of *Lydia, Queen of Palestine,* by Uri Orlev. Translated from the Hebrew by Hillel Halkin. Houghton Mifflin Company, 1993. Jacket art © 1993 by Todd Doney. All rights reserved. Reproduced by permission./ Orlev, Uri, photograph. © Aliza Auerbach. Reproduced by permission.

**PAYNE, NINA.** Payne, Adam S., illustrator. From an illustration in *Four in All,* by Nina Payne. Front Street, 2001. Illustration copyright © 2001 by Adam S. Payne. Reproduced by permission.

**RANSOM, CANDICE F.** Ransom, Candice F. From a cover of her *Children of the Civil War.* Carolrhoda, 1998. The Library of Congress./ Beier, Ellen, illustrator. From an illustration in *The Promise Quilt,* by Candice F. Ransom. Walker and Company, 1999. Illustration copyright © 1999 by Ellen Beier. Reproduced by permission./ Ransom, Candice F., photograph. Reproduced by permission.

**RICHARDS, JEAN.** Richards, Jean, photograph. Reproduced by permission.

**RUBEL, NICOLE.** Rubel, Nicole, illustrator. From a cover of *Rotten Ralph,* by Jack Gantos. Reproduced by permission of Nicole Rubel./ Rubel, Nicole. From an illustration in her *A Cowboy Named Ernestine.* Dial, 2001. Copyright © 2001 by Nicole Rubel. Reproduced by permission of Dial Books for Young Readers, a division of Penguin Putnam Inc./ Rubel, Nicole, illustrator. Drawing of two alligators standing on beach, illustration copyright © 1988 by Nicole Rubel. Reproduced by permission./ Rubel, Nicole, photograph © Richard Langsen. Reproduced by permission of Nicole Rubel.

**SALTZBERG, BARNEY.** Saltzberg, Barney, illustrator. From an illustration in his *Baby Animal Kisses.* Red Wagon Books, 2001. © 2001 by Barney Saltzberg. Reproduced in the United Kingdom by permission of the author, in the rest of the world by permission of Harcourt, Inc./ Saltzberg, Barney, illustrator. From an illustration in *There's a Zoo in Room 22,* by Judy Sierra. Gulliver Books, 2000. Illustrations © 2000 by Barney Saltzberg. Reproduced in the United Kingdom by permission of the author, in the rest of the world by permission of Harcourt, Inc./ Saltzberg, Barney, photograph by Linda Vanoff. Reproduced by permission of the author.

**SCHMIDT, GARY D.** Nielsen, Cliff, illustrator. From a jacket of *Straw into Gold,* by Gary D. Schmidt. Houghton Mifflin, 2001. Jacket illustration copyright © 2001 by Cliff Nielsen. Reproduced by permission of Houghton Mifflin Company.

**SCHUR, MAXINE ROSE.** All photographs reproduced by permission of the author.

**SILVEY, DIANE F.** Silvey, Joe, illustrator. From an illustration in *Spirit Quest,* by Diane F. Silvey. Beach Holme Publishing, 1997. Illustration copyright © 1997 by Joe Silvey. Reproduced by permission.

**TAYLOR, MILDRED D.** Baracca, Sal, illlustrator. From a cover of *Roll of Thunder, Hear My Cry,* by Mildred D. Taylor. Bantam Books, 1984. Cover art © 1984 by Sal Baracca. Reproduced by permission of Bantam Books, a division of Random House, Inc.

**WALKER, SALLY M(ACART).** David B. Fleetham/Visuals Unlimited, photographer. From a photograph in *Dolphins,* by Sally Walker. Carolrhoda, 1999. Reproduced by permission.

**WEBB, SOPHIE.** From an illustration in her *My Season with Penguins.* Houghton Mifflin, 2000. Copyright © 2000 by Sophie Webb. Reproduced by permission of Houghton Mifflin Company.

**WEGMAN, WILLIAM (GEORGE).** Wegman, William, photographer. From a photograph in his *Wegmanology.* Hyperion Books for Children, 2001. © 2001 by William Wegman. Reproduced by permission of the author./ Wegman, William, photograph by Steven Senne. AP/Wide World Photos. Reproduced by permission.

**WESTON, CAROL.** Roth, Marci, illustrator. From a cover of *The Diary of Melanie Martin: Or How I Survived Matt the Brat, Michelangelo, and the Leaning Tower of Pizza,* by Carol Weston. Yearling Books, 2001. Reproduced by permission of Dell Publishing, a division of Random House, Inc./ Weston, Carol, photograph by Pierre du Four. Reproduced by permission of the author.

**WHITMAN, SYLVIA (CHOATE).** Whitman, Sylvia. From a photograph in her *Get Up and Go!* Lerner, 1996. The Library of Congress./ Whitman, Sylvia, photograph by Mohamed Ben Jemaa. Reproduced by permission of Sylvia Whitman.

**WILHELM, HANS.** Wilhelm, Hans, illustrator. From a cover of *Dinofours: Let's Go Sledding!,* by Steve Metzger. Scholastic, 2002. Cover illustration copyright © 2002 by Han Wilhelm, Inc. Reproduced by permission./ Wilhelm, Hans. From an illustration in his *I'll Always Love You!* Crown Publishers, 1985. Copyright © 1985 by Hans Wilhelm, Inc. Reproduced by permission of Crown Publishers, a division of Random House, Inc./ Wilhelm, Hans, illustrator. From an illustration in his *I Hate My Bow!* Scholastic, 1995. Copyright © 1995 by Hans Wilhelm, Inc. Reproduced by permission./ Wilhelm, Hans. From an illustration in his *It's Too Windy!* Cartwheel Books, a division of Scholastic Inc., 2000. Copyright © 2000 by Hans Wilhelm. Reproduced by permission./ Wilhelm, Hans. Photographs reproduced by permission of the author.

**WILLIAMS, SOPHY.** Williams, Sophy, illustrator. From an illustration in *The Night You Were Born,* by Wendy McCormick. Peachtree, 2000. Illustration copyright © 2000 by Sophy Williams. Reproduced by permission.

**YOUD, (CHRISTOPHER) SAM(UEL).** Guay, Rebecca, illustrator. From a cover of *A Dusk of Demons,* by John Christopher. Aladdin Paperbacks, 1996. Cover illustration © 1996 by Rebecca Guay. Reproduced by permission of Rebecca Guay./ Cover of *The Pool of Fire,* by John Christopher. Collier Books, 1970. Reproduced by permission of Simon & Schuster Books for Young Readers, an imprint of Simon & Schuster Children's Publishing Division./ Youd, Sam, photograph by A. Vaughan Kimber. Reproduced by permission of the Literary Estate of A. Vaughan Kimber.

# SOMETHING ABOUT THE AUTHOR

## ALEXANDER, Lloyd (Chudley) 1924-

### Personal

Born January 30, 1924, in Philadelphia, PA; son of Alan Audley (a stockbroker and importer) and Edna (Chudley) Alexander; married Janine Denni, January 8, 1946; children: Madeleine. *Education:* Attended West Chester State Teachers College and Lafayette College; attended the Sorbonne, University of Paris. *Hobbies and other interests:* Music (particularly violin, piano, and guitar) and printmaking.

### Addresses

*Home*—1005 Drexel Ave., Drexel Hill, PA 19026. *Agent*—Brandt & Hochman, 1501 Broadway, New York, NY 10036.

### Career

Writer and translator, 1946—. Author-in-residence, Temple University, 1970-74. Worked as a cartoonist, layout artist, advertising copywriter, and editor of an industrial magazine. *Military service:* U.S. Army, Intelligence, 1942-46; became staff sergeant.

### Awards, Honors

National Jewish Book Award, 1959, for *Border Hawk: August Bondi;* notable book citation, American Library Association (ALA), 1964, for *The Book of Three;* Newbery Honor Book, ALA, 1966, for *The Black Cauldron;* "Best Books" citations, *School Library Journal,* 1967, for *Taran Wanderer,* 1971, for *The King's Fountain,* and 1982, for *Westmark;* citation from American Institute of Graphic Arts Children's Books, 1967-68, for *The Truthful Harp;* "Children's Book of the Year" citation, Child Study Association of America, 1968, for *The High King,* 1971, for *The King's Fountain,* 1973, for *The Cat Who Wished to Be a Man,* 1974, for *The Foundling and Other Tales of Prydain,* 1975, for *The Wizard in the Tree,* 1982, for *The Kestrel,* and 1985, for *The Black Cauldron* and *Time Cat;* Newbery Medal, ALA, and National Book Award nomination, both 1969, both for *The High King;* "Best Books of the Year" citation, Library of Congress, 1970, and National Book Award, 1971, both for *The Marvelous Misadventures of Sebastian;* Drexel Award, 1972 and 1976, for outstanding contributions to literature for children; *Boston Globe-Horn Book* Award, 1973, for *The Cat Who Wished to Be a Man,* and 1993, for *The Fortune-Tellers;* "Outstanding Books of the Year" citation, *New York Times,* 1973, for *The Foundling and Other Tales of Prydain;* Laura Ingalls Wilder Award nomination, 1975; CRABbery Award, Oxon Hill Branch of Prince George's County Library (Maryland), 1979, National Book Award nomination, 1979, Silver Pencil Award, 1981, and Austrian Children's Book Award, 1984, all for *The First Two Lives of Lukas-Kasha.*

American Book Award nomination, 1980, for *The High King,* and 1982, for *The Wizard in the Tree;* "Best Books for Young Adults" citation, ALA, 1981, for *Westmark,* 1982, for *The Kestrel,* and 1984, for *The Beggar Queen;* American Book Award, 1982, for

*Lloyd Alexander*

*Westmark;* Parents' Choice Award, 1982, for *The Kestrel,* 1984, for *The Beggar Queen,* 1986, for *The Illyrian Adventure,* 1991, for *The Remarkable Journey of Prince Jen,* and 1993, for *The Fortune-Tellers;* Golden Cat Award, Sjoestrands Foerlag (Sweden), 1984, for excellence in children's literature; Regina Medal, Catholic Library Association, 1986; Church and Synagogue Library Association Award, 1987; Field Award, Pennsylvania Library Association, 1987, for *The Illyrian Adventure;* Lifetime Achievement Award, Pennsylvania Center for The Book in Philadelphia, 1991; Otter Award, Northern California Booksellers Association, 1993; New Atlantic Independent Booksellers Association, 1998; 100 Books that Shaped the Twentieth Century, School Library Award, 2000; Parent's Choice Lifetime Achievement Award, 2001.

## Writings

### JUVENILE

*Border Hawk: August Bondi* (biography), illustrated by Bernard Krigstein, Farrar, Straus (New York, NY), 1958.
*The Flagship Hope: Aaron Lopez* (biography), illustrated by B. Krigstein, Jewish Publication Society, 1960.
*Time Cat: The Remarkable Journeys of Jason and Gareth,* illustrated by Bill Sokol, Holt (New York, NY), 1963,

published as *Nine Lives,* Cassell (London, England), 1963.
*Coll and His White Pig,* illustrated by Evaline Ness, Holt (New York, NY), 1965.
*The Truthful Harp,* illustrated by Evaline Ness, Holt (New York, NY), 1967.
*The Marvelous Misadventures of Sebastian,* Dutton (New York, NY), 1970.
*The King's Fountain,* illustrated by Ezra Jack Keats, Dutton (New York, NY), 1971.
*The Four Donkeys,* illustrated by Lester Abrams, Holt (New York, NY), 1972.
*The Foundling and Other Tales of Prydain,* illustrated by Margot Zemach, Holt (New York, NY), 1973.
*The Cat Who Wished to Be a Man,* Dutton (New York, NY), 1973.
*The Wizard in the Tree,* illustrated by Laszlo Kubinyi, Dutton (New York, NY), 1975.
*The Town Cats and Other Tales,* illustrated by Laszlo Kubinyi, Dutton (New York, NY), 1977.
*The First Two Lives of Lukas-Kasha,* Dutton (New York, NY), 1978.
*The Remarkable Journey of Prince Jen,* Dutton (New York, NY), 1991.
*The Fortune-Tellers,* illustrated by Trina Schart Hyman, Dutton (New York, NY), 1992.
*The Arkadians,* Dutton (New York, NY), 1995.
*The House Gobbaleen,* illustrated by Diane Goode, Dutton (New York, NY), 1995.
*The Iron Ring,* Dutton (New York, NY), 1997.
*The Gypsy Rizka,* Dutton (New York, NY), 1999.
*How the Cat Swallowed Thunder,* illustrated by Judith Byron Schachner, Dutton (New York, NY), 2000.
*The Gawgon and the Boy,* Dutton (New York, NY), 2001.
*The Rope Trick,* Dutton (New York, NY), 2002.

### THE "PRYDAIN CHRONICLES" SERIES

*The Book of Three,* Holt (New York, NY), 1964.
*The Black Cauldron,* Holt (New York, NY), 1965.
*The Castle of Llyr,* Holt (New York, NY), 1966.
*Taran Wanderer,* Holt (New York, NY), 1967.
*The High King,* Holt (New York, NY), 1968.

### THE WESTMARK TRILOGY

*Westmark,* Dutton (New York, NY), 1981.
*The Kestrel,* Dutton (New York, NY), 1982.
*The Beggar Queen,* Dutton (New York, NY), 1984.

### THE VESPER HOLLY ADVENTURES

*The Illyrian Adventure,* Dutton (New York, NY), 1986.
*The El Dorado Adventure,* Dutton (New York, NY), 1987.
*The Drackenberg Adventure,* Dutton (New York, NY), 1988.
*The Jedera Adventure,* Dutton (New York, NY), 1989.
*The Philadelphia Adventure,* Dutton (New York, NY), 1990.

### TRANSLATOR FROM THE FRENCH

Jean-Paul Sartre, *The Wall and Other Stories,* New Directions (New York, NY), 1948, published as *Intimacy and Other Stories,* Peter Nevill (London, England), 1949, New Directions (New York, NY), 1952.

Jean-Paul Sartre, *Nausea,* New Directions (New York, NY), 1949, published as *The Diary of Antoine Roquentin,* Lehmann, 1949.

Paul Eluard, *Selected Writings,* New Directions (New York, NY), 1951, published as *Uninterrupted Poetry: Selected Writings,* 1975.

Paul Vialar, *The Sea Rose,* Neville Spearman (London, England), 1951.

Paul Eluard, *Ombres et Soleil—Sun and Shadows: Writings of Paul Eluard, 1913-1953,* Oyster River Press, 1992.

*OTHER*

*And Let the Credit Go* (novel), Crowell (New York, NY), 1955.

*My Five Tigers,* Crowell (New York, NY), 1956.

*Janine Is French,* Crowell (New York, NY), 1958.

*My Love Affair with Music,* Crowell (New York, NY), 1960.

(With Dr. Louis Camuti) *Park Avenue Vet,* Holt (New York, NY), 1962.

*Fifty Years in the Doghouse,* Putnam (New York, NY), 1963, published as *Send for Ryan!,* W. H. Allen (London, England), 1965.

*My Cats and Me: The Story of an Understanding,* Running Press, 1989.

Also author of afterword to E. Nesbit's *Five Children and It.* Work included in New Directions anthologies. Contributor to books, including, *Cricket's Choice,* Open Court (New York, NY), 1974. Contributor to periodicals, including *Contemporary Poetry, School Library Journal, Harper's Bazaar,* and *Horn Book.* Member of editorial board, *Cricket.*

## Adaptations

Stage versions of *The Cat Who Wished to Be a Man* and *The Wizard in the Tree,* produced in Japan; television serial version of *The Marvelous Misadventures of Sebastian,* produced in Japan; *The Book of Three* and *The Black Cauldron* were adapted to film, Walt Disney Productions, 1985.

## Sidelights

Lloyd Alexander is widely regarded as a master of twentieth-century children's literature. He is best-known for his fantasy fiction and modern fables: imaginative and adventurous stories, often rooted in historical fact and legend, which explore universal themes such as good versus evil and the quest of individuals for self-identity. Among Alexander's best-known works are the five novels which comprise his "Prydain Chronicles"—culminating with *The High King,* which in 1969 received the Newbery Medal for children's literature. Among Alexander's numerous other awards are the National Book Award for *The Marvelous Misadventures of Sebastian* and the American Book Award for his imaginative 1981 novel, *Westmark.* "At heart, the issues raised in a work of fantasy are those we face in real life," Alexander stated in his Newbery Award acceptance speech printed in *Horn Book.* "In whatever guise—our own daily nightmares of war, intolerance, inhumanity; or

the struggles of an Assistant Pig-Keeper against the Lord of Death—the problems are agonizingly familiar. And an openness to compassion, love, and mercy is as essential to us here and now as it is to any inhabitant of an imaginary kingdom."

Alexander was born in 1924 in Philadelphia, Pennsylvania. His father, a former stockbroker who was bankrupted by the Stock Market Crash of 1929, struggled to support the Alexander family through a number of largely unsuccessful business ventures. Alexander became impassioned with books, scouring the odd assortment that lay about his household. "I learned to read quite young and have been an avid reader ever since, even though my parents and relatives were not great readers," he was quoted by Lee Bennett Hopkins in *More Books by More People.* "I was more or less left to my own devices and interests, which, after all, may not be such a bad idea." Alexander became very fond of Greek and Celtic mythologies, in addition to the Welsh tales and legends contained in the *Mabinogion.* He also discovered the novels of Charles Dickens, and was particularly impressed with *David Copperfield.* "Dickens was one of many authors who helped me grow up

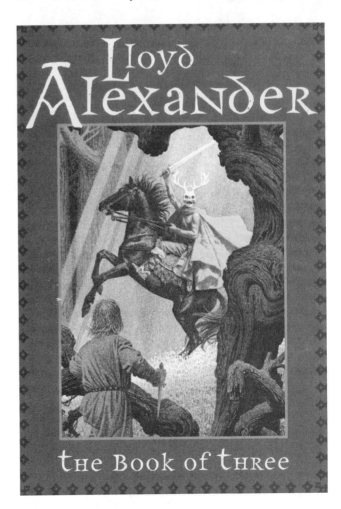

*Chasing a runaway pig leads Taran on a dangerous journey to fight the evil threatening his home in Alexander's first book of the Prydain Chronicles, inspired by Welsh legend.*

*Taran and his friends again face danger in their quest to destroy the black cauldron, birthplace of an evil army threatening Prydain.*

(and are still helping)," Alexander wrote in *Top of the News.* "For a long while he was both refuge and encouragement. If he helped me escape from my daily life, ... he also sent me back somehow better able to face up to it."

At the age of fifteen, Alexander announced to his parents that he wished to become a poet—a decision which greatly concerned his father. As Alexander recalled in *More Books by More People,* "Poetry, my father warned, was no practical career; I would do well to forget it." His mother interceded, however, and it was agreed upon that Alexander could pursue poetry—granted he also find practical work. "For my part, I had no idea how to find any sort of work—or, in fact, how to go about being a poet. For more than a year I had been writing long into the night and studying verse forms to the scandalous neglect of my homework." Upon graduation, Alexander's poor grades and his family's limited finances ruled out the possibility of college, and his prospects of becoming a successful writer looked equally dim. "In addition to poor marks, I collected rejection slips," Alexander recollected in *My Love Affair with Music.* "My goal was to become an author and it appeared that I would reach it only if I inserted the qualifying word 'unpublished'." Alexander was able to

find work as a messenger boy in a bank, a job which, although it was low-paying and he found it miserable, allowed him to continue writing.

Alexander eventually saved enough money to enroll in a local college to formally study writing, yet he found the course work inadequate. Instead, as he wrote in *My Love Affair with Music,* he decided that "adventure . . . was the best way to learn about writing," and he enlisted in the army. The year was 1942 and the United States was already in World War II. Alexander was eventually assigned to military intelligence, and his unit was sent off to the country of Wales for combat training. "Wales was an enchanted world," Alexander once stated. "The Welsh language fascinated me, as did English spoken with a Welsh lilt, more song than speech.... It seemed I recognized faces from all the hero tales of my childhood.... The Companions of Arthur might have galloped from the mountains with no surprise to me. Wales, to my eyes, appeared still a realm of bards and heroes; even the coal-tips towered like dark fortresses. Not until years afterwards did I realize I had been given, without my knowing, a glimpse of another enchanted kingdom."

Alexander was assigned to the Seventh Army in the Alsace-Lorraine region of France, and worked as an interpreter-translator. When the war ended in 1945, he was sent to work with a counter-intelligence unit in Paris, and, as he wrote in *My Love Affair with Music,* he "fell in love with the city at first sight and sound." The same year he met his future wife, a young Parisian named Janine Denni, and the two were married three months later in January of 1946. Alexander requested a discharge from the army to resume his education, and received a scholarship from the French Foreign Ministry, with which he attended the Sorbonne, University of Paris. Feeling, however, that he needed to be closer to his roots if he were to succeed as a writer, Alexander returned to the United States with his wife and her small daughter Madeleine, whom he had adopted. The three initially lived with Alexander's parents, until they were moved into their own home, an old farmhouse in Drexel Hill, just outside of Philadelphia.

Alexander began writing novels, the first three of which were promptly rejected by publishers. Between 1948 and 1955, he worked a variety of jobs to support his family, including being a cartoonist, advertising writer, layout artist, and an associate editor for an industrial magazine; he also translated several works from French, including Jean-Paul Sartre's *The Wall* and *Nausea.* Alexander was on the verge of giving up on writing when his fourth novel, *And Let the Credit Go,* was published. Based on his own experiences as a struggling writer, the book launched a number of biographical-based adult books by Alexander. "One thing I had learned during those seven years was to write about things I knew and loved," he explained in *Horn Book.* "Our cats delighted me. So did music; I had ... tried to learn the violin, piano, and guitar. I relished Janine's war with the English language and her bafflement at the peculiar customs of Americans. All this found its way into books and was published. I was writing out of my own life and experience. But nearly ten years passed before I learned a writer could know and love a fantasy world as much as his real one."

Alexander made his first venture into children's fantasy with *Time Cat: The Remarkable Journeys of Jason and Gareth.* The story of a magical black cat which is able to transport a young boy into different historical periods, *Time Cat* brought Alexander into contact once again with ancient Wales. "Surely everyone cherishes a secret, private world from the days of childhood. Mine was Camelot, and Arthur's Round Table, Malory, and the *Mabinogion,"* Alexander wrote in *Horn Book.* "The Welsh research brought it all back to me. Feeling like a man who has by accident stumbled into an enchanted cavern lost since boyhood, both terrified and awestruck, I realized I would have to explore further." Originally intending to include a Welsh episode in *Time Cat,* Alexander decided to replace it with an Irish one, and began plans to devote a future book to his beloved Wales. "Not to the beautiful land of Wales I knew in reality," he told *Horn Book,* "but an older, darker one."

Alexander didn't expect that his exploration would result in the five-novel Prydain Chronicles. In the first novel, *The Book of Three,* Alexander's intent was to retell the convoluted tales of the *Mabinogion.* "I tried this at first, but strange things happened to me," he stated in an interview for *The Pied Pipers.* "I found I had been kidding myself: I didn't want simply to retell anybody's mythology. What I really wanted to do was invent my own, or at least use my own in some way.... The more I worked on *The Book of Three* the more I realized the personal importance it was taking on.... It was a tremendously liberating decision. I found myself, to my amazement, tapping into various areas of my personality that I never even knew existed." The subsequent books of the series, *The Black Cauldron, The Castle of Llyr, Taran Wanderer,* and *The High King,* relate the adventures of a young hero, Taran, on a quest which leads him to understand the true meaning of heroism, goodness, and also evil. "Prydain grew into something much more than a thinly disguised ancient Wales," Laura Ingram commented in *Dictionary of Literary Biography.* "Undeniably, it was similar to that land, but reshaped by the addition of contemporary realism, modern values, and a generous dose of humor, as well as the special depth and insight provided by characters who not only act, but think, feel, and struggle with the same kinds of problems that confuse and trouble people in the twentieth century." An essayist for the *St. James Guide to Fantasy Writers* wrote: "The series is impressive, atmospheric and, despite a few slightly too convenient short cuts of plotting, ... avoids all options of easy wish-fulfillment." *The Black Cauldron* was a runner-up for the Newbery Medal in 1966, and *The High King* received the prestigious honor in 1969.

Alexander followed the Prydain Chronicles with several simpler tales geared more towards younger children. Some of these books, including *Coll and His White Pig, The Truthful Harp,* and *The Foundling and Other Tales of Prydain,* are special introductions for young readers

into the world of Prydain. In 1970, Alexander went in a different direction with another children's book, *The Marvelous Misadventures of Sebastian,* which was honored with the National Book Award. The story, set in a country similar to eighteenth-century Europe, charts the adventures of a young fiddler as he assists an orphaned princess who is trying to escape marriage to the repressive ruler of the land. As Alexander described in *The Pied Pipers,* the boy "comes into the possession of a fiddle that allows him to play and hear music as he has never done before. It changes his life." Alexander added that the story has parallels to his own discovery of the joys of writing for children. "The fiddle ... is a mixed blessing because it also drains his life away the more he understands his magnificent discovery. Without being pretentious about it, I suppose *Sebastian* attempts to say something about what it feels like to be an artist."

In 1981, Alexander published a new novel, *Westmark,* the first of a trilogy which includes *The Kestrel* and *The Beggar Queen.* These novels became known as "The Westmark Trilogy," through which Alexander explores the political development of an imaginary land called Westmark, "a cross between colonial America and feudal Europe," wrote Ingram. "Quite different in tone and setting from the *Prydain* series," according to Jill P. May in *Twentieth Century Children's Writers,* Alexander's Westmark trilogy depicts "the horrors of revolution

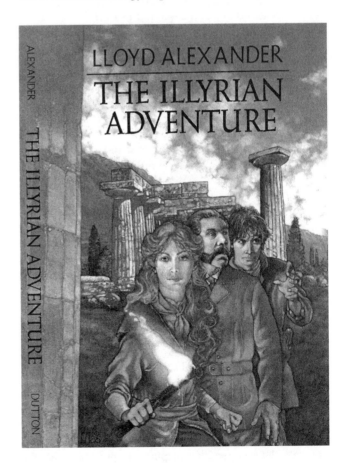

*Alexander's popular heroine, Vesper Holly, faces deadly adversaries on her quest for the legendary treasure of the small, rebellion-torn country of Illyria.*

and unrest, and the conflicts caused by corrupt leadership."

A subsequent series of five books by Alexander recounts the adventures of a spirited young character named Vesper Holly. The first novel in the series, *The Illyrian Adventure,* was "in every way different from anything I'd written before," Alexander explained. "It was intended as an entertainment—for its author as much as anyone—with a gloriously fearless heroine, legendary heroes, inscrutable mysteries, and fiendish villains. What surprised me shouldn't have surprised me at all. In what was meant as sheer amusement, below the surface I realized that my own concerns and questions were still there, even though set in different terms." An essayist for the *St. James Guide to Young Adult Writers,* wrote that the series "boasts a fast-paced vitality reminiscent of the best Victorian adventures; it's as if Sherlock Holmes and Dr. Watson were racing Captain Nemo to King Solomon's mines."

Exotic locales also characterize Alexander's novel *The Remarkable Journey of Prince Jen* and the picture book *The Fortune-Tellers.* The *Remarkable Journey of Prince Jen,* the story of a Chinese prince's voyage to study the way to govern a happy kingdom, "is a classic quest novel and classic Alexander," noted Kathleen Beck in *Voice of Youth Advocates,* continuing, "The adventures are exciting, the message subtly conveyed, and the characters as quirky and engaging as ever." *Horn Book* reviewer Ann A. Flowers concurred, writing that "Alexander's forte is the coming-of-age novel, and he skillfully uses symbolism and humor to reinforce his theme." *The Fortune-Tellers* is set in the West African country of Cameroon, and tells of a young carpenter's visit to find out his future, which unexpectedly turns into an adventure. "The trickster's hand is hidden here," remarked Betsy Hearne of the *Bulletin of the Center for Children's Books;* "it is the author's, and a clever tale he has turned, proving as adept at a picture book text as he is at complex fantasy series." A contributor to *Kirkus Reviews* observed, "Alexander narrates his original tale with folkloric verve and his own mellow brand of irony." Linda Boyles of *School Library Journal* noted, "Visual details ... add an authenticity to the story."

In her book *The Green and Burning Tree: On the Writing and Enjoyment of Children's Books,* Eleanor Cameron described Alexander as "a perfect example of one who, before he could come into his own as a writer, had to discover that place which was, for him, the spiritual symbol or expression of something hidden." Alexander's varied contributions to children's literature have earned him not only many awards and critical accolades, but also a devoted and diverse readership. "I am amazed and delighted by how many adults read the 'Prydain Chronicles,'" Alexander was quoted in *The Pied Pipers.* "I don't think adults stop growing, or at least they shouldn't. If you stop growing you're dead. At any rate, I've never tried to pull any punches with the kids." For Alexander, the world of the imagination and fantasy has been a way to explore that which is most real. "Using the device of an imaginary world allowed

me in some strange way to go to the central issues," he added in *The Pied Pipers.* "In other worlds I used the imaginary kingdom not as a sentimentalized fairyland, but as an opening wedge to express what I hoped would be some very hard truths. I never saw fairy tales as an escape or a cop out.... On the contrary, speaking for myself, it is the way to understand reality."

## Biographical and Critical Sources

*BOOKS*

*Authors and Artists for Young Adults,* Gale (Detroit, MI), Volume 1, 1989, Volume 27, 1998.
Cameron, Eleanor, *The Green and Burning Tree: On the Writing and Enjoyment of Children's Books,* Little, Brown (Boston, MA), 1969, p. 185.
*Children's Literature Review,* Gale (Detroit, MI), Volume 1, 1976, Volume 5, 1983.
*Contemporary Literary Criticism,* Gale (Detroit, MI), Volume 35, 1985.
*Dictionary of Literary Biography,* Volume 52: *American Writers for Children since 1960; Fiction,* Gale (Detroit, MI), 1986, pp. 3-21.
Hopkins, Lee Bennett, *More Books by More People,* Citation (New York, NY), 1974.
Jacobs, James S. and Tunnell, Michael O., *Lloyd Alexander: A Bio-Bibliography,* Greenwood (Westport, CT), 1989.
May, Jill P., *Lloyd Alexander,* Twayne (Boston), 1991.
*St. James Guide to Children's Writers,* 5th edition, St. James Press (Detroit, MI), 1999.
*St. James Guide to Fantasy Writers,* St. James Press (Detroit, MI), 1996.
*St. James Guide to Young Adult Writers,* 2nd edition, St. James Press (Detroit, MI), 1999.
*Something about the Author Autobiography Series,* Volume 19, Gale (Detroit, MI), 1995.
Tunnell, Michael O., *The Prydain Companion,* Greenwood Press (New York, NY), 1989.
*Twentieth Century Children's Writers,* 3rd edition, St. James Press (Detroit, MI), 1989, pp. 16-18.
Tymm, Marshall B., Kenneth J. Zahorski, and Robert H. Boyer, *Fantasy Literature: A Core Collection and Reference Guide,* Bowker (New York, NY), 1979, pp. 39-44.
Wintle, Justin, and Emma Fisher, *The Pied Pipers: Interviews with the Influential Creators of Children's Literature,* Paddington Press, 1974.

*PERIODICALS*

*Book Links,* March, 1994, pp. 30-39.
*Bulletin of the Center for Children's Books,* September, 1992, Betsy Hearne, review of *The Fortune-Tellers,* pp. 4-5.
*Chicago Tribune Book World,* November 26, 1967, p. 16.
*Christian Science Monitor,* May 2, 1968, p. B8; November 7, 1973, p. B5.
*Cricket,* December, 1976.
*Elementary English,* December, 1971, pp. 937-945.
*Horn Book,* April, 1965, Lloyd Alexander, "The Flat-Heeled Muse," pp. 141-146; August, 1969, Lloyd Alexander, "Newbery Award Acceptance Speech";

March, 1992, Ann A. Flowers, review of *The Remarkable Journey of Prince Jen,* pp. 200-201.

*Kirkus Reviews,* August 1, 1992, review of *The Fortune-Tellers,* p. 985.

*Language Arts,* April, 1984.

*The Lion and the Unicorn,* Volume 9, 1985.

*Los Angeles Times,* July 24, 1985; July 27, 1985.

*New York Times Book Review,* December 3, 1964; June 19, 1966, p. 36; April 9, 1967, p. 26; March 28, 1968, p. 38; November 15, 1970, p. 42; November 13, 1977, p. 37; April 25, 1982, p. 47; June 7, 1987.

*Publishers Weekly,* July 12, 1999, "Revisiting Prydain," p. 96; July 3, 2000, review of *How the Cat Swallowed Thunder,* p. 70; May 14, 2001, review of *The Gawgon and the Boy,* p. 83.

*School Library Journal,* May, 1967, p. 61; February, 1968, p. 86; September, 1992, Linda Boyles, review of *The Fortune-Tellers,* p. 196.

*Times Literary Supplement,* November 24, 1966, p. 1089; May 25, 1967, p. 451; October 3, 1968, p. 1113; April 6, 1973, p. 379.

*Top of the News,* November, 1968, Lloyd Alexander, "A Personal Note by Lloyd Alexander on Charles Dickens."

*Voice of Youth Advocates,* February, 1992, Kathleen Beck, review of *The Remarkable Journey of Prince Jen,* p. 378.

*Washington Post Book World,* August 21, 1966; November 8, 1970, p. 10; November 12, 1978, p. E4; May 10, 1981; January 9, 1983.

*Writer's Digest,* April, 1973.

OTHER

*Meet the Newbery Author: Lloyd Alexander* (filmstrip/cassette), Miller-Brody, 1975.

\*          \*          \*

# ALTER, Anna 1974-

## Personal

Born October 10, 1974, in Charlottesville, VA; daughter of Gary (a businessman) and Lee (a massage therapist and painter) Alter. *Nationality:* American. *Education:* Rhode Island School of Design, B.F.A. (with honors), 1997. *Hobbies and other interests:* Traveling, camping, reading, yoga.

## Addresses

*Home*—35 Parkton Rd., Apt. No. 2, Jamaica Plain, MA 02130. *E-mail*—annaalter@hotmail.com.

## Career

Houghton Mifflin, Boston, MA, design assistant, 1998-2000; Boston Children's School, Boston, MA, preschool teacher, 2000—. Freelance writer and illustrator.

## Writings

(And illustrator) *Estelle and Lucy,* Greenwillow (New York, NY), 2001.

(Illustrator and reteller) *The Three Little Kittens,* Henry Holt (New York, NY), 2001.

(Illustrator) Patrick Jennings, *The Bird Shadow* ("Ike and Mem" chapterbook series), Holiday House (New York, NY), 2001.

(Illustrator) Patrick Jennings, *The Tornado Watches* ("Ike and Mem" chapterbook series), Holiday House (New York, NY), 2002.

(Illustrator) Patrick Jennings, *The Weeping Willow* ("Ike and Mem" chapterbook series), Holiday House (New York, NY), 2002.

## Work in Progress

Illustrating *The Purple Ribbon,* by Sharelle Byars Moranville, for Henry Holt, 2003, and *The Ears of Corn* and *The Lightning Rings,* both by Patrick Jennings, for Holiday House; writing and illustrating *Francine's Day* for Greenwillow, 2003.

## Sidelights

Anna Alter is the author of several picture books for young readers, her gentle pen-and-ink and watercolor renderings creating soft, soothing accompaniments to her own texts as well as those of other writers. Beginning with her 2001 picture book debut, *Estelle and Lucy,* Alter has a number of projects in the works, both in the picture book and chapter book genres.

Born in 1974, Alter began drawing at an early age. "Both my parents are artists," she explained to *SATA,* "and we were often working on creative projects together. As I child I didn't differentiate between the art on walls and in museums, and the art in children's books. I was always surrounded by wonderful books and have wanted to illustrate children's books as long as I can remember." Among Alter's favorite illustrators are Beatrix Potter, Maurice Sendak, Garth Williams, Arnold Lobel, and James Marshall.

By the time she was in high school, Alter was writing and illustrating her own stories. Enrolling in the prestigious Rhode Island School of Design's illustration program, she studied drawing and painting, which Alter found to be "a wonderful point of departure" in preparation for a career as a professional illustrator. "In addition to illustration courses (mainly figurative drawing), I also did a lot of printmaking, mainly etching and linocut," she explained. In school she also came to appreciate the works of artists such as Rembrandt, Leonardo da Vinci, Käthe Kollwitz, Edvard Munch, and Georges Seurat.

Alter's first published book, *Estelle and Lucy,* is a picture book that introduces an interesting set of siblings: Estelle is a growing kitten, while little sister Lucy is a mouse. As the story progresses, Estelle lists her many accomplishments, including baking biscuits and being able to wear her father's slippers, while little sister Lucy tags along, her efforts clearly on a smaller scale than those of her big sister. Calling Alter's debut "a charmer," *Booklist* contributor Ilene Cooper added that "Alter shows strong talent as both a storyteller and an artist." A *Publishers Weekly* reviewer had reservations about the future friendship between the cat and mouse, but praised the book's "buttery-toned, cross-hatched watercolor and ink artwork that harks back to times past." Reviewing *Estelle and Lucy* for *School Library Journal,* Karen Scott called the illustrations "a joy to look at" and noted that they are "perfectly suited" to Alter's text.

In addition to writing and illustrating her own books, Alter has contributed her artistic talents to books by other authors, including the "Ike and Mem" series of chapterbooks by author Patrick Jennings. She has also adapted a traditional story in *The Three Little Kittens,* which reveals the true reason for the kittens' lost mittens: a family of mice who make off with the mittens despite the kittens' best efforts to snatch them back. "Humor injects vitality into Alter's entertaining take on the traditional nursery rhyme," noted Ellen Mandel in her *Booklist* review, while in *School Library Journal,* Jane Marino dubbed *The Three Little Kittens* a "worthy" adaptation.

"I have always enjoyed representative imagery and meticulous observation of life in drawing, something I try to imitate in my work," explained Alter in discussing her role as an illustrator. "I find books a unique and interesting medium due to their ability to absorb and transport the child reader."

## Biographical and Critical Sources

### PERIODICALS

*Booklist,* April 1, 2001, Ilene Cooper, review of *Estelle and Lucy,* p. 1470; Ellen Mandel, October 1, 2001, review of *The Three Little Kittens,* p. 320.
*Publishers Weekly,* April 16, 2001, review of *Estelle and Lucy,* p. 64.
*School Library Journal,* July, 2001, Karen Scott, review of *Estelle and Lucy,* p. 72; November, 2001, Jane Marino, review of *The Three Little Kittens,* p. 110.

\*    \*    \*

# APPERLEY, Dawn 1969-

## Personal

Born April 26, 1969, in Southampton, England; daughter of Norman (a computer designer) and Lorrain (a special-needs teacher) Apperley. *Nationality:* British. *Education:* Middlesex University (London, England), B.A. (with honors; graphic design).

## Addresses

*Home*—32 Penshurst Rd., London E9 7DT, England.

## Career

Freelance designer in London, England, 1991-98; freelance author/illustrator, 1998—.

## Awards, Honors

Sheffield Book Award, 2001, for *There's an Octopus under My Bed.*

## Writings

### SELF-ILLUSTRATED

*Shape Sorter,* David & Charles (New York, NY), 1996.
*Christmas Story,* David & Charles (New York, NY), 1997.
*Noah's Ark,* David & Charles (New York, NY), 1998.
*Animal Noises: A Pull-Tab Book,* Little, Brown (Boston, MA), 1998.
*Animal Moves: A Pull-Tab Book,* Little, Brown (Boston, MA), 1998.
*Wakey-wakey* (board book), Little, Brown (Boston, MA), 1999.
*Nighty-night* (board book), Little, Brown (Boston, MA), 1999.
*Hello Little Lamb,* David & Charles (New York, NY), 2000.
*Hello Little Pig,* David & Charles (New York, NY), 2000.
*Hello Little Ducklings,* David & Charles (New York, NY), 2000.

*Dawn Apperley*

*Hello Little Chicks,* David & Charles (New York, NY), 2000.

*There's an Octopus under My Bed,* Bloomsbury (London, England), 2000.

*Flip and Flop,* Orchard (London, England), 2000, Scholastic (New York, NY), 2001.

*Crash Bang Thud,* Hodder Headline (London, England), 2000.

*Good Night, Sleep Tight, Little Bunnies,* Scholastic (New York, NY), 2001.

*Don't Wake the Baby!,* Bloomsbury (London, England), 2001.

*Blossom and Boo: A Story about Best Friends,* Little, Brown (Boston, MA), 2001.

*Blossom and Boo Stay up Late,* Little, Brown (Boston, MA), 2002.

*Someone's Coming Tonight,* Scholastic (New York, NY), 2002.

*SELF-ILLUSTRATED; "HIDE AND SEEK" SERIES*

*In the Ocean,* Little, Brown (Boston, MA), 1996.
*In the Sand,* Little, Brown (Boston, MA), 1996.
*In the Snow,* Little, Brown (Boston, MA), 1996.
*In the Jungle,* Little, Brown (Boston, MA), 1996.

*ILLUSTRATOR*

Kate Burns, *How Does Your Garden Grow,* David & Charles (New York, NY), 1997.

*Kira the Koala,* Picadilly Press (London, England), 2000.

*Best Tea Party Ever!,* Penguin Putnam (New York, NY), 2000.

*Easter Basket,* Simon & Schuster (New York, NY), 2002.

*Easter Egg,* Simon & Schuster (New York, NY), 2002.

*Sparkle and Twinkle Christmas,* Simon & Schuster (New York, NY), 2002.

*Sparkle and Twinkly Channaka,* Simon & Schuster (New York, NY), 2002.

## Sidelights

Dawn Apperley is an illustrator and graphic designer who has also created numerous picture book texts to accompany her watercolor renderings. Animal characters figure prominently in Apperley's stories, such as *Flip and Flop,* about two penguin brothers, and *Don't Wake the Baby!,* which shows readers that, like their human counterparts, young squirrels have difficulty keeping quiet while infant siblings are sleeping. Her illustrations have been praised by reviewers for their uncomplicated style, with *Booklist* contributor Ilene Cooper noting of *Flip and Flop* that "the simply designed artwork is just right for children, who will see themselves" in Apperley's anthropomorphic animal characters.

Born in England, Apperley earned her art degree at London's Middlesex University before beginning her career as a freelance illustrator and designer. She has since gone on to create several series of board and pop-up books for the pre-reading set, including the four titles in the "Hello Little . . ." series: *Hello Little Lamb, Hello Little Chicks, Hello Little Ducklings,* and *Hello Little Pig.* Praising Apperley's rhyming text as "spare" and "melodious," *School Library Journal* contributor Olga R. Barnes added that the series focuses on "familiar objects" and features brightly colored illustrations. And in her *Blossom and Boo: A Story about Best Friends,* a bunny and bear show affection and caring toward each other while engaged in everything from making a daisy chain to preparing for Boo bear's hibernation. "Apperley's unadorned, at times childlike, watercolor and pencil illustrations convey the chums' changeable emotions," noted a *Publishers Weekly* contributor.

Apperley told *SATA:* "I work with watercolor and colored pencil for my illustrations. The stories always come first. They are mostly inspired by children themselves, as I spend time observing children and the pickles they get themselves into. I love endings to stories that you don't expect, and I often come up with such endings when I least expect to."

## Biographical and Critical Sources

*PERIODICALS*

*Booklist,* January 1, 2002, Ilene Cooper, review of *Flip and Flop,* p. 862.

*Books for Keeps,* July, 1999, review of *Wakey-wakey* and *Nighty-night,* p. 19.

*Publishers Weekly,* March 5, 2001, review of *Blossom and Boo: A Story about Best Friends,* p. 78.

*School Library Journal,* May, 1999, Marsha McGrath, review of *Nighty-night* and *Wakey-wakey,* p. 79; September, 1999, Mary M. Hopf, review of *Animal Moves: A Pull-Tab Book* and *Animal Noises: A Pull-Tab Book,* p. 174; February, 2001, Olga R. Barnes, review of "Hello Little . . ." series, p. 92; May, 2001, Roxanne Burg, review of *Blossom and Boo,* p. 108; December, 2001, Bina Williams, review of *Don't Wake the Baby!,* p. 88.*

\*          \*          \*

# AYE, A. K.
## See EDWARDS, Hazel (Eileen)

# B

## BARTOLETTI, Susan Campbell 1958-

### Personal

Born November 18, 1958, in Harrisburg, PA; married Joseph Bartoletti (a history teacher), June 25, 1977; children: Brandy, Joey. *Education:* Marywood College, B.A. (English and secondary education), 1979; University of Scranton, M.A. (English), 1982; additional graduate work at Marywood College; Binghamton University, State University of New York—Binghamton, Ph.D., 2001.

### Addresses

*Home*—Moscow, PA. *Agent*—Curtis Brown, Ltd., 10 Astor Place, New York, NY 10003.

### Career

Writer. North Pocono Middle School, Moscow, PA, English teacher, 1979-97; educational consultant, 1983—; Keystone Junior College, adjunct faculty, 1984-86; International Correspondence School, commissioned author and editor, 1990—; University of Scranton, Scranton, PA, instructor in children's literature, 1997-98; Binghamton University, State University of New York—Binghamton, Binghamton, NY, instructor in creative writing, 1997-2001; Hollins University, Roanoke, VA, visiting associate professor in creative writing, Graduate Program in Children's Literature, 1999—. North Pocono Middle School, Moscow, PA, Faculty Advisory Committee, North Pocono Middle School literary magazine (past advisor), Student Assistance Program counselor.

### Member

Society of Children's Book Writers and Illustrators (co-regional advisor, 1992-1999), Children's Literature Association, National Council of Teachers of English, Rutgers Council on Children's Literature (board member, 2001).

*Susan Campbell Bartoletti*

### Awards, Honors

Special Achievement Cinema in Industry (CINDY) award, for *Wooden Angel*, 1988; winner, *Highlights for Children* fiction contest, 1993, for "No Man's Land;" Jane Addams Children's Book Award, American Library Association Award (ALA) Notable Book, ALA

*Vintage photographs and Bartoletti's detailed account portray the harsh and dangerous life of coal mining in Pennsylvania.* (*Photo from* Growing Up in Coal Country.)

Best Book for Young Adults, Golden Kite Honor Book for Nonfiction, Society of Children's Book Writers and Illustrators, Carolyn Field Award, Pennsylvania Library Association, Editor's Choice Award, *Booklist,* Notable Children's Trade Book in the Field of Social Studies, National Council for the Social Studies/Children's Book Council (NCSS/CBC), Orbis Pictus Recommended Title, National Council of Teachers of English (NCTE), Lamplighter Award, and Parents Gold Choice Award Winner, all for *Growing Up in Coal Country;* Best Books of 1999, *School Library Journal,* Best Book for Young Adults, ALA, Notable Book, *Smithsonian* magazine, Books for the Teen Age, New York Public Library, Jane Addams Children's Book Honor Award, Carolyn Field Honor Award, Pennsylvania Library Association, Orbis Pictus Recommended Title, NCTE, Notable Children's Trade Book in the Field of Social Studies, NCSS/CBC, and Jefferson Cup Recommended Title, all for *Kids on Strike!;* Notable Children's Trade Book in the Field of Social Studies, NCSS/CBC, 1999, for *No Man's Land: A Young Soldier's Story;* Books for the Teen Age, New York Public Library, 2000, for *A Coal Miner's Bride: The Diary of Anetka Kaminska;* Robert F. Sibert Award, ALA/Bound to Stay Bound Books, 2002, for *Black Potatoes: The Story of the Great Irish Famine, 1845-1850.* Graduate Student Excellence in Research Award, Binghamton University, 2001; Outstanding Pennsylvania Author of the Year, Pennsylvania Library Association, 2001.

## Writings

(With Elaine Slivinski Lisandrelli) *Easy Writer, Levels G and H* (textbook), ERA/CCR, Inc., 1987.
(With Elaine Slivinski Lisandrelli) *The Study Skills Workout* (textbook), Scott, Foresman, 1988.
*Silver at Night* (picture book), Crown Books (New York, NY), 1994.
*Growing Up in Coal Country* (nonfiction), Houghton (Boston, MA), 1996.
*Dancing with Dziadziu* (picture book), Harcourt (San Diego, CA), 1997.
*Kids on Strike!,* Houghton Mifflin (Boston, MA), 1999.
*No Man's Land: A Young Soldier's Story,* Blue Sky Press (New York, NY), 1999.
*A Coal Miner's Bride: The Diary of Anetka Kaminska,* Scholastic (New York, NY), 2000.
*Black Potatoes: The Story of the Great Irish Famine, 1845-1850,* Houghton Mifflin (Boston, MA), 2001.
*The Christmas Promise,* illustrated by David Christiana, Blue Sky Press (New York, NY), 2001.
*Nobody's Nosier Than a Cat* (picture book), Harcourt (San Diego, CA), in press.

Also author of numerous textbooks, commissioned by the National Education Corporation, on composition, grammar, child abuse, medical assistance, and other topics. Author of two screenplays, *Wooden Angel* (1988) and *The Seed* (1989), produced on CTVN. Stories have appeared in *Highlights for Children* and *Turtle Magazine;* and "Backyard Zoo" appeared in *The Favorites* (Institute of Children's Literature, 1991). Stories and educational articles have appeared in *Middle School Journal,* in Kendall/Hunt anthologies, and in *Highlights for Children* anthologies.

## Sidelights

Susan Campbell Bartoletti writes stories that empower the young, and novels, nonfiction, and picture books that inspire and nudge young readers to look into history and see themselves in its reflection. Often using her native Pennsylvania as the setting for her books, Bartoletti has made a specialty of labor history, more specifically of tales from the coal mines that warren the underworld of Pennsylvania.

Hers are not the usual tales of the coal miner himself, or of the rapacious coal owners; rather Bartoletti focuses on what she terms the "gaps" in history—untold stories of the women and children of the coal mining era. With her nonfiction books, *Growing Up in Coal Country* and *Kids on Strike!,* she delves into the world of child labor in the anthracite coal industry. In fiction titles such as *A Coal Miner's Bride: The Diary of Anetka Kaminska,* Bartoletti relates the hardships and political turmoil of one coal mining community through the eyes of a young immigrant girl. In her debut picture book, *Silver at Night,* she tells the story of her husband's grandfather who immigrated from Italy and spent nearly half a century in the mines.

But the versatile Bartoletti has gone further afield for both fiction and nonfiction: to the American Civil War for *No Man's Land: A Young Soldier's Story,* and to Ireland for *Black Potatoes: The Story of the Great Irish Famine, 1845-1850.* "I let my instinct tell me whether the story is fiction or nonfiction, picture book or novel," Bartoletti noted in *Meet Authors and Illustrators.* But regardless of the genre, Bartoletti's message remains the same: "Many books show kids as disenfranchised victims," Bartoletti related in an interview with *Authors and Artists for Young Adults (AAYA).* "But that is not the whole story. In the coal mines, in the Civil War, there were many who fought for their rights. They weren't powerless. They did not always need adults to lead the way. And it's important that kids get that message. For their future, they need to see that other kids have power and can be powerful."

Born in Harrisburg, Pennsylvania, in 1958, Bartoletti and her family moved several times after the death of the father of the family in 1959. Basically, she grew up in the countryside outside of Scranton, Pennsylvania, enjoying the freedom of open land with few urban restrictions placed on her. Two main pastimes ordered her young life. "I loved to read and draw as a kid," Bartoletti told *AAYA.* "Those were my main passions. Writing was secondary to any art that I was working on at the moment." Ironically, for a writer who would later make her mark mining the ore of the past, history was not Bartoletti's favorite subject in school. "I used to complain a lot about history class," Bartoletti recalled in her interview. "I was a real whiner. I guess it serves me right that later I not only chose to write history, but I also married a history teacher and have a history teacher for a son-in-law."

Bartoletti took early encouragement in reading from her mother, who started reading to her children before they could even hold a book. Favorite titles included *Tom Sawyer, The Jungle Book, Little Women, Harriet the Spy,* the "Nancy Drew" books, and "The Little House on the Prairie" books. "But I would read anything," Bartoletti noted. "When you really love to read you'll read lists, even cereal boxes. And even though I complained about history class, I read lots of history as a kid, both nonfiction and fiction." The world of art and books were her domain.

A good student in school, Bartoletti also had an independent mind and was not afraid to speak up for herself and others. "My mother would say that I was not afraid to stand up for a person who needed a friend. There was so much that I remember about growing up. I also loved horses and the space and time I had growing up in the country. Today parents tend to fill up their kids' lives with all sorts of activities. Children don't get enough time to be alone, to enjoy solitude and develop fantasy in their lives."

By eighth grade, Bartoletti was beginning to show a talent for writing, becoming editor of her school newspaper. However, her interest in art was not left behind: she also designed the masthead for the paper.

"It's funny, though," Bartoletti recalled, "I never had a teacher from grade school through high school tell me that I was a good writer. I was always winning awards and contests for my art; I was recognized for my art." Growing weary of the high school routine, Bartoletti decided as a sixteen-year-old junior to enter college. "I majored in art in college. But suddenly there were lots of other kids who had won contests, and seeing their work I quickly became less confident. I got good grades in my art classes, but I could see the difference in talent between me and some of the others." Meanwhile she was earning high praise from her composition instructor, with her essays read aloud as models. "So I switched majors," Bartoletti recalled. "I became an English major. It was meant to be."

Bartoletti's life proceeded in overdrive. Sixteen when she entered college, she was eighteen and a junior in college when she married, a student teacher by nineteen, and out of college in her first teaching job by age twenty. "I didn't think I was going to like teaching in a junior high where I got my first job," Bartoletti told *AAYA.* "I figured I would rather teach older kids. And it was a strange beginning. Here I was not much older than

*Ridden with guilt for not saving his father from an alligator attack, fourteen-year-old Thrasher joins the Okefinokee Rifles to fight alongside General Stonewall Jackson and prove his manhood. (Cover painting by David Shannon.)*

some of the kids who had been held back a year or two. But I loved the teaching. I stayed with it for eighteen years."

Bartoletti soon was blending her enjoyment of writing with her teaching, creating textbooks which employed techniques she developed. "I didn't usually like the teacher packets that accompanied many of our reading materials," Bartoletti recalled. "I liked the way I developed my courses better, and soon I saw that in fact there were gaps in the curriculum. That's what any writer does, actually. Sees where something is needed and then does it. That's how I got started with textbooks." She has written and coauthored a score of texts on subjects from study skills and writing to grammar and medical assistance.

"I enjoyed writing texts," Bartoletti commented, "and selling those books whetted my appetite for other kinds of writing. But there is no real story or narrative there, and I love story. So I began writing short stories. I love the challenge of writing fiction." Soon Bartoletti began selling this short fiction to various magazines, including *Highlights for Children.* When one of her stories, "No Man's Land," won a fiction contest in that magazine, Bartoletti began to think seriously about writing book-length fiction for children. Though she later adapted her award-winning short story into a juvenile novel, Bartoletti chose the picture book format for her first longer work. And for that work, she chose a subject that she had learned about from many dinner conversations with her husband's grandfather.

"*Silver at Night* was inspired by my husband's family, who were immigrant coal miners. His grandfather, Massimino Santarelli, came to the United States from Italy when he was nine, and he quit school at age eleven to work in the coal industry." This grandfather was full of stories of working in the mines, and the grandmother, Pearl, also had tales of being a miner's wife. Bartoletti gathered some of these stories for her picture book, and then shopped it to ten publishers before finding a home for it at Crown. *Silver at Night* tells the story of Massimino who leaves his country to make his fortune in the New World. He departs from his village and his one true love, promising that some day he will be a rich man with "gold in the morning and silver at night." In his new country, Massimino works in the coal mines by day and indeed at night he counts the silver coins he earns, and longs for his lost love. "First-time author Bartoletti throngs the simple story with an avalanche of fulsome imagery," noted a reviewer for *Publishers Weekly.*

"The reviews for that first book were not all that promising," Bartoletti related. "In fact, they stopped me creatively for several months. I started a quilt for my daughter as a creative outlet. But in the end, the quilt went unfinished and I went back to my writing." It took, however, another two years before her second book was published.

*A young girl and her father get a taste of hobo life in the 1930s in their search for a home.* (From Bartoletti's The Christmas Promise, *illustrated by David Christiana.*)

Bartoletti's first book led to an interest in the anthracite coal industry in general. As she read about the industry, she discovered one of those historical "gaps" she is always eager to fill with her own words. "As I began to read more and more about coal mining, I found that most books concentrated on what it was like to be a wealthy and powerful coal operator, or what the hardships were of being a miner. However, few told what it was like to be a child in that industry, and fewer still what it was like to be a female then." Bartoletti began reading newspapers of the period, magazines, autobiographies, diaries, interview transcripts of oral histories, and she also examined collections of photographs and even began collecting her own oral history interviews. These first-hand accounts of life in the coal fields excited her and showed her the way to new books.

In *Growing Up in Coal Country,* she writes "a concise, thoroughly researched account of working and living conditions in Pennsylvania coal towns," observed *Horn Book*'s Anne Deifendeifer. In the first half of the book, Bartoletti describes the various jobs around a coal camp, from those performed by young boys to those of the adult miners. In the next half of the book she details life in the company town. Much of this comes from first-person source material which "provides a refreshing . . . frame of reference," Deifendeifer noted. Full of anecdotes and personal histories, the book is also well illustrated with "compelling black-and-white photographs of children at work in the coal mines of northeastern Pennsylvania about 100 years ago," according to *Booklist*'s Hazel Rochman. These photos came from the well-known photographer Lewis Hine, who was hired by the National Child Labor Committee to document child labor in early twentieth-century America. Rochman also drew attention to the "heartfelt memories of long hours, hard labor, and extremely dangerous working conditions, as well as lighter accounts" in Bartoletti's transcripts and interviews. "As with most fine juvenile nonfiction," Rochman concluded, "this will also have great appeal for adults." *Growing Up in Coal Country* won numerous awards, including a Golden Kite Honor Book Award for Nonfiction, and continues to attract a readership that bridges the generations.

Turning her hand to picture books once again, Bartoletti tells the story of Gabriella, who dances for her beloved grandmother, Babci. *Dancing with Dziadziu* is another book dealing with family history, this time with the impending death of a cherished grandmother. "Far from sad," wrote a contributor for *Publishers Weekly,* "the story is largely a celebration of Babci's life as a Polish immigrant." The same reviewer called this picture book a "mellifluously written tale" with a "motif of rebirth" woven into it with the family's early Easter celebration before the death of Babci. Reviewing the picture book in *Booklist,* Karen Morgan noted, "In direct and uncomplicated language and through a series of flashbacks, Bartoletti captures the spirit of love and caring across generations." Further picture books from Bartoletti include *The Christmas Promise,* about a Depression-era father and daughter in search of a home, and *Nobody's Nosier Than a Cat.*

In 1998 Bartoletti quit teaching eighth-grade English to commit herself to writing full time and to earn her doctorate in creative writing. One of her first publications thereafter was the reworking of her prize-winning short story, "No Man's Land," about a makeshift baseball game between young Rebel and Yankee soldiers under a private truce during the Civil War. In the novel *No Man's Land,* she tells the story of fourteen-year-old Thrasher McGee who lies about his age to join the army to fight for the Confederacy. Searching for heroic adventures, Thrasher at first finds mostly boredom waiting for the battle. Arriving too late for one battle, Thrasher and his comrades are detailed the gory job of burying the dead. Echoing the original short story, one chapter details friendly relations between Yanks and Rebels until they are forced to fight each other once again. In the final climactic battle, Thrasher loses his arm and what little illusions he has left about the glory of warfare. "Bartoletti compellingly and carefully crafts her characters," noted a writer for *Publishers Weekly,* "especially the boys-turned-soldiers Thrasher, Baylor Frable and Trim LaFaye." The same reviewer concluded that Bartoletti "spins a history as fresh as the day it happened." *Booklist*'s Rochman also praised the novel,

calling attention to Bartoletti's "careful historical research."

With *Kids on Strike!* Bartoletti again deals with young kids facing difficult adult circumstances, this time in a nonfiction format. A further extension of her initial coal industry research, this book examines child labor from 1836 to the early twentieth century told through the stories of kids who rebelled against unfair working conditions. "I found the true stories of kids who discovered power when they banded together for a common cause," Bartoletti wrote in *Book Links.* "Sometimes they won big.... Sometimes they helped their parents win.... Sometimes they won small.... Often they did not win at all." Examining strikes from the New York bootblack action of 1899 to the Pennsylvania anthracite coals strikes of 1900 and 1902 and the mill workers' strike in Lawrence, Massachusetts of 1913, Bartoletti focuses on the roles children played in such labor disputes. "Bartoletti has a gift for collecting stories with telling details," noted a contributor for *Publishers Weekly.* "Her dense but highly readable prose brings individual children and the struggles in which they engaged vividly to life." The same reviewer called *Kids on Strike!* "accessible and engrossing," and "tangible proof for would-be activists that children have made and continue to make a difference." Writing in *Booklist,* Hazel Rochman concluded, "Along with unforgettable photos by Lewis Hine and others on nearly every page, Bartoletti dramatizes the politics with individual stories of hardship and struggle." "As memorable as their inspiring stories are," commented a reviewer for *Horn Book,* "they represent just a few of the children who worked and battled for better lives."

Returning to fiction with *A Coal Miner's Bride: The Diary of Anetka Kaminska,* Bartoletti takes a "vivid and compelling look at the lives of Pennsylvania's immigrant coal miners and their families at the turn of the last century," wrote Valerie Diamond in a *School Library Journal* review. "I wrote about a spirited thirteen-year-old-girl," Bartoletti noted in *Book Links,* "whose father has arranged a marriage for her to ... a man she does not know in Lattimer, Pennsylvania." Anetka thus immigrates to America in 1896 and keeps a diary of her experiences in her new country. Anetka becomes a miner's wife and the stepmother to three children, recording the hardships of her life all the while. When her husband is killed soon after the marriage, Anetka must take in boarders to care for her small stepdaughters. Anetka soon falls in love with a labor organizer, Leon Nasevich, and things all come to a crisis during the Lattimer Massacre in which nineteen miners were killed during a march on September 10, 1987. "Bartoletti paints an accessible and evocative picture of life in a harsh era," Diamond concluded. Reviewing the novel in *Booklist,* Hazel Rochman commended this "dramatic" history, but found problems with the "format," wondering when the busy Anetka could find time to write in her diary. Rochman, however, went on to note that Bartoletti's historical note at the end "authenticates the account of the immigration, the labor struggle, the massacre, and the role of strong women."

Further approaches to nonfiction include *Black Potatoes: The Story of the Great Irish Famine, 1845-1850,* which also served as Bartoletti's doctoral dissertation. Researching the records and transcripts of oral history interviews in Dublin, she put together a presentation of the famine with a folklore basis, focusing again on personal stories, historical records and documents, and photographic illustrations to bring history alive for young readers. According to *Booklist*'s Hazel Rochman, "Bartoletti humanizes the big events by bringing the reader up close to the lives of ordinary people."

"Story comes first for me," Bartoletti, who gets up before five a.m. each day to begin writing, concluded in the *AAYA* interview. "I need to look at history in a way that makes sense, and one way of making sense is by following story, which is not always about chronology. . . . I choose a character or characters and I think that if I develop them honestly and truly, then readership will follow. But in the end, it is up to the individual reader to decide if I have succeeded. With these stories of hard times from another era, my primary goal is not just to let kids of today see how easy they have it. Rather my hope is that I can give kids hope and courage with these stories."

## Biographical and Critical Sources

### BOOKS

Bartoletti, Susan Campbell, *Silver at Night,* Crown Books (New York, NY), 1994.
Bartoletti, Susan Campbell, interview with J. Sydney Jones for *Authors and Artists for Young Adults,* Volume 44, Gale (Detroit, MI), 2002.

### PERIODICALS

*Book Links,* August-September, 2000, Susan Campbell Bartoletti, "Exploring the Gaps in History," pp. 16-21.
*Booklist,* November 1, 1994, p. 505; December 1, 1996, Hazel Rochman, review of *Growing Up in Coal Country,* p. 652; March 15, 1997, Karen Morgan, review of *Dancing with Dziadziu,* p. 1238; April 1, 1999, Hazel Rochman, review of *No Man's Land: A Young Soldier's Story,* p. 1424; December 1, 1999, Hazel Rochman, review of *Kids on Strike!,* p. 691; April 1, 2000, Hazel Rochman, review of *A Coal Miner's Wife: The Diary of Anetka Kaminska,* p. 1473; September 15, 2001, GraceAnne A. DeCandido, review of *The Christmas Promise,* p. 234; October 15, 2001, Hazel Rochman, review of *Black Potatoes: The Story of the Great Irish Famine,* p. 394.
*Horn Book,* March-April, 1997, Anne Deifendeifer, review of *Growing Up in Coal Country,* pp. 210-211; January-February, 2000, review of *Kids on Strike!,* p. 91; January-February, 2002, Margaret A. Bush, review of *Black Potatoes,* p. 91.
*Publishers Weekly,* November 14, 1994, review of *Silver at Night,* p. 67; February 10, 1997, review of *Dancing with Dziadziu,* p. 83; May 31, 1999, review of *No Man's Land: A Young Soldier's Story,* p. 94; November 29, 1999, review of *Kids on Strike!,* p. 72; September 24, 2001, review of *The Christmas Promise,* p. 53.

*School Library Journal,* November, 1994, p. 72; February, 1997, p. 109; May, 1997, p. 92; December, 1999, pp. 144-45; August, 2000, Valerie Diamond, review of *A Coal Miner's Bride: The Diary of Anetka Kaminska,* p. 177; October, 2001, review of *The Christmas Promise,* p. 62; November, 2001, Mary R. Hoffmann, review of *Black Potatoes,* p. 168.
*Scientific American,* December, 1997, p. 124.

### OTHER

*Meet Authors and Illustrators,* http://www.childrenslit.com/ (June 30, 2001).*

*　　*　　*

# BENDICK, Jeanne 1919-

## Personal

Born February 25, 1919, in New York, NY; daughter of Louis Xerxes (an inventor) and Amelia Maurice (Hess) Garfunkel; married Robert Louis Bendick (a television and film producer-director), November 24, 1940; children: Robert Louis, Jr., Karen Ann Watson Holton. *Education:* New York High School of Arts and Music; Parsons School of Design, B.A. 1939. *Politics:* Democrat. *Religion:* Jewish. *Hobbies and other interests:* Sailing, beachcombing, science, history and mysteries, cooking, Inuit art.

## Addresses

*Home*—80 Sea View #19, Guilford, CT 06437. *E-mail*—rlbendick@snet.net.

## Career

Author and illustrator. Trustee, Rye (NY) Free Reading Room. Illustrator for *Jack and Jill* and a fabric designer during the 1930s. Volunteer in American Women's Voluntary Services (AWVS) during World War II.

## Member

Authors Guild, Authors League of America, Writers Guild, National Science Teachers Association, American Library Association, Society of Children's Book Writers and Illustrators.

## Awards, Honors

Boy's Club Junior Book Awards, 1949, for *How Much and How Many: The Story of Weights and Measures,* and 1975; New York Academy of Sciences Children's Science Honor Book Awards, 1943, for *Let's Find Out: A Picture Science Book,* 1947, for *The First Book of Space Travel,* and 1974, for *Discovering Cycles;* Eva L. Gordon Award, American Nature Society, 1975.

## Writings

### BOOKS FOR CHILDREN

*The Future Explorers' Club Meets Here,* illustrations by Joan Paley, Ginn (Boston, MA), 1973.

*Why Things Change: The Story of Evolution,* illustrations by daughter, Karen Bendick Watson, Parents' Magazine Press (New York, NY), 1973.

(With husband, Robert L. Bendick) *The Consumer's Catalog of Economy and Ecology,* illustrations by K. B. Watson, McGraw (New York, NY), 1974.

*Ginn Science Program* (teacher's edition for grades K-4), Volumes 1-3, Ginn (Boston, MA), 1975.

*Exploring an Ocean Tide Pool,* photographs by R. Bendick, Garrard (Champaign, IL), 1976, revised and enlarged edition, Holt (New York, NY), 1992.

*The Big Strawberry Book of Astronomy,* illustrations by Sal Murdocca, Strawberry Books/Larouse (New York, NY), 1979.

*The Big Strawberry Book of the Earth: Our Ever-Changing Planet,* illustrations by M. Luppold Junkins, McGraw (New York, NY), 1980.

*Caves! Underground Worlds,* illustrated by Todd Telander, Henry Holt (New York, NY), 1995.

(With Robert L. Bendick) *Markets: From Barter to Bar Codes,* F. Watts (New York, NY), 1997.

### AUTHOR AND ILLUSTRATOR; CHILDREN'S FICTION

*The Good Knight Ghost,* F. Watts (New York, NY), 1956.

*The Blonk from beneath the Sea,* F. Watts (New York, NY), 1958.

### AUTHOR AND ILLUSTRATOR; CHILDREN'S NONFICTION

*Electronics for Boys and Girls,* McGraw (New York, NY), 1944, published as *Electronics for Young People,* 1947, revised edition with R. J. Lefkowitz, 1972.

(With Robert L. Bendick) *Making the Movies,* McGraw (New York, NY), 1945, rewritten as *Filming Works like This,* McGraw (New York, NY), 1970.

*How Much and How Many: The Story of Weights and Measures,* McGraw (New York, NY), 1947, revised edition, 1960, revised edition, F. Watts (New York, NY), 1989.

(With Robert L. Bendick) *Television Works like This,* McGraw (New York, NY), 1948, revised edition, 1965.

*All around You: A First Look at the World,* McGraw (New York, NY), 1951.

*What Could You See?: Adventures in Looking,* McGraw (New York, NY), 1957.

(With Barbara Berk) *How to Have a Show,* F. Watts (New York, NY), 1957.

(With Candy Bendick and Rob Bendick, Jr.) *Have a Happy Measle, a Merry Mumps, and a Cheery Chickenpox,* McGraw (New York, NY), 1958.

*Lightning,* Rand McNally (Chicago, IL), 1961.

(With Marcia Levin) *Take a Number; New Ideas + Imagination = More Fun,* McGraw (New York, NY), 1961.

*Archimedes and the Door of Science,* F. Watts (New York, NY), 1962, reprinted, Bethlehem Books (Warsaw, ND), 1995.

(With Marcia Levin) *Take Shapes, Lines, and Letters: New Horizons in Mathematics,* McGraw (New York, NY), 1962.

*A Fresh Look at Night,* F. Watts (New York, NY), 1963.

*Sea So Big, Ship So Small,* Rand McNally (Chicago, IL), 1963.

(With Marcia Levin) *Pushups and Pinups: Diet, Exercise, and Grooming for Young Teens,* McGraw (New York, NY), 1963.

(With Leonard Simon) *The Day the Numbers Disappeared,* McGraw (New York, NY), 1963.

*The Wind,* Rand McNally (Chicago, IL), 1964.

*The Shape of the Earth,* Rand McNally (Chicago, IL), 1965.

(With Marcia Levin) *Illustrated Mathematics Dictionary,* McGraw (New York, NY), 1965, revised edition published as *Mathematics Illustrated Dictionary: Facts, Figures, and People,* F. Watts (New York, NY), 1989.

(With M. Levin) *New Mathematics Workbooks: Sets and Addition; Sets and Subtraction; Sets and Multiplication; Sets and Division,* Grosset (New York, NY), 1965.

*The Emergency Book,* Rand McNally (Chicago, IL), 1967.

*Shapes,* F. Watts (New York, NY), 1967.

(With Marian Warren) *What to Do?: Everyday Guides for Everyone,* McGraw (New York, NY), 1967.

*The Human Senses,* F. Watts (New York, NY), 1968.

*Space and Time,* F. Watts (New York, NY), 1968.

*Living Things,* F. Watts (New York, NY), 1969.

*Why Can't I?,* McGraw (New York, NY), 1969.

*A Place to Live: A Study of Ecology,* Parents' Magazine Press (New York, NY), 1970.

*Adaptation,* F. Watts (New York, NY), 1971.

*How to Make a Cloud,* Parents' Magazine Press (New York, NY), 1971.

*Measuring,* F. Watts (New York, NY), 1971.

*Names, Sets, and Numbers,* F. Watts (New York, NY), 1971.

*What Made You You?,* McGraw (New York, NY), 1971.

*Motion and Gravity,* F. Watts (New York, NY), 1972.

*Observation,* F. Watts (New York, NY), 1972.

*Why Things Work: A Book about Energy,* additional illustrations by daughter, Karen Bendick, Parents' Magazine Press (New York, NY), 1972.

*Heat and Temperature,* F. Watts (New York, NY), 1974.

*Solids, Liquids, and Gases,* F. Watts (New York, NY), 1974.

*Ecology,* F. Watts (New York, NY), 1974.

*How Heredity Works: Why Living Things Are as They Are,* Parents' Magazine Press (New York, NY), 1975.

*How Animals Behave,* Parents' Magazine Press (New York, NY), 1976.

*The Mystery of the Loch Ness Monster,* McGraw (New York, NY), 1976.

(With R. Bendick) *Finding out about Jobs: TV Reporting,* Parents' Magazine Press (New York, NY), 1976.

*Putting the Sun to Work,* Garrard (Champaign, IL), 1980.

*Super People: Who Will They Be?,* McGraw (New York, NY), 1980.

*Elementary Science* (teacher's edition with activities book), Volume 6, Ginn (Boston, MA), 1980.

*Scare a Ghost, Tame a Monster,* Westminster Press (Philadelphia, PA), 1983.

*Egyptian Tombs,* F. Watts (New York, NY), 1987.

*Tombs of the Early Americans,* F. Watts (New York, NY), 1992.

*Markets,* F. Watts (New York, NY), 1995.

*Along Came Galileo,* Beautiful Feet (Sandwich, MA), 1999.

*Galen and the Door to Medicine,* Bethlehem Books (Warsaw, ND), 2003.

*"FIRST BOOK" SERIES FOR CHILDREN*

(Illustrator) Campbell Tatham (pseudonym of Mary Elting), *The First Book of Boats,* F. Watts, 1945, rewritten by Margaret Gossett, 1953.

(Illustrator) Campbell Tatham, *The First Book of Trains,* F. Watts (New York, NY), 1948, rewritten by Russell Hamilton, 1956.

(Illustrator) Campbell Tatham, *The First Flying Book,* F. Watts (New York, NY), 1948, new edition by Mary Elting published as *The First Flying Book by Campbell Tatham,* 1948, published as *The First Book of Flight,* F. Watts (New York, NY), 1958.

*Bendick's self-illustrated biography of this ancient Greek mathematician, his principles, and inventions includes the experiment that resulted in his famous shout of "Eureka!"*

(Illustrator) Campbell Tatham, *The First Book of Automobiles,* F. Watts (New York, NY), 1949, revised edition written and illustrated by Bendick, 1966, revised again as *Automobiles,* 1984.

(Illustrator) Benjamin Brewster (pseudonym of Mary Elting), *First Book of Baseball,* F. Watts (New York, NY), 1950, revised edition by Franklin Folsom published as *Baseball by Benjamin Brewster,* 4th revised edition, F. Watts (New York, NY), 1970.

(Author and illustrator) *The First Book of Airplanes,* California State Department of Education (Sacramento, CA), 1950, revised edition, F. Watts (New York, NY), 1976, published as *Airplanes,* 1982.

(Illustrator) Benjamin Brewster, *The First Book of Firemen,* F. Watts (New York, NY), 1951.

(Author and illustrator) *The First Book of Space Travel,* F. Watts (New York, NY), 1953, revised edition published as *Space Travel,* 1969.

(Illustrator) *The First Book of Supermarkets,* F. Watts (New York, NY), 1954.

(Illustrator) *The First Book of Ships,* F. Watts (New York, NY), 1959.

(Author, with Barbara Berk, and illustrator) *The First Book of Costume and Makeup,* F. Watts (New York, NY), 1960.

(Author, with Barbara Berk, and illustrator) *The First Book of How to Fix It,* F. Watts (New York, NY), 1961.

(Author and illustrator) *The First Book of Time,* F. Watts (New York, NY), 1963.

(Author and illustrator) *The First Book of Fishes,* F. Watts (New York, NY), 1965.

(Author and illustrator) *Artificial Satellites,* F. Watts (New York, NY), 1983.

*"EARLY BIRD ASTRONOMY" SERIES*

(And illustrator) *Artificial Satellites: Helpers in Space,* Millbrook Press (Brookfield, CT), 1991.

(And illustrator) *Comets and Meteors: Visitors from Space,* Millbrook Press (Brookfield, CT), 1991.

(And illustrator) *Moons and Rings: Companions to the Planets,* Millbrook Press (Brookfield, CT), 1991.

*The Planets: Neighbors in Space,* illustrated by Caroline Brodie, Millbrook Press (Brookfield, CT), 1991.

*The Stars: Lights in the Night Sky,* illustrated by Caroline Brodie, Millbrook Press (Brookfield, CT), 1991.

*The Sun: Our Very Own Star,* illustrated by Caroline Brodie, Millbrook Press (Brookfield, CT), 1991.

*The Universe: Think Big,* illustrated by Caroline Brodie, Millbrook Press (Brookfield, CT), 1991.

*ILLUSTRATOR OF BOOKS FOR CHILDREN*

Carol Lynn, *Modeling for Money,* Greenberg (New York, NY), 1937.

Charles F. Martin and George M. Martin, *At West Point,* Heath (Boston, MA), 1943.

Mary Elting and Robert T. Weaver, *Soldiers, Sailors, Fliers, and Marines,* Doubleday (New York, NY), 1943.

Katherine Britton, *What Makes It Tick?,* Houghton (Boston, MA), 1943.

Mary Elting and Robert T. Weaver, *Battles: How They Are Won,* Doubleday (New York, NY), 1944.

Mary McBurney Green, *Everybody Has a House*, W. R. Scott (New York, NY), 1944.

Shirley Matthews, *The Airplane Book*, W. Roberts (Washington, DC), 1945.

Jeffrey Roberts, *The Fix-It Book*, W. Roberts (Washington, DC), 1945.

Eleanor Clymer, *The Grocery Mouse*, R. McBride (New York, NY), 1945.

Elizabeth Kinsey, *Teddy*, R. McBride (New York, NY), 1945.

Mary Elting and Margaret Gossett, *We Are the Government*, Doubleday (New York, NY), 1945.

Mary Elting, *The Lollypop Factory*, Doubleday (New York, NY), 1946.

Herman and Nina Schneider, *Let's Find Out: A Picture Science Book*, Scott (New York, NY), 1946.

Eleanor Clymer, *The Country Kittens*, McBride (New York, NY), 1947.

Herman and Nina Schneider, *Your Telephone and How It Works*, McGraw (New York, NY), 1947.

John Ernest Bechdolt, *Going Up: The Story of Vertical Transportation*, Abingdon-Cokesbury (New York, NY), 1948.

Will Rogow, *The Fix-It Book: Big Pictures and Little Stories about Carpenters, Mechanics, Welders, Tailors, and Lots of Others*, W. Roberts (Washington, DC), 1949.

Herman Schneider, *Everyday Machines and How They Work*, McGraw (New York, NY), 1950.

Herman Schneider, *Everyday Weather and How It Works*, McGraw (New York, NY), 1951.

Dorothy Canfield Fisher, *A Fair World for All*, McGraw (New York, NY), 1952.

Joseph Leeming, *Real Book about Easy Music-Making*, Garden City Books (New York, NY), 1952.

Lynn Poole, *Today's Science and You*, McGraw (New York, NY), 1952.

Herman and Nina Schneider, *Science Fun with Milk Cartons*, McGraw (New York, NY), 1953.

Glenn Orlando Blough, *The Tree on the Road to Turntown*, McGraw (New York, NY), 1953.

Glenn Orlando Blough, *Not Only for Ducks: The Story of Rain*, McGraw (New York, NY), 1954.

Julius Schwartz, *Through the Magnifying Glass*, McGraw (New York, NY), 1954.

Glenn Orlando Blough, *Wait for the Sunshine: The Story of Seasons and Growing Things*, McGraw (New York, NY), 1954.

Lynn Poole, *Diving for Science*, McGraw (New York, NY), 1955.

Glenn Orlando Blough, *Lookout for the Forest: A Conservation Story*, McGraw (New York, NY), 1955.

John Perry, *Our Wonderful Eyes*, McGraw (New York, NY), 1955.

Glenn Orlando Blough, *After the Sun Goes Down: The Story of Animals at Night*, McGraw (New York, NY), 1956.

Herman and Nina Schneider, *Let's Find Out*, W. Scott, 1956.

(With Bob Beane) William Harry Crouse, *Understanding Science*, McGraw (New York, NY), 1956, 4th edition, 1973.

Glenn Orlando Blough, *Who Lives in This House?: A Story of Animal Families*, McGraw (New York, NY), 1957.

Glenn Orlando Blough, *Young People's Book of Science*, McGraw (New York, NY), 1958.

George Barr, *Young Scientist Takes a Walk: A Guide to Outdoor Observations*, McGraw (New York, NY), 1959.

Glenn Orlando Blough, *Soon after September: The Story of Living Things in Winter*, McGraw (New York, NY), 1959.

Earl Schenck Miers, *The Storybook of Science*, Rand McNally (Chicago, IL), 1959.

George Barr, *Young Scientist Takes a Walk*, McGraw (New York, NY), 1959.

Glenn Orlando Blough, *Christmas Trees and How They Grow*, McGraw (New York, NY), 1961.

Glenn Orlando Blough, *Who Lives in This Meadow?: A Story of Animal Life*, McGraw (New York, NY), 1961.

Glenn Orlando Blough, *Who Lives at the Seashore?: Animal Life along the Shore*, McGraw (New York, NY), 1962.

Glenn Orlando Blough, *Bird Watchers and Bird Feeders*, McGraw (New York, NY), 1963.

Glenn Orlando Blough, *Discovering Plants*, McGraw (New York, NY), 1966.

Glenn Orlando Blough, *Discovering Insects*, McGraw (New York, NY), 1967.

Glenn Orlando Blough, *Discovering Cycles*, McGraw (New York, NY), 1973.

Sam and Beryl Epstein, *Saving Electricity*, Garrard (Champaign, IL), 1977.

*"EARLYBIRD ASTRONOMY" SERIES*

*Artificial Satellites: Helpers in Space*, illustrated by Mike Roffe, Millbrook (Brookfield, CT), 1991.

*Comets and Meteors: Visitors from Space*, illustrated by Mike Roffe, Millbrook (Brookfield, CT), 1991.

*The Planets: Neighbors in Space*, illustrated by Mike Roffe, Millbrook (Brookfield, CT), 1991.

*The Stars: Lights in the Night Sky*, illustrated by Chris Forsey, Millbrook (Brookfield, CT), 1991.

*The Sun: Our Very Own Star*, illustrated by Mike Roffe, Millbrook (Brookfield, CT), 1991.

*The Universe: Think Big!*, illustrated by Mike Roffe and Lynne Willey, Millbrook (Brookfield, CT), 1991.

*"INVENTING" SERIES; ILLUSTRATED BY SAL MURDOCCA*

*Eureka! It's an Airplane*, Millbrook (Brookfield, CT), 1992.

*Eureka! It's an Automobile*, Millbrook (Brookfield, CT), 1992.

*Eureka! It's a Telephone*, Millbrook (Brookfield, CT), 1993.

(With Robert Bendick) *Eureka! It's Television*, Millbrook (Brookfield, CT), 1993.

Author of filmstrips, *The Seasons* for the Society for Visual Education, and *You and Me and Our World, Monsters and Other Science Mysteries,* and *Dreams and Other Science Mysteries,* for Miller-Brody. Also author of multi-media educational program "Starting Points" for Ginn. Story editor and script writer of television programs for the National Broadcasting Company

(NBC-TV), *The First Look,* 1965-66, and *Giant Step,* 1968, plus a segment for *20/20* for the American Broadcasting Companies (ABC-TV) entitled "Evolution/Creation"; associate producer of documentary for public television, *Fight for Food.* Contributor to *Britannica Junior Encyclopaedia, Book of Knowledge,* and other publications.

## Sidelights

An acclaimed author and illustrator of children's books, Jeanne Bendick is especially regarded for her introductory science books. Comprehensive research combined with clearly written text and simple illustrations mark her work, much of which clarifies the areas of television, movies, time, shapes, numbers, ecology, astronomy, heredity and science history for young readers, and encourages them toward higher levels of understanding.

Bendick's mother was sixteen when her family, some of whom had emigrated from France to settle in the Louisiana Territory, moved from Alabama to New York, where Bendick was born. Both of her maternal grandfathers were veterans of the U.S. Civil War; and her paternal grandfather emigrated from Europe when he was fourteen, adopting the name of the childless couple to whom the immigration officer had assigned him. By the time he was nineteen, though, he had learned the English language, saved a considerable sum of money, married, and opened a restaurant—one of the first cafeterias, which later became a chain. It is to her mother's father, however, that Bendick owes special gratitude. He was an artist who taught her how to draw, demanding her best efforts. He also spent countless hours drawing for her and escorting her to the American Museum of Natural History on Sundays. "Grandpa Charley was my hero," Bendick once recalled, adding that he was "a scholar and an artist, gentle, patient, full of humor, and endlessly generous with his time."

Bendick has fond memories of living in New York City. Her father, who had dreams of becoming a writer before he eventually entered the restaurant business with his father, graduated in 1917 from Columbia with such luminaries as George Gershwin. "I'm told that one night, when I was very small, George Gershwin was at the house, playing *An American in Paris,* which he had just written," recalls Bendick. "I put my hands over my ears, said firmly, 'Too noisy!' and marched out of the room." She also remembers the summer weeks her family would vacation at a farm in the mountains. It was there that she met a woman who opened up her enormous library to her. "I read my way up one shelf and down another," says Bendick. "I read books I understood and books whose meanings only glimmered in my head, but I loved the words."

The 1930s were difficult times for most people, including Bendick's family. Her father's father maintained a bread line throughout that period but lost most of his own restaurants before the Depression was over. Bendick helped teach a children's class in art on weekends and illustrated a children's magazine, *Jack and Jill,* to

help pay her tuition to the Parsons School of Design. She graduated in 1939, winning a scholarship to study in Paris for a year; but with war raging in Europe, she decided against leaving home. She had also become engaged that year to Robert Bendick, whom she married a year later. Her husband, a photographer, entered the field of television by becoming one of the first three cameramen at the emerging CBS-TV network. Soon after the United States entered the war, though, he enlisted in the Army Air Forces and Bendick offered her services to the American Women's Voluntary Services (AWVS). According to Bendick, she and her husband decided to work jointly on a project while he was away—*Making the Movies,* which they rewrote twenty-five years later as *Filming Works like This.* Through the years, Bendick has worked with her husband, who is an illustrator, on other projects, as well as with her son and daughter.

It was while her husband was in the service, though, that she developed an interest in the new science of electronics. An inability to find a simple, instructive book on electronics prompted her to write *Electronics for Boys and Girls,* which she has since revised, like several other books, to keep pace with the advances of technology. Bendick has worked closely with the "First Book" science series for children by Franklin Watts, which served as the basis for NBC-TV's series *The First Look,* on which she was also story editor and script writer. In addition to working extensively on the "Early Bird Astronomy" series for Millbrook Press, she has written three volumes for the Ginn science program. Author and/or illustrator of more than one hundred books, Bendick has not only helped to introduce young readers to the field of science, but she has helped to make that field less intimidating as well.

In an essay in *Science and Children,* Bendick expressed her belief that "text and pictures should complement, not duplicate each other," adding that "one of the best things any illustrator can give to a picture is his own viewpoint—the special way he sees things." Before Bendick draws any picture to illustrate a scientific principle, she always builds a model of what she will be drawing to make sure that it really works. And she admits that although she is "certainly not the best artist in the world," children respond well to her illustrations. She once commented, "Children sometimes write to me saying that they like my pictures because I've drawn things the way *they* would draw them. Children do see things in another way from adults. I think that's because they look for different things. So when I draw and when I write, I try to look at the world their way and my way so that I end up with *our* way of seeing the world around us."

In a review of *A Place to Live,* Bendick's book about conservation and the environment, Della Thomas wrote in *School Library Journal,* "As usual, this author's simple but expressive pictures of active children keep readers' attention and help them to better appreciate the ideas in the text." Beryl B. Beatley concluded in her *Appraisal* review of *How Animals Behave,* "Bendick is a born teacher for she knows how to stimulate interest and make a book both interesting and attractive without boring the reader." Carolyn Phelan, a reviewer in *Booklist,* recommended Bendick's collaboration with her husband, *Markets: From Barter to Bar Codes* as having "some strengths for social studies units."

"I am not, by training, a scientist," Bendick once said. "Maybe what I am is a translator. I enjoy taking a complex science concept, breaking it down into components simple enough for *me* to understand, and then writing it that way for young people." Bendick indicated that she has tried to help children grasp the mysteries of the natural. "One part of the job I set for myself is to make those young readers see that everything is connected to everything—that science isn't something apart. It's a part of everyday life. It has been that way since the beginning. The things the earliest scientists learned were the building blocks for those who came after. Sometimes they accepted earlier ideas. Sometimes they questioned them and challenged them. I want to involve readers directly in the text so they will ask themselves questions and try to answer them. If they can't answer, that's not really important.... Questions are more important than answers. Who knows, in science, what will happen next to change everything? If I were a fairy godmother, my gift to every child would be curiosity."

## Biographical and Critical Sources

### BOOKS

*Books for Children, 1960-65,* American Library Association (Chicago, IL), 1966.
*The Children's Bookshelf,* Child Study Association of America/Bantam (New York, NY), 1965.
*Children's Literature Review,* Volume 5, Gale (Detroit, MI), 1983.
Fisher, Margery, *Matters of Fact: Aspects of Non-Fiction for Children,* Harper (New York, NY), 1972.
*Good Books for Children,* edited by Mary K. Eakin, Phoenix Books (Chicago, IL), 1966.
Hopkins, Lee Bennett, *Books Are by People,* Citation Press (New York, NY), 1969.
*Illustrators of Children's Books: 1957-1966,* Horn Book (Boston, MA), 1968.
Larrick, Nancy, *A Teacher's Guide to Children's Books,* Merrill (Columbus, OH), 1966.
Larrick, Nancy, *A Parent's Guide to Children's Reading,* 3rd edition, Doubleday (New York, NY), 1969.
*Something about the Author Autobiography Series,* Volume 4, Gale (Detroit, MI), 1987.
Sutherland, Zena, *The Best in Children's Books,* University of Chicago Press (Chicago, IL), 1973.
Sutherland, Zena, Diane L. Monson, and May Hill Arbuthnot, *Children and Books,* 6th edition, Scott, Foresman (Glenview, IL), 1981.

### PERIODICALS

*Appraisal,* spring 1972; fall 1972; spring 1977, Beryl Beatley, review of *How Animals Behave,* pp. 12-13; spring 1980; winter 1981.
*Atlantic,* December, 1947.
*Children's Book Review,* February, 1971.

*Library Journal,* November 1, 1949; May 15, 1969; March, 1973.
*New York Times Book Review,* November 11, 1945.
*School Librarian and School Library Review,* July, 1964.
*School Library Journal,* November, 1970, Della Thomas, review of *A Place to Live,* p. 96.
*Science and Children,* April, 1973, Jeanne Bendick, "Illustrating Science Books for Children," pp. 20-21.
*Science Books,* September, 1973; March, 1974; March, 1975.
*Science Books and Films,* March-April, 1981.

\*      \*      \*

## BENSON, Mildred Augustine Wirt 1905-2002

*OBITUARY NOTICE*—See index for *SATA* sketch: Born July 10, 1905, in Ladora, IA; died May 28, 2002, in Toledo, OH. Author and journalist. Mildred Augustine Wirt Benson authored more than 130 books, including many popular series under other pseudonyms. She is best known for creating the Nancy Drew character, whose series is still in print and has sold over 200 million books. Benson, who wrote 23 of the 30 stories in the original Nancy Drew series, signed contracts stipulating she was not to receive any royalties from the series, was legally bound to keep her identity as the author a secret, and received about 125 dollars per book. She earned her master's degree in journalism from the University of Iowa in 1927 and married Asa Wirt, an Associated Press journalist. Around this time she penned the "Ruth Fielding Mystery Stories," the "Ruth Darrow Flying Stories," the "Mildred A. Wirt Mystery Stories," "Trailer Stories for Girls," half the "Penny Parker" mysteries, and the "Doris Force," "Madge Sterling," "Kay Tracey," "Penny Nichols," and "Honeybunch" series. In 1944 she began reporting for Toledo newspapers, but continued to write prolifically under her own name and various pseudonyms, including the male pseudonym Don Palmer for her "Boy Scouts Explorers" series. Three years after Wirt's death in 1947, Mildred married George Benson, editor of the *Toledo Times;* he died in 1959. She continued working as a journalist, held commercial, private, seaplane, and instrument pilot licenses, and cultivated an avid interest in pre-Columbian archaeology. Benson wrote a daily column for the *Toledo Blade* up until the day she died.

*OBITUARIES AND OTHER SOURCES:*

*PERIODICALS*

*Houston Chronicle* (Houston, TX), May 30, 2002, p. 1.
*New York Times,* May 30, 2002, p. A23.
*San Francisco Chronicle,* June 1, 2002, p. D3.
*USAToday.com,* http://www.usatoday.com (June 2, 2002).

# BERENSTAIN, Jan(ice) 1923-

## Personal

Born July 26, 1923, in Philadelphia, PA; daughter of Alfred J. and Marian (Beck) Grant; married Stanley Berenstain (an author and illustrator), April 13, 1946; children: Leo, Michael. *Education:* Attended Philadelphia College of Art, 1941-45.

## Addresses

*Home*—Bucks County, PA. *Agent*—Sterling Lord, Sterling Lord Literistic Inc., 65 Bleecker St., New York, NY 10012.

## Career

Author and illustrator. Creator, with husband, Stan Berenstain, of "It's All in the Family," an illustrated feature first published in *McCall's,* (1956-69) and then in *Good Housekeeping,* (1970-90). *Exhibitions:* Work exhibited in Metropolitan Museum of Art international exhibition of cartoons, and in an exhibition of British and American humorous art in London, England. Works represented in the Albert T. Reid Cartoon Collection at the University of Kansas, the Farrell Library Collection at Kansas State University, and Syracuse University in New York.

## Awards, Honors

School Bell Award, National Education Association, 1960, for distinguished service in the interpretation of education in a national magazine; British Book Centre honor book, 1968, for *Inside, Outside, Upside Down;* Best Book Award, American Institute of Graphic Arts, 1970, for *The Bear Scouts;* University of Chicago Center for Children's Books named *Bears in the Night* a best book of 1972, and *He Bear, She Bear* a best book of 1974; Philadelphia Library Children's Reading Round Table honor book, 1972, for *Bears in the Night,* 1973, for *The Bears' Almanac: A Year in Bear Country— Holidays, Seasons, Weather, Actual Facts about Snow, Wind, Rain, Thunder, Lightning, the Sun, the Moon, and Lots More,* 1974, for *He Bear, She Bear,* 1976, for *The Bears' Nature Guide,* 1980, for *The Berenstain Bears and the Missing Dinosaur Bone,* 1982, for *The Berenstain Bears Visit the Dentist,* 1983, for *The Berenstain Bears in the Dark, The Berenstain Bears Go to Camp,* and *The Berenstain Bears and the Truth,* 1984, for *The Berenstain Bears and Too Much TV,* 1985, for *The Berenstain Bears Learn about Strangers,* 1987, for *The Berenstain Bears Go Out for the Team,* 1988, for *The Day of the Dinosaur,* and 1989, for *After the Dinosaurs;* Children's Book of the Year, Child Study Association of America, 1977, for *The Berenstain Bears' Science Fair,* and 1982, for *The Berenstain Bears Go to the Doctor, The Berenstain Bears Visit the Dentist, The Berenstain Bears and the Sitter,* and *The Berenstain Bears' Moving Day.*

Silver Diploma, International Film and Television Festival (Naples, Italy), 1980, for *The Berenstain Bears' Christmas Tree;* Silver Award, International Film and Television Festival (New York, NY), 1980, for *The Berenstain Bears' Christmas Tree,* 1982, for *The Berenstain Bears' Comic Valentine,* and 1987, for *The Berenstain Bears' CBS Show;* Young Readers' Award, Michigan Council of Teachers of English, 1981, for *Bears in the Night;* Drexel Citation, Drexel University, School of Library and Information Science, 1982, for "contributions to children's literature"; Children's Classic Award, International Reading Association, 1982, for *The Berenstain Bears Go to the Doctor* and *The Berenstain Bears Visit the Dentist,* 1983, for *The Berenstain Bears Get in a Fight, The Berenstain Bears Go to Camp,* and *The Berenstain Bears in the Dark,* 1984, for *The Berenstain Bears and the Messy Room,* and *The Berenstain Bears and the Truth,* and 1987, for *The Berenstain Bears: No Girls Allowed;* Buckeye Award, Ohio State Library Association, Teachers of English, and International Reading Association, 1982, for *The Berenstain Bears and the Spooky Old Tree,* and 1985, for *The Berenstain Bears and the Messy Room;* Arizona Children's Choice Book Award nomination, and Arizona Young Reader's Award, both 1985, both for *The Berenstain Bears and the Messy Room;* Colorado Children's Choice Book Award nomination, 1985, for *The Berenstain Bears in the Dark;* Humanitas Certificate, 1987, for the television adaptation of *The Berenstain Bears Forget Their Manners;* Ludington Award, 1989, for "contributions to children's literature." The "Berenstain Bears" books have also won numerous awards from state library and reading associations.

## Writings

*AUTHOR AND ILLUSTRATOR WITH HUSBAND, STAN BERENSTAIN*

*The Berenstain's Baby Book,* Macmillan (New York, NY), 1951.
*Sister* (cartoons), Schuman, 1952.
*Tax-Wise,* Schuman, 1952.
*Marital Blitz,* Dutton (New York, NY), 1954.
*Baby Makes Four,* Macmillan (New York, NY), 1956.
*Lover Boy,* Macmillan (New York, NY), 1958.
*It's All in the Family,* Dutton (New York, NY), 1958.
*Bedside Lover Boy,* Dell (New York, NY), 1960.
*And Beat Him When He Sneezes,* McGraw (New York, NY), 1960, published as *Have a Baby, My Wife Just Had a Cigar,* Dell (New York, NY), 1960.
*Call Me Mrs.,* Macmillan (New York, NY), 1961.
*It's Still in the Family,* Dutton (New York, NY), 1961.
*Office Lover Boy,* Dell (New York, NY), 1962.
*The Facts of Life for Grown-ups,* Dell (New York, NY), 1963.
*Flipsville-Squaresville,* Dial (New York, NY), 1965.
*Mr. Dirty vs. Mr. Clean,* Dell (New York, NY), 1967.
*You Could Diet Laughing,* Dell (New York, NY), 1969.
*Be Good or I'll Belt You,* Dell (New York, NY), 1970.
*Education Impossible,* Dell (New York, NY), 1970.
*Never Trust Anyone over 13,* Bantam (New York, NY), 1970.

*Stan and Jan Berenstain*

*How to Teach Your Children about Sex without Making a Complete Fool of Yourself,* Dutton (New York, NY), 1970.

*How to Teach Your Children about God without Actually Scaring Them out of Their Wits,* Dutton (New York, NY), 1971.

*Are Parents for Real?,* Bantam (New York, NY), 1972.

*What Your Parents Never Told You About Being a Mom or Dad,* Crown, 1995.

*"BERENSTAIN BEARS" SERIES; AUTHOR AND ILLUSTRATOR WITH HUSBAND, STAN BERENSTAIN*

*The Big Honey Hunt* (also see below), Beginner Books (New York, NY), 1962.

*The Bike Lesson* (also see below), Beginner Books (New York, NY), 1964, reissued with cassette, 1987.

*The Bears' Picnic* (also see below), Beginner Books (New York, NY), 1966.

*The Bear Scouts* (also see below), Beginner Books (New York, NY), 1967.

*The Bears' Vacation* (also see below), Beginner Books (New York, NY), 1968, published in England as *The Bears' Holiday,* Harvill, 1969, reissued with cassette, Random House (New York, NY), 1987.

*Inside, Outside, Upside Down,* Random House (New York, NY), 1968.

*Bears on Wheels* (also see below), Random House (New York, NY), 1969.

*The Bears' Christmas* (also see below), Beginner Books (New York, NY), 1970, reissued with cassette, Random House (New York, NY), 1988.

*Old Hat, New Hat* (also see below), Random House (New York, NY), 1970.

*Bears in the Night* (also see below), Random House (New York, NY), 1971.

*The B Book,* Random House (New York, NY), 1971.

*C Is for Clown,* Random House (New York, NY), 1972, revised edition published as *Berenstain's C Book,* Beginner Books (New York, NY), 1997.

*The Bears' Almanac: A Year in Bear Country—Holidays, Seasons, Weather, Actual Facts about Snow, Wind, Rain, Thunder, Lightning, the Sun, the Moon, and Lots More* (also see below), Random House (New York, NY), 1973, published as *The Berenstain Bears' Almanac: A Year in Bear Country—Holidays, Seasons, Weather, Actual Facts about Snow, Wind, Rain, Thunder, Lightning, the Sun, the Moon, and Lots More,* 1984.

*The Berenstain Bears' Nursery Tales,* Random House (New York, NY), 1973.

*He Bear, She Bear* (also see below), Random House (New York, NY), 1974.

*The Berenstain Bears' New Baby* (also see below), Random House (New York, NY), 1974, reissued with cassette, 1985.

*The Bears' Nature Guide,* Random House (New York, NY), 1975, published as *The Berenstain Bears' Nature Guide,* 1984.

*The Bear Detectives: The Case of the Missing Pumpkin* (also see below), Random House (New York, NY), 1975, reissued with cassette, 1988.

*The Berenstain Bears' Counting Book,* Random House (New York, NY), 1976.

*The Berenstain Bears' Science Fair,* Random House (New York, NY), 1977.

*The Berenstain Bears and the Spooky Old Tree,* Random House (New York, NY), 1978.

*Papa's Pizza: A Berenstain Bear Sniffy Book,* Random House (New York, NY), 1978.

*The Berenstain Bears Go to School,* Random House (New York, NY), 1978, reissued with cassette, 1985.

*The Bears' Activity Book,* Random House (New York, NY), 1979.

*The Berenstain Bears and the Missing Dinosaur Bone,* Random House (New York, NY), 1980.

*The Berenstain Bears' Christmas Tree* (also see below), Random House (New York, NY), 1980.

*The Berenstain Bears and the Sitter* (also see below), Random House (New York, NY), 1981, reissued with cassette, 1985, reissued with puppet package, 1987.

*The Berenstain Bears Go to the Doctor* (also see below), Random House (New York, NY), 1981, reissued with cassette, 1985, reissued with puppet package, 1987.

*The Berenstain Bears' Moving Day,* Random House (New York, NY), 1981.

*The Berenstain Bears Visit the Dentist* (also see below), Random House (New York, NY), 1981, reissued with cassette, 1985, reissued with puppet package, 1987.

*The Berenstain Bears Get in a Fight,* Random House (New York, NY), 1982, reissued with puppet package, 1987, reissued with cassette, 1988.

*The Berenstain Bears Go to Camp,* Random House (New York, NY), 1982, reissued with cassette, 1989.

*The Berenstain Bears in the Dark* (also see below), Random House (New York, NY), 1982.

*The Berenstain Bears and the Messy Room* (also see below), Random House (New York, NY), 1983, reissued with puppet package, 1987.

*The Berenstain Bears and the Truth,* Random House (New York, NY), 1983, reissued with puppet package, 1988.

*The Berenstain Bears and the Wild, Wild Honey,* Random House (New York, NY), 1983.

*The Berenstain Bears' Soccer Star,* Random House (New York, NY), 1983.

*The Berenstain Bears Go Fly a Kite,* Random House (New York, NY), 1983.

*The Berenstain Bears to the Rescue,* Random House (New York, NY), 1983.

*The Berenstain Bears' Trouble with Money,* Random House (New York, NY), 1983.

*The Berenstain Bears' Make and Do Book,* Random House (New York, NY), 1984.

*The Berenstain Bears and the Big Election,* Random House (New York, NY), 1984.

*The Berenstain Bears and Too Much TV* (also see below), Random House (New York, NY), 1984, reissued with cassette, 1989.

*The Berenstain Bears Shoot the Rapids,* Random House (New York, NY), 1984.

*The Berenstain Bears and the Neighborly Skunk,* Random House (New York, NY), 1984.

*The Berenstain Bears and the Dinosaurs,* Random House (New York, NY), 1984.

*The Berenstain Bears Meet Santa Bear,* Random House (New York, NY), 1984, reissued with puppet package, 1988, reissued with cassette, 1989.

*The Berenstain Bears and Mama's New Job,* Random House (New York, NY), 1984.

*The Berenstain Bears and Too Much Junk Food,* Random House (New York, NY), 1985.

*The Berenstain Bears on the Moon,* Random House (New York, NY), 1985.

*The Berenstain Bears Learn about Strangers,* Random House (New York, NY), 1985, reissued with cassette, 1986.

*The Berenstain Bears' Take-Along Library* (includes *The Berenstain Bears Visit the Dentist, The Berenstain Bears and Too Much TV, The Berenstain Bears and the Sitter, The Berenstain Bears in the Dark,* and *The Berenstain Bears and the Messy Room*), Random House (New York, NY), 1985.

*The Berenstain Bears' Toy Time,* Random House (New York, NY), 1985.

*The Berenstain Bears Forget Their Manners,* Random House (New York, NY), 1985, reissued with cassette, 1986, reissued with puppet package, 1988.

*The Berenstain Bears' Bath Book,* Random House (New York, NY), 1985.

*The Berenstain Bears Get Stage Fright,* Random House (New York, NY), 1986.

*The Berenstain Bears: No Girls Allowed,* Random House (New York, NY), 1986.

*The Berenstain Bears and the Week at Grandma's,* Random House (New York, NY), 1986, reissued with puppet package, 1990.

*The Berenstain Bears and Too Much Birthday,* Random House (New York, NY), 1986.

*The Berenstain Kids: I Love Colors,* Random House (New York, NY), 1987.

*The Berenstain Bears Go Out for the Team,* Random House (New York, NY), 1987, reissued with cassette, 1991.

*Berenstain Bears: Coughing Catfish,* Random House (New York, NY), 1987.

*The Berenstain Bears Blaze a Trail,* Random House (New York, NY), 1987.

*The Berenstain Bears on the Job,* Random House (New York, NY), 1987.

*The Berenstain Bears and the Trouble with Friends,* Random House (New York, NY), 1987.

*The Berenstain Bears and the Missing Honey,* Random House (New York, NY), 1987.

*The Berenstain Bears and the Big Road Race,* Random House (New York, NY), 1987.

*The Berenstain Bears and the Bad Habit,* Random House (New York, NY), 1987.

*The Berenstain Bears' Trouble at School,* Random House (New York, NY), 1987, reissued with puppet package, 1990.

*After the Dinosaurs,* illustrated by Michael Berenstain, Random House (New York, NY), 1988.

*The Berenstain Bears and the Ghost in the Forest,* Random House (New York, NY), 1988.

*The Berenstain Bears Get the Gimmies,* Random House (New York, NY), 1988, reissued with cassette, 1990.

*The Berenstain Bears and the Double Dare,* Random House (New York, NY), 1988.

*The Berenstain Bears and the Bad Dream,* Random House (New York, NY), 1988.

*The Berenstain Bears Ready, Get Set, Go!,* Random House (New York, NY), 1988.

*The Berenstain Bears and Too Much Vacation,* Random House (New York, NY), 1989, reissued with cassette, 1990.

*The Berenstain Bears' Trick or Treat,* Random House (New York, NY), 1989.

*The Berenstain Bears and the In-Crowd,* Random House (New York, NY), 1989.

*The Berenstain Bears and the Slumber Party,* Random House (New York, NY), 1990.

*The Berenstain Bears and the Prize Pumpkin,* Random House (New York, NY), 1990.

*The Berenstain Bears' Trouble with Pets,* Random House (New York, NY), 1990.

*The Berenstain Bears Are a Family,* Random House (New York, NY), 1991.

*The Berenstain Bears at the Super-Duper Market,* Random House (New York, NY), 1991.

*The Berenstain Bears Say Good Night,* Random House (New York, NY), 1991.

*The Berenstain Bears' Four Seasons,* Random House (New York, NY), 1991.

*The Berenstain Bears Don't Pollute (Anymore),* Random House (New York, NY), 1991.

*The Berenstain Bears and the Trouble with Grownups,* Random House (New York, NY), 1992.

*The Berenstain Bears and Too Much Pressure,* Random House (New York, NY), 1992.

*The Berenstain Bears and the Bully,* Random House (New York, NY), 1993.

*The Berenstain Bears Get a Checkup,* Random House (New York, NY), 1993.

*The Berenstain Bears and the Green-Eyed Monster,* Random House (New York, NY), 1994.

*The Berenstain Bears' New Neighbors,* Random House (New York, NY), 1994.

*The Berenstain Bears and Too Much Teasing,* Random House (New York, NY), 1995.

*The Berenstain Bears Count Their Blessings,* Random House (New York, NY), 1995.

*The Berenstain Bears Grow-It,* Random House (New York, NY), 1996.

*The Berenstain Bears' Yike! Yike! Where's My Trike,* Random House (New York, NY), 1996.

*The Berenstain Bears Cook-It,* Random House (New York, NY), 1996.

*The Berenstain Bears in Big Bear City,* Random House (New York, NY), 1996.

*The Berenstain Bears Draw-It,* Random House (New York, NY), 1996.

*The Berenstain Bears Fly-It,* Random House (New York, NY), 1996.

*The Berenstain Bears Home Sweet Tree,* Random House (New York, NY), 1996.

*The Berenstain Bears' Sampler: The Best of Bear Country* (includes *The Berenstain Bears' New Baby, The Berenstain Bears and the Sitter, The Berenstain Bears in the Dark, The Berenstain Bears Go to the Doctor,* and *The Berenstain Bears and the Messy Room*), Random House (New York, NY), 1996.

*The Berenstain Bears The Whole Year Through: With Earthsaver Tips and Things to Do for Each and Every Month of the Year,* Scholastic (New York, NY), 1997.

*Berenstain's A Book,* Beginner Books (New York, NY), 1997.

*The Berenstain Bears and the Blame Game,* Random House (New York, NY), 1997.

*The Berenstain Bears and the Homework Hassle,* Random House (New York, NY), 1997.

*The Berenstain Bears' Big Book of Science and Nature,* Random House (New York, NY), 1997.

*The Berenstain Bears' Thanksgiving,* Scholastic (New York, NY), 1997.

*The Berenstain Bears' Big Bear, Small Bear,* Random House (New York, NY), 1998.

*The Berenstain Bears by the Sea,* Random House (New York, NY), 1998.

*The Berenstain Bears Get the Don't Haftas,* Random House (New York, NY), 1998.

*The Berenstain Bears Ride the Thunderbolt,* Random House (New York, NY), 1998.

*The Berenstain Bears' Comic Valentine* (also see below), Scholastic (New York, NY), 1998.

*The Berenstain Bears Easter Surprise* (also see below), Scholastic (New York, NY), 1998.

*The Berenstain Bears Play Ball* (also see below), Scholastic (New York, NY), 1998.

*The Berenstain Bears Get the Screamies,* Random House (New York, NY), 1998.

*The Berenstain Bears Get Their Kicks,* Random House (New York, NY), 1998.

*The Berenstain Bears Lend a Helping Hand,* Random House (New York, NY), 1998.

*The Birds, the Bees and the Berenstain Bears,* Random House (New York, NY), 1999.

*The Berenstain Bears Mad, Mad, Mad Toy Craze,* Random House (New York, NY), 1999.

*The Berenstain Bears Go up and Down,* Random House (New York, NY), 1999.

*The Berenstain Bears Catch the Bus,* Random House (New York, NY), 1999.

*The Berenstain Bears Think of Those in Need,* Random House (New York, NY), 1999.

*The Berenstain Bears and the Big Question,* Random House (New York, NY), 1999.

*The Berenstain Bears Get the Noisies,* Random House (New York, NY), 1999.

*The Berenstain Bears Get the Scaredies,* Random House (New York, NY), 1999.

*The Berenstain Bears in the House of Mirrors,* Random House (New York, NY), 1999.

*The Berenstain Bears Go in and Out,* Random House (New York, NY), 2000.

*The Berenstain Bears and the Big Blooper,* Random House (New York, NY), 2000.

*The Berenstain Bears and Baby Makes Five,* Random House (New York, NY), 2000.

*The Berenstain Bears Get the Twitchies,* Random House (New York, NY), 2000.

*The Berenstain Bears and the Escape of the Bogg Brothers,* Random House (New York, NY), 2000.

*The Berenstain Bears' That Stump Must Go!,* Random House (New York, NY), 2000.

*The Goofy, Goony Guy,* Random House (New York, NY), 2001.

*The Berenstain Bears and the Excuse Note,* Random House (New York, NY), 2001.

*The Berenstain Bears and the Tic-Tac-Toe Mystery,* Random House (New York, NY), 2001.

*The Berenstain Bears and the Wrong Crowd,* Random House (New York, NY), 2001.

*The Berenstain Bears Dollars and Sense,* Random House (New York, NY), 2001.

*Runamuck Dog Show,* illustrated by Michael Berenstain, Random House (New York, NY), 2001.

*The Berenstain Bears and the Missing Watermelon Money,* Random House (New York, NY), 2001.

*The Berenstain Bears and the Haunted Lighthouse,* Random House (New York, NY), 2001.

*The Berenstain Bears and the Real Easter Eggs,* Random House (New York, NY), 2002.

*Ride Like the Wind,* Random House (New York, NY), 2002.

*The Berenstain Bears Report Card Trouble,* Random House (New York, NY), 2002.

*Mama and Papa Bear help Brother Bear adjust to the family latest "addition" in* **The Berenstain Bears' New Baby,** *written and illustrated by Stan and Jan Berenstain.*

Also creators of coloring books published by Random House, including *Berenstain Bears' around the Clock-Coloring Book,* 1987, *Berenstain Bears' Bear Scout-Coloring Book,* 1987, *Berenstain Bears' Count on Numbers Coloring Book,* 1987, *Berenstain Bears' on the Farm Coloring Book,* 1987, *Berenstain Bears' Safety First-Coloring Book,* 1987, and *Berenstain Bears Story-time Color Book,* 1989. Works have also been recorded into audio format, including *The Berenstain Bears' Read Along Library* (includes *He Bear, She Bear; The Bear Scouts; The Bear Detectives; The Big Honey Hunt; Old Hat, New Hat;* and *The Bears' Christmas*), Random House (New York, NY), 1977; *The Bears' Picnic and Other Stories* (includes *The Bears' Picnic; The Bear Scouts; Bears in the Night; The Bears' New Baby; The Bears' Vacation;* and *The Big Honey Hunt*), Caedmon (New York, NY), 1977; *The Bears' Christmas and Other Stories* (includes *The Bears' Christmas; He Bear, She Bear; The Bear Detectives; The Bears' Almanac;* and *The Bike Lesson*), Random House (New York, NY), 1982; and *He Bear, She Bear* [and] *Bears on Wheels,* Random House (New York, NY), 1989.

*"BERENSTAIN BEARS CUB CLUB" SERIES*

*The Berenstain Bears and the Spooky Fun House,* Western Publishing (Racine, WI), 1991.

*The Berenstain Bears and the Spooky Old House,* Western Publishing (Racine, WI), 1991.

*The Berenstain Bears and the Broken Piggy Bank,* Western Publishing (Racine, WI), 1992.

*The Berenstain Bears Hug and Make Up,* Western Publishing (Racine, WI), 1992.

*The Berenstain Bears Visit Fun Park,* Western Publishing (Racine, WI), 1992.

*The Berenstain Bears' Big Rummage Sale,* Western Publishing (Racine, WI), 1992.

*The Berenstain Bears Perfect Fishing Spot,* Western Publishing (Racine, WI), 1992.

*The Berenstain Bears All Year 'Round,* Western Publishing (Racine, WI), 1993.

*The Berenstain Bears Family Get-Together,* Western Publishing (Racine, WI), 1993.

*The Berenstain Bears and the Wishing Star,* Western Publishing (Racine, WI), 1993.

*The Berenstain Bears Visit Farmer Ben,* Western Publishing (Racine, WI), 1993.

*The Berenstain Bears Learn about Colors,* Western Publishing (Racine, WI), 1993.

*The Berenstain Bears' Pet Show,* Western Publishing (Racine, WI), 1993.

*The Berenstain Bears and the Baby Chipmunk,* Western Publishing (Racine, WI), 1993.

*The Berenstain Bears and the Good Deed,* Western Publishing (Racine, WI), 1993.

*The Berenstain Bears and the Hiccup Cure,* illustrated by Michael Berenstain, Western Publishing (Racine, WI), 1993.

*The Berenstain Bears and the Bedtime Battle,* Western Publishing (Racine, WI), 1993.

*The Berenstain Bears with Nothing to Do,* Western Publishing (Racine, WI), 1993.

*The Berenstain Bears and the Jump Rope,* Western Publishing (Racine, WI), 1993.

*The Berenstain Bears and the Summer Job,* Western Publishing (Racine, WI), 1994.

*The Berenstain Bears Visit Uncle Tex,* Western Publishing (Racine, WI), 1994.

*The Berenstain Bears Lost in a Cave,* Western Publishing (Racine, WI), 1994.

*The Berenstain Bears' Birthday Boy,* Western Publishing (Racine, WI), 1994.

*The Berenstain Bears at Big Bear Fair,* Western Publishing (Racine, WI), 1994.

*The Berenstain Bears and the Big Picture,* Western Publishing (Racine, WI), 1994.

*"BERENSTAIN BEAR SCOUTS" SERIES; AUTHOR WITH HUSBAND, STAN BERENSTAIN*

*The Berenstain Bear Scouts and the Humongous Pumpkin,* illustrated by Michael Berenstain, Scholastic (New York, NY), 1995.

*The Berenstain Bear Scouts in the Giant Bat Cave,* illustrated by Michael Berenstain, Scholastic (New York, NY), 1995.

*The Berenstain Bear Scouts and the Coughing Catfish,* illustrated by Michael Berenstain, Scholastic (New York, NY), 1996.

*The Berenstain Bear Scouts and the Sci-Fi Pizza,* illustrated by Michael Berenstain, Scholastic (New York, NY), 1996.

*Ghost Versus Ghost,* illustrated by Michael Berenstain, Scholastic (New York, NY), 1996.

*The Berenstain Bear Scouts and the Sinister Smoke,* illustrated by Michael Berenstain, Scholastic (New York, NY), 1997.

*The Berenstain Bear Scouts and the Search for Naughty Ned,* illustrated by Michael Berenstain, Scholastic (New York, NY), 1998.

*The Berenstain Bear Scouts and the Missing Merit Badges,* illustrated by Michael Berenstain, Scholastic (New York, NY), 1998.

*The Berenstain Bear Scouts and the Ripoff Queen,* illustrated by Michael Berenstain, Scholastic (New York, NY), 1998.

*The Berenstain Bear Scouts Scream Their Heads Off,* illustrated by Michael Berenstain, Scholastic (New York, NY), 1998

*The Berenstain Bear Scouts and the Stinky Milk Mystery,* illustrated by Michael Berenstain, Scholastic (New York, NY), 1999.

*The Berenstain Bear Scouts and the White-Water Mystery,* illustrated by Michael Berenstain, Scholastic (New York, NY), 1999.

*"BERENSTAIN BABY BEARS" SERIES; AUTHOR AND ILLUSTRATOR WITH HUSBAND, STAN BERENSTAIN; BOARD BOOKS*

*My New Bed: From Crib to Bed,* Random House (New York, NY), 1999.

*My Potty and I: A Friend in Need,* Random House (New York, NY), 1999.

*My Trusty Car Seat: Buckling Up for Safety,* Random House (New York, NY), 1999.

*Pacifier Days: A Fond Farewell,* Random House (New York, NY), 1999.

*Me First! Me First!,* Random House (New York, NY), 2000.

*My Every Day Book: A Day in the Life,* Random House (New York, NY), 2000.

*"BIG CHAPTER BOOKS" SERIES; AUTHOR WITH HUSBAND, STAN BERENSTAIN, AND SON LEO BERENSTAIN*

*The Berenstain Bears and the Red-Handed Thief,* illustrated by Michael Berenstain, Random House (New York, NY), 1993.

*The Berenstain Bears and the Nerdy Nephew,* illustrated by Michael Berenstain, Random House (New York, NY), 1993.

*The Berenstain Bears Gotta Dance,* illustrated by Michael Berenstain, Random House (New York, NY), 1993.

*The Berenstain Bears and the Drug Free Zone,* illustrated by Leo and Michael Berenstain, Random House (New York, NY), 1993.

*The Berenstain Bears and the Female Fullback,* illustrated by Michael Berenstain, Random House (New York, NY), 1993.

*The Berenstain Bears and the New Girl in Town,* illustrated by Michael Berenstain, Random House (New York, NY), 1993.

*The Berenstain Bears and the Wheelchair Commando,* illustrated by Leo and Michael Berenstain, Random House (New York, NY), 1993.

*The Berenstain Bears Accept No Substitutes,* illustrated by Michael Berenstain, Random House (New York, NY), 1993.

*The Berenstain Bears and the Dress Code,* illustrated by Michael Berenstain, Random House (New York, NY), 1994.

*The Berenstain Bears at Camp Crush,* illustrated by Michael Berenstain, Random House (New York, NY), 1994.

*The Berenstain Bears and the Galloping Ghost,* illustrated by Michael Berenstain, Random House (New York, NY), 1994.

*The Berenstain Bears and the School Scandal Sheet,* illustrated by Michael Berenstain, Random House (New York, NY), 1994.

*The Berenstain Bears and the Giddy Grandma,* illustrated by Michael Berenstain, Random House (New York, NY), 1994.

*The Berenstain Bears Media Madness,* illustrated by Michael Berenstain, Random House (New York, NY), 1995.

*The Berenstain Bears and the Showdown at Chainsaw Gap,* illustrated by Michael Berenstain, Random House (New York, NY), 1995.

*The Berenstain Bears in the Freaky Funhouse,* illustrated by Michael Berenstain, Random House (New York, NY), 1995.

*The Berenstain Bears at Teen Rock Café,* illustrated by Michael Berenstain, Random House (New York, NY), 1996.

*The Berenstain Bears in Maniac Mansion,* illustrated by Michael Berenstain, Random House (New York, NY), 1996.

*The Berenstain Bears and Queenie's Crazy Crush,* illustrated by Michael Berenstain, Random House (New York, NY), 1997.

*The Berenstain Bears and the Haunted Hayride,* illustrated by Michael Berenstain, Random House (New York, NY), 1997.

*The Berenstain Bears and the Bermuda Triangle,* illustrated by Michael Berenstain, Random House (New York, NY), 1997.

*The Berenstain Bears and the Ghost of the Auto Graveyard,* illustrated by Michael Berenstain, Random House (New York, NY), 1997.

*The Berenstain Bears Go Platinum,* illustrated by Michael Berenstain, Random House (New York, NY), 1998.

*The Berenstain Bears and the Love Match,* illustrated by Michael Berenstain, Random House (New York, NY), 1998.

*The Berenstain Bears and the Big Date,* illustrated by Michael Berenstain, Random House (New York, NY), 1998.

*The Berenstain Bears and the Perfect Crime (Almost),* illustrated by Michael Berenstain, Random House (New York, NY), 1998.

*The Berenstain Bears Lost in Cyberspace,* illustrated by Michael Berenstain, Random House (New York, NY), 1999.

*The Berenstain Bears in the Wax Museum,* illustrated by Michael Berenstain, Random House (New York, NY), 1999.

*The Berenstain Bears Go to Hollywood,* illustrated by Michael Berenstain, Random House (New York, NY), 1999.

*The Berenstain Bears and the G-Rex Bones,* illustrated by Michael Berenstain, Random House (New York, NY), 1999.

*The Berenstain Bears No Guns Allowed,* illustrated by Michael Berenstain, Random House (New York, NY), 2000.

*The Berenstain Bears and the Great Ant Attack,* illustrated by Michael Berenstain, Random House (New York, NY), 2000.

*The Berenstain Bears—Phenom in the Family,* illustrated by Michael Berenstain, Random House (New York, NY), 2001.

*TELEVISION SCRIPTS; WITH HUSBAND, STAN BERENSTAIN*

*The Berenstain Bears' Christmas Tree,* National Broadcasting Company, Inc. (NBC-TV), 1979.

*The Berenstain Bears Meet Bigpaw,* NBC-TV, 1980.

*The Berenstain Bears' Easter Surprise,* NBC-TV, 1981.

*The Berenstain Bears' Comic Valentine,* NBC-TV, 1982.

*The Berenstain Bears Play Ball,* NBC-TV, 1983.

*The Berenstain Bears' CBS Show,* Columbia Broadcasting System, Inc. (CBS-TV), 1986-87.

*OTHER*

*The Day of the Dinosaur* ("Berenstain Bears" series), illustrated by son, Michael Berenstain, Random House (New York, NY), 1987.

(With Stan Berenstain) *What Your Parents Never Told You about Being a Mom or Dad,* Crown (New York, NY), 1995.

(With Stan Berenstain) *Down a Sunny Dirt Road* (autobiography), Random House (New York, NY), 2002.

A Janice and Stanley Berenstain manuscript collection is housed at Syracuse University. Many of the "Berenstain Bears" books have been translated into Spanish.

## Adaptations

Writings which have been adapted for filmstrips and released by Random House include: *The Bears' Nature Guide,* 1976, *The Berenstain Bears' Science Fair,* 1978, *The Bear Detectives; The Bears' Almanac; The Bears' Vacation; Bears in the Night; The Bear Scouts; The Bike Lesson; The Bears' Picnic; Inside, Outside, Upside Down; Old Hat, New Hat; The Berenstain Bears and the Spooky Old Tree; He Bear, She Bear; C Is for Clown; The Berenstain Bears' B Book* (book titled *The B Book*); *The Big Honey Hunt;* and *The Bears' Christmas,* all 1986. *The Berenstain Bears Forget Their Manners* was adapted for videocassette and released by Random House Home Video, 1989. Several books have been adapted as multimedia presentations for computer by Living Books (Novato, CA), including *The Berenstain Bears Get in a Fight,* 1995, and *The Berenstain Bears in the Dark,* 1996.

## Work in Progress

*Down a Sunny Dirt Road,* Random House, October of 2002.

## Sidelights

The husband and wife team behind the immensely popular "Berenstain Bears" series, Jan and Stan Berenstain teach children about everyday occurrences through the use of slapstick humor. The books in the series feature a family of bears, each member having a distinct personality—the children are intelligent and alert, the mother is often imparting moralistic wisdom, and the father is portrayed as a sincere, but bumbling and inept expert. Although the characterization of Papa Bear is seen as demeaning by some critics, most critics also recognize the series' merits, such as the easily attainable information and guidance it offers. "Our world is family humor," explains Stan in an interview with Joyce Hoffman for the *Chicago Sunday Tribune Magazine of Books.* "I see us in the Peter Rabbit mold, popular, gentle, straightforward and noncontroversial—yet we don't sugar-coat life. We deal with reality." The popularity of the Berenstain Bears is "indisputable," maintains Hoffman, adding that they are "the hottest ticket in children's publishing today."

Both Jan and Stan were born in Philadelphia, Pennsylvania, but did not meet until they entered the Philadelphia College of Art. Jan's childhood was filled with books; and her love of the Sunday comics often prompted her to reproduce them. Stan similarly found books at an early age, and those which taught how to paint and draw were among his favorites. "When we were young," said Stan in an interview for *Something about the Author* (*SATA*), "we each aspired to draw like the old masters—we never got there, but at least they were good models." By the time the two met in college, they were both somewhat accomplished artists with similar interests. "We painted and did all the things that art kids do, becoming good buddies," recalled Stan in his *SATA* interview. "I don't know whether we were ever formally engaged, but we planned to marry after World War II." Stan was drafted and remained in the army for about three-and-a-half years, and Jan continued her education, eventually teaching at the same school she had attended. Humorous art had always interested Stan, and toward the end of his army career he submitted four cartoons to Norman Cousins, then editor-in-chief of the *Saturday Review of Literature.* "The fact that he bought them came as a great shock," revealed Stan in his *SATA* interview. "So I figured that unless I was going to continue to study painting under the GI Bill, Jan and I could make a little money here, and our collaboration evolved."

The Berenstains married on April 13, 1946, and their collaboration continued to develop as they began doing cartoons for the family magazine market. "I really started contributing them because we had to do domestic subjects, and I just horned my way in," explained Jan in her *SATA* interview. Stan, though, points out in his interview that Jan's contributions were invited and encouraged. "It never occurred to me that it wouldn't be a good idea. We got along well and Jan drew good, funny stuff. We developed the cartoon style jointly, though not as part of any big plan. As a matter of fact, we didn't even think there was anything unusual about our collaboration. It wasn't until after we'd sold a lot of work to the major magazines that people even knew there were two of us because originally, I had signed the cartoons just 'Berenstain.' Then, when an editor in New York met us in person, he said, 'You mean there's two of you?' We said, 'Sure,' and he suggested that we change our signature to 'The Berenstains,' because it would be terrific marketing. So we did and it attracted some attention."

When the magazine industry began to decline, the Berenstains, through an association with Theodore Geisel (also known as Dr. Seuss), began to focus on juvenile books. By this time they had children of their own who enjoyed reading, especially humorous books. "So we began buying Dr. Seuss books because they were among the few funny books being done for kids," remembered Stan in his *SATA* interview. "Once we perceived that there weren't many robust, laugh-out-loud books for kids, we thought, 'There's a niche that might be fun to enter.'" The couple was doing a magazine feature entitled "It's All in the Family" at the time, and thought they could do family humor for children just as well as they were doing it for adults.

The first books the Berenstains did were "Beginner Books," which Dr. Seuss originated with *The Cat in the Hat.* These books strove to encourage young children to read by using a combination of rhyme and humor. The Berenstains' first "Bear" book, *The Big Honey Hunt,* was published in 1962, and although they had no say in the matter, they hoped a series would ensue. Originally instructed by their editor to try something else, the Berenstains wrote a book about a penguin at the South

*Brother and Sister Bear lie about breaking Mama's favorite lamp in* The Berenstain Bears and the Truth, *written and illustrated by Stan and Jan Berenstain.*

Pole. When they delivered the sketches for this book, however, they were told that *The Big Honey Hunt* was doing well, and were asked for another "Bear" book. "After that it was just bears, bears, bears," said Stan in his *SATA* interview.

Bears were chosen as the main characters by the Berenstains for a variety of reasons. "The most popular creatures in children's books are bunnies and bears," related Jan in her *SATA* interview. "Bunnies because they're cuddly and cute and bears because they tend to do things standing up. Part of the reason we chose bears is that they look good in clothes! You can dress them up and they're fun to draw." The bears received their creators' name when the Berenstains' second book, *The Bike Lesson,* was published. "Ted decided to put a slug line on the cover: 'Another adventure of the Berenstain Bears,'" recalled Jan in her *SATA* interview. "That's really how our bears were named. We never really would have thought of it."

These early books, particularly their design, had a definite influence on the Berenstains' style. "Dr. Seuss had wanted very simple, schematic illustrations with nothing in the background because the purpose of the books was to help kids tie the pictures in with the words," explained the Berenstains in their *SATA* interview. "He had a wild and wacky approach that we liked and went along with. The pages of the books had to be very simple." Although this style was different from the magazine covers and cartoons the Berenstains were used to doing, they adapted quickly and their bears came to life. "If you look through one of our books," claimed Stan in his *SATA* interview, "there are probably hundreds of bear faces and I doubt that two of them would be the same, which is not the usual technique for children's books. Normally those animals are expressionless or smiling, and are portrayed realistically: a rabbit looks like a rabbit. Our bears are created totally out of our own vision and methods. They don't look like real bears at all, nor do they look like teddy bears. But letters from kids say that they can always tell how our bears feel or what they're going through. It's just been a long … process of finding what works for the kinds of stories we want to do."

In the late 1970s, the Berenstains began their "First Time" series. A departure from their earlier Berenstain Bears books, the books in this series describe "first time" experiences that children can identify with. A nuclear family is depicted, and the slapstick quality of the "Beginner Books" is left out. Stan asserted in his *SATA* interview that "The 'First Time' books are partly intended to give children some idea of what to expect from an experience, since what scares them most is their own unfamiliarity with what's going to happen next (even if it seems perfectly obvious to their parents). If these books lay out what may happen at a certain time of life, like the first day of school, then kids will feel better prepared for the event before it happens. I think there should be more books like that for grown-ups."

The pictures, along with the subject matter, are also different in the "First Time" series. The landscapes are very realistic, and there is a definite foreground, middle ground, and background. "We try never to skimp on detail in our pictures either, because readers enjoy getting as much information as they can from illustrations," professed the Berenstains in their *SATA* interview. "Creating a real place with clarity and a good balance between words and pictures is equally important. We work very hard to make our pictures 'read,' and apparently they do because when kids write they often comment on our pictures. They're more alert to the content of pictures than adults, because the first reading they do is of pictures—they don't get to language and words for a long time."

The topics discussed in the books are carefully selected, as are the words used to convey them. "We try not to dictate to parents how they should react in situations which should be a parent's prerogative," noted the authors in their *SATA* interview. "For instance, we stay away from religious issues. We were even reluctant to do something about strangers until we found a way to do it that would help parents without scaring children. We get a lot of requests to do books on tough subjects like divorce, drugs, people dying, but we have a lot of humor in our books, and there's nothing funny about those situations." Many of the topics that do make it into the books come from personal experiences the Berenstains have had with their own children. Others come from discussions with young parents, who encounter different situations today than the Berenstains did when raising their children.

In addition to the two series they have already done, the Berenstains have also written a series similar to the "First Time" books, but aimed at a younger audience. These books are relatively short and use rhyme to get across a concept, such as the seasons or bedtime. Other series include the "Stepping Stones" books, a collection of easy-to-read chapter books intended for children who have graduated from the "Berenstain Bears" picture books, but who still enjoy reading about the family. Meanwhile, their bears are popping up everywhere. A number of television shows have been made, as have filmstrips and cassettes of the books, and several multimedia adaptions of their books for the computer. The Berenstains remarked in their *SATA* interview that they're "also doing a lot of merchandising: games, clothing, and toys based on our characters. We just want to make sure that it's done carefully, that's why we design everything ourselves."

Although their books, and the bears themselves, are enormously successful, the Berenstains continue to see themselves as an "old-fashioned Mom and Pop operation in which both partners do whatever needs to be done— writing, illustrating, cooking, bottle washing. We find our work (and our bears) tremendously stimulating and enjoyable and, while we don't always agree on every dot and line, we have managed to harmonize successfully over … years of working together as cartoonists-writers and … as author-illustrators of children's books," they wrote in *Publishers Weekly*. "Back in the cartoon days," explained Stan in his *SATA* interview, "we had to come up with twenty, twenty-five cartoons a week—week in and week out. So we were depending upon ideas coming, and if they didn't, we were out of business. That training was probably helpful. Besides, what we are doing isn't exotic. Our family is a very normal one, and our bear family is very much like us. As life goes on," he concludes, "it keeps proposing new ideas."

## Biographical and Critical Sources

### BOOKS

*Children's Books and Their Creators,* edited by Anita Silvey, Houghton (Boston, MA), 1995.
*St. James Guide to Children's Writers,* 5th edition, St. James Press (Detroit, MI), 1999.
*Something about the Author,* Volume 64, interview with Jan and Stan Berenstain by Marc Caplan, Gale (Detroit, MI), 1991, pp. 31-41.

### PERIODICALS

*Appraisal: Science Books for Young People,* fall, 1982.
*Booklist,* January 1, 1982; February 1, 1995, Denise Perry Donavin, review of *What Your Parents Never Told You about Being a Mom or Dad,* p. 981.
*Books for Your Children,* spring, 1988.
*Bulletin of the Center for Children's Books,* April, 1974; November, 1980.
*Chicago Sunday Tribune Magazine of Books,* November 4, 1984, Joyce Hoffman, "Bear Facts: What the Berenstain Bears Teach America's Kids about Life," pp. 16-22, 31.
*Children's Book Review Service,* winter, 1982.

*Junior Bookshelf,* December, 1977; February, 1979.
*Kirkus Reviews,* September 1, 1972; October 15, 1975.
*Los Angeles Times Book Review,* April 13, 1986.
*Modern Maturity,* December, 1989; January, 1990.
*New York Times Book Review,* November 25, 1973; July 21, 1985; November 10, 1985; May 20, 1990.
*People,* January 22, 1979.
*Publishers Weekly,* October 24, 1977; *Publishers Weekly,* February 27, 1981, Jan and Stan Berenstain, "You Can't Animate a Plaid Shirt," pp. 99-100; June 17, 1983; June 7, 1993, review of *The Berenstain Bears and the New Girl in Town,* December 19, 1994, review of *What Your Parents Never Told You about Being a Mom or Dad,* p. 42.
*School Librarian,* September, 1977.
*School Library Journal,* December, 1974; January, 1976; December, 1978; May, 1980; October, 1980; November, 1983; October, 1985.
*Science Books and Films,* May, 1976; December, 1976; September, 1978; November-December, 1985.
*Times Literary Supplement,* July 14, 1972.

OTHER

*Berenstain Bears Web Site,* http://www.berenstainbears. com/ (December 20, 2001).

\* \* \*

# BERENSTAIN, Stan(ley) 1923-

## Personal

Born September 29, 1923, in Philadelphia, PA; son of Harry and Rose (Brander) Berenstain; married Janice Grant (an author and illustrator), April 13, 1946; children: Leo, Michael. *Education:* Attended Philadelphia College of Art, 1941-42, and Pennsylvania Academy of Fine Arts, 1946-49.

## Addresses

*Home*—Bucks County, PA. *Agent*—Sterling Lord, Sterling Lord Literistic Inc., 65 Bleecker St., New York, NY 10012.

## Career

Author and illustrator. Creator, with wife, Jan Berenstain, of "It's All in the Family," an illustrated feature first published in *McCall's,* (1956-69) and then in *Good Housekeeping,* (1970-90). *Exhibitions:* Work exhibited in Metropolitan Museum of Art international exhibition of cartoons, and in an exhibition of British and American humorous art in London. Works represented in the Albert T. Reid Cartoon Collection at the University of Kansas, the Farrell Library Collection at Kansas State University, and Syracuse University in New York.

## Awards, Honors

School Bell Award, National Education Association, 1960, for distinguished service in the interpretation of education in a national magazine; British Book Centre honor book, 1968, for *Inside, Outside, Upside Down;* Best Book Award, American Institute of Graphic Arts, 1970, for *The Bear Scouts;* University of Chicago Center for Children's Books named *Bears in the Night* a best book of 1972, and *He Bear, She Bear* a best book of 1974; Philadelphia Library Children's Reading Round Table honor book, 1972, for *Bears in the Night,* 1973, for *The Bears' Almanac: A Year in Bear Country—Holidays, Seasons, Weather, Actual Facts about Snow, Wind, Rain, Thunder, Lightning, the Sun, the Moon, and Lots More,* 1974, for *He Bear, She Bear,* 1976, for *The Bears' Nature Guide,* 1980, for *The Berenstain Bears and the Missing Dinosaur Bone,* 1982, for *The Berenstain Bears Visit the Dentist,* 1983, for *The Berenstain Bears in the Dark, The Berenstain Bears Go to Camp,* and *The Berenstain Bears and the Truth,* 1984, for *The Berenstain Bears and Too Much TV,* 1985, for *The Berenstain Bears Learn about Strangers,* 1987, for *The Berenstain Bears Go Out for the Team,* 1988, for *The Day of the Dinosaur,* and 1989, for *After the Dinosaurs;* Children's Book of the Year, Child Study Association of America, 1977, for *The Berenstain Bears' Science Fair,* and 1982, for *The Berenstain Bears Go to the Doctor, The Berenstain Bears Visit the Dentist, The Berenstain Bears and the Sitter,* and *The Berenstain Bears' Moving Day.*

Silver Diploma, International Film and Television Festival, Naples, Italy, 1980, for *The Berenstain Bears' Christmas Tree;* Silver Award, International Film and Television Festival, New York City, 1980, for *The Berenstain Bears' Christmas Tree,* 1982, for *The Berenstain Bears' Comic Valentine,* and 1987, for *The Berenstain Bears' CBS Show;* Young Readers' Award, Michigan Council of Teachers of English, 1981, for *Bears in the Night;* Drexel Citation, Drexel University, School of Library and Information Science, 1982, for "contributions to children's literature"; Children's Classic Award, International Reading Association, 1982, for *The Berenstain Bears Go to the Doctor* and *The Berenstain Bears Visit the Dentist,* 1983, for *The Berenstain Bears Get in a Fight, The Berenstain Bears Go to Camp,* and *The Berenstain Bears in the Dark,* 1984, for *The Berenstain Bears and the Messy Room,* and *The Berenstain Bears and the Truth,* and 1987, for *The Berenstain Bears: No Girls Allowed;* Buckeye Award, Ohio State Library Association, Teachers of English, and International Reading Association, 1982, for *The Berenstain Bears and the Spooky Old Tree,* and 1985, for *The Berenstain Bears and the Messy Room;* Arizona Children's Choice Book Award nomination, and Arizona Young Reader's Award, both 1985, both for *The Berenstain Bears and the Messy Room;* Colorado Children's Choice Book Award nomination, 1985, for *The Berenstain Bears in the Dark;* Humanitas Certificate, 1987, for the television adaptation of *The Berenstain Bears Forget Their Manners;* Ludington Award, 1989, for "contributions to children's literature."

# Writings

*AUTHOR AND ILLUSTRATOR WITH WIFE, JAN BERENSTAIN*

*The Berenstain's Baby Book,* Macmillan (New York, NY), 1951.

*Sister* (cartoons), Schuman, 1952.

*Tax-Wise,* Schuman, 1952.

*Marital Blitz,* Dutton (New York, NY), 1954.

*Baby Makes Four,* Macmillan (New York, NY), 1956.

*Lover Boy,* Macmillan (New York, NY), 1958.

*It's All in the Family,* Dutton (New York, NY), 1958.

*Bedside Lover Boy,* Dell (New York, NY), 1960.

*And Beat Him When He Sneezes,* McGraw (New York, NY), 1960, published as *Have a Baby, My Wife Just Had a Cigar,* Dell (New York, NY), 1960.

*Call Me Mrs.,* Macmillan (New York, NY), 1961.

*It's Still in the Family,* Dutton (New York, NY), 1961.

*Office Lover Boy,* Dell (New York, NY), 1962.

*The Facts of Life for Grown-ups,* Dell (New York, NY), 1963.

*Flipsville-Squaresville,* Dial (New York, NY), 1965.

*Mr. Dirty vs. Mr. Clean,* Dell (New York, NY), 1967.

*You Could Diet Laughing,* Dell (New York, NY), 1969.

*Be Good or I'll Belt You,* Dell (New York, NY), 1970.

*Education Impossible,* Dell (New York, NY), 1970.

*Never Trust Anyone over 13,* Bantam (New York, NY), 1970.

*How to Teach Your Children about Sex without Making a Complete Fool of Yourself,* Dutton (New York, NY), 1970.

*How to Teach Your Children about God without Actually Scaring Them out of Their Wits,* Dutton (New York, NY), 1971.

*Are Parents for Real?,* Bantam (New York, NY), 1972.

*What Your Parents Never Told You About Being a Mom or Dad,* Crown, 1995.

*"BERENSTAIN BEARS" SERIES; AUTHOR AND ILLUSTRATOR WITH WIFE, JAN BERENSTAIN*

*The Big Honey Hunt* (also see below), Beginner Books (New York, NY), 1962.

*The Bike Lesson* (also see below), Beginner Books (New York, NY), 1964, reissued with cassette, 1987.

*The Bears' Picnic* (also see below), Beginner Books (New York, NY), 1966.

*The Bear Scouts* (also see below), Beginner Books (New York, NY), 1967.

*The Bears' Vacation* (also see below), Beginner Books (New York, NY), 1968, published in England as *The Bears' Holiday,* Harvill, 1969, reissued with cassette, Random House (New York, NY), 1987.

*Inside, Outside, Upside Down,* Random House (New York, NY), 1968.

*Bears on Wheels* (also see below), Random House (New York, NY), 1969.

*The Bears' Christmas* (also see below), Beginner Books (New York, NY), 1970, reissued with cassette, Random House (New York, NY), 1988.

*Old Hat, New Hat* (also see below), Random House (New York, NY), 1970.

*Bears in the Night* (also see below), Random House (New York, NY), 1971.

*The B Book,* Random House (New York, NY), 1971.

*C Is for Clown,* Random House (New York, NY), 1972, revised edition published as *Berenstain's C Book,* Beginner Books (New York, NY), 1997.

*The Bears' Almanac: A Year in Bear Country—Holidays, Seasons, Weather, Actual Facts about Snow, Wind, Rain, Thunder, Lightning, the Sun, the Moon, and Lots More* (also see below), Random House (New York, NY), 1973, published as *The Berenstain Bears' Almanac: A Year in Bear Country—Holidays, Seasons, Weather, Actual Facts about Snow, Wind, Rain, Thunder, Lightning, the Sun, the Moon, and Lots More,* 1984.

*The Berenstain Bears' Nursery Tales,* Random House (New York, NY), 1973.

*He Bear, She Bear* (also see below), Random House (New York, NY), 1974.

*The Berenstain Bears' New Baby* (also see below), Random House (New York, NY), 1974, reissued with cassette, 1985.

*The Bears' Nature Guide,* Random House (New York, NY), 1975, published as *The Berenstain Bears' Nature Guide,* 1984.

On the night before the Bears' big day, they look at the moon, far, far away.

*Brother and Sister Bear and their dog experience weightlessness and meteor showers as they travel to the moon and back in their colorful spaceship. (From* The Berenstain Bears on the Moon, *written and illustrated by Stan and Jan Berenstain.)*

*The Bear Detectives: The Case of the Missing Pumpkin* (also see below), Random House (New York, NY), 1975, reissued with cassette, 1988.

*The Berenstain Bears' Counting Book,* Random House (New York, NY), 1976.

*The Berenstain Bears' Science Fair,* Random House (New York, NY), 1977.

*The Berenstain Bears and the Spooky Old Tree,* Random House (New York, NY), 1978.

*Papa's Pizza: A Berenstain Bear Sniffy Book,* Random House (New York, NY), 1978.

*The Berenstain Bears Go to School,* Random House (New York, NY), 1978, reissued with cassette, 1985.

*The Bears' Activity Book,* Random House (New York, NY), 1979.

*The Berenstain Bears and the Missing Dinosaur Bone,* Random House (New York, NY), 1980.

*The Berenstain Bears' Christmas Tree* (also see below), Random House (New York, NY), 1980.

*The Berenstain Bears and the Sitter* (also see below), Random House (New York, NY), 1981, reissued with cassette, 1985, reissued with puppet package, 1987.

*The Berenstain Bears Go to the Doctor* (also see below), Random House (New York, NY), 1981, reissued with cassette, 1985, reissued with puppet package, 1987.

*The Berenstain Bears' Moving Day,* Random House (New York, NY), 1981.

*The Berenstain Bears Visit the Dentist* (also see below), Random House (New York, NY), 1981, reissued with cassette, 1985, reissued with puppet package, 1987.

*The Berenstain Bears Get in a Fight,* Random House (New York, NY), 1982, reissued with puppet package, 1987, reissued with cassette, 1988.

*The Berenstain Bears Go to Camp,* Random House (New York, NY), 1982, reissued with cassette, 1989.

*The Berenstain Bears in the Dark* (also see below), Random House (New York, NY), 1982.

*The Berenstain Bears and the Messy Room* (also see below), Random House (New York, NY), 1983, reissued with puppet package, 1987.

*The Berenstain Bears and the Truth,* Random House (New York, NY), 1983, reissued with puppet package, 1988.

*The Berenstain Bears and the Wild, Wild Honey,* Random House (New York, NY), 1983.

*The Berenstain Bears' Soccer Star,* Random House (New York, NY), 1983.

*The Berenstain Bears Go Fly a Kite,* Random House (New York, NY), 1983.

*The Berenstain Bears to the Rescue,* Random House (New York, NY), 1983.

*The Berenstain Bears' Trouble with Money,* Random House (New York, NY), 1983.

*The Berenstain Bears' Make and Do Book,* Random House (New York, NY), 1984.

*The Berenstain Bears and the Big Election,* Random House (New York, NY), 1984.

*The Berenstain Bears and Too Much TV* (also see below), Random House (New York, NY), 1984, reissued with cassette, 1989.

*The Berenstain Bears Shoot the Rapids,* Random House (New York, NY), 1984.

*The Berenstain Bears and the Neighborly Skunk,* Random House (New York, NY), 1984.

*The Berenstain Bears and the Dinosaurs,* Random House (New York, NY), 1984.

*The Berenstain Bears Meet Santa Bear,* Random House (New York, NY), 1984, reissued with puppet package, 1988, reissued with cassette, 1989.

*The Berenstain Bears and Mama's New Job,* Random House (New York, NY), 1984.

*The Berenstain Bears and Too Much Junk Food,* Random House (New York, NY), 1985.

*The Berenstain Bears on the Moon,* Random House (New York, NY), 1985.

*The Berenstain Bears Learn about Strangers,* Random House (New York, NY), 1985, reissued with cassette, 1986.

*The Berenstain Bears' Take-Along Library* (includes *The Berenstain Bears Visit the Dentist, The Berenstain Bears and Too Much TV, The Berenstain Bears and the Sitter, The Berenstain Bears in the Dark,* and *The Berenstain Bears and the Messy Room*), Random House (New York, NY), 1985.

*The Berenstain Bears' Toy Time,* Random House (New York, NY), 1985.

*The Berenstain Bears Forget Their Manners,* Random House (New York, NY), 1985, reissued with cassette, 1986, reissued with puppet package, 1988.

*The Berenstain Bears' Bath Book,* Random House (New York, NY), 1985.

*The Berenstain Bears Get Stage Fright,* Random House (New York, NY), 1986.

*The Berenstain Bears: No Girls Allowed,* Random House (New York, NY), 1986.

*The Berenstain Bears and the Week at Grandma's,* Random House (New York, NY), 1986, reissued with puppet package, 1990.

*The Berenstain Bears and Too Much Birthday,* Random House (New York, NY), 1986.

*The Berenstain Kids: I Love Colors,* Random House (New York, NY), 1987.

*The Berenstain Bears Go Out for the Team,* Random House (New York, NY), 1987, reissued with cassette, 1991.

*Berenstain Bears: Coughing Catfish,* Random House (New York, NY), 1987.

*The Berenstain Bears Blaze a Trail,* Random House (New York, NY), 1987.

*The Berenstain Bears on the Job,* Random House (New York, NY), 1987.

*The Berenstain Bears and the Trouble with Friends,* Random House (New York, NY), 1987.

*The Berenstain Bears and the Missing Honey,* Random House (New York, NY), 1987.

*The Berenstain Bears and the Big Road Race,* Random House (New York, NY), 1987.

*The Berenstain Bears and the Bad Habit,* Random House (New York, NY), 1987.

*The Berenstain Bears' Trouble at School,* Random House (New York, NY), 1987, reissued with puppet package, 1990.

*After the Dinosaurs,* illustrated by Michael Berenstain, Random House (New York, NY), 1988.

*The Berenstain Bears and the Ghost in the Forest,* Random House (New York, NY), 1988.

*The Berenstain Bears Get the Gimmies,* Random House (New York, NY), 1988, reissued with cassette, 1990.

*The Berenstain Bears and the Double Dare,* Random House (New York, NY), 1988.

*The Berenstain Bears and the Bad Dream,* Random House (New York, NY), 1988.

*The Berenstain Bears Ready, Get Set, Go!,* Random House (New York, NY), 1988.

*The Berenstain Bears and Too Much Vacation,* Random House (New York, NY), 1989, reissued with cassette, 1990.

*The Berenstain Bears' Trick or Treat,* Random House (New York, NY), 1989.

*The Berenstain Bears and the In-Crowd,* Random House (New York, NY), 1989.

*The Berenstain Bears and the Slumber Party,* Random House (New York, NY), 1990.

*The Berenstain Bears and the Prize Pumpkin,* Random House (New York, NY), 1990.

*The Berenstain Bears' Trouble with Pets,* Random House (New York, NY), 1990.

*The Berenstain Bears Are a Family,* Random House (New York, NY), 1991.

*The Berenstain Bears at the Super-Duper Market,* Random House (New York, NY), 1991.

*The Berenstain Bears Say Good Night,* Random House (New York, NY), 1991.

*The Berenstain Bears' Four Seasons,* Random House (New York, NY), 1991.

*The Berenstain Bears Don't Pollute (Anymore),* Random House (New York, NY), 1991.

*The Berenstain Bears and the Trouble with Grownups,* Random House (New York, NY), 1992.

*The Berenstain Bears and Too Much Pressure,* Random House (New York, NY), 1992.

*The Berenstain Bears and the Bully,* Random House (New York, NY), 1993.

*The Berenstain Bears Get a Checkup,* Random House (New York, NY), 1993.

*The Berenstain Bears and the Green-Eyed Monster,* Random House (New York, NY), 1994.

*The Berenstain Bears' New Neighbors,* Random House (New York, NY), 1994.

*The Berenstain Bears and Too Much Teasing,* Random House (New York, NY), 1995.

*The Berenstain Bears Count Their Blessings,* Random House (New York, NY), 1995.

*The Berenstain Bears Grow-It,* Random House (New York, NY), 1996.

*The Berenstain Bears' Yike! Yike! Where's My Trike,* Random House (New York, NY), 1996.

*The Berenstain Bears Cook-It,* Random House (New York, NY), 1996.

*The Berenstain Bears in Big Bear City,* Random House (New York, NY), 1996.

*The Berenstain Bears Draw-It,* Random House (New York, NY), 1996.

*The Berenstain Bears Fly-It,* Random House (New York, NY), 1996.

*The Berenstain Bears Home Sweet Tree,* Random House (New York, NY), 1996.

*The Berenstain Bears' Sampler: The Best of Bear Country* (includes *The Berenstain Bears' New Baby, The Berenstain Bears and the Sitter, The Berenstain Bears in the Dark, The Berenstain Bears Go to the Doctor,*

and *The Berenstain Bears and the Messy Room*), Random House (New York, NY), 1996.

*The Berenstain Bears The Whole Year Through: With Earthsaver Tips and Things to Do for Each and Every Month of the Year,* Scholastic (New York, NY), 1997.

*Berenstain's A Book,* Beginner Books (New York, NY), 1997.

*The Berenstain Bears and the Blame Game,* Random House (New York, NY), 1997.

*The Berenstain Bears and the Homework Hassle,* Random House (New York, NY), 1997.

*The Berenstain Bears' Big Book of Science and Nature,* Random House (New York, NY), 1997.

*The Berenstain Bears' Thanksgiving,* Scholastic (New York, NY), 1997.

*The Berenstain Bears' Big Bear, Small Bear,* Random House (New York, NY), 1998.

*The Berenstain Bears by the Sea,* Random House (New York, NY), 1998.

*The Berenstain Bears Get the Don't Haftas,* Random House (New York, NY), 1998.

*The Berenstain Bears Ride the Thunderbolt,* Random House (New York, NY), 1998.

*The Berenstain Bears' Comic Valentine* (also see below), Scholastic (New York, NY), 1998.

*The Berenstain Bears Easter Surprise* (also see below), Scholastic (New York, NY), 1998.

*The Berenstain Bears Play Ball* (also see below), Scholastic (New York, NY), 1998.

*The Berenstain Bears Get the Screamies,* Random House (New York, NY), 1998.

*The Berenstain Bears Get Their Kicks,* Random House (New York, NY), 1998.

*The Berenstain Bears Lend a Helping Hand,* Random House (New York, NY), 1998.

*The Birds, the Bees and the Berenstain Bears,* Random House (New York, NY), 1999.

*The Berenstain Bears Mad, Mad, Mad Toy Craze,* Random House (New York, NY), 1999.

*The Berenstain Bears Go up and Down,* Random House (New York, NY), 1999.

*The Berenstain Bears Catch the Bus,* Random House (New York, NY), 1999.

*The Berenstain Bears Think of Those in Need,* Random House (New York, NY), 1999.

*The Berenstain Bears and the Big Question,* Random House (New York, NY), 1999.

*The Berenstain Bears Get the Noisies,* Random House (New York, NY), 1999.

*The Berenstain Bears Get the Scaredies,* Random House (New York, NY), 1999.

*The Berenstain Bears in the House of Mirrors,* Random House (New York, NY), 1999.

*The Berenstain Bears Go in and Out,* Random House (New York, NY), 2000.

*The Berenstain Bears and the Big Blooper,* Random House (New York, NY), 2000.

*The Berenstain Bears and Baby Makes Five,* Random House (New York, NY), 2000.

*The Berenstain Bears Get the Twitchies,* Random House (New York, NY), 2000.

*The Berenstain Bears and the Escape of the Bogg Brothers,* Random House (New York, NY), 2000.

*The Berenstain Bears' That Stump Must Go!*, Random House (New York, NY), 2000.

*The Goofy, Goony Guy*, Random House (New York, NY), 2001.

*The Berenstain Bears and the Excuse Note*, Random House (New York, NY), 2001.

*The Berenstain Bears and the Tic-Tac-Toe Mystery*, Random House (New York, NY), 2001.

*The Berenstain Bears and the Wrong Crowd*, Random House (New York, NY), 2001.

*The Berenstain Bears Dollars and Sense*, Random House (New York, NY), 2001.

*Runamuck Dog Show*, illustrated by Michael Berenstain, Random House (New York, NY), 2001.

*The Berenstain Bears and the Missing Watermelon Money*, Random House (New York, NY), 2001.

*The Berenstain Bears and the Haunted Lighthouse*, Random House (New York, NY), 2001.

*The Berenstain Bears and the Real Easter Eggs*, Random House (New York, NY), 2002.

*Ride Like the Wind*, Random House (New York, NY), 2002.

*The Berenstain Bears Report Card Trouble*, Random House (New York, NY), 2002.

Also creators of coloring books published by Random House, including *Berenstain Bears' around the Clock-Coloring Book*, 1987, *Berenstain Bears' Bear Scout-Coloring Book*, 1987, *Berenstain Bears' Count on Numbers Coloring Book*, 1987, *Berenstain Bears' on the Farm Coloring Book*, 1987, *Berenstain Bears' Safety First-Coloring Book*, 1987, and *Berenstain Bears Story-time Color Book*, 1989. Works have also been recorded into audio format, including *The Berenstain Bears' Read Along Library* (includes *He Bear, She Bear; The Bear Scouts; The Bear Detectives; The Big Honey Hunt; Old Hat, New Hat;* and *The Bears' Christmas*), Random House (New York, NY), 1977; *The Bears' Picnic and Other Stories* (includes *The Bears' Picnic; The Bear Scouts; Bears in the Night; The Bears' New Baby; The Bears' Vacation;* and *The Big Honey Hunt*), Caedmon (New York, NY), 1977; *The Bears' Christmas and Other Stories* (includes *The Bears' Christmas; He Bear, She Bear; The Bear Detectives; The Bears' Almanac;* and *The Bike Lesson*), Random House (New York, NY), 1982; and *He Bear, She Bear* [and] *Bears on Wheels*, Random House (New York, NY), 1989.

### "BERENSTAIN BEARS CUB CLUB" SERIES

*The Berenstain Bears and the Spooky Fun House*, Western Publishing (Racine, WI), 1991.

*The Berenstain Bears and the Spooky Old House*, Western Publishing (Racine, WI), 1991.

*The Berenstain Bears and the Broken Piggy Bank*, Western Publishing (Racine, WI), 1992.

*The Berenstain Bears Hug and Make Up*, Western Publishing (Racine, WI), 1992.

*The Berenstain Bears Visit Fun Park*, Western Publishing (Racine, WI), 1992.

*The Berenstain Bears' Big Rummage Sale*, Western Publishing (Racine, WI), 1992.

*The Berenstain Bears Perfect Fishing Spot*, Western Publishing (Racine, WI), 1992.

*The Berenstain Bears All Year 'Round*, Western Publishing (Racine, WI), 1993.

*The Berenstain Bears Family Get-Together*, Western Publishing (Racine, WI), 1993.

*The Berenstain Bears and the Wishing Star*, Western Publishing (Racine, WI), 1993.

*The Berenstain Bears Visit Farmer Ben*, Western Publishing (Racine, WI), 1993.

*The Berenstain Bears Learn about Colors*, Western Publishing (Racine, WI), 1993.

*The Berenstain Bears' Pet Show*, Western Publishing (Racine, WI), 1993.

*The Berenstain Bears and the Baby Chipmunk*, Western Publishing (Racine, WI), 1993.

*The Berenstain Bears and the Good Deed*, Western Publishing (Racine, WI), 1993.

*The Berenstain Bears and the Hiccup Cure*, illustrated by Michael Berenstain, Western Publishing (Racine, WI), 1993.

*The Berenstain Bears and the Bedtime Battle*, Western Publishing (Racine, WI), 1993.

*The Berenstain Bears with Nothing to Do*, Western Publishing (Racine, WI), 1993.

*The Berenstain Bears and the Jump Rope*, Western Publishing (Racine, WI), 1993.

*The Berenstain Bears and the Summer Job*, Western Publishing (Racine, WI), 1994.

*The Berenstain Bears Visit Uncle Tex*, Western Publishing (Racine, WI), 1994.

*The Berenstain Bears Lost in a Cave*, Western Publishing (Racine, WI), 1994.

*The Berenstain Bears' Birthday Boy*, Western Publishing (Racine, WI), 1994.

*The Berenstain Bears at Big Bear Fair*, Western Publishing (Racine, WI), 1994.

*The Berenstain Bears and the Big Picture*, Western Publishing (Racine, WI), 1994.

### "BERENSTAIN BEAR SCOUTS" SERIES; AUTHOR WITH WIFE, JAN BERENSTAIN

*The Berenstain Bear Scouts and the Humongous Pumpkin*, illustrated by Michael Berenstain, Scholastic (New York, NY), 1995.

*The Berenstain Bear Scouts in the Giant Bat Cave*, illustrated by Michael Berenstain, Scholastic (New York, NY), 1995.

*The Berenstain Bear Scouts and the Coughing Catfish*, illustrated by Michael Berenstain, Scholastic (New York, NY), 1996.

*The Berenstain Bear Scouts and the Sci-Fi Pizza*, illustrated by Michael Berenstain, Scholastic (New York, NY), 1996.

*Ghost Versus Ghost*, illustrated by Michael Berenstain, Scholastic (New York, NY), 1996.

*The Berenstain Bear Scouts and the Sinister Smoke*, illustrated by Michael Berenstain, Scholastic (New York, NY), 1997.

*The Berenstain Bear Scouts and the Search for Naughty Ned*, illustrated by Michael Berenstain, Scholastic (New York, NY), 1998.

*The Berenstain Bear Scouts and the Missing Merit Badges*, illustrated by Michael Berenstain, Scholastic (New York, NY), 1998.

*Papa Bear reads a story about being too friendly with strangers in Stan and Jan Berenstain's* **The Berenstain Bears Learn about Strangers.**

*The Berenstain Bear Scouts and the Ripoff Queen,* illustrated by Michael Berenstain, Scholastic (New York, NY), 1998.

*The Berenstain Bear Scouts Scream Their Heads Off,* illustrated by Michael Berenstain, Scholastic (New York, NY), 1998

*The Berenstain Bear Scouts and the Stinky Milk Mystery,* illustrated by Michael Berenstain, Scholastic (New York, NY), 1999.

*The Berenstain Bear Scouts and the White-Water Mystery,* illustrated by Michael Berenstain, Scholastic (New York, NY), 1999.

*"BERENSTAIN BABY BEARS" SERIES; AUTHOR AND ILLUSTRATOR WITH WIFE, JAN BERENSTAIN; BOARD BOOKS*

*My New Bed: From Crib to Bed,* Random House (New York, NY), 1999.

*My Potty and I: A Friend in Need,* Random House (New York, NY), 1999.

*My Trusty Car Seat: Buckling Up for Safety,* Random House (New York, NY), 1999.

*Pacifier Days: A Fond Farewell,* Random House (New York, NY), 1999.

*Me First! Me First!,* Random House (New York, NY), 2000.

*My Every Day Book: A Day in the Life,* Random House (New York, NY), 2000.

*"BIG CHAPTER BOOKS" SERIES; AUTHOR WITH WIFE, JAN BERENSTAIN, AND SON LEO BERENSTAIN*

*The Berenstain Bears and the Red-Handed Thief,* illustrated by Michael Berenstain, Random House (New York, NY), 1993.

*The Berenstain Bears and the Nerdy Nephew,* illustrated by Michael Berenstain, Random House (New York, NY), 1993.

*The Berenstain Bears Gotta Dance,* illustrated by Michael Berenstain, Random House (New York, NY), 1993.

*The Berenstain Bears and the Drug Free Zone,* illustrated by Leo and Michael Berenstain, Random House (New York, NY), 1993.

*The Berenstain Bears and the Female Fullback,* illustrated by Michael Berenstain, Random House (New York, NY), 1993.

*The Berenstain Bears and the New Girl in Town,* illustrated by Michael Berenstain, Random House (New York, NY), 1993.

*The Berenstain Bears and the Wheelchair Commando,* illustrated by Leo and Michael Berenstain, Random House (New York, NY), 1993.

*The Berenstain Bears Accept No Substitutes,* illustrated by Michael Berenstain, Random House (New York, NY), 1993.

*The Berenstain Bears and the Dress Code,* illustrated by Michael Berenstain, Random House (New York, NY), 1994.

*The Berenstain Bears at Camp Crush,* illustrated by Michael Berenstain, Random House (New York, NY), 1994.

*The Berenstain Bears and the Galloping Ghost,* illustrated by Michael Berenstain, Random House (New York, NY), 1994.

*The Berenstain Bears and the School Scandal Sheet,* illustrated by Michael Berenstain, Random House (New York, NY), 1994.

*The Berenstain Bears and the Giddy Grandma,* illustrated by Michael Berenstain, Random House (New York, NY), 1994.

*The Berenstain Bears Media Madness,* illustrated by Michael Berenstain, Random House (New York, NY), 1995.

*The Berenstain Bears and the Showdown at Chainsaw Gap,* illustrated by Michael Berenstain, Random House (New York, NY), 1995.

*The Berenstain Bears in the Freaky Funhouse,* illustrated by Michael Berenstain, Random House (New York, NY), 1995.

*The Berenstain Bears at Teen Rock Café,* illustrated by Michael Berenstain, Random House (New York, NY), 1996.

*The Berenstain Bears in Maniac Mansion,* illustrated by Michael Berenstain, Random House (New York, NY), 1996.

*The Berenstain Bears and Queenie's Crazy Crush,* illustrated by Michael Berenstain, Random House (New York, NY), 1997.

*The Berenstain Bears and the Haunted Hayride,* illustrated by Michael Berenstain, Random House (New York, NY), 1997.

*The Berenstain Bears and the Bermuda Triangle,* illustrated by Michael Berenstain, Random House (New York, NY), 1997.

*The Berenstain Bears and the Ghost of the Auto Graveyard,* illustrated by Michael Berenstain, Random House (New York, NY), 1997.

*The Berenstain Bears Go Platinum,* illustrated by Michael Berenstain, Random House (New York, NY), 1998.

*The Berenstain Bears and the Love Match,* illustrated by Michael Berenstain, Random House (New York, NY), 1998.

*The Berenstain Bears and the Big Date,* illustrated by Michael Berenstain, Random House (New York, NY), 1998.

*The Berenstain Bears and the Perfect Crime (Almost),* illustrated by Michael Berenstain, Random House (New York, NY), 1998.

*The Berenstain Bears Lost in Cyberspace,* illustrated by Michael Berenstain, Random House (New York, NY), 1999.

*The Berenstain Bears in the Wax Museum,* illustrated by Michael Berenstain, Random House (New York, NY), 1999.

*The Berenstain Bears Go to Hollywood,* illustrated by Michael Berenstain, Random House (New York, NY), 1999.

*The Berenstain Bears and the G-Rex Bones,* illustrated by Michael Berenstain, Random House (New York, NY), 1999.

*The Berenstain Bears No Guns Allowed,* illustrated by Michael Berenstain, Random House (New York, NY), 2000.

*The Berenstain Bears and the Great Ant Attack,* illustrated by Michael Berenstain, Random House (New York, NY), 2000.

*The Berenstain Bears—Phenom in the Family,* illustrated by Michael Berenstain, Random House (New York, NY), 2001.

*TELEVISION SCRIPTS; WITH WIFE, JAN BERENSTAIN*

*The Berenstain Bears' Christmas Tree,* National Broadcasting Company, Inc. (NBC-TV), 1979.

*The Berenstain Bears Meet Bigpaw,* NBC-TV, 1980.

*The Berenstain Bears' Easter Surprise,* NBC-TV, 1981.

*The Berenstain Bears' Comic Valentine,* NBC-TV, 1982.

*The Berenstain Bears Play Ball,* NBC-TV, 1983.

*The Berenstain Bears' CBS Show,* Columbia Broadcasting System, Inc. (CBS-TV), 1986-87.

*OTHER*

*The Day of the Dinosaur* ("Berenstain Bears" series), illustrated by son, Michael Berenstain, Random House (New York, NY), 1987.

(With Jan Berenstain) *What Your Parents Never Told You about Being a Mom or Dad,* Crown (New York, NY), 1995.

(With Jan Berenstain) *Down a Sunny Dirt Road* (autobiography), Random House (New York, NY), 2002.

A Janice and Stanley Berenstain manuscript collection is housed at Syracuse University. Many of the "Berenstain Bears" books have been translated into Spanish.

## Adaptations

Writings which have been adapted for filmstrips and released by Random House include: *The Bears' Nature Guide,* 1976, *The Berenstain Bears' Science Fair,* 1978, *The Bear Detectives; The Bears' Almanac; The Bears' Vacation; Bears in the Night; The Bear Scouts; The Bike Lesson; The Bears' Picnic; Inside, Outside, Upside*

*Down; Old Hat, New Hat; The Berenstain Bears and the Spooky Old Tree; He Bear, She Bear; C Is for Clown; The Berenstain Bears' B Book* (book titled *The B Book*); *The Big Honey Hunt;* and *The Bears' Christmas,* all 1986. *The Berenstain Bears Forget Their Manners* was adapted for videocassette and released by Random House Home Video, 1989. Several books have been adapted as multimedia presentations for computer by Living Books (Novato, CA), including *The Berenstain Bears Get in a Fight,* 1995, and *The Berenstain Bears in the Dark,* 1996.

## Work in Progress

*Down a Sunny Dirt Road,* Random House, October of 2002.

## Sidelights

See entry on wife, Jan Berenstain, for joint "Sidelights" on Stan and Jan Berenstain.

## Biographical and Critical Sources

*PERIODICALS*

*Appraisal: Science Books for Young People,* fall 1982.
*Booklist,* January 1, 1982.
*Books for Your Children,* spring 1988.
*Bulletin of the Center for Children's Books,* April, 1974; November, 1980.
*Children's Book Review Service,* winter 1982.
*Junior Bookshelf,* December, 1977; February, 1979.
*Kirkus Reviews,* September 1, 1972; October 15, 1975.
*Los Angeles Times Book Review,* April 13, 1986.
*Modern Maturity,* December, 1989; January, 1990.
*New York Times Book Review,* November 25, 1973; July 21, 1985; November 10, 1985; May 20, 1990.
*People,* January 22, 1979.
*Publishers Weekly,* October 24, 1977; June 17, 1983.
*School Librarian,* September, 1977.
*School Library Journal,* December, 1974; January, 1976; December, 1978; May, 1980; October, 1980; November, 1983; October, 1985.
*Science Books and Films,* May, 1976; December, 1976; September, 1978; November-December, 1985.
*Times Literary Supplement,* July 14, 1972.

\*　　　\*　　　\*

# BOWERMASTER, Jon 1954-

## Personal

Born June 29, 1954, in Normal, IL; son of Ralph E. (a school administrator) and Barbara (a teacher; maiden name, Cryer) Bowermaster; married Debra Goldman (a photographer), September 4, 1982. *Nationality:* American. *Education:* Drake University, B.A., 1976; American University, M.A., 1977.

## Addresses

*Home*—Box 730, Stone Ridge, NY 12484. *Agent*—(literary) Stuart Krichevsky, Sterling Lord Literistic, 1 Madison Avenue, New York, NY 10010.

## Career

Rockford Newspaper Co., Rockford, IL, reporter, 1974-75; *Des Moines Register,* Des Moines, IA, reporter, 1975-76; *Planet,* Des Moines, IA, editor, 1977-82; Busby Productions, Des Moines, IA, film producer, 1982-84; *Record,* New York, NY, managing editor, 1985, contributing editor, *Outside, American Photo;* freelance writer, 1985—.

## Writings

*Governor: An Oral Biography of Robert D. Ray,* Iowa State Press (Ames, IA), 1987.
(With Will Steger) *Saving the Earth: A Citizen's Guide to Environmental Action,* Knopf (New York, NY), 1990.
(With Will Steger) *Crossing Antarctica,* Knopf (New York, NY), 1992.
*The Adventures and Misadventures of Peter Beard in Africa,* Little, Brown (Boston, MA), 1993.
(With Will Steger) *Over the Top of the World: Explorer Will Steger's Trek across the Arctic,* Scholastic (New York, NY), 1997.
*Birthplace of the Winds: Storming Alaska's Islands of Fire and Ice,* National Geographic Society (Washington, DC), 2000.
*Aleutian Adventure: Kayaking in the Birthplace of the Winds,* photographs by Barry Tessman, National Geographic Society (Washington, DC), 2001.

*Jon Bowermaster collaborated with explorer Will Steger on* **Over the Top of the World,** *chronicling Steger's trek across the Arctic. (Photo by Gordon Wiltsie.)*

Contributor to periodicals, including *New York Times, National Geographic, Rolling Stone,* and *Playboy.*

## Sidelights

Jon Bowermaster is a professional adventurer whose skill as an author has allowed him to share his exploits around the world with less hardy souls. His books range in focus from a trip to an island cluster in Alaska's remote Bering Sea in *Birthplace of the Winds: Storming Alaska's Islands of Fire and Ice* to the environmental handbook *Saving the Earth: A Citizen's Guide to Environmental Action.* In addition, Bowermaster has collaborated with fellow adventurer Will Steger to produce accounts of Steger's journeys to the Earth's coldest regions. Bowermaster's *Over the Top of the World: Explorer Will Steger's Trek across the Arctic* was praised by *Booklist* reviewer Susan Dove Lempke as "written with . . . crispness and immediacy," while *Crossing Antarctica,* coauthored with Steger, was cited by a *Publishers Weekly* contributor as "a story of hardship and endurance as men . . . from different cultures . . . fight to survive in the harshest wilderness on earth." Called "a straightforward and informative story-teller" by *Washington Post Book World* contributor Elizabeth Grossman, Bowermaster "likes the nuts-and-bolts aspect of an expedition: gear, transportation, aspects of athletic skill and personality," according to the critic in a review of *Birthplace of the Winds.*

*Birthplace of the Winds* recounts a trip taken in the summer of 1999 by Bowermaster and three fellow travelers. Kayaking across the Bering Sea to the Islands of Four Mountains, the men found themselves not only in an area rarely traveled, but also facing snow squalls, strong tides, fog, and high winds during their twenty-five-day-long exploration of the region. Bowermaster also includes a history of the volcanic islands, which were once inhabited by Aleuts, his prose written in what *Booklist* contributor Gilbert Taylor described as "dramatic tones, paralleled by evocative and meditative moods that infuse his observations of the rocky, treeless, sulfurous scenery." Finding *Birthplace of the Winds* to be a "remarkable narrative," a *Publishers Weekly* contributor praised in particular the author's "clear vision and clean prose," which "make for many pleasing, writerly moments." Calling Bowermaster's book about the expedition "engrossing," Linda M. Kaufmann added in her *Library Journal* review that "this energetic travel narrative will appeal to both armchair and active adventurers."

"It has taken several years for me to come up with a response to the inevitable 'What do you do?' question," Bowermaster once told *SATA.* "I've finally come up with a reply that will have to do, even though it prompts even more queries: I am a writer who travels."

## Biographical and Critical Sources

### PERIODICALS

*Booklist,* April 15, 1997, Susan Dove Lempke, review of *Over the Top of the World: Explorer Will Steger's Trek*

*across Africa,* p. 1425; February 1, 2001, Gilbert Taylor, review of *Birthplace of the Winds: Storming Alaska's Islands of Fire and Ice,* p. 1035.

*Book Report,* November-December, 1990, Linda Nichols Haring, review of *Saving the Earth: A Citizen's Guide to Environmental Action,* p. 54; May-June, 1992, Arne Handley, review of *Crossing Antarctica,* p.62.

*Country Journal,* January-February, 1992, Patrice Crowley, review of *Saving the Earth,* p. 81.

*Library Journal,* April 15, 1990, Sue McKimm, review of *Saving the Earth,* p. 119; January, 1992, J. F. Husband, review of *Crossing Antarctica,* p. 162; October 1, 1993, Nancy Moeckel, review of *The Adventures and Misadventures of Peter Beard in Africa,* p. 102; February 15, 2001, Linda M. Kaufmann, review of *Birthplace of the Winds,* p. 188.

*Publishers Weekly,* November 22, 1991, review of *Crossing Antarctica,* p. 43; January 29, 2001, review of *Birthplace of the Winds,* p. 82.

*School Library Journal,* August, 1992, Susan B. McFaden, review of *Crossing Antarctica,* p. 192; April, 1997, Roz Goodman, review of *Over the Top of the World,* p. 160.

*Sewanee Review,* spring, 1992, Sam Pickering, review of *Crossing Antarctica,* p. 331.

*Washington Post Book World,* April 15, 2001, Elizabeth Grossman, review of *Birthplace of the Winds,* p. 13.*

\*       \*       \*

## BRADFORD, Richard (Roark) 1932-2002

*OBITUARY NOTICE*—See index for *SATA* sketch: Born May 1, 1932, in Chicago, IL; died of lung cancer March 23, 2002, in Santa Fe, NM. Editor, screenwriter, and author. Bradford is remembered primarily as the author of the novel *Red Sky at Morning,* a coming-of-age story that was compared by some reviewers to J. D. Salinger's *The Catcher in the Rye.* A graduate of Tulane University, where he received his B.A. in 1952, Bradford spent the 1950s as a staff writer for the New Mexico State Tourist Bureau and then as an editor for the New Orleans Chamber of Commerce. In the early 1960s he continued working as an editor for Zia Co. in Los Alamos, NM, before becoming a research analyst in Santa Fe at the New Mexico Department of Development. Bradford completed *Red Sky at Morning* while working as a screenwriter for Universal Pictures, a job he left in 1970. His first novel was followed in 1973 with the less critically successful *So Far from Heaven.* Suffering from writer's block, the author never penned another novel, making his living as a medical transcriber and as a freelance book reviewer and contributor of humorous articles to various periodicals.

*OBITUARIES AND OTHER SOURCES:*

*BOOKS*

*The Writers Directory,* 16th edition, St. James Press (Detroit, MI), 2001.

PERIODICALS

*Los Angeles Times,* March 29, 2002, p. B12.
*New York Times,* March 30, 2002, p. A15.
*Washington Post,* March 28, 2002, p. B7.

\*       \*       \*

# BUZZEO, Toni 1951-

## Personal

Born October 4, 1951, in Dearborn, MI; daughter of Anthony and Jeanne (Mackey) Buzzeo; married Kenneth Cyll; children: Christopher. *Nationality:* American. *Education:* University of Michigan—Dearborn, B.A. (English), 1976; University of Michigan, M.A. (English), 1978; University of Rhode Island, M.L.I.S., 1990.

## Addresses

*Home*—Back Nippin Rd., Buxton, ME 04093. *Office*—Library Media Center, Longfellow Elementary School, 432 Stevens Ave., Portland, ME 04103. *E-mail*—tonibuzzeo@tonibuzzeo.com.

## Career

Library media specialist, author, and book reviewer. Baxter Memorial Library, Gorham, ME, children's librarian, beginning 1988; Margaret Chase Smith School, Sanford, ME, library media specialist, beginning 1990; Longfellow Elementary School, Portland, ME, library media specialist, 1993—. Lecturer at schools; conducts workshops and training sessions at conferences and in school districts.

## Member

International Library Science Honor Society, American Library Association, American Association of School Librarians, National Education Association, Society of Children's Book Writers and Illustrators, Maine Writers and Publishers Alliance, Maine Educational Media Association, Maine Education Association, Beta Phi Mu.

## Awards, Honors

Maine Library Media Specialist of the Year, Maine Association of School Libraries, 1999; Barbara Karlin grant, Society of Children's Book Writers and Illustrators, 2000, for *The Sea Chest.*

## Writings

(With Jane Kurtz) *Terrific Connections with Authors, Illustrators, and Storytellers: Real Space and Virtual Links,* Libraries Unlimited (Englewood, CO), 1999.
(With Jane Kurtz) *Thirty-five Best Books for Teaching U.S. Regions: Using Fiction to Help Students Explore the Geography, History, and Cultures of the Seven U.S. Regions—And Link to Social Studies,* Scholastic Professional (New York, NY), 1999.

*Toni Buzzeo*

*Collaborating to Meet Standards, Teacher/Librarian Partnerships for K-6,* Linworth Publishers (Worthington, OH), 2002.
*The Sea Chest* (for children), illustrated by Mary GrandPré, Dial (New York, NY), 2002.
*Dawdle Duckling* (for children), illustrated by Margaret Spengler, Dial (New York, NY), 2003.
*Collaborating to Meet Standards, Teacher/Librarian Partnerships for 7-12,* Linworth Publishers (Worthington, OH), 2002.

Contributor of book reviews to *Southern Maine Library District Children's Book Review* and of audio reviews to *AudioFile.*

## Work in Progress

*The Imagining Walk,* a picture book; *The Rogue Pine,* a middle-grade novel.

## Sidelights

Toni Buzzeo is a library media specialist whose involvement in libraries extends to both sides of the librarian's desk. On the one hand, she is well known for her work in bringing young children together with inspiring authors and illustrators through her work as both a librarian and as an author of professional books and articles. On the other hand, Buzzeo has written several picture books for children to read, among them *The Sea Chest* and *Dawdle Duckling.* As she noted on her Web site, the time not devoted to her job as a media specialist is devoted to her second job as a children's book author, "so that someday my books will be lined up in the children's libraries that have nurtured me so much all of my life."

Born and raised in Dearborn, Michigan, Buzzeo attended Sacred Heart School and haunted the Dearborn Public Library as a child. As a teen she began what she considers her writing apprenticeship by copying favorite poems into spiral notebooks, then rereading them to learn the cadences of the poems and develop a love and a habit for lyrical language. In high school she continued to frequent libraries, shelving books as a library page, and then at age eighteen the author began working as a full-time library clerk to earn money for college tuition. While attending the University of Michigan, Buzzeo had several of her own poems published in the school's literary magazine. It was at this point, as she noted on her Web site, that she "began to think of myself as a *real* writer. Since then I have always written, in one way or another."

Buzzeo's first published book, *Terrific Connections with Authors, Illustrators, and Storytellers: Real Space and Virtual Links,* penned with coauthor Jane Kurtz, contains a wealth of information for educators desiring to host author and illustrator visits. Noting the book's wealth of "common sense" and "practical hints," *Booklist* contributor Todd Morning had special praise for Buzzeo and Kurtz's inclusion of "the section on 'virtual visits,' which explores ways in which students and authors can communicate online or by using television/satellite links." Her first book for children, *The Sea Chest,* was published in 2002 and features illustrations by Mary GrandPré.

## Biographical and Critical Sources

### PERIODICALS

*Booklist,* March 15, 2000, Todd Morning, review of *Terrific Connections with Authors, Illustrators, and Storytellers: Real Space and Virtual Links,* p. 1391.

### OTHER

*Toni Buzzeo Web Site,* http://www.tonibuzzeo.com (March 4, 2002).*

# C

## CARTER, Anne Laurel 1953-

### Personal

Born September 22, 1953, in Toronto, Ontario, Canada; daughter of Norm and Ruth (Bringloe) Ovenden; married Craig Carter (a lawyer), 1986; children: David, Geordie, James, Kaitlyn. *Education:* University of Toronto, B.Ed., 1978, M.Ed., 1984. *Hobbies and other interests:* Classical piano.

### Addresses

*Home*—14 Send Ave., Toronto, Ontario, Canada. *Agent*—Leona Trainer, Transatlantic Literary Agency, Inc., 72 Glengowan Rd., Toronto, Ontario MAN 164, Canada. *E-mail*—annelaurelcarter@sympatico.ca.

### Career

Teacher of English as a second language and of French.

### Member

International Board on Books for Youth, Canadian Society of Children's Authors, Illustrators and Performers, Canadian Children's Book Centre, Writers Union of Canada.

### Awards, Honors

*Toronto Star* Short Story Competition Second Prize, 1997, for "No Missing Parts"; Vicky Metcalf Award, 1999, for "Leaving the Iron Lung"; Pick of the List selection, American Booksellers Association, 1999, for *Tall in the Saddle;* Thistledown Young Adult Short Story Competition Winner, 2001, for "The Piano Lesson"; *In the Clear* was nominated for the Ontario Silver Birch Award, 2002.

*Anne Laurel Carter*

### Writings

*Tall in the Saddle,* illustrated by David McPhail, Orca Books (Custer, WA), 1999.
*From Poppa,* illustrated by Kasia Charko, Lobster Press (Montreal, Canada), 1999.

*The Girl on Evangeline Beach* (young adult novel),
    Stoddart (Don Mills, Canada), 2000.
*In the Clear,* Orca Books (Custer, WA), 2001.
*Elizabeth: Bless This House* ("Our Canadian Girl" series),
    Penguin (Toronto, Canada), 2002.
*Under a Prairie Sky,* Orca Books (Custer, WA), 2002.
*No Missing Parts,* Red Deer Press (Calgary, Canada), 2002.
*Circus Play,* Orca Books (Custer, WA), 2002.
*My Home Bay,* Red Deer Press (Calgary, Canada), in press.
*The F Team,* Orca Books (Custer, WA), in press.

Contributor of stories to periodicals.

## Work in Progress

*Dr. Smart Stories,* "humorous tales about a female
muskrat dentist who invents new techniques for her
patients in the swamp"; *Call It a Miracle,* "a role-
reversal story about a mother who doesn't want to get up
and go to work and her young daughter, who must find a
plan so she can work at home."

## Sidelights

Anne Laurel Carter often looks to both contemporary
life and Canadian history for the inspiration that fuels
her creation of picture books, stories, and novels. She
first came on the scene with short stories, such as the
award-winning "No Missing Parts," then the picture
books *Tall in the Saddle* and *From Poppa.* In *Tall in the
Saddle,* which *Quill & Quire* reviewer Arlene Perly Rae
called "a rollicking cowboy fantasy," a father and son
play cowboy together. Rae commented that "both
drawings and text reflect the overwhelming love" the
two share, and in *Resource Links* a reviewer also
described the work as "a gentle affirmative story,"
dubbing it a "winning picture book." In a similar vein,
*From Poppa* also deals with a special relationship, this
time between a grandfather who has to leave his home to
winter in a warmer climate and his granddaughter, who
will feel his absence. This work caught the attention of
critics. A reviewer for *Resource Links* found the work to
be "charming and true to life." So too, a *Quill & Quire*
writer, while noting some instances of "awkward"
writing, judged the story's "great strength" to lie in
Carter's portrayal of the grandfather-granddaughter relationship, with "all the nuanced detail of real life."

Carter's debut novel, *Girl on Evangeline Beach,* demon-
strated the author's interest in Canadian history. A time-
slip fantasy, the novel revolves around the efforts of a
teenage boy, Michael, to rescue an Acadian girl from
1755, whom he had previously met as a ghost in the
twentieth century and whom he meets again in the past.
According to a *Resource Links* critic, with this novel
"Anne Carter weaves historical events with modern day
circumstances to bring a story gripping with adventure,
excitement and romance."

Carter told *SATA:* "Although I didn't notice history as a
child, I certainly do now. My first three novels are all
historical: a time-travel back to Acadia; a girl's struggle
with polio in the 1950s; and the settling of Nova Scotia

by New England 'Planters' after the deportation of the
Acadians. I find history speaks to me. Our world is
constantly changing, yet some part of human experience
always stays the same. In my collection of short stories,
I look at the pivotal experiences a teenaged girl can
have: love, loss, adventure, peer pressure. Each girl is
given a different setting and time period, yet she could
be any girl anywhere. A refugee in 1756 probably felt
many of the same things a refugee feels now, and I find
stories a wonderful way to try to understand and capture
the essence of our experiences."

## Biographical and Critical Sources

*PERIODICALS*

*Books in Canada,* February, 2000, review of *Tall in the
    Saddle,* p. 34; July, 2001, review of *In the Clear,*
    pp. 31-32.
*Canadian Children's Literature,* summer, 2000, review of
    *From Poppa,* p. 109; spring, 2001, review of *Girl on
    Evangeline Beach,* pp. 180-181.
*Quill & Quire,* July, 1999, Arlene Perly Rae, review of *Tall
    in the Saddle,* p. 51; November, 1999, review of *From
    Poppa,* p. 45.
*Resource Links,* December, 1999, review of *Tall in the
    Saddle,* p. 4; February, 2000, review of *From Poppa,*
    p. 2; April, 2000, review of *From Poppa,* p. 50;
    February, 2001, review of *Girl on Evangeline Beach,*
    p. 29.
*Toronto Star,* March 17, 2002, Deirdre Baker, "Uncertain
    History."

*        *        *

# CHOLDENKO, Gennifer 1957-

## Personal

Born October 20, 1957, in Santa Monica, CA; daughter
of Jimmy (a business executive) and Ann (a physical
therapist) Johnson; married to Jacob Brown; children:
Ian and Kai Brown. *Education:* Brandeis University,
B.A.; Rhode Island School of Design, B.F.A.

## Addresses

*Agent*—c/o Author Mail, Putnam, 345 Hudson St., New
York, NY 10014. *E-mail*—choldenko@earthlink.net.

## Career

Author.

## Awards, Honors

California Book Award Silver Medal for YA, School
Library Journal Best of 2001 list, Junior Library Guild,
IRA/CBC Children's Choice, all for *Notes from a Liar
and Her Dog.*

# Writings

*Moonstruck: The True Story of the Cow Who Jumped over the Moon,* illustrated by Paul Yalowitz, Hyperion (New York, NY), 1997.

*Notes from a Liar and Her Dog,* Putnam (New York, NY), 2001.

*Al Capone Does My Shirts,* Putnam (New York, NY), in press.

*Notes from a Liar and Her Dog* has been translated into German.

# Adaptations

*Notes from a Liar and Her Dog* was adapted for audiocassette, Listening Library, 2001.

# Work in Progress

*Tales of a Second-Grade Giant,* illustrated by Amy Walrod, for Putnam.

# Sidelights

Gennifer Choldenko made quite a splash on the children's picture book scene with her humorous take on the traditional nursery rhyme "Hey Diddle Diddle." Her *Moonstruck: The True Story of the Cow Who Jumped over the Moon* brings new light to bear on the perplexing line "And the cow jumped over the moon," which has puzzled young and old listeners alike. According to the story's narrator—a horse, of course—the black-and-white bovine in question accomplished the high-flying task after training with a group of agile horses that regularly made the leap into the night sky to skim the top of the moon and return to Earth. Calling the picture book "a giggle from beginning to end," a *Publishers Weekly* contributor noted that the author "clearly had fun setting tradition on its ear, and her glee is evident throughout." In *Booklist* Ilene Cooper dubbed *Moonstruck* "fractured and funny" and called it "a fun read-aloud—and a tribute to hard work."

*Moonstruck* was Choldenko's debut, and she has followed up its success with several more books for children. *Notes from a Liar and Her Dog,* the author's 2001 book for middle-grade readers, introduces preteen Antonia "Ant" MacPherson, a middle sister who finds herself constantly on the outs with her two bookend ballerina sisters—the perfect "Your Highness Elizabeth" and the equally perfect "Katherine the Great"—as well as her parents. Ant's only confidants are a Chihuahua named Pistachio and best friend Harrison, an artist who is obsessed with poultry. Ant resorts to fabricating elaborate falsehoods as a way to mask her unhappiness until a sixth-grade teacher sensitive to the girl's emotional problems steps in and helps Ant face responsibility for contributing to the problems within her family. Noting that Choldenko "vividly captures the feelings of a middle child torn between wanting to be noticed and wanting to be invisible," a *Publishers Weekly* contributor praised *Notes from a Liar and Her Dog* as a "funny and touching novel." Connie Tyrrell Burns added in *School Library Journal* that the author's "first-person narrative is humorous, tongue-in-cheek, and as irreverent as her independent heroine."

# Biographical and Critical Sources

*PERIODICALS*

*Booklist,* March 1, 1997, Ilene Cooper, review of *Moonstruck: The True Story of the Cow Who Jumped over the Moon,* p. 1169; October 15, 2001, Lolly Gepson, review of *Notes from a Liar and Her Dog* (audio review), p. 428.

*Publishers Weekly,* February 10, 1997, review of *Moonstruck,* p. 83; May 14, 2001, review of *Notes from a Liar and Her Dog,* p. 82.

*School Library Journal,* April, 1997, Patricia Pearl Doyle, review of *Moonstruck,* p. 91; April, 2001, Connie Tyrrell Burns, review of *Notes from a Liar and Her Dog,* p. 139.

*OTHER*

*Gennifer Choldenko Web Site,* http://www.choldenko.com (March 5, 2002).

\*     \*     \*

# CHRISTOPHER, John
## See YOUD, (Christopher) Sam(uel)

\*     \*     \*

# COTTLE, Joan 1960-

## Personal

Born July 29, 1960, in Brooklyn, NY; daughter of Peter (an electrical engineer) and Alice (an English professor; maiden name, Bonander) Cavanaugh; children: two. *Nationality:* American. *Education:* Boston University, B.F.A., 1982, M.F.A., 1985.

## Addresses

*Home*—Northern California. *Agent*—Elizabeth Harding, Curtis Brown, Ltd., 10 Astor Pl., New York, NY 10003. *E-mail*—joancottle@home.com.

## Career

Author and illustrator. Santa Clara University, Santa Clara, CA, instructor. Visiting artist/author at schools.

## Member

Authors Guild, Authors League of America, Society of Children's Book Writers and Illustrators.

## Awards, Honors

Kid's Pick of the List, American Booksellers Association, 2001, for *Miles away from Home.*

*Joan Cottle*

# Writings

*No Nap for Ned* (phonics reader), Scott-Foresman (Glenview, IL), 1999.

*The Queen and the Quilt!* (phonics reader), Scott-Foresman (Glenview, IL), 1999.

*Those Amazing Animals* (phonics reader), Scott-Foresman (Glenview, IL), 1999.

(And illustrator) *Emily's Shoes*, Children's Press (New York, NY), 1999.

(And illustrator) *Miles away from Home*, Harcourt (San Diego, CA), 2001.

Contributor to *Whatever the Weather* (poetry anthology), Scholastic Professional (New York, NY), 2001.

*ILLUSTRATOR*

Katherine Lewis, *Cassie's Cast*, Macmillan (New York, NY), 1997.

Shelley Tucker, *Word Weavings: Writing Poetry with Young Children*, Good Year Books (Glenview, IL), 1997.

Larry Dane Brimner, *How Many Ants?*, Children's Press (New York, NY), 1997.

Chuck Lawrence, *You Can't Judge a Book by Its Cover*, Macmillan (New York, NY), 1999.

# Work in Progress

More books for children.

# Sidelights

Joan Cottle credits her decision to become a children's book author and illustrator with her mother's gift of one hundred sheets of drawing paper, a big box of sharp new crayons, and a "Nancy Drew" mystery novel. That very day, which she spent alternating between becoming lost in the adventures of the spunky girl detective and creating colorful drawings, Cottle "fell in love with words and pictures," as she noted on her Web site.

After studying painting and earning an advanced degree in fine art from Boston University, Cottle began her career as an author/illustrator and has gone on to help others refine their writing skills as an instructor at California's Santa Clara University. Her first published work was as an illustrator of elementary grade readers, and in 1999 she made her authorial debut with a series of readers that include *Those Amazing Animals, The Queen and the Quilt!,* and *No Nap for Ned.* Also published in 1999, *Emily's Shoes* was Cottle's first book to showcase her talents as both writer and illustrator.

In *Emily's Shoes* a young girl finishing her bath muses on what her mother means by calling out, "Emily, it's time!" In imagining where she and her family might be going, Emily also speculates what kind of shoes she will need to put on, in a book that *Booklist* contributor Carolyn Phelan praised for both its "lighthearted" watercolor and ink drawings and "upbeat mood." Cottle's picture book *Miles away from Home* features the same whimsical artwork by Cottle as it recounts the over-the-top efforts of Miles the dog to take care of his family during a summer vacation at the beach. First, an effort at being helpful by applying too much sun screen turns the children green. Then, he accidentally breaks the beach umbrella and hits a nearby beachgoer in the head with a ball. After gobbling up another family's picnic lunch, Miles causes his owners to rethink their decision not to leave the canine in a kennel during their vacation. Fortunately, the pup's swimming skills save the day and make all else forgotten when he saves a swimmer from drowning in the surf. Noting that the story is "full of sly humor," *Booklist* reviewer Ilene Cooper added that Cottle's lightly drawn illustrations for *Miles away from Home* "find the fun in the text and expand on it." As an acknowledgment of the book's popularity among readers, *Miles away from Home* was named a Kid's Pick of the List by the American Booksellers Association.

# Biographical and Critical Sources

*PERIODICALS*

*Booklist,* October 1, 1999, Carolyn Phelan, review of *Emily's Shoes,* p. 364; May 15, 2001, Ilene Cooper, review of *Miles away from Home,* p. 1756.

*Publishers Weekly,* April 16, 2001, review of *Miles away from Home,* p. 64.

*School Library Journal,* June, 2001, Patti Gonzales, review of *Miles away from Home,* p. 111.

*OTHER*

*Joan Cottle Web Site,* http://www.joancottle.com (November 14, 2001).*

*   *   *

# CULLINAN, Bernice E(llinger) 1926-

## Personal

Born October 12, 1926, in Hamilton, OH; daughter of Lee Alexander (a small business owner) and Hazel (a nutritionist; maiden name, Berry) Dees; married George Webb Ellinger (a school superintendent), June 5, 1948 (died, 1966); married Paul Anthony Cullinan (a professor), June 9, 1967 (divorced, October 2, 1990); married Kenneth S. Giniger (a publisher), April 13, 2002; children: Susan Jane Ellinger Carley, James Webb Ellinger, Jonathan Cullinan (deceased). *Nationality:* American. *Education:* Ohio State University, B.Sc., 1948, M.A., 1951, Ph.D., 1964. *Politics:* Republican. *Religion:* Episcopalian.

## Addresses

*Home and office*—1045 Park Ave., New York, NY 10028. *E-mail*—bernicecullinan@Worldnet.att.com.

## Career

Elementary school teacher, Ohio, 1946-59; Ohio State University, Columbus, OH, instructor, 1959-64; USOE Critical Reading Project, study director, 1964-67; Ohio State University, Columbus, OH, assistant professor, 1964-67; New York University, New York, NY, associate professor, 1967-72, professor of reading, 1972-97, professor emeritus, adjunct, 1998—; Wordsong/Boyds Mills Press, Honesdale, PA, editor-in-chief, 1990—. Huck Professor of Children's Literature, Ohio State University, 1996-97. Educational consultant to Viking Penguin, 1977-87. Teacher on *Sunrise Semester,* broadcast by Columbia Broadcasting System (CBS), spring, 1978. Member of the advisory board for the *Arthur* children's series, WGBH Public Television (Boston, MA), 1998, and a number of other boards relating to children's literature and education. Member of award selection committees, including the Caldecott Award Selection Committee, 1982-83, and the Ezra Jack Keats Award Selection Committee, 1984-2000.

## Member

International Reading Association (member of board of directors, 1979-84; president, 1984-85), Reading Hall of Fame (president, 1999), National Council of Teachers of English (co-chair of National Language Arts Conference, 1978-79; member of literature commission, 1979-82), American Library Association (member of committee on teaching children's literature, 1982-84).

*Bernice E. Cullinan*

## Awards, Honors

Reading Hall of Fame inductee, International Reading Association (IRA), 1989; Arbuthnot Award for Outstanding Teacher of Children's Literature, IRA, 1989; Jeremiah Ludington Award, EPA Contribution to Educational Publishing, 1992; President's Club inductee, Ohio State University, 1993; Citation for Outstanding Contribution to Children's Literacy, Indiana University, 1995; College of Education's Hall of Fame inductee, Ohio State University, 1995.

## Writings

*Literature for Children: Its Discipline and Content,* W. C. Brown (Dubuque, IA), 1971.
(With John Bierhorst) *American Indian Folklore* (sound recording and booklet), Children's Book Council (New York, NY), 1979.
(With Mary K. Karrer and Arlene M. Pillar) *Literature and the Child,* Harcourt (New York, NY), 1981, 5th edition (with Lee Galda), Wadsworth Publishers (Belmont, CA), 2002.
*Read to Me: Raising Kids Who Love to Read,* Scholastic (New York, NY), 1992.
*Let's Read About—: Finding Books They'll Love to Read,* Scholastic (New York, NY), 1993.

(With Lee Galda and Dorothy S. Strickland) *Language, Literacy and the Child,* Harcourt (Fort Worth, TX), 1993.

(With Brod Bagert) *Helping Your Child Learn to Read,* U.S. Department of Education/OERI (Washington, DC), 1993.

(With Marilyn Scala, Virginia Schroder) *Three Voices: An Invitation to Poetry across the Curriculum,* Stenhouse Publishers (York, ME), 1995.

(With David L. Harrison) *Easy Poetry Lessons That Dazzle and Delight,* illustrated by Julie Durrell, Scholastic (New York, NY), 1999.

*Future Poets Guide: Techniques to Help Kids Fall in Love with Poetry,* Children's Book Council (New York, NY), 1999.

Also author of videotape series "Teaching Reading and Literature," New York University, 1981. Contributor to professional magazines, including *School Library Journal* and *Journal of Research Development in Education.*

*EDITOR*

*Black Dialects and Reading,* ERIC Clearinghouse on Reading and Communication Skills (Urbana, IL), 1974.

(With Carolyn W. Carmichael) *Literature and Young Children,* National Council of Teachers of English (Urbana, IL), 1977.

(With M. Jerry Weiss) *Books I Read When I Was Young: The Favorite Books of Famous People,* Avon (New York, NY), 1980.

*Children's Literature in the Reading Program,* International Reading Association (Newark, DE), 1987.

(With Janet Hickman) *Children's Literature in the Classroom—Weaving Charlotte's Web,* Christopher-Gordon Publishers (Needham Heights, MA), 1989.

*Invitation to Read: More Children's Literature in the Reading Program,* International Reading Association (Newark, DE), 1992.

*Children's Voices: Talk in the Classroom,* International Reading Association (Newark, DE), 1993.

*Pen in Hand: Children Become Writers,* International Reading Association (Newark, DE), 1993.

*Fact and Fiction: Literature across the Curriculum,* International Reading Association (Newark, DE), 1993.

*A Jar of Tiny Stars: Poems by NCTE Award-Winning Poets,* illustrated by Andi MacLeod and Marc Nadel, Wordsong (Honesdale, PA), 1996.

(With Diane G. Person) *The Continuum Encyclopedia of Children's Literature,* Continuum (New York, NY), 2001.

General editor of *Sleeping Beauty* (adapted from the German fairy tale by the Brothers Grimm), retold by Sharon Fear and illustrated by Linda Graves; *The Elves and the Shoemaker* (adapted from the German fairy tale by the Brothers Grimm), retold by Seva Spanos and illustrated by Yoshi Miyake; *Goldilocks and the Three Bears* (adapted from an English folktale), retold by Seva Spanos and illustrated by Chi Chung; *The Three Little Pigs* (adapted from an English folktale), retold by Seva Spanos and illustrated by James Eugene Sutton; and

*Thumbelina's Song* (inspired by Hans Christian Andersen's *Thumbelina*), retold by Seva Spanos and illustrated by Lydia Geretti Halverson; all for World Book (Chicago, IL), 1992.

## Work in Progress

*The Continuum Encyclopedia of Young Adult Literature; Language Arts: Learning and Teaching.*

## Sidelights

Bernice E. Cullinan told *SATA:* "I spent most of my life as a teacher, first of young children and then as a teacher of teachers. My background as a teacher and later as a parent led me into the world of children's books. There I discovered firsthand the delight of watching children's eyes light up and smiles cover their faces when a good story enchanted them.

"When I studied at Ohio State University, I became Charlotte S. Huck's first doctoral student. Charlotte, a nationally known expert on children's literature, sent me back to my kindergarten classroom each week with poems by A. A. Milne. I read the poems to my students and they began to say them along with me. By the end of the year, they could recite at least twenty-five Milne poems by heart. Charlotte sent books home with me for my own children. When I read her gift of *Charlotte's*

*Cullinan coauthored* Easy Poetry Lessons That Dazzle and Delight, *a book that helps teach children how to write poetry. (Illustrated by Julie Durrell.)*

*In this revised guide, reading specialist Cullinan advises parents on how to make their children love books.*

*Web,* it brought tears and everlasting memories. Charlotte Huck played an important role in my life. In November, 1975, my son Jonathan was killed on his bicycle in front of our house. At that time Charlotte was president of the National Council of Teachers of English (NCTE). Charlotte, Alvina Treut Burrows, a colleague at New York University, John Donovan, head of the Children's Book Council, and Sister Rosemary Winkeljohann head of the elementary section at NCTE, joined together and said, 'There must be some beauty that comes from this tragedy. There is no award for poetry for children. One must be established in memory of Jonathan's Life.'

"The NCTE award was given annually for the first six years. The first was given in 1977 to David McCord; the others to Aileen Fisher, Karla Kuskin, who drew the medallion, Myra Cohn Livingston, Eve Merriam, and John Ciardi. The award was given every three years to the following recipients: Lilian Moore, Arnold Adoff, Valerie Worth, Barbara Esbensen, Eloise Greenfield, and X. J. Kennedy. The next award will be presented in 2002.

"Poetry for children has become the center of my interests. Kent L. Brown asked me in 1990 to become poetry editor for Boyds Mills Press. We named the imprint Wordsong, the Japanese word for a poem, a word song. I spent lots of time nurturing new poets and encouraging teachers to use poetry with children. I still teach at New York University and, with Paul Janezcko, write the poetry column in *Scholastic Instructor.*"

A noted scholar in the field of children's literature, Cullinan has made a career of teaching others how to develop a love of reading in young people. The author of over forty books, Cullinan is particularly well known for her works that help educators to incorporate children's literature into a classroom setting. Books such as *Children's Literature in the Reading Program, Read to Me: Raising Kids Who Love to Read,* and *Three Voices: An Invitation to Poetry across the Curriculum* all provide useful information, according to reviewers, for teachers, parents, and librarians trying to inspire young readers. In *Children's Literature in the Reading Program,* edited by Cullinan, the author offers her ideas on how to get children in kindergarten through eighth grade interested in reading by incorporating children's literature into the school's reading program. Described as an "easy-to-read, concise book," by *Language Arts* contributor Eileen Tway, *Children's Literature in the Reading Program* "gives a fresh look at children's literature in the classroom." *Booklist*'s Barbara Elleman found the book to be "a helpful resource" for those who wish "to expose children to good books."

Parents as educators are the focus of Cullinan's *Read to Me.* Thinking that parents play an important role in how a youngster views reading, the author gives advice on how to encourage children to sit down, enjoy a book, and develop an appreciation for the written word. *Read to Me* "is designed to appeal to the busy parent who needs a starting point," claimed *School Library Journal* critic Gwen Porter. *Booklist* writer Stephanie Zvirin remarked on Cullinan's "sensible advice," going on to write that the author's "warm anecdotal style makes her book a genuine pleasure to read."

In *Three Voices* Cullinan concentrates on making poetry interesting for children. Here the author gives suggestions on how to incorporate poems into classroom lessons, including using poetry in subjects such as science, math, and social studies. Joan Hamilton, writing in *School Library Journal,* predicted that for "anyone interested in helping children acquire a lifelong love of poetry, this is a gold mine." Similar sentiments were offered by *New Advocate* contributors Lee Galda and Jane West, who found *Three Voices* to be "written with verve and an obvious love for poetry." The two further commented that "this resource sparks instructional imaginations."

For the 1996 work *A Jar of Tiny Stars: Poems by NCTE Award-Winning Poets,* students were polled about their favorite poems written by winners of the National Council of Teachers of English Award for Poetry for Children. Over fifty of the most popular poems are included, as is biographical information about each author, illustrations, and a brief quote from the poet. Calling the book's format "accessible," *Bulletin of the Center for Children's Books* reviewer Betsy Hearne felt "this neatly packaged anthology will make it easy for teachers to incorporate poetry into a preset curriculum."

Cullinan has also coedited a well-received reference book, *The Continuum Encyclopedia of Children's Literature,* with Diane G. Person, a work which "represents the most comprehensive basic reference work on children's literature currently available," according to *Library Journal*'s Karen E. S. Lempert. *The Continuum Encyclopedia of Children's Literature* features entries on over 1,200 author and illustrators of interest to young readers, as well as essays on specific aspects of children's literature and an index. Critics had strong words of praise for the quality of the volume, with *Reference & User Services Quarterly* reviewer Charlotte Decker finding "the text ... easy to read and comprehend," and *Booklist*'s Deborah Rollins and Barbara Bibel claiming that "all entries are well written."

Cullinan continued to *SATA,* "I seldom think of myself as a writer even though I have written over forty books. I consider myself a teacher and editor. The only time I've written a book is when someone asked me to write it. I think of writing as being a part of my job. My hope is that parents, teachers, and librarians will read aloud to children from the day they are born. Only then can we develop the kind of audience that will become a nation of readers."

## Biographical and Critical Sources

*PERIODICALS*

*Booklist,* July, 1987, Barbara Elleman, review of *Children's Literature in the Reading Program,* p. 1684; August, 1992, Stephanie Zvirin, review of *Read to Me: Raising Kids Who Love to Read,* p. 1982; January 1, 1996, Hazel Rochman, review of *A Jar of Tiny Stars: Poems by NCTE Award-Winning Poets,* p. 823; September 15, 2001, Barbara Bibel and Deborah Rollins, review of *The Continuum Encyclopedia of Children's Literature,* p. 254.

*Bulletin of the Center for Children's Books,* February, 1996, Betsy Hearne, review of *A Jar of Tiny Stars,* p. 186.

*Horn Book,* May, 2001, Cathryn M. Mercier, review of *Read to Me,* p. 289.

*Kirkus Reviews,* December 15, 1995, review of *A Jar of Tiny Stars,* p. 1768.

*Language Arts,* March, 1988, Eileen Tway, "The Resource Center: Literary Discourse," pp. 322-324.

*Library Journal,* March 15, 2001, Karen E. S. Lempert, review of *The Continuum Encyclopedia of Children's Literature,* p. 70.

*New Advocate,* winter, 1996, Lee Galda and Jane West, "Ways of Implementing Literature-Based Instruction," pp. 75-78.

*Reference & User Service Quarterly,* fall, 2001, Charlotte Decker, review of *The Continuum Encyclopedia of Children's Literature,* p. 72.

*School Library Journal,* September, 1992, Gwen Porter, review of *Read to Me,* p. 152; March, 1996, Joan Hamilton, review of *Three Voices,* p. 132; June, 2001, Sue Burgess, review of *The Continuum Encyclopedia of Children's Literature,* p. 190.

# E–F

## EDWARDS, Hazel (Eileen) 1945-
## (A. K. Aye)

### Personal

Born September 21, 1945, in Melbourne, Australia; daughter of David (an engineer) and Hazel Grace (a homemaker; maiden name, Abbott) Muir Moir; married Garnet George Edwards (a hospital manager), January 6, 1967; children: Kimberlea, Trevelyan. *Education:* Toorak Teachers College (now Deakin University), Trained Primary Teacher's Certificate, 1965; Monash University, B.A., 1971, B.Ed., 1974, M.Ed., 1980.

### Addresses

*Home*—28 Lana St., Blackburn S., 3130 Victoria, Australia. *Agent*—Fran Bryson, Bryson Literary Agency, First Floor, 313 Flinders Ln., Melbourne, Australia. *E-mail*—hazele@netspace.net.au.

### Career

Frankston and Toorak Teaching Colleges, Malvern, Australia, lecturer in English, 1969-72; Council of Adult Education, Melbourne, Australia, lecturer, 1973-85; freelancer writer and lecturer in women's issues, 1986—. Member of Victoria College Council, 1982-86. Writer in residence in primary schools, 1982; leader of seminars and workshops for children and adults, 1987—; Australian Antarctic Research Expedition, Casey Station, Australia, writer in residence, 2000-01.

### Member

Australian Society of Authors (member of management committee, 2002), Australian Writers Guild.

### Awards, Honors

Commendation by the Australian Book Publishers Association Design Awards, 1980-81, and bronze medal, Leipzig International Book Fair, 1982, both for *There's a Hippopotamus on Our Roof Eating Cake;* Literature Board grant, 1985; nominated for AWGIE Children's Original Scripts, 1992, for *Hip Hip Hippo,* and 1994, for *The Best School in the Galaxy.*

### Writings

*General Store,* Hodder (Sydney, Australia), 1977.
*Kendall, Min, and Temporary Fred,* Hodder (Sydney, Australia), 1980.
*Mum on Wheels,* Hodder (Sydney, Australia), 1980.
*Pancake Olympics,* Rigby (Adelaide, Australia), 1981.
*The Billycart Battle,* Rigby (Adelaide, Australia), 1982.
*Quirky the Ex,* Rigby (Adelaide, Australia), 1982.
*Mystery Twin,* Hodder (Sydney, Australia), 1983.
*Skin Zip Me,* Kangaroo Press (Kenthurst, Australia), 1984.
*Stupendous Speewah Antics,* Edward Arnold (Sydney, Australia), 1984.
*The O Gang,* Ashton Scholastic (Sydney, Australia), 1985.
*Storycraft* (short stories), Harcourt (Sydney, Australia), 1985.
*Stowaway,* Hodder (Sydney, Australia), 1987.
*A Hairy Question,* Blake Education (Glebe, Australia), 1999.
*Kalo Li's New Country,* Blake Education (Glebe, Australia), 1999.
*Stalker* (young adult), Lothian (Melbourne, Australia), 2000.
*Seiko to Watch Dog,* Shortlands, 2000.

*PICTURE BOOKS*

*There's a Hippopotamus on Our Roof Eating Cake,* illustrated by Deborah Niland, Hodder (Sydney, Australia), 1980.
*Honey the Hospital Dog,* photographs by Jane Chisholm, Buttercup Hodder (Sydney, Australia), 1984.
*The Imaginary Menagerie,* illustrated by Rod Clement, Lothian (Melbourne, Australia), 1985.
*Tolly Leaves Home,* illustrated by Rosemary Wilson, Hodder (Sydney, Australia), 1985.
*Stickybeak,* illustrated by Rosemary Wilson, Nelson (South Melbourne, Australia), 1986.

*Snail Mail,* illustrated by Rod Clement, Collins (Sydney, Australia), 1986.

*Fish and Chips and Jaws,* illustrated by Rae Dale, Nelson (South Melbourne, Australia), 1987.

*Grandma Zed,* illustrated by Carolyn Johnston, Lothian (Melbourne, Australia), 1987.

*The Hundreds and Thousands Kid,* illustrated by Rosemary Wilson, Collins (Sydney, Australia), 1988.

*My Hippopotamus Is on Our Caravan Roof Getting Sunburnt,* illustrated by Deborah Niland, Hodder (Sydney, Australia), 1990.

*Hey Hippopotamus, Do Babies Eat Cake Too?,* illustrated by Deborah Niland, Hodder (Sydney, Australia), 1992.

*Look, There's a Hippopotamus in the Playground, Eating Cake,* illustrated by Deborah Niland, Hodder (Sydney, Australia), 1994.

*Guess What: There's a Hippo on the Hospital Roof Eating Cake,* illustrated by Deborah Niland, Hodder (Sydney, Australia), 1997.

(Created with Michael Salmon) *Just in Case ... You Visit the Children's Court,* Victoria Legal Aid (Melbourne, Australia), 2000.

Also author of *Feymouse,* illustrated by Kilmeny Niland, Penguin Puffin; *Astrid the Mind Reading Chook,* Macmillan; *The Judge, the Cheat, the Bribe and the Part-Time Pet,* Macmillan; *Hat-Tricks, Red Day,* and *That Bird,* Cambridge University Press series; *Winning a Giraffe called Geoffrey,* Random House; *Birds on the Brain,* Random House; *Mindspaces,* Random House; *Axminster the Carpet Snake,* illustrated by Rosemary Wilson, Penguin; *Fish and Chips and Jaws,* illustrated by Rae Dale, Penguin; *Not Lost, Just Somewhere Else,* Hill of Content; *A Hairy Question,* Blake; *Kalo Li's New Country,* Blake; and *The Giant Traffic Jam,* Macmillan.

*PLAYS*

*Playing with Ideas,* Nelson (South Melbourne, Australia), 1980.

*Playing with More Ideas,* Nelson (South Melbourne, Australia), 1981.

*Primary Plays,* Nelson (South Melbourne, Australia), 1981.

*More Primary Plays,* Nelson (South Melbourne, Australia), 1981.

*Playpack One,* Nelson (South Melbourne, Australia), 1983.

*Enact One,* Longman Cheshire (Melbourne, Australia), 1983.

*Enact Two,* Longman Cheshire (Melbourne, Australia), 1984.

*Workplays,* Longman Cheshire (Melbourne, Australia), 1984.

*Playpack Two,* Nelson (South Melbourne, Australia), 1984.

*Playpack Three,* Nelson (South Melbourne, Australia), 1985.

*Snails on Stage* (classroom script), Bookshelf (Malvern, Australia), 1987.

*Our Cake-Eating Hippo Plays* (songs and scripts) Bushfire Press (Donvale, Australia), 1997.

(With Goldie Alexander) *Excuse Me!,* Longman (Melbourne, Australia), 1998.

*OTHER*

*Women Returning to Study,* Primary Education, 1975.

*An imaginative girl takes her invisible friend on a vacation by the sea in Hazel Edwards's* **My Hippopotamus Is on Our Caravan Roof Getting Sunburnt.** *(Illustrated by Deborah Niland.)*

*Houseworking: The Unsuperperson's Guide to Sharing the Load,* Dove Communications (Blackburn, Australia), 1984.

(With Pam Chessell) *Being Your Own Boss,* Penguin (Ringwood, Australia), 1984.

*Second Start: Challenge and Change in Mid Life,* Penguin (Ringwood, Australia), 1987.

(Under pseudonym A. K. Aye) *Formula for Murder,* BLMH Publisher (Blackburn, Australia), 1995.

*Writing a Non-boring Family History,* Hale & Iremonger (Sydney, Australia), 1997.

(With Goldie Alexander) *The Business of Writing for Young People,* Hale & Ironmonger (Sydney, Australia), 1998.

(With Helen McGrath) *Creative Kaleidoscope: Strategies for Developing Creativity,* Horwitz Martin (St. Leonards, Australia), 1999.

(With Helen McGrath) *Friends: A Practical Guide to Understanding Relationships,* Choice Books (Marrickville, Australia), 1999.

(With Helen McGrath) *Difficult Personalities: Managing the Hurtful Behavior of Others (and Maybe Your Own),* Choice Books (Marrickville, Australia), 2000.

*Non-boring Travel Writing,* Common Ground (Altona, Australia), 2001.

*Healthy Women: Getting the Balance Right,* Choice Books (Marrickville, Australia), 2001.

*Antarctic Writer on Ice,* Common Ground (Altona, Australia), 2002.

Also author of *E-Mail Murder Mystery,* with Goldie Alexander, and "Travelling On" (series), Council of Adult Education, 1988. Contributor to books, including *Australian Writers of Children's Literature,* Educational Media, 1980; *Discussing Literature,* Sorrett, 1980; *Do Elephants Ever Forget?,* Longman Cheshire, 1987. Author of television script "I'm Going to Bed with Shakespeare." Contributor of reviews to various periodicals. Some of Edwards' work has been translated into Finnish, Braille, Japanese and Chinese.

## Adaptations

*There's a Hippopotamus on Our Roof Eating Cake* has been adapted for video by Box Hill, Technical and Further Education College, 1985.

## Work in Progress

*Duty Free,* a young adult crime and espionage novel, for Lothian; *Fake ID,* a young adult crime novel, for Lothian; *Stickybill: TV Duckstar* and *Cyberfarm,* both coauthored with Christine Anketell, for Oxford Press.

## Sidelights

Author of numerous children's books and as well as adult nonfiction, Hazel Edwards often uses the setting of her native Australia as background for her stories. *General Store,* for instance, features the tale of a young girl named Josie and her family as they settle into life in a small town in the country. Edwards uses "local color" to good effect noted a critic for *Junior Bookshelf.*

Of her picture books, Edwards is best known for her "Hippo" series, the first of which was *There's a Hippopotamus on Our Roof Eating Cake.* Followed by *My Hippopotamus Is on Our Caravan Roof Getting Sunburnt* and *Hey Hippopotamus, Do Babies Eat Cake, Too?,* the stories are mostly a monologue by a young girl who has an imaginary hippopotamus to help her through the challenging times in her life, including a spanking from her father, a family vacation, and even the birth of a new sibling.

In addition to children's books, Edwards has also written several nonfiction works, including *The Business of Writing for Young People.*

## Biographical and Critical Sources

PERIODICALS

*Books for Keeps,* May, 1992, Judith Sharman, review of *My Hippopotamus Is on Our Caravan Roof Getting Sunburnt,* p. 11.
*Junior Bookshelf,* April, 1978, review of *General Store,* pp. 101-102.
*Magpies,* September, 1991, Cynthia Anthony, review of *Not Lost, Just Somewhere Else,* p. 25; September, 1992, Karen Jameyson, reviews of *Stickybeak* and *Axminster the Carpet Snake,* p. 28; July, 1993, Kim Caraher, review of *Hey Hippopotamus, Do Babies Eat Cake Too?,* p. 26; March, 1998, Fran Knight, review of *E-Mail Murder Mystery,* p. 36; November, 1998, Fran Knight, review of *The Business of Writing for Young People,* p. 43.
*School Librarian,* November, 1993, review of *Hey Hippopotamus, Do Babies Eat Cake Too?,* p. 148.
*School Library Journal,* June, 1989, Gale W. Sherman, review of *Stickybeak,* p. 87.
*Times Literary Supplement,* March 27, 1981, Joy Chant, "Pictures for the Very Young," p. 342.

\*     \*     \*

# FARNSWORTH, Bill 1958-

## Personal

Born October 11, 1958, in Norwalk, CT; son of John M. and Gloria (Mulcahy) Farnsworth; married Deborah M. Jajer (a school teacher), October 6, 1984; children: Allison Marie, Caitlin Elizabeth. *Education:* Ringling School of Art, graduated with honors, 1980.

## Addresses

*Office*—1396 Roosevelt Dr., Venice, FL 34293. *E-mail*—bookillustrator@aol.com.

## Career

Illustrator, 1980—.

## Illustrator

*The Illustrated Children's Bible,* Harcourt (San Diego, CA), 1993, selection printed as *The Illustrated Children's Old Testament,* Harcourt (San Diego, CA), 1993.
Dorothy and Thomas Hoobler, *French Portraits,* Raintree Steck-Vaughn (Austin, TX), 1994.
Sanna Baker, *Grandpa Is a Flier,* Albert Whitman (Morton Grove, IL), 1995.
Cheryl Ryan, *Sally Arnold,* Cobblehill Books/Dutton (New York, NY), 1995.
Janice Cohn, *The Christmas Menorahs: How a Town Fought Hate,* Albert Whitman (Morton Grove, IL), 1995.
Ronald Kidd, *Grandpa's Hammer,* Habitat for Humanity International (Americus, GA), 1995.
Mary Quattlebaum, reteller, *Jesus and the Children,* Time-Life Kids (Alexandria, VA), 1995.
Darice Bailer, *The Last Rail: The Building of the First Transcontinental Railroad,* Soundprints (Norwalk, CT), 1996.
Sanna Anderson Baker, *Mississippi Going North,* Albert Whitman (Morton Grove, IL), 1996.
Andrew Gutelle, reteller, *David and Goliath,* Time-Life Kids (Alexandria, VA), 1996.
Nan Ferring Nelson, *My Days with Anica,* Lothrop (New York, NY), 1996.

Peter Roop, *The Buffalo Jump,* Northland (Flagstaff, AZ), 1996.

Kathleen V. Kudlinski, *Shannon: A Chinatown Adventure, San Francisco, 1880,* Aladdin (New York, NY), 1997.

Kathleen V. Kudlinski, *Shannon, Lost and Found: San Francisco, 1880,* Aladdin (New York, NY), 1997.

Kathleen V. Kudlinski, *Shannon: The Schoolmarm Mysteries, San Francisco, 1880,* Aladdin (New York, NY), 1997.

Elizabeth Van Steenwyk, *My Name Is York,* Rising Moon (Flagstaff, AZ), 1997.

Susan Korman, *Horse Raid: An Arapaho Camp in the 1800s,* Soundprints (Norwalk, CT), 1998.

Steven Kroll, *Robert Fulton: From Submarine to Steamboat,* Holiday House (New York, NY), 1999.

Marcia K. Vaughan, *Abbie against the Storm: The True Story of a Young Heroine and a Lighthouse,* Beyond Words (Portland, OR), 1999.

Claire Sidhom Matze, *The Stars in My Geddoh's Sky,* Albert Whitman (Morton Grove, IL), 1999.

Richard Ammon, *Conestoga Wagons,* Holiday House (New York, NY), 2000.

Elizabeth Van Steenwyk, *When Abraham Talked to the Trees,* Eerdmans (Grand Rapids, MI), 2000.

Avi, *Prairie School: A Story,* HarperCollins (New York, NY), 2001.

Linda Oatman High, *A Humble Life: Plain Poems,* Eerdmans (Grand Rapids, MI), 2001.

Janet Beeler Shaw, *Meet Kaya: An American Girl,* Pleasant Company (Middleton, WI), 2002.

Janet Beeler Shaw, *Kaya and Lone Dog: A Friendship Story,* Pleasant Company (Middleton, WI), 2002.

Janet Beeler Shaw, *Kaya Shows the Way: A Sister Story,* Pleasant Company (Middleton, WI), 2002.

Janet Beeler Shaw, *Kaya's Hero: A Story of Giving,* Pleasant Company (Middleton, WI), 2002.

Janet Beeler Shaw, *Changes for Kaya: A Story of Courage,* Pleasant Company (Middleton, WI), 2002.

Janet Beeler Shaw, *Kaya's Escape: A Survival Story,* Pleasant Company (Middleton, WI), 2002.

David A. Adler, *A Hero and the Holocaust; The Story of Janusz Korczak and His Children,* Holiday House (New York, NY), 2002.

Gary D. Schmidt, *The Great Stone Face: A Retelling of a Tale by Nathaniel Hawthorne,* Eerdmans (Grand Rapids, MI), 2002.

Lenice Strohmeier, *Mingo,* Marshall Cavendish (New York, NY), 2002.

## Sidelights

Illustrator Bill Farnsworth has contributed illustrations to numerous works for children written by prominent authors such as Avi, Steven Kroll, and Linda Oatman High. Farnsworth often receives high marks from reviewers for his oil paintings, which are recognized for their harmony with the author's text. In Cheryl Ryan's *Sally Arnold,* the illustrator provides the artwork for a story about young Jenny Fox, a school girl sent to spend the summer with her grandfather in a small West Virginia town. Bored at first by the lack of activity, Jenny soon occupies herself by following around Sally Arnold, the garbage-collecting town eccentric. However,

*Bill Farnsworth's oil-on-linen paintings illustrate the plain life of the Amish and Mennonite communities of Pennsylvania Dutch Country in Linda Oatman High's collection of poems,* **A Humble Life.**

while spying near the woman's home, Jenny accidently slips and falls into a nearby creek. Noticing the commotion, Sally helps the young girl and invites Jenny into her home. Surprised at the old woman's generosity, Jenny accepts the offer and discovers that Sally is not a witch, but an interesting character, and the two develop a lasting friendship. "Farnsworth's beautiful, light-filled paintings steal the show from the quiet story," observed *Booklist*'s Lauren Peterson, while a *Publishers Weekly* critic found that the illustrator's "paintings are hazy, nostalgic affairs . . . , matching the text in its genial use of familiar conventions."

A traditional Native American event is featured in Peter Roop's *The Buffalo Jump,* captured in illustration by Farnsworth. Hoping to earn his adult name, Little Blaze is disappointed when his older brother, Curly Bear, is chosen instead to act as a decoy, leading the buffalo on a chase that ends when the decoy jumps off a cliff, followed by the charging animal. While the boy keeps from plummeting to the ground by dexterously landing on a small ledge underneath the cliff, the lumbering buffalo falls to its death. However, as the end of the buffalo jump nears, Curly Bear tires and stumbles in the path of the charging buffalo. Coming to his brother's rescue, Little Blaze finishes the jump, earning himself the respect and praise of the village elders. According to *School Library Journal* critic Celia A. Huffman, the illustrator's "oil representations depict the culture, setting, and lifestyle of the Blackfeet nation." Also referring to Farnsworth's artwork, a *Publishers Weekly* critic commented that "his dramatic scenes of stampeding buffalo churning up clouds of dust add suspense."

Farnsworth also provided the illustrations for *Abbie against the Storm,* written by Marcia K. Vaughan and based on a true-life story, about a young girl who struggles to keep two important lighthouses lit during a stretch of forbidding weather. Set in 1856, Abbie Burgess and her family have recently moved to a remote island off the coast of Maine. Living with her parents and younger sisters, Abbie enjoys the isolated life of the island and agrees to take charge when her father leaves for the mainland in order to replenish their dwindling supplies. Unexpectedly, a fierce storm overtakes the island and Mrs. Burgess falls ill, leaving only Abbie to care for her sisters as well as to ensure that the lights of the two towers stay lit, providing ships in the ocean safe navigation through the rough waters. For nearly four weeks, the seventeen year old keeps everything working, even as fierce waves wipe away buildings on the island, events depicted in pictures that "make the violently changing moods of the sea so palpable that readers can feel her danger and celebrate her courage," claimed *School Library Journal* critic Margaret A. Chang. Writing in *Publishers Weekly,* a contributor also found that Farnsworth's artwork added to the tale's suspense, saying that his "resplendent paintings of the turbulent seas heighten the drama and lend the tale immediacy."

Moving to quieter country, Farnsworth provided the illustrations for *A Humble Life: Plain Poems,* a book of verse written by Linda Oatman High. Depicting life among the Amish and Mennonites in south-central Pennsylvania, Oatman's poems capture the lifestyles of people who eschew modern conveniences. Sharing, to differing degrees, a religious belief that avoids modern technology, the Amish and Mennonites are celebrated in High's verse, which depicts common Lancaster County features like horse-drawn buggies, barn raisings, and quilting. Both author and illustrator earned high praise from critics about their creation, with *Booklist* reviewer Susan Dove Lempke remarking that "the poems and the paintings offer a quiet, pleasurable reading experience." Similarly, *School Library Journal* contributor Sharon Korbeck found that "the seamless meshing of words and illustrations creates anything but 'plain poems.'"

Farnsworth once told *SATA:* "Real people and events that have in some way influenced our lives are the core of what I paint. From book jackets, children's books, and magazine illustration to private portrait commissions and limited edition prints and plates, the research involved with a particular painting can be quite extensive, especially if it is some kind of historical matter. Whatever the wide variety of subject matter might be, my personal goal is to give the client more than what they asked for and aim for the very best painting I've ever done. The whole process of reading a manuscript, doing the research, and producing the finished art is very exciting and fun. An artist must continually grow with every project in order to improve and sharpen his skills as a draftsman. And what will ultimately make your personal view unique is what you have to say from your heart."

## Biographical and Critical Sources

*PERIODICALS*

*Booklist,* April 1, 1995, Hazel Rochman, review of *Grandpa Is a Flyer,* p. 1422; May 1, 1996, Lauren Peterson, review of *Sally Arnold,* p. 1513; September 15, 1996, Leone McDermott, review of *My Day with Anka,* p. 249; October 15, 1996, Hazel Rochman, review of *The Last Rail: The Building of the First Transcontinental Railroad,* p. 46; May 15, 1999, Hazel Rochman, review of *The Stars in My Geddoh's Sky,* p. 1702; December 15, 2001, Susan Dove Lempke, review of *A Humble Life: Plain Poems,* p. 734.

*Publishers Weekly,* September 18, 1995, review of *The Christmas Menorahs: How a Town Fought Hate,* p. 103; May 13, 1996, review of *Sally Arnold,* p. 76; August 19, 1996, review of *The Buffalo Jump,* p. 67; February 3, 1997, review of *The Last Rail,* p. 46; February 7, 2000, review of *Abbie against the Storm: The True Story of a Young Heroine and a Lighthouse,* p. 85.

*School Library Journal,* July, 1995, Carole D. Fiore, review of *Grandpa Is a Flyer,* p. 54; October, 1995, Jane Marino, review of *The Christmas Menorahs,* p. 103; April, 1996, Jane Marino, review of *Sally Arnold,* p. 116; September, 1996, Leda Schubert, review of *My Day with Anka,* p. 186; October, 1996, Melissa Hudak, review of *Mississippi Going North,* p. 111; February, 1997, Celia A. Huffman, review of *The Buffalo Jump;* April, 1999, Rosie Peasley, review of *Robert Fulton: From Submarine to Steamboat,* p. 115; May, 1999, Diane S. Marton, review of *The Stars in My Geddoh's Sky,* p. 93; July, 2000, Margaret A. Chang, review of *Abbie against the Storm,* p. 89; September, 2000, Anne Chapman, review of *Conestoga Wagons,* p. 213; December, 2000, Marlene Gawron, review of *When Abraham Talked to the Trees,* p. 137; May, 2001, Carol Schene, review of *Prairie School,* p. 108; October, 2001, Sharon Korbeck, review of *A Humble Life,* p. 140.

\*     \*     \*

## FLEMING, Sally
### See WALKER, Sally M(acArt)

\*     \*     \*

## FORD, Hilary
### See YOUD, (Christopher) Sam(uel)

# FOREMAN, Michael 1938-

## Personal

Born March 21, 1938, in Pakefield, Suffolk, England; son of Walter Thomas (a crane operator) and Gladys (Goddard) Foreman; married Janet Charters, September 26, 1959 (divorced, 1966); married Louise Phillips, December 22, 1980; children: (first marriage) Mark; (second marriage) Ben Shahn, Jack. *Education:* Lowestoft School of Art, national diploma in design (painting), 1958; Royal College of Art, A.R.C.A. (with first honors), 1963.

## Addresses

*Home*—5 Church Gate, London SW6, England; Cornwall, England. *Agent*—John Locke, 15 East 76th St., New York, NY 10021.

## Career

Graphic artist and author of children's books. Lecturer in graphics at St. Martin's School of Art, London, England, 1963-66, London College of Printing, London, England, 1966-68, Royal College of Art, London, England, 1968-70, and Central School of Art, London, England, 1971-72. Art director of *Ambit,* 1960—, *Playboy,* 1965, and *King,* 1966-67. *Exhibitions:* Individual show, Royal Festival Hall, London, England, 1985. Work exhibited in Europe, America, and Japan.

## Member

Chelsea Arts.

## Awards, Honors

Schweppes traveling scholarship to United States, 1961-63; Gimpel Fils Prize for young painters, 1962; Festival International du Livre Silver Eagle Award, France, 1972; Francis Williams Memorial awards, Victoria and Albert Museum, 1972, and 1977, for *Monkey and the Three Wizards;* Kate Greenaway Commended Book, British Library Association (BLA), 1978, for *The Brothers Grimm: Popular Folk Tales;* Carnegie Medal, BLA, and Kate Greenaway Highly Commended Book, both 1980, and Graphics Prize, International Children's Book Fair, Bologna, Italy, 1982, all for *City of Gold and Other Stories from the Old Testament;* Kate Greenaway Medal and Kurt Maschler (Emil) Award, Book Trust of England, both 1982, both for *Sleeping Beauty and Other Favourite Fairy Tales;* Kate Greenaway Medal, 1982, for *Longneck and Thunderfoot;* Federation of Children's Book Groups award, England, 1983, for *The Saga of Erik the Viking;* Kate Greenaway Commended Book and *New York Times* Notable Book, both 1985, both for *Seasons of Splendour: Tales, Myths and Legends of India; Signal* Poetry award, 1987, for *Early in the Morning: A Collection of New Poems;* named Royal College of Arts honorary fellow, 1989; Kate Greenaway Medal and W. H. Smith/Books in Canada Award, both 1990, both for *War Boy: A Country Childhood;* Smarties

*Michael Foreman*

Prize for Children's Books, Book Trust (London), 1993, for *War Game;* honorary degree from Plymouth University, 1998.

## Writings

*SELF-ILLUSTRATED*

*The Perfect Present,* Coward (New York, NY), 1967.
*The Two Giants,* Pantheon (New York, NY), 1967.
*The Great Sleigh Robbery,* Hamish Hamilton (London, England), 1968, Pantheon (New York, NY), 1969.
*Horatio,* Hamish Hamilton (London, England), 1970, published as *The Travels of Horatio,* Pantheon (New York, NY), 1970.
*Moose,* Hamish Hamilton (London, England), 1971, Pantheon (New York, NY), 1972.
*Dinosaurs and All That Rubbish,* Hamish Hamilton (London, England), 1972, Crowell (New York, NY), 1973.
*War and Peas,* Crowell (New York, NY), 1974.
*All the King's Horses,* Hamish Hamilton (London, England), 1976, Bradbury Press (Scarsdale, NY), 1977.
*Panda's Puzzle, and His Voyage of Discovery* (also see below), Hamish Hamilton (London, England), 1977, Bradbury Press (Scarsdale, NY), 1978.
*Panda and the Odd Lion* (also see below), Hamish Hamilton (London, England), 1979.
*Trick a Tracker,* Philomel (New York, NY), 1981.
*Land of Dreams,* Holt (New York, NY), 1982.

*Panda and the Bunyips,* Hamish Hamilton (London, England), 1984, Schocken (New York, NY), 1988.

*Cat and Canary,* Andersen (London, England), 1984, Dial (New York, NY), 1985.

*Panda and the Bushfire,* Prentice-Hall (Englewood Cliffs, NJ), 1986.

*Ben's Box* (pop-up book), Hodder & Stoughton (London, England), 1986, Piggy Toes Press (Kansas City, MO), 1997.

*Ben's Baby,* Andersen (London, England), 1987, Harper (New York, NY), 1988.

*The Angel and the Wild Animal,* Andersen (London, England), 1988, Atheneum (New York, NY), 1989.

*One World,* Andersen (London, England), 1990.

(Editor) *Michael Foreman's World of Fairy Tales,* Pavilion (London, England), 1990, Arcade (New York, NY), 1991.

*War Boy: A Country Childhood,* Pavilion (London, England), 1989.

(Editor) *Michael Foreman's Mother Goose,* Harcourt (New York, NY), 1991.

(With Richard Seaver) *The Boy Who Sailed with Columbus,* Arcade (New York, NY), 1992.

*Jack's Fantastic Voyage,* Harcourt (San Diego, CA), 1992.

*Grandfather's Pencil and the Room Full of Stories,* Andersen (London, England), 1993, Harcourt (San Diego, CA), 1994.

*War Game,* Arcade (New York, NY), 1993.

*Dad! I Can't Sleep,* Andersen (London, England), 1994, Harcourt (San Diego, CA), 1995.

*After the War Was Over* (sequel to *War Boy*), Pavilion (London, England), 1995, Arcade (New York, NY), 1996.

*Surprise! Surprise!,* Harcourt (San Diego, CA), 1995.

*Seal Surfer,* Andersen (London, England), 1996, Harcourt (San Diego, CA), 1997.

*The Little Reindeer,* Dial (New York, NY), 1996.

*Look! Look!,* Andersen (London, England), 1997.

*Angel and the Box of Time,* Andersen (London, England), 1997.

*Jack's Big Race,* Andersen (London, England), 1997.

*Chicken Licken,* Andersen (London, England), 1998.

*Panda* (includes *Panda's Puzzle* and *Panda and the Odd Lion*), Pavilion (London, England), 1999.

*Little Red Hen,* Andersen (London, England), 1999.

*Rock-a-Doodle-Do!,* Andersen (London, England), 2000.

*Michael Foreman's Christmas Treasury,* Pavilion (London, England), 2000.

*Cat in the Manger,* Andersen (London, England), 2000, Holt (New York, NY), 2001.

*Saving Sinbad,* Andersen (London, England), 2001.

*Michael Foreman's Playtime Rhymes,* Candlewick Press (Cambridge, MA), 2002.

*ILLUSTRATOR*

Janet Charters, *The General,* Dutton (New York, NY), 1961.

Cledwyn Hughes, *The King Who Lived on Jelly,* Routledge & Kegan Paul (London, England), 1963.

Eric Partridge, *Comic Alphabets,* Routledge & Kegan Paul (London, England), 1964.

Derek Cooper, *The Bad Food Guide,* Routledge & Kegan Paul (London, England), 1966.

Gwen Clemens, *Making Music,* 1966.

Leonore Klein, *Huit enfants et un bébé,* Abelard (London, England), 1966.

*Foreman looks back on his childhood on the Suffolk coast during World War II in his humorous and unusual self-illustrated memoir* **War Boy: A Country Childhood.**

Mabel Watts, *I'm for You, You're for Me,* Abelard (London, England), 1967.

Sergei Vladimirovich Mikalkov, *Let's Fight!, and Other Russian Fables,* Pantheon (New York, NY), 1968.

Donald Davie, *Essex Poems,* 1969.

Janice Elliott, *The Birthday Unicorn,* Penguin (London, England), 1970.

William Ivan Martin, *Adam's Balm,* Bowmar (Los Angeles, CA), 1970.

C. O. Alexander, *Fisher v. Spassky,* Penguin (London, England), 1972.

William Fagg, editor, *The Living Arts of Nigeria,* Studio Vista (Eastbourne, England), 1972.

Barbara Adachi, *The Living Treasures of Japan,* Wildwood House (Aldershot, England), 1973.

Janice Elliott, *Alexander in the Land of Mog,* Brockhampton Press (Leicester, England), 1973.

Sheila Burnford, *Noah and the Second Flood,* Gollancz (London, England), 1973.

Jane H. Yolen, *Rainbow Rider,* Crowell (New York, NY), 1974.

Georgess McHargue, *Private Zoo,* Viking (New York, NY), 1975.

Barbara K. Walker, *Teeny-Tiny and the Witch-Woman,* Pantheon (New York, NY), 1975.

Cheng-en Wu, *Monkey and the Three Wizards,* translated by Peter Harris, Collins & World (London, England), 1976.

Jean Merrill, *The Pushcart War,* 1976.

Alan Garner, *The Stone Book,* Collins & World (London, England), 1976.

Alan Garner, *Tom Fobble's Day,* Collins & World (London, England), 1976.

Alan Garner, *Granny Reardun,* Collins & World (London, England), 1977.

Hans Christian Andersen, *Hans Christian Andersen: His Classic Fairy Tales,* translated by Erik Haugaard, Gollancz (London, England), 1977.

K. Bauman, *Kitchen Stories,* Nord Sud, 1977, published as *Mickey's Kitchen Contest,* Andersen (London, England), 1978.

Alan Garner, *The Aimer Gate,* Collins & World (London, England), 1978.

Bryna Stevens, reteller, *Borrowed Feathers and Other Fables,* Random House (New York, NY), 1978.

Brian Alderson, translator, *The Brothers Grimm: Popular Folk Tales,* Gollancz (London, England), 1978.

Oscar Wilde, *The Selfish Giant,* Kaye & Ward (London, England), 1978.

*Seven in One Blow,* Random House (New York, NY), 1978.

Alan Garner, *Fairy Tales of Gold,* Volume 1: *The Golden Brothers,* Volume 2: *The Girl of the Golden Gate,* Volume 3: *The Three Golden Heads of the Well,* Volume 4: *The Princess and the Golden Mane,* Collins & World (London, England), 1979.

Bill Martin, *How to Catch a Ghost,* Holt (New York, NY), 1979.

Anthony Paul, *The Tiger Who Lost His Stripes,* Andersen (London, England), 1980, 2nd edition, Harcourt (San Diego, CA), 1995.

Ernest Hemingway, *The Faithful Bull,* Emme Italia, 1980.

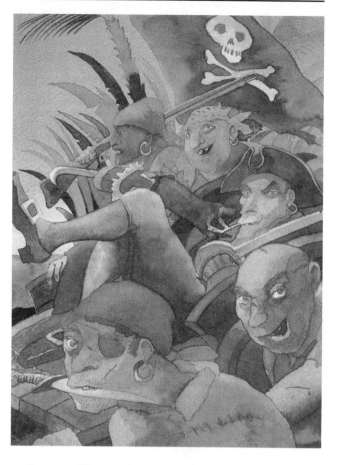

*Foreman illustrated this version of J. M. Barrie's classic tale* **Peter Pan and Wendy.**

Aldous Huxley, *After Many a Summer,* Folio Society (London, England), 1980.

Allen Andrews, *The Pig Plantagenet,* Hutchinson (London, England), 1980.

Peter Dickenson, *City of Gold and Other Stories from the Old Testament,* Gollancz (London, England), 1980.

Terry Jones, *Terry Jones' Fairy Tales,* Pavilion (London, England), 1981, excerpts published separately as *The Beast with a Thousand Teeth, A Fisherman of the World, The Sea Tiger,* and *The Fly-by-Night,* P. Bedrick (New York, NY), 1994.

Oscar Wilde, *The Nightingale and the Rose,* 1981.

John Loveday, editor, *Over the Bridge,* Penguin (London, England), 1981.

Robert McCrum, *The Magic Mouse and the Millionaire,* Hamish Hamilton (London, England), 1981.

Rudyard Kipling, *The Crab That Played with the Sea: A Just So Story,* Macmillan (London, England), 1982.

Angela Carter, selector and translator, *Sleeping Beauty and Other Favourite Fairy Tales,* Gollancz (London, England), 1982, Schocken (New York, NY), 1984.

Helen Piers, *Longneck and Thunderfoot,* Kestrel (London, England), 1982.

Robert McCrum, *The Brontosaurus Birthday Cake,* Hamish Hamilton (London, England), 1982.

Terry Jones, *The Saga of Erik the Viking,* Pavilion (London, England), 1983.

Charles Dickens, *A Christmas Carol,* Dial (New York, NY), 1983.

Nanette Newman, *A Cat and Mouse Love Story,* Heinemann (London, England), 1983.

Robert Louis Stevenson, *Treasure Island,* Penguin (London, England), 1983.

Kit Wright, editor, *Poems for Nine-Year-Olds and Under,* Puffin (London, England), 1984.

Helen Nicoll, editor, *Poems for Seven-Year-Olds and Under,* Puffin (London, England), 1984.

Kit Wright, editor, *Poems for Ten-Year-Olds and Over,* Puffin (London, England), 1985.

Roald Dahl, *Charlie and the Chocolate Factory,* Puffin (London, England), 1985.

Madhur Jaffrey, *Seasons of Splendour: Tales, Myths, and Legends of India,* Pavilion (London, England), 1985.

Robert McCrum, *Brontosaurus Superstar,* Hamish Hamilton (London, England), 1985.

Leon Garfield, adaptor, *Shakespeare Stories,* Gollancz (London, England), 1985, Houghton (Boston, MA), 1991.

William McGonagall, *Poetic Gems,* Folio Society (London, England), 1985.

Robert Louis Stevenson, *A Child's Garden of Verses,* Delacorte (New York, NY), 1985.

*Michael Morpurgo retells the legend of King Arthur and the Knights of the Round Table in* **Arthur, High King of Britain,** *illustrated by Foreman.*

Nigel Gray, *I'll Take You to Mrs. Cole!* (picture book), Bergh, 1986, Kane/Miller (New York, NY), 1992.

Edna O'Brien, *Tales for the Telling: Irish Folk and Fairy Tales,* Pavilion (London, England), 1986.

Eric Quayle, *The Magic Ointment, and Other Cornish Legends,* Andersen (London, England), 1986.

Terry Jones, *Nicobobinus,* Pavilion (London, England), 1986.

Michael Moorcock, *Letters from Hollywood,* Harrap (London, England), 1986.

Charles Causley, *Early in the Morning,* Kestrel (London, England), 1986, Viking (New York, NY), 1987.

Rudyard Kipling, *Just So Stories,* Kestrel (London, England), 1987.

Rudyard Kipling, *The Jungle Book,* Kestrel (London, England), 1987.

Jan Mark, *Fun,* Gollancz (London, England), 1987, Viking (New York, NY), 1988.

Daphne du Maurier, *Classics of the Macabre,* Gollancz (London, England), 1987.

Clement C. Moore, *The Night before Christmas,* Viking (New York, NY), 1988.

Terry Jones, *The Curse of the Vampire's Socks,* Pavilion (London, England), 1988.

J. M. Barrie, *Peter Pan and Wendy,* Pavilion (London, England), 1988.

Martin Bax, *Edmond Went Far Away,* Harcourt (New York, NY), 1989.

David Pelham, *Worms Wiggle,* Simon & Schuster (New York, NY), 1989.

Eric Quayle, editor, *The Shining Princess, and Other Japanese Legends,* Arcade (New York, NY), 1989.

Ann Turnbull, *The Sand Horse* (picture book), Macmillan (New York, NY), 1989.

Christina Martinez, *Once upon a Planet,* 1989.

Roald Dahl, *The Complete Adventures of Charlie and Mr. Willy Wonka,* Puffin (New York, NY), 1990.

Kiri Te Kanawa, *Land of the Long White Cloud,* Arcade (New York, NY), 1990.

Brian Alderson, reteller, *The Arabian Nights; or, Tales Told by Sheherezade during a Thousand and One Nights,* Gollancz (London, England), 1992, Morrow (New York, NY), 1995.

Stacie Strong, adaptor, *Over in the Meadow* (pop-up book), Simon & Schuster (New York, NY), 1992.

Mary Rayner, *The Echoing Green,* 1992.

Terry Jones, *Fantastic Stories,* Viking (New York, NY), 1993.

Roald Dahl, *Charlie and the Great Glass Elevator,* Puffin (New York, NY), 1993.

Troon Harrison, *The Long Weekend,* Andersen (London, England), 1993, Harcourt (San Diego, CA), 1994.

Kit Wright, *Funnybunch,* 1993.

Toby Forward, *Wyvern Spring,* 1993.

Nanette Newman, *Spider the Horrible Cat,* Harcourt (San Diego, CA), 1993.

Nanette Newman, *There's a Bear in the Bath!,* Pavilion (London, England), 1993, Harcourt (San Diego, CA), 1994.

Toby Forward, *Wyvern Summer,* 1994.

Toby Forward, *Wyvern Fall,* 1994.

Michael Morpurgo, *Arthur, High King of Britain,* Pavilion (London, England), 1994, Harcourt (San Diego, CA),. 1995.

Andrew Baynes, *Sarah and the Sandhorse,* 1994.

Sally Grindley, *Peter's Place,* Andersen (London, England), 1995, Harcourt (San Diego, CA), 1996.

Leon Garfield, adaptor, *Shakespeare Stories II,* Houghton (Boston, MA), 1995.

Antoine de Saint-Exupéry, *The Little Prince,* 1995.

Michael Morpurgo, editor, *Beyond the Rainbow Warrior: A Collection of Stories to Celebrate Twenty-five Years of Greenpeace,* Pavilion (London, England), 1996.

Michael Morpurgo, *Robin of Sherwood,* Harcourt (San Diego, CA), 1996.

Michael Morpurgo, *Farm Boy,* Pavilion (London, England), 1997.

James Riordan, *The Songs My Paddle Sings,* 1996.

Louise Borden, *The Little Ships: The Heroic Rescue at Dunkirk in World War II,* Margaret McElderry (New York, NY), 1997.

Ann Pilling, reteller, *Creation: Read-aloud Stories from Many Lands,* Candlewick Press (Cambridge, MA), 1997.

Michael Morpurgo, *Joan of Arc of Domrémy,* Harcourt (San Diego, CA), 1999.

Terry Jones, *The Lady and the Squire,* Pavilion (London, England), 2001.

Kenneth Grahame, *The Wind in the Willows,* Harcourt (San Diego, CA), 2002.

Also illustrator of *The Young Man of Cury* by Charles Causley, Macmillan.

*OTHER*

*Winter's Tales,* illustrated by Freire Wright, Doubleday (New York, NY), 1979.

Also creator of animated films for television in England and Scandinavia.

## Sidelights

British children's author and graphic artist Michael Foreman draws upon his real-life experiences when writing and illustrating books. Calling his writing "in turn serious, whimsical, and poetic," an essayist in the *St. James Guide to Children's Writers* praised Foreman's artwork as "outstanding": "He combines a distinctive style of flowing watercolour with a genius for conveying atmosphere," the essayist commented, "and the visual richness of his work is always a feast for the eye." In addition to illustrating the works of such wide-ranging authors as Rudyard Kipling, Oscar Wilde, and Terry Jones, Foreman has produced a number of solo works, including *Seal Surfer, Jack's Fantastic Voyage, Michael Foreman's Mother Goose,* and the award-winning *War Boy: A Country Childhood.* His artwork, whether rendered in expressive watercolor or more detailed pen-and-ink, was described by *Booklist* contributor Shelley Townsend-Hudson as possessing "a special peaceful, cozy elegance."

Foreman was born in a fishing village on England's east coast in 1938, "and grew up there during [World War II]," he once recalled. Foreman's village, Pakefield, is Britain's closest town to Germany; he once wrote, "The memory of those who passed through our village on the way to war will remain forever with the ghosts of us children in the fields and woods of long ago." Foreman's 1989 book *War Boy,* as well as its sequel, *After the War Was Over,* is a memoir of growing up in England during the war years, as Nazi bombers flew over the Suffolk coast, goods were rationed, fathers and older brothers called to arms, and children played in the wreckage of bombed out buildings. Commented reviewer Christopher Lehmann-Haupt in the *New York Times,* "Though his memories are haunted by enemy bombers and V1 and V2 rockets, the author recalls in delicate watercolors the many joys of being a shopkeeper's child under siege: the licorice comforts that left your teeth stained black, or the millions of flower seeds that were exploded out of gardens and showered around the district so that 'the following spring and summer, piles of rubble burst into bloom.'" "Foreman's recollections are sharp and graphic," added *School Library Journal* reviewer Phyllis G. Sidorsky, "as he poignantly recalls the servicemen who crowded into his mother's shop, grateful for her welcoming cup of tea and a place to chat."

After graduating from the Lowestoft School of Art in the late 1950s, Foreman got his first illustration job, providing pictures to Jane Charters's *The General.* The book, published in 1961, was set in his home town, "and the local people recognised the church, the ice cream hut, and other scenes in the pictures," he later explained. By the time *The General* reached bookstore shelves, however, its illustrator had left Pakefield and was living in London, studying toward the advanced design degree he would receive from the Royal College of Art in 1963. *The Perfect Present,* the first book on which he would be both author and illustrator, contains many scenes from London, where he has continued to make his home.

Although he worked as an art director for several magazines, and also taught at several schools in Great Britain, Foreman has devoted most of his career as a graphic artist to book illustration. Well traveled, he has been inspired by the diversity of culture and surroundings he has seen; "the sketches I bring back become the backgrounds for new books," he explained. A trip to New Mexico and the state of Arizona inspired his artwork for Jane Yolen's 1974 picture book *Rainbow Rider,* while Foreman's own *Panda and the Odd Lion* contains illustrations based on his travels throughout Africa and in the city of Venice, Italy.

"Occasionally, I get the idea for a story while traveling, but usually it takes a long time to get the right place, the right story, and the right character to meet," explained Foreman. "Much of my time I am illustrating the work of other writers, and the subject matter varies from the Bible to Shakespeare to stories set in contemporary Britain or the future. My own books are never really about a place or country, but about an idea which is hopefully common to the dreams of everyone, one which works best, however, against a particular background."

Many of Foreman's works as author/illustrator feature engaging animal characters. In *Dad! I Can't Sleep,* Little Panda's father helps him to fall asleep by counting other animals, while *Seal Surfer* focuses on a handicapped boy living in Cornwall, England, who bonds with the seal he has watched being born on the rocky coast. While building a dramatic storyline—in one scene the boy is almost drowned, while in another the coastal seals are threatened by a particularly harsh winter—Foreman "keeps the tension loose," noted a *Publishers Weekly* contributor, "thereby emphasizing the preeminence of the life cycles that shape his story." One of several Christmas stories written and illustrated by Foreman, *The Little Reindeer* is about what happens when a city boy is accidentally given a young reindeer for a present. "Foreman's touching tale sparkles like a Christmas ornament," noted a *Publishers Weekly* contributor, who also praised the book's "lyrical watercolors."

While many of Foreman's books are inspired by people and places he has seen, some have a more personal basis. His *War Game* is a picture-book tribute to four of his uncles who perished in World War I. In this unusual book he presents the many sides of war—the excitement, the daily grind, the horror—through a combination of original watercolors, archive material, and stark text. The main portion of *War Game* focuses on a hopeful moment where English and German soldiers joined in a game of soccer on Christmas Day, 1914, before the realities of war intrude once again. As *Junior Bookshelf* reviewer Marcus Crouch noted, *War Game* "is a story to be retold to each generation, and it could hardly have been told to deeper effect." Writing in *Publishers Weekly,* a reviewer commented that Foreman "transmutes the personal experiences of his uncles into a universal story.... History springs to life in this admirable work." Equally appreciative of the value of Foreman's book, *Bulletin of the Center for Children's Books* contributor Deborah Stevenson called *War Game* "an unusual war story [that] would certainly help to humanize a faraway but significant event for young readers."

"My books are not intended for any particular age group," Foreman once commented, "but the type is large and inviting for young readers who like to explore the pages after the story has been read to them. In addition I want the story to have some relevance for the adult reader. Less a question of age—more a state of mind."

## Biographical and Critical Sources

### BOOKS

*Children's Literature Review,* Volume 32, Gale (Detroit, MI), 1994.
*Something about the Author Autobiography Series,* Volume 21, Gale (Detroit, MI), 1996.
*St. James Guide to Children's Writers,* 5th edition, St. James Press (Detroit, MI), 1999.

### PERIODICALS

*Booklist,* March 15, 1998, Karen Hutt, review of *The Songs My Paddle Sings,* p. 1242; December 1, 2000, Shelley Townsend-Hudson, review of *Michael Foreman's Christmas Treasury,* p. 702; February 15, 2001, John Peters, review of *The Lady and the Squire,* p 1137.
*Bulletin of the Center for Children's Books,* October, 1994, Deborah Stevenson, review of *War Game,* p. 43.
*Horn Book,* May-June, 1996, Elizabeth S. Watson, review of *Peter's Place,* p. 323; May-June, 1997, Ann A. Flowers, review of *The Little Ships,* p. 302.
*Isis,* November, 1966.
*Junior Bookshelf,* February, 1994, Marcus Crouch, review of *War Game,* p. 31.
*New Statesman,* November 27, 1987, p. 34.
*New York Times,* December 3, 1990, Christopher Lehmann-Haupt, "Presents of Words, Pictures, and Imagination."
*New York Times Book Review,* April 28, 1985, p. 26.
*Publishers Weekly,* April 25, 1994, review of *War Game,* p. 78; August 12, 1996, review of *Robin of Sherwood,* p. 84; March 24, 1997, review of *Seal Surfer,* p. 83; October 6, 1997, review of *The Little Reindeer,* p. 55; February 22, 1999, review of *Joan of Arc of Domrémy,* p. 95; September 24, 2001, review of *Cat in the Manger,* p. 52.
*School Library Journal,* May, 1990, Phyllis G. Sidorsky, review of *War Boy: A Country Childhood,* p. 116; October, 2000, review of *Michael Foreman's Christmas Treasury,* p. 59; March, 2001, Lisa Prolman, review of *The Lady and the Squire,* p. 250.
*Times* (London), August 29, 1991, p. 14.
*Times Educational Supplement,* November 14, 1986, p. 41; March 11, 1988, p. 24; June 3, 1988, p. 46; October 13, 1989, p. 28; September 21, 1990, p. R22.
*Times Literary Supplement,* November 26, 1982; November 30, 1984, p. 1379; June 6, 1986, p. 630; November 25, 1988, p. 1321; August 3, 1990, p. 833.
*Washington Post Book World,* September 11, 1988, p. 9.

### OTHER

*Andersen Press Web site,* http://www.andersenpress.co.uk/ (December 11, 2001), "Michael Foreman."*

\*        \*        \*

# FRADIN, Dennis
## See FRADIN, Dennis Brindell

\*        \*        \*

# FRADIN, Dennis Brindell 1945-
## (Dennis Fradin)

## Personal

Born December 20, 1945, in Chicago, IL; son of Myron (an accountant) and Selma (a political activist; maiden name, Brindell) Fradin; married Judith Bloom (an author and college English teacher), March 19, 1967; children: Anthony, Diana, Michael. *Education:* Northwestern University, B.A. (creative writing), 1967; graduate study at University of Illinois, 1968. *Politics:* Independent. *Religion:* Jewish. *Hobbies and other interests:* Baseball, astronomy.

## Addresses

*Home and office*—2121 Dobson, Evanston, IL 60202.

## Career

Teacher (mostly second grade) in Chicago, IL, public schools, 1968-79; children's book author, 1976—.

## Awards, Honors

Educator of the Year, National College of Education, 1989; Editor's Choice, *Booklist,* 2000, for *Ida B. Wells: Mother of the Civil Rights Movement;* Flora Steiglitz Straus Nonfiction Book of the Year Award, Bank Street College of Education, 2001, for *Ida B. Wells;* Nonfiction Children's Book of the Year Award, Society of Midland Authors, 2001, for *Bound for the North Star.*

## Writings

*Archaeology,* Children's Press (Chicago, IL), 1983.
*Astronomy,* Children's Press (Chicago, IL), 1983.
*Blizzards and Winter Weather,* Children's Press (Chicago, IL), 1983.
*Droughts,* Children's Press (Chicago, IL), 1983.
*Olympics,* Children's Press (Chicago, IL), 1983.
*Farming,* Children's Press (Chicago, IL), 1983.
*Movies,* Children's Press (Chicago, IL), 1983.
*Comets, Asteroids, and Meteors,* Children's Press (Chicago, IL), 1984.
*Explorers,* Children's Press (Chicago, IL), 1984.
*Pioneers,* Children's Press (Chicago, IL), 1984.
*Skylab,* Children's Press (Chicago, IL), 1984.
*Space Colonies,* Children's Press (Chicago, IL), 1985.
*Halley's Comet,* Children's Press (Chicago, IL), 1985.
*Moon Flights,* Children's Press (Chicago, IL), 1985.
*The Voyager Space Probes,* Children's Press (Chicago, IL), 1985.
*Voting and Elections,* Children's Press (Chicago, IL), 1985.
*Continents,* Children's Press (Chicago, IL), 1986.
*Famines,* Children's Press (Chicago, IL), 1986.
*Space Telescope,* Children's Press (Chicago, IL), 1987.
*The Search for Extraterrestrial Intelligence,* Children's Press (Chicago, IL), 1987.
*Heredity,* Children's Press (Chicago, IL), 1987.
*Nuclear Energy,* Children's Press (Chicago, IL), 1987.
*Remarkable Children: Twenty Who Changed History,* Little, Brown (Boston, MA), 1987.
*Cancer,* Children's Press (Chicago, IL), 1988.
*The Shoshoni,* Children's Press (Chicago, IL), 1988, revised edition, 1993.
*The Flag of the United States,* Children's Press (Chicago, IL), 1988.
*The Declaration of Independence,* Children's Press (Chicago, IL), 1988.
*The Thirteen Colonies,* Children's Press (Chicago, IL), 1988.
*Drug Abuse,* Children's Press (Chicago, IL), 1988.

*Dennis Brindell Fradin*

*The Cheyenne,* Children's Press (Chicago, IL), 1988, revised edition, 1992.
*Ethiopia,* Children's Press (Chicago, IL), 1988.
*Earth,* Children's Press (Chicago, IL), 1989, revised edition, 1993.
*Mars,* Children's Press (Chicago, IL), 1989, revised edition, 1992.
*Venus,* Children's Press (Chicago, IL), 1989, revised edition, 1993.
*Medicine: Yesterday, Today, and Tomorrow,* Children's Press (Chicago, IL), 1989.
*Uranus,* revised edition, Children's Press (Chicago, IL), 1990.
*Amerigo Vespucci,* F. Watts (New York, NY), 1991.
*The Niña, the Pinta, and the Santa Maria,* F. Watts (New York, NY), 1991.
*Hiawatha: Messenger of Peace,* McElderry Books (New York, NY), 1992.
*The Pawnee,* revised edition, Children's Press (Chicago, IL), 1992.
*Jupiter,* revised edition, Children's Press (Chicago, IL), 1992.
*Mercury,* revised edition, Children's Press (Chicago, IL), 1992.
*Neptune,* revised edition, Children's Press (Chicago, IL), 1992.

*Pluto,* revised edition, Children's Press (Chicago, IL), 1993.

*Saturn,* revised edition, Children's Press (Chicago, IL), 1993.

*"We Have Conquered Pain": The Discovery of Anesthesia,* McElderry Books (New York, NY), 1996.

*Louis Braille: The Blind Boy Who Wanted to Read,* illustrated by Robert G. Sauber, Silver Burdett Press (Parsippany, NJ), 1996.

*Searching for Alien Life,* Twenty-First Century Books (New York, NY), 1997.

*The Planet Hunters: The Search for Other Worlds,* Simon & Schuster (New York, NY), 1997.

*Maria de Sautuola: The Bulls in the Cave,* Silver Burdett Press (Parsippany, NJ), 1997.

*Sacagawea: The Journey to the West,* Silver Burdett Press (Parisppany, NJ), 1998.

*Samuel Adams: The Father of American Independence,* Clarion Books (New York, NY), 1998.

*Is There Life on Mars?,* McElderry Books (New York, NY), 1999.

(With Judith Bloom Fradin), *Ida B. Wells: Mother of the Civil Rights Movement,* Houghton Mifflin (Boston, MA), 2000.

*Bound for the North Star: True Stories of Fugitive Slaves,* Houghton Mifflin (Boston, MA), 2000.

*My Family Shall Be Free!: The Life of Peter Still,* HarperCollins (New York, NY), 2001.

*"BEST HOLIDAY BOOK" SERIES*

*Christmas,* Enslow Publishers (Hillside, NJ), 1990.

*Fradin describes the geography, history, sights, and famous people of Arizona. (Cover photo by Jerry Jacka.)*

*Columbus Day,* Enslow Publishers (Hillside, NJ), 1990.

*Halloween,* Enslow Publishers (Hillside, NJ), 1990.

*Hanukkah,* Enslow Publishers (Hillside, NJ), 1990.

*Lincoln's Birthday,* Enslow Publishers (Hillside, NJ), 1990.

*Thanksgiving Day,* Enslow Publishers (Hillside, NJ), 1990.

*Valentine's Day,* Enslow Publishers (Hillside, NJ), 1990.

*Washington's Birthday,* Enslow Publishers (Hillside, NJ), 1990.

*"COLONIAL PROFILES" SERIES*

*Abigail Adams: Adviser to a President,* illustrated by Tom Dunnington, Enslow Publishers (Hillside, NJ), 1989.

*John Hancock: First Signer of the Declaration of Independence,* illustrated by Tom Dunnington, Enslow Publishers (Hillside, NJ), 1989.

*Anne Hutchinson: Fighter for Religious Freedom,* illustrated by Tom Dunnington, Enslow Publishers (Hillside, NJ), 1990.

*Patrick Henry: "Give Me Liberty or Give Me Death,"* Enslow Publishers (Hillside, NJ), 1990.

*King Philip: Indian Leader,* Enslow Publishers (Hillside, NJ), 1990.

*"WORDS AND PICTURES" SERIES; AS DENNIS FRADIN*

*Illinois in Words and Pictures,* illustrated by Richard Wahl, Children's Press (Chicago, IL), 1976.

*Virginia in Words and Pictures,* illustrated by Richard Wahl, Children's Press (Chicago, IL), 1976.

*Alaska in Words and Pictures,* illustrated by Robert Ulm, Children's Press (Chicago, IL), 1977.

*California in Words and Pictures,* illustrated by Robert Ulm, Children's Press (Chicago, IL), 1977.

*Ohio in Words and Pictures,* illustrated by Robert Ulm, Children's Press (Chicago, IL), 1977.

*Wisconsin in Words and Pictures,* illustrated by Richard Wahl, Children's Press (Chicago, IL), 1977.

*Alabama in Words and Pictures,* illustrated by Richard Wahl, Children's Press (Chicago, IL), 1980.

*Arizona in Words and Pictures,* illustrated by Richard Wahl, Children's Press (Chicago, IL), 1980.

*Arkansas in Words and Pictures,* illustrated by Richard Wahl, Children's Press (Chicago, IL), 1980.

*Colorado in Words and Pictures,* illustrated by Richard Wahl, Children's Press (Chicago, IL), 1980.

*Connecticut in Words and Pictures,* illustrated by Richard Wahl and Len Meents, Children's Press (Chicago, IL), 1980.

*Delaware in Words and Pictures,* illustrated by Richard Wahl, Children's Press (Chicago, IL), 1980.

*Florida in Words and Pictures,* illustrated by Richard Wahl, Children's Press (Chicago, IL), 1980.

*Hawaii in Words and Pictures,* illustrated by Richard Wahl, Children's Press (Chicago, IL), 1980.

*Idaho in Words and Pictures,* illustrated by Richard Wahl, Children's Press (Chicago, IL), 1980.

*Indiana in Words and Pictures,* illustrated by Richard Wahl, Children's Press (Chicago, IL), 1980.

*Iowa in Words and Pictures,* illustrated by Richard Wahl, Children's Press (Chicago, IL), 1980.

*Kansas in Words and Pictures,* illustrated by Richard Wahl, Children's Press (Chicago, IL), 1980.

*Maine in Words and Pictures,* illustrated by Richard Wahl, Children's Press (Chicago, IL), 1980.

*Maryland in Words and Pictures,* illustrated by Richard Wahl, Children's Press (Chicago, IL), 1980.

*Michigan in Words and Pictures,* illustrated by Richard Wahl, Children's Press (Chicago, IL), 1980.

*Minnesota in Words and Pictures,* illustrated by Richard Wahl, Children's Press (Chicago, IL), 1980.

*Mississippi in Words and Pictures,* illustrated by Richard Wahl, Children's Press (Chicago, IL), 1980.

*Missouri in Words and Pictures,* illustrated by Richard Wahl, Children's Press (Chicago, IL), 1980.

*Nebraska in Words and Pictures,* illustrated by Richard Wahl, Children's Press (Chicago, IL), 1980.

*New Jersey in Words and Pictures,* illustrated by Richard Wahl, Children's Press (Chicago, IL), 1980.

*North Carolina in Words and Pictures,* illustrated by Richard Wahl, Children's Press (Chicago, IL), 1980.

*Oklahoma in Words and Pictures,* illustrated by Richard Wahl, Children's Press (Chicago, IL), 1980.

*Oregon in Words and Pictures,* illustrated by Richard Wahl, Children's Press (Chicago, IL), 1980.

*Pennsylvania in Words and Pictures,* illustrated by Richard Wahl, Children's Press (Chicago, IL), 1980.

*South Carolina in Words and Pictures,* illustrated by Richard Wahl, Children's Press (Chicago, IL), 1980.

*Tennessee in Words and Pictures,* illustrated by Richard Wahl, Children's Press (Chicago, IL), 1980.

*Utah in Words and Pictures,* illustrated by Richard Wahl, Children's Press (Chicago, IL), 1980.

*Vermont in Words and Pictures,* illustrated by Richard Wahl, Children's Press (Chicago, IL), 1980.

*Washington in Words and Pictures,* illustrated by Richard Wahl, Children's Press (Chicago, IL), 1980.

*West Virginia in Words and Pictures,* illustrated by Richard Wahl, Children's Press (Chicago, IL), 1980.

*Wyoming in Words and Pictures,* illustrated by Richard Wahl, Children's Press (Chicago, IL), 1980.

*Georgia in Words and Pictures,* illustrated by Richard Wahl, Children's Press (Chicago, IL), 1981.

*Kentucky in Words and Pictures,* illustrated by Richard Wahl, Children's Press (Chicago, IL), 1981.

*Louisiana in Words and Pictures,* illustrated by Richard Wahl, Children's Press (Chicago, IL), 1981.

*Massachusetts in Words and Pictures,* illustrated by Richard Wahl, Children's Press (Chicago, IL), 1981.

*Montana in Words and Pictures,* illustrated by Richard Wahl, Children's Press (Chicago, IL), 1981.

*Nevada in Words and Pictures,* illustrated by Richard Wahl, Children's Press (Chicago, IL), 1981.

*New Hampshire in Words and Pictures,* illustrated by Richard Wahl, Children's Press (Chicago, IL), 1981.

*New Mexico in Words and Pictures,* illustrated by Richard Wahl, Children's Press (Chicago, IL), 1981.

*New York in Words and Pictures,* illustrated by Richard Wahl, maps by Len Meents, Children's Press (Chicago, IL), 1981.

*North Dakota in Words and Pictures,* illustrated by Richard Wahl, Children's Press (Chicago, IL), 1981.

*Rhode Island in Words and Pictures,* illustrated by Richard Wahl, maps by Len Meents, Children's Press (Chicago, IL), 1981.

*South Dakota in Words and Pictures,* illustrated by Richard Wahl, Children's Press (Chicago, IL), 1981.

*Texas in Words and Pictures,* illustrated by Richard Wahl, Children's Press (Chicago, IL), 1981.

*"DISASTER!" SERIES*

*Earthquakes,* Children's Press (Chicago, IL), 1982.
*Fires,* Children's Press (Chicago, IL), 1982.
*Floods,* Children's Press (Chicago, IL), 1982.
*Hurricanes,* Children's Press (Chicago, IL), 1982.
*Tornadoes,* Children's Press (Chicago, IL), 1982.
*Volcanoes,* Children's Press (Chicago, IL), 1982.

*"THIRTEEN COLONIES" SERIES*

*The Massachusetts Colony,* Children's Press (Chicago, IL), 1986.

*The Virginia Colony,* Children's Press (Chicago, IL), 1986.

*The New Hampshire Colony,* Children's Press (Chicago, IL), 1987.

*The New York Colony,* Children's Press (Chicago, IL), 1988.

*The Pennsylvania Colony,* Children's Press (Chicago, IL), 1988.

*The Georgia Colony,* Children's Press (Chicago, IL), 1989.

*The Rhode Island Colony,* Children's Press (Chicago, IL), 1989.

*The Connecticut Colony,* Children's Press (Chicago, IL), 1990.

*The Maryland Colony,* Children's Press (Chicago, IL), 1990.

*The New Jersey Colony,* Children's Press (Chicago, IL), 1991.

*The North Carolina Colony,* Children's Press (Chicago, IL), 1991.

*The Delaware Colony,* Children's Press (Chicago, IL), 1992.

*The South Carolina Colony,* Children's Press (Chicago, IL), 1992.

*"FROM SEA TO SHINING SEA" SERIES*

*Georgia,* Children's Press (Chicago, IL), 1991.
*Illinois,* Children's Press (Chicago, IL), 1991.
*Massachusetts,* Children's Press (Chicago, IL), 1991.
*California,* Children's Press (Chicago, IL), 1992.
*Florida,* Children's Press (Chicago, IL), 1992.
*Michigan,* Children's Press (Chicago, IL), 1992.
(With Judith Bloom Fradin) *Montana,* Children's Press (Chicago, IL), 1992.
*New Hampshire,* Children's Press (Chicago, IL), 1992.
*North Carolina,* Children's Press (Chicago, IL), 1992.
*South Carolina,* Children's Press (Chicago, IL), 1992.
*Tennessee,* Children's Press (Chicago, IL), 1992.
*Texas,* Children's Press (Chicago, IL), 1992.
*Virginia,* Children's Press (Chicago, IL), 1992.
*Washington, D.C.,* Children's Press (Chicago, IL), 1992.
*Wisconsin,* Children's Press (Chicago, IL), 1992.
*Alabama,* Children's Press (Chicago, IL), 1993.
*Alaska,* Children's Press (Chicago, IL), 1993.
*Arizona,* Children's Press (Chicago, IL), 1993.
*Colorado,* Children's Press (Chicago, IL), 1993.
*Iowa,* Children's Press (Chicago, IL), 1993.
*Kentucky,* Children's Press (Chicago, IL), 1993.
*New Jersey,* Children's Press (Chicago, IL), 1993.
*New Mexico,* Children's Press (Chicago, IL), 1993.
*New York,* Children's Press (Chicago, IL), 1993.

*Ohio,* Children's Press (Chicago, IL), 1993.

*Utah,* Children's Press (Chicago, IL), 1993.

*Vermont,* Children's Press (Chicago, IL), 1993.

(With Judith Bloom Fradin) *Arkansas,* Children's Press (Chicago, IL), 1994.

(With Judith Bloom Fradin) *Connecticut,* Children's Press (Chicago, IL), 1994.

(With Judith Bloom Fradin) *Delaware,* Children's Press (Chicago, IL), 1994.

*Hawaii,* Children's Press (Chicago, IL), 1994.

(With Judith Bloom Fradin) *Indiana,* Children's Press (Chicago, IL), 1994.

(With Judith Bloom Fradin) *Maryland,* Children's Press (Chicago, IL), 1994.

*Maine,* Children's Press (Chicago, IL), 1994.

*Missouri,* Children's Press (Chicago, IL), 1994.

(With Judith Bloom Fradin) *North Dakota,* Children's Press (Chicago, IL), 1994.

*Pennsylvania,* Children's Press (Chicago, IL), 1994.

(With Judith Bloom Fradin) *Washington,* Children's Press (Chicago, IL), 1994.

(With Judith Bloom Fradin) *West Virginia,* Children's Press (Chicago, IL), 1994.

(With Judith Bloom Fradin) *Wyoming,* Children's Press (Chicago, IL), 1994.

*Idaho,* Children's Press (Chicago, IL), 1995.

(With Judith Bloom Fradin) *Kansas,* Children's Press (Chicago, IL), 1995.

(With Judith Bloom Fradin) *Louisiana,* Children's Press (Chicago, IL), 1995.

(With Judith Bloom Fradin) *Minnesota,* Children's Press (Chicago, IL), 1995.

(With Judith Bloom Fradin) *Mississippi,* Children's Press (Chicago, IL), 1995.

*Nebraska,* Children's Press (Chicago, IL), 1995.

(With Judith Bloom Fradin) *Nevada,* Children's Press (Chicago, IL), 1995.

(With Judith Bloom Fradin) *Oklahoma,* Children's Press (Chicago, IL), 1995.

(With Judith Bloom Fradin) *Oregon,* Children's Press (Chicago, IL), 1995.

(With Judith Bloom Fradin) *Puerto Rico,* Children's Press (Chicago, IL), 1995.

(With Judith Bloom Fradin) *Rhode Island,* Children's Press (Chicago, IL), 1995.

(With Judith Bloom Fradin) *South Dakota,* Children's Press (Chicago, IL), 1995.

*"ENCHANTMENT OF THE WORLD" SERIES*

*The Republic of Ireland,* Children's Press (Chicago, IL), 1984, revised edition, 1994.

*The Netherlands,* Children's Press (Chicago, IL), 1994.

*FICTION; FOR CHILDREN*

*Cara,* illustrated by Joann Daley, Children's Press (Chicago, IL), 1977.

*Cave Painter,* illustrated by John Maggard, Children's Press (Chicago, IL), 1978.

*Bad Luck Tony,* illustrated by Joanne Scribner, Prentice-Hall (Englewood Cliffs, NJ), 1978.

*North Star,* illustrated by William Neebe, Children's Press (Chicago, IL), 1978.

*Beyond the Mountain, beyond the Forest,* illustrated by John Maggard, Children's Press (Chicago, IL), 1978.

*The New Spear,* illustrated by Tom Dunnington, Children's Press (Chicago, IL), 1979.

*How I Saved the World,* Dillon (Minneapolis, MI), 1986.

*OTHER*

Several of Fradin's stand-alone and series titles have been translated into Spanish.

## Sidelights

Author of over two hundred books for young readers, Dennis Brindell Fradin has penned mostly nonfiction titles dealing with historical topics, science, and contemporary discussions of the states of the Union. Contributing to several reference-book series, he has looked at the territorial makeup of this country in "From Sea to Shining Sea" and in "Words and Pictures." Fradin has additionally examined aspects of America's colonial heritage in his "Colonial Profiles" series and in the "Thirteen Colonies" series, and with his "Best Holiday Book" series he turns his inquisitive eye to such important days as Christmas and Hanukkah. And if such series work totaling almost one hundred and fifty titles were not enough, he has also produced over fifty stand-alone titles in works dealing with scientific, historical, and biographical topics. A man who clearly loves his work, Fradin once explained to *Something about the Author* (*SATA*): "I have the time of my life as a children's author. Each day I take about five steps from my bedroom into my office, where I spend my time reading, writing, rewriting, and phoning people for information. Often I travel to do in-person research." In the course of just a couple of weeks in his busy research schedule, for example, he interviewed the ninety-year-old discoverer of the planet Pluto, Clyde Tombaugh, for his *The Planet Hunters,* and then went to Puerto Rico where he saw the biggest radio telescope in the world for a book on the search for extraterrestrial (ET) intelligence. There he talked to a scientist who was taking part in a program listening for signals that ETs may be sending us. "Can you imagine getting to visit places like that and actually making a living at it?" Fradin once remarked. "Every day I'm thrilled when I think that I became what I dreamed of becoming: a children's author."

Born in Chicago, Illinois, in 1945, Fradin started writing in junior high school, but had to learn early on that he must trust his own instincts. "When I was a freshman in high school," the author told *SATA,* "I wrote a science-fiction story that my English teacher said was the best story by a freshman he had ever seen. But then when I was a junior and showed my English teacher some of my stories, he advised me to forget about becoming an author. That was when I realized that if I wanted to become an author I couldn't live and die by other people's opinions but should do it out of my own desire and need to write." Attending Northwestern University, Fradin majored in creative writing, and went on to do graduate study at the University of Illinois. While in college, he married Judith Bloom, herself a writer and

English teacher, and from 1968 to 1979, he worked as an elementary school teacher in the Chicago public schools. During this time Fradin finally began to use his writing skills, penning six titles in the "Words and Pictures" series before giving up teaching to become a full-time writer. In this initial series, Fradin provides a brief history of each state blended with geography and travelogue in forty-eight pages of text and pictures. Reviewing many titles in the series, Gail L. Gunnesh, writing in *School Library Journal,* felt that "the books are easy to follow and comprehend (color photographs and maps help), and there is no other series for beginning readers." Reviewing the Spanish version of the books on California and Texas in the same series, another reviewer for *School Library Journal* reiterated the fact that Fradin's books are unique for not only the age group but also the language group.

Publishing largely with Children's Press in Chicago, Fradin soon found himself writing in numerous series. His work on the states of the Union led also to his "From Sea to Shining Sea" series. Reviewing his title *Hawaii* in the series, Marcia S. Rettig noted in *School Library Journal* that the book was a "clear and concise over-view" containing "readable text" that "holds readers' interest and provides useful information." Reviewing *Georgia, Illinois* and *Massachusetts* in *Booklist,* Denise Wilms felt the titles "will be very useful and especially welcome by middle-grade reluctant readers." Critiquing Fradin's *New York* in the pages of *School Library Journal,* Cheryl Cufari found it to be a "simple overview of the Empire State that includes discussion of its history, industries, sites of interest, and short biographies of prominent New Yorkers."

Writing on colonial America, Fradin has also created books on notable Americans of those times as well as books about the original colonies. In his *The Pennsylvania Colony,* for example, Fradin manages to include history, personalities, and individual topics such as Native American relations. "This title is a rare treat," wrote Pamela K. Bomboy in a *School Library Journal* review, adding that the author writes "with vigor and strength" to provide "an accurate recollection of those exciting days before independence and statehood." In non-series books he has also tackled the founding of this country. Writing for a slightly younger audience in *The Declaration of Independence,* he provides "a valuable resource" for students of U.S. government due to the existence of few books on the topic "that provide material for the primary curriculum," according to *School Library Journal* contributor Becky Rosser. Preparing his biography *Samuel Adams: The Father of American Independence,* Fradin did a large amount of historical research. "For one thing," the author told *SATA,* "I read a very-hard-to-find three-volume, 1,000-page biography of Samuel by his great-grandson. The books were so old that the pages crumbled as I read them. Every day when I was done reading I had to get up pieces of the book with a vacuum cleaner! I also visited many historic sites associated with Samuel in the Boston, Massachusetts, area. For example, I tracked down the site where his house once stood and found out

that a skyscraper now stands on the spot. I got to the point that I felt Samuel was an old friend. I just loved doing that book." Reviewers responded well to Fradin's enthusiasm about his subject. "Fradin's carefully researched and detailed account . . . does much to clarify the importance of Adams's role in history," wrote Shirley Wilton in a *School Library Journal* review of the biography. Wilton concluded, "This much-needed biography focuses on Samuel Adams as an astute politician, able propagandist, and inspired patriot." Writing in *Booklist,* Carolyn Phelan noted favorably upon Fradin's "unusually personal and readable afterword," and further commented that though the author "clearly admires Adams, he doesn't shrink from pointing out the man's flaws." Phelan went on to observe, "In this literary portrait, Adams emerges as a complex man."

Often collaborating with his wife, Judith Bloom Fradin, who sometimes co-authors the works and does the picture research, Fradin is highly professional in his methods. "Each [book] I research extremely carefully and rewrite about five to six times," he explained to *SATA.* "I also check over all my facts line by line to make sure everything is accurate. So all that keeps me pretty busy. I try not to let a day of the year go by without working. Even when I fly on a plane I'm sure to bring along a book to read, just so the day doesn't go by without me doing any work. Not everything always [goes] smoothly, though. I love colonial history—a topic not too many people seem concerned about today." After all his work on the Adams biography, Fradin initially had trouble placing it, but it was eventually picked up by Clarion and published successfully. "One thing about being a writer," Fradin cautioned, "you often have to keep trying to have success because manuscripts often get rejected."

"When I was in school I didn't much like history," Fradin further commented to *SATA,* "but now I *love* history—maybe because I'm so old that I feel I'm part of history." Slave escapes have also piqued Fradin's curiosity, resulting in the book *Bound for the North Star: True Stories of Fugitive Slaves,* a compilation of over a dozen "compelling narratives of slaves' flight[s] to freedom," as *Horn Book* critic Anita L. Burkam noted, stories which include the heroic Harriet Tubman. A critic for *Publishers Weekly* described the same accounts as "riveting," and went on to comment that Fradin's use of such accounts "will likely send many readers on to further volumes." *Booklist* critic Hazel Rochman found the book to be an "inspiring history of those who escaped slavery and their rescuers," and also praised Fradin for his "direct" narrative, "with no rhetoric or cover-up." And critiquing *Bound for the North Star* in the *New York Times Book Review,* Theodore Rosengarten thought that Fradin's "gifts for concision, for suspenseful pacing and for pushing his story to the edge of plausibility before drawing it back and letting the reader catch a breath make the stories feel new even to someone well versed in the sources." On a more individual level, Fradin tells the story of one slave in *My Family Shall Be Free!: The Life of Peter Still.* Reviewing this title in *Booklist,* Roger Leslie felt that Fradin's book "is an engrossing saga that is both sweeping and intensely personal," and one that "remains strong to the very last page." Toniann Scime, writing in *School Library Journal,* found the same book "compelling," as Fradin traces the story of a man and his family ripped apart by the horror of slavery.

In collaboration with his wife, Fradin has produced a biography of the great civil rights leader Ida B. Wells, an outspoken African-American journalist and reformer who was involved in the birth of the National Association for the Advancement of Colored People (NAACP) and who resisted racism of all sorts. *Ida B. Wells* is a book which John Peters, writing in *Booklist,* found to be "by far the most moving and complete" of several contemporary biographies. Leah J. Sparks, reviewing the same title in *School Library Journal,* called it a "stellar biography of one of history's most inspiring women," and one that offers "an excellent overview of Wells's life and contributions." Sparks concluded, "The Fradins' compelling book is one that most libraries will want." *Horn Book* contributor Anita L. Burkam called the

biography "well-substantiated," and also felt that the Fradins "have remained constant to Wells as a person amidst the history."

Fradin told *SATA* that his favorite kinds of writing are history and science. In the latter category, the author has penned numerous volumes as well, astronomy and outer space being among his favorite topics. Reviewing his book *Astronomy* in *School Library Journal,* Frances E. Millhouser noted that Fradin uses a "personal style" to introduce the many scientists and their important discoveries in the field, adding information about "current research, theories, and trends." Looking into space, Fradin examines planets as well as comets, the colonizing of space, and the possibility for intelligent life elsewhere in the universe. For young readers, he provides brief overviews of the planets, including *Uranus* and *Jupiter,* books which are "very basic introductions to the planets," according to Margaret Chatham in *School Library Journal.* "The familiar format, with large type and lots of color photos, may appeal to reluctant readers who must do a report,"

*Fradin's biography* Samuel Adams: The Father of American Independence *includes this illustration of Harvard College in Adams's day. (Illustration from the Library of Congress.)*

Chatham further noted. In *The Planet Hunters: The Search for Other Worlds,* the story of men from Copernicus and Newton through Tombaugh of Pluto fame, the author "makes planetary discovery into an intriguing story with a surprising amount of human interest," wrote *Booklist* reviewer Carolyn Phelan. Fradin has also tackled the question of the existence of other life forms in space in several titles. *Is There Life on Mars?* is a "fascinating, well-researched book," according to Linda Wadleigh, writing in *School Library Journal,* a book in which the "author's genuine enthusiasm for his subject is contagious." "This fusion of science, history, and popular culture says at least as much about life on Earth as it does about the red planet," observed Randy Meyer in a *Booklist* review of the same title. For much younger readers, *The Search for Extraterrestrial Intelligence* "fills the gap between the simplest of introductions and more sophisticated, scientific treatments of this intriguing subject," as *School Library Journal* contributor Ann G. Brouse wrote. Brouse also felt that Fradin's "solid introduction to the topic ... will lead budding astronomers to more advanced works."

From the laws of the land to the laws of outer space, Fradin has covered a wealth of historical and scientific topics in his works. Writing for both beginning readers and middle graders, he has helped keep young readers informed as well as entertained with his books. "One of the great things about writing is that you can do it at any age," Fradin concluded to *SATA.* "I plan to be still writing when I'm 100 years old!"

## Biographical and Critical Sources

*PERIODICALS*

*Booklist,* May 1, 1990, p. 1702; February 1, 1992, Denise Wilms, reviews of *Georgia, Illinois,* and *Massachusetts,* p. 1023; September 15, 1992, p. 143; May 15, 1996, p. 1577; December 1, 1997, Carolyn Phelan, review of *The Planet Hunters,* p. 621; July, 1998, Carolyn Phelan, review of *Samuel Adams: The Father of American Independence,* p. 1877; January 1, 1999, p. 782; December 1, 1999, Randy Meyer, review of *Is There Life on Mars?,* p. 698; February 15, 2000, John Peters, review of *Ida B. Wells,* p. 1105; March 1, 2000, p. 1248; January 1, 2001, Hazel Rochman, review of *Bound for the North Star,* p. 950; February 15, 2001, Roger Leslie, review of *My Family Shall Be Free!,* p. 1147.

*Horn Book,* January, 1993, p. 97; September-October, 1996, p. 613; May-June, 2000, Anita L. Burkam, review of *Ida B. Wells,* p. 331; January-February, 2001, Anita L. Burkam, review of *Bound for the North Star,* p. 108.

*Kirkus Reviews,* August 15, 1992, p. 1060.

*New York Times Book Review,* November 19, 2000, Theodore Rosengarten, review of *Bound for the North Star,* p. 62.

*Publishers Weekly,* August 31, 1992, p. 80; December 13, 1999, p. 50; November 20, 2000, review of *Bound for the North Star,* p. 69.

*School Library Journal,* February, 1977, p. 56; September, 1977, p. 107; April, 1978, p. 68; September, 1978, p. 108; January, 1979, p. 41; September, 1979, p. 136; August, 1980, p. 50; March, 1981, Gail L. Gunnesh, review of *Arkansas in Words and Pictures,* p. 131; October, 1981, p. 128; April, 1983, p. 113; September, 1983, p. 122; October, 1983, p. 145; March, 1984, pp. 142, 144, 159; April, 1984, p. 101; November, 1984, p. 106; April, 1985, p. 78; February, 1986, p. 73; April, 1986, p. 70; January, 1987, pp. 74, 82; August, 1987, p. 82; December, 1987, Frances E. Millhouser, review of *Astronomy,* p. 93; January, 1988, p. 72; February, 1988, review of *California en palabras y fotos* and *Texas en palabras y fotos,* p. 94; October, 1988, p. 132; November, 1988, p. 101; January, 1989, Ann G. Brouse, review of *The Search for Extraterrestrial Intelligence,* p. 70; March, 1989, Becky Rosser, review of *The Declaration of Independence,* p. 173; April, 1989, Pamela K. Bomboy, review of *The Pennsylvania Colony,* p. 111; September, 1989, p. 262; November, 1989, pp. 122, 134; February, 1990, pp. 81, 114; March, 1990, Margaret Chatham, review of *Jupiter* and *Uranus,* p. 206; April, 1990, p. 132; October, 1990, p. 108; February, 1991, p. 79; October, 1991, p. 138; January, 1992, pp. 124, 126; March, 1992, p. 246; August, 1992, p. 164; September, 1992, p. 216; April, 1993, p. 130; January, 1994, p. 121; February, 1994, Cheryl Cufari, review of *New York,* p. 108; November, 1994, Marcia S. Rettig, review of *Hawaii,* p. 114; August, 1995, p. 146; July, 1997, p. 82; July, 1998, Shirley Wilton, review of *Samuel Adams,* p. 105; January, 2000, Linda Wadleigh, review of *Is There Life on Mars?,* p. 144; April, 2000, Leah J. Sparks, review of *Ida B. Wells,* p. 148; November, 2000, p. 168; December, 2000, p. 53; April, 2001, Toniann Scime, review of *My Family Shall Be Free!,* p. 158.

*Social Education,* May, 2001, p. 2S3.

*Voice of Youth Advocates,* August, 1996, p. 176.

# G

## GARLAND, Sarah 1944-

### Personal

Born April 9, 1944, in Herfordshire, England; daughter of Richard A. (a writer) and Charlotte (a writer; maiden name, Woodyatt) Hough; married David Anthony Garland (an artist), May 30, 1964; children: William, Laura, Kitty, Jack. *Nationality:* British. *Education:* Attended Bedales School, Hampshire, England, and the London College of Printing. *Hobbies and other interests:* Growing food, orchid hunting, walking, reading, playing the piano.

### Addresses

*Home and office*—1 The Forge, Chedworth, Gloucestershire, England GL54 4AF. *Agent*—Laura Cecil, 11 Alwyne Villas, London, England N12H6.

### Career

Author, illustrator, and journalist.

### Awards, Honors

Children's Books of the Year selection, Child Study Association of America, 1986, for *Having a Picnic;* Best Baby Books, 1990, for *All Gone!* and *Oh, No!;* runner-up, Smarties Prize, 1991, for *Shadows on the Barn;* UKRA Book Award, 1994, for *Clive and the Missing Finger.*

### Writings

*Rose and Her Bath,* Faber (London, England), 1970.
*The Herb and Spice Book,* Frances Lincoln (London, England), 1979.
(And diagrams illustrator) *Peter Rabbit's Gardening Book,* illustrated by Beatrix Potter, Warne (London, England), 1983.
*The Complete Book of Herbs and Spices,* Reader's Digest Association (Pleasantville, NY), 1993.

*The baby, the dog, the rabbit, and a garden gnome all help with planting in Sarah Garland's self-illustrated* **Doing the Garden.**

*The Herb Garden,* photographs by Pat Hunt, Penguin (New York, NY), 1996.
(Illustrator) Margaret Mahy, *Dashing Dog,* Greenwillow (New York, NY), 2002.

*SELF-ILLUSTRATED*

*Rose, the Bath, and the Merboy,* Faber (London, England), 1970.
*The Joss Bird,* Faber (London, England), 1974, Scribner (New York, NY), 1975.
*Henry and Fowler,* Scribner (New York, NY), 1976.
*Potter Brownware,* Scribner (New York, NY), 1977.
*The Seaside Christmas Tree,* Bodley Head (London, England), 1980.
*Going Shopping,* Bodley Head (London, England), 1982, Little, Brown (Boston, MA), 1985.
*Tex the Cowboy,* Collins (London, England), 1983, Dutton (New York, NY), 1995.

*The ducks, geese and goats thwart Ellie's plans to help Dad make breakfast in Garland's* **Ellie's Breakfast.**

*Tex and Gloria,* Collins (London, England), 1983.
*Tex the Champion,* Collins (London, England), 1983.
*Tex and Bad Hank,* Collins (London, England), 1983.
*Doing the Washing,* Bodley Head (London, England), 1983.
*Having a Picnic,* Bodley Head (London, England), 1984, Little, Brown (Boston, MA), 1985.
*Coming to Tea,* Bodley Head (London, England), 1985.
*Harry and the Digger Lord,* Walker (London, England), 1986.
*Sam's the Name,* Walker (London, England), 1987.
*Sam's Cat,* Walker (London, England), 1987.
*Super Sam,* Walker (London, England), 1987.
*Sam and Joe,* Walker (London, England), 1987.
*Polly's Puffin,* Bodley Head (London, England), 1988, Greenwillow (New York, NY), 1989.
*Tom's Pocket,* Reinhardt (London, England), 1989.
*All Gone!,* Reinhardt (London, England), 1989, Viking (New York, NY), 1990.
*Oh, No!,* Reinhardt (London, England), 1989, Viking (New York, NY), 1990.
*Going Swimming,* Bodley Head (London, England), 1990.
*Shadows on the Barn,* A & C Black (London, England), 1990.
*Going to Playschool,* Bodley Head (London, England), 1990.
*Doing the Garden,* Bodley Head (London, England), 1992.
*Billy and Belle,* Viking (New York, NY), 1992.
*What Am I Doing?,* Reinhardt (London, England), 1993.
*Who Can I Be,* Reinhardt (London, England), 1993.

*Clive and the Missing Finger,* A & C Black (London, England), 1994.
*Pass It, Polly,* Bodley Head (London, England), 1994.
*Madam Sizzers,* A & C Black (London, England), 1994.
*Doing Christmas,* Bodley Head (London, England), 1994.
*Coming and Going,* Bodley Head (London, England), 1995.
*Dad on the Run,* Collins (London, England), 1995.
*The Survival of Arno Mostyn,* Collins (London, England), 1996.
*Seeing Red,* illustrated by Tony Ross, Kane/Miller (New York, NY), 1996.
*Ellie's Shoes,* Bodley Head (London, England), 1997.
*Ellie's Breakfast,* Bodley Head (London, England), 1997.
(Compiler) *Shimmy with My Granny,* Macdonald (Hove, England), 1999.
(Illustrator) *Dashing Dog,* Margaret Mahy, Harper Collins (New York, NY), 2002.

## Sidelights

British author Sarah Garland is known for her picture books designed for very young readers. According to *Junior Bookshelf*'s Marcus Crouch, her strength lies in her skill "at seeking out the small dramas of everyday life and presenting them with honesty and humour." In books like *Oh, No!* and *All Gone!,* Garland introduces toddlers to the concepts of accidents and absence, respectively. Both featuring a curious little boy. *Oh, No!* shows the tot dressing the cat, grabbing grandmother's glasses, and dumping a plate of spaghetti on his head, while *All Gone!* features the trouble-maker discovering that things disappear as he tosses his bear about, witnesses the cat finish its dinner, and watches his balloon explode. Reviewing both books, *Booklist*'s Ilene Cooper found that "these small volumes speak in a simple easy fashion to toddlers."

Other books for the young set include a series of books revolving around two preschoolers and their mother. In *Going to Playschool,* Garland shows the duo having fun in the classroom, while *Doing the Garden* solves the problem of creating a yard which all members of the family—parents, kids, and pets—can enjoy. Mom, big sister, and little brother all decide to go for a dip in the public pool in *Going Swimming.* The youngest is not sure he wants to enter the water, but then, seeing the fun everyone is having, the tot begins to enjoy splashing around. In fact, he enjoys himself so much so that he cries when it is time to leave. In a review of *Going Swimming, Bulletin for the Center of Children's Books* critic Zena Sutherland suggested that Garland's illustrations "show ... clever simplicity," while, speaking of *Doing the Garden* and other entries in the series, a *Junior Bookshelf* reviewer recommended the books "for preschool children who are ready to consider and discuss the events of the day."

Designed for an older reading audience, *Shadows on the Barn* and *Tex the Cowboy* offer newly-independent readers action packed adventurers that feature Garland's cartoon-like illustrations. In *Shadows on the Barn,* Ned and Izzy must figure out why two men suddenly appear in their town and try to buy Ned's mother's barn. Thanks to some detective work, the two discover that the barn's floor is actually an old Roman mosaic. When word of the barn's contents leaks out, the villagers understand its value and the greedy crooks are chased away. According to *Books for Your Children* contributor T. Glazier, "the almost comic strip illustrations are very effective."

Part of a series of books about a bumbling cowboy, his dependable horse Gloria, and the evil Hank Bones, *Tex the Cowboy* "cheerfully lampoons the western genre," observed a *Publishers Weekly* critic. As Tex tries to outwit his nemesis, he generally fails miserably. However, thanks to the trusty Gloria, Tex is credited with solving the problem, being it winning a rodeo prize, stopping a stagecoach robbery, or discovering oil in his parched parcel of land. As clueless as Tex is, he never realizes the extent of his follies or of Gloria's hand in his successes, a running source of humor throughout the book. A contributor to *Kirkus Reviews* admired Garland's "parodic sketches of the Old West, with a cowhand's understated sense of humor."

Garland once told *SATA:* "I write and draw about the domestic life of my family and friends, so my characters are generally cheerful, improvident, rather untidy, often distracted. The children tend to cope with the vagaries of their parents fairly well and get on with their interesting and independent lives despite, rather than because of, parental interruptions. I also write adult books on herbs and spices and herb gardening and work as a journalist."

## Biographical and Critical Sources

*PERIODICALS*

*Booklist,* February 15, 1990, Ilene Cooper, review of *All Gone!* and *Oh, No!,* p. 1168; September, 1993, Alice Joyce, review of *The Complete Book of Herbs and Spices,* p. 20.

*Books for Keeps,* March, 1991, review of *Polly's Puffin,* p. 6; July, 1992, review of *Going Swimming,* p. 8; January, 1997, review of *Madam Sizzers,* p. 22; November, 1999, review of *Coming to Tea, Going Swimming, Going to Playschool,* and *Doing the Garden,* pp. 19-20.

*Books for Your Children,* autumn, 1992, T. Glazier, review of *Shadows on the Barn,* p. 21; summer, 1994, S. Williams, review of *Clive and the Missing Finger,* p. 13.

*Bulletin of the Center for Children's Books,* July, 1992, Zena Sutherland, review of *Going Swimming,* p. 294.

*Junior Bookshelf,* February, 1991, Marcus Crouch, review of *Going to Playschool,* pp. 14-15; February, 1992, review of *Shadows on the Barn,* p. 17; August, 1992, review of *Doing the Garden,* p. 142; October, 1996, review of *Seeing Red,* p. 184.

*Kirkus Reviews,* June 1, 1995, review of *Tex the Cowboy,* p. 781; July 15, 2002, review of *Dashing Dog.*

*Library Journal,* September, 1993, Virginia A. Henrichs, review of *The Complete Book of Herbs and Spices,* p. 96.

*Magpies,* November, 1994, Nola Allen, review of *Pass It, Polly,* p. 24.

*Observer* (London, England), November 20, 1994, review of *Doing Christmas,* p. 11.

*Publishers Weekly,* February, 1990, review of *Oh, No!* and *All Gone!,* p. 58; August, 1993, review of *The Complete Book of Herbs and Spices,* p. 92; July 3, 1995, review of *Tex the Cowboy,* p. 60.

*School Librarian,* February, 1994, I. Anne Rowe, review of *What Am I Doing?* and *Who Can I Be?,* p. 16.

*School Library Journal,* May, 1990, Virginia Opocensky, review of *Oh, No!,* p. 85; September, 1992, Anna DeWind, review of *Billy and Belle,* p. 203.

\*          \*          \*

## GODFREY, William
### See YOUD, (Christopher) Sam(uel)

\*          \*          \*

## GRAAF, Peter
### See YOUD, (Christopher) Sam(uel)

\*          \*          \*

## GUEST, Jacqueline 1952-

### Personal

Born November 27, 1952, in Turner Valley, Alberta, Canada; daughter of James and Violet (Hocking) Tourond; married Gordon Guest (a geologist); children: Vanessa Simmons, Kristina.

### Addresses

*Home*—Box 522, Bragg Creek, Alberta T0L 0K0, Canada. *E-mail*—writer@jacquelineguest.com.

### Career

Author. Speaker at schools and libraries.

### Member

Canadian Society of Children's Authors, Illustrators, and Performers, Canadian Children's Book Centre, Writers' Guild of Alberta.

### Awards, Honors

Children's Book Centre Choice selection, for *Hat Trick, Free Throw,* and *Rookie Season.*

### Writings

*Hat Trick,* James Lorimer (Toronto, Canada), 1997.
*Free Throw,* James Lorimer (Toronto, Canada), 1999.
*Triple Threat* (sequel to *Free Throw*), James Lorimer (Toronto, Canada), 1999.
*Rookie Season* (sequel to *Hat Trick*), James Lorimer (Toronto, Canada), 2000.

*Sixteen-year-old January tries to prove that her brother is not a bike thief in Jacqueline Guest's first novel for young adults. (Cover illustration by Jeff Domm.)*

*Lightning Rider,* James Lorimer (Toronto, Canada), 2000.

*Rink Rivals,* James Lorimer (Toronto, Canada), 2001.
*A Goal in Sight,* James Lorimer (Toronto, Canada), 2002.

## Sidelights

An author of Métis descent, Jacqueline Guest writes children's books that feature sports themes and examine how youngsters handle difficult social situations, such as adapting to blended families, competition between siblings, and overcoming physical challenges. In addition, Guest frequently creates characters of Métis background for her stories. These male and female protagonists must overcome racial prejudice as well as other obstacles in the course of the story. Covering several different sports in her books, her first work, *Hat Trick,* deals with the game of hockey, as does its sequel, *Rookie Season,* and *Rink Rivals.* Basketball is the focus of both *Free Throw* and its follow up, *Triple Threat,* while *Lightning Rider,* a young adult mystery, features the sport of motorcycle racing. After her brother Gray survives a serious motorcycle accident, sixteen-year-old January Fournier, a Métis girl, learns that a local police sergeant known for his prejudice against Native people wants to prosecute Gray for stealing the vehicle. Knowing that her brother would never steal a bike, January must work to clear her brother's name, a problem made more difficult because Gray remains in a coma after the crash and cannot offer any information in his defense. Fortunately, the town's police constable does not harbor the same racist assumptions as does the sergeant, and at some risk to her own life, January discovers the culprits who actually stole the motorcycle.

## Biographical and Critical Sources

### PERIODICALS

*Resource Links,* April, 2001, Brenda Dillon, review of *Lightning Rider,* p. 23.

### OTHER

*Jacqueline Guest's Web Site,* http://www.jacquelineguest. com/ (August 2, 2002).

# H

## HAAS, (Katherine) Jessie 1959-

### Personal

Born July 27, 1959, in Westminster, VT; daughter of Robert Joseph (a truck driver and freight manager) and Patricia Anne (a farmer and housewife; maiden name, Trevorrow) Haas; married Michael Joseph Daley (a writer and educator), April 25, 1981. *Education:* Wellesley College, B.A. (English), 1981. *Politics:* Progressive Democrat. *Hobbies and other interests:* Horseback riding, animals, cooking, knitting, drawing, reading, Scottish dancing, politics.

### Addresses

*Home*—367 Lettier Road, Putney, Vermont 05346.

### Career

Writer, 1981—. Worker at a vegetable stand, early 1980s; yarn mill laborer, mid-1980s to 1991. Trustee, Westminster West Library, 1984-87; member of board of directors, Vermont Public Interest Research Group; Westminster Cares (Meals-on-Wheels delivery).

### Member

Society of Children's Book Writers and Illustrators, Vermont Citizens Campaign for Health (president of board).

### Awards, Honors

Dorothy Canfield Fisher Award Master List, Volunteer State Book Award Master List, 1983, for *Keeping Barney*, 1993-94, for *Skipping School*, 1995-96, for *Uncle Daney's Way*, 1996-97, for *A Blue for Beware*, 1997-98, for *Be Well, Beware*, 2000, for *Unbroken*, and for *Runaway Radish;* Northwest Territories (Australia) Children's Choice Award Master List, 1983, for *Keeping Barney;* Pick of the Lists, *American Bookseller*, 1993, for *Beware the Mare*, 1994, for *Busybody Brandy*, 1995, for *No Foal Yet*, and 1996, for *Clean House;* Sequoyah Children's Book Award Master List, 1995-96, for *Beware the Mare;* Children's Book of the Year, Child Study Association, 1996, for *Be Well, Beware* and for *Clean House*, and 1997, for *Sugaring;* Bluebonnet Award Master List, Mark Twain Award Master List, and South Carolina Children's Book Award Master List, all 1996-97, all for *Uncle Daney's Way;* Notable Children's Book in the Field of Social Studies, NCSS/CBC, 1997, for *Sugaring;* West Virginia Children's Book Award Master List, 1997-98, for *A Blue for Beware;* Volunteer State Book Award Master List, 1998-99, for *Clean House;* Garden State Award Master List, *Publishers Weekly* Best Book citation, and *School Library Journal* Best Book citation, all 1999, CCBC Choice, 2000, Notable Children's Trade Book in Social Studies, Parent's Choice Gold Award, and *Voice of Youth Advocates* Outstanding Book for Middle School Students, all for *Unbroken; Bulletin* Blue Ribbon Book, *Horn Book* Fanfare list, and American Library Association Notable book, all for *Runaway Radish*. Several of Haas's books have been chosen as Junior Literary Guild titles.

### Writings

*Keeping Barney,* Greenwillow (New York, NY), 1982.
*Working Trot,* Greenwillow (New York, NY), 1983.
*The Sixth Sense and Other Stories,* Greenwillow (New York, NY), 1988.
*Skipping School,* Greenwillow (New York, NY), 1992.
*Beware the Mare,* illustrated by Martha Haas, Greenwillow (New York, NY), 1993.
*Chipmunk!,* illustrated by Joseph A. Smith, Greenwillow (New York, NY), 1993.
*A Horse Like Barney,* Greenwillow (New York, NY), 1993.
*Mowing,* illustrated by Joseph A. Smith, Greenwillow (New York, NY), 1994.
*Uncle Daney's Way,* Greenwillow (New York, NY), 1994.
*Busybody Brandy,* illustrated by Yossi Abolafia, Greenwillow (New York, NY), 1994.

*Safe Horse, Safe Rider: A Young Rider's Guide to Responsible Horsekeeping,* Storey Communications (Pownal, VT), 1994.

*Getting Ready to Drive a Horse and Cart,* illustrated by Christine Erickson, Storey Communications (Pownal, VT), 1995.

*A Blue for Beware,* illustrated by Joseph A. Smith, Greenwillow (New York, NY), 1995.

*No Foal Yet,* illustrated by Joseph A. Smith, Greenwillow (New York, NY), 1995.

*Be Well, Beware,* illustrated by Joseph A. Smith, Greenwillow (New York, NY), 1996.

*Clean House,* illustrated by Yossi Abolafia, Greenwillow (New York, NY), 1996.

*Sugaring,* illustrated by Joseph A. Smith, Greenwillow (New York, NY), 1996.

*Westminster West,* Greenwillow (New York, NY), 1997.

*Fire!: My Parents' Story,* Greenwillow (New York, NY), 1998.

(And illustrator) *Beware and Stogie,* Greenwillow (New York, NY), 1998.

*Unbroken,* Greenwillow (New York, NY), 1999.

*Hay in the Barn,* Greenwillow (New York, NY), 1999.

*Hurry!,* illustrated by Joseph A. Smith, Greenwillow (New York, NY), 2000.

*Will You, Won't You?,* Greenwillow (New York, NY), 2000.

*Runaway Radish,* illustrated by Margot Apple, Greenwillow (New York, NY), 2001.

*Appaloosa Zebra: A Horse Lover's Alphabet,* illustrated by Margot Apple, Greenwillow (New York, NY), 2002.

*Shaper,* Greenwillow (New York, NY), 2002.

*Horse Show Colors,* illustrated by Margot Apple, Greenwillow (New York, NY), in press.

Haas's works have been translated into Swedish, Finnish, Danish, and German.

## Work in Progress

*Ride Back with Me,* poems about the history of horses; *Uncle Charlie's Ride,* an "I Can Read" story "based on a real-life adventure my uncle had with our childhood horse"; and *Bareback,* a middle-grade novel about three friends with two horses between them.

## Adaptations

Sound recordings of *Unbroken* were produced by Recorded Books (Prince Frederick, MD), 1999, and by American Printing House for the Blind (Louisville, KY), 2000; sound recordings of *Uncle Daney's Way* and *No Foal Yet* were produced by American Printing House for the Blind in 1996 and 1997, respectively.

## Sidelights

Jessie Haas is the author of some twenty novels and picture books for children, most of which deal with one of Haas's reigning passions—horses. In award-winning titles such as *Keeping Barney, Beware the Mare, Uncle Daney's Way, A Blue for Beware,* and *Sugaring,* Haas illuminates the life of farming and working with farm animals. The topic comes naturally for Haas, who was raised on a Vermont farm that she still calls home.

"My childhood was full of haying, gardening, horseback riding, and animals," Haas once commented. "I trained my own horse. I was given a goat for my sixteenth birthday. My mother was the town pound-keeper, so we had an endless stream of stray cats and dogs coming through. Lots of them stayed." But if animals were a vital part of Haas's growing up, so was reading, an activity that was not limited to the confines of an easy chair. Haas read everywhere, even, as she once explained, "in the bathtub. I read all the horse stories ever written, as first choice, and then anything else printed on a page." This magpie curiosity stood her in good stead when she went to college, at Wellesley, to study English literature and writing.

Influenced by the British novelist Jane Austen and by the loads of horse stories she had earlier consumed, Haas wrote her first novel while still a college student. One of her teachers recommended that she try to publish the book and gave her the name of a former student who had become editor-in-chief at Greenwillow Books. The novel, *Keeping Barney,* was initially rejected, but with helpful suggestions which Haas followed, the novel was accepted by Greenwillow upon its second submission, a month before Haas graduated from college.

That same month, Haas married and settled on property near her parents' farm, building a simple cabin. "We had one room at first," Haas once said, "with no insulation, no phone, no plumbing, and no electricity—but a very small mortgage. The little house gave us—still gives us—the freedom to pursue our interests without having to get 'real jobs.' I've worked at a vegetable stand, a village store, and a yarn mill, all part-time, while concentrating mainly on my writing."

Meanwhile, *Keeping Barney* was published to favorable reviews, earning several awards to boot. Barney is a cranky and stubborn horse who causes his young owner no end of trouble. Sarah Miles is thirteen and has long waited for the day she would have her own horse, imagining a lovely partnership between human and animal. But Barney is a far cry from the sleek stallion of her imagination, and his feistiness is intimidating. Finally, Sarah learns that the "secret of success is frequently self-control," as Mary M. Burns wrote in *Horn Book,* and the realization that Barney "would never really be hers was not only the moment of demarcation between childhood and adolescence but is also the climax of the story." *Booklist* critic Denise M. Wilms noted that "there is much truth in the portrayal of Sarah's struggles with a real rather than a dream horse, and her girlish joy in horses and riding will surely be communicated to readers." Calling the story "satisfying and sustaining," a *Kirkus Reviews* contributor dubbed this first novel a "nicely managed girl-gets-horse story—with individuated characters and some unexpected twists."

Haas's second title, *Working Trot,* again features horses, but this time her protagonist is a young man. James graduates from high school with plans far different from those of his parents, who want him to attend college and pursue a business career. Instead James wants to train as a dressage rider, working with a somewhat dilapidated Lipizzan stallion at his uncle's riding establishment in Vermont. The demands of a professional riding career prove greater than James first imagined, however, and he struggles to balance his study with his social life, attempting to fit in with a young equestrian who wants to ride on the Olympic team. Pat Harrington, writing in *School Library Journal,* observed that "Haas conveys an impressive knowledge of her subject" and that she "has written a novel that is realistic and satisfying."

Haas turned to the short story format for her next work, *The Sixth Sense and Other Stories,* a collection of nine "wonderful stories," according to *Horn Book* reviewer Elizabeth Watson. Haas employs two main characters, James and Kris, who tie together many of these stories about cats, dogs, and horses, and she examines the relationship between humans and animals through themes of loyalty, death, responsibility, love, and understanding. Watson concluded that this is a "superb collection with deeply felt emotion for animal lovers." Betsy Hearne noted in *Bulletin of the Center for Children's Books* that Haas's tales "make a real contribution to the short story genre, being both resonant and readable."

With *Skipping School,* Haas left horses behind for the time being. Fifteen-year-old Phillip feels isolated and confused as he learns to cope with his father's terminal illness. Still reeling from the move from a farm to the suburbs, Phillip skips school and finds solace at a nearby abandoned farmhouse, where he spends afternoons chopping wood and caring for a pair of kittens. Skipping school ultimately pays off, for Phillip slowly comes to terms with his father's impending death. A *Publishers Weekly* reviewer commended Haas on her "eye for telling details," which "give this heartwarming novel its subtle power," and concluded that "this is a book to savor." *Horn Book* critic Watson observed that Haas has created "a provocative, satisfying novel that contrasts the value of life against the constant presence of death.... A wonderful book to read and discuss— probably the only time skipping school resulted in an A+."

Haas returned to her initial equine creation with *A Horse Like Barney,* a sequel to *Keeping Barney* in which Sarah continues the search for a horse of her own. Again, the search is more difficult than Sarah imagined: Should she pick the lively Roy or the older and needier Thunder? Watson, writing in *Horn Book,* felt that the story has "depth and texture, provided by insights into the emotions Sarah feels," while Hazel Rochman, writing in *Booklist,* noted that Haas's short chapters make the book ideal "for young readers ready to go beyond illustrated fiction. A wholesome, introspective novel, just right for horse enthusiasts."

In the novel *Uncle Daney's Way,* young Cole learns important lessons about life and managing a workhorse when his disabled uncle moves into the family's barn. Watson noted in *Horn Book* that the "middle-grade reader will identify with Cole's growing enthusiasm fueled by increasing accomplishment in this refreshing treatment of a loving family's successful attempt to cope with a challenge." Deborah Stevenson observed in *Bulletin of the Center for Children's Books* that the novel is "a good old story told with affection and subtlety."

Haas has also written historical fiction. In *Westminster West,* two sisters in 1884 must deal with their roles as women, both in the family and in society, when an arsonist threatens their Vermont village. "*Westminster West* is based on real events which took place within three miles of my home, over a hundred years ago," Haas once explained. "I fictionalized the story, trying to understand and make convincing one version of why people might have behaved as they did. A story about arson and about taking to one's bed with the vapors, it was poised between melodrama and no drama at all, and required a complex understructure." In any event, Haas's technical efforts with the book proved successful. *Horn Book* reviewer Mary M. Burns concluded that "the book grapples effectively with the conflicting issues of personal freedom and family responsibilities," and Elizabeth Bush noted in *Bulletin of the Center for Children's Books* that "Haas builds a rich and sensitive portrait of a late nineteenth-century Vermont farm family." Another work of historical fiction is *Fire!: My Parents' Story,* the story of the burning of Haas's mother's house when she was eight. Haas tried to write this book for years, "in various complex ways," she once said. "It only worked when I found the way to tell it in the eight-year-old voice, as simply as possible."

In addition to her novels for older children, Haas has created a number of award-winning picture books and beginning chapter readers. *Beware the Mare* was the first of her illustrated books for younger readers, as well as the first in a series to feature the mare named Beware. In this initial title, Gramps gets a good bargain on a seemingly perfect mare for young Lily, though the horse's name does make him suspect something might be wrong. Haas uses this mystery "to provide enough tension to hold this charming vignette together," according to a critic in *Kirkus Reviews.* "Horse lovers who like their fiction short and easy are frequently disappointed," noted Stevenson in *Bulletin of the Center for Children's Books,* "but here's a well-written offering that conveys a flavorful lot in a small space." Lily and her horse Beware continue their adventures in further titles in the "Beware" series. A horse show ribbon is won in *A Blue for Beware,* a book to be "greeted with unbridled enthusiasm," according to Stevenson in *Bulletin of the Center for Children's Books.* A case of colic has to be treated in *Be Well, Beware,* a book in which the "plot takes off from the first page and maintains intensity right until the end," according to Christina Linz in *School Library Journal.* The fourth work in the series is *Beware and Stogie,* for which Haas herself illustrated the chapter headers. She described illustration as "my newest adventure" and finds it "exciting to be learning something completely new, and to go beyond what I thought were limits."

Another early reader is *Clean House,* in which Tess and her mother have to tidy the house for the arrival of Tess's cousin, Kate. The more they clean, the messier things get, but finally the house is spotless. It is also very boring and antiseptic, but once the relatives arrive they help to mess things up nicely again. Roger Sutton noted in *Bulletin of the Center for Children's Books* that the book admits "the little-acknowledged truth about house work: why bother? ... Cognizant of both parent and child demands, this easy chapter book would make a fine intergenerational read-together."

Haas's books aimed at preschool and first-grade readers include the companion volumes *Mowing, No Foal Yet,* and *Sugaring,* featuring the winning duo of Gramp and Nora. Nora helps her grandfather in the first title with horse-drawn mowing, avoiding a fawn and a killdeer nest in the process. A *Kirkus Reviews* critic noted that "the warm interaction between Nora and Gramp grows naturally from their companionable dialogue, while art and text work beautifully together to bring out the story's quiet drama." In *No Foal Yet,* Nora and Gramp are back on the farm waiting for Bonnie to give birth to her foal. Nora helps Gramp make maple syrup and sugar in *Sugaring,* a "satisfying story," according to Caroline Ward in *School Library Journal,* and one that "will be a welcome addition during any season."

Haas has continued to produce a wide variety of books for young readers. In *Unbroken,* for example, Haas tells another story involving horses. When young Harriet, called Model T. Harry, has no way to get to school, a young colt must be trained or Harry will have to quit school. A reviewer for *Publishers Weekly* noted, "Haas has a gift for description and graceful simile ('Night after night I lay still and narrow, like a wrinkle in the blanket'), and her characters are sharply observed, especially honest and wise 13-year-old Harry who can coax compassion from even her frozen Aunt Sarah." Haas uses her interest in politics to tell the story of *Will You, Won't You?* This contemporary novel focuses on young Madison "Mad" Parker and the summer she spends with her grandmother, who happens to be the chair of the Senate Finance Committee in Washington, D.C. Mad ends up speaking out about a bill to ban clear-cut logging. "Haas creates a large cast of well-rounded characters to weave engaging details about political life, Scottish country dancing, horse training, and personal growth," wrote Laura Scott in the *School Library Journal.* Other recent books include *Runaway Radish,* about a pony that grows too big for the girls who own him; *Appaloosa Zebra,* in which a girl dreams about the horses she will have when she gets older; and *Shaper,* a story about a young boy, the family dog, and an animal trainer.

Haas has been able to reduce her other part-time work and concentrate solely on writing. "Car trips, horseback rides, and long walks are times when I ask myself questions about my characters, and when I listen to the answers," Haas once explained. "Bad habits are excess reading and excess public radio, which occupy brain space I should keep free." For Haas, writing is similar to riding—both are processes that demand balance and profound concentration. "Each novel is different and requires a different process," she noted. "Some come inch by inch, arriving in polished sentences which remain the same from first draft to printed book. Others come scattershot; you catch the fragments and press them into shape like a meat loaf."

Literary awards and a growing readership have not greatly changed Haas's lifestyle. She and her husband haul water by hand and heat their Vermont house with wood. However, they do have electricity (supplied primarily by solar power) for lighting and their writing work. "I still live the same kind of life I did growing up," she reported. "I ride a horse I trained myself. A cat sleeps on my desk as I work. I walk to my parents' farm every day and can pick out the exact spot in the pasture where my horse Josey gave me *Beware the Mare.* It's an immense privilege to live this way—to make up stories and people, to spend all day drawing pictures of cows, to find a way to tell a family story so it will reach a wider audience, move perfect strangers, and be preserved. Another great benefit is being master, more or less, of my time, which allows me to be politically active." Much of Haas's political activity is directed at campaigning for a national health care system to cover all citizens.

Haas, who meets her reading public regularly, once commented, "When I speak in schools I show slides of my house, to try and challenge kids' ideas of what's possible and necessary. I show my animals, because that's where many of my ideas come from. It's fascinating to hear their questions, to find out where I'm reaching them and where I miss. Each of us has only one life to live, but a writer gets to try on others, and then send ideas out into the lives of people she will never meet, to affect them in unknown and private ways."

Haas later told *MAICYA:* "In spring 2002 I sold my first book of poetry. It felt like an enormous step to take. I love and respect poetry, and had not dared to write it, but the history of horses I was trying to write demanded a response that was more personal and immediate than mere narrative. I dared, after a while I dared read some aloud to writer friends, and finally I dared send the poems to Greenwillow. Their acceptance has made me very happy. I go around saying aloud, 'I'm a poet!'

"My other new direction is the books I'm doing with Margot Apple. *Runaway Radish* and *Appaloosa Zebra* are the books I would time-travel with, and give to my second grade self. I didn't know that until I held *Radish,* with Margot's marvelous illustrations, in my hand. What Margot does for my work is to carve the eyes in the pumpkin, so to speak, and let the light shine out. It's a great gift to be working with her, and because we live so close together, see each other occasionally, and share a love of horses, our work cross-fertilizes. I give her picture ideas, she gives me words. The words for L in *Appaloosa*, 'My Lipizzans will perform lively leaps, the lightest of lengthenings, lovely levades,' are Margot's. The concept for the cover is mine. It's a lot of fun!

"A big change in my life has come with the retirement of Susan Hirschman from Greenwillow Books. Susan has been my editor for twenty years; having her retire was like having your mother retire! But Susan made the transition smooth, and the person she chose to replace her, Virginia Duncan, is wonderful. I've been working closely with Rebecca Davis, also new at Greenwillow, and find her an extraordinarily talented editor; hardworking, creative, tenacious, and subtle. So Susan's retirement has not made the difference I feared it would."

## Biographical and Critical Sources

*PERIODICALS*

*Booklist,* June 1, 1982, Denise M. Wilms, review of *Keeping Barney,* p. 1312; September 15, 1993, Hazel Rochman, review of *A Horse Like Barney,* p. 152; April 15, 1997, Ilene Cooper, review of *Westminster West,* p. 1422; May 1, 1998, Linda Perkins, review of *Fire!: My Parents' Story,* p. 1514; August, 1998, Shelle Rosenfeld, review of *Beware and Stogie,* p. 2004; March 15, 1999, Lauren Peterson, review of *Unbroken,* p. 1325; April 15, 2001, Gillian Engberg, review of *Runaway Radish,* p. 1552; September 15, 2001, Lolly Gepson, review of *Unbroken,* p. 240.

*Book Report,* September-October, 1997, Jennifer Schwelik, review of *Westminster West,* p. 35; September-October, 1999, Catherine M. Andronik, review of *Unbroken,* p. 59.

*Bulletin of the Center for Children's Books,* January, 1989, Betsy Hearne, review of *The Sixth Sense and Other Stories,* p. 122; July-August, 1993, Deborah Stevenson, review of *Beware the Mare,* p. 345; April, 1994, Deborah Stevenson, review of *Uncle Daney's Way,* p. 259; March, 1995, Deborah Stevenson, review of *A Blue for Beware,* p. 236; March, 1996, Roger Sutton, review of *Clean House,* p. 227; April, 1997, Elizabeth Bush, review of *Westminster West,* p. 284.

*Horn Book,* August, 1982, Mary M. Burns, review of *Keeping Barney,* p. 403; March-April, 1989, Elizabeth Watson, review of *The Sixth Sense and Other Stories,* p. 216; January-February, 1993, Elizabeth Watson, review of *Skipping School,* p. 90; November-December, 1993, Elizabeth Watson, review of *A Horse Like Barney,* p. 744; July-August, 1994, Elizabeth Watson, review of *Uncle Daney's Way,* p. 452; July-December, 1996, review of *Sugaring,* p. 30; May-June, 1997, Mary M. Burns, review of *Westminster West,* p. 321; September-October, 1998, Elizabeth S. Watson, review of *Beware and Stogie,* p. 608; July, 1999, Bridget T. McCaffrey, review of *Unbroken,* p. 464; July, 2000, review of *Hurry!,* p. 435; May, 2001, Anita L. Burkam, review of *Runaway Radish,* p. 324.

*Kirkus Reviews,* April 1, 1982, review of *Keeping Barney,* p. 417; May 15, 1993, review of *Beware the Mare,* p. 661; May 14, 1994, review of *Mowing,* p. 698; February 1, 1997, review of *Westminster West,* p. 223.

*New York Times Book Review,* December 20, 1998, Andrea Higbie, review of *Fire!,* p. 25; May 16, 1999, Emily Arnold McCully, review of *Unbroken,* p. 25.

*Publishers Weekly,* November 9, 1992, review of *Skipping School,* p. 87; May 11, 1998, review of *Fire!,* p. 69; February 8, 1999, review of *Unbroken,* p. 215; October 2, 2000, review of *Will You, Won't You?,* p. 82.

*School Library Journal,* January, 1984, Pat Harrington, review of *Walking Trot,* p. 86; April, 1996, Christina Linz, review of *Be Well, Beware,* p. 132; October, 1996, Caroline Ward, review of *Sugaring,* p. 94; May, 1997, Wendy D. Caldiero, review of *Westminster West,* p. 133; May, 1998, Anne Chapman Callaghan, review of *Fire!,* p. 133; November 1, 1998, Lee Bock, review of *Beware and Stogie,* p. 85; April, 1999, Christy Norris Blanchette, review of *Unbroken,* p. 134; June, 2000, Lee Bock, review of *Hurry!,* p. 114; October, 2000, Laura Scott, review of *Will You, Won't You?,* p. 160; May, 2001, Lisa Falk, review of *Runaway Radish,* p. 122.

*Stone Soup,* March, 2000, Julia Schuchard, review of *Unbroken,* p. 34.

*　　*　　*

## Autobiography Feature

# Jessie Haas

I was born in 1959 in Westminster, Vermont, the oldest child of Robert and Patricia (Trevorrow) Haas.

Dad was born in Glendale, New York, but had been vacationing in Vermont since early childhood on the farm owned by my mother's family. He attended agricultural college, planning to buy a dairy farm with his father. Unfortunately my grandfather, Aloysius Haas, died before that dream could come true. My father served in the army—he was posted in Germany during the Korean War—and then began working for a trucking company in Bellows Falls, Vermont.

My mother grew up on a farm belonging to her uncle in East Dover, Vermont. My grandfather, Emmanuel Trevorrow (Mandy), worked the farm, and my grandmother, Jessie Atherton, worked in the kitchen. The farm took in summer boarders, and people came to stay and hunt deer in the fall. Mom was an only child; the only other child in the house was a cousin nearly ten years older. But during the summer other children visited. When Mom was a teenager Gram and Gramp adopted P.G., the son of Jessie's sister. He was ten years younger than Mom.

My mother graduated from high school in 1958, and that autumn married Dad. They moved to Westminster West, to a big old circa 1800 farmhouse. The way they found it is a classic family story. They'd been out looking at houses together and hadn't seen anything that was right. Dad needed to pee. He stepped behind some bushes and there was an old house, with a For Sale sign on the overgrown lawn. It was exactly what they'd been looking for.

A few years later the surrounding land came up for sale. With twenty acres and a barn Mom and Dad began to farm, eventually raising all the meat and vegetables and most of the fruit for a family of five. My brother Jim was born in 1961, and my sister Martha in 1965.

One of the first animals to arrive was a horse. Mom had always wanted a riding horse; the pleas of her children made a perfect excuse.

Scamper was a Welsh/Morgan cross, a beautiful little white horse with a mind of his own. He allowed small children to sit on him and pretend to ride, and if they fell off he'd stand carefully, never moving his feet, until they were safely gathered up.

But let an older person get on, with a notion that she knew how to ride, and Scamper was ready to prove otherwise. He had a large bag of tricks, and no show-off

*Jessie Haas*

rider without a strong base of real knowledge could get far with him.

Scamper was joined by Rosie, an Ayshire broodcow who raised many beef calves. We had pigs year after year, chickens, sheep, and eventually, after much pleading, I was given a goat for my sixteenth birthday. Goats had long been a passion of mine. At age two I was taken to see some, and awakened my parents at an early hour the next morning bouncing in my crib and saying, "Want to see a goat! Want to see a goat!"

We always had cats, many wonderful characters down through the years. And there was Shep, a beautiful Border collie who could bark for hours at a stretch, and often did. Shep adored baby animals, even little chicks, and once was spotted sitting in the cow pasture with the twin calves, each sucking one of his ears.

Both of Mom's parents were alive when I was small. They'd finally bought a house and land of their own in East Dover, and we visited on weekends. I remember my grandmother talking on the phone, saying "Ayuh. Ayuh. Ayuh." I stood somewhere near the hem of her dress, imitating her. "Ayuh. Ayuh. Ayuh." I felt very clever.

Gram and Gramp spoke with an old-time Vermont accent which is nearly gone. Echoes of it remain in the hill country and the Northeast Kingdom of Vermont. Whenever I hear it I always feel at home.

Mom, though, was a child of the fifties. My grandparents had an outhouse as well as indoor plumbing. The outhouse was called "the bomb shelter," and that led to a lot of confusion in my young life. I thought that was the name for outdoor toilets, and even after I knew better it was years before I understood the inwardness of the joke.

My brother and I sometimes spent the weekend with Gram and Gramp. Gramp worked at a ski area then. He ate breakfast and left before it was light out. We would wake up too, and come downstairs, and get in bed with Gram. I'm sure she would have liked to go back to sleep, but we made her tell stories, about bears and bobcats and the horses Gramp used to work with; Mom's childhood dog Rover, who would bite anyone who threatened her, even in play; and The Fire.

The Fire was the big family story. When Mom was eight, and Dad eighteen and up in Dover for a visit, the farmhouse burned in the middle of the night. Mom was the one who woke first, and by waking her parents, saved everyone's lives. Dad carried her and her teddy bear down the stairs under one arm, holding up his pants with his free hand—that was the part of the story we liked best.

The family stories connected me with a still older Vermont, one that I see vividly in my mind, where odd old bachelors lived on remote back roads, travelling only by horse and buggy. They could go to town and drink themselves senseless, and the horse would bring them home.

I always had the sense of the glory days passing. We would drive by a dense patch of whipstock saplings, and Mom would recall cutting hay there. Not long before, it had been a field. If the saplings were a little thicker, Dad might remember the days when it was pasture. There were new houses on the road; the country had gone right to hell, in my parents' opinion.

Still, the road was quiet enough that Gram always stepped to the window if she heard a car coming. Even in the 1960s, so few cars passed that chances were she knew who was coming. If she did know the person they stopped in the road and talked to Gram for fifteen or twenty minutes. At other times the collie dog and the black rabbit stretched out in the middle of the road in nearly perfect safety.

By way of contrast we visited my grandmother Haas in Glendale every summer. It always seemed terribly hot, and terribly noisy, in what I see now was a pretty and quiet little neighborhood in Queens. It was a German area, or had been. All my German relatives were terribly perturbed at the recent arrival of Italians—something I remembered with irony when I began dating Irish-Italian Mike Daley.

I liked it much better when Grandma Haas came to visit us. She loved our cats, she loved to dust our house, she never came back from a shopping trip to Brattleboro without a brown box from the bakery, tied up with string, and she took us for walks, to the blackberry bushes, or to throw pebbles into the brook.

Though I was only six when Gram Trevorrow died, I remember her well, and she's gone on influencing my life by her example. Though she had little herself, when she met someone who had less she broke what she had in half and shared. Though she was ill herself, with a bad back and diabetes, she housed and cared for a sister with Huntington's disease. I've never met anyone who had a bad word to say about her.

By contrast Gramp was quarrelsome, smoked heavily, drank beer and tossed the cans out the window as he drove—and was also a wonderful person. He was a trouble maker. A favorite picture from the local newspaper shows him standing up at a town meeting making a point. I have a similar picture of me, at our town meeting, making some kind of trouble for the town fathers. Though I've never sought elected office, I've been involved in some form of political effort or other for most of my adult life, usually activated by indignation at sombody, and I think it traces back to my cantankerous grandfather.

Growing up on our farm, I didn't see other children often. Mom stayed home and cared for us, so there was no such thing as day care. I was shy with other kids, and hated kindergarten. My chief memory is of being sick, often. Children do get sick when exposed to one another's germs; I now know that was normal. Back then I blamed kindergarten. I didn't like the teacher, I didn't like the kids, and I didn't like being sick. It was a bad start.

First and second grades were not much improvement. We had teachers who were cruel and incompetent, not to put too fine a point on it. The first-grade teacher made a child who peed his pants sit in it all day long. She made me dump my crammed-full desk out on the floor in front of all the children and clean it up, and dubbed me "Messy Jessie." None of us ever told our parents about the things she did. We thought teachers got to do whatever they wanted, and so they did.

The second-grade teacher was really a teacher of high school home economics and had no ability to teach younger children. Our whole class was set back in math—almost none of us ever learned to enjoy it or do it well. I wrote on top of one of my math papers, in an early moment of self-expression and protest, "I hate this work." It got me a parent-teacher conference.

In third grade, though, the light came on. Mrs. Metcalf was sweet and pretty in an older-lady way. She was kind, she liked me, she read us stories after recess—a very good way to calm us down—and for the first time I knew that a teacher could be nice, and school could be enjoyable.

I had a best friend now, too: Patty Stebbins. We both loved horses, spent class time watching out the window while the local orthodontist exercised his trotter on a dirt track just thirty feet away, read horse books together, laughed and giggled, and had way too good a time through third and fourth grade.

Books and stories were important from the earliest moment of my life. Mom read stories to me before I was old enough to understand them. *Bambi,* by Felix Salten, is more vividly alive in my mind than any memory of my real life at that age. It's a big, mysterious, terrible, and tender story. I keep coming back to it, and to the other books of my childhood, as a new person, able to appreciate different things. I have loved the style of *Bambi,* the phrasing, the beauty of the way Salten keeps to the animals' points of

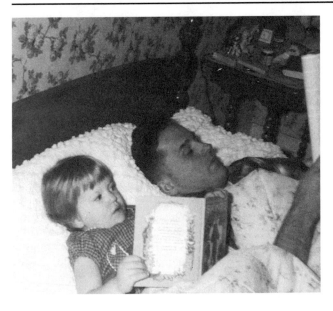

*" 'Reading' in bed with Dad, age two"*

view, so that He, a human being like ourselves, is terrifying.

When I studied herbs and discovered that certain plants have a powerful action to stop bleeding, I remembered Bambi being shot. His father leads him through the woods, forcing him to eat bitter plants, and saves his life.

As someone interested in politics and history, I was startled more recently to notice that *Bambi* was translated by Whittaker Chambers, a central figure in one of the great Cold War spy scandals.

Dad read to me at bedtime. For years it was always *Little Black, a Pony,* or *Little Black Goes to the Circus.* I knew the stories word for word and would often "read" along. It was many years before I noticed that the author of these early favorites was the author of my beloved *The Black Stallion,* Walter Farley. (There's more than one reason I never know exactly what I'm doing. I live a great deal in my imagination, not noticing the real world as much as I should.)

Mom went grocery shopping once every two weeks. I was dropped off at the library, where I devoured books and checked out as many as I could—they needed to last a long time, but they never did. I read all the horse books. Then I read them again. "Try something new," Mom insisted. So I read dog books, cat books, adventure stories—especially Westerns, which at least took place on horseback. Then I read the horse books again. Years later I figured out that I was, in effect, studying them, preparing for my career.

Authors weren't people to me then, just words on the book cover that meant I was in for a certain kind of experience. I never wondered about their lives, and was shocked, as the young author of a horse story, to discover that Marguerite Henry was still alive—my colleague.

Authors didn't speak in schools then, as I do now. I often wonder if it's really such a wonderful thing to do. What I love about reading is the private, magical experience of becoming a different person, in a different place and time. Am I doing anybody a favor by lifting the curtain, and showing the machinery that makes the illusion?

Fortunately, it's impossible to talk about what I really do, how a story really comes about. It remains mysterious, even to me. I can show kids that a real person wrote the story, and give them some tips, but I'm incapable of stripping away the mystery.

In fifth grade the school decided to separate Patty and me. Kids from other schools came to our building for fifth and sixth grades, making the classes large enough to be divided. It was easy to part gigglers and troublemakers. We were together at recess, but it wasn't the same.

In those days parents didn't shuttle children back and forth. My parents only had one car; it just wasn't possible to get Patty and me together as often as we would have liked. As we headed into adolescence and the unionized middle school and high school, we continued to be in separate classes. Pat began to deal with severe depression, though no one knew that's what it was. The friendship was damaged.

In recent years we've gotten back together with the ease and compatibility we felt in grade school, and I understand anew the importance of childhood friendships. Our perceptions were true; we were right for each other. I'm angry at the school system for hurting us, just because we were such good friends.

Often adults, and maybe even children, think that childhood is not real life. Later we're told, Life is not a dress rehearsal. True. Neither is childhood. It's the real deal. As a writer I'm on the kids' side. I know their lives are full of passion and a search for meaning. I remember how important books were in my own passions and searches, and I want to give back to the community some of what was given to me.

In sixth grade our regular teacher fell ill and we had a long term substitute, a young woman named Mrs. Aumand. For the first time we were invited to write about things we cared about. I wrote poems about horses, and then an epic ballad about Billy the Kid. That wasn't an assignment; it was for pleasure, for extra credit, and as a farewell present for Mrs. Aumand.

Those pages of pencilled verse expressed real love and gratitude. Mrs. Aumand changed my life. She showed me that writing was as fun as reading. After sixth grade, I was a writer.

Then came middle school, the worst of my school experiences. We country children were bussed to a big school in neighboring Bellows Falls, a depressed mill town full of tough kids who drank and did drugs and a whole lot more that most of us had never even heard of. I never saw Patty except to pass in the hall. My shyness became more intense.

The only good thing about that school was the library. I lived there. It was the first time in my life that I had my own library card. I could take *The Black Stallion* out once a week if I wanted, without parental comment. I did! I read and read and read.

And I wrote. I began a long Western (Westerns were my favorite kinds of books just then). My story took a group of cowboys up the Chisholm Trail from Texas to Kansas. I crossed them over every river they would really have encountered, and put them through every hazard from Indians to thunderstorms to stampedes. It involved a lot of study of the Old West. I put my friends in, disguised as cowboys, and for a while a few of them got involved and wrote stories of their own. But they were more socially adept than I was, and soon had other fish to fry. I kept writing. The story swelled to two hundred pencilled longhand pages, and kept me alive through eighth grade.

I was helped by the friendship of a new teacher, Winifred Vogt. Bellows Falls was a shock to her, coming from a wealthy school in Connecticut. I stood out for my writing talent, and she made sure I knew it. It was the first time anyone told me that.

Mrs. Vogt encouraged me, introduced me to new and strange and classic things, marvelled at my pitch-perfect parroting of them, and for eighth-grade graduation gave me a copy of *The Elements of Style*: "Omit needless words," became my mantra. She also secretly resolved that I would attend her alma mater, Wellesley College.

I knew nothing of that. I only knew how grateful I was to her, and to Larry Diamond, the young science teacher, for letting me stand beside them in the hall during the free-for-all fifteen minutes before classes began. I don't remember what they said to each other. I only remember standing there, sheltered and welcomed by intelligent adults, rather thrilled and intensely thankful.

For high school I was well prepared. I had *The Elements of Style,* which I read over and over. My parents had given me *The American Heritage Dictionary of the English Language,* which I also read (no kidding!). What I loved most was the section in the back called "Indo-European and the Indo-Europeans," complete with a dictionary of root words.

Why would an incoming freshman be reading the dictionary? I'd just read *Lord of the Rings,* and kept on reading it over and over for quite a while. I was in love with Tolkien's imagined ancient history. Time to abandon my cowboys, still a long way south of Wichita, and begin a fantasy. All characters, including the horses, had Indo-European root names, and I had a shelter, in case high school was even worse than middle school.

For a while it was—bigger and uglier, a vast single-story sheet of a building in shades of orange and green, with no interior walls. It was an open-concept school, and that was a challenge. You could hear other classes going on around you. Paper airplanes and spitballs sailed over the dividers. There were drugs and other social problems, and I was just as lonely, just as shy. At some point I got laryngitis, lost my voice completely, and stayed home for weeks, watching the Senate Watergate hearings on our extremely snowy black-and-white TV.

Could I have regained my voice? I've never been sure. I remember it being a decision I felt I could make, to go to school or to stay home one more week. (I didn't, you may be sure, voice this to my parents.) They became very concerned as time dragged on. There were doctor visits, and eventually they checked me into the hospital where I worked with a speech therapist. It seemed that I *couldn't* force my voice out, and then one day it surprised me, and I could talk. Back to school again.

I had other things to keep me at home besides the Watergate hearings. My childhood was not idyllic; there were many conflicts, from sibling rivalry to struggles with my parents, and farm work I would rather have avoided, like weeding in the hot sun or canning stringbeans. (I hated canned stringbeans, so the work seemed worse than wasted.)

But I also had a horse of my own. I'd gone to summer camp (which I hated; too many kids) and had fallen in love with a palomino mare named Beauty, so much in love that I plucked up the courage to ask my parents if they'd consider buying her for me. They asked, Beauty was not for sale, but they did know by this time that I was motivated and serious about riding.

How did they know? Earlier that year I'd attended a horse camp with old Scamper. He was lame. I spent much of what was supposed to be lesson time standing him in the creek. I had laryngitis and practically the only time I could speak above a whisper was after diving into the icy mill pond at the campground where we children stayed with our 4-H leaders. One morning while I was finishing dressing in the camper the leader packed the kids into the car and drove off to where the horses were staying, leaving me behind, unable to shout to let them know I was there. They came back in about twenty minutes, and off I went to another day of cleaning stalls and standing in cold water. I remember the drive home, feeling very sick, yet knowing I'd had a marvellous time, and hearing my parents say, "I guess she's serious about this."

So, though it was a large request, they took it seriously, and since Beauty was not available we went looking for a different horse for me.

As a family, we tend to fall in love with the first creature we see. We answered an ad for a half-Morgan foal who fit the budget and met Josey, a bold and sociable baby who endeared herself by letting me hold her head in my lap as she slept.

So we bought her—a decision I would never recommend. I was in seventh grade, too young to be training a

*From left, Jessie Trevorrow, Jessie Haas, Katherine Haas, and Bob Haas, 1964*

horse. My parents had worked horses, but never trained one. Having a young, untrained horse meant I couldn't participate in activities my friends were enjoying. Josey and I had a lot of misadventures, and hurt or frightened each other often.

Still, it was fun and we both survived. I planned a grand trip with her, a ride across country to California, or to the tip of South America. At the same age my next door neighbor was building a Friendship sloop in the former milkhouse of his landlocked Vermont farm; both working on means of transport, looking to get away, and both were very clear that real life was what happened outside of school.

David went to Harvard, I went to Wellesley, and we both still live in Westminster West, next door to our parents' farms. I send books out into the world and he sends award-winning sheeps' milk cheese, and it just goes to show something, I don't know exactly what. Maybe that we always were in the best place of all, and had the sense to realize that in time.

High school had one lure; a teacher who read kids' stories—the stories that kids like me wrote for their own pleasure. She wrote, too.

I watched Linda Felch from afar, too shy to approach her. She watched me, having heard that I was a writer. Eventually we connected, and school was good again. Linda and I shared writing, a love of animals, a taste for fantasy and English history, and many long conversations during the abundant study halls that were then built into the Bellows Falls Union High School (BFUHS) day. We designed independent study courses around things we were interested in—writing, obviously, and I remember a course we designed on the English kings as seen through fiction, which meant I got to read things like *The Once and Future King* for credit.

That was an important part of my education, actually; both the books I read with Linda, and the concept of getting credit for doing exactly what I wanted to do. That has stood me in greater stead than anything else I learned in high school. I never learned to do, in a sustained way, things that didn't interest me. I've never held down a full-time job, or acquired the skills that would let me do so. Instead I've done what I wanted, and made that pay.

As well as being a friend, Linda Felch was a rigorous and demanding teacher, a brilliant woman with far greater talents than a school like BFUHS, or perhaps any high school, could use productively. Her high standards kept our self-designed courses from being self-indulgent.

Linda also pushed me onto the stage. How she persuaded me to try out for a one-act I don't remember, but she did, and probably had a hand in casting me, for that, and for a leading role in the senior play. They were terrifying and liberating experiences.

That friendship was the most important of my high school years, but there were others. I had a boyfriend, the wittiest person in our class and one of the smartest. I found out I liked smart people and could hold my own with them. I learned how to be funny, and how being funny is a way of being a leader. The boy and I broke up, but his friends were my friends, so we hung around in the same crowd, somehow managing to never quite speak to each other. It gave social life an extra edge.

Another important experience was the day the French teacher came to our advanced placement history class and conducted a discussion of contemporary politics. I don't remember anything about the subject. I just remember taking part, and trembling uncontrollably with a visceral excitement. The class was full of Young Republicans; I didn't know what I was, but I was sure I wasn't that, and was filled with the joy of opposition.

Meanwhile my eighth grade teacher, Winifred Vogt, was pulling strings. She saw to it that I considered Wellesley. I didn't know anything about colleges, and neither did my parents. We visited Wellesley; I fell in love with the buildings, applied, and was accepted.

As I look back it seems clear to me that nothing has ever been clear, that I have never quite known what I was doing, and that my life has functioned very well that way. Like my father finding the perfect house while taking a leak behind a bush, I found my college through the architecture, and found the perfect publisher through similar chance.

My advisor at Wellesley was Helen Storm Corsa, a professor of English literature. She introduced me to books I loved and responded as Linda Felch had to my enthusiasm. Because I'd been exposed to very little of it (and because they're terrific!) I was wildly impressed with English authors like Austen and Trollope. I loved the way Helen talked about them, with a sharp and slightly cynical slant, and I built my major around taking whatever course she was teaching each semester.

In my junior year I took a semester off. My best friends were spending their junior years at co-ed colleges, but I had already fallen in love with a onetime BFUHS classmate now at Dartmouth, Michael Daley. I decided to stay home a semester (home being closer to Dartmouth) and possibly to provide myself with an excuse, wrote a children's horse story.

*With husband, Michael Daley, on their wedding day,*
*April 25, 1981*

In those days (and sometimes still) I started a story with a vague feeling and some characters. If they went in a promising direction it continued, and if not, not. I had no control. Sarah and Missy and Barney must have gotten themselves started right—and I had, in fact, studied the genre intensively for many years, so it's not suprising that I knew how to do it.

I was also motivated by English literature, with its flawed protagonists like Jane Austen's Emma. In my beloved horse books, the human protagonist was always perfect, possessing miraculous natural abilities in horse-taming and riding. Having struggled with Scamper and Josey, I knew I had few of those qualities. What if I wrote a horse story like the ones I loved, and also like *Emma,* with a main character you weren't supposed to wholly admire?

When I finished the manuscript, I mentioned the project to Helen. "I have a former student who's now the head of a publishing company," she said. "Why don't you send it to Susie Carr Hirschman?"

Susan Hirschman, the founder of Greenwillow Books, was one of the preeminent editors of children's books. I didn't know that, nor did I know that Susan had attended Wellesley for reasons as unsound as my own; a revered camp counselor told stories of gathering at "The Well," which Susan thought was a real well until it was too late to change her mind. ("The Well" was the student center of Susan's day, gone by the time I got there.)

I sent my story, *Keeping Barney,* to Greenwillow. Editor Ann Tobias rejected it, with a letter explaining what was wrong, but also what was right—and much was already right with the story. I was encouraged to submit the story again if I reworked it.

The revision must have dragged on into the fall, because it was only a month or two before graduation when I was called down to the dorm telephone. It was Susan Hirschman. "We love your story, we'll pay you two thousand dollars, and now hang up and call your mother!" Susan said.

I married and graduated, in that order; an exciting couple of months and of course, I thought life would always be that thrilling. We settled in Bellows Falls, Vermont, Michael becoming night-manager of a grocery store and I working at a vegetable stand. These were jobs that would leave our minds free to think about writing, which was our real work. Michael, in his year at BFUHS, had been one of the writers who worked with Miss Felch. Now we lived just down the street from her, starting our careers as real writers. I didn't want to be typecast as an author of horse books, so I wrote something else. It was rejected without invitation to resubmit if I improved it. Fortunately I had a horse story I'd begun as an independant study project at Wellesley. I submitted that, and Greenwillow accepted.

*Keeping Barney,* meanwhile, had done very well, though I didn't understand that. I was very isolated as a writer, with only Michael and Linda Felch to read my work, and no other acquaintances who were experienced authors of childrens' books. An experienced advisor might have told me to consolidate my success by writing more horse books. Left to my own perceptions, I decided horse books were not very respected in the field, and that I would be writing myself into a corner by doing more. I was determined to branch out.

*From left, Brian Sages, Jessie Haas, and Patty Stebbins Sager*

The problem was that I didn't know how to write a novel. I'd accomplished *Keeping Barney* through beginner's luck; it was a type of book I'd studied thoroughly and understood in my bones, but it took me years to know that. Instead I stumbled around with novel after novel, each taking about a year to write, each eliciting a letter from Susan Hirschman that began, "Oh dear!"

Oh dear. Michael and I moved to a farmhouse in Walpole, New Hampshire, for a couple of years, and began to confront a problem. We had money in the bank. We did not have time to write.

Most of our spending was on rent. If we could find a way to live more cheaply, we could work less and write more. We reread *Walden* and started hunting for an affordable piece of land.

Luckily a few acres came up for sale just west of my parents' cow pasture. This was land I used to hike to at least once every spring around twilight, when a certain pleasantly melancholy restlessness would overcome me. I'd climb, look out from the ridgetop, and after a while, walk home.

Now the ridgetop was for sale, and we could afford it, barely. We were left with about $2,000 in the bank, and an urgent desire to change our lives. Could we move, or did we have to wait and accumulate still more money?

We read books about building your own house, and decided to go for it. We built a goat barn first, for practice. It is a badly-constructed building, though still standing. Then we moved on to the house—local rough-sawn lumber, modified post-and-beam, no plumbing, no power, no insulation, and a grand total of 12x16 feet. That was exactly the size of Thoreau's cabin on Walden Pond, and we occupied ours on July 4, the anniversary of Thoreau's move to Walden. A huge thunderstorm welcomed us that night.

The house has changed a lot since then. We've added a tower study for Michael, a study for me, a greenhouse, a wine-cellar, and a bedroom. We've insulated, and gotten solar electricity, laptop computers, a telephone—it's not very different from a lot of people's homes. The bathroom is still outdoors, and a midnight trip to the john gives us a chance to look at the stars or whatever blizzard happens to be passing. Running water is seasonal and comes via garden hose. The refrigerator runs on propane, as does the cooking stove, and heating comes from a little Morso parlor stove with a squirrel on the side.

Children who've done web-searches on me prior to a school visit are often mystified: Why would you want to live in a house like that? Economics, is the first answer. The house was ridiculously cheap, and that has bought us time we'd otherwise have spent working for other people, doing things we didn't want to do.

It's empowering to discover that you can do something as important as build your own shelter. We didn't know how; we didn't know if we could; but as I write this it is raining outside and I am dry, under a roof my husband and I put up board by board.

And my house is beautiful. I can see no other house—just woods and birds and the flowers in my garden. It's quiet, it's peaceful, and light comes in through many windows. My house is great. I didn't know I would love it this much, but then, I didn't know we would do this good a job.

Another important reason, though, has to do with my childhood reading. I loved books about people finding or making shelter; *My Side of the Mountain,* where the boy lives in a tree-trunk; *The Ark,* where a refugee family makes a home in an old railroad car; the "Little House" books; *The House at World's End,* where a family of children goes to live in a derelict mill. Whether the books caused the attraction, or I loved the books because I already loved little handmade unusual houses, I don't know. I just know it's completely in character for me to be living here in this way.

After we moved, Michael got a job working for an antinuclear organization. I took part-time work at a local food co-op, and later at a yarn mill, rode my horse, and meanwhile wrote wrote wrote. And was rejected consistently. It was bewildering, because I knew the writing was good.

In desperation, I decided to change what I was doing. I'd been writing novels; I would write short stories instead and try to gain some control over the shape of what I was writing.

I loved the work. It was exciting and strong and quite different than the baggy, self-indulgent novels I'd been trying. With considerable trepidation—it had been five years since *Working Trot* was accepted—I submitted *The Sixth Sense,* and was astonished to have it bought immediately.

A YA collection of short stories about animals, *The Sixth Sense* was far from a commercial success, but it got wonderful reviews and saved a dog's life. A *Horn Book* reviewer, Elizabeth Watson, was inspired by one of the stories to adopt a racing greyhound as a pet, thereby saving her from being euthanized.

Well, I was published again, and felt I'd learned something. I embarked on another novel, a time-travel story, only to have it soundly rejected.

Tremendously disheartened, I took a friend's advice and sought an agent; maybe I was too dependant on Greenwillow. Maybe they weren't treating me well.

Susan discovered I was doing that, and insisted that I stop in to see her after I'd seen the agent.

It was a dreadful trip to New York City. Two days before, our beloved cat was killed by a wild animal. I tracked it over the snow and found his body. The agent didn't want to represent me; I hadn't published enough to interest her (which was precisely why I wanted an agent, of course!). In the old days, she told me, an author in my situation might be offered an open contract: an advance on whatever you might write next. But that was in the old days.

I stumbled around the corner to the Greenwillow office, where Susan told me firmly that I didn't need an agent. "If it's money you need," she said, "we'll give you an open contract."

It was a stunning affirmation of faith in an author who had sent them many unpublishable manuscripts. Essentially Susan didn't even want to know what I was working on. That was for the future. I went home and got back to work.

What I sent Susan next was an enormous baggy novel—I was a *very* slow learner!—that followed one of the characters in *The Sixth Sense.* Susan sent back a letter saying that she thought there were two novels there, and one of them was good. Panic! The advance was spent, and though I was free to submit a different manuscript, I didn't have one ready. And Susan wasn't right, was she? I sat down with letter and manuscript to prove it.

To my astonishment the story came apart, as neatly as two-ply yarn. I made numerous cuts and sent the messy manuscript back to Susan. (This was before I owned a printer, and producing a new, clean copy was virtually impossible.)

Back it came. "You did a great job! Now cut it!"

I thought I had cut it, but I bit the bullet and cut again.

Back it came. "You did a great job! Now cut!"

That manuscript—it became *Skipping School*—was my real writing education. I finally, really, understood how to cut, and how powerful a tool that is. It's like weeding; it leaves space around your beautiful plant so you can see it.

Now I edit myself spatially. The amount of white space on the page is important to me. I break up long paragraphs. I put paragraph islands in the middle of long conversations. All of this must make sense to the story, and it must make people sense. It must be what people—*these* people—would say and do. Yet it must be easy for the reader; not in a way that condescends to children. These are basic courtesies, I believe, between any writer and her readers. I appreciate them in all kinds of writing.

I also learned to enjoy cutting, and changing my work. And I learned that the agony a writer undergoes does not show in the final product. *Skipping School* got excellent reviews. No one could see the tortuous process of getting it written.

When I was a kid in school revision meant erasing, and the marks you'd erased always showed, an ugly mark on the paper. As writers, I think we bear the scars of those smears. We think it means we're bad writers if we don't get it right the first time.

But the story doesn't care how often you erase, as long as you get it right in the end. The only bad writer is the one who fails to keep at it till it's perfect. It doesn't matter if you enjoy it or not; if it's hard or easy; if you see the problems yourself, or only when others point them out. All that matters is that in the end, you do the work that's needed. Nobody will ever know how hard it was. When you've done your job well, it will look easy.

That's why the next step in my education as a writer was so crucial. In the summer of 1991 I resubmitted the manuscript that became *Skipping School,* and it was accepted. It felt like a graduation.

Simultaneously, Michael took a leave of absence from the yarn mill where we both worked to experiment with working in renewable energy education. The mill then turned around and laid me off.

It was a shock, as this was a small, friendly, progressive workplace that was supposed to have better values than that. In fact, we were explicitly told when we signed on that the last hired would be the first fired if layoffs were needed, and I had worked at the mill for six years.

Left high and dry, I finally decided to try out a children's book critique group I'd seen advertized in the paper for years.

I hated it, I thought. I was wary of group-think and didn't believe it made for good stories, and I was put off by hearing the two or three published writers opine about unpublished people's work. At the same time it was electrifying to suddenly be around a lot of people who were doing the same work I was; who knew the inner workings of the children's book world, and the names of lots of editors. I was hungry for that kind of detail.

Even more important, I heard many people reading picture book manuscripts, and I could tell that they weren't good enough. I had never tried or thought about picture books, but a sort of "tilt" alarm went off in my mind, like the buzzer on a pinball machine. Not like that, I thought, like *this*!

My neighbor had told me a story about a killdeer stopping him as he was mowing hay. That could be a picture book, I thought. I wanted simplicity, and beauty of language, and something young, and I wrote *Mowing.* In terror I took it to the critique group and read it aloud. They loved it. Send it in, they said, and I did, and in three days Susan called and said, "Congratulations on your new career!"

It was a new career. That summer I wrote another picture book, *Chipmunk!,* and one of my most successful young novels, *Beware the Mare.* Suddenly I was prolific. Suddenly I was solvent. I didn't need to look for a new job. I could just stay home and write.

*"Our little house in the woods"*

What made the difference? Part of it was losing the job. Luckily, I respond well to financial pressure. It makes me work hard, and it makes me creative, though never about things like finding a better job. I never once got a well-paying job, or even remembered to ask what the wages were when applying for work. But in writing, pressure makes me deeply creative. That is my enormous good fortune.

The free time was also important. I'd only been working twenty hours a week and hadn't suspected that was a drain, but it was. From earliest childhood I've resented every moment spent doing things other people wanted me to do. I am not naturally an employee. After a period of adjustment I gained a delightful sense of having elbow room again—and I loved not having to get up early in the morning and organize myself.

But most important of all was the critique group. I'd spent ten years writing on my own, and had gained from that, but I had a lot to learn. At the group I heard stories in all stages. I heard mistakes, and I heard a lot of people's opinions on what writers could do to fix those mistakes. I was exposed to picture book and younger fiction attempts; I'd never even considered doing things like that, and I doubt I'd have learned very quickly by studying finished books. Remember, the mistakes become invisible, and it's mistakes that you learn from.

The critique group multiplied my experience of stories in progress, and my exposure to narrative strategies. It gave me ideas of what to avoid, and what to try.

Since joining that group I've made many friends in children's books. That's been a blessing, but also a source of concern. It isn't always a gentle world. I learned to be intensely grateful for Susan Hirschman at Greenwillow, who read manuscripts as fast as was humanly possible, made fair offers, sent checks promptly, and always called to read particularly good reviews aloud. She was the best possible editor, and I wish all my friends could have had her, or someone like her.

Susan became a friend over the course of the 1990s; she would have earlier, if I'd had the self-confidence to respond to her that way. I've learned so much from her. She has a direct simplicity in speech that is essentially childlike, and is my idea of what picture-book diction should be. She demands honesty. She demands stories she believes, and the most devastating critique of Susan's, applied both to stories I've sent her and to popular Newbery winners, is: I didn't believe it for a minute! She strongly dislikes sentimentality, as do I. (The market, and the juries for major awards, have disagreed with us time after time!)

But most important is Susan's enthusiasm, for books, food, good weather, all kinds of festivities—for life. I am a New England person, reserved even with myself at times, saving of my enthusiasm. I often think, Susan would be enjoying this more than I am. And I try to live up to her example. I think of her when I sit down to a good meal. I've heard her say so often, "This makes me happy!" It does me, too, but I didn't know it out loud until I heard Susan say it.

But I am thirty years younger than Susan, and inevitably, she has retired on me. Her replacement, Virginia Duncan, is wonderful, as is Rebecca Davis, with whom I've worked closely on books such as *Shaper* and *Appaloosa Zebra.* Rebecca is a fantastic editor, who works in great detail and definitely brings out the best in me. Maybe she is an even better editor for me, for a novel, than Susan. Still, I miss the single word scrawled beside a tricky paragraph that doesn't work: Fix!

I had a marvellous time with Jos. A. Smith on the Gramp and Nora books: *Mowing, No Foal Yet, Sugaring,* and *Hurry!* Joe visited the farm of my friend Jay Bailey to take pictures for reference when he began *Mowing;* when I got a look at the sketches, there was Jay starring as Gramp, and when Jay saw the book he said, "Those are my horses. That's my harness!" The series has been popular in local schools, and the children who go to Jay's farm on field trips know the name of each piece of farm equipment—and these machines are things of the past. Jay does all his farming with horses, using machinery that was current at the turn of the *last* century.

That's the kind of farm equipment I grew up using, too. The only difference was that we hitched it to a tractor. When I was writing *Unbroken,* the haying scenes circa 1910 required no research, just memory.

There's a lot of haying in my books. "Nothing's more important on this farm than hay," Gramp says in *Hurry!* In my childhood we seemed to hay all summer, on every single pleasant day when we could have been going swimming or staying cool in the shade. I hate getting hot. I am not fond of hard physical work. I did not love every minute of haying, and I don't today, when we get it in baled instead of loose.

But haying is central. Haying is the reason for the broad open fields I love, the fields so many ignorant people regard as mere vacant space to put a house on. Hay smells

*With Josey, 1993*

*"November 1998 on the front steps as Haas-e-n-da Farm," back row from left, husband Michael Daley, Jim Robert Haas; front row from left, Katherine "Jessie" Haas, Martha Doreen Haas (holding Bonnie) and Bob and Pat Haas*

wonderful. Hay in the barn is an intense perfume for months. It's the sweat of your brow, and how many times you handle it! Fork it down from the mow, then down into the manger. Throw the manure onto the pile, then into the manure spreader. Run the spreader over the field. Cut the hay, ted it (that means fluff it up so the sun can dry it all), rake it, bale it, throw it onto the wagon, stack it on the wagon, throw it into the haymow, stack it in the mow, check it a couple of days later to be sure it isn't overheating, and then, come September or October, start throwing it down out of the mow again. No wonder it becomes an obsession! Nothing can ruin your day more thoroughly than hay on the ground and a storm coming. Nothing feels better than sitting down with that cold drink, a tired back, and all the winter's hay under the barn roof.

So I understood exactly why the Westminster West firebug, back in 1883, chose October to torch people's barns.

I read the story in a collection of vignettes my father discovered at the local library. This wasn't in book form; just typed stories and paragraphs on loose sheets of paper. On one page was the story of the firebug who burned several barns over a two-year period. He burned a house next, and was caught, identified by a footprint bearing a distinctive patch on the sole of the boot.

A few pages farther on was the story of two sisters, one of whom took to her bed with a mysterious illness—the vapors, so common among women in the 1800s. Nothing was apparently wrong with her, and her mother and sister waited on her hand and foot. Then one night in October the barn was discovered to be on fire—the firebug! The bedridden girl Susan got up to help her family. The well sister, Clara, took to her own bed that very night, and never resumed a normal life.

I knew immediately that it was a novel, though it took a long time to figure out what the novel was. It was difficult, a balance between melodrama and no drama at all. At first it didn't work. I remember an hour-long conversation with Susan about everything wrong with it, and lying awake that night thinking I would have to become a waitress, because I'd done the best writing I had in me to do and it wasn't enough.

But thanks to Susan's intelligent questions, I had better in me, and the book *Westminster West* was finally published.

Intelligent questions are sometimes the greatest gift a writer can receive. Another historical, fire-centered book became possible for me through a question of Susan's. I had long struggled to write an account of the house fire my parents were both in, when my mother was eight and my father eighteen. I told Susan about it. "Are you writing it for the eight year old or the eighteen year old?" she asked. Brilliant! Immediately I knew it was for the eight year old, and I knew what that meant about the narrative; simplicity, directness, no necessity to deal with the genealogy and history I'd always struggled to include.

I learned a couple of valuable things from that book. In the process of writing it I asked my parents dozens of questions. I had heard the story of the fire all my life, but there were details I didn't know, details that don't become important until you are trying to tell exactly how they came down the stairs, and around a corner, and could see—what?

"But Jessie, that was fifty years ago!" my parents said.

I wrote a draft, making guesses where their memories failed, and had them read that.

Immediately they could remember everything! The wrongness in my narrative stirred their memories; it's a classic prosecutorial technique, according to a lawyer friend. "So you broke into the pickup and stole the tools?"

"*And* the CD-player!" the perp corrects proudly.

I now believe this is one reason why writing a crappy first draft is so useful. Deep down, your mind has certain intentions, certain knowledge about your story. That knowledge is hard to bring to the surface. When you write a crappy first draft, what teachers like to call a "sloppy copy," you trigger that sense of wrongness. "Not like *that!*" your deep mind says. "Like *this!*"

The other thing I learned was about structuring for suspense. The first chapter begins in moonlight and peace, with smoke rising from the kitchen wall of a house. I must introduce the people in the house, and there are more than I'd have if it were fiction—a lot of names to keep track of. I introduce them in a spiral, from least important to most central, my mother Patty. At intervals I remind the reader that these people are sleeping, and I strike the word "smoke," like a bell. Finally Patty coughs herself awake, and calls for her mother, asleep in the same room. "Mom?" Mom doesn't answer. "Mom? Mom? Mo-om!" (*Fire: My Parents' Story,* Greenwillow, 1998.)

When I read the chapter aloud to groups of kids, the inevitable scuffle of noise dims at each repeat of the word "smoke," hushes when Patty coughs and is introduced.

When Patty calls "Mom?" and Mom doesn't answer, the room goes dead silent. You can hear a feather fall. That gives me an intense thrill. I have their attention, and they hear as fully as I wanted them to my grandmother's remarkable words when she struggled awake and realized what was happening. "Don't be afraid; the house is afire."

When I read stories about Dorothy Canfield Fisher's family I feel I knew them, that she's given them to me. I want to give my people to others, and the deepest praise someone can give me is to tell me they know these people, these Vermonters. My real family, and the fictional Vermonters I've extrapolated from them, Uncle Daney, Uncle Clayton, and Uncle Truman from *Unbroken,* Jeep, the grandfather in *Shaper,* Aunt Sarah, old Mrs. Braley in *Westminster West*—all form an extended family of fictional Vermonters for me, stretching far back in time.

*The author on her farm, Westminster West, Vermont*

In 1989 I went looking for an understudy for Josey, my childhood horse. I wanted a Morgan, and answered a few ads (I got the material for *A Horse Like Barney* doing this.) Then one morning I pulled into the yard of an old dairy farm. A beautiful dark stallion was playing in the pen. I was dazzled. Several of his foals were for sale and I knew I had to have one if I could afford it. I was staring at the stallion when a woman and her young son walked around the corner of the barn. Cheryl Rivers introduced herself, and I barely noticed; I was too star struck.

The stallion was Portledge Steven, the fastest Morgan of the twentieth century. He had offspring ranging from four years old down to one month. They went down in price as they went down in age, and soon I had negotiated to buy the month-old colt.

A year later Cheryl became a state senator, and the year after that she introduced a bill to create a single payer health care system in Vermont. I didn't know anything about health care reform, but Cheryl had become a friend, and her bold move was unpopular with many politicians. Cheryl was attacked, I got mad, and the next thing I knew I was neck-deep in the fight for health care reform. My writing talents and inherited cussedness make me a wicked letter-to-the-editor writer; I may be as famous for that, locally, as for my books.

Currently I'm the president of Vermont Citizens Campaign for Health, an organization still working for single payer health care. We still need it, the situation is only getting worse, and I believe it's only a matter of time.

Having a friend in the senate was an education for me. I got to see the inside workings of state politics. It was thrilling, fascinating, heartbreaking, demoralizing, and a lot of other things. In a small state like Vermont, the individual matters. I've been yelled at over the telephone by the president pro tem. of the senate, and yelled right back. I've conferred in the Speaker of the House's office, talked to the lieutenant governor, I'm on a first-name basis with the state auditor, and (soon to be former) governor Howard Dean once said to the chairman of the House Health and Welfare committee—"Jessie Haas! She hates me!" An exaggeration, governor, I assure you.

It's fun to be a sort of insider; fun enough for me to see the seduction. I understand how you can start to compromise what you believe in for the sake of your own power and position. Not many politicians resist that. It was a source of pride to me that my friend was one of the few who did.

The horse turned out fine too!

Out of these experiences came many of the events and indeed the characters—heavily disguised—in *Will You, Won't You?*, in which one of the main characters is a state senator.

Another element of my real life that went into *Will You, Won't You?* is Scottish Country dancing, which has been a great joy in our lives since the early 1980s. Originally it was a way to reconnect with neighbors when I moved back to my hometown as a new adult. It was difficult for a shy person who had always avoided team sports or in any way drawing attention, to reach across the set and take someone's hand, and skip down the middle of a line of people—more like running the gauntlet than dancing. But we persisted, became excellent dancers, and enjoy the togetherness, the music, the motion, and the precision that good dancing demands. Bernie McGrath is just the latest in a long line of fabulous teachers I've had, in all realms of life.

I've rarely known what I was really doing in life. What was supposed to be important was often fleeting, and my goofing off, daydreaming, playing, have turned out to be central to how I earn my living. Certainly it mattered far more that I played horses with Patty Stebbins than that I learned long division. I wrote a book about our game: *Appaloosa Zebra: A Horse Lover's Alphabet.* On rainy-day recesses Patty and I planned our future horse farm. When I wanted a premise to hang a horse alphabet on, there was that childhood game.

It mattered more to me to read *Little Women* under cover of my desk than to study social studies in the 1960s. The countries we were supposed to learn about have dissolved, but *Little Women* remains, and I write children's books.

With horses, I have often felt like a failure. I had a hard time training Josey, and later Atherton. I didn't do a professional job—no wonder!—and often forget to notice that I did in fact train them, all by myself. They are nice horses, and quite ridable.

I'm increasingly a timid rider. At one time I desperately wanted to compete in dressage. By the time I finally had a suitable horse, the ambition had evaporated. I trail ride and dub around on horseback, but not having a friend or my sister to ride with, I avoid scary situations. Also, just as I was training Atherton, I wrote a book called *Safe Horse, Safe Rider,* about handling horses so you don't hurt them and they don't hurt you. Focusing on safety made me even more chicken. That keeps me riding close to home and not thinking well of myself for that. On the other hand, it's rich for fiction. A horse seen through the lens of fear and the need for control is an elemental force as well as a personality. The speed, the potential for violence, the powerful emotional response of human characters ... this all works for me in a way I doubt it would had I become a better and more confident rider.

In 2002 I discovered I was a poet. I had begun writing poems earlier than that; a few, furtively, on random subjects, which remained hidden and half-forgotten in notebooks. In 2000 I began writing a horse history for kids and quickly discovered two things. One, there were plenty of horse histories out there, and two, I wasn't enjoying myself. I didn't want to proceed consecutively and connect all the dots. I didn't want to tell all the old stories every book about horses and history tells. I wanted to write something more personal, react to what I was learning in my research, and explore the byways rather than what everyone else seemed to regard as the main event. "Could this be poetry?" I wrote on top of a page, and began to try it.

It took a long time before I dared read my poems in a critique group. Poetry was scary. I didn't know the rules, and it felt much more personal. I was putting myself on the page, unscreened by invented characters. It took a lot of courage to eventually send the poems to Greenwillow; the first long manuscript I'd submitted since Susan Hirschman's retirement, and one of the most serious manuscripts of my life. The stakes were high. Fortunately, Greenwillow wants to publish them. I'm at work on the manuscript now, and looking for a title.

I've been lucky all my life in the people and the animals I've found. My friends, my teachers, my horses, my editors, have all been wonderful. I married a fellow writer who is my best critic, and a lively mind to engage with. (And he's cute!) And almost by accident I found the most satisfying work to do, always challenging, almost always fun. I hope to keep doing it forever.

# HARLAN, Judith 1949-

## Personal

Born February 3, 1949, in Albany, NY; daughter of Jack (a military officer) and Ruth Harlan; married Terry Tintorri (a real estate agent), December 10, 1988. *Education:* University of Arizona, B.A., 1971; San Francisco State University, M.A., 1979.

## Addresses

*Agent*—c/o Author Mail, Feminist Press, 365 Fifth Ave., Ste. 5406, New York, NY 10016. *E-mail*—judith_harlan@yahoo.com.

## Career

Freelance journalist and author. *Harbor Times* (a beach and harbor weekly), editor, 1980-81; Murphy Organization (advertising agency), news copywriter, 1982-83; *Freebies* (magazine), editor, 1984-85; Oxnard College, instructor, 1991—. Has also worked as a feature and news stringer for the *Los Angeles Times,* Los Angeles, CA.

## Member

Society of Professional Journalists, Society of Children's Book Writers and Illustrators.

## Awards, Honors

Notable Book citation, National Council for Social Studies and Children's Book Council, 1987, for *American Indians Today;* Carter G. Woodson Outstanding Merit Award, National Council for Social Studies, 1989, for *Hispanic Voters.*

## Writings

*American Indians Today: Issues and Conflicts,* Franklin Watts (New York, NY), 1987.
*Hispanic Voters: Gaining a Voice in American Politics,* Franklin Watts (New York, NY), 1988.
*Sounding the Alarm: A Biography of Rachel Carson,* Dillon Press (Minneapolis, MN), 1989.
*Bilingualism in the United States: Conflict and Controversy,* Franklin Watts (New York, NY), 1991.
*Puerto Rico: Deciding Its Future,* Twenty-First Century Books (New York, NY), 1996.
*Girl Talk: Staying Strong, Feeling Good, Sticking Together,* illustrated by Debbie Palen, Walker (New York, NY), 1997.
*Feminism: A Reference Handbook,* ABC-CLIO (Santa Barbara, CA), 1998.
*Mamphela Ramphele: Ending Apartheid in South Africa,* Feminist Press (New York, NY), 2000.

Also contributor to numerous periodicals, including *Alternative Energy Retailer, American Way, Art Business News, Business Travelers International, L.A. Par-*

*Judith Harlan offers girls advice on the topics of friends, boys, sports, fashion, school, and more in* **Girl Talk.** *(Illustrated by Debbie Palen.)*

*ent,* and *Entree;* West Coast editor and author of monthly column for *Earnshaw's* magazine.

## Sidelights

Judith Harlan is the author of several nonfiction works geared toward young adults. Much of the Harlan's work has concentrated on topics important to the Hispanic community, including *Hispanic Voters: Gaining a Voice in American Politics, Bilingualism in the United States: Conflict and Controversy,* and *Puerto Rico: Deciding Its Future.* Additionally, Harlan has created titles featuring the accomplishments of women, writing a reference book on feminism, *Feminism: A Reference Handbook,* an advice book for teenagers, *Girl Talk: Staying Strong, Feeling Good, Sticking Together,* and two biographies about important females on the world stage, *Sounding the Alarm: A Biography of Rachel Carson* and *Mamphela Ramphele: Ending Apartheid in South Africa.*

The efforts of Puerto Ricans to decide whether or not to declare themselves an independent state fill the pages of *Puerto Rico: Deciding Its Future.* Here, the author shares with readers the country's long history, beginning with the conquest by the Spanish of the original Indian inhabitants, the island's relationship with the United States, and efforts to declare itself independent of the United States. Using books, newspaper articles, and interviews, among other research methods, Harlan presents the reasons why some Puerto Ricans wish to abandon the commonwealth status they currently enjoy and why others support Puerto Rico becoming the fifty-first state of the United States. Calling the information "interesting and timely," *Booklist* reviewer Susan Dove Lempke thought that the author "fairly assesses the points in favor of each side," while *School Library*

*Journal* critic Linda Greengrass found that "the language is clear and the discussion straightforward." In her positive review of the book, Greengrass specifically praised "the clarity and simplicity with which the statehood-commonwealth-independence question is presented."

Focusing on the emotional needs of young females, *Girl Talk: Staying Strong, Feeling Good, Sticking Together* offers teenage girls support in developing a healthy self-image as they make the transition to adulthood. In a "conversational text that is full of asides and funny musings," as a *Kirkus Reviews* contributor described it, Harlan offers advice about how to make the adolescent years a positive experience by participating in sporting activities, learning about important feminists, and planning for a satisfying career after school. Additionally, she offers tips on how to handle the pressures of teen life, giving suggestions "on how to enjoy life while trying new, positive experiences," remarked Debbie Earl in *Voice of Youth Advocates*. Earl described the book as "bubbly, informative and easily read," while the *Kirkus Reviews* contributor called it a "lightweight but kind-hearted guide."

Other books featuring women's themes include *Feminism*, a reference work about modern feminism, and *Mamphela Ramphele*, a biography of the black South African doctor. The first title, called "a convenient beginning guide to contemporary feminism" by *Choice* reviewer J. Ariel, presents a large amount of information about various aspects of feminism, including short biographies of important women leaders, discussion of the impact of women's rights in society, and a history of the feminist movement. In *Mamphela Ramphele*, Harlan focuses on the life of one woman who overcame gender and racial bias to become a leading figure in the movement to dismantle the Apartheid regime in South Africa. In addition to her work as a physician, Ramphele also worked as a teacher and an anthropologist before the end of Apartheid allowed her to serve as an advisor to the first post-Apartheid president, Nelson Mandela. Writing in *School Library Journal*, Ann G. Brouse declared that in her biography, Harlan "provide[s] more information for this age group than other single sources."

Harlan once told *SATA*: "I have always been a sucker for a good story, always interested in reading, writing, and people. In elementary school, I was an outdoors, rough-and-tumble kind of girl during the day; in the evenings, I was a silent adventurer, discovering the worlds far away inside books.... I read all the adventures and wanted to be just like the heroes in them. When I was a teenager, I noticed that I enjoyed writing stories almost as much as reading them. I've been writing them ever since, from newspaper and magazine articles to advertising copy to children's books. And children's books are what I enjoy most, what takes me back to those faraway places I used to go as a child.

"I hope that the books I have written ... have been helpful and informative for young readers.... I wanted to know all sides of the issues, to present those sides as objectively as is humanly possible. Three of the books involve the study of multiculturalism in the United States, a topic about people, a topic of interest to me; [a] fourth one is about one of my heroes, Rachel Carson."

## Biographical and Critical Sources

*PERIODICALS*

*Booklist,* January, 1997, Susan Dove Lempke, review of *Puerto Rico: Deciding Its Future,* p. 836; December 1, 1997, Stephanie Zvirin, review of *Girl Talk: Staying Strong, Feeling Good, Sticking Together,* p. 620.

*Choice,* December, 1998, J. Ariel, review of *Feminism: A Reference Handbook,* p. 668.

*Horn Book Guide,* spring, 2001, Anita L. Burkam, review of *Mamphela Ramphele: Ending Apartheid in South Africa,* p. 145.

*Kirkus Reviews,* October 15, 1997, review of *Girl Talk,* p. 1582.

*Publishers Weekly,* November 24, 1997, review of *Girl Talk,* p. 76.

*School Library Journal,* December, 1988, Oralia Garza de Cortes, review of *Hispanic Voters: Gaining a Voice in American Politics,* p. 127; November, 1989, Amy Adler, review of *Sounding the Alarm: A Biography of Rachel Carson,* p. 123; December, 1991, Kathryn Harvis, review of *Bilingualism in the United States: Conflict and Controversy,* p. 142; July, 1997, Linda Greengrass, review of *Puerto Rico,* p. 105; December, 2000, Ann G. Brouse, review of *Mamphela Ramphele,* p. 162.

*Voice of Youth Advocates,* February, 1998, Debbie Earl, review of *Girl Talk,* pp. 400, 402.*

\*        \*        \*

# HARRIS, Carol Flynn 1933-

## Personal

Born June 19, 1933, in Boston, MA; daughter of William B. (a chauffeur) and Emily (a bookkeeper; maiden name, Rourke) Flynn; married George H. Harris (a banker), June 9, 1957. *Education:* Attended high school in Watertown, MA. *Hobbies and other interests:* Gardening, golf, travel.

## Addresses

*Home and office*—16 Nyack St., Watertown, MA 02472. *E-mail*—chghwat@mediaone.net.

## Career

Watertown Public Library, Watertown, MA, head of circulation at North Branch Library, 1968-85; writer, 1985—.

## Member

Society of Children's Book Writers and Illustrators, New England Society of Children's Book Writers and Illustrators.

## Awards, Honors

*A Place for Joey* was named among the "best children's books of 2001" by the *Boston Herald.*

## Writings

*A Place for Joey,* Boyds Mills Press (Honesdale, PA), 2001.

Work represented in anthologies and textbooks. Contributor of articles and stories to magazines, including *Boys Life, Brio, Children's Digest, My Friend, Highlights,* and *Hopscotch,* and to the Internet web site *Our Creative Space.*

## Work in Progress

Two teen novels, *Island Melody* and *A Pebble in the Water.*

## Sidelights

Carol Flynn Harris told *SATA:* "I started writing for children very late in life, after I 'retired' from the Watertown Public Library after twenty years of working in a branch library. My husband had retired, and I now had the time to pursue a long-held (and long-deferred) dream. Children have always been my favorite people. I wanted to write stories for all the children I had met, sometimes briefly, who captured my heart. I wanted to write for children I'd never met, but whose dreams I imagined.

"My first publication came in 1991 and brought me the thrill of knowing I *could* write something that children would want to read. I continued to write and publish stories and articles in children's magazines. I wrote books that sometimes got me a hand-written rejection, but no publication. Still I persisted. Ten years after I first saw my name in print, my book *A Place for Joey* was accepted. In 2001, at the age of sixty-eight, I realized my dream as I held my newly published book in my hand.

"*Joey* is about a twelve-year-old Italian/American immigrant boy who lives in the North End of Boston, loves it there, and is determined to stay in the city despite his family's plans to buy a farm in the country. He has a dream. The book was named one of the three 'best children's books of 2001' by the *Boston Herald.* More important to me are the responses I get from children, such as 'Are you going to write a sequel?' Maybe I will, but right now I'm working on two other novels, plus writing some short pieces for an educational publisher, pieces that will be used in school reading assessment programs. It's great to have a dream, no matter what your age!"

Harris added, "My education beyond high school has been for my own edification. It consists of non-degree courses in library reference training, English, American history, and writing for children."

## Biographical and Critical Sources

### PERIODICALS

*Arizona Daily Sun,* December 2, 2001, Anne Pisacano, "Children's Novel Tackles 'Immigration Problem.'"

*Booklist,* September, 2001, Roger Leslie, review of *A Place for Joey.*

*Boston Globe,* September 27, 2001, review of *A Place for Joey.*

*Lorgnette,* October, 2001, Susan Carruth, review of *A Place for Joey.*

*Midwest Book Review,* September, 2001, review of *A Place for Joey.*

*Multicultural Review,* December, 2001, Ruth G. Becker, review of *A Place for Joey.*

*School Library Journal,* September, 2001, Diane S. Marton, review of *A Place for Joey.*

*Voice of Youth Advocates,* October, 2001, review of *A Place for Joey.*

### OTHER

*Our Creative Space,* http://www.ourcreativespace.com/ (March 6, 2002).*

\*      \*      \*

# HEINE, Helme 1941-

## Personal

Born April 4, 1941, in Berlin, Germany. *Education:* Studied art and business management.

## Addresses

*Agent*—c/o M. K. McElderry/Simon & Schuster Children's Publishing, 1230 Avenue of the Americas, New York, NY 10020.

## Career

Writer and illustrator. Has also worked in a cabaret as decorator, actor, and director, Johannesberg, South Africa, 1966-76; writer and illustrator for the television program *Sauerkraut* in Germany.

## Awards, Honors

Outstanding Books of the Year selection, *New York Times,* 1979, for *The Pig's Wedding;* Best Illustrated Books of the Year, *New York Times,* 1980, for *Mr. Miller the Dog; Boston Globe-Horn Book* Honor Book for Illustration, 1983, and Owl Prize from Japan's Shiko-sha and Maruzen Co., 1984, both for *Friends;* Children's Choice Book selection, Children's Book Council and the International Reading Association, 1981, for *Mr. Miller the Dog,* 1984, for *The Most Wonderful Egg in the World,* and 1986, for *The Pearl;*

Bologna Fair Graphic Prize, International Children's Book Fair; Hans Christian Andersen Award runner-up, 1984.

## Writings

*IN ENGLISH TRANSLATION; SELF-ILLUSTRATED*

*Na Warte, sagte Schwarte,* Middlehauve, 1978, published as *The Pig's Wedding,* Atheneum (New York, NY), 1979.

*Der Hund Herr Muller,* Unterhaching, 1979, published as *Mr. Miller the Dog,* Atheneum (New York, NY), 1980.

*Freunde,* Middlehauve, 1981, published as *Friends,* Atheneum (New York, NY), 1982.

*Konig Hupf der 1,* Middlehauve, 1981, published as *King Bounce the First,* Neugebauer Press, 1982.

*Das Schoenste Ei der Welt,* Middlehauve, 1983, published as *The Most Wonderful Egg in the World,* Atheneum (New York, NY), 1983.

*Der Rennwagen,* Middlehauve, 1983, published as *The Racing Car,* Atheneum (New York, NY), 1985.

*Der Wecker,* Middlehauve, 1983, published as *The Alarm Clock,* Atheneum (New York, NY), 1986.

*Die Perle,* Middlehauve, 1984, published as *The Pearl,* Dent (London, England), 1985.

*Der Besuch,* Middlehauve, 1985, published as *The Visitor,* Atheneum (New York, NY), 1985.

*Samstag in Paradies,* Middlehauve, 1986, published as *One Day in Paradise,* Atheneum (New York, NY), 1986.

*Prinz Baer,* Middlehauve, 1988, published as *Prince Bear,* M. K. McElderry (New York, NY), 1989.

*Seiben Wilde Schweine,* Middlehauve, 1988, published as *Seven Wild Pigs: Eleven Picture Book Fantasies,* M. K. McElderry (New York, NY), 1988.

*The Marvelous Journey through the Night,* translated by Ralph Mannheim, Farrar, Straus (New York, NY), 1990.

*Mollywoop,* translated by Ralph Mannheim, Farrar, Straus (New York, NY), 1991.

*Friends Go Adventuring,* M. K. McElderry (New York, NY), 1995.

*The Boxer and the Princess,* M. K. McElderry (New York, NY), 1998.

Also author of untranslated children's books, including *Tante Nudel, Onkel Ruhe, und Herr Schlau: Ein Bilderbuch,* Middlehauve, 1979.

*IN ENGLISH; SELF-ILLUSTRATED*

*Superhare,* Barron's (Hauppauge, NY), 1979.

*Merry-Go-Round,* Barron's (Hauppauge, NY), 1980.

*OTHER*

*Uhren haben keine Bremse* (humor), Diogenes, 1985.

## Sidelights

Author and illustrator Helme Heine is best known for creating picture books that are both thought-provoking and entertaining. While his work covers a wide range of subjects and themes, Heine specializes in retelling classic fables and fairytales from a humorous point of view. Many of Heine's books feature playful and inventive watercolor illustrations of animals and nature. Despite the often whimsical nature of his illustrations and stories, Heine tries to put a bit of seriousness in all his tales. "I like to put in something that continues to grow when the book is closed—a moral, or a different way to think about something," Heine told Margaret Carter in an interview for *Books for Your Children.* He added: "Language and illustration are after all two sides of the same coin. Language creates pictures but an illustrator shouldn't follow the author—it is his job to create between the lines—what the author has *not* written. . . . Language is the opposite—the picture builds up gradually word by word so that sometimes it isn't until the end of the story that you recognize the landscape."

Born in Berlin, Heine completed his art studies in West Germany before traveling in Europe and Asia, with an extended stay in Africa. He has acted, designed stage settings, and directed plays for the theater, written film scripts, and at one time operated a cabaret and published a humorous magazine. Heine writes and illustrates picture books from his home in Munich, in the lake country of Bavaria. Several of his works have been adapted for television presentations. Anthea Bell, writing in *Twentieth-Century Children's Writers,* observed that picture books are "the easiest [way] in which to achieve internationalism, the pictures mattering as much as, or more than, the words" and remarked that "the

*Beaver finds a valuable pearl and is afraid of angering his neighbors by keeping it for himself in* **The Pearl,** *a self-illustrated work by Heine.*

*Watercolors depict the bicycle adventure of Charlie Rooster, Johnny Mouse, and Fat Percy the pig in* **Friends Go Adventuring,** *written and illustrated by Heine.*

bucolic humour of Helme Heine's picture books strikes a particularly German note."

Heine's first book, *The Pig's Wedding,* named one of the *New York Times* Outstanding Books for 1979, is a "dotty tale ... executed in swirling swathes of paint that express comedy, while pleasantly natural backgrounds of sky, trees and flowering meadows set off the grotesque figures of the pigs," according to Margery Fisher in *Growing Point.* Denise M. Wilms characterized Heine's "porcine menagerie" as "a comedic triumph: rotund, flop-eared, and guileless, they pose their way uninhibitedly across the pages." And Harold C. K. Rice noted in the *New York Times Book Review,* "despite the awkward text, the pictures had the kids in my house snorting with glee."

*Mr. Miller the Dog,* Heine's second book, is a role-reversal fantasy where a night watchman changes places with his dog, Murphy. A critic for *Kirkus Reviews* observed that Heine's sketches are reminiscent of James Thurber and went on to praise his "offbeat idea" as "properly proportioned, the performance by Mr. Miller and Murphy never overstated, always on cue." This book was named one of *New York Times* Best Illustrated Books for 1980. As Ethel Heins concluded in *Horn Book:* "To an adult the book might seem like a Kafkaesque spoof, to a child, pure fun."

The text of Heine's award-winning 1982 book, *Friends,* relates the adventures of Percy the pig, Johnny Mouse, and Charlie Rooster, who spend a happy day together bicycling, sailing, and picking cherries, then spend the night apart. The pictures, however, reveal a contrasting story: an overturned boat, unfairly divided cherries, and a night together. "None of these experiences are outlandish or even out of the ordinary," Kenneth

Marantz stated in a *School Library Journal* review. "But Heine's visual imagination makes the images extraordinary." Eileen Colwell described the book's atmosphere in *Junior Bookshelf* as "one of innocence and friendship and childlike fun." Heine reprised the cheerful, indomitable barnyard trio in the 1995 *Friends Go Adventuring,* in which Charlie Rooster, Johnny Mouse, and Fat Percy the pig once again hit the road on their bicycle, searching for adventure and fun. En route, they manage to perform a daring rescue, deal with wicked pirates and a cannibal cook, and finally return home safely full of tales with which to alternately regale and bore their friends. Reviewing the title in *Booklist,* Susan Dove Lempke felt that Heine's watercolors are "zesty and lyrical," though she was also fearful that young readers might find "nightmare material" in the cannibal cook. However, Lempke concluded, "Children who relish the thrills and chills of adventure ... will be well pleased."

In another of Heine's early works, *King Bounce the First,* the artist uses colorful collage patterns which, as Olga Richard and Donnarae McCann noted in *Wilson Library Bulletin,* "may remind the viewer of illustrations by Ezra Jack Keats or Eric Carle." The reviewers appreciated the "serious zaniness in Heine's work which has no close antecedent—a zaniness of concept plus an unusually high standard of execution," and concluded that "value contrasts in the color and ingenious shape arrangements make the static cut-outs look animated."

In another *Wilson Library Bulletin* review, McCann and Richard commended Heine for his consistent excellence: "Whether the subject is a celebration or a variation on the friendship theme ... or a comment on vain chickens, Heine makes good use of humor, suspense, and strong design." They also praised the "spontaneity, balance, vitality, expressiveness, and effortlessness" of his work, noting that he "demonstrates an appreciation of childhood's spirit that is probably unattainable if one doesn't have it from the start." As George A. Woods concluded in the *New York Times Book Review,* "What [Heine] gives us most is a sense of joy, of irrepressible glee, of fellowship and delight."

In two titles translated by Ralph Mannheim, *The Marvelous Journey through the Night* and *Mollywoop,* Heine again makes use of his zany take on life. In the former title, "a rather odd discourse on the pleasures of sleep," according to a reviewer for *Publishers Weekly,* Heine details a dream journey full of animals which are "as always ... whimsical." In *Mollywoop,* Heine introduces "three animal friends in ... breezy snippets of verse," according to another *Publishers Weekly* writer, who went on to conclude that each of these vignettes, "aided by perky, endearing" illustrations, reinforces the book's underlying theme about "the importance of friendship."

In the 1998 title, *The Boxer and the Princess,* Heine relates a "gentle, funny fantasy/fable," according to *Booklist*'s Hazel Rochman, along with illustrations "that make you laugh and feel." Max the Rhinoceros is scolded by his father for being too sensitive, for having skin much too thin. So Max proceeds to don boxing gloves, a helmet, and armor to protect himself from the world. He goes out into the cold world to slay dragons and rescue a beautiful princess with whom he falls in love. But no luck; the princess wants nothing to do with a boxer. So in love is Max that he sheds he armor and learns to pick flowers to win the hand of his princess fair. "There's a wonderful light tone to the exaggerated story and the wry pictures," Rochman remarked. Reviewing the same title in *Publishers Weekly,* a contributor concluded, "Heine's watercolors convey a courageous young hero whose posture belies tenderness no matter how thick his shell."

## Biographical and Critical Sources

*BOOKS*

*Twentieth-Century Children's Writers,* 3rd edition, St. James Press (Detroit, MI), 1989, p. 1121.
*Children's Literature Review,* Volume 18, Gale (Detroit, MI), 1989.
Holtze, Sally Holmes, editor, *Sixth Book of Junior Authors and Illustrators,* H. W. Wilson (New York, NY), 1989, pp. 120-122.

*PERIODICALS*

*Booklist,* March 1, 1979, Denise M. Wilms, review of *The Pig's Wedding,* pp. 1091-1092; January 1, 1983; January 1, 1996, Susan Dove Lempke, review of *Friends Go Adventuring,* p. 845; October 15, 1998, Hazel Rochman, review of *The Boxer and the Princess,* p. 427.
*Books for Your Children,* spring, 1985, Margaret Carter, "Helme Heine," p. 9.
*Growing Point,* January 1979, Margery Fisher, review of *The Pig's Wedding,* p. 3449.
*Horn Book,* February, 1981, Ethel L. Heins, review of *Mr. Miller the Dog,* pp. 42-43.
*Junior Bookshelf,* October, 1982, Eileen Colwell, review of *Friends,* p. 181.
*Kirkus Reviews,* November 1, 1980, review of *Mr. Miller the Dog,* p. 1392.
*New York Times Book Review,* April 29, 1979, Harold C. K. Rice, review of *The Pig's Wedding,* p. 29; November 28, 1982, George A. Woods, review of *Friends,* p. 24; November 13, 1983, p. 55; September 22, 1985, p. 32; September 21, 1986, p. 22; November 19, 1995, p. 37.
*Publishers Weekly,* November 19, 1982; June 20, 1986; July 28, 1989, p. 219; October 12, 1990, review of *The Marvelous Journey through the Night,* p. 63; August 16, 1991, review of *Mollywoop,* p. 57; October 23, 1995, p. 68; September 28, 1998, review of *The Boxer and the Princess,* p. 101.
*School Library Journal,* February, 1983, Kenneth Marantz, review of *Friends,* p. 66; August, 1988, p. 66; October, 1989, p. 86; March, 1990, p. 206; February, 1996, p. 84; November, 1998, p. 85.
*Times Literary Supplement,* March 26, 1982; September 17, 1982.
*Wilson Library Bulletin,* September, 1982, Donnarae McCann and Olga Richard, review of *King Bounce the First,* pp. 58-59; February, 1984, Donnarae McCann and Olga Richard, "Picture Books for Children," pp. 435-436; December, 1985; February, 1991, pp. 114-116.

\*　　\*　　\*

# HERRIOT, James 1916-1995

## Personal

Given name, James Alfred Wight; born October 3, 1916, in Sunderland, County Tyne, and Werr, England; died February 23, 1995, of prostate cancer, in Thirsk, Yorkshire, England; son of James Henry (a musician) and Hannah (a professional singer; maiden name, Bell) Wight; married Joan Catherine Danbury, November 5, 1941; children: James, Rosemary Page. *Education:* Glasgow Veterinary College, M.R.C.V.S., 1938. *Religion:* Protestant. *Hobbies and other interests:* Music, walking with his dog.

## Career

Veterinarian and author. Sinclair & Wight, Thirsk, Yorkshire, England, partner and general practitioner in veterinary medicine, 1938-92; writer, 1966-95. *Military service:* Royal Air Force, 1943-45.

## Member

British Veterinary Association (honorary member), Royal College of Veterinary Surgeons (fellow).

## Awards, Honors

Best Young Adult Book citations, American Library Association, 1974, for *All Things Bright and Beautiful,* and 1975, for *All Creatures Great and Small;* Order of the British Empire, 1979; D.Litt., Watt University, Scotland, 1979; honorary D.Vsc., Liverpool University, 1984; *Redbook* Award, 1988, for *Blossom Comes Home;* James Herriot Award established by Humane Society of America.

## Writings

*If Only They Could Talk* (also see below), M. Joseph (London, England), 1970.
*It Shouldn't Happen to a Vet* (also see below), M. Joseph (London, England), 1972.
*All Creatures Great and Small* (contains *If Only They Could Talk* and *It Shouldn't Happen to a Vet*), St. Martin's Press (New York, NY), 1972.
*Let Sleeping Vets Lie* (also see below), M. Joseph (London, England), 1973.
*Vet in Harness* (also see below), M. Joseph (London, England), 1974.
*All Things Bright and Beautiful* (contains *Let Sleeping Vets Lie* and *Vet in Harness*), St. Martin's Press (New York, NY), 1974.
*Vets Might Fly* (also see below), M. Joseph (London, England), 1976.

*James Herriot*

*Vet in a Spin* (also see below), M. Joseph (London, England), 1977.

*All Things Wise and Wonderful* (contains *Vets Might Fly* and *Vet in a Spin*), St. Martin's Press (New York, NY), 1977.

*James Herriot's Yorkshire,* illustrated with photographs by Derry Brabbs, St. Martin's Press (New York, NY), 1979, revised edition published as *James Herriot's Yorkshire Revisited,* 1999.

(With others) *Animals Tame and Wild,* Sterling (New York, NY), 1979, published as *Animal Stories: Tame and Wild,* 1985.

*The Lord God Made Them All,* St. Martin's Press (New York, NY), 1981.

*The Best of James Herriot,* St. Martin's Press (New York, NY), 1983.

*James Herriot's Dog Stories,* illustrated by Victor G. Ambrus, St. Martin's Press (New York, NY), 1986.

*Every Living Thing,* St. Martin's Press (New York, NY), 1992.

*James Herriot's Cat Stories,* illustrated by Lesley Holmes, St. Martin's Press (New York, NY), 1994.

*James Herriot's Favorite Dog Stories,* illustrated by Lesley Holmes, G. K. Hall (Boston, MA), 1996.

*James Herriot's Yorkshire Stories,* illustrated by Lesley Holmes, M. Joseph (London, England), published as *James Herriot's Animal Stories,* St. Martin's Press (New York, NY), 1997.

Contributor of stories to *Greatest Cat Stories,* F. A. Thorpe (Austey, Leicester, England), 1997, *A Dog's*

*World,* Travelers' Tales Guides (San Francisco, CA), 1997, and *Love of Spaniels,* Voyageur Press, 2000. Also author of *James Herriot's Yorkshire Calendar.*

*FOR CHILDREN*

*Moses the Kitten,* illustrated by Peter Barrett, St. Martin's Press (New York, NY), 1984.

*Only One Woof,* illustrated by Peter Barrett, St. Martin's Press (New York, NY), 1985.

*The Christmas Day Kitten,* illustrated by Ruth Brown, St. Martin's Press (New York, NY), 1986.

*Bonny's Big Day,* illustrated by Ruth Brown, St. Martin's Press (New York, NY), 1987.

*Blossom Comes Home,* illustrated by Ruth Brown, St. Martin's Press (New York, NY), 1988.

*The Market Square Dog,* illustrated by Ruth Brown, St. Martin's Press (New York, NY), 1990.

*Oscar, Cat-about-Town,* illustrated by Ruth Brown, M. Joseph (London, England), 1990.

*Smudge, the Little Lost Lamb,* illustrated by Ruth Brown, St. Martin's Press (New York, NY), 1991.

*James Herriot's Treasury for Children,* St. Martin's Press (New York, NY), 1992.

*James Herriot's Yorkshire Village: A Pop-up Book,* St. Martin's Press (New York, NY), 1995.

## Adaptations

*All Creatures Great and Small* was filmed by EMI Production, 1975; was presented on the *Hallmark Hall of Fame,* NBC-TV, 1975; was adapted as a television series by BBC-TV, 1978; and recorded on audio cassette by Listen for Pleasure, 1980. *All Things Bright and Beautiful* was filmed by BBC-TV, 1979 (also released as *It Shouldn't Happen to a Vet*), and recorded as an audio cassette by Listen for Pleasure, 1980. Audio cassette versions were recorded by Cassette Book for *All Things Wise and Wonderful,* and by Listen for Pleasure for *The Lord God Made Them All,* 1982; Listen for Pleasure also released an audio cassette titled *Stories from the Herriot Collection;* Audio Renaissance released audio cassette versions of *If Only They Could Talk,* 1994, *James Herriot's Favorite Dog Stories,* 1995, and *James Herriot's Animal Stories,* 1997, all read by Christopher Timothy; *It Shouldn't Happen to a Vet* was released as an audio cassette, read by Christopher Timothy, 1995, Chivers North America; various short stories were adapted for audio cassette as *James Herriot's World of Animals: A Collection of Stories from the World's Most Beloved Veterinarian,* Audio Renaissance, 2000.

## Sidelights

James Herriot, vet-turned best-selling author, penned twenty books in his lifetime, selling over sixty million copies. His gentle, humorous, heartwarming narratives of the life of a veterinary in England's Yorkshire Dales during the 1940s and 1950s touched a vein in readers of the late twentieth century. As Mitzi Brunsdale noted in her *James Herriot,* "an audience buffeted by brushfire wars, continent-spanning plagues, voice mail, E-mail, lost mail, MTV, and the Information Superhighway can still find solace in the disarming tales a gentle veterinarian from a Yorkshire town ... and a ... world far removed from the horrors of the nightly news, yet as intimate as the decency and compassion of the human heart." Brunsdale further noted that Herriot's work "charms his readers with a healthy nostalgia for what used to be best in our world as well as an unquenchable hope for what we want to think—in spite of ourselves—remains a constant good in what Mark Twain called 'the damned human race.'"

Herriot's story collections, including 1972's *All Creatures Great and Small* and 1974's *All Things Bright and Beautiful,* not only topped the best-seller charts, but were also turned into movies and hugely successful television series, making his pen name a household word on both sides of the Atlantic Ocean. Herriot—born James Alfred Wight—liked to say he was just a simple country veterinarian. But readers and critics alike appreciated the joy he found in his hard work, laughed at his humorous anecdotes, marveled at the curative practices he explained, and relaxed with his descriptions of the English countryside. In Herriot's later years, to the delight of children and adults alike, he transformed some of his most endearing vignettes into picture book stories. Although these tales are short and uncomplicated, their emotional content is vintage Herriot: they exude love, humor, and, at times, elicit tears. They have, in fact, the same peculiar magic that his adult fiction has, a blend according to Mary Ann Grossmann, writing in the *Chicago Tribune,* of "finely drawn and colorful characters, empathy for humans and animals, a good story set in a gentler time, humor, respect for uneducated but hard-working people and an appreciation of the land." Grossmann further commented, "there's something else in Herriot's writing that I can't quite articulate, a glow of decency that makes people want to be better humans. I guess we'd call it 'spirituality' these days, this profound belief of Herriot's that humans are linked to all animals, whether they be the cows he helped birth or pampered pets like Tricki Woo, Mrs. Pumphrey's lovable but overfed Pekinese."

Herriot rejected the idea that his work was extraordinary. He once reflected to William Foster in *Scotsman,* "I know some writers dream of best sellerdom and the best table in the restaurants and all that, but not me. I just had this compulsion to write down what it was like to be a vet in those funny old days in the 1930s before I forgot. If I could find a publisher and my stories amused a few people well, that was the summit of my ambition." In his opinion, Herriot told David Taylor of *Radio Times,* Americans "read ... all kinds of weighty, humanitarian, sociological meanings" into his work that he could not see and did not have time to wonder about. "I'm much too busy being a vet."

Herriot grew up in Hillhead, a small town near Glasgow, Scotland. He once told *SATA:* "I had what I can only describe as an idyllic childhood, because, although I grew up in the big city of Glasgow, my home was only a few miles from the beauties of Loch Lomond and the Scottish hills. I spent much of my childhood and adolescence walking along with my dog, camping and climbing among the highlands of Scotland so that at an early age three things were implanted in my character: a love of animals, reading, and the countryside."

Herriot was just thirteen years old when he decided to become a veterinarian. By the time he received a degree from Glasgow Veterinary School, however, England was in the midst of the Great Depression. He was fortunate to find a job as an assistant vet in North Yorkshire, England, in the practice of Dr. John Sinclair. Although Herriot had always assumed he would be a small-animal surgeon and own his own modern office, this job involved house calls to treat horses, cows, pigs, and other livestock. It was not long before Herriot realized he loved what he did, and soon he revised his high-tech vision of what his ideal career path should be.

He wrote in *All Creatures Great and Small,* "Maybe it was something to do with the incredible sweetness of the air which still took me by surprise when I stepped out into the old wild garden at Skeldale House every morning. Or perhaps the daily piquancy of life in the graceful old house with my gifted but mercurial boss, Siegfried, and his reluctant student brother, Tristan. Or it could be that it was just the realization that treating cows and pigs and sheep and horses had a fascination I had never even suspected; and this brought with it a new concept of myself as a tiny wheel in the great machine of British agriculture. There was a kind of solid satisfaction in that."

Herriot was made a partner in the Yorkshire practice and married Joan Catherine Danbury—known as Helen in his books—on the same day in 1941. The couple lived together in the house Herriot called Skeldale House in his books, where Herriot was disturbed at all times of the night to tend sick animals. His rigorous practice and his happy life with his new wife were interrupted when he was called, at twenty-seven years of age, into active duty with the Royal Air Force (RAF) in 1943. After reporting to the Lords Cricket Ground at St. John's Wood in London for his initial training, Herriot was posted to Scarborough, Yorkshire, not too far from home. He was able to visit home when his son, James, was born.

Herriot was sent to flying school in Windsor and was then posted to Manchester. A subsequent operation made him unfit to fly, and he returned home to Yorkshire for good. Herriot had time to reflect on his career, and decided he was happy as a country vet. He wrote in *All Things Bright and Beautiful,* "I had no regrets, the life which had been forced on me by circumstances had turned out to be a thing of magical fulfillment. It came to me with a flooding certainty that I would rather spend my days driving over the unfenced roads of the high country than stooping over that operating table."

A second child, daughter Rosemary, was born in 1947. Well established in his profession, Herriot made a trip to the USSR in 1961 as a sheep veterinarian; another professional trip, to Istanbul, Turkey, in 1966 as a cattle veterinarian, followed. That same year, at age fifty,

**James Herriot's Animal Stories** *offer a fitting introduction to Herriot's writing. (Illustrated by Lesley Holmes.)*

Herriot began to write. He once told Foster of *Scotsman,* "The life of a country vet was dirty, uncomfortable, sometimes dangerous. It was terribly hard work and I loved it. I felt vaguely that I ought to write about it and every day for twenty-five years I told my wife of something funny that had happened and said I was keeping it for the book. She usually said, 'Yes, dear' to humour me but one day, when I was fifty, she said: 'Who are you kidding? Vets of fifty don't write first books.' Well, that did it. I stormed out and bought some paper and taught myself to type.

"Then I started to put it all down and the story didn't work. All I managed to pick out on the machine was a very amateur school essay. So I spent a year or two learning my craft, as real writers say. I read *How to Be a Writer* and *Teach Yourself to Write* and I bombarded newspapers, magazines and the BBC with unreadable short stories. They came back, every one, without a word of comment. Not even 'You show promise.'" Herriot began to study and learn from his favorite writers, like Charles Dickens, Arthur Conan Doyle, Ernest Hemingway, and J. D. Salinger, and kept on writing.

Although Herriot was still working as a vet, he wrote when he found time, sometimes in front of the television. He wrote his first book in eighteen months. *If Only They Could Talk* was published in 1970 under the name James Herriot because Herriot thought it would be akin to advertising to publish under his own name. He had to choose a pseudonym. "I was sitting in front of the TV tapping out one of my stories and there was this fellow James Herriot playing such a good game of soccer for Birmingham that I just took his name," Herriot explained to Arturo F. Gonzalez in *Saturday Review.*

Herriot's first book sold only 1,200 copies. "I thought it would stop at one book and nobody would ever discover the identity of the obscure veterinary surgeon who had scribbled his experiences in snatched moments of spare time," he wrote in *James Herriot's Yorkshire.* However, the writing bug had bitten deeply, and soon a second, 1972's *It Shouldn't Happen to a Vet,* appeared. By chance, Thomas McCormack, president of St. Martin's Press, was in London on a buying trip and picked up the first Herriot titles and saw real possibilities for them in the American market. Thus the first two novels were bound together in the U.S. edition, *All Creatures Great and Small.* A best seller and an immediate success, *All Creatures Great and Small* recalls moments from Herriot's career: assisting in the birth of calves, relieving Tricki Woo (an obese Pekinese dog pampered by her owner), and diagnosing and treating the ailments of numerous other dogs, cats, cows, horses, pigs, and sheep. Herriot also describes the people he worked with, including his boss, Siegfried Farnon, and his boss's brother, Tristan. In real life, these characters were J. Donald Sinclair and Brian Sinclair, and the Darrowby of the novels was a composite of several villages in Yorkshire, including Thirsk, where Herriot and his family lived.

Warmly received by readers, the critical reception of *All Creatures Great and Small* was also glowing. According to Nelson Bryant of the *New York Times Book Review,* Herriot's *All Creatures Great and Small* "shines with love of life" and "there is humor everywhere." Bryant further commented, "Herriot's book is more than a collection of well-told anecdotes and sharply drawn personalities.... Herriot charms because he delights in life, embraces it with gusto and writes with grace." Other reviewers found the book to be a breath of fresh air in the over-mechanized modern world. "What the world needs now, and does every so often," wrote William R. Doerner in *Time* magazine, "is a warm, G-rated, down-home, and unadrenalized prize of a book that sneaks onto the bestseller lists for no apparent reason other than a certain floppy-eared puppy appeal." Doerner went on to note, however, that it was only partly because of the "warm puppies" of Herriot's fiction that his book "qualifies admirably." Phoebe Adams, reviewing the novel in *Atlantic Monthly,* noted that it is "full of recalcitrant cows, sinister pigs, neurotic dogs, Yorkshire weather, and pleasantly demented colleagues. It continues to be one of the funniest and most likable books around."

1974's *All Things Bright and Beautiful* is a compilation of Herriot's next two books, *Let Sleeping Vets Lie* and *Vet in Harness.* It provides new stories about treating animals as well as tales of his courtship of Helen. Tristan's exploits are also related with humor. Once again, Herriot's tales of veterinary and social adventures on the Yorkshire Dales were welcomed by reviewers and fans alike. As Edward Weeks of *Atlantic Monthly* observed, the "laughter and fidelity in the writing arise from the fact that Dr. Herriot loves his work." Eugene J. Linehan of *Best Sellers* asserted that even those who don't like children, pets, and animals will like *All Things Bright and Beautiful:* "It's a joy." And writing in the *New York Times Book Review,* Paul Showers described the book as Herriot's "enthusiastic endorsement of a simple, unpretentious lifestyle." Showers further remarked: "No wonder the earlier book was so popular. Here is a man who actually enjoys his work without worrying about the Protestant Ethic; he finds satisfaction in testing his skill against challenges of different kinds. Beyond that, he delights in the day-to-day process of living even when things aren't going too well."

Herriot began *All Things Wise and Wonderful*—which contains *Vets Might Fly* and *Vet in a Spin*—with his training in the RAF at the beginning of World War II. The focus of this book is on Herriot's homesickness, memories, and desires rather than his RAF duties; the vet misses his wife, family, practice, and the Yorkshire countryside, and recalls events and moments of times at home with flashbacks. At the end of the book, Herriot has received his discharge and is happily marching home. Although Richard R. Lingeman of *New York Times Book Review* concluded that *All Things Wise and Wonderful* is "ingratiating," he sensed "formula creeping into the stories." Writing in the *English Journal,* Joy K. Roy, however, found curative powers in the book: "Herriot's writings epitomize the process of bibliotherapy; they can be used to inspire, to nurture, to brighten and to help the reader endure." For Roy, a reading of Herriot could "patch up the human spirit."

With 1981's *The Lord God Made Them All* Herriot takes up a new narrative "as if the others had never ended, the same way old friends meet again and talk, at once forgetting they have been apart," according to Lola D. Gillebaard in *Los Angeles Times Book Review.* More heartwarming and humorous tales of the Farnon household and of the odd cast of characters—two-legged and four-legged—in the Dales are brought center stage. Vic Sussman, reviewing the novel in *Washington Post Book World,* wrote, "This is Herriot at his best, the Buster Keaton of veterinary medicine, able to make us laugh, cry or nod in agreement with some snippet of universal truth." After writing *The Lord God Made Them All,* Herriot insisted that he would never write another "big" book. He had grandchildren to visit, gardens to tend, and walks to take. He also wanted to mitigate his popularity: since two of his books had been adapted as motion pictures and one had been transformed into a BBC television series in the 1970s, desperate fans found him despite his attempts to lead them astray on Yorkshire's winding roads. Herriot needed to rest. He did not write

another large book until *Every Living Thing,* published in 1992.

In the meantime, and fortunately for fans of all ages, Herriot began to adapt some of the stories he had told in his books for adults as stories for children. *Moses the Kitten* is based on an anecdote in *Vet in Harness.* Moses is a small black kitten rescued by Dr. Herriot from icy death among the frozen rushes of a pond. Herriot gives the kitten to a farm family, who warm it in an oven and allow it to live with the pigs in their barn. Bertha, a sow, nurses and cares for Moses like one of her own. Although Bertha's piglets grow up and leave her, she and Moses become fast friends. "Patience, kindness and caring are the dominant themes here," wrote Mary Lou Budd of *School Library Journal.*

Another stray cat figures in *The Christmas Day Kitten.* Based on a tale from *All Things Wise and Wonderful,* the book tells how Debbie, a roving female cat, refuses to live with kind Mrs. Pickering. Nevertheless, Mrs. Pickering continues to offer love and food to the cat when she calls. Early one Christmas morning, Debbie arrives sick and dying at Mrs. Pickering's home, carrying a tiny kitten. While Dr. Herriot cannot save Debbie, the kitten grows up to be Mrs. Pickering's beloved pet, Buster. According to Ann A. Flowers of *Horn Book, The Christmas Day Kitten* is "warm, compassionate, and very suitable for the season." Writing in the *Los Angeles Times,* Jack Miles also had praise for Herriot's children's book, describing it a "yarn of the sort Herriot spins so effectively, a memory shared, this time, as a doctor might share it with a child on his knee." Miles concluded, "I think the average kid would be all ears."

Dogs have also starred in Herriot's books for children. Gyp and Sweep are sheep dog siblings parted as puppies in *Only One Woof.* Gyp lives with the Wilkins', his mother's owners, and Sweep is a sheepherder on another farm. Gyp never barks until, at a sheep dog competition with his owners, he recognizes the winner of the competition as Sweep and barks once to say hello. The "woof" is the only one of his life. Ethel R. Twichell of *Horn Book* commented that Herriot's "affection and respect for animals warm the tale; yet the story avoids cuteness and sentimentality." Another special dog story, *The Market Square Dog* "tugs at the heartstrings as only a Herriot tale can," in the words of a *Publishers Weekly* critic. In this story, Herriot notices a dog begging for food from vendors in the market. He tries to help the dog, but it runs away. Days later, a policeman brings the injured dog to the vet, who saves him. The dog is finally adopted by the policeman and his family.

Farm animals and their special relationship with their masters have also inspired Herriot's books for children. Although his carthorses have worked for twelve years, farmer John Skipton takes Herriot's advice to enter his carthorse Dolly in the pet show in *Bonny's Big Day.* Skipton's love and care revives the horse enough to win first prize in the family pet category. Tom S. Hurlburt of *School Library Journal* wrote that readers "are bound to be moved ... as Herriot again shows the deep feelings" animals and humans share. According to *Horn Book* reviewer Karen Jameyson, the "curmudgeonliness, humor, and down-to-earth qualities of the community shine right through." Similarly, when the aging bovine heroine of *Blossom Comes Home* can no longer produce large quantities of milk, Mr. Dakin hands her over to the cattle drover. Blossom, however, has a mind of her own and escapes from the drover's herd. Upon her surprising arrival back home, Mr. Dakin decides to let the determined cow stay to feed calves. *School Library Journal* reviewer Eldon Younce proclaimed that "Herriot has again done a superb job of describing one of his many experiences."

Herriot's last two picture books feature wanderers. The feline protagonist of 1990's *Oscar, Cat-about-Town* is a stray who seems to find the village's social events, especially soccer matches, fascinating. Herriot makes friends with the stray only to learn that he has a home and a loving owner. *Smudge, the Little Lost Lamb* tells the story of a little lamb who manages to escape under Farmer Cobb's fence. When the hungry Smudge tries to return home, a dog and bull frighten him. A little girl finds the lamb in the midst of a blizzard, and takes him home for a drink of warm milk. The next day, she returns Smudge to his mother. Karen Hutt wrote in *Booklist* that young children would "appreciate" *Smudge, the Little Lost Lamb,* "especially because Smudge is rescued by a child."

Children may also enjoy Herriot's adult compilations of stories about dogs and cats. *James Herriot's Dog Stories* collects many of Herriot's dog stories from *All Creatures Great and Small* and *All Things Bright and Beautiful,* along with some stories which have never been published in the United States. The fifty stories discuss Herriot's own dogs, how he cured dogs with various ailments and injuries, and how the dogs reacted to treatment. According to a *Kirkus Reviews* critic, the stories "bear witness to [Herriot's] own good character and sensibility." Mary Wadsworth Sucher of *School Library Journal* asserted that many of the stories will "bring a smile or a tear to the eyes of dog lovers." Similarly, a contributor to *Time* magazine noted that "Herriot's style is unadorned, his message is affectionate, and his four-footed characters are irresistible." And refuting Herriot's own admission that he was sometimes "soppy" in these canine yarns, Donald McCaig wrote in the *Washington Post Book World,* "I suppose there's someone who will find this 'soppy.' Me, I think it's true."

*James Herriot's Cat Stories,* written after Herriot's retirement as a veterinarian, offers new stories. As Michele Slung of *New York Times Book Review* noted, this book features a "large cast of mostly impassive furry creatures who never for an instant question the devotion they inspire or the havoc they create." Children familiar with Herriot's picture books about cats will recognize the story of Moses, the black kitten found almost frozen and adopted by a sow, as well as the story of Debbie, who brought a kitten home to Mrs. Ainsworth before the

cat died on Christmas day. There is a story about a cat living in a candy store, and another about a cat living in a tarpaulin house. Herriot also tells about Olly and Ginny, his own cats, who refused to live indoors. Reviewers warmed to Herriot's feline tales. "These heartwarming stories should make an ideal gift for cat lovers," remarked a critic for *Publishers Weekly*. "A must for Herriot followers and cat lovers alike," concluded a *Kirkus Reviews* critic. And echoing that praise, *Booklist* contributor Barbara Duree wrote that "Herriot's devotees, especially cat lovers, will applaud this encore."

When *Every Living Thing* was published in 1992, Herriot fans were finally provided with updated information about Herriot's personal life. Herriot even discussed his struggle against an infection that left him feverish and depressed. A *Kirkus Reviews* critic asserted that *Every Living Thing* was a "smashingly good sequel to the beloved veterinarian's earlier memoirs, and well worth the ten-year-wait since *The Lord God Made Them All.*" A contributor for *Publishers Weekly* noted that there were no surprises in the book, "just the expected mix of gentle humor and compassion for animals and people alike." The same reviewer promised that Herriot's "many fans will not be disappointed." Writing in the *Detroit Free Press,* Cathy Collison noted that the book "offers more of Herriot's personal life," and concluded that it "is enough to keep the reader hoping Herriot, now retired from surgery, will turn his hand to one more volume." However, *Every Living Thing* was Herriot's last original book.

In the winter of 1995, Herriot died at home in England, leaving his son James, who worked in the same practice Herriot had entered in 1938, and his daughter, Rosemary, a doctor. Before he died, Herriot insisted that he had everything he wanted. "If you get married and have kids, that's the main thing, isn't it?" he asked Claudia Glenn Dowling in a *Life* magazine profile. "And I've lived in this beautiful district, having the great pleasure of being associated with animals. Oh aye, it's been a marvelous life."

The Herriot legacy included two unexpected spin-offs: England's veterinary schools were flooded with applicants as a result of his books, and his practice and home in Thirsk continues to be besieged by tourists from around the world. Since Herriot's death, two posthumous volumes of stories have appeared, *James Herriot's Favorite Dog Stories* and *James Herriot's Animal Stories.* The first title reprints nine previously published stories, tales of Tricki Woo, and "Rags to Riches" in which an amateur vet nurses a starving dog back to health, among others. "[F]ans of Herriot's previous works and animal lovers everywhere will enjoy this collection," wrote *Booklist* contributor Kathleen Hughes in a review of *Favorite Dog Stories.* The nine dogs in the book "provide material for lively, heartwarming stories," according to a reviewer for *Publishers Weekly.* The same critic dubbed the illustrations by Lesley Holmes as "endearing," and the book appeared in a first printing of almost a million copies, a testimony to the lasting popularity of Herriot's work. *James Herriot's Animal Stories* appeared two years after the author's death, again with illustrations by Holmes and "includes ten of the prolific author's most popular tales of animal husbandry," according to *Booklist*'s Hughes. Here are more stories of the quirky characters and animals of the Dales with Herriot's signature brief yet poignant style. Hughes felt that fans of Herriot "will not be disappointed."

Brunsdale noted in her 1997 critical study that Herriot's words "remain bright" even after his death. Readership of his books remains high with both young and old in many parts of the world. Brunsdale attempted a partial explanation for such enduring popularity: "By depicting the stability of a rural society revolving around the virtues of integrity and hard work, Herriot's stories offer the healing security to love and be loved for all creatures, great and small. Herriot's wise portrayals of character, his self-portrait most of all, illustrate the human need to belong; to achieve victories little or great; to change for good reason, not for the sake of change alone; and to grasp as well as human beings can an orderly meaning for their existence. Finally, by celebrating the bright and beautiful Yorkshire Dales he loved, James Herriot allowed his readers to share the sense of wonder he felt at creation, reflected in every living thing."

## Biographical and Critical Sources

### BOOKS

Brunsdale, Mitzi, *James Herriot,* Twayne (New York, NY), 1997.

*Contemporary Literary Criticism,* Volume 12, Gale (Detroit, MI), 1980.

Herriot, James, *All Creatures Great and Small,* St. Martin's Press (New York, NY), 1972.

Herriot, James, *All Things Bright and Beautiful,* Pan (London, England), 1978.

Herriot, James, *James Herriot's Yorkshire,* illustrated with photographs by Derry Brabbs, St. Martin's Press (New York, NY), 1979.

Lord, Graham, *James Herriot: The Life of a Country Vet,* Carroll & Graf (New York, NY), 1997.

Rossi, Michael J., *James Herriot: A Critical Companion,* Greenwood Press (Westport, CT), 1997.

*St. James Guide to Young Adult Writers,* 2nd edition, St. James Press (Detroit, MI), 1999.

Sternlicht, Sanford, *All Things Herriot: James Herriot and His Peaceable Kingdom,* Syracuse University Press (Syracuse, NY), 1999.

Wight, Jim, *The Real James Herriot,* Ballantine (New York, NY), 2000.

### PERIODICALS

*Atlantic Monthly,* August, 1974, Phoebe Adams, review of *All Creatures Great and Small;* October, 1974, Edward Weeks, review of *All Things Bright and Beautiful,* pp. 114-115.

*Best Sellers,* October 1, 1974, Eugene J. Linehan, review of *All Things Bright and Beautiful,* pp. 304-305.

*Booklist,* January 15, 1992, Karen Hutt, review of *Smudge, the Little Lost Lamb,* p. 951; July, 1994, Barbara

Duree, review of *James Herriot's Cat Stories,* p. 1891; September 15, 1996, Kathleen Hughes, review of *James Herriot's Favorite Dog Stories,* p. 194; October 15, 1997, Kathleen Hughes, review of *James Herriot's Animal Stories,* p. 371; March 15, 1998, p. 1256; June 1, 2001, p. 1906.

*Bulletin of the Center for Children's Books,* February, 1985, p. 107.

*Detroit Free Press,* September 28, 1992, Cathy Collison, review of *Every Living Thing;* February 24, 1995.

*English Journal,* December, 1973; March, 1979, Joy K. Roy, review of *All Things Wise and Wonderful,* p. 57.

*Horn Book,* March-April, 1986, Ethel R. Twichell, review of *Only One Woof,* p. 192; January-February, 1987, Ann A. Flowers, review of *The Christmas Day Kitten,* p. 46; January-February, 1988, Karen Jameyson, review of *Bonny's Big Day,* p. 54.

*Junior Bookshelf,* December, 1990, p. 266.

*Kirkus Reviews,* May 1, 1986, review of *James Herriot's Dog Stories,* pp. 695-696; July 1, 1992, review of *Every Living Thing,* p. 827; July 1, 1994, review of *James Herriot's Cat Stories,* p. 903.

*Library Journal,* October 1, 1992, p. 110; August, 1994, p. 112; March 1, 1998, p. 142.

*Life,* March, 1988, Claudia Glenn Dowling, "Herriot Country," pp. 66-69.

*Los Angeles Times,* December 25, 1986, Jack Miles, review of *The Christmas Day Kitten.*

*Los Angeles Times Book Review,* June 7, 1981, Lola D. Gillebaard, review of *The Lord God Made Them All,* p. 4.

*Maclean's,* May 29, 1978.

*National Observer,* December 28, 1974.

*New York Times,* December 14, 1972; September 24, 1974; April 18, 1982.

*New York Times Book Review,* February 18, 1973, Nelson Bryant, "A Place Where the Wind Blows Clean," p. 10; November 3, 1974, Paul Showers, review of *All Things Bright and Beautiful,* p. 61; September 18, 1977, Richard R. Lingeman, "Animal Doctor," p. 13; June 8, 1980, pp. 46-47; April 15, 1981, p. 35; April 18, 1982, p. 43; October 21, 1984, p. 35; December 14, 1986, p. 29; May 3, 1987, p. 2; September 6, 1992, p. 5; September 11, 1994, Michelle Slung, "Hairballs and Havoc," p. 12.

*People,* March 18, 1985; July 18, 1994, p. 47.

*Publishers Weekly,* January 1, 1986; October 14, 1988, p. 69; October 13, 1989, review of *The Market Square Dog,* p. 51; July 20, 1992, review of *Every Living Thing,* p. 238; July 18, 1994, review of *James Herriot's Cat Stories,* p. 228; July 15, 1996, review of *James Herriot's Favorite Dog Stories,* p. 61.

*Radio Times,* January, 1978, David Taylor, "It Could Only Happen to a Vet."

*Saturday Review,* May-June, 1986, Arturo F. Gonzalez, interview with James Herriot.

*School Library Journal,* December, 1984, Mary Lou Budd, review of *Moses the Kitten,* p. 71; September, 1986, Mary Wadsworth Sucher, review of *James Herriot's Dog Stories,* p. 154; December, 1986, p. 88; May, 1988, Tom S. Hurlburt, review of *Bonny's Big Day,* p. 91; August, 1989, Eldon Younce, review of *Blos-*

*som Comes Home,* p. 136; March, 1995, p. 108; March, 1997, pp. 143-144; May, 1997, p. 167.

*Scotsman,* October 16, 1981, William Foster, "James Herriot Talking to William Foster."

*Smithsonian,* November, 1974.

*Time,* February 19, 1973, William R. Doerner, review of *All Creatures Great and Small;* June 29, 1981; July 7, 1986, review of *James Herriot's Dog Stories,* p. 60; July 18, 1994, p. 15.

*Times* (London, England), July 23, 1976.

*Washington Post Book World,* December 8, 1974; December 5, 1976; September 11, 1977; June 21, 1981, Vic Sussman, review of *The Lord God Made Them All;* p. 11; May 25, 1988, Donald McCaig, review of *James Herriot's Dog Stories,* p. 4.

*OTHER*

*James Alfred Wight OBE,* http://www.thirsk.org.uk/herriot1 (February 21, 2002).

## Obituaries

*PERIODICALS*

*Chicago Tribune,* March 1, 1995, Mary Ann Grossmann, "Remembering James Herriot Fondly."

*Entertainment Weekly,* March 10, 1995, p. 13.

*Independent,* February 24, 1995, p. 16.

*New York Times,* February 24, 1995, p. C16.

*People Weekly,* March 13, 1995, p. 104.

*Time,* March 6, 1995, p. 31.*

\*　　\*　　\*

# HOLABIRD, Katharine 1948-

## Personal

Born January 23, 1948, in Cambridge, MA; daughter of John Augur (an architect) and Donna (an actress; maiden name, Smith) Holabird; married Michael Haggiag (a publisher), June 15, 1974; children: Tara, Alexandra, Adam. *Education:* Bennington College, B.A., 1969.

## Addresses

*Home*—17 Corringham Rd., London NW11 7BS, England.

## Career

*Bennington Review* (magazine), Bennington, VT, assistant editor, 1969-70; freelance journalist in Rome, Italy, 1970-72; nursery school teacher in London, England, 1973-76; writer.

## Member

Women Writers Network.

## Awards, Honors

Notable Book, American Library Association (ALA), 1984, for *Angelina and the Princess,* and 1985, for *Angelina at the Fair* and *Angelina's Christmas;* Kentucky Bluegrass Award, University of Kentucky, 1984, for *Angelina Ballerina;* Children's Books of the Year, Child Study Association of America, 1987, for *Angelina's Christmas.*

## Writings

*FOR CHILDREN*

*The Little Mouse ABC,* illustrated by Helen Craig, Simon & Schuster (New York, NY), 1983.

*The Little Mouse One Two Three,* illustrated by Helen Craig, Simon & Schuster (New York, NY), 1983.

*Angelina Ballerina,* illustrated by Helen Craig, C. N. Potter (New York, NY), 1984.

*Angelina and the Princess,* illustrated by Helen Craig, C. N. Potter (New York, NY), 1984.

*Angelina at the Fair,* illustrated by Helen Craig, C. N. Potter (New York, NY), 1985.

*Angelina's Christmas,* illustrated by Helen Craig, C. N. Potter (New York, NY), 1985.

*Angelina on Stage,* illustrated by Helen Craig, C. N. Potter (New York, NY), 1986.

*Angelina and Alice,* illustrated by Helen Craig, C. N. Potter (New York, NY), 1987.

*Katie's Feelings,* C. N. Potter (New York, NY), 1987.

*Alexander and the Dragon,* illustrated by Helen Craig, C. N. Potter (New York, NY), 1988.

*Angelina's Birthday Surprise,* illustrated by Helen Craig, C. N. Potter (New York, NY), 1989.

*Alexander and the Magic Boat,* illustrated by Helen Craig, C. N. Potter (New York, NY), 1988.

*Angelina's Baby Sister,* illustrated by Helen Craig, C. N. Potter (New York, NY), 1991.

*Angelina Dances,* illustrated by Helen Craig, Random House (New York, NY), 1992.

*Christmas with Angelina* (board book), illustrated by Helen Craig, Random House (New York, NY), 1992.

*Angelina Ice Skates,* illustrated by Helen Craig, C. N. Potter (New York, NY), 1993.

*Angelina's Halloween,* illustrated by Helen Craig, Pleasant Company Publications (Middleton, WI), 2000.

*Angelina's Ballet Class,* illustrated by Catherine Kanner, Pleasant Company Publications (Middleton, WI), 2001.

*Angelina and Henry,* illustrated by Helen Craig, Pleasant Company Publications (Middleton, WI), 2002.

(Adapter) *Angelina and the Butterfly* (from the TV series written by Sally-Ann Lever), illustrated by Helen Craig, Pleasant Company Publications (Middleton, WI), 2002.

(Adapter) *Angelina and the Rag Doll* (from the TV series written by Sally-Ann Lever), illustrated by Helen Craig, Pleasant Company Publications (Middleton, WI), 2002.

*Angelina Ballerina's 123,* illustrated by Helen Craig, Pleasant Company Publications (Middleton, WI), 2002.

*Angelina Ballerina's ABC,* illustrated by Helen Craig, Pleasant Company Publications (Middleton, WI), 2002.

*Angelina's new best friend laughs at her because she can't do perfect handstands, but their teamwork in the gymnastics show renews the friendship. (From* Angelina and Alice, *written by Katharine Holabird and illustrated by Helen Craig.)*

*Angelina Ballerina's Colors,* illustrated by Helen Craig, Pleasant Company Publications (Middleton, WI), 2002.

*Angelina Ballerina's Shapes,* illustrated by Helen Craig, Pleasant Company Publications (Middleton, WI), 2002.

## Adaptations

*Angelina Ballerina* has been adapted for audio cassette as *Angelina Ballerina and Other Stories,* with music by Don Heckman, Caedmon, 1986; an animated series based on *Angelina Ballerina* appeared on television in 2001 from HTI Entertainment; many spin-offs from Angelina and her friends are available, including dolls, coloring books, activity and sticker books, calendars, and videos.

## Sidelights

Katharine Holabird is the author of the popular "Angelina" stories about a little dancing mouse. An American

living in England, Holabird has also written popular picture books about Little Mouse and a boy named Alexander, but it is the mouse in dancing shoes that remains her most popular creation. Over two and a half million copies of the books in print, and various spin-off merchandise, from dolls to calendars, has also appeared. In 2001, the ballet-loving mouse was even adapted for a television series. Holabird once commented, "I have always loved children and writing. When I started reading to my own children, I found that many children's books were too sophisticated. They were actually written for adults. I wanted to write something for young children that would mirror their own experiences in their own words. *Angelina Ballerina* was written when my own daughters became fascinated with dance."

Born in Cambridge, Massachusetts in 1948, Holabird was the second of four daughters. She grew up in Chicago, living in a tall wooden house, "a San Francisco steamboat captain's fantasy that survived the Chicago fire and looked a bit like something Hansel and Gretel might have found in the woods, though it was squeezed between a seedy hotel and a dark rooming house by the time we lived there," Holabird commented to *SATA*. Her father was from a long line of architects and was also a painter, while her mother was an actress. Other members of the family were artistic, as well. "From an early age we scribbled and drew and painted with utter abandon," the author continued. Her parents were also actively involved in the theater while Holabird was growing up, with her mother acting and her father directing and designing sets. "My mother recited romantic poetry and loved to dress up with us and dance to anything from Louis Armstrong to the 'Nutcracker Suite,'" Holabird recalled. It was during these years also that Holabird became interested in dance and the world of ballerinas. "Sometimes, looking back on the strange obsessions of our childhood, we see that they were actually archetypal rites of passage that everyone goes through ... and it seems to me that ballerinas are an almost archetypal symbol for little girls, awakening a longing to grow and change into beautiful womanhood."

Another early interest was animals. Holabird's sisters were usually content with more typical pets such as parakeets or kittens, but she was a "mad collector of anything wild and unusual," as she told *SATA*. She had a

baby skunk, a raccoon, and even a baby crocodile. "Thanks to my parents bemused tolerance, no one paid much attention to my menagerie. I was allowed to keep them all as pets in my bedroom for a time, and well remember the raccoon's furry little arms entwined around my head at night."

A third passion Holabird had as a child was reading. She read voraciously about animals in such books as *Charlotte's Web* and *My Friend Flicka*. E. B. White's *Stuart Little* also made a lasting impression on her, though as she later commented, "I certainly never dreamt that I would be writing about a little mouse myself when I was in my thirties."

Holabird attended Bennington College, worked as a freelance writer in Rome during the early 1970s, and in 1974 married the publisher Michael Haggiag and began her family. Later, they moved to London, where Holabird taught nursery school for a couple of years. After several years in London the idea of the "Angelina" books was developed. Holabird's husband had published the work of illustrator Helen Craig and her "Mouse House" books, and Holabird and she had become good friends. When the publishers asked Craig to work on a large format book, Craig in turn asked Holabird if she

*Angelina is overcome with jealousy following the birth of her baby sister in Holabird's* **Angelina's Baby Sister,** *illustrated by Helen Craig.*

wanted to write it. "At the time my eldest daughter was a four-year-old prima ballerina," Holabird told *SATA,* "pink tutu, fairy wings and all. I was delighted by Tara's balletomania, so similar to my own dreams of grandeur at her age, and knew that I wanted to write about the great passions that little hearts can have." In the first draft, the little ballerina-mouse was called Primrose, but when it was discovered there was already a little mouse called Primrose in another book, the character's name was changed to Angelina.

That first title, *Angelina Ballerina,* about a little mouse who more than anything else in the world wants to become a ballerina, became an instant success and spawned numerous sequels. Angelina and her crew of friends and relatives, including cousin Henry and buddy Alice, experience county fairs, birthdays, holidays, and dance recitals at Miss Lilly's ballet school together, overcoming small obstacles in life with aplomb and ingenuity.

Often Holabird's own children provided the inspiration for a story, as with *Angelina and Alice,* the result of her daughter Alexandra's fights with her best friend. Reviewing that title in *Books for Keeps,* a contributor found it "well written, acutely observed and safely distanced" by having mice as the characters in this story about the defection of a best friend. In *Angelina's Baby Sister,* sibling relations are explored. Angelina promises herself that she will be a good big sister when baby Polly is born, but soon sibling rivalry begins to rear its ugly head when Polly continually gets the limelight. Angelina begins to act out her aggressions and throws tantrums for a time, until her family brings her around and she vows to teach the young Polly to dance when she gets older. *Booklist*'s Carolyn Phelan felt that the title was a "pleasant addition to a popular series."

In *Angelina Ice Skates,* the balletic mouse proves she is as adept on the ice as she is the ballet studio and organizes a New Year's Eve figure skating show. She even manages to deal with a couple of pesky hockey players who keep interrupting rehearsals. A reviewer for *Publishers Weekly* praised Craig's illustrations in this title and further noted that Holabird's narrative "percolates steadily, and words and pictures culminate in a jubilant final scenario."

Holabird explained her working relationship with Craig to *SATA:* "Every Angelina has a slow gestation, then suddenly seems to pour out onto the page, full-blown. . . . I always confer with Helen [Craig] after I've written a first draft for myself. Then I write several drafts longhand before sending a word-processed story to out editor. . . . Working with an illustrator like Helen Craig is an author's dream. She has a great sense of humor, and intuitively grasps the essence of the story, and makes her characters jump off the page even in the first rough drafts. Many writers never meet their illustrator, which seems to me a real waste of potential inspiration and collaboration."

The birth of her son Adam prompted Holabird to write another set of books, this one about a boy named Alexander. In this case the inspiration was the way in which her young son "swaggered around the house with his sword and shield, battling with invisible dragons," Holabird told *SATA.* The resulting book, *Alexander and the Dragon,* introduced this young character, who makes another appearance in *Alexander and the Magic Boat.* The youthful protagonist uses his imagination to take him into adventures; this time out he takes his mother on a sea cruise on two armchairs pushed together to resemble a boat. Alexander proves a hero when they land on an island populated by stranded pirates and again when the magic boat hits a storm on the voyage home. "The story is a testimony to how far one can go with just a few everyday props," wrote Martha Topol in a *School Library Journal* review of *Alexander and the Magic Boat.*

"Children's stories are a form of magic—full of dreams and mystery," Craig once commented, "and children are a most challenging and intelligent audience to write for."

## Biographical and Critical Sources

*PERIODICALS*

*Booklist,* January 15, 1992, Carolyn Phelan, review of *Angelina's Baby Sister,* p. 951.
*Books for Keeps,* November, 1990, review of *Angelina and Alice,* p. 9.
*Horn Book,* January-February, 1985, Anita Silvey, review of *Angelina and the Princess,* p. 46; November-December, 1985, Anita Silvey, review of *Angelina's Christmas,* p. 720.
*Newsweek,* December 16, 1991, Laura Shapiro, review of *Angelina's Baby Sister,* p. 72.
*New York Times Book Review,* October 9, 1983, Selma G. Lanes, review of *The Little Mouse ABC,* p. 38.
*Publishers Weekly,* July 19, 1993, p. 63; November 8, 1993, review of *Angelina Ice Skates,* p. 74; July 18, 1994, p. 160; February 28, 2000, "Licensing Hotline," p. 33, April 2, 2001, review of *Angelina and Alice,* p. 67.
*School Library Journal,* January, 1988, p. 58; March, 1991, Martha Topol, review of *Alexander and the Magic Boat,* p. 174; October, 1992, review of *Christmas with Angelina,* p. 41.
*Wilson Library Bulletin,* June, 1984, p. 739.*

\*       \*       \*

# HOWARD, Todd 1964-

## Personal

Born March 17, 1964, in Long Beach, CA; son of Thomas Gerald Howard (a sales broker) and Nancy Diane McBride (in human resources). *Education:* California State University—Long Beach, B.A., 1995, M.A., 1999. *Politics:* Green Party. *Religion:* "Hybrid." *Hobbies and other interests:* Playing guitar and piano, hiking, swimming.

## Addresses

*Agent*—c/o Author Mail, Lucent Books, P.O. Box 289011, San Diego, CA 92198-9011.

## Career

Freelance writer and editor, 1994—. English instructor, California State University—Long Beach and California State University—Dominguez Hills, 1995-2000. Story analyst for the motion picture industry.

## Writings

*Ether* (novel), California State University—Long Beach (Long Beach, CA), 1999.
(Editor) *William J. Clinton* (nonfiction), Greenhaven Press (San Diego, CA), 2001.
*Understanding The Outsiders* (nonfiction), Lucent Books (San Diego, CA), 2001.
(Editor) *Mark Twain* (nonfiction), Greenhaven Press (San Diego, CA), 2002.
*Heroin* (nonfiction), Lucent Books (San Diego, CA), 2002.

Contributor of poetry to journals, including *Beyond Baroque Literary Arts* and *Sheila-na-gig*.

## Work in Progress

Several screenplays, including "a drama that takes place in America during World War II."

## Sidelights

Todd Howard told *SATA:* "Reading and writing were always my strong suits in school, and I have always loved to write both poetry and fiction in my spare time. However, it was only after trying everything from business to firefighting that I came to recognize that writing is my dream career, and I now feel a tremendous sense of urgency to write about a multitude of topics of both personal and global importance. Though I have dabbled in the amazing field of multi-media writing in order to create educational Web sites and CD-ROMs, and am learning to write motion-picture screenplays, I sense that my greatest challenges and rewards shall always come from working in the good, old-fashioned realm of books."

## Biographical and Critical Sources

*PERIODICALS*

*Booklist,* February 15, 2001, Todd Morning, review of *William J. Clinton,* p. 1128.
*School Library Journal,* April, 2001, Mary Mueller, review of *William J. Clinton,* p. 161; July, 2001, Susan Riley, review of *Understanding The Outsiders,* p. 125.

# HUTCHINS, Hazel J. 1952-

## Personal

Born August 9, 1952, in Calgary, Alberta, Canada; daughter of Wilmot (a farmer) and Peggy (a farmer; maiden name, McKibbin) Sadler; married Ted Hutchins (a warehouse supervisor), January 13, 1973; children: Wil, Leanna, Ben. *Education:* Attended the University of Calgary. *Hobbies and other interests:* Skiing, hiking, biking, reading, canoeing.

## Addresses

*Office*—Box 185, 521 4th St., Canmore, Alberta, Canada T0L 0M0. *E-mail*—hjhutch@telusplanet.net.

## Career

Writer. Lectures and gives readings at schools.

## Member

Writers' Union of Canada, Canadian Children's Book Centre, Canadian Society of Children's Authors, Illustrators, and Performers, Alberta Writers' Guild.

## Awards, Honors

White Raven Selection, International Youth Library (Munich, Germany), 1987, for *Leanna Builds a Genie Trap;* Reading Magic Award, *Parenting* magazine, 1988, for *The Three and Many Wishes of Jason Reid;* R. Ross Annett Award, Writers Guild of Alberta, 1992, for *A Cat of Artimus Pride,* and 1998, for *The Prince of Tarn;* Christie Award, Storyteller's Award, and shortlist, Governor General's Award, all 1996, and all for *Tess.*

## Writings

*FOR CHILDREN*

*The Three and Many Wishes of Jason Reid,* illustrated by John Richmond, Annick (Toronto, Ontario, Canada), 1983, illustrated by Julie Tennent, Viking (New York, NY), 1988.
*Anastasia Morningstar,* illustrated by John Prater, Annick (Toronto, Ontario, Canada), 1984, published as *Anastasia Morningstar and the Crystal Butterfly,* illustrated by Julie Tennent, Viking (New York, NY), 1990.
*Leanna Builds a Genie Trap,* illustrated by Catharine O'Neil, Annick (Toronto, Ontario, Canada), 1986, published as *Leanna and the Genie Trap,* Oxford University Press (New York, NY), 1987.
*Ben's Snow Song,* illustrated by Lisa Smith, Annick (Toronto, Ontario, Canada), 1987.
*Casey Webber the Great,* illustrated by John Richmond, Annick (Toronto, Ontario, Canada), 1988.
*Norman's Snowball,* illustrated by Ruth Ohi, Annick (Toronto, Ontario, Canada), 1989.
*Nicholas at the Library,* illustrated by Ruth Ohi, Annick (Toronto, Ontario, Canada), 1990.
*A Cat of Artimus Pride,* illustrated by Ruth Ohi, Annick (Toronto, Ontario, Canada), 1991.

*Katie's Babbling Brother,* illustrated by Ruth Ohi, Annick (Toronto, Ontario, Canada), 1991.

*And You Can Be the Cat,* illustrated by Ruth Ohi, Annick (Toronto, Ontario, Canada), 1992.

*The Best of Arlie Zack,* illustrated by Ruth Ohi, Annick (Toronto, Ontario, Canada), 1993.

*The Catfish Palace,* illustrated by Ruth Ohi, Annick (Toronto, Ontario, Canada), 1993.

*Within a Painted Past,* Annick (Toronto, Ontario, Canada), 1994.

*Tess,* illustrated by Ruth Ohi, Annick (Toronto, Ontario, Canada), 1995.

*Cookies,* Whitman (Morton Grove, IL), 1995.

*Believing Sophie,* A. Whitman (Morton Grove, IL), 1995.

*A Cat Named Cortez,* Annick (Toronto, Ontario, Canada), 1995.

*Yancy and Bear,* illustrated by Ruth Ohi, Annick (Toronto, Ontario, Canada), 1996.

*The Prince of Tarn,* Annick (Toronto, Ontario, Canada), 1997.

*Shoot for the Moon, Robyn,* Formac (Halifax, Nova Scotia, Canada), 1997.

*It's Raining, Yancy and Bear,* Annick (Toronto, Ontario, Canada), 1998.

*Robyn's Want Ad,* Formac Publishing (Halifax, Nova Scotia, Canada), 1998.

*One Duck,* Annick (Toronto, Ontario, Canada), 1999.

*Robyn Looks for Bears,* Formac Publishing (Halifax, Nova Scotia, Canada), 2000.

*Two So Small,* illustrated by Ruth Ohi, Annick (Toronto, Ontario, Canada), 2000.

*The Wide World of Suzie Mallard,* illustrated by Dominick Catalano, Ducks Unlimited (Memphis, TN), 2000.

*One Dark Night,* illustrated by Susan Kathleen Hartung, Viking (New York, NY), 2001.

*Robyn's Best Idea,* Formac Publishing (Halifax, Nova Scotia, Canada), 2001.

*TJ and the Cats,* Orca Book Publishers (Custer, WA), 2002.

*Leanna Builds a Genie Trap* and *A Cat of Artimus Pride* have been published in French; *Norman's Snowball* and *Katie's Babbling Brother* have been published in Mandarin Chinese. Contributor to *Mini-Book Fun Pack,* Annick Press, 2002.

## Adaptations

*The Three and Many Wishes of Jason Reid* is available on cassette.

## Sidelights

Canadian author Hazel J. Hutchins has written many books for children and young adults. Her works are known both for their humorous take on the world and their inclusion of magical elements. "Ok—I admit it," Hutchins noted in a biographical essay for *St. James Guide to Children's Literature.* "I love to write. I *have* to write. I'm addicted to the strange habit of putting words, ideas, people, places and happenings onto that blank, white landscape known as paper." This passion for writing can be seen in Hutchins's best known titles, such as *The Three and Many Wishes of Jason Reid, Anastasia Morningstar and the Crystal Butterfly, Casey Webber the Great, Leanna Builds a Genie Trap, Within a Painted Past, Tess,* the "Yancy and Bear" books, *The Prince of Tarn* and *One Dark Night.* Whether picture book or novel, Hutchins's works draw readers in with their "elemental power and high drama," as a *Horn Book* reviewer noted in a review of *One Dark Night.*

Born in 1952 in Calgary, Alberta, Hutchins is the daughter of farmers. As she once told *SATA:* "My home was a farm in southern Alberta and I loved living there. I can remember walking out across the fields singing at the top of my lungs just to hear my voice alive on the prairie air. Living on a farm was fun, but I must have been lonely sometimes, for as a young child I invented several imaginary friends to entertain me while my older sisters and brother were at school. I named my imaginary friends Valerie, Barette, and Witch Hazel. And I used to daydream. When I became old enough to go to school I left my imaginary friends at home but I took the day-dreaming with me. I remember sitting at my desk in the classroom and staring out the window—lost in another world entirely. My first book grew out of some of those day-dreams, recalled many years later."

After college at the University of Calgary, Hutchins married, had a family, and worked at various jobs, including being a store and office clerk and a waitress, before turning to writing in 1983. Hutchins's first work, *The Three and Many Wishes of Jason Reid,* is a modern reworking of the story of the genie who comes out of a magic lantern and grants three wishes to the first person he sees. In Hutchins's rendition, eleven-year-old Jason decides to wish for more wishes in order to give himself the time to think of something important enough to warrant the intervention of a genie. *Bulletin of the Center for Children's Books* reviewer Betsy Hearne described the result of Jason's wishes as "ecological, suspenseful, and convincing." Critics praised *The Three and Many Wishes of Jason Reid* for its fresh rendering of an old tale; as Julia Marriage, writing in *School Librarian,* observed, "The story-line may not be original, but it is accessible, well presented and boldly written." Other critics emphasized the well-developed relationships between Jason and the genie and between Jason and his friend Penny, who helps him decide what he should wish for. A *Kirkus Reviews* critic remarked, "Hutchins has devised believable characters and a moral problem that has its analogue in the larger world, with plenty of funny dialogue and comic situations."

Several of Hutchins's subsequent novels for middle-grade readers also feature characters with magical powers in realistic settings. In *Anastasia Morningstar,* Sarah and Ben discover that the clerk at the corner store can perform magic when they see her turn Derek into a frog as punishment for shoplifting. When they decide to feature Anastasia in their science project they encounter resistance from a skeptical science teacher. Many reviewers found Hutchins's characters charming, although *Junior Bookshelf* contributor Marcus Crouch felt that they had little room to develop in such a short novel:

*Yancy and Bear trade places for the day in Hazel J. Hutchins's* **Yancy and Bear.** *(Illustrated by Ruth Ohi.)*

"We ... lament that the author's fine and delicate writing, her abundant fun, and her shrewd view have to operate within such a restricting framework." On the other hand, Pamela K. Bomboy remarked in *School Library Journal:* "This tale successfully combines realism with fantasy to produce a celebration of the wonders of the natural world."

*Casey Webber the Great* also relies on magic to propel its plot. In this story for middle graders, Jason and his sister Morgan discover a magic coat that makes them invisible. This "simple, humorous fantasy" was certain to be popular among reluctant readers, Roger Sutton noted in the *Bulletin of the Center for Children's Books.* Similarly, in *The Best of Arlie Zack,* a novel for preteens, a boy is tempted to compromise his values in order to fit in at a new town. Only after he receives three special objects from the mysterious Mrs. Sphinx—that may or may not be magic—is he reminded of his inner strength. A *Books in Canada* critic recommended the book, noting: "Hutchins's prose never lags nor is its momentum contrived. In this it mirrors the preferred rhythms of 12-year-olds, temporally bound to their inexorable, hormonal press toward adolescence."

More magic is served up in *Within a Painted Past,* in which a picture becomes a time travel vehicle for twelve-year-old Allison while she is visiting her aunt in Banff. In *The Prince of Tarn,* eleven-year-old Fred awakens in his apartment to the clamor of the Prince of Tarn calling out for the Captain of the Guard. Fred realizes that he has somehow slipped into the fantasy story his mother had written, but not published, shortly before her death. Fred helps the prince to return to his kingdom by reversing an enchantment, and in doing so,

Fred is able to lay to rest some of his own pain at his mother's death. "Hutchins creates some memorable scenes," noted Carolyn Phelan in a *Booklist* review, while Janet McNaughton, writing in *Books in Canada,* found much larger implications in the novel. "Hutchins takes on big questions about art and life," McNaughton wrote. "In doing so, she touches the hearts of her characters in ways that change them forever. This book will touch the hearts and funny bones of many readers as well." And John Wilson, reviewing *The Prince of Tarn* in *Quill and Quire,* felt that this coming-of-age tale "is overall a wonderful story: fast-paced, thoughtful, and imaginative. It will engross readers even younger than its target market and gain new fans for Hutchins."

Hutchins has also written a series of books featuring young Robyn. These longer novels for young readers include *Robyn's Want Ad, Shoot for the Moon, Robyn, Robyn Looks for Bears,* and *Robyn's Best Idea.* In the last-named title, Robyn finds a stray kitten but knows she cannot keep it, as their apartment has a no-pets rule. Instead, she tries to find a good home for the cat. Mavis Holder, reviewing the title in *Resource Links,* commented that the children in Robyn's class "find ways of including and accepting all the children."

Hutchins has also written the text for several picture books in which the only magic is that of the imagination. In *Leanna Builds a Genie Trap,* a little girl decides that all of the things that she has lost have been taken by a genie hiding in her house, so she devises several traps to capture the spirit before she discovers the real culprit. Although Carol McMichael in *School Library Journal* found the vocabulary and illustrations potentially "confusing" for its intended audience, *Quill and Quire* reviewer Bernie Goedhart concluded that Hutchins "has created another imaginative, funny, and well-constructed tale in this book for younger children." *Nicholas at the Library* tells of a reluctant reader who finds a monkey in the stacks and is lured into making his way through many books as he and a librarian try to find the story where the monkey belongs. *Junior Bookshelf* reviewer Crouch stated that "the idea is excellent," while Jennifer Taylor remarked in *School Librarian* that the concept of books as magical "comes over well in this nicely humorous and satisfying text."

Real world situations common to children form the basis of other Hutchins books. *The Catfish Palace* focuses on the efforts of a little girl to learn about the mistreatment of animals and what she can do to help stop it. A little girl is annoyed by her younger sibling's nonsensical chatter in *Katie's Babbling Brother,* but in sharing her feelings with her mother she finds a surprising solution. *Quill and Quire* contributor Chris Mousseau believed the story would produce a "responsive chord" in its readers, and concluded that the work "is one of those books that begs to be shared with all members of the family."

Another picture book, *And You Can Be the Cat,* tells of a youngest child who uses his imagination to create a more satisfying role for himself than the older children usually allow him to play. A moral dilemma is at the center of the picture book *Believing Sophie,* in which young Sophie must prove that she did not steal from the local store. *Booklist* writer Julie Corsaro called this a "buoyantly illustrated picture book."

In the award-winning *Tess,* Hutchins packs a lot of story into thirty-two pages. The young protagonist loves her new prairie home, but when she and her brother are sent to gather cow dung to supplant their dwindling fuel supply, she is embarrassed and ultimately scorned by one neighbor. Later, Tess saves this neighbor's dog, and thereafter he helps to supply Tess's family with fuel. *Quill and Quire*'s Janet McNaughton felt that both Hutchins and her illustrator, Ruth Ohi, "combine their talents skillfully in this book." McNaughton further dubbed the book a "fine tale." *Booklist* contributor Kay Weisman similarly felt that Hutchins's "sparsely told story, set in the 1930s, vividly portrays both the desolation and the allure of frontier life."

In her "Yancy and Bear" titles, Hutchins "puts a different twist on the favourite toy coming to life," according to Gwyneth Evans in a *Quill and Quire* review of *Yancy and Bear.* Toddler Yancy and his toy teddy, Bear, actually change places by dressing in each other's clothes. Subsequently Bear is the one carrying the little inanimate Yancy around, and the child can communicate with Bear only by sending special thought waves. "This is the sort of fantasy that a young child may enter with glee," Evans further observed. Silvana DeFonzo Bartlett called the same title in *Books in Canada* a "pleasant handling of a familiar theme." With *It's Raining, Yancy and Bear,* the bear and boy once again trade places and this time Grandfather takes the pair to the museum on a rainy day. "The text and illustrations blend well, making this a friendly read-aloud," remarked Pam Hopper Webb in *School Library Journal.*

Other picture books from Hutchins include *Two So Small* and *One Dark Night.* In the former title, Hutchins presents a story with the feeling of a folktale. A boy and his goat are off to visit Grandmother, but they do not follow the directions that they have been given. Nothing looks familiar, and soon it seems they are in the land of the giants. Meeting a sad baby giant, the boy decides that there must be a mother giant close by, and that perhaps the mother giant can direct him towards his Grandmother's house. Ultimately this is the case in this "clever story [that] is satisfying and tests listeners' memory in a fun way," according to Jean Gaffney in *School Library Journal.*

In *One Dark Night* Jonathan is happy to be inside at his grandparent's during a summer storm. However, a cat family seeking shelter from the storm brings Jonathan back out to help. "Simple, lyrical prose conveys the intensity and sometimes the spookiness of thunderstorms," wrote *Booklist*'s Shelle Rosenfeld. Writing in *School Library Journal,* Shara Alpern also had praise for the title, noting that children "will share Jonathan's concern for the cats and will take comfort in the story's

resolution." A contributor for *Kirkus Reviews* commented that the combination of "suspense, compassion, kittens, and safety" was sure to be popular with children.

"People often ask me where I get my ideas," Hutchins once told *SATA.* "Sometimes they grow out of feelings I myself remember having as a child—the importance of friendship, a love of magic, and a fascination for the game of baseball even though I was a terrible player and was always picked last for any team. Other times ideas jump alive and clear out of my own young family—a special winter ski outing, the time my youngest son threw up his arms while playing with the older children and announced he was sick and tired of having to be the cat, the joy of rolling snowballs bigger, and Bigger and BIGGER! I like words—how they sound and feel. I love the way ideas in fiction open so many doors in the mind. The most rewarding part is making the words say exactly what I want. When that happens, it's wonderful!"

A contributor for *St. James Guide to Children's Writers* concluded that Hutchins's stories "are both light and serious, humorous and profound. The magic in them relates to fantasies, such as unlimited wishes or invisibility, in which most children have indulged. However, it does not overwhelm the stories; it is an intriguing and entertaining plot device that enhances the events, but more important, provides a means of examining the personalities of the people it touches."

## Biographical and Critical Sources

*BOOKS*

*St. James Guide to Children's Writers,* 5th edition, St. James Press (Detroit, MI), 1999.

*PERIODICALS*

*Booklist,* July, 1990, p. 2090; September 1, 1995, Julie Corsaro, review of *Believing Sophie,* p. 87; December 15, 1995, Kay Weisman, review of *Tess,* pp. 704-705; February 15, 1998, Carolyn Phelan, review of *The Prince of Tarn,* p. 1011; November 15, 2000, Catherine Andronik, review of *Two So Small,* p. 648; May 15, 2001, Shelle Rosenfeld, review of *One Dark Night,* p. 1758.

*Books in Canada,* December, 1983, p. 16; July, 1991, p. 58; September, 1993, review of *The Best of Arlie Zack,* p. 58; October, 1996, Silvana DeFonzo Bartlett, review of *Yancy and Bear,* p. 32; October, 1997, Janet McNaughton, review of *The Prince of Tarn,* p. 34.

*Bulletin of the Center for Children's Books,* June, 1988, Betsy Hearne, review of *The Three and Many Wishes of Jason Reid,* p. 208; January, 1989, Roger Sutton, review of *Casey Webber the Great,* p. 124.

*Canadian Children's Literature,* summer, 1996, Joann Wallace, review of *Within a Painted Past,* p. 89; spring, 1999, Lissa Paul, review of *Yancy and Bear,* p. 66; summer, 2000, Deborah L. Begoray, review of *Shoot for the Moon, Robyn,* p. 103.

*Christian Science Monitor,* May 6, 1988, p. B2.

*Horn Book,* July, 2001, review of *One Dark Night,* p. 440.

*Junior Bookshelf,* August, 1986, p. 147; February, 1988, Marcus Crouch, review of *Anastasia Morningstar,* p. 29; June, 1991, Marcus Crouch, review of *Nicholas at the Library,* p. 94.

*Kirkus Reviews,* February 15, 1988, review of *The Three and Many Wishes of Jason Reid,* p. 279; September 1, 1999, review of *One Duck,* p. 1424; April 15, 2001, review of *One Dark Night,* p. 586.

*Quill and Quire,* February, 1984, p. 39; April, 1986, Bernie Goedhart, review of *Leanna Builds a Genie Trap,* p. 26; November, 1990, p. 12; April, 1991, Chris Mousseau, review of *Katie's Babbling Brother,* p. 18; December, 1991, p. 24; March, 1992, p. 66; July, 1993, p. 56; August, 1995, Janet McNaughton, review of *Tess,* p. 34; October, 1996, Gwyneth Evans, review of *Yancy and Bear,* p. 62; June, 1997, John Wilson, review of *The Prince of Tarn,* p. 64.

*Resource Links,* October, 2001, Mavis Holder, review of *Robyn's Best Idea,* p. 12.

*School Librarian,* June, 1986, Julia Marriage, review of *The Three and Many Wishes of Jason Reid,* p. 150; August, 1991, Jennifer Taylor, review of *Nicholas at the Library,* p. 101.

*School Library Journal,* January, 1987, Carol McMichael, review of *Leanna Builds a Genie Trap,* p. 65; May, 1988, p. 97; August, 1990, Pamela K. Bomboy, review of *Anastasia Morningstar,* p. 148; March, 1995, Lucinda Lockwood, review of *Within a Painted Past,* pp. 204-205; January, 1996, Carol Schene, review of *Believing Sophie,* p. 85; February, 1998, Robin L. Gibson, review of *The Prince of Tarn,* p. 109; January, 1999, Pam Hopper Webb, review of *It's Raining, Yancy and Bear,* p. 95; October, 1999, Arwen Marshall, review of *One Duck,* p. 116; October, 2000, Jean Gaffney, review of *Two So Small,* p. 127; June, 2001, Shara Alpern, review of *One Dark Night,* p. 118.

OTHER

*Annick Press—Authors and Illustrators—Hazel Hutchins,* http://www.annickpress.com/ (June 4, 2002).

*Hazel Hutchins Home Page,* http://www.telusplanet.net/public/hjhutch/ (June 4, 2002).*

# J

## JOHNSON, Neil 1954-

### Personal

Born September 1, 1954, in Shreveport, LA; son of Melvin F., Jr. (a physician) and Lea (in book sales; maiden name, Morton) Johnson; divorced, children: Bradford, Hannah. *Education:* Washington and Lee University, B.A., 1976. *Politics:* Independent. *Religion:* Lutheran.

### Addresses

*Office*—1301 Louisiana, Shreveport, LA 71101. *Agent*—Mary Jack Wald, 111 East 14th, New York, NY 10003.

### Career

Photo-lab technician, Shreveport, LA, 1976-80; freelance photographer and writer, 1980—; Centenary College of Louisiana, Shreveport, LA, photography instructor, 1981—. Marjorie Lyons Playhouse, official photographer, 1987—; Red River Rally (hot air balloon festival), founder and co-chair, 1991 and 1992. Created Portrait 2000, a community public art project to celebrate the millennium.

### Member

American Society of Media Photographers.

### Awards, Honors

Rising Young Business Leader award, 1991; Shreveport-Bossier Ambassador Award, 2002.

### Writings

#### PHOTO-ILLUSTRATOR AND AUTHOR

*Step into China,* Simon & Schuster (New York, NY), 1988.
*Born to Run: A Racehorse Grows Up,* Scholastic (New York, NY), 1988.

*The Battle of Gettysburg,* Macmillan (New York, NY), 1989.
*All in a Day's Work,* Little, Brown (Boston, MA), 1989.
*Batter Up!,* Scholastic (New York, NY), 1990.
*Fire & Silk: Flying in a Hot Air Balloon,* Little, Brown (Boston, MA), 1991.
*The Battle of Lexington and Concord,* Macmillan (New York, NY), 1992.
*Jack Creek Cowboy,* Dial (New York, NY), 1993.
*Big-Top Circus,* Dial (New York, NY), 1995.
*Shreveport and Bossier City,* Louisiana State University Press (Baton Rouge, LA), 1995.
*Ghost Night: An Adventure in 3-D,* Dial (New York, NY), 1996.
*Louisiana Journey,* Louisiana State University Press (Baton Rouge, LA), 1997.
*National Geographic Photography for Kids,* National Geographic Society (Washington, DC), 2001.

Also contributor of text and photos to *Louisiana Life.*

#### PHOTOGRAPHER

Charlotte Moser, *Clyde Connell: The Art & Life of a Louisiana Woman,* University of Texas Press (Austin, TX), 1989.
Millicent E. Selsam, *How Puppies Grow,* revised edition, Scholastic (New York, NY), 1990.
Millicent E. Selsam, *How Kittens Grow,* revised edition, Scholastic (New York, NY), 1992.

Also contributor of photos to periodicals, including *Time, Audubon, National Geographic World, Art Forum, Travel and Leisure, SB Magazine,* and *USA Today.*

### Sidelights

Children's author and photographer Neil Johnson is well regarded by critics for his nonfiction books, which educate young readers with exciting text and exceptional photographs. These books cover a wide range of places, from far-away China to the Revolutionary War to a modern circus, and Johnson has been praised for his ability to capture the atmosphere of such varied events. In his 1993 work, *Jack Creek Cowboy,* Johnson explores life on a ranch in Wyoming through the activities of two brothers who help their ranch-hand father during the summer. The younger sibling, Justin, not only must prove his abilities as a cowboy but also must learn how to care for the animals during the summer grazing season. Through the boys' experiences, Johnson relates the hard work that accompanies a ranch hand's life and captures the beauty of the Shoshone National Forest where the cows graze. Reviewing *Jack Creek Cowboy* in *New Advocate,* M. Jean Greenlaw predicted that "many will find this informational book fascinating," while a critic from *Kirkus Reviews* found the book "an attractive, realistic portrayal of present practice in an occupation where ... the myths are still strong."

The festive atmosphere of the circus is featured in Johnson's *Big-Top Circus,* a 1995 offering that gives youngsters a close-up view of the events that take place under the big top. Offering a brief history of the traveling circus, Johnson shows children how a traditional circus under a large tent is conducted. The lives of circus performers both in and out of the ring are highlighted, as is the treatment of trained animals in the show, an aspect that *Booklist* contributor Mary Harris Veeder thought would "interest children of the 1990's." Some critics noted that one important aspect of the book is how Johnson offers the technical names, definitions, and photos of the unique activities that take place in a circus, including such features as the elephant long mount. "This title will delight and inform young audiences," claimed *School Library Journal* critic Nancy E. Curran.

Special effects heighten the spookiness of Johnson's ghost story, *Ghost Night: An Adventure in 3-D.* Here the author challenges readers to spend the night in a house haunted by a family said to have died during a yellow fever outbreak just after the Civil War. However, as the reader finds out, a forbidden romance caused the demise of the Delancy family. Now, the ghosts of the lovers look to the reader for help in solving the mystery of what actually happened to the members of the household. Accompanied by a pair of 3-D glasses, *Ghost Night* chills viewers through a series of "elaborately staged and manipulated stereo photos," in the words of *School Library Journal* contributor John Peters, who noted that the subjects, when properly viewed, "jump out in exquisitely sharp detail." Though many critics commented that the book's plot offered little to readers, many did compliment Johnson on his ability to create interest in the story though his use of eerie photographs, which a *Publishers Weekly* critic felt were "well-suited to the spooky theme."

Johnson once told *SATA:* "Buzzing along in a two-seater ultra-light aircraft (like a big tricycle with wings), circling a hot air balloon 1000 feet over a cotton field, it hit me: This is a JOB?! I was photographing the balloon for *Fire & Silk: Flying in a Hot Air Balloon.* I would have gladly paid someone for the chance to do what I was doing. Just like the Elephant's Child, I have an insatiable curiosity for the world around me and I love to ask questions. I am a journalist, but the main medium for putting out what I learn is not the usual print journalism media—newspapers or magazines—it is books for young readers."

After a few years working at a photo-lab, learning from other photographers and refining his abilities, Johnson quit his job to become a freelance photographer. "I realized I had *two* skills: writing *and* photography," he commented. "Why not put them together? I managed to sell these double talents to our city magazine, which hired me to do a story on an art center and then on conditions in the worst local inner city neighborhood. This latter story took me into some fairly miserable places with my camera. It surprised me to find out later that many people who read my story and viewed the photos had no idea how bad the situation was ... until it confronted them out of the pages of the magazine. This was a very satisfying feeling." Johnson also did freelance work for a Louisiana state magazine, including a story on thoroughbred horses and another that involved a trip to China.

"But the city and state magazine jobs did not come very often," Johnson continued. "I was forced to constantly go out searching for any kind of photography work. And many times, there simply was no work. I challenged myself to go for the national magazines. I had friends in New York City (where most national magazines are published) to stay with and a car to drive me there. My plan was to go there once a year for five years, to knock on doors and show my portfolio.

"On one of my long drives to New York ... I thought about how fun it would be to actually write a book, and how similar a nonfiction children's book and a long magazine story were. The ideas for books started coming immediately. While in New York, a friend gave me the name of an agent and within a year, my agent was hustling me around introducing me to editors at various publishers where we emphasized nonfiction books. One editor studied a batch of my China photos, and I soon had a contract to introduce children to China in a book. A month later, another editor looked at my thoroughbred horse photos and began discussing what kind of horse book we could do. Boom, boom! Two books directly from magazine stories! Today, I still enjoy doing magazine work, but doing book and commercial photography takes most of my time."

Two of Johnson's book projects stemmed from his interest in historical reenactments. When an editor proposed a book based on a famous Civil War battle illustrated with photographs of reenactors, his response was enthusiastic. Of the actual photography process he related: "At one point during the photographing of *The Battle of Gettysburg* at the largest-ever Civil War reenactment in 1988, I was very close to thousands of 'soldiers' facing each other in long lines and all shooting blanks at each other as fast as they could. The deafening, continuous noise and the strong, acrid smell of black powder smoke was almost overwhelming! For a few seconds, I was shocked to actually feel like I was witnessing the horrifying tragedy of a real battle. It was both exciting and very, very scary.

"We were extremely proud of *The Battle of Gettysburg* and followed up a few years later with *The Battle of Lexington and Concord,* published in 1992. Half of the illustrations in both books were photographed during actual reenactments for the public and the other half I staged. I have always been fascinated by the process of making movies, and here I was doing something very similar. I was dealing with actors, costumes, props, strict schedules, and even special effects. For one image in *The Battle of Lexington and Concord,* I gathered about thirty 'Redcoats' on a dirt road and directed them for an illustration of the British retreat from Concord to Boston, which had been along that very dirt road in 1775. When I yelled, 'Action!,' there was a lot of running and shooting—all for a single still image. Then, we repeated the action twice to make sure I got just the image I wanted. I owe a lot to these 'living historians' for the help they gave me.

"Writing two history books made me realize how important historians are and how difficult their job can be. Numerous authors had already written about both battles in many books. As a historian, I had the responsibility to read as many of these [accounts] as I could and then compare the detailed descriptions which did not always agree with one another. There turned out to be certain information on Lexington and Concord that was accepted as American *history,* but was actually American *myth.* I also wanted to present the Americans and the British as real people, not as 'bigger-than-life' heroes and villains. It was also very important for me to remember that I was telling a *story* to my readers. My job was to bring these two war stories to life and make the stories flow quickly and dramatically, so that learning about history would also be an enjoyable experience to readers.

"I am fascinated with the constant flow of drama and beauty in the world around me. My favorite topic is whatever subject I happen on that grabs my interest and flips on my curiosity switch. But it also has to catch my eye—like majestic hot air balloons in the sky or cowboys in the Rocky Mountains—for a subject to become one of my books. Luckily, there is an unending supply of interesting and visual topics in the world, and I plan to be asking questions about them and pointing my camera at them for many years to come. My goal is always to produce books that I would enjoy reading. Working is a part of life and I feel very fortunate to absolutely love my work. I also love to get feedback. It is especially enjoyable then to give talks on what I do to groups of young readers, and find that they have read, enjoyed, and even learned something new about the world from my books."

## Biographical and Critical Sources

### BOOKS

Wyatt, Flora R., Margaret Coggins, and Jane Hunter Imber, *Popular Nonfiction Authors for Children,* Libraries Unlimited (Englewood, CO), 1998.

### PERIODICALS

*Booklist,* January 15, 1995, Mary Harris Veeder, review of *Big-Top Circus,* p. 932.
*Kirkus Reviews,* April 1, 1993, review of *Jack Creek Cowboy,* p. 457; February 15, 1995, review of *Big-Top Circus,* p. 226; September 1, 1996, review of *Ghost Night: An Adventure in 3-D,* p. 1331.
*New Advocate,* summer, 1993, M. Jean Greenlaw, review of *Jack Creek Cowboy,* p. 218.
*Publishers Weekly,* September 23, 1996, review of *Ghost Night,* p. 78.
*School Library Journal,* March, 1993, Charlene Strickland, review of *Jack Creek Cowboy,* p. 212; March, 1995, Nancy E. Curran, review of *Big-Top Circus,* p. 214; September, 1996, John Peters, review of *Ghost Night,* p. 202; October, 1997, Carolyn Jenks, review of *A Field of Sunflowers,* p. 100; September 1, 2001, Susan Lissim, review of *National Geographic Photography for Kids,* p. 247.

\*        \*        \*

# JONAS, Ann 1932-

## Personal

Born January 28, 1932, in Flushing, NY; daughter of Herbert (a mechanical engineer) and Dorothy (a homemaker and artist; maiden name, Ireland) Jonas; married Donald Crews (an author and illustrator), January 28, 1963; children: Nina, Amy. *Education:* Cooper Union for the Advancement of Science and Art, art certificate, 1959.

## Addresses

*Home and office*—New York, NY. *Agent*—c/o Greenwillow Books, 1350 Ave. of the Americas, New York, NY 10019.

## Career

Rudolph de Harak, Inc. (design company), New York, NY, designer, 1959-62; Advertis, Inc. (advertising agency), Frankfurt, Germany, designer, 1962-63; Donald & Ann Crews (design company), New York, NY, designer, 1964—; author and illustrator of children's books, 1981—.

## Awards, Honors

*Round Trip* was an American Library Association (ALA) Notable Book, one of the *New York Times* Best Illustrated Books of the Year, one of *Booklist*'s Children's Editors' Choice books, and cited on the *Horn Book* honor list, all 1983, included in American Institute

*Ann Jonas*

of Graphic Arts Book Show, 1984, and received Golden Sower Book Award from Nebraska Library Association, 1985; *Holes and Peeks* and *The Quilt* were both chosen as Notable Children's Books by the ALA; *Holes and Peeks* was chosen as one of *School Library Journal*'s Best Books, 1984; *The Trek* was chosen as an ALA Notable Book, as one of *School Library Journal*'s Best Books, and one of Child Study Association of America's Children's Books of the Year, all 1985, and was a *Boston Globe-Horn Book* Award honor book, 1986; *Color Dance* was selected one of the *New York Times* Best Books of the Year, c. 1989.

## Writings

*SELF-ILLUSTRATED CHILDREN'S BOOKS*

*When You Were a Baby,* Greenwillow (New York, NY), 1982.
*Two Bear Cubs,* Greenwillow (New York, NY), 1982.
*Round Trip,* Greenwillow (New York, NY), 1983.
*Holes and Peeks,* Greenwillow (New York, NY), 1984.
*The Quilt,* Greenwillow (New York, NY), 1984.
*The Trek,* Greenwillow (New York, NY), 1985.
*Now We Can Go,* Greenwillow (New York, NY), 1986.
*Where Can It Be?,* Greenwillow (New York, NY), 1986.
*Reflections,* Greenwillow (New York, NY), 1987.
*Color Dance,* Greenwillow (New York, NY), 1989.
*Aardvarks, Disembark!,* Greenwillow (New York, NY), 1990.

*The Thirteenth Clue,* Greenwillow (New York, NY), 1992.
*Splash!,* Greenwillow (New York, NY), 1995.
*Watch William Walk,* Greenwillow (New York, NY), 1997.
*Bird Talk,* Greenwillow (New York, NY), 1999.

## Adaptations

*Round Trip* has ben recorded on audiocassette published by Live Oak Media.

## Sidelights

A creator of children's picture books, Ann Jonas is especially admired for skillful illustrations influenced by her training in graphic design. Using uncomplicated shapes, bright colors, and clean lines, Jonas forms illusionary watercolor worlds that intrigue young children. Though possessing an underlying sophistication, her illustrations are praised for their simplicity and warmth. Her books, which address issues of concern to preschoolers, such as losing objects, going on trips, and having scary dreams, both comfort and entertain. Noting her ability to render the familiar from a fresh perspective, critics have considered Jonas one of the most inventive creators of picture books today. *Round Trip, The Quilt, Reflections, Color Dance,* and *Aardvarks, Disembark!* are a few of the several works that Jonas has both written and illustrated.

Jonas grew up on New York's Long Island; she once told *Something about the Author* (*SATA*) that "it seems that my brother and I spent all of our free time out of doors." She continued, "There were open fields and things to be discovered everywhere." The theme of discovery is evident in Jonas's books for children, most notably in *The Trek,* in which a suburb is transformed into several different landscapes as a girl walks to school. Through the eyes of the protagonist, gorillas are disguised as bushes, tigers are hidden in tall grass, stone chimneys become giraffes, and garbage bags look like rhinos—examples of Jonas's ability to create the exotic from the ordinary.

Drawing was a rather ordinary pursuit in Jonas's childhood environment. Her industrious family "attached great importance to knowing how to do as many things as possible, from skiing to cabinetmaking to repairing the family car. Everyone always had several projects going at once, and drawing was considered an incidental skill, a tool for planning a project rather than an end in itself," the author told *SATA.* Yet she decided to make art her career. Jonas explained to *SATA* her initial move into that field: "I went to work after high school, without seriously considering college. After a few years, while working in the advertising department of a department store, I realized how much I needed to know if I was to build a career in art. I attended Cooper Union, learned a lot, and, during summers and after graduation, worked in the design office of my former graphic design instructor."

Jonas met her husband, author and illustrator Donald Crews, at Cooper Union. When Crews was inducted into the army in the early 1960s, the couple moved to Germany, where he was stationed. After an unsuccessful attempt at working as a freelance artist, Jonas obtained a position as a designer at an advertising agency. Eighteen months later, the pair returned to the United States and decided to start their own graphic design firm. Their in-home office gave Jonas the freedom to work while taking care of their two young daughters.

Jonas was encouraged to write children's books by Crews, who had written and illustrated several himself. She described for *SATA* how she became involved in the field: "Through [my husband] I met and got to know his publisher, Susan Hirschman. They both urged me to try my hand at a book. The result was *When You Were a Baby,* which Susan liked and published. Since then, writing and illustrating children's books seems to have become a full-time occupation."

Indeed, Jonas has been creating unique children's books regularly since 1981. She remarked in *SATA* that as a result of her design background, "I find that I approach each book quite differently. Each idea seems to need a specific technique and style to most clearly illustrate the point I'm trying to make. Since I'm not really an illustrator and don't have a style as such, I feel free to let each book look as different from the next as necessary."

Jonas's experimentation led to the award-winning *Round Trip,* a book with stark black-and-white illustrations that serve a double function; once the end of the book is reached, it can be flipped upside down and read backwards. The first pass through the book details a trip from the country to the city; when the book is reversed, the return trip is featured. "I had been thinking that it would be wonderful to do a book that went from beginning to end and then back to the beginning again, if I could find a way to do it.... I drew on my graphic design experience to stylize the images sufficiently to make this reversal possible," Jonas commented on *Round Trip* in a *Horn Book* interview with Sylvia and Kenneth Marantz. She noted that she made numerous mistakes in the beginning stages of *Round Trip:* "I had to make many changes before it worked," she explained. Her effort was applauded by critics, many of whom enthusiastically praised the ingenuity of the book's illustrations and concept.

Jonas particularly likes to create visual effects "against the background of a believable situation, to involve the child on an emotional level as well," she remarked in *SATA.* The *Quilt* is an example of this approach; in it a quilt given to a girl by her parents becomes a variety of patterned landscapes in her dreams. The girl, concerned about her lost toy dog, searches for it through each dream landscape. Upon awakening, she is pleased to find the stuffed dog beside her. Jonas noted in the interview with the Marantzes that "*The Quilt* ... is my daughter Nina's book. I made her a quilt using scraps

*In Jonas's self-illustrated* **Round Trip,** *readers read forward to see the first half of a journey, then flip the book over to see different sights on the way home.*

from other things I had made for her, and she used to have very vivid dreams about it." Reviewers praised the comforting manner in which Jonas addresses the common night fears and scary dreams of young children as well as her clever transformation of quilt to landscape.

Commenting on the kind of books she enjoys writing and illustrating most, Jonas remarked in *SATA* that "the books that have been the most fun to do are the ones that involve some sort of visual game, as do *Round Trip, The Quilt,* and *The Trek.* Children are so inundated with images that require nothing of them that it is a pleasure to do something that demands their involvement, that makes them work a little. I hope that they can then get the satisfaction of solving it, of mastering it."

Jonas takes a decidedly educational approach in *Aardvarks, Disembark!,* which lists many of the world's unusually-named animals as they leave Noah's Ark after the biblical story's famous flood. Jonas had originally intended to make *Aardvarks, Disembark!* an alphabet book of atypical animals. When she researched each animal, however, she discovered that, as she noted in the book, "Many animals that existed at the time of the story of Noah are now extinct. Many more are endangered. If we are to keep them from extinction, we must work to protect them." The book includes a glossary that defines each animal, tells if it is endangered, and gives clues to name pronunciation. "Is this a new interpretation of the biblical story, a spur to conservation, or an alphabet book?," asked Ellen Fader in a *Horn Book* review. She continued, declaring that "from any perspective, it's a masterpiece." Other works by Jonas teach how colors can be combined to make other colors, detail a child's preparation for a trip, and tell of a search for a favorite blanket.

With her typical inventiveness, Jonas continues to challenge young readers in her more recent books. In *Watch William Walk,* for example, Jonas depicts a not-so-simple walk on the beach taken by William and his dog, Wally, and by Wilma and her duck, Wanda, all of whom wander, waddle, and whirl in the playfully alliterative text. What's more, the illustrations give the reader a view from above the walkers' heads, allowing their footprints and silhouettes to trace their paths. A "tongue-twisting, mind-expanding romp," observed *Horn Book*'s Marilyn Bousquin, who also commented on the subtle illustrations that "create an aerial view that loosens and frees the tight text." In her review for *Booklist,* Hazel Rochman noted that "if there isn't quite a story, Jonas does manage to spin out quite a lot of

action. The clear pen-and-watercolor pictures are dramatic, all seen from above, the figures simple and bright, their shadows and footprints in silhouettes of widening circles."

In her interview with Sylvia and Kenneth Marantz, Jonas commented on children's reactions to her work: "It is wonderful to get feedback from children. Every once in a while you meet a child who has a really well-thought-out question, his or her own particular concern. I don't really get book ideas from children, just a sense of what they like best." Jonas is most pleased when her work challenges children to use their imaginations or reassures them about concerns they might have. "But I don't want the message to get the upper hand.... I want to entertain, not preach."

## Biographical and Critical Sources

*BOOKS*

*Children's Literature Review,* Volume 12, Gale (Detroit, MI), 1987.
*St. James Guide to Children's Writers,* 5th edition, St. James Press (Detroit, MI), 1999.
Silvey, Anita, editor, *Children's Books and Their Creators,* Houghton Mifflin (Boston, MA), 1995.

*PERIODICALS*

*Booklist,* November 15, 1990, p. 664; November 15, 1992, review of *The Thirteenth Clue,* p. 609; June 1, 1995, review of *Splash!,* p. 1756; April 1, 1997, review of *Watch William Walk,* p. 1338; June 1, 1999, review of *Bird Talk,* p. 1842.
*Horn Book,* January-February, 1986, p. 49; May-June, 1986, p. 319; November-December, 1986, p. 735. May-June, 1987, Sylvia and Kenneth Marantz, "Interview with Ann Jonas," pp. 308-313; November, 1990, Ellen Fader, review of *Aardvarks, Disembark!,* p. 759; November-December, 1992, review of *The Thirteenth Clue,* p. 714; May, 1994, p. 366; September-October, 1995, review of *Splash!,* p. 589; July-August, 1997, Marilyn Bousquin, review of *Watch William Walk,* p. 444.
*New York Times Book Review,* December 23, 1984, p. 20; March 16, 1986, p. 30; November 30, 1989, review of *Color Dance,* p. C22.
*School Library Journal,* November, 1984, p. 110; October, 1990, p. 110; September, 1992, review of *The Thirteenth Clue,* p. 206; June, 1995, review of *Splash!,* p. 88; April, 1997, review of *Watch William Walk,* p. 112; April, 1999, review of *Bird Talk,* p. 99.*

# K

## KANEFIELD, Teri 1960-

### Personal

Born June 25, 1960, in St. Louis, MO. *Education:* University of Pennsylvania, B.A., 1985; Harvard University, graduate study, 1987-89; University of California—Davis, M.A., 1993; University of California—Boalt Hall, doctoral study.

### Addresses

*Home*—1970 Curtis St., No. 2, Berkeley, CA 84702. *E-mail*—Tkanefield@aol.com.

### Career

Harvard University, Cambridge, MA, copyright officer for Sourcebook Publications, 1988-89; Los Rios Community College District, Sacramento, CA, began as adjunct instructor, became instructor in English, 1993-2000; writer, 2000—. University of California—Davis, instructor in fiction writing, 1994-98. Harvey Siskind Jacobs (law firm), summer associate, 2001. Volunteer American sign language interpreter; writing contest judge; presenter of seminars and lectures.

### Awards, Honors

First prize scholarship, Squaw Valley Writers Convention, 1993; first prize, Focus on Writers Contest, 1995.

### Writings

*Rivka's Way* (novel), Cricket Books/Front Street Books (Chicago, IL), 2001.

Contributor of short stories, essays, and reviews to periodicals, including *Recorder, Jewish Currents, Macguffin, American Literary Review, Iowa Review, Education Week,* and *Writers' Forum.*

### Work in Progress

*The Family Liar,* a young adult novel.

### Sidelights

Teri Kanefield told *SATA:* "*Rivka's Way* was inspired by a trip to Prague in 1985. I have always enjoyed historical fiction, and when I fell in love with Prague—as so many visitors do—I knew I had to write something set there. The story developed naturally when I wondered what it would be like to be a girl living in the Jewish quarter when the Jews still lived behind locked gates. I chose the eighteenth century because so little has been done with this era in Europe, and few people know much about the historical context of the Holocaust.

"People are always asking me why I resigned a tenured college teaching position to go to law school, so perhaps I should say something about this. I loved teaching, and I learned much about writing during the years I taught composition, literature, and creative writing. Teaching gave me valuable time to write, but I feel I need to keep trying new things and learning about the world.

"For two years in my twenties I worked as a sign language interpreter, and the experience gave me material for my writing. I visited the eastern part of Germany and Prague in 1995, and ended up with material for a novel and two travel essays. I imagine my experiences in the legal field, too, will give me much to write about."

### Biographical and Critical Sources

PERIODICALS

*Booklist,* April 1, 2000, Kay Weisman, review of *Rivka's Way.*
*Hadassah,* December, 2001, review of *Rivka's Way.*
*Jewish Bulletin,* March 30, 2001, Joe Eskenazi, "Novel Explores Life in—and out—of Jewish Quarter," pp. 42-43.
*Kliatt,* July 15, 2001, review of *Rivka's Way.*
*Lilith,* fall, 2001, review of *Rivka's Way,* p. 40.

*School Library Journal,* March, 2001, Kathleen Isaacs, review of *Rivka's Way,* p. 252.*

\* \* \*

# KENYON, Kate
## See RANSOM, Candice F.

\* \* \*

# KING-SMITH, Dick 1922-

## Personal

Born March 27, 1922, in Bitton, Gloucestershire, England; son of Ronald (a paper mill director) and Grace (Boucher) King-Smith; married Myrle England, February 6, 1943; children: Juliet Clare (Mrs. Jeremy Hurst), Elizabeth Myrle (Mrs. David Rose), Giles Anthony Beaumont. *Education:* Attended Marlborough College, 1936-40; Bristol University, B.Ed., 1975.

## Addresses

*Home*—Diamond's Cottage, Queen Charlton, near Keynsham, Avon BS18 2SJ, England. *Agent*—Caradoc King, A. P. Watt & Son, 26/28 Bedford Row, London WC1R 4HL, England.

## Career

Farmer in Gloucestershire, England, 1947-67; sold asbestos suits and worked in a shoe factory; Farmborough Primary School, near Bath, Avon, England, teacher, 1975-82; writer, 1978—. Writer and presenter of Yorkshire Television's *Tumbledown Farm* series for children, beginning 1983; presenter of *Rub-a-Dub-Dub* for TVAM and *Pob's Programme* for Channel 4. *Military service:* Grenadier Guards, 1941-46; became lieutenant; mentioned in dispatches.

## Awards, Honors

Guardian Award runner-up, 1981, for *Daggie Dogfoot;* American Library Association Notable Book citations, 1982, for *Pigs Might Fly,* 1985, for *Babe: The Gallant Pig,* and 1987, for *Harry's Mad;* Guardian Award, 1984, for *The Sheep-Pig; Boston Globe-Horn Book* Honor Book, and Parents' Choice Award for Literature, both 1985, both for *Babe: The Gallant Pig;* Children's Author of the Year, British Book Awards, 1991; Reading Magic Award, *Parenting* magazine, 1995, for *Harriet's Hare.*

## Writings

### FOR CHILDREN

*The Fox Busters,* illustrated by Jon Miller, Gollancz (London, England), 1978, Delacorte (New York, NY), 1988.

*Daggie Dogfoot,* illustrated by Mary Rayner, Gollancz (London, England), 1980, published as *Pigs Might Fly,* Viking (New York NY), 1982.

*The Mouse Butcher,* illustrated by Wendy Smith, Gollancz (London, England), 1981, illustrated by Margot Apple, Viking (New York, NY), 1982.

*Magnus Powermouse,* illustrated by Mary Rayner, Gollancz (London, England), 1982, Harper (New York, NY), 1984.

*The Queen's Nose,* illustrated by Jill Bennett, Gollancz (London, England), 1983, Harper (New York, NY), 1985.

*The Sheep-Pig,* illustrated by Mary Rayner, Gollancz (London, England), 1983, published as *Babe: The Gallant Pig,* Crown (New York, NY), 1985.

*Harry's Mad,* illustrated by Jill Bennett, Gollancz (London, England), 1984, Crown (New York, NY), 1987.

*Saddlebottom,* illustrated by Alice Englander, Gollancz (London, England), 1985.

*Lightning Fred,* illustrated by Michael Bragg, Heinemann (London, England), 1985.

*Noah's Brother,* illustrated by Ian Newsham, Gollancz (London, England), 1986.

*Pets for Keeps* (nonfiction), illustrated by Alan Saunders, Penguin (London, England), 1986.

*H. Prince,* illustrated by Martin Honeysett, Walker Books (London, England), 1986.

*Yob,* illustrated by Abigail Pizer, Heinemann (London, England), 1986.

*E.S.P.,* illustrated by Peter Wingham, Deutsch (London, England), 1986.

*Dumpling,* illustrated by Jo Davies, Hamish Hamilton (London, England), 1986.

*Farmer Bungle Forgets,* illustrated by Martin Honeysett, Walker (London, England), 1986.

*Town Watch* (nonfiction), illustrated by Catherine Bradbury, Penguin (London, England), 1987.

*Country Watch: Animals to Look out for in the Countryside* (nonfiction), illustrated by Catherine Bradbury, Penguin (London, England), 1987.

*Tumbleweed,* illustrated by Ian Newsham, Gollancz (London, England), 1987.

*The Hodgeheg,* illustrated by Linda Birch, Hamish Hamilton (London, England), 1987.

*Cuckoobush Farm,* illustrated by Kazuko, Orchard (London, England), 1987, Greenwillow (New York, NY), 1988.

*Friends and Brothers,* illustrated by Susan Hellard, Heinemann (London, England), 1987.

*Martin's Mice,* illustrated by Jez Alborough, Gollancz (London, England), 1988, Crown (New York, NY), 1989.

*George Speaks,* illustrated by Judy Brown, Viking (London, England), 1988, Roaring Brook Press (Brookfield, CT), 2002.

*The Jenius,* illustrated by Peter Firmin, Gollancz (London, England), 1988, published as *Jenius: The Amazing Guinea Pig,* illustrated by Floca, Hyperion (New York, NY), 1996.

*Emily's Legs,* illustrated by Katinka Kew, Macdonald (London, England), 1988.

*Water Watch* (nonfiction), illustrated by Catherine Bradbury, Penguin (London, England), 1988.

*Dodo Comes to Tumbledown Farm,* illustrated by John Sharp, Heinemann (London, England), 1988.

*The Greatest!,* Heinemann (London, England), 1988.

*The Toby Man,* illustrated by Ian Newsham, Gollancz (London, England), 1989, illustrated by Lynette Hemmant, Crown (New York, NY), 1991.

*Alice and Flower and Foxianna,* Heinemann (London, England), 1989.

*Beware of the Bull!,* Heinemann (London, England), 1989.

*Henry Pond Poet,* Hodder & Stoughton (London, England), 1989.

*Dodos Are Forever,* illustrated by David Parkins, Viking (London, England), 1989.

*Sophie's Snail,* illustrated by Claire Minter-Kemp, Delacorte (New York, NY), 1989.

*The Trouble with Edward,* Hodder & Stoughton (London, England), 1989.

*Ace: The Very Important Pig,* illustrated by Lynette Hemmant, Crown (New York, NY), 1990.

*Dick King-Smith's Alphabeasts,* illustrated by Quentin Blake, Gollancz (London, England), 1990, Macmillan (New York, NY), 1992.

*The Jolly Witch,* Simon & Schuster (London, England), 1990.

*Paddy's Pot of Gold,* illustrated by David Parkins, Crown (New York, NY), 1990.

*The Water Horse,* illustrated by David Parkins, Viking (London, England), 1990, Crown (New York, NY), 1998.

*The Whistling Pig,* Walker (London, England), 1990.

*Caruso's Cool Cats,* BBC/Longman (London, England), 1991.

*Horace and Maurice,* Doubleday (London, England), 1991.

*Lightning Strikes Twice,* Mammoth (London, England), 1991.

*Sophie's Tom,* illustrated by David Parkins, Candlewick Press (Cambridge, MA), 1991.

*The Cuckoo Child,* illustrated by Leslie Bowman, Hyperion (New York, NY), 1991.

*The Animal Parade: A Collection of Stories and Poems,* illustrated by Jocelyn Wild, Tambourine Books (New York, NY), 1992.

*Blessu and Dumpling,* Penguin (London, England), 1992.

*Farm Tales,* Mammoth (London, England), 1992.

*The Finger Eater,* Walker (London, England), 1992.

*The Ghost at Codlin Castle,* Viking (London, England), 1992.

*The Guard Dog,* Corgi (London, England), 1992.

*Jungle Jingles,* Corgi (London, England), 1992.

*Pretty Polly,* illustrated by Marshall Peck, Crown (New York, NY), 1992.

*Triffic Pig Book,* Gollancz (London, England), 1992, published as *Triffic, the Extraordinary Pig,* illustrated by Cary Pillo, Troll (Mahwah, NJ), 1998.

*The Topsy-turvy Storybook,* illustrated by John Eastwood, Gollancz (London, England), 1992.

*Dragon Boy,* illustrated by Jocelyn Wild, Viking (London, England), 1993.

*Horse Pie,* Doubleday (London, England), 1993.

*A Narrow Squeak, and Other Animal Stories,* Viking (London, England), 1993.

*Sophie Hits Six,* illustrated by David Parkins, Candlewick Press (Cambridge, MA), 1993.

*Lady Daisy,* illustrated by Jan Naimo Jones, Delacorte (New York, NY), 1993.

*The Invisible Dog,* illustrated by Roger Roth, Crown (New York, NY), 1993.

*Find the White Horse,* illustrated by Larry Wilkes, Chivers (London, England), 1993.

*All Pigs Are Beautiful,* illustrated by Anita Jeram, Candlewick Press (Cambridge, MA), 1993.

*The Merrythought,* illustrated by Mike Reid, Puffin (London, England), 1993.

*Uncle Bumpo,* Deutsch (London, England), 1993.

*Bobby the Bad,* illustrated by Julie Anderson, Deutsch (London, England), 1994.

*Connie and Rollo,* illustrated by Judy Brown, Doubleday (London, England), 1994.

*The Excitement of Being Ernest,* illustrated by Nigel McMullen, Simon & Schuster (London, England), 1994.

*The Swoose,* illustrated by Maire Corner, Hyperion (New York, NY), 1994.

*Happy Mouseday,* Doubleday (London, England), 1994.

*Harriet's Hare,* illustrated by Valerie Littlewood, Doubleday (London, England), 1994, illustrated by Roger Roth, Crown (New York, NY), 1995.

*Mr. Potter's Pet,* illustrated by Hilda Offen, Viking (London, England), 1994, illustrated by Mark Teague, Hyperion (New York, NY), 1996.

*Sophie in the Saddle,* illustrated by David Parkins, Candlewick Press (Cambridge, MA), 1994.

*Three Terrible Trins,* illustrated by Mark Teague, Crown (New York, NY), 1994.

*The Schoolmouse,* illustrated by Phil Garner, Viking (London, England), 1994, illustrated by Cynthia Fisher, Hyperion (New York, NY), 1995.

*Sophie Is Seven,* illustrated by David Parkins, Candlewick Press (Cambridge, MA), 1995.

*I Love Guinea Pigs,* illustrated by Anita Jeram, Candlewick Press (Cambridge, MA), 1995.

*King Max the Last: A Second Hodgeheg Story,* illustrated by Birch, Hamish Hamilton (London, England), 1995.

*Warlock Watson,* Hippo (London, England), 1995.

*All Because of Jackson,* illustrated by John Eastwood, Doubleday (London, England), 1995.

*The Stray,* illustrated by Wayne Parmenter, Crown (New York, NY), 1996.

*Dick King-Smith's Animal Friends: Thirty-one True Life Stories,* illustrated by Anita Jeram, Candlewick Press (Cambridge, MA), 1996.

*Sophie's Lucky,* illustrated by David Parkins, Candlewick Press (Cambridge, MA), 1996.

*Clever Duck,* illustrated by Mike Terry, Viking (London, England), 1996.

*Hogsel and Gruntel and Other Animal Stories,* illustrated by Liz Graham-Yooll, Gollancz (London, England), 1996, Orchard (New York, NY), 1999.

*Godhanger,* illustrated by Andrew Davidson, Doubleday (London, England), 1996.

*Mrs. Jollipop,* illustrated by Frank Rodgers, Macdonald (London, England), 1996.

*Treasure Trove,* illustrated by Paul Howard, Viking (London, England), 1996.

*Omnibombulator,* illustrated by Jim and Peter Kavanagh, Corgi (London, England), 1996.

*Smasher,* illustrated by Michael Terry, Viking (London, England), illustrated by Richard Bernal, Random House (New York, NY), 1997.

*Animal Stories,* illustrated by Michael Terry, Puffin (London, England), 1997.

*The Spotty Pig,* illustrated by Mary Wormell, Farrar, Straus (New York, NY), 1997.

*A Mouse Called Wolf,* illustrated by Jon Goodell, Crown (New York, NY), 1997.

*Puppy Love,* illustrated by Anita Jeram, Crown (New York, NY), 1997.

*What Sadie Saw,* illustrated by Julie Anderson, Scholastic (London, England), 1997.

*The Crowstarver,* Doubleday (London, England), 1998, published as *Spider Sparrow,* illustrated by Peter Bailey, Crown (New York, NY), 2000.

*Mr. Ape,* illustrated by Roger Roth, Crown (New York, NY), 1998.

*How Green Was My Mouse,* illustrated by Robert Bartelt, Viking (London, England), 1998, published as *Charlie Muffin's Miracle Mouse,* illustrated by Lina Chesak, Crown (New York, NY), 1999.

*The Merman,* illustrated by Roger Roth, Crown (New York, NY), 1999.

*The Witch of Blackberry Bottom,* illustrated by Ann Kronheimer, Viking (London, England), 1999, published as *Mysterious Miss Slade,* Crown (New York, NY), 2000.

*A lonely farmer wins a bride by breeding a green mouse that wins the Grand Mouse Championship Show in King-Smith's* **Charlie Muffin's Miracle Mouse.** *(Illustrated by Lina Chesak.)*

*The Roundhill,* illustrated by Sian Bailey, Crown (New York, NY), 2000.

*Lady Lollipop,* illustrated by Jill Barton, Candlewick Press (Cambridge, MA), 2001.

*Chewing the Cud: An Extraordinary Life Remembered by the Author of Babe, the Gallant Pig* (autobiography), illustrated by Harry Horse, Viking (London, England), 2001.

*Billy the Bird,* illustrated by Susie Jenkin Pearce, Hyperion (New York, NY), 2001.

*Funny Frank,* illustrated by Roger Roth, Knopf (New York, NY), 2001.

Contributor to periodicals, including *Punch, Blackwood's Magazine,* and *Field.*

## Adaptations

*The Sheep-Pig* (also published as *Babe: The Gallant Pig*) was adapted for film as *Babe,* Universal Pictures/Kennedy Miller Productions, 1995. *Lady Daisy* was adapted to audio in 1996 by Listening Library. Chivers North America adapted the following to audio: *The Fox Busters,* 1987, *The Sheep-Pig, Magnus Powermouse,* and *Tumbleweed,* all 1988, and *Ace, the Very Important Pig,* 1991. Also adapted to audio were *The Hodgeheg* and *The Mouse Butcher,* 1989; *Jungle Jingles, The Schoolmouse,* and *Three Terrible Trins,* 1996; *The Stray,* 1997; *The Merman,* 1999; *Spider Sparrow,* 2000; and *The Witch of Blackberry Bottom,* 2001, among others.

## Sidelights

Take a cast of improbable animal protagonists, from pigs to mice and dogs; add a dose of anthropomorphism, a pinch of human affection, and a sprinkling of adversity to overcome. The result is the winning formula in the books of British author Dick King-Smith, perhaps best known for his *Babe: The Gallant Pig,* from which the 1995 Academy Award-winning movie *Babe* was adapted. With eight million copies of his books sold worldwide, King-Smith has become a one-man cottage industry in children's literature. "Helped by years of classical education in the best tradition of the English public-school system," wrote *Guardian* contributor Julia Eccleshare, King-Smith's "stories have heroic resonances, as well as being written in perfectly shaped classical sentences, which makes them a joy to read—and especially out loud." Eccleshare further remarked, "More than that, [his books] are written with the humorous, civilised view of human or animal interaction so reflective of King-Smith himself."

Often compared to British writers of past generations, such as Beatrix Potter, Kenneth Grahame, E. B. White, and Rudyard Kipling, King-Smith mines the same vein of rich animal stories, never fearing to give his pigs, dogs, hamsters, parrots, and other critters human characteristics while also making sure to retain the characteristics of the animal as well. "I allow them some human ones, especially speech, because it is such fun putting words into their mouths," King-Smith explained to a group of online grammar-school interviewers on *Young Writer.*

Most amazing about King-Smith's prodigious achievement is that he began writing for children later in life, after pursuing careers in farming and teaching. He has been prolific since the late 1970s, and has earned acclaim for his novels about animals, including *Pigs Might Fly, Babe: The Gallant Pig, Harry's Mad, Dodos Are Forever, The Water Horse, The Schoolmouse, The Spotty Pig,* and *Charlie Muffin's Miracle Mouse,* among a host of others. King-Smith is widely admired for a witty and often parodic writing style that appeals to both children and adults, as well as for his ability to portray his subjects affectionately without becoming too whimsical or sentimental. Combining exciting adventures with witty dialogue and subtly drawn but strong characters, King-Smith presents his readers with specific moral lessons without being overly didactic. In his novels, animal protagonists—usually underdogs—manage to triumph through some extraordinary ability, supplemented by the help of friends. His humor ranges from high-spirited to absurd and is often punctuated by wordplay.

"I write for the simplest and best of reasons—because I enjoy it," King-Smith once observed. "I write for children for a number of reasons: My level of humor is pretty childish (both my grandfathers were punsters of the worst kind, which is the best kind); I think I know what children like to read (teaching helps here); I like to write about animals (farming helps here), whereas adults on the whole prefer to read novels about people; I think an ounce of fantasy is worth a pound of reality; and anyway I wouldn't possibly write a modern sort of novel for grown people—I should get the giggles."

Born in 1922, in Bitton, Gloucestershire, England, King-Smith grew up in a "comfortably off West Country family," according to Eccleshare. The son of a paper mill director, his education was primarily in the classics, and he attended Marlborough College as a teen. But his early life also revolved around animals. "As a child I had pets—rabbits, tortoises, rats, mice—and a toy farm which I played with endlessly," King-Smith told Eccleshare. "It was a pretty eccentric collection—I never minded much what went with what, so I included a giraffe among the dairy herd—but it absorbed me completely." With the advent of World War II in 1939, King-Smith knew it was only a matter of time before he was called up, so he tried his hand at his dream—farming—while waiting. In 1940 he began a year of work on a farm where all the labor was done by men and animals, something of a relic even at the time.

When England entered the war, King-Smith served in the Grenadier Guards, and in 1943, while still in the service, he married his childhood sweetheart Myrle England. Wounded severely in Italy, King-Smith became a lieutenant and served with distinction until 1946, when he left the military. With wife and children in tow and in need of an occupation, he took over a small farm owned by his father's paper mill, and for the next twenty years he and his family lived his dream of farming. Milk

*Eight-year-old Patsy and her brother Jim befriend a neighbor, as well as her dogs, cats, goats, and chickens.* (From Mysterious Miss Slade, *written by King-Smith and illustrated by Ann Kronheimer.*)

and eggs were the product of his farm; there were no great expectations for it. But farming had undergone a revolution during the war years; the age of mechanization had arrived. King-Smith began to gather a motley assortment of animals on the farm, just as with his youthful collection of animals. There was Ben the bull who made a heroic bid for freedom one day, a goat who enjoyed riding in the passenger seat of the farm van, and a bevy of pigs—one of King-Smith's favorite animals. "I ran my farm in much the same way [as the childhood animal collection]. I had animals that I liked," the author told Eccleshare. "Now I see that it was rather a stupid way to run a farm, but at the time I felt I didn't have to conform." In addition to housing this bizarre menagerie, the King-Smiths also ran their home as if from a different age, even hosting country balls in which male guests wore white ties and tails.

In the end, the numbers did not tally. Over the years on Woodlands Farm, profits continually dropped. "If I'd had the sense to let my wife keep the accounts ... I suppose we might be farming still," King-Smith noted in a *Junior Literary Guild* article, "but my lack of any head for business ensured our financial downfall." In 1967, after twenty years of farming, King-Smith had to call it quits. For a time he sold asbestos suits for firefighters, and then for three years worked in a shoe factory, until he finally went to university and earned a bachelor's degree in education. He would give teaching a go.

Thus began King-Smith's second career, at age fifty-three, as an elementary school teacher in the Farmborough Primary School near Bath, Avon, England. It was during his years of teaching that King-Smith began tinkering with stories. Although he explained in a *Junior Literary Guild* article that he had written "reams of what might most comfortably be called verse, ranging from the romantically pastoral to vulgar lampoonery," he did not begin his career as a novelist until the mid-1970s. Though his teaching career provided insight into the type of material children like to read, he received equal inspiration from his days as a farmer, for the tales he most enjoys creating concern farm animals. In 1978 King-Smith published his first book for children, *The Fox Busters,* which centers on a family of chickens who plot to drive the local foxes away from their hen house. Explaining the inspiration for this tale to *Young Writer,* King-Smith recalled that when he was a farmer a fox once killed many of his chickens. "One day, I thought, I'll have a go at writing a story where the weak are the winners, not the strong. About ten years later, I did have

*Lollipop, the smartest pig in the kingdom, transforms the spoiled Princess Penelope in King-Smith's chapter book* **Lady Lollipop.** *(Illustrated by Jill Barton.)*

a go, and that became *The Fox Busters.*" Anne Carter in the *Times Literary Supplement* labeled the book "a good, fast-moving story with sound characterization and an ability to be funny without condescension or whimsicality."

King-Smith continued to teach and write for several years, but as with farming, the numbers were his undoing as a teacher. He could not do long division, and so was moved from teaching middle graders to teaching younger children where he only had to manage simple addition. In 1982, at age sixty, he retired from teaching to write full time. Many of King-Smith's animal novels for children focus on "a single hero, whom we grow to love, [who] fights desperately against a terrifying enemy in a genuinely exciting plot, while the style, dialogue, and characterization remain light and playful," commented Stephanie Nettell in *Twentieth-Century Children's Writers.* For instance, Daggie Dogfoot, the piglet protagonist of *Pigs Might Fly* whose unusually webbed feet allow him to become a skilled swimmer, saves the entire farm, including the slaughterer, during a flood by swimming for help. His actions ensure that he will never be butchered by the farmer for food and serve to educate other characters metaphorically about inner values versus exterior appearances. About *Pigs Might Fly,* Arthur Arnold remarked in *Children's Literature in Education* that "King-Smith's writing stands comfortably alongside the more celebrated E. B. White's, sustained by his own inimitable wry sense of humour." Another of King-Smith's noteworthy animal books, *Harry's Mad,* chronicles the adventures of Madison, an intelligent, talking African gray parrot bequeathed by his American professor owner to a young English boy. Karla Kuskin of the *New York Times Book Review* observed that "King-Smith, as articulate in English as Madison is in American, is mostly to be congratulated. The characters in *Harry's Mad* have wit and are good, lively company."

King-Smith is perhaps best known for the award-winning *Babe: The Gallant Pig,* the novel first published in England as *The Sheep-Pig* and on which the popular film *Babe* was based. Nettell wrote that in this book King-Smith "succeeds in balancing in one story the strongest qualities of all the others, and it is clearly right to award it that often overworked encomium, 'a modern classic.'" The story focuses on Babe, a piglet who is won at a fair by a farmer. Adopted by the mother sheepdog, Fly, Babe comes to understand that the best way to get sheep to obey is to speak politely to them. In the process, he saves the sheep from rustlers, not to mention saving his own life as the farmer realizes he is more valuable as a sheep-pig than as a meal. In fact, the farmer has so much confidence in Babe that he enters him in the local sheep-dog trials, which he wins. King-Smith's own experience as a farmer enables him to depict farm life with accuracy and affection.

Critics universally praised *Babe: The Gallant Pig.* Nettell called it "deftly constructed, the animal and human characters are marvelously defined in dialogue, the suspense remains strong and quite unbullied by the joke, and the style is so clean and economic that our hero wins through to a frenzy of cheers without a hint of soppiness." Denise M. Wilms of *Booklist* was particularly impressed with the book's characterization. She wrote, "The relationship between Fly and Babe is fresh, and Babe's sensitivities, which are the key to his success, give the novel a richness that's impossible to resist." In *Observer,* Naomi Lewis suggested, "The dialogue couldn't be bettered. There's a readymade classroom play here for the taking." Lewis's observation turned out to be prophetic indeed, though on a much greater scale than she imagined. In 1995, the film adapted from the book was nominated for several 1996 Academy Awards, and won the award for best visual effects. The success of the film led to a 1998 sequel, *Babe, Pig in the City,* not based on King-Smith's work.

More rich animal tales are served up in *The Animal Parade,* a compilation of stories and poems, including retellings of five of Aesop's fables. A *Publishers Weekly* critic found that book to be an "ideal compendium for introducing readers to animal tales." Teaming up with illustrator Quentin Blake, King-Smith produced the alphabet book, *Dick King-Smith's Alphabeasts,* an "entertaining and quotable" book, according to *Horn Book* contributor Ann A. Flowers. In 1993's *The Invisible Dog,* King-Smith tells a tale of a girl who desperately wants a dog, but whose parents can not afford to buy her one. Imagination takes over, and she enjoys the companionship of an invisible pooch until an unexpected inheritance allows her to purchase a real canine. Writing in *Publishers Weekly,* a reviewer dubbed this a book "chock-full of warmth, zany imagination and soft-hearted irony." Another animal-smitten child takes center stage in *The Cuckoo Child,* in which a boy steals an ostrich egg and places it with a family of geese. Upon the ostrich's birth, the geese are surprised, but soon accept this strange new cousin. However, the boy sees that as the ostrich grows it needs to be back with its own family, and returns it to the park where he stole it as an egg. Writing in *School Library Journal,* Virginia Golodetz felt that *The Cuckoo Child* will "grace the author's long list of well-loved animal fantasies." More of King-Smith's ebullient porcine friends are presented in *All Pigs Are Beautiful,* an "affectionate, amusing and informative" book, according to Kay McPherson writing in *School Library Journal.* And with *Ace: The Very Important Pig,* King-Smith provides something of a sequel to *Babe,* for the pig in question is Babe's great-grandson. Ace is a talking pig who enjoys watching educational television and visiting the local pub. Fame arrives, but does not go to Ace's head in this "winsome story ... sure to warm hearts and bring smiles," according to a *Publishers Weekly* contributor.

Mice are at the center of *Three Terrible Trins,* the tale of an often-widowed mouse, Mrs. Gray, who vows never to marry again but instead devote herself to the upbringing of her three "trins" or triplets. "With his customary panache," wrote a reviewer for *Publishers Weekly,* "King-Smith grabs the reader's attention from his opening sentence" and incorporates the same "understated humor and rollicking pace." *Horn Book* contributor

*Although he can't speak or learn like other children, Spider perfectly imitates animal sounds and lives happily on a farm in World War II England. (Cover illustration by Brad Yeo.)*

Ann Flowers called the book a "wildly comic view of the world in microcosm." More mice appear in *The Schoolmouse* in which a young mouse uses her reading skills to save her parents. "With a heroic main character that will surely remind kids of the lovely gray spider in *Charlotte's Web,* this is a fine book for instilling in children the importance of reading," wrote *Booklist* contributor Lauren Peterson. And in *Charlie Muffin's Miracle Mouse,* a lonely mouse farmer breeds a green mouse and wins best of show at the Grand Mouse Championship Show in an "offbeat, gently humorous story," according to *Booklist* critic Carolyn Phelan.

King-Smith also presents a menagerie of animals in *Dick King-Smith's Animal Friends,* thirty-one true stories about animals he has met during his life. *Booklist* reviewer Ellen Mandel called the compilation a "delightful gift to his fans." *Puppy Love* is another title dealing with personal anecdotes of the dogs King-Smith and his family have enjoyed over the years. *Hogsel and Gruntel and Other Animal Stories* present fifteen tales about animals from pigs to bees, and in *Animal Stories,* the author presents eight tales in an "upbeat medley [that] is ... a treat for animal lovers of all ages," according to a reviewer for *Publishers Weekly.* With the 2001 title *Funny Frank,* King-Smith tweaks the ugly duckling story with a tale of a barnyard chick who longs to be a duck. "Chipper dialogue, generous helpings of humor and lickety-spit plot add up to an amusing chapter book," commented a *Publishers Weekly* critic.

Not all of King-Smith's juvenile novels center on animal characters, however. The well-received *Noah's Brother* takes liberties with the biblical tale to present the story of Noah's brother, Hazardikladoram, who is ordered about and otherwise abused by his family and in particular, Noah. Alice H. G. Phillips noted in the *Times Literary Supplement* that "the majority of parents will smile at the biblical jokes and approve King-Smith's gentle revisionism. Children ... will appreciate in Noah's brother the eternal myth of wicked authority figures making life hard for an innocent child (in this case, for a childlike 708-year-old man)." Phillips described the book's moral as "funny and true: Count your blessings—you're alive, you have your animal friends, and your family has left you."

King-Smith's personal favorites for non-animal stories are his tales of Sophie, a rambunctious young girl who wants to be a farmer. Inaugurated in 1989 with *Sophie's Snail,* the "Sophie" books take her from four to the age of eight. *Booklist* reviewer Mary Harris Veeder compared Sophie to Beverly Cleary's invention for her spunk: "Think of Sophie as a slightly plump, more determined, British Ramona," wrote Veeder in a review of *Sophie Is Seven.* In *Sophie's Tom,* she befriends a cat named Tom who later, to everyone's surprise, produces a litter of kittens. Sophie has proved a winner with critics. Reviewing *Sophie's Tom* in *Publishers Weekly,* a contributor noted that "Sophie's spirit is sure to win readers' admiration." The reviewer also felt that the young girl's mischief "will keep laughs coming." *Horn Book* reviewer Ann Flowers felt that while "Tom is a terrific cat ... it is Sophie who takes center stage in an endearing picture of a sturdy, self-reliant small girl." In *Sophie in the Saddle,* the protagonist gets hand-on practice with farming when she and her family vacation on a farm. In her *Booklist* review, Kay Weisman felt the book will "charm young and old alike." And in *Sophie's Lucky,* the young protagonist is eight and getting closer to achieving her agrarian dream when she goes to visit a relation in Scotland.

Fantasy takes the fore in many King-Smith titles. *The Queen's Nose* concerns a little girl who receives a magic wishing coin from her uncle and how she manages the seven wishes allotted by the coin. In *Paddy's Pot of Gold,* young Brigid inherits a pot of gold from the leprechaun Paddy O'Brien. When she turns eight, Brigid meets the leprechaun, visible only to herself. Soon they are friends, with Paddy teaching the young girl animal sounds, but the friendship ends when the leprechaun dies. Betsy Hearne, reviewing the book in *Bulletin of the Center for Children's Books,* found that it "makes cozy holiday reading." Likewise, fantasy is integral to *Lady Daisy,* in which a Victorian wax doll comes alive, informing a nine year old about days of old. *School Library Journal* reviewer Yvonne Frey felt that this book provided "good light reading." In *Harriet's Hare,* science fiction and animal stories combine when young Harriet discovers an alien from outer space—in the disguise of a hare—in her backyard. *Booklist* reviewer Peterson declared the book to be "another surefire hit for the prolific King-Smith." *The Water Horse* deals with the origins of the Loch Ness Monster in a "just-shy-of believable fantasy," according to a reviewer for *Publishers Weekly.*

Historical fantasy is at the heart of *The Roundhill,* the tale of a fourteen-year-old boy on holidays in 1936. On a pilgrimage to a local peak, the boy meets a mysterious young girl, Alice, who bears a striking resemblance to the main character in *Alice's Adventures in Wonderland.* A contributor to *Publishers Weekly* found this tale to be "served up with a measure of suspense and King-Smith's usual flair," resulting in "satisfying fare" for young readers. Reviewing the same novel in *School Library Journal,* Beth Wright concluded, "More than just a skillfully told ghost story, this is a thoughtful exploration of the transforming power of friendship, however unusual its circumstance." *Spider Sparrow* deals with a most unusual foundling who has the power to charm animals. *Horn Book* reviewer Kristi Beavin felt this novel was a departure from the author's usual animal fantasies in that it deals in "the magic of the ordinary world." Set in the agrarian world of pre-World War II England, the book abounds in details with which King-Smith himself is all too familiar. Linda L. Plevak, writing in *School Library Journal,* called the book "heartwarming" and one "filled with memorable characters." A reviewer for *Publishers Weekly* joined the chorus of praise for the novel, noting King-Smith's "pitch-perfect prose," and concluding, "Poignant and wise, this deeply moving tale is not to be missed." In the 2001 title *Billy the Bird,* young Mary Bird is amazed to discover that her little brother—who is seemingly a typical child in other respects—can fly when the moon is full. "King-Smith's fans will enjoy this ... title and wish they could share the experience," wrote Anne Connor in a *School Library Journal* review.

The versatile King-Smith, equally at home with the novel, short stories, picture books, and nonfiction, has also penned a trio of books featuring elderly protagonists. In *The Stray,* a lady escapes from an old-folks home and is taken in by a family with five red-haired children, wins the lottery, and catches a burglar. A contributor to *Publishers Weekly* called this a "cozy, old-fashioned novel." *Mr. Ape* presents a crusty, aged male protagonist who turns his house into a mini-zoo, aided by a Gypsy boy and his father. When Mr. Ape's house is burned down, these two help him to save the animals. This novel found praise from a reviewer for *Publishers Weekly* who noted that, "Once again adding a well-calculated measure of pathos to his comedy, King-Smith delivers another memorable animal tale." And in *The Witch of Blackberry Bottom,* an elderly woman who lives alone in Blackberry Bottom with an odd assortment of animals is thought to be a local witch, yet proves to be the daughter of a baron. "Shot through with themes of redemption and compassion," wrote a reviewer for *Publishers Weekly* of the American edition titled *Mysterious Miss Slade*, "the story carries King-Smith's dependable dose of adventure, humor and warm, believable characters (of both the two-legged and four-legged variety)."

It continues to be the qualities of adventure, humor, and warmth of characterization that gain King-Smith legions of new fans. He once commented about his reasons for writing: "If there is a philosophical point behind what I write, I'm not especially conscious of it; maybe I do stress the need for courage, something we all wish we had more of, and I also do feel strongly for underdogs. As for trying to fill a need in children's literature, if I am, it is to produce books that can afford adults some pleasure when they read to their children. I write for fun." Into his eighties, King-Smith continues to pursue his third career as a writer diligently, rising early, writing by longhand, and retyping drafts in the afternoon. At night he reads aloud what he has written to his wife of sixty years. As he noted in an interview on the *Random House Web Site*, "I live in a beautiful old cottage in a tiny village; don't like nuts, turnips or pineapples; love the English countryside and would probably die immediately if forced to live in a town; and am a very happy man doing what is in effect my hobby for a living, i.e., writing stories for children."

## Biographical and Critical Sources

*BOOKS*

*Children's Literature Review*, Volume 40, Gale (Detroit, MI), 1996.

King-Smith, Dick, *Dick King-Smith's Animal Friends: Thirty-one True Life Stories*, Candlewick Press (Cambridge, MA), 1996.

King-Smith, Dick, *Puppy Love*, Candlewick Press (Cambridge, MA), 1997.

King-Smith, Dick, *Chewing the Cud*, Viking (London, England), 2001.

*Twentieth-Century Children's Writers*, 4th edition, St. James Press (Detroit, MI), 1995.

*PERIODICALS*

*Booklist*, August, 1985, Denise Wilms, review of *Babe: The Gallant Pig*; April 1, 1994, Kay Weisman, review of *Sophie in the Saddle*, p. 1448; November 15, 1994, p. 594; January 15, 1995, p. 929; April 15, 1995, Lauren Peterson, review of *Harriet's Hare*, p. 1499; July 15, 1995, Marry Harris Veeder, review of *Sophie Is Seven*, p. 1880; October 15, 1995, Lauren Peterson, review of *The Schoolmouse*, p. 303; April 1, 1996, p. 1366; May 1, 1996, p. 1506; September 15, 1996, p. 238; October 1, 1996, p. 352; December 1, 1996, Ellen Mandel, review of *Dick King-Smith's Animal Friends*, p. 650; March 1, 1997, p. 1172; January 1, 1998, p. 813; May 1, 1998, p. 1518; September 15, 1998, p. 230; March 1, 1999, p. 1202; April 15, 1999, Carolyn Phelan, review of *Charlie Muffin's Miracle Mouse*, p. 1528; January 1, 2000, p. 924; August, 2000, p. 2140; April 15, 2001, p. 1552; July, 2001, Carolyn Phelan, review of *Billy the Bird*, p. 2006;

January 1, 2002, Ilene Cooper, review of *Funny Frank*, p. 858; February 15, 2002, Stephanie Zvirin, review of *George Speaks*, p. 1014.

*Bulletin of the Center for Children's Books*, July-August, 1984; July-August, 1985; May, 1987; June, 1992, Betsy Hearne, review of *Paddy's Pot of Gold*, p. 266; March, 1993, p. 215; April, 1993; May, 1993.

*Children's Literature in Education*, Volume 19, number 2, 1988, Arthur Arnold, review of *Pigs Might Fly*, p. 81.

*Horn Book*, September-October, 1992, Ann A. Flowers, review of *Dick King-Smith's Alphabeasts*, p. 595; March-April, 1993, Ann A. Flowers, review of *Sophie's Tom*, pp. 208-209; July-August, 1993, p. 478; November-December, 1994, Ann A. Flowers, review of *Three Terrible Trins*, pp. 733-734; July-August, 1995, pp. 478-479; January-February, 1997, pp. 60-61; March-April, 1997, pp. 211-212; May-June, 1998, pp. 372-373; November-December, 1998, p. 733; July-August, 1999, p. 467; July-August, 2000, p. 458; January-February, 2001, Kristi Beavin, review of *Spider Sparrow*, p. 122; May-June, 2001, p. 327.

*Junior Literary Guild*, March, 1984.

*Kirkus Reviews*, November 1, 1992, p. 1379; April 1, 1993, p. 458.

*New York Times Book Review*, May 17, 1987, Karla Kuskin, review of *Harry's Mad;* November 12, 1995.

*Observer* (London, England), December 11, 1983, Naomi Lewis, review of *The Sheep-Pig*.

*Publishers Weekly*, June 29, 1990, review of *Ace: The Very Important Pig*, p. 102; June 29, 1992, review of *Sophie's Tom*, p. 63; October 19, 1992, review of *The Animal Parade*, p. 79; May 31, 1993, review of *The Invisible Dog*, p. 55; October 17, 1994, review of *The Terrible Trins*, pp. 81-82; March 13, 1995, review of *Harriet's Hare*, p. 70; September 11, 1995, p. 86; August 5, 1996, review of *The Stray*, p. 442; March 19, 1997, p. 65; March 16, 1998, review of *Mr. Ape*, p. 64; July 6, 1998, review of *Animal Stories*, p. 61; July 13, 1998, review of *The Water Horse*, p. 78; February 22, 1999, p. 96; December 6, 1999, review of *Spider Sparrow*, p. 77; June 26, 2000, p. 77; June 26, 2000, review of *Mysterious Miss Slade*, p. 75; November 20, 2000, review of *The Roundhill*, p. 69; April 23, 2001, review of *Billy the Bird*, p. 78; June 4, 2001, p. 80; July 9, 2001, p. 70; December 10, 2001, review of *Funny Frank*, pp. 70-71; April 1, 2002, review of *George Speaks*, p. 83.

*School Library Journal*, July, 1992, Yvonne Frey, review of *Lady Daisy*, p. 62; April, 1993, Virginia Golodetz, review of *The Cuckoo Child*, p. 121; October, 1993, Kay McPherson, review of *All Pigs Are Beautiful*, p. 118; November, 1994, p. 105; January, 1995, p. 108; May, 1995, p. 100; July, 1995, p. 65; December, 1995, p. 82; April, 1996, p. 112; September, 1996, p. 165; November, 1996, p. 87; January, 1997, p. 37; May, 1997, p. 102; December, 1997, p. 94; September, 1998, p. 204; November 1, 1998, p. 88; February, 1999, p. 108; June, 1999, p. 132; January, 2000, pp. 105-106; March, 2000, Linda L. Plevak, review of *Spider Sparrow*, p. 239; July, 2000, p. 81; December, 2000, Beth Wright, review of *The Roundhill*, p. 145; June, 2001, Anne Connor, review of *Billy the Bird*, p. 121; July, 2001, p. 61.

*Times Educational Supplement,* July 31, 1992; September 18, 1992; November 12, 1993; March 15, 1996; October 14, 1996; May 30, 1997; June 15, 2001.

*Times Literary Supplement,* July 7, 1978, Anne Carter, review of *The Fox Busters,* p. 770; November 30, 1984, p. 1383; August 16, 1985; January 3, 1986; October 17, 1986, Alice H. G. Phillips, review of *Noah's Brother.*

*Washington Post Book World,* May 7, 1995.

OTHER

*BBC—Radio 4,* http://www.bbc.co.uk/ (February 12, 2002), "Authors: Dick King-Smith Audio Interview."

*Guardian,* http://books.guardian.co.uk/ (November 10, 2001), Julia Eccleshare, "How to Make Millions from Pigs."

*Random House Web Site,* http://www.randomhouse.com/ (February 12, 2002), "Dick King-Smith."

*Young Writer,* http://www.mystworld.com/ (February 12, 2002), "Issue 4: Dick King-Smith."*

*—Sketch by J. Sydney Jones*

\* \* \*

# KROLL, Steven 1941-

## Personal

Born August 11, 1941, in New York, NY; son of Julius (a diamond merchant) and Anita (a business executive; maiden name, Berger) Kroll; married Edite Niedringhaus (a children's book editor), April 18, 1964 (divorced, 1978); married Abigail Aldridge (a milliner), June 3, 1989 (divorced, 1994); married Kathleen Beckett (a journalist), October 4, 1997. *Education:* Harvard University, B.A., 1962. *Politics:* "Committed to change." *Religion:* Jewish. *Hobbies and other interests:* Walking, traveling, and playing tennis.

## Addresses

*Home and Office*—64 West Eleventh St., New York, NY 10011.

## Career

*Transatlantic Review,* London, England, associate editor, 1962-65; Chatto & Windus, London, reader and editor, 1962-65; Holt, Rinehart & Winston, New York, NY, acquiring editor, adult trade department, 1965-69; freelance writer, 1969—. Instructor in English, University of Maine at Augusta, 1970-71.

## Member

PEN American Center (former chairman of children's book authors' committee and former member of executive board), Authors Guild, Authors League of America, Society of Children's Book Writers and Illustrators, Harvard Club (New York, NY).

## Writings

FOR CHILDREN

*Is Milton Missing?,* illustrated by Dick Gackenbach, Holiday House (New York, NY), 1975.

*That Makes Me Mad!,* illustrated by Hilary Knight, Pantheon (New York, NY), 1976, illustrated by Christine Davenier, SeaStar Books (New York, NY), 2002.

*The Tyrannosaurus Game,* illustrated by Tomie de Paola, Holiday House (New York, NY), 1976.

*Gobbledygook,* illustrated by Kelly Oechsli, Holiday House (New York, NY), 1977.

*If I Could Be My Grandmother,* illustrated by Lady McCrady, Pantheon (New York, NY), 1977.

*Sleepy Ida and Other Nonsense Poems,* illustrated by Seymour Chwast, Pantheon (New York, NY), 1977.

*Santa's Crash-Bang Christmas,* illustrated by Tomie de Paola, Holiday House (New York, NY), 1977.

*T. J. Folger, Thief,* illustrated by Bill Morrison, Holiday House (New York, NY), 1978.

*Fat Magic,* illustrated by Tomie de Paola, Holiday House (New York, NY), 1979.

*The Candy Witch,* illustrated by Marylin Hafner, Holiday House (New York, NY), 1979.

*Space Cats,* illustrated by Friso Henstra, Holiday House (New York, NY), 1979.

*Amanda and the Giggling Ghost,* illustrated by Dick Gackenbach, Holiday House (New York, NY), 1980.

*Dirty Feet,* illustrated by Toni Hormann, Parents Magazine Press (New York, NY), 1980.

*Monster Birthday,* illustrated by Dennis Kendrick, Holiday House (New York, NY), 1980.

*Friday the Thirteenth,* illustrated by Dick Gackenbach, Holiday House (New York, NY), 1981.

*Giant Journey,* illustrated by Kay Chorao, Holiday House (New York, NY), 1981.

*Are You Pirates?,* illustrated by Marylin Hafner, Pantheon (New York, NY), 1982.

*Banana Bits,* illustrated by Maxie Chambliss, Avon (New York, NY), 1982.

*Bathrooms,* illustrated by Maxie Chambliss, Avon (New York, NY), 1982.

*The Big Bunny and the Easter Eggs,* illustrated by Janet Stevens, Holiday House (New York, NY), 1982.

*The Goat Parade,* illustrated by Tim Kirk, Parents Magazine Press (New York, NY), 1982.

*One Tough Turkey,* illustrated by John Wallner, Holiday House (New York, NY), 1982.

*The Hand-me-down Doll,* illustrated by Evaline Ness, Holiday House (New York, NY), 1983.

*Otto,* illustrated by Ned Delaney, Parents Magazine Press (New York, NY), 1983.

*Pigs in the House,* illustrated by Tim Kirk, Parents Magazine Press (New York, NY), 1983.

*Toot! Toot!,* illustrated by Anne Rockwell, Holiday House (New York, NY), 1983.

*Woof, Woof!,* illustrated by Nicole Rubel, Dial (New York, NY), 1983.

*The Biggest Pumpkin Ever,* illustrated by Jeni Bassett, Holiday House (New York, NY), 1984.

*Loose Tooth,* illustrated by Tricia Tusa, Holiday House (New York, NY), 1984.

*Happy Mother's Day,* illustrated by Marylin Hafner, Holiday House (New York, NY), 1985.

*Mrs. Claus's Crazy Christmas,* illustrated by John Wallner, Holiday House (New York, NY), 1985.

*Annie's Four Grannies,* illustrated by Eileen Christelow, Holiday House (New York, NY), 1986.

*The Big Bunny and the Magic Show,* illustrated by Janet Stevens, Holiday House (New York, NY), 1986.

*I'd Like to Be,* illustrated by Ellen Appleby, Parents Magazine Press (New York, NY), 1987.

*I Love Spring,* illustrated by Kathryn E. Shoemaker, Holiday House (New York, NY), 1987.

*It's Groundhog Day!,* illustrated by Jeni Bassett, Holiday House (New York, NY), 1987.

*Don't Get Me in Trouble!,* illustrated by Marvin Glass, Crown (New York, NY), 1988.

*Happy Father's Day,* illustrated by Marylin Hafner, Holiday House (New York, NY), 1988.

*Looking for Daniela: A Romantic Adventure,* illustrated by Anita Lobel, Holiday House (New York, NY), 1988.

*Newsman Ned Meets the New Family,* illustrated by Denise Brunkus, Scholastic (New York, NY), 1988.

*Oh, What a Thanksgiving!,* illustrated by S. D. Schindler, Scholastic (New York, NY), 1988.

*Big Jeremy,* illustrated by Donald Carrick, Holiday House (New York, NY), 1989.

*The Hokey-Pokey Man,* illustrated by Deborah Kogan Ray, Holiday House (New York, NY), 1989.

*Newsman Ned and the Broken Rules,* illustrated by Denise Brunkus, Scholastic (New York, NY), 1989.

*Branigan's Cat and the Halloween Ghost,* illustrated by Carolyn Ewing, Holiday House (New York, NY), 1990.

*Gone Fishing,* illustrated by Harvey Stevenson, Crown (New York, NY), 1990.

*It's April Fools' Day!,* illustrated by Jeni Bassett, Holiday House (New York, NY), 1990.

*Annabelle's Un-Birthday,* illustrated by Gail Owens, Macmillan (New York, NY), 1991.

*Howard and Gracie's Luncheonette,* illustrated by Michael Sours, Holt (New York, NY), 1991.

*Mary McLean and the St. Patrick's Day Parade,* illustrated by Michael Dooling, Scholastic (New York, NY), 1991.

*Princess Abigail and the Wonderful Hat,* illustrated by Patience Brewster, Holiday House (New York, NY), 1991.

*The Squirrels' Thanksgiving,* illustrated by Jeni Bassett, Holiday House (New York, NY), 1991.

*The Magic Rocket,* illustrated by Will Hillenbrand, Holiday House (New York, NY), 1992.

*Andrew Wants a Dog,* illustrated by Molly Delaney, Hyperion Books (New York, NY), 1992.

*The Hit and Run Gang,* volumes 1-4, illustrated by Meredith Johnson, Avon (New York, NY), 1992.

*The Pigrates Clean Up,* illustrated by Jeni Bassett, Henry Holt (New York, NY), 1993.

*Queen of the May,* illustrated by Patience Brewster, Holiday House (New York, NY), 1993.

*Will You Be My Valentine?,* illustrated by Lillian Hoban, Holiday House (New York, NY), 1993.

*I'm George Washington and You're Not!,* illustrated by Betsy Lewin, Hyperion Books (New York, NY), 1994.

*By the Dawn's Early Light: The Story of the Star-Spangled Banner,* illustrated by Dan Andreasen, Scholastic (New York, NY), 1994.

*Patrick's Tree House,* illustrated by Roberta Wilson, Macmillan (New York, NY), 1994.

*The Hit and Run Gang,* volumes 5-8, illustrated by Meredith Johnson, Avon (New York, NY), 1994.

*Lewis and Clark: Explorers of the American West,* illustrated by Richard Williams, Holiday House (New York, NY), 1994.

*Doctor on an Elephant,* illustrated by Michael Chesworth, Henry Holt (New York, NY), 1994.

*Eat!,* illustrated by Diane Palmisciano, Hyperion Books (New York, NY), 1995.

*Ellis Island: Doorway to Freedom,* illustrated by Karen Ritz, Holiday House (New York, NY), 1995.

*Pony Express!,* illustrated by Dan Andreasen, Scholastic (New York, NY), 1996.

*The Boston Tea Party,* illustrated by Peter Fiore, Holiday House (New York, NY), 1998.

*Oh, Tucker!,* illustrated by Scott Nash, Candlewick Press, 1998.

*Robert Fulton: From Submarine to Steamboat,* illustrated by Bill Farnsworth, Holiday House (New York, NY), 1999.

*William Penn: Founder of Pennsylvania,* illustrated by Ronald Himler, Holiday House (New York, NY), 2000.

*Patches Lost and Found,* illustrated by Barry Gott, Winslow Press, 2001.

*YOUNG ADULT BOOKS*

*Take It Easy!,* Four Winds (Bristol, FL), 1983.

*Breaking Camp,* Macmillan (New York, NY), 1985.

*Multiple Choice,* Macmillan (New York, NY), 1987.

*Sweet America,* Jamestown Publishers (Chicago, IL), 2000.

*When I Dream of Heaven,* Jamestown Publishers (Chicago, IL), 2000.

*Dear Mr. President: John Quincey Adams' Letters from a Southern Planter's Son,* Winslow Press, 2001.

*OTHER*

Also contributor of book reviews to *Book World, Commonweal, Village Voice, Listener, New York Times Book Review, Spectator, Times Literary Supplement,* and *London Magazine.* Contributor to poetry anthologies. Some of Kroll's works have been translated into French, Spanish, Dutch, Danish, Italian, and Japanese.

## Work in Progress

"A revised edition of *That Makes Me Mad!,* just published by North South Sea Star; a new picture book story, *A Tale of Two Dogs,* to be published by Marshall Cavendish in 2004. Other picture books, a book of poems, and a YA novel."

## Adaptations

*The Biggest Pumpkin Ever and Other Stories* (includes *The Biggest Pumpkin Ever; Sleepy Ida and Other Nonsense Poems; T. J. Folger, Thief;* and *Woof, Woof!*) has been recorded on audiocassette for Caedmon, 1986;

*The Biggest Pumpkin Ever, The Big Bunny and the Easter Eggs, Will You Be My Valentine?,* and *Oh, Tucker!* have been recorded on audiocassette for Scholastic.

## Sidelights

According to reviewers, children's author Steven Kroll possesses a unique ability to view his stories as a child would, so he understands what interests and entertains his young audience. Even though it took him years to commit himself to writing and he fell into children's writing by chance, the author has never regretted his career choice. Writing for children grants Kroll a special connection with his own youth—something he values greatly. "What is most important is the feeling that I am somehow in touch with my own childhood," Kroll told *SATA.* "To be in touch with your own childhood is to be, in some way, touched with wonder, and when I write for children, that is what I feel."

As a child in New York City, Kroll entertained himself with imaginative games, baseball, and trips to the local candy store. When he was older, he would visit the Museum of Modern Art on Tuesday afternoons to study sculpture. Naturally, people thought Kroll would become a sculptor. "But I turned to writing instead," Kroll admitted in the *Junior Literary Guild* magazine. "It happened quite by accident. Appointed editor of *Panorama,* his secondary school literary journal, Kroll discovered "there wasn't much to publish. Someone had to fill the gap. I sat down and wrote two stories and I've been hooked on writing ever since."

Kroll never set out to write children's stories. Following his graduation from Harvard University in 1962, he worked as an editor of adult trade books in both London, England, and in New York City. In 1969 he moved to Maine so he could write full time. He was contributing book reviews to magazines and writing adult short stories and novels during the early 1970s when his former wife, a children's book editor, and other friends in children's book publishing suggested he try writing for children. "I said, 'Oh, no. I couldn't possibly. I don't know how to do that,'" Kroll recalled in *Behind the Covers.* But "one night at a dinner party I got an idea for a children's story. I wrote it and it was bad. But I discovered an important thing: I liked doing it."

After spending a few years writing unsuccessful children's picture-book stories, Kroll moved back to New York City, where he met Margery Cuyler. She became his editor at Holiday house and published his first book, *Is Milton Missing?,* published in 1975. Since then Kroll has steadily produced at least two books per year, once as many as nine, for Holiday House and other publishers. He has now written more than eighty books for children.

For his story ideas and settings Kroll sometimes recalls places and instances from his own childhood. "When I write about a child's room, that room is often my own—the one in the Manhattan apartment house where I grew up," Kroll commented. "When I write about an urban street or an urban school, it is often my street or my school, taken out of time into a situation I have invented. And sometimes," the author continued, "if I'm writing about a suburb or a small town, that place will resemble the home of a summer camp friend I visited once, and longed to see again."

Kroll's stories appeal greatly to young readers, evidenced by the number of letters the author constantly receives. His favorites are those from children who are not afraid to share their enthusiasm. "The best letter I ever got was from a first grader in Connecticut where I was going to speak the following week," Kroll recollected in *Behind the Covers.* "This one read, 'Dear Mr. Kroll, My heart is beating because it's so anxious to see what you look like.' The little girl was wonderful! She signed everything she wrote with her name and 'Made in U.S.A.'"

Kroll's collection of works includes several that help bring to life stories from American history. From *The Boston Tea Party* to *Pony Express!,* these colorful volumes are designed for readers of various elementary school levels. *The Boston Tea Party,* for example, is geared toward the third-to sixth-grade set and uses vivid impressionistic illustrations to recount the events leading up to the famous uprising of December 16, 1773. Setting the protest in context, *The Boston Tea Party* opens with an explanation of how the Seven Years War placed England in debt, and how the country planned to raise money by taxing the colonies. Carolyn Phelan noted in a *Booklist* review that the lack of a central character makes the narrative more difficult for young readers, but observed that Kroll still does a "credible job of summarizing history."

Another colonial-era story is recounted in Kroll's picture book, *William Penn: Founder of Pennsylvania.* Aimed at a slightly older audience (ages 9-12), *Penn* focuses on the rebellious personality of a man who, though born to privilege, chose a more challenging path of spreading religious and political freedom. In another *Booklist* review, Phelan expressed concern that the subject matter may be too advanced for the young readership, citing Penn's background of civil disobedience and debt problems. Still, she recommends the book to school libraries as "a useful and certainly handsome addition" to history collections. An article in *Kirkus Reviews* singled out Kroll's "highly event-oriented and [information-]packed" text as notable. Kroll is also the author of the biography *Robert Fulton: From Submarine to Steamboat,* which a *Kirkus Reviews* critic called "a handsomely illustrated biography" that "will make readers yearn for more information" on the visionary marine designer.

In 2001, Kroll published *Dear Mr. President: John Quincy Adams, Letters from a Southern Planter's Son.* Instead of simply writing a biography of Adams, Kroll puts the historical context into perspective by having Adams correspond with William Pratt, a young boy from Georgia. Much of the story discusses treatment of Native

Americans during Adams's presidency. "Despite the implausibility of the correspondence, this offers an effective way for young people to learn about history," wrote Todd Morning of *Booklist.*

Kroll invited youngsters in grades three and older to saddle up with the *Pony Express!* Oil paintings underline the text as the hunt for "young skinny wiry fellows not over eighteen, orphans preferred" brought scores of riders to the fledgling mail delivery system of 1860-61. The book earned high marks from *Horn Book, Booklist* and *Publishers Weekly,* all of whom found the depth of information (detailed route maps are provided), sharp graphic detail, and compelling narrative valuable for its intended audience. "An absorbing and enlightening dose of history and adventure," *Publishers Weekly* elaborated.

History for older readers is served up in Kroll's novel-length titles for young adults, including *Sweet America* and *When I Dream of Heaven.* In the former title, Kroll presents an immigrant's story in the guise of fourteen-year-old Tonio who gradually is transformed into Tony in late nineteenth-century New York. In *When I Dream of Heaven,* "the appalling conditions of the New York City sweatshops at the turn of the 20th century and the plight of young immigrant girls come to life," according to Linda Bindner, writing in *School Library Journal.* In this piece of historical fiction, Gina Petrosino tries to balance her familial duties with her own wishes to continue her education.

On a lighter note, Kroll has also created contemporary picture books for young readers. His 2001 title, *Patches Lost and Found,* "is a masterful blend of text and illustration," according to Barbara Buckley in *School Library Journal.* Jenny would much rather draw than write stories, so when her beloved guinea pig, Patches, goes missing, she designs "missing" posters for the pet and distributes them all over town. The posters do the trick—her pet is found and returned. This incident happily coincides with a difficulty at school: Jenny has been unable to come up with a writing assignment for her teacher, but has been drawing pictures of what might have happened to Patches. Now her mother points out that Jenny's pictures tell a story; all she needs to do is add some words to complete her assignment. Buckley found *Patches Lost and Found* "a suspenseful, kid-friendly picture book that works on several levels," while *Booklist*'s Phelan noted that the book was written "with a sure sense of narrative and an understanding of the concerns and the learning styles of children." Phelan concluded, "A fresh, fine offering." Judy Freeman of *Instructor* commented, "For many of the artists in your group, this story will be a godsend." *Patches Lost and Found* won a *Booklist* editor's choice award.

For still younger readers, Kroll has published such whimsical stories as *The Biggest Pumpkin Ever, The Squirrel's Thanksgiving* and, in 1998, *Oh, Tucker!* In the 1998 work, young children are introduced to a playful, oversized pup whose ability to generate household havoc is matched only by his loving personality. "Wherever he goes—'WHAM!'—he creates a trail of disaster," proclaimed a *Publishers Weekly* critic, who went on to predict that early readers were likely to "get swept up in the momentum" of Tucker's well-meaning rampages. *Booklist*'s Ellen Mandel noted that Tucker's "slapstick race through the house" led straight "into readers' hearts."

Kroll never regrets leaving his full-time job to become a children's author. "I really love writing for children," he remarked. "I love starting the fireworks, love that explosion of emotion, of excitement, terror, and enthusiasm that comes with putting those words on paper and sometimes, if the mood is right, doing a draft of a whole picture-book story in one sitting. I've been doing a lot more picture books, but I've also become much more involved in writing chapter books, American history for middle grade readers, and historical fiction for young adults." Writing for children is what Kroll feels most content doing. "It's part of me now," the author concluded, "and I'd like other adults to let down the barriers and feel the wonder in their own lives that I feel in these books."

## Biographical and Critical Sources

*BOOKS*

*Behind the Covers: Interviews with Authors and Illustrators of Books for Children and Young Adults,* Libraries Unlimited (Littleton, CO), 1985.

*PERIODICALS*

*Booklist,* March 1, 1996, review of *Pony Express!,* p. 177; May 1, 1998, Ellen Mandel, review of *Oh, Tucker!,* p. 521; September 15, 1998, Carolyn Phelan, review of *The Boston Tea Party,* p. 222; February 15, 2000, Carolyn Phelan, review of *William Penn: Founder of Pennsylvania,* p. 1108; March 1, 2001, Carolyn Phelan, review of *Patches Lost and Found,* p. 1277; January 1, 2002, Todd Morning, review of *Dear Mr. President: John Quincy Adams, Letters from a Southern Planter's Son,* p. 858.

*Horn Book,* September-October, 1996, review of *Pony Express!,* p. 616; July-December, 2001, review of *Dear Mr. President.*

*Instructor,* April, 2002, Judy Freeman, review of *Patches Lost and Found,* p. 17.

*Junior Literary Guild,* September, 1975, review of *Is Milton Missing?,* p. 7.

*Kirkus Reviews,* February 1, 1999, review of *Robert Fulton: From Submarine to Steamboat;* January 1, 2000, review of *William Penn: Founder of Pennsylvania,* p. 60.

*Publishers Weekly,* February 5, 1996, review of *Pony Express!,* p. 90; May 4, 1998, review of *Oh, Tucker!,* p. 212.

*School Library Journal,* March, 2000, p. 234; September, 2000, Linda Bindner, review of *When I Dream of Heaven,* p. 233; May, 2001, Barbara Buckley, review of *Patches Lost and Found,* p. 126.

                                        *          *          *

---

## Autobiography Feature

# Steven Kroll

To my great surprise last year—had it really been that long?—I found myself invited to my Harvard twenty-fifth reunion. Before these festivities were to take place—and I ended up enjoying them tremendously—a form was sent out to all the old grads. We were asked to provide the relevant details of our lives—occupation, marital status, children, etc.—but we were also asked to write a one-page account of what had happened to us since graduation and, if we wished, include how we felt about the world. Each of these accounts was to appear in a fat red book, to be published and distributed among the classmates before we returned to Cambridge in June.

Summing up twenty-five years in a page seemed, at best, a perilous task. (Commenting on the state of the world was clearly out of the question.) But as I wondered what to do, Holiday House, my principal publisher, and I were asked permission to have three of my books for younger children appear as part of a new Holt reading series. The "unit" devoted to my work was to be called "Surprises," and at first I couldn't understand why. Many of my books are about things going wrong and getting put right, but the element of surprise didn't seem particularly strong in them. Then I had a revelation. Not only was most of my work preoccupied with surprise. My entire life since college had been *nothing but* surprises!

So that's what I wrote my page about. I included the important details of becoming an editor and getting married and divorced and struggling to become a writer, but surprise—how little of my life had gone according to plan—is what I emphasized. And now, as I begin this essay, I am preoccupied with it once again, because even the most conservative among us are continually surprised by life, and no one ever teaches us how to cope. We grow up thinking we are in control, and what a shock it can be when we learn we are not.

Then again, there was nothing at all surprising about my arrival in the world on August 11, 1941, in the Harkness Pavilion of Columbia Presbyterian Hospital in New York City. My father, Julius Kroll, and some friends of my parents were already waiting, and when the baby had successfully made his appearance and they had gone to see him, they adjourned to the hospital cafeteria for a champagne party. For years afterward, my mother would occasionally mention how much she missed being at that party.

There was nothing atypical in that response. My mother, Anita Berger Kroll, was always a genuine enthu-siast. Throughout my childhood, it was she who became den mother of the Cub Scout troop, supported me in everything I did, and gave me the confidence to do well.

Even after my father died, when I was thirteen, the enthusiasm never dimmed. Instead, it found new paths to follow. My father had been a diamond importer, with offices at 580 Fifth Avenue in Manhattan. For a year after his death, my mother ran the business. Then, having decided not to continue, she realized she would have to get a job. Enthusiastically, she decided to attend the Speedwrit-ing Institute and learn their ABC shorthand.

The school liked her so much that when she finished the course, they offered her a job as a registrar. For the next twenty years, as registrar, director of the Brooklyn school, and eventually regional director of the New York office, my mother was the force behind Speedwriting's success. When she finally retired—because ITT had bought the company and they discovered she was over sixty-five—the place went into an instant decline.

But even in retirement, my mother continued her enthusiasms. Always a liberal Reform Jew, she became active in the Community Church, a nonsectarian Unitarian/ Universalist church in New York City. For several years, she was chairperson of the Church Council, and up until she died, at eighty in 1984, she continued to do all the publicity for a little Off-Off-Broadway theater, attached to and sponsored by the church, called the Theater Off Park.

I'd be at home relaxing, and the phone would ring. "Steven," I would hear, "there's an opening next week and a party afterwards. You have to come."

The play would sound a little questionable, not quite my sort of thing. "Well, Mother ..." I would say.

"Come on," she'd say, "you'll love it. We'll go out for coffee afterwards, or maybe some dinner."

And I would go, of course, and sometimes it would be great and sometimes it would be terrible, but what it actually was never mattered a bit. My mother's affection for the cast, the play, the occasion, the young people doing something creative, would transform the evening and make it terrific.

Of course this kind of enthusiasm spilled over into everything. Mother was always finding the latest, interest-ing, out-of-the-way restaurant, the most exciting, undiscov-ered Off-Broadway play, the fabulous movie that just happened to be showing around the corner. And of course she wanted to tell you about it because part of the fun was in letting the people she cared about know.

An extension of that excitement involved her love of family. To her, the family came first. She was always close to my grandmother. She maintained a lifelong friendship with her older sister, Beryl. My sister, June, and I were more important than anyone else. And every year at Thanksgiving, the gala family dinner was held at her apartment.

Because my mother felt so strongly about family, the coolness of my father's family toward her was a frequent source of pain. Both my paternal grandparents, Lazar and Bertha Kroll, died before I was born, but pictures of them reveal a stern, unbending couple. He was Prussian, she Viennese, and they had come to this country with their eldest son, Charles, several years before my father's birth in 1895. The best-known story about Lazar was that my father had been forced to drop out of City College after his second year and join the family diamond business, then located on Maiden Lane right off Wall Street, because he refused to become a doctor. (Supposedly, my father had been interested in that most precarious of professions, writing. I often feel I have, in some way, turned that blighted dream into reality.)

But if Lazar and Bertha Kroll had a somewhat sinister quality hovering just beyond my reach, Uncle Charles, Aunt Janet, and Aunt Eve, in all their humorlessness, were very real. I almost never saw them—they were certainly not included at what I thought of as family gatherings—but Charles and Janet shared an apartment in—of all places—our apartment building! This was 277 West End Avenue, a large, gracious, pre-World War II building on Manhattan's Upper West Side. There were two lines of apartments, one off an elevator in the front, one off an elevator in the rear, with a long lobby corridor dividing them. We lived in the front. Charles and Janet lived in the back. During my entire childhood, we never moved. Unfortunately, Charles and Janet never moved either.

Charles was a dogmatic, well-to-do stockbroker. Janet, who seemed not to do anything, was best known for stocking up on horrid little items in Europe, then packaging them up in special department-store boxes and passing them off as gifts from Saks or Lord and Taylor. Occasionally I would be told I had to visit them.

Not at all happy, I would slouch the distance between the two apartments. Upon arrival, the door would open and Aunt Janet would usher me into what felt like total darkness.

Beyond the entrance foyer was a long, dark hallway flanked, on either side, by mahogany bookshelves with glass doors. All the bookshelves were filled with leather-bound books. All the glass doors were locked. Midway along was a small marble table. On the table was a replica of a Greek bronze called *The Discus Thrower.*

Reaching the end of the hallway, I would be sat down in the dark and formal living room and offered "smelly" cheese, usually Port du Salut. This was the one thing Janet knew I liked, and in her only gesture of affection toward me, she always offered it. There was a highly polished piano, but it was never played. Charles would appear, and he and Janet would quiz me about my schoolwork, my parents, and how things were at home. Then I would be allowed to leave.

All of this would seem to indicate that not even the Queen of England would have met with a very warm

*Steven Kroll*

reception in the Kroll family. Given my mother's history, she never had a chance.

Born in 1903, she had been a beauty in her youth and danced at more than one elegant New York party. She married a wealthy young man, gave birth to my sister, June, and was divorced early. For several years after that, she and June lived on West Eighty-sixth Street in Manhattan with my aunt Beryl, my uncle, Manny Kaufman, their son, Jay, and my grandmother, Libby Silman Berger.

When she eventually married my father, my mother was already thirty-four and June eight. My father was forty-two, a bachelor and man-about-town who had always lived with his parents. It was time my father got out of his parents' house, and my mother was very charming. But attitudes were different then, and my father's family didn't see things that way. Not even his formal adoption of my sister or my arrival four years later made any difference. All the family saw was that my father had married a divorced woman with a child.

Just how much the Kroll family's attitude bothered my mother, it was never possible to say. The subject was never discussed at home, everyone remained cordial, and the Krolls were not very likeable anyway, but my mother's generosity of spirit and love of being liked were obviously wounded.

How could she have Kroll-family stories to tell if none were forthcoming? The question would have been on her mind, because more than anything, I realized long after childhood, my mother was a storyteller.

I did my first piece of real writing when I was in the sixth grade. It was an autobiography (complete with pictures), and my teacher, Mrs. Carey, told me afterwards that if I wanted to be a journalist when I grew up, she knew some people I should contact. I wrote my first fiction when I was thirteen and went for a walk in the rain along the outer edge of Central Park. The glistening streets looked as if they were made of glass, and I rushed home and without removing my raincoat pulled out the old Remington portable and wrote a story that began, "The world is made of glass, layer upon layer of glass, like the glass in the doors of the West End Plaza Hotel."

Even though I went for years believing I couldn't be a writer because writers were like gods and I wasn't at all like a god, I always felt that those two moments were the ones that put me in touch with what it meant to be a writer. They made me understand how delicious it was to put words on paper and how much I enjoyed telling stories. Only much later did I realize I was wrong, that although those two moments had been important, it was really my mother's storytelling that had piqued my interest in language and stories and begun my lifelong fascination with the written and spoken word.

Around the dinner table, at holiday gatherings and on lazy winter afternoons, my mother told stories. Needless to say, the stories she enjoyed telling most were about her family.

Her mother, my grandmother, had grown up in St. Mary's, Pennsylvania. She was one of nine children, and

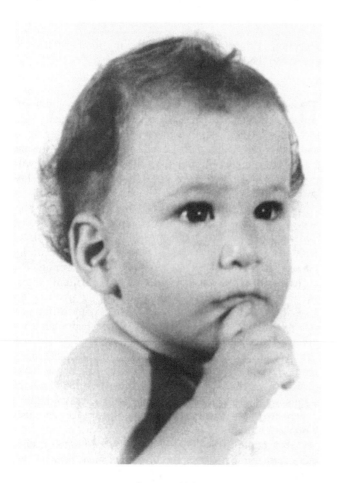

*Steven, 1941*

her father, my great-grandfather, had founded the first department store in town. The only Jewish family in Catholic St. Mary's, all the girls were educated at the local convent. Years later, when I went to visit my great-uncle, Jack Silman, I found him living alone in the big old Silman-family house on Main Street. In his seventies and with five or six choices available, he still slept in the smallest bedroom. He had been the youngest in the family, and that had always been his room.

My mother's father, my grandfather Simon Berger, had come to work in the store. Mother had been born in St. Mary's, but Simon moved his family to New York—and an apartment in the Bronx—when she was three. By then there were three daughters: Beryl, Anita, and the eldest, Reva, who would die of diphtheria at eleven. Simon had a men's clothing store in the Bronx and was beloved by everyone. I always wished I'd been able to meet him.

Stories galore came out of all this, but the one my mother liked telling most was about her grandfather, Hyman Silman.

It began with his arrival in New York from a village in Russia called Romshashock. He hated New York—the crowds, the dirt, the noise—and decided to leave. But he had only twenty dollars in his pocket. Where could he possibly go?

He went down to Grand Central Station, strode up to the ticket counter, and asked the clerk: "Where can I go for twenty dollars?"

"Where would you like to go?" the clerk replied.

"Where can I go for twenty dollars?" Grandfather Silman asked again.

"Sir," said the clerk, "you must tell me where you'd like to go. Then I will sell you a ticket."

Grandfather Silman drew himself up. "Where can I go for twenty dollars?" he asked once more.

At this point the clerk was totally exasperated. He looked at his chart. "St. Mary's, Pennsylvania," he declared.

"Fine," said Grandfather Silman. "That's where I'll go."

I'd like to think that the spirit that allowed me to struggle through years of rejection to my particular success as a writer was based, at least in part, on the kind of peculiar determination revealed in this story. But then, my mother showed her own kind of determination when she was widowed in her fifties, and my father had his special strengths as well.

My father was a man who knew what he wanted. Thwarted in his choice of career, he wanted to do well for his family. At the same time, he wanted his family to do well for him.

Sometimes this fierce desire to succeed became too much. In his insistence that my sister and I do well, he could make us feel that nothing we did was ever good enough. Even though I followed through and was always a top student, there were times when my mother had to take my father aside and say, "Go easier."

There was a special kind of love between my parents, but my father's principles were so strong, his determination and integrity so great, that there were moments when he would get terribly frustrated. There were arguments,

*The Kroll family in New York City, about 1925: from left, Gilbert and Eve Kroll Kellner; Julius; Lazar and Bertha; Charles; Janet Kroll Wolff and her husband*

seldom in front of me but often within hearing distance of my room. It is a legacy I have managed to overcome, though that fierce devotion to principle and that desire to continue doing well, I will carry with me always.

My father was a tall man, and quite robust in his later years. He had a mustache and wore three-piece suits, a homburg, a watch chain, and a Patek-Philippe watch with an alligator band that is now my own. Always handsome and elegant in a way I don't mind emulating, he spent a lot of time traveling, mostly to Antwerp and Amsterdam, to buy diamonds. Toward the end, he sometimes went by plane, but mostly he traveled by ocean liner. The romantic names of ships—the *Rotterdam,* the *Statendam,* the *Mauretania*—floated through my consciousness. Frequently my mother went along on these journeys, and there were always champagne parties in the staterooms before sailing. Of course I was too young to attend these parties. I stayed home and was looked after by my sister, who at twelve years older than I was more like a second mother than a sister, or by our housekeeper, Ayrie Smith.

My sister, June, was never very happy about these absences of our parents. When she went to the shipboard parties, she was often uncomfortable. I remember the ship

names and the visits of glamorous European friends. I remember my father being away and my mother sometimes going, too, but for some reason it doesn't seem as if anyone was ever away for very long. I never had any of that sense of deprivation or abandonment that comes with having parents not at home. Perhaps it's because my sister, by being there, did such a good job.

And when my parents were around, my mother was always attentive—and sometimes there were terrific things to do with my father.

The best was baking. For some reason, my dapper, world-traveling father was an avid baker. He loved nothing more on a Sunday afternoon than to put on his apron and get down to the delectable business of baking his famous sand torte or orange chocolate-chip cake or brown edge cookies. Mother was always called on to assist—she continued baking these specialties herself after my father's death—and I, though also given the title of assistant, was really there to lick the mixing bowl. My father's favorite expression was "When there's a boy in the house, have a cake in the house," and there almost always was.

Second best was going to the office. Because my father imported diamonds, his office at 580 Fifth Avenue had a

*"My grandmother Libby Silman Berger, with my mother, Anita, before she became a Kroll," Atlantic City, about 1925*

bulletproof door. You rang the bell, opened a normal, clouded glass, office door, and stepped into a little vestibule. My father's secretary slid up a panel that revealed a bulletproof window. She scrutinized you to be sure you were okay and then painstakingly unlocked the heavy inner door.

Inside was the view of Fifth Avenue and my father's mahogany desk with the black-enamel and gold pen set and the pictures of the family and the cream-colored clay mouse I had made and glazed in sculpture class. There was the Deer Park water cooler with the spigot that turned and the dome filled with water that gurgled as you turned the spigot. And then there were the scales.

They were jeweler's scales. They were small and delicate, and my father weighed diamonds on them. I would watch him weigh the stones, never quite understanding the meaning of carats, and I would be enthralled.

As marvelous as these moments were, there never seemed enough of them. As much as I felt my mother's involvement in my life, I felt my father's remoteness. He seemed always to be there urging me to succeed but seldom there just for fun. I remember a special walk along the Hudson River one cold and sunlit winter afternoon. I remember a night game at the old Polo Grounds, the first night baseball game I had ever been to. But there isn't too much more.

Part of this was due to the fact that as I grew older and more interested in being with my father, my father grew less and less well. He developed a heart condition, had several heart attacks, and eventually died of one in 1955, at the age of fifty-nine. I always felt that his inability to control his temper had played a part in his condition, but for many years, I also felt, quite mistakenly, that I had been indirectly responsible for his death.

This was how I remembered my father's last day.

The two of us spent a quiet Sunday afternoon at home alone. For some reason, we decided to have soft-boiled eggs and toast for dinner. After eating, we sat in the living room—a comfortable, warm room with bookshelves, a red couch, and two blue easy chairs—and talked. I said something—I don't know what—that angered my father. He got so angry he began having a heart attack. My mother rushed in and helped him to bed. She called the doctor. The doctor came. There was some commotion and muffled conversation. When I woke up the next morning, I was told my father was dead.

Years later, when I was almost thirty, I wrote the second of three wildly experimental, unpublished, adult novels. In the book was a character called The General, who might or might not have been dead. The General was based on my father, and the way in which he might or might not have died was more or less the description I have given.

I showed the manuscript to my mother, to whom I showed everything I wrote. When she had finished her reading and we sat down in her apartment to talk, she immediately brought up The General and his death.

For the first time, we actually discussed what had happened the day my father died. I had never discussed my fears or feelings of guilt with anyone, and although I hadn't intended the subject to come up in this way, I was both pleased and relieved that it had.

My mother said that I was entirely wrong, that my father's last day had been totally different from what I had imagined. It had rained, she said, and we'd spent time looking out the window. The three of us had baked a cake together and had felt very close. The heart attack had been completely unexpected, and my father had died peacefully in his sleep.

Of course I realized that my mother might have been saying these things to make me feel better, but once I'd gone over them in my mind, I knew she had not. If my fears had had any foundation, she would have wanted me to deal with them.

This conversation eliminated any feelings of blame I might have had with regard to my father's death, but it wasn't until 1983 and the publication of *Take It Easy,* my first novel for young adults, that I really came to terms with that death.

I came to writing for young adults by a route both circuitous and—incredibly—connected to my childhood. Alice Miller Bregman, a longtime children's book editor now turned children's book reviewer, had grown up at 277 West End Avenue at the same time I had. Our parents had known each other, and we were about the same age. Somewhere there was even a photograph of the two of us side by side in our baby carriages. Alice and I had known each other only slightly during those growing up years. Mostly we had run into each other visiting with Tony, the night doorman in the building, on our way home from weekend dates in high school. It was completely by coincidence that we both found ourselves in children's books.

In the late 1970s, I was back in New York from four years in Maine and starting to make a reputation as a writer of picture books. I was living on West Eleventh Street in Greenwich Village, in the same cozy apartment I'm living in now. One morning the telephone rang. It was Alice, then an editor at Delacorte Press. Would I like to have lunch?

I hadn't seen her in a long time and wondered what this might be about. But a struggling writer is not too likely to refuse a nice lunch with a friendly editor. Besides, I was flattered. Of course I said yes.

Alice took me to lunch at Le Bistro, one of the classier New York restaurants. We had a marvelous talk, and in the midst of it, she began asking me about those adolescent years when we kept running into each other visiting Tony. She'd never really known what was going on with me then, she said. She wanted me to tell her now.

So I told her, and when I was through, she said, "You know, a lot of that would make a wonderful novel."

I was struck dumb, remembering my earlier failed experiments. "But I'm not writing novels," I said. "I'm writing picture books."

"You should think about doing a novel," said Alice.

I went home, thought about it, and got distracted by picture-book projects. A year later the telephone rang. It was Alice. Would I like to have lunch?

We had another marvelous lunch. Again Alice asked if I would write the novel. Again I said I would think about it.

And once again I thought about it and did nothing.

Another year passed, and the phone rang a third time. By now I was starting to get embarrassed. When, over lunch, Alice said she thought she might be able to get me some option money from Delacorte if I would send her a proposal letter for a novel, what could I do but agree?

I wrote the proposal letter, but it was too late for the option money. Alice was just leaving Delacorte and could do nothing about the project. But at this point I was hooked. I wrote the book anyway, and it caught up with Alice at Scholastic/Four Winds Press. She bought it for them, and after a lot of rewriting and careful editing, it was eventually published.

*Take It Easy!* is a fiction. Only a few of the incidents have any basis in reality. But on a gut level, the novel is about the horrible time I had in high school and the boy who made my life miserable during those years. Thrown into the middle is the question of how, as a teenager, you cope with your father's death.

Nick Warner, the central character in the book, is fifteen when his father dies. I was thirteen, but thirteen going on twenty-one. Nick's father is a hard-driving, perfectionist New York lawyer in his forties. My father was

*"My parents, Julius and Anita Kroll, on their honeymoon," April 1937*

fifty-nine but fit all those other characteristics except lawyer. Nick's father seems as remote as mine always did, and when he dies, Nick is forced to deal with the same feelings of loss and humiliation I had to deal with. Like me, Nick refuses to go to the cemetery after attending his father's funeral. Like me, he runs off and—without thinking—goes back to school.

*Take It Easy!* went through a number of rewrites. New material was written for the beginning. Other parts of the book were moved around. The whole last section, set in a summer camp, was dropped—and eventually became the basis for my second young-adult novel, *Breaking Camp*. Through all the rewriting, the portion of the book that deals with Nick's father's death never changed. It got moved around a bit, but I had finally come so fully to terms with my father's death and the feelings surrounding it that my expression of those feelings came out whole, all of a piece, immutable.

With so much of my emotional life as a teenager coming into focus in *Take It Easy!*, the one thing that was missing was a relationship with a sister. The book had no need of a sister and no room for one, but my own relationship with my sister was very important to my growing up.

By the time I was old enough to be aware of her, June was herself a teenager. A few years after that, she was a college student, playing Titania in *A Midsummer Night's Dream* at Hollins College and then returning home, for her final two years, at the Columbia School of Painting and Sculpture.

*Steven, with his sister, June, on Riverside Drive, New York City, 1942*

My sister was going to be a painter (though she eventually became and remains a highly successful fabric designer). She was a red-haired free spirit who wore bizarre costumes to costume balls, had strange, intriguing boyfriends, and took me everywhere, sometimes even on her dates.

But best of all were the times we spent in her room. I was allowed to sit in a plaid chair and read or strum my guitar (which I was never very good at practicing) while June painted and talked to me about art and adventure. To prove the point, there is even a June Kroll portrait of Steven Kroll in chair with guitar. I think it was there and then that I got my earliest introduction to art and culture and first saw the possibility of becoming an artist. And even though it took me years to make that choice, it was in my sister's room that I think I realized I had one.

Early on, however, the whole question of our rooms involved a different kind of choice.

The apartment at 277 West End Avenue was large and spacious, with seven rooms. Through the front door, you entered an ample foyer, with the kitchen, pantry, dining room, and maid's room on the right and the living room on the left. On the other side of the foyer was a long hallway, with two bedrooms (the first with its own bathroom) on the left and another bedroom at the end on the right. All the rooms on the left faced West End Avenue. All the rooms on the right faced a back courtyard, though if you looked out the window of the back bedroom on the right, you could glimpse, through a crack between buildings, Riverside Drive and the Hudson River. The two back bedrooms, left and right, shared a bathroom between them.

I dwell on the details of the apartment because it occupies an important place in my imagination. Whenever an urban apartment or child's room appears in a story of mine, more often than not it resembles where I grew up. In two illustrated books—*Is Milton Missing?* (my first published picture book) and *T. J. Folger, Thief* (an easy-to-read mystery)—the apartment was consciously in my mind as I wrote, though inevitably the artists involved represented it differently in the pictures. In *Take It Easy!*, the apartment is more or less there, but it's located not at Seventy-third Street and West End Avenue but in a building at Seventy-ninth and Broadway.

When I was little, my bedroom was the one in the front on the left, the one with its own bathroom. I really loved this room. It had lots of light, a dark-blue linoleum floor, and two closets. I would set up a row of chairs, install myself in a blue leather one at the end, and imagine I was in a boat sailing on a deep blue sea. When I got a few years older, I would climb up the shelves along the side of one of the closets, reach the top shelf that ran all the way across, stretch out around the light bulb, and daydream for hours. Sometimes my mother would come into the room and wonder where I was.

In those years, my sister's room was the back bedroom on the right. It was a bit smaller and a lot darker. It had that weird, almost nonexistent view of the Drive and the Hudson and a bathroom to share with our parents. When I was about five, my sister decided she wanted my room.

Somehow she convinced me that this was a good idea. Her reason, as I recall, was that she needed more light for her painting, but I was so devoted to her, the reason wouldn't have mattered.

*"With my green-and-white bike," West End Avenue and Seventy-third Street, 1952*

And I took immediately to my new room. It was more out of the way, more private, and it became my sanctuary. Once I had permission, it was where I listened Friday nights to "The Lone Ranger" and "The Fat Man" on the radio and later—under the covers, with the volume turned low so no one could hear—to Johnny Addy announcing "The Friday Night Fights." It was where, on Sunday afternoons, I listened to "The Shadow" and "True Detective Mysteries" and imagined that the escaped criminal announced as "somewhere in your vicinity" at the beginning of "True Detective Mysteries" was climbing through my window. It was where I hung my horse-show ribbons (won at summer camp) and kept my rows of plastic antique cars (made out of Revel model kits) and my model airplanes. It was also where I kept my green-and-white bike and did my studying and had my bookcase full of books.

In retrospect, my childhood reading was a little unorthodox. The first book I can remember loving was Dr. Seuss's first picture book, *And to Think That I Saw It on Mulberry Street.* I never owned a copy, but I spent hours, at the age of six, poring over the text and the pictures at a large oak table in the children's section of the public library at Amsterdam Avenue and Eighty-first Street.

It was the fantasy I loved, and even though I have written as many realistic stories as I have those that are not, fantasy remains especially close to my heart.

After *Mulberry Street,* my favorite book became an odd little story by Al Graham called *Timothy Turtle.* (I'd always thought this book was about a turtle who triumphed over adversity and climbed a mountain. When I looked at it again last year, it turned out to be about a turtle who didn't quite climb the mountain but believed the publicity that said he had!) And then there were the Grimm and Andersen fairy tales and *Millions of Cats* and *The Little Engine That Could* and *Ferdinand the Bull* and *Tubby the Tuba* (which was also on a record) and *Little Toot* and of course *Winnie-the-Pooh* and eventually *Bambi* and *Alice in Wonderland.*

But before I graduated to *The Adventures of Huckleberry Finn, The Catcher in the Rye,* and *The Great Gatsby,* books I first read around the age of twelve and still count among my favorites and most important influences, I took a detour into dog and horse stories.

I had two dogs growing up. The first, a delightful, fuzzy, little mutt called Suzette, was given away when I was at summer camp and my father had one of his heart attacks. The second, a cocker spaniel puppy called Spike, was given away after he nipped my father's ankle. Those reasons provided the official explanations for the dogs' departures, but it always seemed to me that the real reasons were that my mother didn't especially like animals and was probably afraid of them. It was perhaps out of this knowledge that I became absorbed in the novels of Albert Payson Terhune.

There were many of them, and I had over a dozen. Terhune had a collie breeding farm in New Jersey, and almost all the books were about collies who did heroic things. All these collies—precursors of Lassie that they were—seemed pretty much the same dog, but that didn't bother me. As I recall, the most famous of the books was the first: *Lad: A Dog.*

Then there were the horse stories. I'd become very involved with horses at summer camp, so it seemed natural for me to want to weep through *Black Beauty.* From there, it was an easy leap to Walter Farley and the "Black Stallion" books.

I had all of them. *The Black Stallion, The Black Stallion Returns,* and *The Island Stallion* were magical to me. I loved the adventures of these spectacular horses, loved the dignity and glamour of their personalities. I wished, over and over again, that I could be part of their world. Just like other kids, I had a whole cabinet full of *Superman, Batman,* and *Archie* comic books (though I hated horror comics and still hate them and horror films even now). But Walter Farley and Albert Payson Terhune were my literary heroes.

Though I never found either one of them at the Corner Book Store, which was on Seventy-second Street between West End and Broadway. It was just down the street and around the corner from my building and across from Manbro's Drug Store, where I drank the best ice-cream sodas in the world.

Mr. and Mrs. Kramer owned the Corner Book Store. They sold books, comic books, magazines, and candy. In what was actually a terribly small space, they also had a lending library. They would let me sit on the floor near the shelves of comic books and look at anything I liked for as long as I liked. Their kindness and the coziness of their store were just the right kind of introduction to the world of books I would eventually want to join.

But even as I enjoyed my reading, I was also an athletic, outdoor kid. West End Avenue in the 1940s and 1950s was a sedate, mostly residential avenue. Except for the tearing down of the Schwab mansion across the street from 277, a sad event that took place when I was about three, zoning regulations have kept it pretty much as it was. But zoning regulations haven't kept the traffic from becoming impossible or, ironically, the increasingly upscale neighborhood from becoming less safe. When I was growing up, you could play, almost unsupervised, on West End Avenue until dark.

The boys and girls from 277 seemed to do exactly that, at least during the months when it wasn't too cold and no one was away at summer camp. Everyone gathered in front of the building after school and on weekends. There were kids from about seven to about twelve. They all more or less knew one another, and many of them played together.

The girls played hopscotch around the corner. The boys played stickball in the side street. There were games of catch and a lot of hanging out on the fenders of parked cars under the occasionally watchful eye of Gordon, the day doorman. But for some reason, what captured the most attention was a narrow ledge that ran along the front of the building.

*"With my mother, appearing in a movie short on cameras,"* 1947

At its highest point, the ledge was about five feet above the pavement; at its lowest—because the building was on a slight hill—it practically met the ground. It was set at about a forty-five-degree angle to the building, and the idea was to throw a pink rubber ball, called a Spaldeen, in the direction of the angle. If you hit it, the ball would pop up in the air. There were records for who had hit the most pop-ups, who had hit the most in a row, and so on. This endlessly boring activity occupied us for hours.

But I wasn't always hanging out in front of the building. Sometimes I was up in the penthouse with my friend Arthur Gordon, dropping water bombs on unsuspecting passersby. (Fortunately we never hit anyone. The penthouse was sixteen floors up!) Sometimes I was learning how to play gin rummy with my friend Paul Funt and his little brother, Butch. And sometimes I was in Riverside Park, just a block away.

I went there to play baseball and to ride my bike along the river, where lots of elderly ladies and gentlemen sat on benches, nodding in the sun. There was a spectacular view of New Jersey and what was then still Palisades Park, an amusement park I loved going to with my Saturday day camp. Sometimes I rode up past the softball diamonds to the boat basin, where fancy yachts and cabin cruisers were always tied up at the dock.

But mostly, in the years before I was twelve, I went to the park to climb my favorite tree and to play cops and robbers. The tree was always wonderfully difficult to climb. Near the top, it had a horizontal branch, almost totally covered in leaves, where I could sit and dream. (I had a similar spot in Central Park, a little nest near the transverse at Eighty-first Street and Central Park West, but I wasn't there so often and it wasn't as special as the tree.) When I was through dreaming, it was always fun to jump from the branch to the ground, though the distance seemed fairly great and I had to be careful how I landed.

Years later, as an adult, I went back to look at my favorite tree. It was very small, but my memories of that special branch and summoning the courage to jump down were in no way diminished by the discovery.

When we played cops and robbers, I was always the robber. When we played cowboys and Indians, I was always the Indian. Cops and cowboys had to chase robbers and Indians. Robbers and Indians got to figure out where to run and where to hide. Cops and cowboys seemed dull and unimaginative. Robbers and Indians were the artists of Riverside Park.

When I got to be older than twelve, and especially when I reached high-school age, the park took on a different dimension. By then a playground had been built and in the midst of the playground a group of basketball courts. Basketball was the one sport I was never good at, but the kids in the neighborhood all seemed to hang out at the courts and that was where the girls were. So frequently on weekend afternoons, I would be found trying to get into a game and talking to the girls, most of whom were much more interested in the big-time jocks scoring the baskets.

The world of the courts was never my world. I was always too much of a loner. Except for my position as center halfback on my high-school soccer team, the sports I liked best were individual sports: tennis and horseback riding. Though I loved the illusion of being part of the gang and loved going to the Optimo candy store on Seventy-eighth and Broadway to talk about the games, the moments I loved best at the courts were when someone suggested going to play stickball—one-on-one—at the baseball diamond down by the railroad yards.

The cement diamond was so old and full of cracks, it was almost never used for baseball anymore. Behind it was a fence concealing abandoned New York Central railroad cars. Above them, mounted on huge pillars, soared an expanse of the West Side Highway. You would stand at home plate with your broomstick bat. Your opponent would stand at the pitcher's mound and hurl a Spaldeen across the plate. There were various rules for hits, but the only way you could hit a home run was to loft that Spaldeen onto the highway.

There were several of us who played, and the only statistic we ever kept was for home runs. I never hit the most in a season, but I was second once, with fifty-two. Even now, my mind reels as I imagine all those Spaldeens bouncing onto cars on the West Side Highway.

When I wasn't in the park or in front of my building, there were all the stores on Broadway, there was tennis in Central Park, and then, of course, there were the movies.

The neighborhood had two fabulous movie theaters within walking distance of my apartment building. They were cavernous and old and filled with the elaborate ornament and detailing of a bygone era. They were the Loew's Eighty-third Street (now torn down and rebuilt as an antiseptic six-plex) and the Beacon at Seventy-fourth and Broadway (defunct as a movie house for years and now constantly in danger of passing into history). As a teenager and before, these were the places I spent rainy Saturday afternoons.

I saw *Kismet* and *The Red Badge of Courage.* I saw *Gentlemen Prefer Blondes, Three Coins in the Fountain, The Day the Earth Stood Still, The Boy with Green Hair* (which terrified me), *The Red Shoes* (which terrified me even more), *High Noon, Shane,* and a million other westerns (all of which I loved). I found movies wonderfully entertaining, but I could never take them seriously the way

I could books. Of course, once I was a teenager, the movie was no longer the point anyway.

The trouble with the movie theaters was they both had children's sections. Until you were sixteen, you were not allowed to sit anywhere else, and if you did, there was a stout, muscular matron in a white uniform, carrying a flashlight, whose specific job it was to track you down. Everyone tried to sneak into the balcony to make out. At one time or another, everyone got caught and endured the humiliation of being summarily dispatched downstairs to you know where.

By the early 1950s, of course, TV was beginning to compete with the movies. At the age of ten or eleven, I remember watching early children's shows like "The Magic Cottage," "Captain Video and His Video Rangers," and "Kukla, Fran, and Ollie" on my friend Arthur's small set with its round screen. But for me and my family, TV in those years seemed curiously irrelevant. It was a kind of reverse snobbery, but I remember being very proud to be the last one in my seventh-grade class to get a TV. And then we only got one because my sister, with money, from one of her first jobs, gave it to our parents as a present.

After the TV arrived, we all watched a little. We watched "Playhouse 90" and "Robert Montgomery Presents" and the "Hallmark Hall of Fame." We watched and were appalled by the Army-McCarthy hearings, and then there were the ritual, Sunday-night "TV suppers" when we would all gather round for "Lassie" and Ed Sullivan.

But TV never really became important to us. Even toward the end of her life, my mother hardly watched. My sister and I don't watch very much now. We have always been too busy, and in those years, for reasons unknown, I would much prefer to come home from school, spread some Arnold Brick Oven white toast with butter, pour myself a Coke, stretch out on the green chaise lounge in my mother's bedroom, and listen to those late-afternoon radio programs—"Sky King," "Stella Dallas," and "Lorenzo Jones and His Wife Belle."

But I was seldom home from school early enough for such indulgences. I spent nursery school and kindergarten at the Walden School, still a progressive private school here in New York City. After that, I went to P.S. 87, still on Seventy-seventh Street and Amsterdam Avenue (though in a new building), for first and second grades. By the time I had skipped third grade and reached Hunter College Elementary School, a school for so-called "gifted children," I was already committed to extracurricular activities.

At Hunter, I played punchball and kickball after school. I helped put together a school paper and joined a radio workshop, where we taped our own radio programs and at one point I got to play the part of Oscar, the talking seal. I was the captain of the monitors, class president several times, and Santa Claus in the sixth-grade play, though I was absolutely mortified when my sleigh carrying the presents got caught in the curtain and no amount of tugging would jar it loose.

In school and out, these years were quite idyllic for me. I was surrounded mostly by smart kids. I did my famous autobiography and got praised for it. My principal at P.S. 87 had liked some clay ducks I had made and told my parents I should go to sculpture class at the Museum of Modern Art; I did that, too, every Tuesday afternoon, and even had a piece on display in the museum. One day my mother and I were walking on Fifth Avenue when a man came running up and insisted I be in a movie short on cameras. We both ended up in the short, I was given my first camera (a Brownie), and a few months later, we were on view at our local newsreel theater! I had many friends and even—from fourth through sixth grade—a girlfriend whom I accompanied to school every day. (The boys I knew were not happy about this. They told me I would have to stop seeing Linda Berman or they would no longer be my friends. I stood my ground and prevailed.)

My one bad memory of this time concerns the flooding of the boys' bathroom when I was in sixth grade. No one knew who had done it, but for reasons that were never made clear, I was accused and marched up to the principal's office. The principal, Florence Brumbaugh, was a haughty woman who loved cats and drew a picture of one whenever she signed her name. When it became obvious I knew nothing, she sent me back to class.

Because the culprit was never caught, the stigma of suspicion never quite left me the rest of the year. Since then, except for my closest friends, I have never quite trusted human nature.

But I still loved Hunter. It was with great sadness that at the end of the sixth grade, I prepared myself for McBurney School.

*Harvard graduation, June 1962*

At that time, Hunter didn't allow boys to continue past sixth grade. My parents didn't like the local public junior high school. They didn't have the money for one of the fancy private schools in the city or in Riverdale. McBurney was considered good academically. It was at Sixty-third Street off Central Park West, just a little more than ten blocks from my home. It was under the auspices of the YMCA and eager to have me from seventh grade through high school.

The school was dark and dreary. It was all boys, and half of them were thugs. The atmosphere was relentlessly repressive, and the teachers all seemed incredibly unimaginative or, at best, eccentric.

During my seventh-grade year, the principal of the lower school, who was also the math teacher, decided we would do nothing but math. Most of our other subjects were canceled. We spent endless hours on drills and speed tests in arithmetic. When this fellow was finally fired at the end of the year, he threw open the classroom window and threatened to jump out in front of us.

And so it went. There was the history teacher who rapped you on the knuckles with his pointer if you misbehaved. There was the headmaster who wore white gloves because he had "athlete's foot of the hands," and the martinet of a gym teacher who had no respect for personal privacy, and the English teacher who asked me to grade his papers because he couldn't be bothered. There was the history teacher who always stood with his hands clasped as if in prayer, and briefly, and for me endearingly, another English teacher who loved to talk about how he'd once met Dylan Thomas in a men's room at Princeton.

With rare exceptions, my impression of these teachers was that they didn't much care about what they were doing, that they were just going through the motions. What seems amazing to me is that having such a feeling, I continued to excel.

But I was a very motivated student. I'd been pushed by my father and been told that if I wanted to get into a good college, I would have to do well. I'd decided I wanted to go to Harvard. I set out to do everything I could to get there.

I was valedictorian of my class. I was editor of the school literary magazine, business manager of the newspaper, chairman of the social committee, the leading actor in the drama group, and, as I've mentioned, center halfback on the soccer team. I was a member of every club and honor society. I was also arrogant, self-assured, and not very well liked.

The arrogance, however, concealed a feeling that there was no one in that place whose intelligence I could trust, no one on whose word I could rely. On examinations, I could never be sure what a teacher might mark me down for. So when I answered an essay question, I included not just the material that was requested but everything I knew about the subject as well. Sometimes I'd be told I didn't need to do this, but it took me a long time to stop.

I also began to notice that the stories I was starting to write at home came out sounding very different from the papers I wrote for school. The writing in the stories was relaxed and economical. The writing in the papers was stiff, contorted, filled with clumsy locutions and subordinate clauses. Without being able to do anything about it at the time, I recognized that a point was being made here, that

*The author in Paley Park, New York City, 1978*

my way of being in the world was different from the way I was at school.

And outside of school, I seemed to fare better. In my early teens, I was the well-liked recording secretary of a neighborhood boys' group called the Stags. I was bar mitzvahed and confirmed at Temple Rodeph Sholom and made some friends there. Later on, I had other neighborhood friends and girlfriends and went to dances and parties, but what made the biggest impression on me was *Venture* magazine.

*Venture* was a small, "bohemian," literary magazine published in Greenwich Village. Their editorial board met every other Friday night to read manuscripts out loud and consider them. In my senior year of high school, through a friend of a friend, I was invited to one of their meetings, got invited back, and became an unofficial member of the board.

It was the time of the Beats and smoky coffee-houses and proliferating jazz clubs. After the meetings, most of us would end up at a dive called Emilio's for pizza and beer or at Paul and Dorothy Ryan's on Grove Street. The Ryans were members of the board. They had a tiny apartment, a tiny baby, and Briscoe, a Dalmatian named after the Jewish Lord Mayor of Dublin (because Paul was Irish and Dorothy was Jewish). Paul would make his famous Dagwood sandwiches for all of us, and of course he would have beer, too.

Wherever the group ended up, the talk was of literature and philosophy and went on till dawn. As the sun rose, usually around 6:00 a.m., Paul and I, still talking of Sartre or Kerouac or Mailer, would take Briscoe for a walk in Washington Square Park.

There was no need and no place for arrogance here. These writers were serious professionals, and I was delighted and honored to be accepted by them. There were some big egos and some poor talents to go with the good, but this was my first real exposure to the world of writing, and despite having convinced myself I was going to be a lawyer, I was right at home. My mother didn't even complain about my coming in so late on those special Friday nights.

How splendid it would have been to have been able to transfer those feelings of belonging back to school. But even had that been possible, it would have been made doubly difficult by one boy.

This boy was in my class. Everyone admired him and thought he was terribly smart. He was the ringleader of a clique of smarter, more sophisticated boys called, affectionately, the "Tweed Ring," because they all wore tweedy Brooks Brothers clothes. He had a lot of power in the school, but he was below me in the class standings. He hated me for this and for my arrogance and did everything he could to make my life miserable.

When I first wrote *Take It Easy!*, Kurt Barnes defeated Nick Warner the way this boy always defeated me. By the time I had finished rewriting the book, the novelist's art had taken over from real life. Sticking it to Kurt provided a much more satisfying ending, and as I wrote the words, I felt like cheering.

How I hated McBurney School! But what's extraordinary to me is that I never told my parents. Had I said something, another school would have been found. Instead I—perhaps afraid of risking my number-one ranking—kept on slogging away.

But if there might have been a reason for my saying nothing about how I felt about school, there was really no excuse for my refusal to object to what went on at summer camp. I had gone off to my first sleep-away camp, Alderkill, in Rhinebeck, New York, just before my sixth birthday. I was never homesick, and I loved learning how to ride and play tennis at such an early age. During my third summer at Alderkill, one of the other campers told me about a special riding camp in New Milford, Pennsylvania, called Susquehanna.

Immediately I wanted to go! My parents were impressed that I'd found my own camp. The director came over with interesting slides, and for the next six summers, four as a "horseman" with my own horse to look after and one as a counselor in training, I went.

At first I wasn't popular there either. Eventually I won a best camper award. But even as my fortunes fell and rose, the riding program and the camp's facilities remained terrific. There was just a whole lot else that wasn't so terrific.

On Saturdays, there was a forced dip in a freezing cold lake at 6:00 a.m. There were late-night ritual visits to "haunted houses," where kids were purposely scared and mistreated. There was an annual, late-night walk down the Old Harmony Road, where you were shocked by dangling electric wires and, if you were unlucky, thrown naked into a stockade filled with horse manure.

When I came to write about these things in *Breaking Camp,* I pushed them one step further into evil and invented a villain to take the blame. But even now it's hard for me to make sense out of my willingness to accept what went on, summer after summer, for six years. I mentioned it in letters home, but I was never alarmed and never critical enough to make anyone take action.

After the vicissitudes of school and camp, it was a pleasure for me to get to Harvard in the fall of 1958. Cambridge was beautiful, and I was on my own. Just about everyone I met was smart. I had two odd freshman roommates, but I didn't have to spend much time with them. There were fascinating courses, interesting Radcliffe girls, and Widener Library. There were professors whose very names held me in awe, scholars like Perry Miller, Howard Mumford Jones, and Arthur Schlesinger, Jr.

Having begun to realize that I might want in some way to be involved with writing, I decided I needed a firm grounding in things American and took as my major American history and literature. But that was as close as I got to any sort of commitment. When I went to an open meeting of the *Advocate,* Harvard's distinguished literary magazine, the whole staff seemed incredibly effete and I decided not to try out. I became active in the Young Democratic Club and the drama society instead. And when it came to writing courses, I wouldn't go near one.

The writing courses were led by important people. There was even the special English S, led by Archibald MacLeish. I dismissed them all with the excuse that no one could teach you how to write.

Of course there was some truth in that notion, but the real reason why I wouldn't take a writing course at Harvard was my fear that someone would tell me I wasn't any good. Instead, on a fluke, I went to work part-time at Harvard University Press.

All through college, I held a part-time job to help pay my way. At the end of sophomore year, weary of linen delivery and dining-hall cleanup, I stopped by the university employment office. They told me the Press was looking for a "faculty aide."

It meant assisting in every department, and for the next year, that's what I did. Senior year, I did nothing but read manuscripts part-time, but the whole experience, coupled with two weeks' reading manuscripts at the *Atlantic Monthly* at the end of my junior-year summer, convinced me that what I wanted to be was an editor and critic!

My tutor/advisor junior and senior year was Walker Cowen, who later became director of the University Press of Virginia. We had become great friends and even written a paper together one Easter vacation. He was the first to really encourage me in my writing and the most important teacher I ever had. When I told Walker about my decision, he said, "Don't be an editor, my boy! Do the writing yourself!"

I wasn't ready to listen. I'd been a dean's-list student but never felt I had a handle on psyching out the professors, the way friends of mine intent on becoming academics seemed able to do. Excluding my friendship with Walker, I seemed in much the same position I'd been in in high school. What I learned outside the classroom seemed much more profitable than what I learned within it. So when graduation rolled around in June of 1962, I was eager to leave for London on the nearest plane and in the spirit of adventure begin a career in publishing!

My contacts at the Harvard Press and the *Atlantic* had given me a list of people to see in New York. Those people had given me a list for London. George Plimpton had offered me an assistant's job in the Paris office of *Paris Review,* but they weren't going to pay me and I wanted to be in London anyway. It took me three weeks of interviewing to turn up several book-reviewing assignments, an associate editorship of *Transatlantic Review,* a full-time manuscript-reader's position at Chatto and Windus Limited (publishers of Aldous Huxley, Iris Murdoch, and Henry Green), and a bed/sitting room in Chelsea (though I later moved to South Kensington and then Hampstead).

I stayed three years. C. Day-Lewis, soon to be poet laureate, was a director at Chatto. He and I became friends. Chatto had bought Leonard and Virginia Woolf's Hogarth Press after World War II. Leonard, in his eighties, was still running it, and I got to know him, too. I got invited to T. S. Eliot's memorial service at Westminster Abbey and saw Ezra Pound, wizened and alone, step out of a Bentley. I was invited to the Society of Bookmen dinner in honor of the American publisher Alfred Knopf's seventy-fifth birthday

*At the Great Wall of China, 1998*

and heard Knopf thank his hosts while confessing it was only his seventieth birthday. I went to dinner and cocktail parties at the home of Joe McCrindle, editor of *Transatlantic Review,* and met Muriel Spark, William Trevor, and L. P. Hartley. I did book reviews for the *Listener,* the *Times Literary Supplement,* the *Spectator,* and the *London Magazine.* I got promoted to reader/editor at Chatto and traveled around Europe on vacations. I got married.

Her name was Edite Niedringhaus. She was German but had become a British citizen. She was director of foreign and subsidiary rights at Chatto, but before very long and with no background in the field, she was appointed editor of children's books.

Edite and I had been a couple for a year and a half when I got drafted. It was the beginning of the Vietnam build-up, but there was still a Kennedy ruling that said no married men. Neither one of us believed in the war. The recurring growth in my right eye that we thought might get me a medical deferment failed. We made the decision to get married.

A year later, I decided to return to the States. I'd become very comfortable in England, but I'd been reviewing a lot of American books and realized I was getting out of touch. If I was ever going to do any writing, I knew it would have something to do with America. It seemed time to return to New York or Boston.

Edite, of course, came with me. The best job offer I got was as an editor at Holt, Rinehart, and Winston in New York. She became a children's book editor at Pantheon/Knopf and later at Holt. The moment we started work, the Kennedy ruling was rescinded. I got called up by the army once again, but this time the growth in my eye (now long since disappeared) got me off.

With me when I arrived in New York was the manuscript of my first adult novel. I had finished it that summer at Edite's parents' home in Germany. Walker Cowen had written to me frequently in London, saying I must write fiction. I had followed his lead. With high hopes, I got myself an agent and the book went nowhere.

During the three-and-a-half years I spent at Holt, I wrote another novel, over a series of Sundays. It, too, failed to find a publisher. Finally I found myself in a crisis of conscience and had to decide what to do with my life.

We had a new editor in chief at Holt. Shortly after his appointment, I received a manuscript of poems everyone in the department loved. But the editor in chief didn't want management to think he was going to publish books that wouldn't sell a lot of copies. He refused to let me publish (though Random House eventually did and the book was named one of the twenty best of the year by the *New York Times*).

I was furious, but I had to understand that until I became the boss, decisions like this would be made against me regularly. I had a long talk with my agent at the time. He said he believed in me, that I should get out of the business and go away and write while I was still young and unencumbered. Edite and I talked things over. At my suggestion and completely on a whim, we decided to move to Maine the following spring.

Coincidentally, we fell into a big house in North Yarmouth for eighty dollars a month. And for four years I

wrote my experimental novels and did book reviews for the *New York Times Book Review* and *Book World.* One year I taught writing at the University of Maine in Augusta, and one summer I taught riding at the local inn, where there was also a stable. Edite did translations from the German, free-lance editing, even worked in a private library in Portland. We kept on struggling and I knew I wouldn't give up, but in all that time, nothing happened with my books.

It became clear we would have to return to New York. Because Edite and other people we knew in children's books had encouraged me, I was now writing for children as well as adults. I needed to be closer to editors. Edite wanted to be back in children's book publishing. I found us an apartment, and she began looking for a job (which she found first at M. Evans and later at Harper before going out on her own as an agent).

One of the people Edite saw on her job hunt was Margery Cuyler, then children's editor at Walker and Company, soon to move to Holiday House. Edite was sure Margery would like my work.

I went to see her. After years of crossed signals, here was instant rapport. Margery took away several of my stories, came back and said she liked my imagination and what I was trying to do in *Is Milton Missing?* and *The Tyrannosaurus Game.* If I would strip those stories back to their original ideas and rewrite them according to her suggestions, she would be interested in publication.

I was overwhelmed. I also went back and did the work. *Is Milton Missing?* (1975) and *The Tyrannosaurus Game* (1976) became my first published books and my first books at Holiday House. Holiday House itself, with John and Kate Briggs at the helm, became like family. Since 1976, I have published books with several other houses, but only at Holiday House have I gone on regularly publishing two books a year. It is also wonderful to be able to count Margery, John, and Kate among my closest personal friends.

In other respects, however, my personal life was not going so wonderfully. Edite and I were divorced in 1978, and the years that followed were not easy. Now, to my delight, everything has turned around again.

In recent years, artists have been coming to me with illustrations and asking if I might write stories to go with them. *Woof, Woof!* began with a picture of a Victorian little girl and a barking bullterrier by Nicole Rubel. *Don't Get Me in Trouble!* began with a dog-food ad Marvin Glass did for the *New York Times.* And the just-published *Looking for Daniela* began with a sketchbook full of drawings by Anita Lobel.

This past Valentine's Day, I was moping in my apartment. I was sick, and I was alone. The telephone rang. It was Anita. She had just that minute finished the artwork for *Daniela!* Could she bring it over?

I wasn't about to say no. Anita arrived in half an hour, and of course the artwork was beautiful. When I had finished marveling, as we sat and talked about our lives, she said out of the blue, "I think you should meet my friend, Abby."

Abby was Abigail Aldridge, a Broadway costumer and milliner. Anita was having dinner with her that night. Why didn't I bring out a copy of one of my books with my picture on it? Anita would show the book to Abby and ask if it was okay for me to call.

It was okay. I called. We met and are now planning for the future. Could anything be a better surprise than that?

## POSTSCRIPT (Summer of 2002)

The surprises have continued. The Walden School and McBurney no longer exist in New York City. I still have that cozy, little apartment on West 11th Street in Greenwich Village; now it is just my office, not my home. The marriage to Abigail did not work out. We were divorced in 1994, but that made possible another meeting and another marriage, in 1997, to the woman I now share my life with, Kathleen Beckett. My work has broadened, deepened and moved in new directions. I have now traveled all over the world, speaking about my books and my life as a writer.

The divorce was painful, but I was fortunate because a lot was happening to distract me. In 1989 I had become Chairman of the Children's Book Authors Committee of PEN American Center, the American branch of the international writers group that works worldwide to keep free expression alive and controversial writers out of jail. I had also become a member of the PEN Executive Board.

As chair of the committee, I ran frequent meetings, planned parties, and each year organized a reading and a larger program, usually a panel discussion involving children's books. My proudest achievement was a program on censorship that incorporated the talents of students from three very different New York City schools: one public, one private, and one alternative. Each school was given a unit on censorship during the fall term. Each chose three students to participate in a panel that would discuss and then vote on whether a particular book should be censored. That discussion took place after a group of experts on both sides of the argument had made their own presentations. Held at the Bank Street College of Education auditorium, the event was a source of comment for years after.

As a member of the PEN Executive Board, I was able to help promote children's books as serious literature, something many authors of adult books (and PEN board members) were reluctant to acknowledge. This role I was eager to fill, and to my delight and surprise, the result was that both children's books and authors became a more significant—as well as a more relevant—part of PEN. Along the way, I got to know many authors, both children's and adult, as well as illustrators, and I began to think of myself as something of an impresario for children's books, a position I would like to think I continue to occupy today.

I remained the chair of the committee for seven years and a member of the board for six until we board members had rewritten the PEN by-laws and substantially changed the make-up of the organization. By the end of the seven years, I was doing a lot of traveling and was ready to move on.

But in those intervening years, my work had also blossomed. Up until then, and primarily with Margery Cuyler as my editor, I had written mostly picture books, many of them with holiday themes. They had included *One Tough Turkey* (which brought me an invitation to the White House when Barbara Bush read it on her radio show one Thanksgiving), *The Tyrannosaurus Game,* and *The Biggest Pumpkin Ever* (my most popular book ever, with a half million copies sold in the Scholastic paperback edition).

True, I had written three YA novels as well, but unfortunately, for the most part, they had been ignored.

I continued to write the picture books—*It's April Fools' Day!, The Squirrels' Thanksgiving, The Magic Rocket*—but I also began moving in the direction of chapter books and nonfiction with American historical themes.

The first chapter book was *Annabelle's Un-Birthday*. It began with my memory of inviting my entire kindergarten class home for a party without telling my mother, only to have my mother give the party as if nothing were amiss. As a book, that memory was transformed into a story about a little girl who liked her first day at a new school so much she just had to tell everyone it was her birthday and invite them all to a party at her grandma's (where she was going that afternoon).

The YA novels had been mostly about my difficult adolescence. The stories were invented, but the main characters were boys and the experiences and the pain were remembered. Now I had not only reinvented an experience of my own. I had created a main character who was a girl, given her depth and written her longer than a picture book.

I was elated, so over the next few years, I wrote more chapter books, though, for reasons unknown, I went back to focusing on boys. There were *I'm George Washington and You're Not!* (about a boy too shy to portray George Washington in the school play) and *Eat!* (about a boy who is a vegetarian). And there was my favorite: *Andrew Wants a Dog,* in which a boy whose parents will not let him have a dog becomes one for a day!

And in the middle of it all, still writing the picture books, I was invited to write an early chapter book series for Avon. The editor-in-chief was a baseball fan, and so was I. (I had grown up rooting for the underdog Boston Red Sox because my hometown Yankees always won). I had proposed an idea for a multicultural series about a group of kids on a hometown baseball team. The editor, Ellen Krieger, had loved it and gotten it approved. I found myself with a four-book contract and no stories to go with it.

I got busy. I created characters (both boys and girls) and their positions on the field. I came up with stories and wrote them around the team's games. (There's nothing like trying to construct a baseball game that will be exciting and still end up where you want it to end up). Each book focused on a different player, and the players were as multicultural as they could be. I found myself writing stories about African American, Latino, Chinese Jewish, and WASP kids. I found myself loving these kids and loving developing them from book to book, something I had not had the opportunity to do before. A second four-book contract followed the first.

By this time, I was also writing nonfiction. Back in 1988, I had written a book for Scholastic called *Oh, What a Thanksgiving!,* which combined a made-up story about a boy going to his grandma's for Thanksgiving with the real story of the first Thanksgiving. Then Scholastic asked me to write a picture book about St. Patrick's Day, and I wrote *Mary McLean and the St. Patrick's Day Parade,* in which an imagined Irish immigrant girl, new to Manhattan, eventually got to ride down Fifth Avenue in the St. Patrick's Day Parade of 1850.

Comfortable now with combining fact and fiction, I was ready when Scholastic wanted a nonfiction book about

*Steven and his wife Kathleen, cruising past the Strom-boli volcano, 1999*

the Star-Spangled Banner. The result was *By the Dawn's Early Light: The Story of the Star-Spangled Banner,* a kind of narrative history in picture book form, complete with a facsimile of Francis Scott Key's original poem. The book became so popular that the Smithsonian invited me down to Washington, D.C., to do a program when they were celebrating the start of the restoration of the flag Key had seen flying from Fort McHenry the morning after the Battle of Baltimore.

The book's popularity also inspired me to write more American history, and I did Lewis *and Clark: Explorers of the American West* and *Ellis Island: Doorway to Freedom* for Holiday House. For *Lewis and Clark,* I found myself not only exploring many avenues of research, but when it came time to do the writing, I sat surrounded by five different accounts of the journey, trying to figure out what really happened. For *Ellis Island,* I spent a lot of time on the island, absorbing the wonderful exhibition on immigration, raiding the archives, and relishing a special private tour, given by one of the librarians, of the still-abandoned hospital buildings on islands two and three.

It was around this time, in 1995, that I was invited, along with my friends—the young adult novelists Norma Fox Mazer and Harry Mazer—to speak about my work at the American school in Nairobi, Kenya. For years I had been speaking at schools and conferences all over America. This was the first time I had been invited to another country. I had always wanted to go to Africa. I was very excited.

The experience was both magical and scary. The kids were great—we were with them for a week giving talks and readings and leading workshops. Every afternoon and evening we did something wonderful. What I remember best was bargaining at the Blue Kiosks in downtown Nairobi and going, with the Mazers, to an extraordinary Ethiopian dinner at a restaurant in a private house, with white-robed Ethiopian dancers performing at the tables.

The scary part was the continual background conversation about car-jacking and other violence, as well as the police officers carrying assault rifles on the street downtown.

We were there for a second week on our own! One day I went to Isak Dinesen's house while Norma and Harry went to Lake Victoria. We spent the rest of the time on two safaris, first to the broad, open plain that is the Maasai Mara and then, farther north, to the more rugged region of Samburu. Flying in on private planes, we slept in both places in marvelous, elaborate tents and rolled out in Land Rovers to view an incredible array of animals and birds.

The couple I stayed with in Nairobi was transferring to the American Embassy School in New Delhi the following year. Before I left, they asked if I would like to visit there. Of course I said yes, never expecting an actual invitation. Imagine my surprise when I was asked to come for three weeks the following spring.

I loved India from the very first moment, when an elephant loomed up along the highway as we drove from the airport to New Delhi. The kids were great again. I had a full two weeks with this group, and every afternoon I got to explore New and Old Delhi with school staff members who knew them well. I especially liked the old city, with its narrow, crowded streets and a hidden Jain temple that looked like a giant Fabergé egg. And then there was the long weekend when I was taken to Agra to see the Taj Mahal, and on to Jaipur so I could ride up to the Amber Fort on the back of an elephant!

This was all very lovely, but my personal life was suffering. Then, in February 1997, mutual friends introduced me to Kathleen Beckett.

We were a classic New York story. We had lived around the corner from one another in Greenwich Village for twenty years and never met. Now, here we were, in a totally different part of town, meeting and liking each other.

She was smart and gorgeous. I was smitten. By spring, we were engaged. On October 4, 1997, we were married in the enchanted Gordon Reading Room at the Harvard Club of New York City, where I had done research for several books. I moved into Kathy's larger apartment on lower Fifth Avenue and kept my little place as an office. During the summer and whenever else we can, we share a two-hundred-year-old stone carriage house in Bucks County, Pennsylvania. It is in my sun porch study at the house, overlooking an expanse of green lawn, that I am writing this piece.

When I was in Nairobi, I bought a beaded African necklace. In Old Delhi, I bought a silk scarf trimmed in gold. I knew that one day both the necklace and the scarf would be for the special someone in my life. Kathy is that someone, and she wears them beautifully.

Kathy is a freelance journalist specializing in fashion, food, style, and travel. The last few years, she has done a lot of travel writing, and as a result, we have done a good deal of traveling together.

When I am invited to speak somewhere exotic, Kathy can usually turn up an assignment for that place, and off we go together, she to do her research and I to attend the conference or visit the schools. Sometimes, when Kathy is on assignment, I get to go along, either for moral support or, on a few occasions, as an on-site photographer. (My photographs have now appeared in the *Los Angeles Times* and *House Beautiful*.)

In the spring of 1998—and thanks to Marvin Terban, another children's author—I was invited to speak at schools in São Paulo and Campinas, Brazil. Kathy came along, and with her assignments, we also got to see Rio and the delectable seacoast resort town, Buzios. In November 1998, we landed in China as guests of Scholastic. I had been asked to speak at a conference in Shanghai and at schools in Shanghai and Hong Kong, but in between, we took our own trip to Beijing, where the Forbidden City and the Great Wall dazzled us.

Since then, my speaking has kept me in the States, but who could complain about trips to New Orleans, Los Angeles, San Diego, and most recently, San Francisco, with a detour, thanks to Kathy, to the Napa and Sonoma valleys.

And, of course, on her account, there have been many other adventures. In the last few years, we have been to Paris, London, Provence, Monaco, Portofino, Florence, Rome, Barcelona, the olive country of Catalonia, Mexico, the Caribbean, British Columbia, Scotland, Vietnam and the Maldive Islands (where we stayed at a fabulously exclusive resort called Soneva Fushi). Just two weeks ago, we returned from Venice and spent two days at a beautifully restored art nouveau villa on Lake Garda.

Travel or no, I had been writing new picture books and recently, what is another new departure for me, historical novels. Jamestown, the educational publisher, had decided to commission a series of eleven novels to be published in both trade and educational editions that would cover all of American history. They asked me to do two about immigration at the end of the nineteenth century. The books are called *Sweet America* and *When I Dream of Heaven*. They are about an Italian immigrant family in New York City. The first is about the eldest son, who becomes a newsboy, and the second about the daughter, who becomes a sweat shop girl. Now I was combining longer stories with history! I like both books very much.

But in between the writing of these two novels came a quite flagrant surprise. My father had died of a heart attack at fifty-nine. At fifty-seven, after a game of squash, I suffered my own heart attack and had to have quintuple bypass surgery. Kathy looked after me, and in a month, I was up and ready to speak at the International Reading Association Convention in San Diego. Then, fifteen months later, the narrowest of the five grafts blocked up and I had to have an angioplasty.

The doctors say I recovered so well and so quickly because I was in such good shape. I had played squash three times a week for decades and had none of the nasty habits or afflictions associated with heart attacks. Within weeks of the angioplasty, I was back doing what I do— traveling, speaking, and most importantly, writing. A newly illustrated version of my book *That Makes Me Mad!* has just been published by North-South/SeaStar. Last week I signed a contract with Marshall Cavendish and my long-time editor, Margery Cuyler, for a new picture book called *A Tale of Two Dogs*.

I'm looking for new challenges.

# L–M

## LAWRENCE, Iain 1955-

### Personal

Born February 25, 1955, in Sault Ste. Marie, Ontario, Canada; son of Raymond Lawrence and Margaret (Smart) Lawrence; lives with Kristin Miller (a writer). *Education:* Studied journalism in Vancouver, British Columbia, Canada.

### Addresses

*Home*—RR #1, S16, C26, Gabriola Island V0R 1XO, Canada. *Agent*—Jane Jordan Browne, Multimedia Product Development, 410 South Michigan Ave., Suite 724, Chicago, IL 60605. *E-mail*—iain@nanaimo.ark.com.

### Career

Writer. Worked as a journalist for newspapers in northern British Columbia, including the *Prince Rupert Daily News;* became editor of the *Prince Rupert Daily News.*

### Awards, Honors

Best Books for Young Adults citation, American Library Association (ALA), Quick Pick, ALA, Geoffrey Bilson Award Winner for Historical Fiction for Young People, Edgar Allan Poe Award nominee for Best Children's Mystery, Books for the Teen Age citation, New York Public Library, Editors' Choice, *Booklist,* Best Books of the Year citation, *School Library Journal,* Blue Ribbon Book, *Bulletin of the Center for Children's Books,* all 1999, all for *The Wreckers;* Best Books for Young Adults citation, ALA, Quick Pick, ALA, Blue Ribbon Book, *Bulletin of the Center for Children's Books,* Books for the Teen Age citation, New York Public Library, all 2000, all for *The Smugglers;* Notable Book, ALA, Best Books for Young Adults citation, ALA, Best Books citation, *School Library Journal,* Best Books citation, *Publishers Weekly,* Books for the Teen Age citation, New York Public Library, all 2001, all for

*Ghost Boy;* Best Children's Books citation, *Publishers Weekly,* 2001, for *Lord of the Nutcracker Men.*

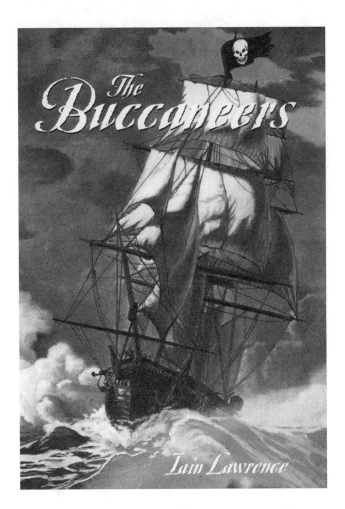

*Seventeen-year-old John and his crew encounter pirates and a mysterious sailor in a high-seas adventure set in the early nineteenth century. (Cover illustration by Patrick Whelan.)*

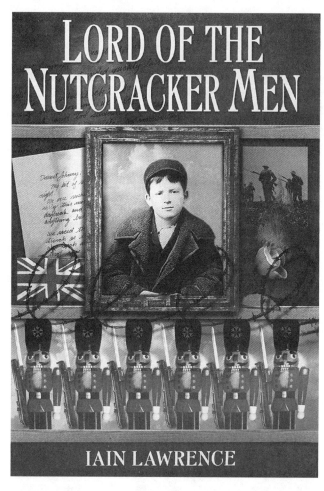

*Ten-year-old Johnny believes that the battles he enacts with his nutcracker soldiers foretell the real-life battles of his father, a World War I soldier. (Cover illustration by Steve McAfee.)*

## Writings

*YOUNG ADULT NOVELS*

*The Wreckers* ("High Seas" trilogy), Delacorte (New York, NY), 1998.
*The Smugglers* ("High Seas" trilogy), Delacorte (New York, NY), 1999.
*Ghost Boy,* Delacorte (New York, NY), 2000.
*The Buccaneers* ("High Seas" trilogy), Delacorte (New York, NY), 2001.
*Lord of the Nutcracker Men,* Delacorte (New York, NY), 2001.
*The Lightkeeper's Daughter,* Delacorte (New York, NY), 2002.

*NONFICTION*

*Far-Away Places: Fifty Anchorages on the Northwest Coast,* Orca Books (Victoria, British Columbia, Canada), 1995.
*Sea Stories of the Inside Passage: In the Wake of the Nid,* Fine Edge Productions (Bishop, CA), 1997.

## Work in Progress

Research on the Royal Air Force Bomber Command in the early years of World War II, for a story about young airmen.

## Adaptations

The novels *The Smugglers, The Wreckers,* and *Ghost Boy* are all available as audio books.

## Sidelights

With several novels and two books of nonfiction to his credit, Canadian writer Iain Lawrence has already "created an *oeuvre* that will appeal to a variety of readers," as Jeannette Hulick noted in the online *Bulletin of the Center for Children's Books.* "His books stand out from the crowd," continued Hulick, "thanks to his masterful pacing, his memorable and unusual characters, and his uncanny ability to capture the atmosphere of very specific times and places. I can't wait to see where he'll take us next."

Lawrence takes readers on high seas adventures in his trilogy of books featuring young John Spencer. Set in the late eighteenth and early nineteenth centuries, *The Wreckers, The Smugglers* and *The Buccaneers* supply "edge-of-your-seat action," according to Hulick, as well as realistically rendered settings. More history is served up in *Ghost Boy,* about an albino youth who works for a circus in the American West shortly after World War II, and *Lord of the Nutcracker Men,* which features a young boy who thinks that he controls his father's fate and the outcome of battles in France during World War I. Lawrence's 2002 novel, *The Lightkeeper's Daughter,* though set contemporaneously, also deals with the past.

Born in northern Ontario, Lawrence is the second of four children. Before he was two, the family moved to Toronto, and then proceeded to travel from home to home around Canada from Calgary to Victoria, British Columbia, so that by the time Lawrence left school, he had, as he noted on his Web site, "lived in eleven different houses and gone to nine different schools." Lawrence further noted, "It was hard at the time, as I was very shy and quite friendless, but now I think I was lucky to have grown up like that." One fond memory from his childhood is his father reading to him and his brother at bedtime. "He used funny voices for the characters," Lawrence recalled on his Web site, "and made the stories seem utterly real. I remember being enchanted with Stuart Little, and being terrified by old Blind Pew and his roguish lot from *Treasure Island.* It gave me a love of books, and of reading." Encouraged by a third-grade teacher in his writing, he also wrote picture books for his younger brother about a beloved stuffed duck.

Lawrence dropped out of high school during his last year and worked in a logging camp for a while. By the time he went back to school, he knew he wanted to be a writer. "Over the next couple of years I churned out short stories that nobody liked, a book that nobody published, and historical articles that I did sell, to a newspaper supplement," Lawrence noted on his Web site. "I lived at home, working at odd jobs that never lasted terribly long; fishing for salmon off the west coast; picking daffodils at Easter; inflating balloons and setting up skittles at a carnival; clearing streams in the Rockies; fighting forest fires on Vancouver Island; taking down the bigtop tent of a traveling circus."

Finally Lawrence saw that he was not progressing with his writing as he wished and went to journalism school for a time in Vancouver, British Columbia, and then took jobs at various small-town newspapers in northern British Columbia for the next ten years. One of these reporting stints was at the *Prince Rupert Daily News.* "For the most part I enjoyed it immensely," Lawrence reported in the biographical sketch on his Web site. "I learned a lot about writing: how to do it quickly without fretting over every word; how deadlines could be inspiring, and how to tell a story in as few words as possible. I worked my way up to become the editor of the daily paper in Prince Rupert."

Meanwhile, Lawrence was keeping up his twin passions of writing and sailing. At a writer's group, he met Kristin Miller, who became his partner, a fellow writer and quilter who lived on a remote island with no telephone or electricity. He liked this lifestyle better than his own, and finally decided to make a break with journalism. As he noted on *Teens@Random,* "journalism has a way of sponging creativity." Taking a job at a fish farm, he devoted his free time to writing and sailing. When the fish farm went bankrupt, he became a caretaker for the radio transmitter on the island.

Books were taking shape for Lawrence as well, in particular an adult title about a boy who was shipwrecked and then captured by the wreckers. When an agent suggested he rework that novel for a teen audience, he did so and the book—which had made the rounds of publishers for a couple of years as an adult title—sold within a few months as a young adult work. Lawrence's tale is set on the barren Cornwall coast of England where a community makes its living by luring ships onto the rocks near their shore. When the ships subsequently sink, the villagers loot what is left of the wreck, using tools as well as clothing from the dead sailors. When the ship *Isle of Skye* crashes on the rocks, a fourteen-year-old survives. However, will young John Spencer be able to survive the wreckers?

John watches horrified as one of the villagers approaches a half-drowned sailor and proceeds to hold the man's head under water to kill him. Escaping from these evil villagers up the cliffs, John makes his way cross country, using his wits and physical stamina, staying one step ahead of those who must kill him to keep their secret. Searching for his father, the boy stumbles across another very villainous sort, the legless Stumps, who makes threats on John's and his father's lives. "Not knowing whom he can trust," noted a contributor for

*Publishers Weekly,* "John has to feel his way through a web of intrigue and treachery."

This debut novel was greeted with widespread praise from reviewers. *Booklist*'s Carolyn Phelan compared it to the adventure novels of Robert Louis Stevenson, pointing to the book's "graceful prose, vivid details, and fast-paced action." *Horn Book Magazine*'s Mary M. Burns found the novel to be "[f]ast-moving, mesmerizing," and a tale "in the grand tradition," while Starr E. Smith concluded in *School Library Journal,* "The author expertly weaves maritime lingo and details into the narrative, creating an entertaining and engrossing nautical adventure."

The adventures of John Spencer are continued in *The Smugglers,* another "riveting high-sea adventure featuring swashbuckling characters, salty dialogue and a taut succession of cliffhangers," as described by a reviewer for *Publishers Weekly.* In this installment, John and his father buy the *Dragon,* a ship they hope to use for the wool trade. John is entranced by the vessel, but soon father and son seemed to be cursed by the schooner: their captain is murdered before they can set sail for London and the replacement they hire turns out to be a real rogue who brings on board a crew of criminal types. John also receives a mysterious message to watch out for harm from an unlikely quarter. John, now sixteen, becomes alarmed by hints at smuggling and must quickly learn to make his way among these experienced con men.

Reviewing this second book in the "High Seas Trilogy," *Booklist*'s Phelan remarked that "John makes a stalwart, sympathetic Everyman, surrounded by a cast of memorable and wildly colorful characters." Phelan concluded that the second volume of this trilogy is "a well-written period adventure." A *Horn Book Magazine* reviewer similarly praised this "thrilling adventure with enough gore and mayhem to satisfy devotees of the genre." The same reviewer concluded, "Avast, ye lubbers, for a great read!" Writing in *School Library Journal,* Smith declared *The Smugglers* a "real page-turner."

Lawrence completed his trilogy in 2001 with publication of *The Buccaneers,* in which the now seventeen year old John and the crew of the *Dragon* unwittingly put themselves in harm's way by rescuing a mysterious man in a lifeboat. This man has already crossed paths with the feared Captain Bartholomew Grace once, and, as the story progresses, Grace ultimately pursues the *Dragon.* When the captain of the *Dragon* is taken sick, it is up to John to sail the ship and bring it home safely.

Once again, reviewers applauded Lawrence's adventure yarn. This high-seas tale "offers plenty of full-blooded salty characters, cunning dialogue, surprises around every corner and a classic battle between good and evil," according to a *Publishers Weekly* contributor. Similarly, a contributor for *Kirkus Reviews* wrote, "Heavily scented with blood, gunpowder, and bracing sea air, this nautical episode makes riveting reading." Burns, writing in *Horn Book Magazine,* felt that this third installment matched the other two "for edge-of-the-seat adventure and feats of derring-do." Burns concluded that this was a "voyage not to be missed." Adding to the chorus of praise, Connie Tyrrell Burns, writing in *School Library Journal,* stated that this story "will be gobbled up by readers of the first books in the trilogy." And Phelan remarked that *The Buccaneer* was a "fine conclusion, sure to please the many readers of this richly atmospheric trilogy."

From the high seas, Lawrence turns his attention to the American Northwest shortly after World War II in a tale of belonging and learning how to fit in. Harold Kline is fourteen, extremely tall and nearly blind, as well as being an albino. It is that last characteristic that has earned him the name Ghost Boy. When a circus comes to town, he takes the first chance he gets to run off with it and escape the small town of his birth where he has been ridiculed all his life. Slowly he wins acceptance with all the other "freaks" in the circus, and when he trains the circus elephants how to play baseball, even the circus owner learns to accept Harold.

Once again, critics reacted positively to Lawrence's combination of insight and action. *Booklist*'s Frances Bradburn called it a "surprising book," one full of "pain and poignancy, with gratifying undercurrents of love and humor." A reviewer for *Publishers Weekly* remarked that this "poignant adventure invites readers to look beyond others' outer appearances and into their souls." And Toni D. Moore, reviewing *Ghost Boy* in *School Library Journal,* felt that this "touching novel will speak especially to readers who consider themselves different, flawed, or misunderstood."

Lawrence's novel *Lord of the Nutcracker Men* deals with World War I from the point of view of a ten-year-old son of one of the combatants. Before Johnny's father enlists in the English Army, he carves his son a set of toy soldiers. Now that his father is away in France, letters arrive to announce how ugly the war actually is. Also enclosed are new toy soldiers that the boy's father has carved. Increasingly, Johnny plays with these soldiers, arranging them in German and English armies, and the battles Johnny stages seem to be a foreshadowing of those his father fights in real life. Johnny suddenly begins to think that he controls the fate of his father and the entire English Army.

"This will be a fine introduction to World War I," *Booklist*'s Hazel Rochman thought, "both for personal interest and curriculum use." For Susan P. Bloom, writing in *Horn Book Magazine, Lord of the Nutcracker Men* is a "poignant, believable tale told with the sure touch of someone who shapes his craft with the same precision, imagination, and intensity as Johnny's ingenious father." In a starred *School Library Journal* review, Cheri Estes also praised Lawrence's "vivid language," further noting that through the use of first-person narration, "readers travel the heights and depths with Johnny's emotions and feel present in the story." And a critic for *Washington Post Book World* called the

book an "impressively original take on the idea that war and madness are closely allied."

In 2002, Lawrence published his sixth novel in five years. *The Lightkeeper's Daughter* is the story of seventeen-year-old Squid McCrae, who returns to the remote lighthouse island off the coast of British Columbia where she grew up. She has come to introduce her daughter to her parents, and it is a hard journey home for her. She remembers her idyllic childhood, when she and her brother Alastair explored Lizzie Island. Her brother wanted desperately to leave the island, but Squid's father would not allow it. Because of this, Squid blames her father for Alastair's subsequent death. Now, returning to this childhood home, the past and present collide as Squid strives to make sense of the death of her brother years ago.

Lawrence wrote on his Web site: "We have a home now in the Gulf Islands. We have a dog and a cat, a sailboat at the dock. We don't seem to go sailing as much as we used to; suddenly, we're too busy for that. Kristin has a quilting studio, and I have my writing. And I wouldn't change places with anyone."

## Biographical and Critical Sources

### PERIODICALS

*Booklist,* June 1 & 15, 1998, Carolyn Phelan, review of *The Wreckers;* January 1, 1999, review of *The Wreckers,* p. 782; April 1, 1999, Carolyn Phelan, review of *The Smugglers,* p. 1424; May 1, 2000, Stephanie Zvirin, review of *The Wreckers,* p. 1606; November 1, 2000, Frances Bradburn, review of *Ghost Boy,* p. 526; May 15, 2001, Carolyn Phelan, review of *The Buccaneers,* p. 1753; November 1, 2001, Hazel Rochman, review of *Lord of the Nutcracker Men,* p. 474.

*Bulletin of the Center for Children's Books,* October, 2000, Elizabeth Bush, review of *Ghost Boy,* pp. 70-71; October, 2001, Elizabeth Bush, review of *Lord of the Nutcracker Men,* pp. 64-65; July-August, 2001, Elizabeth Bush, review of *The Buccaneers,* p. 413.

*English Journal,* November, 1999, Chris Crowe, review of *The Wreckers,* p. 149; November, 2000, Ken Donelson, review of *The Smugglers,* p. 153.

*Horn Book Magazine,* July-August, 1998, Mary M. Burns, review of *The Wreckers,* p. 491; May, 1999, review of *The Smugglers,* p. 331; July, 2001, Mary M. Burns, review of *The Buccaneers,* p. 455; November-December, 2001, Susan P. Bloom, review of *Lord of the Nutcracker Men,* pp. 752-753.

*Kirkus Reviews,* May 15, 2001, review of *The Buccaneers.*

*New York Times Book Review,* April 15, 2001, review of *Ghost Boy,* p. 24; March 10, 2002, Elizabeth Devereaux, review of *Lord of the Nutcracker Men,* p. 20.

*Publishers Weekly,* June 1, 1998, review of *The Wreckers,* p. 48C; June 29, 1998, Bella Stander, "Iain Lawrence," p. 26; March 22, 1999, review of *The Smugglers,* p. 93; November 8, 1999, review of *The Wreckers,* p. 71; October 30, 2000, review of *The Smugglers,* p. 68; July 30, 2001, review of *The Buccaneers,* p. 86; March 4, 2002, review of *Ghost Boy* (audio book), p. 82.

*Resource Links,* October, 2001, K. V. Johansen, review of
*The Buccaneers,* p. 39.

*School Library Journal,* June, 1999, Starr E. Smith, review
of *The Smugglers,* p. 132; July, 2000, Pat Griffith,
review of *The Wreckers* (audio book), p. 55; September, 2000, Toni D. Moore, review of *Ghost Boy,*
p. 233; July, 2001, Connie Tyrrell Burns, review of
*The Buccaneers,* p. 110; November, 2001, Cheri Estes,
review of *Lord of the Nutcracker Men,* p. 160;
December, 2001, Claudia Moore, review of *Ghost Boy*
(audio book), pp. 74-75.

*Washington Post Book World,* January 27, 2002, review of
*Lord of the Nutcracker Men.*

OTHER

*Bulletin of the Center for Children's Books,* http://
www.lis.uiuc.edu/puboff/bccb/ (December 1, 2001),
Jeanette Hulick, "Rising Star: Iain Lawrence."

*Iain Lawrence Home Page,* http://www.randomhouse.com/
Features/iainlawrence/ (June 5, 2002).

*Red Cedar Awards,* http://www.redcedar.swifty.com/ (January 9, 2002), author profile of Iain Lawrence.

*Teens@Random,* http://www.randomhouse.com/ (June 5,
2002).*

\*      \*      \*

# McCLUNG, Robert M(arshall) 1916-

## Personal

Born September 10, 1916, in Butler, PA; son of Frank
A. (a banker) and Mary A. (Goehring) McClung;
married Gale Stubbs (an editor), July 23, 1949; children:
William Marshall, Thomas Cooper. *Education:* Princeton University, A.B., 1939; Cornell University, M.S.,
1948. *Religion:* Protestant.

## Addresses

*Agent*—c/o Linnet Books, an imprint of The Shoe String
Press, Inc., 2 Linsley St., North Haven, CT 06473.

## Career

McCann, Erickson, Inc. (advertising agency), New
York, NY, copywriter, 1940-41, 1946-47; New York
Zoological Park, New York, NY, assistant in animal
departments, 1948-52, curator of mammals and birds,
1952-55; National Geographic Society, Washington,
DC, editor, 1958-62; freelance writer and illustrator of
children's books, 1955-58, 1962—. *Military Service:*
U.S. Naval Reserve, active duty as deck officer and
naval aviator, 1941-46; became lieutenant commander.

## Awards, Honors

Eva L. Gordon Award, American Nature Study Society,
1966, for outstanding achievement in children's science
literature; American Library Association (ALA) notable
book citation, and *School Library Journal* best book
citation, both 1969, both for *Lost Wild America;*
National Science Teachers Association outstanding sci-

*Robert M. McClung documents the past, present, and
future of America's wildlife and the American
conservation movement in* Lost Wild America, *illustrated by Bob Hines.*

ence books for children citations, 1972, for *Scoop, Last
of the Brown Pelicans,* 1974, for *Gypsy Moth: It's
History in America,* 1975, for *Sea Star,* 1977, for
*Peeper, First Voice of Spring,* 1980, for *Green Darner:
The Story of a Dragonfly,* 1981, for *Vanishing Wildlife
of Latin America,* 1982, for *Rajpur, Last of the Bengal
Tigers,* 1984, for *Gorilla,* 1987, for *Whitetail,* and 1988,
for *Lili: A Giant Panda of Sichuan;* Children's Science
Book Award honorable mention, New York Academy of
Sciences, 1975, for *Gypsy Moth: Its History in America;*
Golden Kite Award, Society of Children's Book Writers,
1977, for *Peeper, First Voice of Spring;* Golden Kite
honor book, Society of Children's Book Writers, 1979,
for *America's Endangered Birds: Programs and People
Working to Save Them;* Spur Award second-place honor,
Western Writers of America, 1990, for *Hugh Glass,
Mountain Man.*

## Writings

*Vulcan: The Story of a Bald Eagle,* illustrated by Lloyd
Sandford, Morrow (New York, NY), 1955.

*Little Burma,* illustrated by Hord Stubblefield, Morrow
(New York, NY), 1958.

*Whooping Crane,* illustrated by Lloyd Sandford, Morrow
(New York, NY), 1959.

*Otus: The Story of a Screech Owl,* illustrated by Lloyd
Sandford, Morrow (New York, NY), 1959.

*Shag, Last of the Plains Buffalo,* illustrated by Louis
Darling, Morrow (New York, NY), 1960, new edition,
Linnet Books (Hamden, CT), 1991.

*Mammals and How They Live,* illustrated with photographs,
Random House (New York, NY), 1963.

*Screamer, Last of the Eastern Panthers,* illustrated by
Lloyd Sandford, Morrow (New York, NY), 1964.

*Honker: The Story of a Wild Goose,* illustrated by Bob
Hines, Morrow (New York, NY), 1965.

*The Swift Deer,* illustrated with photographs, Random
House (New York, NY), 1966.

*The Mighty Bears,* illustrated with photographs, Random House (New York, NY), 1967.

*Black Jack, Last of the Big Alligators,* illustrated by Lloyd Sandford, Morrow (New York, NY), 1967, new edition, Linnet Books (Hamden, CT), 1991.

*Lost Wild America: The Story of Our Extinct and Vanishing Wildlife,* illustrated by Bob Hines, Morrow (New York, NY), 1969, revised edition published with additional illustrations by McClung, Linnet Books (Hamden, CT), 1993.

*Thor, Last of the Sperm Whales,* illustrated by Bob Hines, Morrow (New York, NY), 1971.

*Treasures in the Sea,* illustrated with photographs, National Geographic Society (Washington, DC), 1972.

*Samson, Last of the California Grizzlies,* illustrated by Bob Hines, Morrow (New York, NY), 1973, new edition, Linnet Books (Hamden, CT), 1992.

*How Animals Hide,* illustrated with photographs, National Geographic Society (Washington, DC), 1973.

*Creepy Crawly Things: Reptiles and Amphibians,* illustrated with photographs, National Geographic Society (Washington, DC), 1974.

*Lost Wild Worlds: The Story of Extinct and Vanishing Wildlife of the Eastern Hemisphere,* illustrated by Bob Hines, Morrow (New York, NY), 1976, revised edition, Shoe String Press (Hamden, CT), 1993.

*Animals That Build Their Homes,* illustrated with photographs, National Geographic Society (Washington, DC), 1976.

*Peeper, First Voice of Spring,* illustrated by Carol Lerner, Morrow (New York, NY), 1977.

*Hunted Mammals of the Sea,* illustrated by William Downey, Morrow (New York, NY), 1978.

*America's Endangered Birds: Programs and People Working to Save Them,* illustrated by George Founds, Morrow (New York, NY), 1979.

*Snakes, Their Place in the Sun,* illustrated with photographs, Garrard (Easton, MD), 1979, revised edition, illustrated by David M. Dennis, Holt (New York, NY), 1991.

*Vanishing Wildlife of Latin America,* illustrated by George Founds, Morrow (New York, NY), 1981.

*Rajpur, Last of the Bengal Tigers,* illustrated by Irene Brady, Morrow (New York, NY), 1982.

*Mysteries of Migration,* illustrated with photographs, Garrard (Easton, MD), 1983.

*Gorilla,* illustrated by Irene Brady, Morrow (New York, NY), 1984.

*The True Adventures of Grizzly Adams,* illustrated with old prints, Morrow (New York, NY), 1985.

*Whitetail,* illustrated by Irene Brady, Morrow (New York, NY), 1987.

*Lili: A Giant Panda of Sichuan,* illustrated by Irene Brady, Morrow (New York, NY), 1988.

*Hugh Glass, Mountain Man,* illustrated with old prints and paintings, Morrow (New York, NY), 1990, published as *Hugh Glass, Mountain Man: Left for Dead,* Beech Tree Books (New York, NY), 1993.

*America's First Elephant,* illustrated by Marilyn Janovitz, Morrow (New York, NY), 1991.

*Old Bet and the Start of the American Circus,* illustrated by Laura Kelly, Morrow (New York, NY), 1993.

*Last of the Wild: Vanished and Vanishing Giants of the Animal World,* illustrated by Bob Hines, Linnet Books (Hamden, CT), 1997.

*SELF-ILLUSTRATED*

*Wings in the Woods,* Morrow (New York, NY), 1948.

*Sphinx: The Story of a Caterpillar,* Morrow (New York, NY), 1949, revised edition, illustrated by Carol Lerner, 1981.

*Ruby Throat: The Story of a Hummingbird,* Morrow (New York, NY), 1950.

*Stripe: The Story of a Chipmunk,* Morrow (New York, NY), 1951.

*Spike: The Story of a Whitetail Deer,* Morrow (New York, NY), 1952.

*Tiger: The Story of a Swallowtail Butterfly,* Morrow (New York, NY), 1953.

*Bufo: The Story of a Toad,* Morrow (New York, NY), 1954.

*Major: The Story of a Black Bear,* Morrow (New York, NY), 1956.

*Green Darner: The Story of a Dragonfly,* Morrow (New York, NY), 1956, revised edition, illustrated by Carol Lerner, 1980.

*Leaper: The Story of an Atlantic Salmon,* Morrow (New York, NY), 1957.

*Luna: The Story of a Moth,* Morrow (New York, NY), 1957.

*All about Animals and Their Young,* Random House (New York, NY), 1958.

*Buzztail: The Story of a Rattlesnake,* Morrow (New York, NY), 1958.

*Whitefoot: The Story of a Woodmouse,* Morrow (New York, NY), 1961.

*Possum,* Morrow (New York, NY), 1963.

*Spotted Salamander,* Morrow (New York, NY), 1964.

*Caterpillars and How They Live,* Morrow (New York, NY), 1965.

*Ladybug,* Morrow (New York, NY), 1966.

**JAGUAR**
*Panthera onca*

*McClung examines the reasons for the destruction or threatened destruction of sixty species in America, in* **Last of the Wild.** *(Illustrated by Bob Hines.)*

*Moths and Butterflies and How They Live,* Morrow (New York, NY), 1966.

*Horseshoe Crab,* Morrow (New York, NY), 1967.

*Redbird: The Story of a Cardinal,* Morrow (New York, NY), 1968.

*Blaze: The Story of a Striped Skunk,* Morrow (New York, NY), 1969.

*Aquatic Insects and How They Live,* Morrow (New York, NY), 1970.

*Bees, Wasps, and Hornets, and How They Live,* Morrow (New York, NY), 1971.

(With Lloyd Sandford) *Scoop, Last of the Brown Pelicans,* Morrow (New York, NY), 1972.

*Mice, Moose, and Men: How Their Populations Rise and Fall,* Morrow (New York, NY), 1973.

*Gypsy Moth: Its History in America,* Morrow (New York, NY), 1974.

*Sea Star,* Morrow (New York, NY), 1975.

*The Amazing Egg,* edited by Emilie McLeod, Dutton (New York, NY), 1980.

*OTHER*

Also editor and contributor to books published by the National Geographic Society, including *Wild Animals of North America; Song and Garden Birds of North America; Water, Prey and Game Birds of North America;* and *Vacationland U.S.A.;* contributor to *Grolier's New Book of Knowledge,* and to magazines.

McClung's manuscripts and papers are held at the Princeton University Library and the Jones Library in Amherst, MA.

## Sidelights

Robert M. McClung presents the world of science and its many inhabitants to young people through fictionalized stories based on facts. His books, many of which are self-illustrated, deal with specific species and their life cycles, conservation, and the threat of extinction. Much of McClung's success stems from his ability to blend the facts of nature into the shape of a story. He gives names to the animals he discusses and incorporates elements of drama and emotion into the narratives. McClung "is a natural story teller, with a flair for making a child feel he knows the animals as friends," asserted *Christian Science Monitor* contributor Millicent Taylor. He does not avoid the harshness of reality or give the animals human characteristics, though. "McClung may be the best interpreter of natural science now writing for young people," maintained Don Lessem in *Appraisal: Science Books for Young People.*

McClung has been interested in animals, and in writing and illustrating, for as long as he can remember. As a small boy he became an enthusiastic collector of butterflies and moths, and always kept a few wild pets of one kind or another around the house. He also wrote and illustrated many wild adventure stories for his own amusement. His interest in the insect world provided the theme, and his grandfather's farm the setting for his first book, *Wings in the Woods.* Along with telling the story of ten-year-old Dan's first year spent living on a farm,

*Wings in the Woods* also introduces young people to the world of butterflies and moths. Anne Thaxter Eaton pointed out in the *Christian Science Monitor* that the story gives an authentic "feeling of country life" which will invite young people to experience it for themselves.

In many of his books, McClung singles out one particular animal, whether a salmon or a hummingbird, and takes readers through part of its life cycle, usually from birth to maturity. "I try to interest kids in an animal and get them to appreciate it for what it is," explained McClung in a *Hartford Courant* interview with Pam Luecke. In *Spike: The Story of a Whitetail Deer,* McClung narrates the first year of a young fawn's life and the many learning experiences he encounters. Although he portrays the deer frolicking in the meadow and feeding on lily pads, McClung also includes such threats to their lives as hunters, forest fires, and other animals. Spike's story is "presented in dramatic style" and is accompanied by "lively" illustrations, commented *Library Journal* contributor Elizabeth Hodges.

*Bufo: The Story of a Toad* introduces a character not as familiar to children. The story begins with Bufo as a tadpole and follows his life as he matures to a toad. McClung reveals Bufo's characteristics and the threats to his existence as the story progresses. Louise S. Bechtel wrote in the *New York Herald Tribune Book Review* that upon seeing a toad for the first time, a child "should hear read aloud this delightful, short nature book." *Lili: A Giant Panda of Sichuan* develops in the same manner as the story of Bufo. The book begins at Lili's birth and follows her as she grows into adulthood, and finally into motherhood. McClung adds historical information, though, and includes a chapter on man's interests in the panda over the years. He also discusses the threat of extinction and the measures being taken to prevent it. "The physical descriptions provide a keenly evocative visual image of a panda's natural habitat," observed *School Library Journal* contributor Susan Nemeth McCarthy. And Melissa Greene commented in the *Washington Post Book World:* "The book is well-written, fast-moving and engrossing, and Irene Brady's wonderful pen-and-ink drawings bring Lili and the bamboo forest vividly to life."

McClung further pursues his interest in endangered animals and conservation in such books as *Lost Wild America: The Story of Our Extinct and Vanishing Wildlife, Lost Wild Worlds: The Story of Extinct and Vanishing Wildlife of the Eastern Hemisphere,* and *America's Endangered Birds: Programs and People Working to Save Them.* He traces man's effect on nature and its inhabitants over a period of many years in *Lost Wild America,* and his discussion of animal extinction adds to what *School Library Journal* contributor Elizabeth F. Grave called "a thorough and sobering account of wild life in America." The book went on to become "a staple on library shelves," in the words of *Booklist's* Carolyn Phelan, who welcomed its 1993 updated and expanded edition as a "useful, readable book." Other reasons for vanishing species, such as the movement of predators and the destruction of suitable habitat, are also mentioned, as are the difficulties of preservation legislation. *Lost Wild Worlds* deals with similar information, covering a different location—the eastern hemisphere. Through Europe, Africa, Asia, Australia, New Zealand, and Indian Ocean islands, McClung traces man's arrival and his instant as well as gradual effects on the animals' environment. Sarah Gagne, writing in *Horn Book,* saw *Lost Wild Worlds* as providing "a welcome source of information on the status of over fifty species of animals." And Sophie Jakowska asserted in *Science Books and Films* that McClung plays the "role of informing and alerting the reader to the history of wildlife destruction and to the various practices used to help endangered wildlife." McClung continues that role in his most recent book, *Last of the Wild: Vanished and Vanishing Giants of the Animal World.* Here he details more than sixty species of animals that have been destroyed or are immediately threatened across the globe. "Part travelogue and part history," as Randy Meyer described it in *Booklist,* the book examines the conditions that have led to the animals' plight as well as successful programs of captive breeding, hunting bans, and wildlife refuges. "The scope is broad," Meyer observed, "and the book will be an excellent starting point for research projects as well as good browsing material for animal lovers."

In *The True Adventures of Grizzly Adams,* McClung takes on the role of biographer, narrating the events of the adult life of Grizzly Adams. McClung gives a realistic portrait of the man and what he was; unlike the television image, Adams was a fierce hunter who often killed unnecessarily. Adams came from the East during the California gold rush and became a trapper, animal trainer, and performer, spending the last part of his life in New York with P. T. Barnum. "Adams' activities were so extraordinary that they read as if created expressly to be the substance of dime novels," claimed *School Library Journal* contributor George Gleason. Ethel R. Twichell, writing in *Horn Book,* maintained: "The good, solid account of Adams's adventures brings him into a more accurate focus but in no way diminishes his skill in hunting, his respect for the animals he both killed and trained, and his incredible toughness."

McClung once commented on the content and purpose of his works: "Practically all my books deal with wild animals and the natural environment. Unfortunately, more and more of the vital habitat that wildlife needs for survival is being polluted or destroyed by the actions of *Homo sapiens.* Through the years I have increasingly stressed in my writings the importance of a healthy environment and the conservation and wise use of all earth's resources. My aim in all of my books is to heighten the reader's awareness and appreciation of nature, and to develop his or her interest in and sympathy for all living things. The sooner a child develops an appreciation of the world he lives in, and realizes that it could be destroyed, the better prepared he will be to make sane and wise choices when he becomes an adult."

## Biographical and Critical Sources

### BOOKS

*Children's Literature Review,* Volume 11, Gale (Detroit, MI), 1986.

Kingman, Lee, and others, editors, *Illustrators of Children's Books: 1967-1976,* Horn Book (Boston, MA), 1978.

*Something about the Author Autobiography Series,* Volume 15, Gale (Detroit, MI), 1993.

Ward, Martha E., and others, editors, *Authors of Books for Young People,* 3rd edition, Scarecrow Press (Metuchen, NJ), 1990.

### PERIODICALS

*Appraisal: Science Books for Young People,* spring, 1971, p. 24; spring, 1972; winter, 1974, p. 26; fall, 1975, p. 21; fall, 1976, p. 29; winter, 1979, pp. 26-27; spring, 1980, p. 48; fall, 1980, pp. 45-46; fall, 1981, pp. 27-28; winter, 1982, p. 43; spring-summer, 1983, Don Lessem, review of *Rajpur, Last of the Bengal Tigers,* p. 36; fall, 1983, p. 40; summer, 1985, p. 22; winter, 1988.

*Booklist,* November 15, 1972, p. 302; November 15, 1974, p. 344; February 15, 1981, p. 810; June 15, 1981, p. 1403; July, 1983; January 15, 1985, p. 719; February 1, 1986, p. 811; January 1, 1994, Carolyn Phelan, review of *Lost Wild America: The Story of Our Extinct and Vanishing Wildlife,* revised edition, p. 823; July, 1997, Randy Meyer, review of *Last of the Wild: Vanished and Vanishing Giants of the Animal World,* p. 1808.

*Book Report,* November-December, 1985, p. 43.

*Bulletin of the Center for Children's Books,* January, 1972, p. 76; June, 1972, p. 159; September, 1973, p. 12; June, 1974, p. 160; January, 1978, p. 82; May, 1981, p. 176; October, 1982, p. 31; December, 1985, p. 72; June, 1987; July-August, 1988, p. 234.

*Childhood Education,* February, 1978, p. 198; September-October, 1981, p. 51.

*Children's Book Review Service,* January, 1977, p. 48.

*Christian Science Monitor,* December 16, 1948, Anne Thaxter Eaton, "Year on a Farm," p. 19; May 10, 1956, Millicent Taylor, "Bird and Animal Tales," p. 15; May 3, 1978, p. 85.

*Hartford Courant,* April 11, 1976, Pam Luecke, "Children's Author Chronicles Lives of Ladybugs, Skunks."

*Horn Book,* June, 1977, Sarah Gagne, review of *Lost Wild Worlds: The Story of Extinct and Vanishing Wildlife of the Eastern Hemisphere,* p. 339; February, 1979, p. 93; February, 1980, p. 85; October, 1981, p. 558; November-December, 1985, Ethel R. Twichell, review of *The True Adventures of Grizzly Adams,* pp. 751-752; September-October, 1993, review of *Old Bet and the Start of the American Circus,* p. 625.

*Kirkus Reviews,* September 1, 1969, p. 934; April 1, 1971, p. 374; August 15, 1971, p. 879; April 1, 1972, p. 407; September 1, 1974, p. 947; February 1, 1980, p. 139; February 15, 1981, p. 217.

*Library Journal,* October 15, 1952, Elizabeth Hodges, review of *Spike: The Whitetail Deer,* p. 1823; February 1, 1977, p. 398.

*New Yorker,* December 12, 1988, p. 158.

*New York Herald Tribune Book Review,* October 10, 1954, Louise S. Bechtel, review of *Bufo: The Story of a Toad,* p. 10.

*Publishers Weekly,* July 26, 1976, p. 79.

*School Library Journal,* September, 1969, Elizabeth F. Grave, review of *Lost Wild America,* p. 169; May, 1970, p. 90; November, 1970; October, 1971; September, 1973; November, 1973, p. 52; March, 1975, p. 98; October, 1975, p. 100; November, 1976, p. 71; September, 1978, p. 131; October, 1979, p. 160; September, 1980, p. 75; April, 1981, p. 128; January, 1982; November, 1982, p. 102; August, 1983, p. 68; January, 1985, p. 77; November, 1985, George Gleason, review of *The True Adventures of Grizzly Adams,* pp. 99-100; September, 1987, p. 189; September, 1988, Susan Nemeth McCarthy, review of *Lili: A Giant Panda of Sichuan,* p. 192; November, 1990, p. 145.

*Science Books,* September, 1969, p. 181; December, 1969, p. 257; December, 1970, p. 241; March, 1972, p. 312; September, 1972, p. 155.

*Science Books and Films,* May, 1976, pp. 40-41; September, 1977, Sophie Jakowska, review of *Lost Wild Worlds,* p. 82; September, 1978, pp. 112, 161; September, 1979, pp. 89-90; September-October, 1980, p. 33; March-April, 1982, p. 216; September-October, 1983, p. 34; May-June, 1985, p. 309; November-December, 1987; November-December, 1988, p. 100.

*Voice of Youth Advocates,* December, 1985, pp. 33-34.

*Washington Post Book World,* March 20, 1977, p. H4; May 8, 1988, Melissa Greene, "Stalking on the Wild Side," p. 21.*

\*            \*            \*

# McELLIGOTT, Matt(hew) 1968-

## Personal

Born December 8, 1968, in Albany, NY. *Education:* Alfred University, B.F.A., 1990; State University of New York—Buffalo, M.A.H., 1992.

## Addresses

*Agent*—c/o Author Mail, McGraw-Hill Companies, 1221 Avenue of the Americas, New York, NY 10020. *E-mail*—matt@mcegraphics.com.

## Career

Sage Colleges, Albany, NY, assistant professor, beginning 1998; children's book author and illustrator.

## Writings

(And illustrator) *The Truth about Cousin Ernie's Head,* Simon & Schuster (New York, NY), 1996.

(And illustrator) *Uncle Frank's Pit,* Viking (New York, NY), 1998.

(Illustrator) Steve Patschke, *The Spooky Book,* Walker & Co. (New York, NY), 1999.

(Illustrator) Norton Juster, *The Phantom Tollbooth,* McGraw-Hill (New York, NY), 2000.

## Work in Progress

*Absolutely Not!,* for Walker & Co. (New York, NY), expected in 2004.

## Biographical and Critical Sources

*OTHER*

*Matt McElligott,* http://www.mattmcelligott.com/ (April 6, 2002).*

\*            \*            \*

# MILELLI, Pascal 1965-

## Personal

Born 1965, in Madrid, Spain; immigrated to Canada, 1967. *Education:* Graduated from Alberta College of Art, 1988; attended the University of Calgary.

*Pascal Milelli illustrates one spring day in the life of a boy and his dog on an island in the Pacific Northwest. (From* Rainbow Bay, *written by Stephen Eaton Hume.)*

## Addresses

*Home*—Vancouver, British Columbia, Canada. *Office*—#609, 402 West Pender St., Vancouver, British Columbia, Canada V6B 1T6. *E-mail*—pascal@ pascalmilelli.com.

## Career

Artist and freelance illustrator. Has worked with the British Columbia Securities Commission, the University of British Columbia, the Vancouver Opera, Kniepp Netherlands, and Brew King. Apprenticed at CBC Television, the *Calgary Herald,* and Cal Graphica.

## Awards, Honors

Elizabeth Mrazik-Cleaver Canadian Picture Book Award, 1997, Amelia Frances Howard-Gibbon Illustrator's Honour Book, Canadian Association of Children's Librarians, 1998, and Our Choice selection, Canadian Children's Book Center, 1998-99, all for *Rainbow Bay.*

## Illustrator

Stephen Eaton Hume, *Rainbow Bay,* Raincoast Books (Vancouver, Canada), 1997.
Susan Vande Griek, *The Art Room,* Douglas & McIntyre (Toronto, Canada), 2002.

Milelli's illustrations have appeared in the *Vancouver Sun, Harper's, Atlantic Monthly, Sunday Express* (England), and *Éditions du Seuil* (France).

## Biographical and Critical Sources

*OTHER*

*Pascal Milelli Web Site,* http://www.pascalmilelli.com/ (February 27, 2002).
*Raincoast Books,* http://www.raincoastkids.com/ (January 17, 2002).*

# N

## NAIDOO, Beverley 1943-

### Personal

Born May 21, 1943, in Johannesburg, South Africa; daughter of Ralph (a composer and music copyright manager) and Evelyn (a broadcaster and theater critic; maiden name, Levison) Trewhela; married Nandhagopaul Naidoo (a solicitor), February 1, 1969; children: Praveen, Maya. *Education:* University of Witwatersrand, South Africa, B.A., 1963; University of York, B.A. (with honors), 1967, Certificate of Education, 1968; University of Southampton, Ph.D., 1991.

### Addresses

*Home*—13 Huntly Rd., Bournemouth, Dorset BH3 7HF, England. *Agent*—Gary Carter, Roger Hancock Ltd., 4 Water Lane, London NW1 8NZ, England.

### Career

Kupugani Non-Profit Nutrition Corporation, Johannesburg, South Africa, field worker; primary and secondary teacher in London, England, 1969-79; writer, 1985—; researcher, 1988-91; Advisory Teacher for Cultural Diversity and English, Dorset, England, 1988—; visiting fellow, University of Southampton.

### Member

British Defence and Aid Fund for Southern Africa's Education Committee, Writers' Guild for Great Britain, National Association for Teachers of English.

### Awards, Honors

Other Award, *Children's Book Bulletin,* 1985, Children's Book Award, Child Study Book Committee at Bank Street College of Education, 1986, Children's Books of the Year selection, Child Study Association of America, 1987, Parents' Choice Honor Book for Paperback Literature, Parents' Choice Foundation, 1988, and

*Beverley Naidoo*

Notable Children's Trade Book in the Field of Social Studies, National Council for the Social Studies/Children's Book Council (NCSS/CBC), all for *Journey to Jo'burg: A South African Story;* Notable Children's Trade Book in the Field of Social Studies, NCSS/CBC, 1990, and Best Book for Young Adults selection, American Library Association, 1991, both for *Chain of Fire;* Carnegie Medal, 2000, short-listed for the Smarties Prize in the age 9-11 category, 2000, Top of the List winner for Youth Fiction, *Booklist,* 2001, both for *The Other Side of Truth.*

## Writings

### FOR CHILDREN

*Journey to Jo'burg: A South African Story,* illustrated by Eric Velasquez, Longman (London, England), 1985, Lippincott (Philadelphia, PA), 1986.

(Editor) *Free As I Know,* Bell & Hyman (London, England), 1987.

*Chain of Fire,* Collins (London, England), 1989.

*Letang's New Friend,* illustrated by Petra Rohr-Rouendaal, Longman (London, England), 1994.

*No Turning Back: A Novel of South Africa,* HarperCollins (London, England), 1997.

*The Other Side of Truth,* HarperCollins (New York, NY), 2001.

### FOR ADULTS

(Editor) *Censoring Reality: An Examination of Books on South Africa,* ILEA Centre for Anti-Racist Education and British Defence/Aid Fund for Southern Africa, 1985.

(Editor) *Through Whose Eyes? Exploring Racism: Reader, Text and Context,* Trentham Books (London, England), 1992.

Contributor to academic journals, including *English in Education* and *Researching Language and Literature.*

## Sidelights

South African expatriate Beverley Naidoo's books about the evils of the apartheid system and of homelessness in "the new South Africa" brought her and the issues she writes about into the international spotlight. Prior to the May 1994 election of the first black majority government headed by African National Congress leader Nelson Mandela, Naidoo wrote a series of groundbreaking books, including *The Journey to Jo'burg* and *Chain of Fire,* intended to educate young people on the evils of racism in her homeland. In the years since the dismantling of apartheid, Naidoo has turned her attentions to more general concerns. One of these is the plight of homeless street children, which she discussed in *No Turning Back: A Novel of South Africa,* and she has also covered the issue of racism in her own adopted country, England, in *The Other Side of Truth.* She commented in *Twentieth-Century Young Adult Writers* that she now writes to challenge herself by broadening her perspective and to inform, educate, and entertain her readers, particularly children. "Writing is a journey. It is a way of exploring the country of my childhood from the perspective of the child I was not," she explained.

Beverley Naidoo was born into an upper middle-class family in Johannesburg, South Africa. She grew up in a world of privilege where whites patronizingly referred to African males—of any age—as "boys" and females as "girls." Naidoo was raised by a black nanny whom she knew only as "Mary." As a girl, young Beverley was happily oblivious to the fact that her care giver had three

young children of her own who lived nearly two hundred miles away. Mary seldom saw her own family because she had to work in town to support them. One particular incident that occurred when Naidoo was eight or nine has stayed with her: "Mary received a telegram and collapsed. The telegram said that two of her three young daughters had died. It was diphtheria—something for which, I as a white child, had been vaccinated," Naidoo stated in her acceptance speech for the 1986 Award of the Child Study Children's Book Committee, reprinted in *School Library Journal.* It took Naidoo years to realize the significance of that event. She continued, "I must have continued to spout with the arrogance of white youth the customary rationalizations—that Mary and those who followed her, were lucky because we gave them jobs, sent presents to their children at Christmas, and so on. I still feel intensely angry about the racist deceptions and distortions of reality which the adult society passed on to me as a child."

Following her high school graduation, Naidoo attended the University of Witwatersrand, but what she learned outside of the classroom proved to be far more important than anything she learned in it. "It was a period of growing state repression and as I gradually began to see for the first time some of the stark reality all around me, I became intensely angry not only at the narrowness of my schooling, but at its complicity in perpetuating apartheid through not previously challenging my blinkered vision," Naidoo wrote in *Through Whose Eyes? Exploring Racism: Reader, Text and Context.* She became politicized and joined in the anti-apartheid movement. Although she was a "small fish," as she puts it, Naidoo was detained by police in 1964 under the "Ninety Days" solitary confinement law. That experience forever changed the way she viewed life in South Africa. The following year, Naidoo moved to England to study at the University of York, supporting herself for a time by teaching school.

Naidoo had always resisted her mother's suggestion that she should become a teacher. Now, having seen and experienced for herself the impact of education as a tool in the fight against apartheid, Naidoo pursued a career in the classroom. Almost as important, she continued to expand her own horizons by reading about what she terms "the reality [that] she had left behind" in South Africa. Two of the books that Naidoo found to be particularly influential in her own life were *The African Child* by Camara Laye and *Roaring Boys* by Edward Blishen.

"The contexts were so different—Laye's memories of a West African childhood and Blishen's semi-autobiographical novel of a young teacher's initiation into the violence of schooling and youth culture in London's East End," Naidoo stated. "Within each of [these books] I hear a strong, implicit commitment to education as a process of opening out and questions being raised about the nature of schooling, power, young people and society." Inspired by these messages, Naidoo earned a B.A. with honors from York in 1967 and then received her teaching certificate the following year. For the next decade, she taught primary and secondary school in London. She also became involved with an anti-apartheid group and began to look for ways to educate young people about the dangers of racism in general and of the South African apartheid system in particular.

During the 1980s, Naidoo began doing research for the Education Group of the British Defence and Aid Fund for Southern Africa, an activist organization that aided victims of apartheid and worked to raise the world's awareness of human rights abuses in South Africa. Naidoo's efforts helped make people aware of the alarming shortage of suitable teaching materials about apartheid and resulted in the publication of a critical bibliographical study called *Censoring Reality: An Examination of Books on South Africa,* which Naidoo edited. When the Education Group decided to commission a work of "informed and helpful fiction" on apartheid, she volunteered to write it. "I wrote the text simply, quite deliberately," she explained. Naidoo penned the story as if she were telling it to her own children, she recalled, because "it seemed important to be able to explain at their level what was happening in South Africa."

The fruit of Naidoo's efforts was a juvenile novella called *Journey to Jo'burg: A South African Story.* The story deals with the adventures that a young black girl named Naledi and her younger brother Tiro have when they travel to Johannesburg in search of their mother, who works there in a white household as a domestic servant—just as Naidoo's own care giver Mary had done. The children set out on the three-day journey because their baby sister is critically ill and their grandmother, who cares for them in their mother's absence, has no money for medicine or a doctor. The journey is an eye-opener for the children as they encounter the ugly realities of life for black people under apartheid.

Reviews for *Journey to Jo'burg* were mixed. In *School Library Journal* JoAnn Butler Henry said that she appreciated the book. "A short story with a wealth to share, this well-written piece has no equal," she wrote. Gillian Klein, writing in the *Times Educational Supplement,* found the novel a work of "uncompromising realism." In *Booklist,* however, Hazel Rochman stated, "This is not great fiction: story and characters are thinly disguised mechanisms for describing the brutal social conditions and the need for change." Whatever they thought of the quality of Naidoo's writing, critics and readers alike agreed that her subject material was as powerful as it was shocking. As a result, the book achieved the desired effect: it helped to draw the world's attention to the anti-apartheid struggle. *Journey to Jo'burg* was banned by the South African government, and it won several children's book awards in the United States and the United Kingdom.

Encouraged by the success of her first book, Naidoo pressed ahead in her literary efforts. She edited an anthology of poems, short stories, and extracts for young people called *Free As I Know.* Reviewer Bill Deller in

the *Times Educational Supplement* explained the three criteria behind the selections: "The idea of the seminal experience whereby young people gain insight into themselves and society; the concentration on perspectives that may be passed over in a white monocultural society and the desire to include 'stimulating literature of an international character.'"

In 1989 Naidoo produced a sequel to *Journey to Jo'burg,* an adolescent novel called *Chain of Fire.* In it, Naidoo revisits Naledi, the central character in *Journey to Jo'burg,* who is now fifteen years old. *Chain of Fire* tells of the ordeal of Naledi, her family, and their neighbors as they face eviction and enforced resettlement to a "black homeland" called Bophuthatswana. Apartheid laws prevented Naidoo from living in South Africa, so she did all of her research for *Chain of Fire* by interviewing other South African expatriates and by reading whatever books and articles she could find about the government's ethnic cleansing policies. "I immersed myself in the devastating data on the mass destruction of the homes and lives of millions of South Africans by the apartheid regime through its program of 'Removals' to [these] so-called 'Homelands,'" Naidoo once commented. "*Chain of Fire* is dedicated to all those who have struggled to resist and I hope it will enable young people in various parts of the world to feel links of both heart and mind to Naledi and others like her who refuse to let the flames of justice be smothered."

Many reviewers praised *Chain of Fire.* "The work flows effortlessly, with power and grace, as it succeeds in making a foreign culture immediate and real," wrote Marcia Hupp in *School Library Journal.* "*Chain of Fire* is not easy reading, nor should it be; it tackles tough issues head-on and presents them with superb dramatic tension," Diane Roback declared in *Publishers Weekly.* The book's "chief strength lies in the moving representation of family and village life," said Peter Hollindale of the *Times Educational Supplement.* And reviewing the novel in *Kliatt,* Sherri Forgash Ginsberg felt that it would be "uplifting" for young adults to read a book about their peers "who have the courage to stand up for what they believe."

Naidoo's next book was *Through Whose Eyes? Exploring Racism,* a collection of articles by English schoolchildren who were writing about literature they had read and about their own interactions with black visitors to their mostly white school; Naidoo served as editor. In 1994, she wrote a children's book entitled *Letang's New Friend.*

Naidoo's next book for young readers was *No Turning Back: A Novel of South Africa.* This story is about the adventures of a twelve-year-old African boy named Sipho who flees an abusive stepfather and runs away to a new life on the mean streets of Johannesburg. Sipho quickly learns about survival in the "new South Africa." He gets involved with a street gang, sleeps in the gutters, begs for food, and experiments with glue sniffing in an effort to escape his misery. In the end, he finds refuge in a shelter where he has the chance to go to school. "The problems [Sipho] faces are those experienced by street children internationally. However they are also those of a child struggling to make sense of his world at a time of turbulent historical change," Naidoo said in the *Seventh Book of Junior Authors and Illustrators. No Turning Back* is a stark, powerful, uncompromising look at the plight of abused and homeless street children, according to numerous reviewers.

Amy Chamberlain praised *No Turning Back* in her *Horn Book* review as "a can't put down account of an impoverished South African boy." In *Publishers Weekly,* Diane Roback and Elizabeth Devereaux felt that the book was written "effortlessly from the boy's point of view, so that his confusion, eagerness and naive wishes unfold naturally." A contributor for *Kirkus Reviews* was less impressed, describing the book as "bland [and] uninvolving" and noting "the story lacks the fire that made *Journey to Jo'burg* so compelling." Elizabeth Bush, reviewing the novel in *Bulletin of the Center for Children's Books,* also felt that Naidoo "toned down" Sipho's struggles "for middle-grade consumption," shepherding the youth through street danger like a "literary guardian angel." However, Hazel Rochman, writing in *Booklist,* felt that the book did have the power of Naidoo's earlier novels, and something more. "This time the social realism is just as authentic," wrote Rochman, "but there is more personal focus." *Voice of Youth Advocates* critic Beth E. Anderson also noted that Naidoo "brings to her readers the reality of homeless children," and ends her tale with a "glimmer of hope," as Sipho seeks a place at a children's shelter. And *Magpies* contributor Nola Allen called the novel "eloquent and compassionate."

In the post-apartheid era, Beverley Naidoo has persisted in her struggle for human rights. She delivers lectures and holds workshops on anti-racist and multicultural themes. She also conducts creative writing seminars and has said that she intends to continue writing about life in the land of her birth. "South Africa is now in the process of great historical change but, as in the U.S., the rifts and scars of racism run deep. Writing allows me to use my imagination to challenge the segregation of experience caused through discrimination," Naidoo stated in *Twentieth-Century Young Adult Writers.*

Naidoo moved beyond the boundaries of South Africa both politically and geographically with her 2001 title, *The Other Side of Truth.* A pair of Nigerian children, Sade and her younger brother Femi, find themselves in great danger after assassins accidently shoot their mother. The assassins meant to kill their father, an outspoken journalist in this tale set during the political unrest in Nigeria of the 1990s. Shipped off to London, the children soon discover that their university professor uncle has abandoned them and gone into hiding after being threatened himself. Detained and interviewed by the police and immigration authorities, the two remain silent, frightened to reveal anything about themselves in case they would put their father in jeopardy.

Sade and her brother are placed in a foster home, but the kindness experienced there cannot compensate for their sense of dislocation and for the harassment they experience at school. Soon their father manages to enter England illegally; at first overjoyed, the children's jubilation turns to fear when he is arrested and subsequently goes on a hunger strike. Sade manages to get on the evening news to tell her father's harrowing story, and once public attention is drawn to the case, he is released. But this is not the happy end for them. Sade, her brother, and her father must learn to find a way in their new life.

*The Other Side of Truth* was warmly received by critics. Gerry Larson, writing in *School Library Journal,* thought that Naidoo "captured and revealed the personal anguish and universality of the refugee experience" in her novel. Other reviewers had similar praise. *Horn Book* reviewer Nell D. Beram, for example, dubbed the novel a "scrupulously well-observed narrative," and further commented that it not only "honors its political and ethical engagements," but also "succeeds as a first-rate escape-adventure story." *Booklist*'s Rochman similarly noted that *The Other Side of Truth* "brings the news images very close," while Stephanie Zvirin, also writing in *Booklist,* felt that Naidoo "raises tough questions." The book was also honored with a prestigious British award, the Carnegie Medal.

Interviewing Naidoo in *Booklist,* Rochman asked how the author was able to maintain the child's viewpoint in *The Other Side of Truth.* "I think that's the transformation process," Naidoo explained. "I spend a lot of time doing research. But then I dump most of the documentary stuff, get away from it, and imagine one child's story. I'm very interested in the experience of the child of political parents.... Yes, the adults have courage and integrity, but what is the cost to their children?" Naidoo further explained that she wanted to do a book set in London. "I was getting tired of readers pointing fingers at South Africa.... I wanted to look at things right here, including the increasing racism." With *The Other Side of Truth,* as in her earlier novels, Naidoo shows, but does not preach. "That's the great thing about fiction," she concluded to Rochman. "There is no one answer. There are no blueprints."

## Biographical and Critical Sources

*BOOKS*

*Children's Literature Review,* Volume 29, Gale (Detroit, MI), 1993.

Gallo, Donald R., editor and compiler, *Speaking for Ourselves, Too,* National Council of Teachers of English (Urbana, IL), 1993.

Holtze, Sally Holmes, editor, *Seventh Book of Junior Authors and Illustrators,* H. W. Wilson (New York, NY), 1996.

Naidoo, Beverley, *Through Whose Eyes? Exploring Racism: Reader, Text and Context,* Trentham Books (London, England), 1992.

*Twentieth-Century Young Adult Writers,* first edition, St. James Press (Detroit, MI), 1994.

*PERIODICALS*

*ALAN Review,* spring, 1997.

*Booklist,* March 15, 1986, Hazel Rochman, review of *Journey to Jo'burg,* p. 1086; March 15, 1990, p. 1430; October 1, 1990, p. 351; March 15, 1991, p. 1478; December 15, 1996, Hazel Rochman, review of *No Turning Back,* p. 724; December 15, 2001, Hazel Rochman, review of *The Other Side of Truth,* p. 723; January 1, 2002, Hazel Rochman, "The Booklist Interview: Beverly Naidoo," p. 830; February 15, 2002, Stephanie Zvirin, review of *The Other Side of Truth,* p. 1034.

*Book Report,* September-October, 1997, Karen Sebesta, review of *No Turning Back,* pp. 38-39.

*Bulletin of the Center for Children's Books,* May, 1986, p. 175; May, 1990, p. 223; February, 1997, Elizabeth Bush, review of *No Turning Back,* p. 217.

*Children's Literature Association Quarterly,* summer, 1988, pp. 57-60.

*English Journal,* September, 1986, p. 81; March, 1995, p. 55.

*Five Owls,* May, 1990, p. 90; March, 1991, p. 70.

*Horn Book,* September-October, 1990, p. 607; March-April, 1997, Amy Chamberlain, review of *No Turning Back,* p. 203; November-December, 2001, Nell D. Beram, review of *The Other Side of Truth,* pp. 756-757.

*Journal of Reading,* April, 1991, pp. 574-578.

*Kirkus Reviews,* March 15, 1990, p. 428; December 1, 1996, review of *No Turning Back.*

*Kliatt,* May, 1993, Sherri Forgash Ginsberg, review of *Chain of Fire,* p. 10.

*Los Angeles Times Book Review,* January 28, 1990, p. 15.

*Magpies,* March, 1996, Nola Allen, review of *No Turning Back,* p. 36; September, 2002, Sophie Masson, "Know the Author: Beverley Naidoo," pp. 10-12.

*Publishers Weekly,* May 30, 1986, p. 67; March 30, 1990, Diane Roback, review of *Chain of Fire,* p. 64; January 25, 1993, p. 88; December 16, 1996, Diane Roback and Elizabeth Devereaux, review of *No Turning Back,* p. 60.

*School Librarian,* May, 1989, p. 75; February, 1996, p. 31; August, 1996, p. 96.

*School Library Journal,* August, 1986, JoAnn Butler Henry, review of *Journey to Jo'burg,* p. 96; May, 1987, Beverly Naidoo, "The Story behind 'Journey to Jo'burg,'" p. 43; May, 1990, Marcia Hupp, review of *Chain of Fire,* pp. 108, 113; February, 1997, p. 104; September, 2001, Gerry Larson, review of *The Other Side of Truth,* p. 231.

*Times Educational Supplement,* April 26, 1985, Gillian Klein, review of *Journey to Jo'burg,* p. 26; May 20, 1988, Bill Deller, "Breadth of Vision," p. B21; March 10, 1989, Peter Hollindale, "Bound to Protest," p. B15; October 2, 1992, p. 9; July 7, 1995, p. 20; July 5, 1996, p. R8.

*Tribune Books* (Chicago), February 26, 1989, p. 8.

*Voice of Youth Advocates,* August, 1986, p. 148; June, 1990, p. 108; October, 1996, p. 199; October, 1997, Beth E. Anderson, review of *No Turning Back,* p. 246.

*Wilson Library Bulletin,* November, 1990.*

\*    \*    \*

# NICHOLS, Peter
## See YOUD, (Christopher) Sam(uel)

# O–P

## ORLEV, Uri 1931-

### Personal

Original name Jerzy Henryk Orlowski; given name changed to Uri, 1945, surname changed to Orlev, 1958; born February 24, 1931, in Warsaw, Poland; son of Maksymilian (a physician) and Zofia (Rozencwaig) Orlowski; immigrated to Palestine (now Israel), 1945; married Erella Navin, 1956 (divorced, 1962); married Ya'ara Shalev (a dance therapist), November 19, 1964; children: Li (daughter; first marriage), Daniella, Itamar (son), Michael (second marriage).

### Addresses

*Home*—Yemin Moshe, 4 Ha-berakhah, Jerusalem, Israel.

### Career

Writer, 1962—. Member of Kibbutz in Lower Galilee, Israel, 1950-62. *Military service:* Israeli Army, 1949-51.

### Member

Hebrew Writers Association.

### Awards, Honors

Awards from Israeli Broadcast Authorities, 1966, for "The Great Game," 1970, for "The Beast of Darkness," and 1975, for "Dancing Lesson"; Television Prize, 1979, for youth program *Who Will Ring First?,* and Television Prize, 1991, for television script, "The Dream of the Chinese Crown Prince"; prize from Youth Alia, 1966, for *The Last Summer Vacation;* Prime Minister Prize (Israel), 1972 and 1989, for body of work; Ze-ev Prize, Israel Ministry of Education and Culture, 1977, and International Board on Books for Young People (IBBY) Honor List (Israel), 1979, both for *The Beast of Darkness;* Haifa University Prize for Young Readers, 1981; IBBY Honor List (Israel), 1982, *Horn Book* Books of 1984 honor list citation and American Library

*Uri Orlev*

Association (ALA) Notable Book of the Year, both 1984, Sydney Taylor Book award, Association of Jewish Libraries, Mildred L. Batchelder Award, ALA, Edgar Allan Poe Award runner-up, Mystery Writers of America, and Jane Addams Children's Book Award Honor Book, Jane Adams Peace Association, all 1985, Silver

Pencil Prize (Holland), for best book translated to Dutch, 1986, Honor Award, Ministry of Youth, Family, Women, and Health of the Federal Republic of Germany and West Berlin, 1987, and first recipient of Janusz Korczak International Literary Prize (Poland), 1990, all for *The Island on Bird Street;* high commendation, Collective Promotion of the Dutch Book (CPNB), 1989, honor list, Auswahlliste Deutscher Jugendliteraturepreis, 1991, honor list, Catholic Youth Book Prize, 1991, Blue Ribbons list, *Bulletin of the Center for Children's Books,* 1991, Mildred L. Batchelder Award, ALA, 1991, Story Book Honor Title, Parent's Choice, 1991, and National Jewish Book Award, Children's Literature category, Jewish Book Council, 1992, all for *The Man from the Other Side;* Notable Book list, *New York Times Book Review,* 1993, and Book Parade Prize, Ministry of Science and Art and Ministry of Education, Culture, and Sport, Israel, 1995, for *Lydia, Queen of Palestine;* 1995 Honor Award, Jane Addams Peace Association and Women's International League for Peace and Freedom; Notable Children's Books citation, *Booklist,* and Mildred L. Batchelder Award, ALA, both 1996, both for *The Lady with the Hat;* Hans Christian Andersen Award, IBBY, 1996, for body of work; Yad Vasham Brune Brandt Award, and Zeew Prize, Ministry of Education, both 1997, both for *The Sandgame;* Holon Municipality Prize, 1997, for *The Song of the Whales.*

## Writings

*FICTION; IN ENGLISH TRANSLATION*

*Hayale-oferet* (adult novel), Sifriat Paolim, 1956, reprinted, Keter (Jerusalem), 1989, translation from the original Hebrew by Hillel Halkin published as *The Lead Soldiers,* P. Owen, 1979, Taplinger, 1980.

*ha-I bi-Rehov ha-tsiporim,* Keter, 1981, translation from the original Hebrew by Hillel Halkin published as *The Island on Bird Street,* Houghton, 1984.

*Ish min ha-tsad ha-aher,* Keter, 1988, translation from the original Hebrew by Hillel Halkin published as *The Man from the Other Side,* Houghton, 1991.

*Lidyah, malkat Erets Yisra'el* (based on the life of the Israeli poet Arianna Haran), Keter, 1991, translation from the original Hebrew by Hillel Halkin published as *Lydia, Queen of Palestine,* Houghton, 1993.

*Hagueret Im Hamigbaat,* Keter, 1990, translation from the original Hebrew by Hillel Halkin published as *The Lady with the Hat,* Houghton, 1995.

*FOR CHILDREN; IN HEBREW*

*The Beast of Darkness* (also see below), Am Oved (Tel Aviv, Israel), 1976.

*The Big-Little Girl,* Keter (Jerusalem, Israel), 1977.

*The Driving-Mad Girls,* Keter (Jerusalem, Israel), 1977.

*Noon Thoughts,* Sifriat-Poalim (Tel Aviv, Israel), 1978.

*How Mr. Cork Made the Brain Work,* Givatayim, Massada, 1979.

*It's Hard to Be a Lion,* Am Oved (Tel Aviv, Israel), 1979.

*The Lion Shirt,* Givatayim, Massada, 1979.

*Siamina,* Am Oved (Tel Aviv, Israel), 1979.

*The Good Luck Passy,* Am Oved (Tel Aviv, Israel), 1980.

*Granny Knits,* Givatayim, Massada, 1980.

*Mr. Meyer, Let Us Sing,* Givatayim, Massada, 1980.

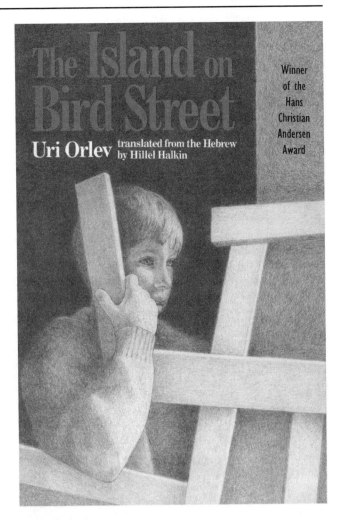

*A Jewish boy must survive on his own for months in a Warsaw ghetto during World War II. (Cover illustration by Jeanne Titherington.)*

*Wings Turn* (short stories), Givatayim, Massada, 1981.

*Big Brother,* Keter (Jerusalem, Israel), 1983.

*The Dragon's Crown* (science-fiction novel), Keter, 1985.

*Journey to Age Four,* Am Oved (Tel Aviv, Israel), 1985.

*Shampoo on Tuesdays,* Keter (Jerusalem, Israel), 1986.

*The Wrong Side of the Bed,* Keter (Jerusalem, Israel), 1986.

*Mouthful of Meatball,* Keter (Jerusalem, Israel), 1995.

*The Sandgame,* Elefanten Press (Berlin, Germany), 1995.

*Last of Kin,* Keter (Jerusalem, Israel), 1996.

*The Wandering Family,* Keter (Jerusalem, Israel), 1997.

*The Song of the Whales,* Keter (Jerusalem, Israel), 1997.

*Run Boy, Run,* Keter (Jerusalem, Israel), 2001.

*FOR ADULTS; IN HEBREW*

*Til Tomorrow* (novel), Am Oved (Tel Aviv, Israel), 1958.

*The Last Summer Vacation* (short stories), Daga, 1967.

*SCRIPTS; IN HEBREW*

*The Great Game* (juvenile), Israel Broadcasting Authority, 1966.

*Dancing Lesson,* Israel Broadcasting Authority, 1970.

*The Beast of Darkness* (juvenile), Israel Broadcasting Authority, 1975.

*Who Will Ring First* (juvenile), Israel Broadcasting Authority, 1979.

*TRANSLATOR; FROM POLISH TO HEBREW*

Henryk Sienkiewicz, *In the Desert and Jungle,* Y. Marcus (Paris), 1970.

*The Stories of Bruno Schulz,* Schocken, 1979.

Janusz Korczak, *King Matthew I,* Keter, 1979.

Janusz Korczak, *King Matthew on a Lonely Island,* Keter, 1979.

Stanislaw Lem, *Eden,* Massada, 1980.

Stanislaw Lem, *Pirx the Pilot,* Schocken, 1981.

Stanislaw Lem, *The Invincible,* Schocken, 1981.

Janusz Korczak, *The Little Jack's Bankruptcy,* Hakibutz Hameuchad, 1985.

Janusz Korczak, *Kajtus the Wizard,* Am Oved, 1987.

Stanislaw Lem, *Return from the Stars,* Keter, 1988.

Stanislaw Lem, *The Star Diaries,* Keter, 1990.

Kornel Makuszinski, *The Devil of the Junior Year,* Zmora-Bitan, 1990.

Kornel Makuszynski, *Journey in the Sign of Dog,* Zmora-Bitan, 2000.

Henryk Sienkiewicz, *Quo Vadis,* Zmora-Bitan, 2002.

*Orlev tells the true story of Israeli poet Arianna Haran, who as a girl played fantasy games with her dolls in which she was the Queen of Palestine. (Cover illustration by Todd Doney.)*

## Sidelights

"Uri Orlev's life and works are a testimony to the indomitable spirit of childhood," wrote Meena Khorana in *Bookbird.* Khorana's article celebrates the Polish-born Israeli author's 1996 Hans Christian Andersen Award, the most prestigious of all international prizes given to an author for young people. Although Orlev writes in Hebrew, translations of his works, which include three adult novels and more than a dozen novels for children and young adults, have garnered him an admiring audience worldwide. The handful of his books available in English translation have won him numerous prizes, including three Mildred L. Batchelder awards for best foreign language book translated into English. When granting the Hans Christian Andersen Award, the prize jury commended Orlev's work, in a statement quoted by Khorana. "Whether his stories are set in the Warsaw Ghetto or his new country Israel," they observed, "he never loses the view of the child he was. His stories have integrity and humour, while his characters learn a loving, accepting attitude towards others—the lesson of how to accept being different in an alien world."

The alien world of which Orlev writes so eloquently in his novels is a nightmare realm of childhood memories of war-torn Poland. When Nazi leader Adolf Hitler became chancellor of Germany in 1933, the author was a toddler living in Warsaw, as yet unaware of his Jewish identity. In the years that followed, the true horror of Hitler's anti-Jewish policies became evident even to children. Jews living in Germany, and then other countries occupied by the German army, were forced to endure multiple injustices, including losing their jobs or their businesses because of their heritage. In 1939, Hitler's troops invaded Poland, marking the beginning of World War II and the onset of severe persecution of Polish Jews.

Orlev's family, like Jewish families throughout Poland, was forced to leave their home and move into a wall-enclosed section of the city, called the ghetto. There, the living accommodations were crowded, with food rationed and unemployment widespread. In an effort to eliminate the European Jewish population, the Germans soon built concentration camps, some with facilities for gassing inmates, and began mass deportations of the Jews out of the ghettos and into the camps. By the war's end, millions of Jews and other persons considered detrimental to German society had been killed in the camps and elsewhere. Although a child, Orlev was spared none of the brutality of the war; his mother was murdered by the Nazis and he and his brother and the aunt who cared for them spent nearly two years in a concentration camp at Bergen-Belsen, Germany.

The horrors of the war would ultimately give Orlev material for future writing projects, but his talent as a storyteller grew out of the awful, surreal existence of his childhood. "From an early age, I read a lot," Orlev said in his acceptance speech for the Hans Christian Andersen Award. "My favorites were war and adventure stories. The more I read, the more jealous I became.

Why did such exciting things happen to the heroes of the books, while all that ever happened to me was being forced to eat by my nanny, to take my afternoon nap, and to go to school every day? School was what I hated most."

When the realities of what was going on around him became too much for the boy, his imagination provided a refuge from the uncertainty of daily existence. In *Something about the Author Autobiography Series* (*SAAS*), Orlev described how his imagination created a buffer between his feelings and reality as he and his relatives fled a burning building during the bombing of Warsaw. "After a month of German shelling, my family found itself fleeing a building that had gone up in flames," Orlev said in his Hans Christian Andersen Award speech. "Fire shot out the windows, timbers cracked from the heat, walls came crashing down, screaming women jumped from the top story."

As they fled, the stark reality of the situation brought a realization to Orlev. "Every now and then," he recalled in *SAAS,* "we stopped to stare at the unbelievable sight of the large city burning in the quiet night, the flames lighting the lower half of the sky. It dawned on me that I was now living in a book myself." Being a character in a book somehow made the unbearable easier to bear. In a similar example, Orlev excuses himself for referring to episodes in his life that happened during the war as "adventures." "I talk about adventures," Orlev explained, "because that's how it seemed to me: I thought of myself as the hero of a thriller who had to survive until the happy ending on the book's last page, no matter who else was killed in it, because he was the main character."

Luckily for Orlev, fate provided the dreamed-of happy ending. Orlev's wartime experiences concluded in April 1945 when the U.S. Army rescued him, his brother, and his aunt from a train at Bergen-Belsen. Orlev and his relatives were among only 350 survivors of the 3,000 Jews brought to the camp from Warsaw. After the war, with their mother dead and their father captured on the Russian front while serving in the Polish Army, Orlev and his brother were sent to Palestine with a group of other Jewish children whose relatives hoped for a better life there for their offspring. Both boys completed their education at a kibbutz, or farming collective, in their new home, and, after the State of Israel was created by a United Nations mandate in 1948, fulfilled their required service in the Israeli army. Orlev and his brother were not reunited with their father until 1954. While Orlev's brother later chose to move to the United States, the author decided to stay in Israel. There he attempted to again write the poetry that he had begun to produce during the war, but, as he once commented in *Twentieth-Century Young Adult Writers,* "When I tried to write poetry, I found that I was no longer able to. So I began to write stories, and later, books for adults. Not until I was forty-five did I write my first book for young people, *The Beast of Darkness.*"

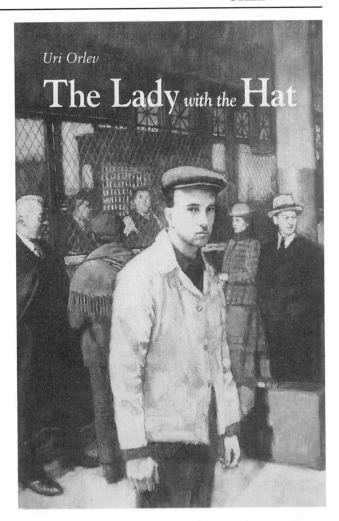

*A young man leaves his Polish homeland after World War II and tries to enter Palestine to begin a new life.* (*Cover illustration by Todd Doney.*)

While Orlev has become best known for his books for young people, his first novel as well as his first work translated into English, *The Lead Soldiers,* was aimed at adults. The story is very close to being an autobiography. The protagonists are two Jewish boys, Yurik and his younger brother Kazik, who live in Warsaw during World War II. After their mother dies, the boys are cared for by their aunt. Eventually, the threesome end up in the concentration camp at Bergen-Belsen, but survive the war and are saved from their German captors by members of the U.S. Army. Critics found the description of the war through the eyes of the children especially powerful. In *New York Times Book Review,* reviewer Leslie Epstein expressed admiration for the novel, while presenting the belief that Orlev "used [the book] to teach himself his craft." The constant dialogue between the brothers, according to Epstein, "are the very tissue of the novel, and they secure for it, I think, a place in the gallery of holocaust literature only a little below that reserved for the finest portraits of children." In *New Statesman,* reviewer Victoria Neumark asserted, "*The Lead Soldiers* touches one of the most poignant stories of the Holocaust, the story of the butterflies children drew on the walls before they went into the gas chambers, keeping faith with their imaginary worlds in the optimism of a Stoic who can't see beyond the moment." A *Publishers Weekly* reviewer called the novel "an unforgettable story that makes its mark as literature."

Orlev's next novel to be translated into English is the acclaimed *The Island on Bird Street.* It, too, is autobiographical, but to a lesser degree. The story takes place in a Jewish ghetto, but not necessarily the Warsaw ghetto, during World War II. It follows the activities of eleven-year-old Alex, who is awaiting the return of his father from a labor camp. Alex must somehow manage to survive by himself in a bombed out building on Bird Street, a street filled with vacant buildings. In the author's introduction to the novel, Orlev explained how Alex's hideaway is in many ways similar to the island on which Daniel Defoe's fictional hero Robinson Crusoe found himself. "[Alex] must survive by himself for many months," Orlev commented, "taking what he needs from other houses the way Robinson Crusoe took what he needed from the wrecks of other ships that were washed up on the beach. The difference is that Alex can't grow his own food, that he has to hide, and that he has no spring to get water from." Orlev also noted that while Alex has no man Friday to keep him company, he does enjoy the companionship of his pet mouse, who even helps to find him food. "And, yes," Orlev added, "one more thing: Alex has hope."

The optimism that Neumark found in Orlev's *The Lead Soldiers* plays a major role in this novel as well. "The power of the book comes through Alex's unwavering hope," maintained Gary D. Schmidt in *Twentieth-Century Young Adult Writers,* "his sense that he will do whatever it takes to survive and wait for his father." In his *Christian Science Monitor* review of the book, Randy Shipp also mentioned "the thread of hope that runs throughout the book," making it stand out from other similar war stories. Orlev's ability to blend recollections of his own experiences with the fictional exploits of his hero garners praise from other reviewers of the work. "The physical details are fascinating," noted Zena Sutherland in *Bulletin of the Center for Children's Books.* The author's familiarity with the life he is writing about, according to Margery Fisher in *Growing Point,* gave "a stark reality" to the prose and allows him to let the reader enter "right into a boy's mind." By "drawing on his own World War II experiences as a child in the Warsaw ghetto," Kate M. Flanagan observed in *Horn Book Magazine,* Orlev produced "a first-rate survival story."

In Orlev's next work translated into English, *The Man from the Other Side,* the author again tells a story of a boy who must survive in a Polish ghetto during World War II. This time Orlev brings to life a friend's story instead of drawing on his own background. In the prologue to the book, entitled "A Word about My Friend Marek," Orlev explained that the novel is a fictionalized version of the life of a Polish photojournalist whom he met in Israel. The photojournalist made Orlev promise not to tell his story publicly until after he was dead; the author wrote the novel after the man died in the crash of a Polish jetliner just months after their conversation. In *The Man from the Other Side,* Orlev presents the photojournalist as fourteen-year-old Marek, a boy who is finally deemed old enough to be of help to Antony, his stepfather. Antony smuggles food through the sewers of Warsaw to the Jews living in the ghetto. Marek dislikes Antony and wishes his father—who was killed in prison for being a communist—was still alive. One day Marek and two of his friends rob a Jew who has escaped from the ghetto. Marek's mother is enraged when she discovers what her son has done. Tearfully, she reveals to him that although he has not been raised a Jew, his biological father was Jewish. Marek is troubled by his mother's disclosure and he vows to make amends for his actions by giving his ill-gotten money to another Jew. Eventually, the boy befriends a Jew and ends up trapped in the Jewish ghetto during the uprising of 1943. Over the course of time, Marek finds his feelings towards his stepfather changing to admiration, and by the end of the story Marek agrees to let the man adopt him.

Many reviewers of *The Man on the Other Side* applauded Orlev's re-creation of Marek's story. "The scenes and dialogue come to life," Sue Rosenzweig stated in *Voice of Youth Advocates,* "in a realistic portrayal of Marek's experiences and emotions." A *Kirkus Reviews* critic wrote with special admiration of the characters Orlev developed in the book, calling them "sobering, believable blends." The reviewer also found the book as a whole "subtle, beautifully crafted, altogether compelling." A *Publishers Weekly* reviewer in particular admired Orlev's main character and narrator Marek, "The voice of [the] 14-year-old narrator, Marek, would be gripping given any plot." Betsy Hearne in *Bulletin of the Center for Children's Books* and Dan Dailey in *Five Owls* both highlighted the gradual change in Marek's feelings toward Jews as well as the change in his relationship with his stepfather. "The sewers through which Marek travels," noted Hearne, "are a naturally apt metaphor for his journey through the under-world of self-knowledge." Putting even more emphasis on Marek's character development, Dailey praised Orlev's portrait "of the individual change of heart that is needed to erase prejudice, promote understanding, and foster cooperation and love in human affairs."

Orlev's next translated novel, *Lydia, Queen of Palestine,* is a retelling of a true story, in this case the life of Israeli poet Arianna Haran, whom Orlev met as a teenager. Like Marek, Lydia undergoes a change of heart in regard to her relationship with the adults in her life. "I was born in 1933 in Bucharest, Romania, and during the war I went to Palestine," Lydia summarized her life in the first sentence of the novel. An only child, who seems to be alone much of the time, Lydia spends hours playing with her dolls in elaborate fantasy games in which she is the queen of Palestine. When Lydia's parents begin to have marital difficulties and the child hears conversations between her mother and her grandmother about someone they call "That Woman," Lydia gives one of her dolls the same name and declares her an official enemy. She explains that even as a pre-schooler she knew—much like the Jews in the lands dominated by Hitler's armies—that "once you were an official enemy, anything could be done to you." Her realization is symbolized by her plaything. "That Woman was my ugliest doll," she comments. "I liked to put her to death."

For Lydia, the break-up of her parents' marriage is much more devastating than any of the events of the war happening around her. Conditions in Romania for Jews worsen, however, so Lydia's mother decides to send her daughter to Palestine, where Lydia's father has already fled. There, Lydia lives on a kibbutz and eventually is reunited with her mother and father. While at first angry at them when she discovers they both have remarried, she learns to accept them. Now a spirited but thoughtful sixth grader, Lydia declares in an official ceremony with her dolls that both That Woman and That Man, her male counterpart, are no longer her enemies.

Mary M. Burns in *Horn Book Magazine* and Robin Tzannes in the *New York Times Book Review* gave Orlev high marks for his female creation, Lydia. "Ingenious, self-confident, energetic, and bright, she is a force to be reckoned with—and a character no one can ignore," Burns wrote of Lydia. "In Lydia," Tzannes commented, "Mr. Orlev has created a real hero, one that wins our admiration but never our pity. Children will love her, will cheer her on in her battles and be uplifted by her triumphs." The reviewer found Lydia an "indomitable, free-spirited child, a genuine original." Schmidt, in *Twentieth-Century Young Adult Writers,* stated that Lydia possesses, like characters from Orlev's other novels, characteristics that help her persevere where other less audacious individuals might perish. He called her "manipulative, assertive, and dominant" and commented, "These are not qualities particularly useful on a kibbutz, but they are ones useful in surviving."

*The Lady with the Hat,* winner of the 1996 Batchelder Award, is another story of survival, but in several ways it is different from Orlev's previously translated works. Yulek, Orlev's main character in this novel, is older than the young protagonists encountered in *The Lead Soldiers, The Man from the Other Side, The Island on Bird Street,* or *Lydia, Queen of Palestine.* In another contrast with those works, *The Lady with the Hat* deals with the post-war Jewish experience rather than the period of World War II itself. The novel begins two years after the end of the war, when Yulek, whose family perished in concentration camps, decides to return to his former home in Poland. Once there, he finds another family living in the family house and all traces of the Jews eliminated. His only sense of hope comes when a former neighbor mentions that an Englishwoman in a hat had been looking for his family and him. Confused at first, Yulek realizes the woman must be his Aunt Malka, who had gone to England and married a British lord. As was the Jewish custom, his aunt's marriage to a Christian caused her to be pronounced dead by her conservative parents, and so Yulek's family and she had seldom had contact over the years. It had all happened so long ago, Yulek could not remember his aunt's married name, nor did he have any idea of how to get in touch with her.

*The Lady in the Hat* marks a departure from Orlev's typical straight-forward narration, deviated from only briefly in *The Lead Soldiers,* among his works in English translation. After the first couple of chapters of *The Lady in the Hat,* Orlev switches from Yulek's story to that of Lady Melanie Faulkner in her home in postwar London. Melanie, the reader learns, is actually Yulek's Aunt Malka and, as Yulek suspected, it was she who was inquiring about his family in Poland. Throughout the rest of the story, the chapters alternate between Yulek's attempt to get into Palestine despite a British blockade around the area and Melanie's efforts to find her nephew after seeing his picture printed in a London newspaper article about young Jewish refugees. Melanie's encounters with holocaust survivors during her frantic search for Yulek causes her to examine her own Jewish identity and her relationship with her husband. Yulek, in the meantime, falls in love with Theresa, a Jewish girl brought up by a group of Catholic nuns during the war, and stands by her as she similarly struggles to come to terms with her Jewish self. The novel ends with five letters written by important figures in the narrative, including Theresa, Yulek, and Melanie, telling how their experiences have changed their lives.

Several reviewers commented on the spirit of adventure present in the story, with Betsy Hearne in *Bulletin of the Center for Children's Books* comparing the events in the novel to a puzzle, stating, "there's suspense in the missing pieces." *Voice of Youth Advocates* contributor Bunni Union mentions other equally important elements of the work, noting, "A love story, a survival story, adventure, search and suspense all combine into the absorbing tale of a Holocaust survivor and his new friends and newfound relative." In *School Library Journal,* Marilyn Makowski compared *The Lady with the Hat* with *The Man from the Other Side* and stated, "Both books go beyond the Jewish issues—they have non-Jewish characters who are crucial to plot development and who add balance." In this regard, *The Lady with the Hat* exemplified the traits the Hans Christian Andersen Award jury praise so highly. While focusing on the Holocaust and its aftermath, Orlev creates characters who not only speak to Jewish readers as well as non-Jews but who also could move and act in a variety of scenarios. According to Khorana, in Orlev's works "readers ... become aware of the duality of human beings: there are Germans who are good as well as Jews who betray, cheat, or rob. The humanity of Orlev's characters transcends the specifics of the historical situation."

## Biographical and Critical Sources

### BOOKS

*Children's Literature Review,* Volume 30, Gale (Detroit, MI), 1993.

*Something about the Author Autobiographical Series,* Volume 19, Gale (Detroit, MI), 1995.

*Twentieth-Century Young Adult Writers,* St. James Press (Detroit, MI), 1994.

*PERIODICALS*

*Bookbird,* summer 1996, Meena Khorana, "Uri Orlev: Celebrating the Indomitable Spirit of Childhood," pp. 6-8.

*Bulletin of the Center for Children's Books,* June, 1984, Zena Sutherland, review of *The Island on Bird Street,* pp. 189-190; June, 1991, Betsy Hearne, review of *The Man from the Other Side,* pp. 246-247; June, 1995, Betsy Hearne, review of *The Lady with the Hat,* p. 356.

*Christian Science Monitor,* May 4, 1984, Randy Shipp, "Thread of Hope in Wartime Story," p. B4.

*Five Owls,* May-June, 1991, Dan Dailey, review of *The Man from the Other Side,* pp. 104-105.

*Growing Point,* May 1, 1985, Margery Fisher, review of *The Island on Bird Street,* p. 4435.

*Horn Book Magazine,* April, 1984, Kate M. Flanagan, review of *The Island on Bird Street,* pp. 197-198; March, 1994, Mary M. Burns, review of *Lydia, Queen of Palestine,* p. 200.

*Kirkus Reviews,* review of *The Man from the Other Side,* May 1, 1991, p. 608.

*New Statesman,* July 6, 1979, Victoria Neumark, "Boiled Sweets," p. 24.

*New York Times Book Review,* March 23, 1980, Leslie Epstein, "Survivor's Story," pp. 14, 31; November 14, 1993, Robin Tzannes, "Audacity, Thy Name Is Lydia," p. 60.

*Publishers Weekly,* January 18, 1980, review of *The Lead Soldiers,* p. 130; May 31, 1991, review of *The Man from the Other Side,* pp. 75-76.

*School Library Journal,* May, 1995, Marilyn Makowski, review of *The Lady with the Hat,* p. 122.

*Voice of Youth Advocates,* October, 1991, Sue Rosenzweig, review of *The Man from the Other Side,* p. 230; October, 1995, Bunni Union, review of *The Lady with the Hat,* p. 222.

\*        \*        \*

# PAYNE, Nina

## Personal

Female; children: Eric, Jessica, Emily, Adam.

## Addresses

*Home*—54 Snell St., Amherst, MA 01002-2535. *E-mail*—npayne@hampshire.edu.

## Career

Poet and fiber artist. Professor of creative writing at Hampshire College for twenty years. Leader of writing workshops.

## Writings

*All the Day Long* (poems), illustrated by Laurel Schindelman, Atheneum (New York, NY), 1973.

*Four in All,* illustrated by Adam S. Payne, Front Street Books (Asheville, NC), 2001.

*Nina Payne uses only fifty-six common nouns, four at a time, to describe a young girl's imaginative journey in* **Four in All,** *illustrated by the author's son, Adam S. Payne.*

Contributor to journals and anthologies including *Ploughshares* and *The Massachusetts.*

## Sidelights

Fiber artist and poet Nina Payne is the author of two books for children, *All the Day Long* and *Four in All.* In the first work, Payne offers young readers a variety of poems which detail daily activities in the life of a youngster, including skipping rope, chewing gum, and listening to stories before bed.

Twenty-eight years after the appearance of her first published work, Payne teamed up with her son, illustrator Adam S. Payne, to create a second children's work, *Four in All.* Here, a young girl takes a fanciful journey in her imagination to explore the world before returning home for dinner with her family. Told in the form of a poem, each two page spread consists of only four words of text, accompanied by the younger Payne's cut-paper collage pictures. However, noted reviewers, Payne's well-considered words successfully convey the little girl's experience to readers. "The solid language choices," remarked *Booklist* reviewer Ilene Cooper, "show . . . keen inventiveness as they fashion a real story out of simple words." Despite commenting that there is "no logic to the word quartets," *School Library Journal* critic Nancy Palmer nonetheless claimed "there is charm and a nursery-rhyme quality to the cadenced verse." Describing the poem as "exceptionally well-crafted," a *Publishers Weekly* critic predicted that "very young children in particular will delight in the sturdiness of the language."

## Biographical and Critical Sources

*PERIODICALS*

*Booklist,* January 1, 2002, Ilene Cooper, review of *Four in All,* p. 867.

*Kirkus Reviews,* July 1, 1973, review of *All the Day Long,* p. 689; October, 2001, review of *Four in All,* p. 1431.

*Library Journal,* October 15, 1973, Daisy Kouzel, review of *All the Day Long,* p. 3140.

*New York Times Book Review,* November 18, 2001, David Small.

*Publishers Weekly,* October 29, 2001, review of *Four in All,* p. 62.

*School Library Journal,* December, 2001, Nancy Palmer, review of *Four in All,* p. 110.

*OTHER*

*Front Street Books,* http://www.frontstreetbooks.com (March 5, 2002), brief biography of Nina Payne.

# R

**RANDALL, Carrie**
**See RANSOM, Candice F.**

\*     \*     \*

## RANSOM, Candice F. 1952-
### (Kate Kenyon, Carrie Randall)

### Personal

Born July 10, 1952, in Washington, DC; daughter of Thomas Garland and Irene Dellinger (Lightfoot) Farris; married Frank Wesley Ransom (a satellite engineer), February 14, 1979. *Education:* Currently studying for an M.F.A. degree in writing at Vermont College. *Hobbies and other interests:* Horseback riding, dancing.

### Addresses

*Home and office*—6819 Orchid Ln., Fredericksburg, VA 22407.

### Career

Writer.

### Member

Society of Children's Book Writers and Illustrators, Children's Book Guild of Washington, D.C.

### Awards, Honors

IRA/Children's Choice Book for 1987, for *Fourteen and Holding;* Best Science Book for Children, 1994, for *Listening to Crickets: A Story about Rachel Carson;* Best Illustrated Books of the Year, *New York Times,* 1995, and 100 Best Children's Books, New York Public Library, 1995, both for *When the Whippoorwill Calls,* illustrated by Kimberly Bulcken Root; Notable Children's Trade Book in the Field of Social Studies, 1997, for *One Christmas Dawn;* Notable Trade Book in Social Studies, 1998, for *Fire in the Sky;* This Week Kids' Pick of the Spring List, *Booklist,* 2000, for *Danger at Sand Cave;* Hodge-Podge Award for Best Children's Book, 2001, and Virginia Younger Readers List, 2001-2002, for *The Promise Quilt.*

### Writings

*FOR CHILDREN*

*The Silvery Past,* Scholastic (New York, NY), 1982.
*Amanda,* Scholastic (New York, NY), 1984.
*Susannah,* Scholastic (New York, NY), 1984.
*Breaking the Rules,* Scholastic (New York, NY), 1985.
*Emily,* Scholastic (New York, NY), 1985.
*Kathleen,* Scholastic (New York, NY), 1985.
*Blackbird Keep,* Silhouette Books (New York, NY), 1986.
*Cat's Cradle,* Silhouette Books (New York, NY), 1986.
*Nicole,* Scholastic (New York, NY), 1986.
*Sabrina,* Scholastic (New York, NY), 1986.
*Thirteen,* Scholastic (New York, NY), 1986.
(Under pseudonym Kate Kenyon) *The Day the Eighth Grade Ran the School,* Scholastic (New York, NY), 1987.
*Fourteen and Holding,* Scholastic (New York, NY), 1987.
*Fifteen at Last,* Scholastic (New York, NY), 1987.
*Kaleidoscope,* Crosswinds, 1987.
*Going on Twelve,* Scholastic (New York, NY), 1988.
*My Sister, the Meanie,* Scholastic (New York, NY), 1988.
*Millicent the Magnificent,* Scholastic (New York, NY), 1989.
*My Sister, the Traitor,* Scholastic (New York, NY), 1989.
(Under pseudonym Carrie Randall) *The Secret,* Scholastic (New York, NY), 1989.
*Today Fifth Grade, Tomorrow the World,* Willowisp Press (St. Petersburg, FL), 1989.
*Almost Ten and a Half,* Scholastic (New York, NY), 1990.
*My Sister, the Creep,* Scholastic (New York, NY), 1990.
*There's One in Every Family,* Scholastic (New York, NY), 1990.
*Funniest Sixth Grade Video Ever,* Willowisp Press (St. Petersburg, FL), 1991.
*Ladies and Jellybeans,* Bradbury Press (New York, NY), 1991.

*Candice F. Ransom tells about the lives of children and their roles during the "War between the States" in her book* **Children of the Civil War.**

*The Love Charm,* Willowisp Press (St. Petersburg, FL), 1991.

*Sixth Grade High,* Scholastic (New York, NY), 1991.

*Hocus-Pocus after School,* Willowisp Press (St. Petersburg, FL), 1992.

*Shooting Star Summer,* illustrated by Karen Milone, Boyds Mills Press (Honesdale, PA), 1992.

*The Big Green Pocketbook,* illustrated by Felicia Bond, HarperCollins (New York, NY), 1993.

*Listening to Crickets: A Story about Rachel Carson,* illustrated by Shelly O. Haas, Carolrhoda Books (Minneapolis, MN), 1993.

*So Young to Die: The Story of Hannah Senesh,* Scholastic (New York, NY), 1993.

*Third Grade Stars,* Troll (New York, NY), 1993.

*We're Growing Together,* illustrated by Virginia Wright-Frierson, Bradbury Press (New York, NY), 1993.

*Who Needs Third Grade?,* Troll (New York, NY), 1993.

*Between Two Worlds,* Scholastic (New York, NY), 1994.

*Jimmy Crack Corn,* illustrated by Shelly O. Haas, Carolrhoda Books (Minneapolis, MN), 1994.

*The Spitball Class,* Archway/Minstrel (New York, NY), 1994.

*Third Grade Detectives,* Troll (New York, NY), 1994.

*Why Are Boys So Weird?,* Troll (New York, NY), 1994.

*When the Whippoorwill Calls,* illustrated by Kimberly Bulcken Root, Tambourine Books (New York, NY), 1995.

*More Than a Name,* Macmillan (New York, NY), 1995.

*Teacher's Pest,* Troll (New York, NY), 1996.

*In Ransom's* **The Promise Quilt** *a Civil War widower makes a quilt and auctions it off to help her children pay for school supplies and fulfill their father's promise. (Illustrated by Ellen Beier.)*

*One Christmas Dawn,* illustrated by Peter Fiore, Bridgewater, 1996.

*Fire in the Sky,* Carolrhoda Books (Minneapolis, MN), 1996.

*Children of the Civil War,* Carolrhoda Books (Minneapolis, MN), 1998.

*The Christmas Dolls,* illustrated by Moira Fain, Walker (New York, NY), 1998.

*The Promise Quilt,* illustrated by Ellen Beier, Walker (New York, NY), 1999.

*Rescue on the Outer Banks,* illustrated by Karen Ritz, Carolrhoda Books (Minneapolis, MN), 2000.

*Danger at Sand Cave,* illustrated by Den Schofield, Carolrhoda Books (Minneapolis, MN), 2000.

*Maria von Trapp: Beyond the Sound of Music,* Carolrhoda Books (Minneapolis, MN), 2001.

*Mother Teresa,* illustrated by Elaine Verstraete, Carolrhoda Books (Minneapolis, MN), 2001.

*George Washington,* Lerner Publications (Minneapolis, MN), 2002.

*Lewis and Clark,* Lerner Publications (Minneapolis, MN), 2002.

*OTHER*

Contributor of articles and stories to magazines, including *Seventeen, Rural Living, Writer's Digest, Single*
Parent, Highlights for Children, and Lutheran Women. Also contributor to the "Boxcar Children" series.

## Work in Progress

Two biographies: *Clara Barton* and *Martha Washington; Liberty Street,* a picture book; historical fiction books *The Sound of Battle* and *The Day of the Black Blizzard.*

## Sidelights

"When I was fifteen, I decided to become a children's writer, even though I believed people who wrote kids' books were all dead," commented writer Candice F. Ransom on her Web site. The author of over seventy books for young readers, Ransom has made good on this childhood promise. Her books for children include the full gamut of genres, from picture books to novels to history and biography. Childhood memories provide Ransom with the basis for many of her children's and young adult books. Reaching back into her own past, Ransom is able to accurately describe what it feels like to be thirteen, to make new friends, or even to hate your own sister. Although Ransom's first novels were young adult paperbacks, she has since written for a wide spectrum of juvenile readers, bringing the same sense of realism to every book. And each of these books keeps Ransom's dream of being a writer alive. She once told *SATA:* "Now that my dream has come true, I often reflect what a strange world I inhabit, trapped between the floors of childhood and adulthood—not really *there,* but not really *here* either."

Ransom's childhood prepared her well for such a career. "I grew up in rural Fairfax County [Virginia], where there wasn't much to do except read, stay out of my sister's path, and listen to my mother's tales about her childhood in the Shenandoah Valley," Ransom noted on her Web site. Even while doing her math homework in the kitchen, Ransom would listen to her mother's stories and tall tales, some of them involving her grandfather's trade as undertaker. One of her favorites was about how her mom once locked her cousin in an empty coffin. "Anyone's life, even my mother's, was more exciting than mine. In second grade, I began writing stories, with myself as heroine. At last, I found a way to have adventures."

"My first novel," Ransom once recalled for *SATA,* "pencilled on the long bus ride home from school at the age of seven, began with the immortal lines, 'It was dark. Everything was silent. Then in rustling leaves....' The books I wrote in elementary school were feeble imitations of Nancy Drew or *Lassie Come Home,* in which I was always the main character. As a lonely child growing up in rural Fairfax County, I wrote to while away long evenings, and who else would I rather have read about having wonderful adventures than myself?" In high school, Ransom continued to sustain her love of writing and reading, although she found herself wondering about her literary interests, which seemed very different from those of her classmates. As she explained to *SATA,* "In high school, I worried that I had a severe case of arrested development. While other kids were passing around *The Green Berets,* with page 388 marked, I was still reading *The Borrowers.* My English teacher set me straight. 'You're going to be a children's writer,' she said. Relieved that I was not living my life in reverse like Merlin in *The Once and Future King,* I set out to fulfill her prophecy." Ransom did this by writing her first children's novel during her sixteenth summer and sending it off to Harper and Row. At the same time, she began writing and submitting poetry, having her first poem published later that year.

Following her graduation from high school, Ransom began work as a secretary, but she still longed to be a children's book writer. "Whenever I walked into the children's room of a library, memories of myself at nine, wide-eyed and thrilled to be in a roomful of books, overpowered me to the point where I thought I'd faint," she recalled. "I *had* to write. And I did." This writing led to Ransom's first published novel in 1982—*The Silvery Past,* a mystery for the Windswept series of paperback originals. "I am frequently asked why my first book was paperback," Ransom related in an article for a *Society of Children's Book Writers and Illustrators* newsletter. "*Because that's the way it turned out,* I reply. I did not intend to write paperback originals for teens, but that was where my break came." Deciding that the popularity of this market gave her a better chance of being published, Ransom studied these young adult paperbacks, wrote her own, and was successful in getting it published.

"I am embarrassed to admit this, but I must confess that after my first book was accepted and in production, I believed publishers would beat a path to my door for my second book (which I hadn't written or even thought of)," Ransom continued in the newsletter. "When no one did, I grumpily wondered what was taking so *long?* It never occurred to me to sit down and begin *writing* another book." And so Ransom considers herself lucky that her publisher called and offered her the chance to write a four-hundred-page historical young adult novel. At first daunted by such a task, Ransom accepted and ended up writing the first two novels of the highly successful Sunfire series. Since these early books, Ransom has delved into comical works for another paperback series, has written such humorous books for pre-teens as *Ladies and Jellybeans, There's One in Every Family, Thirteen,* and *My Sister, the Meanie,* and tackled an even younger audience with *Shooting Star Summer* and *More Than a Name.* "Much of my material comes from within, drawn from my own past, which I remember vividly," Ransom observed for *SATA.* "A lot of my childhood interests have carried over into my profession."

Such memories and interests inform both *Ladies and Jellybeans* and *There's One in Every Family.* In the former title, it is 1959, and Wendy is just starting the third grade, a year sure to bring huge changes in her life. No more chocolate milk each morning in class, and no more teachers who treat the kids like kindergartners.

Instead, she will be learning cursive writing and dealing with air raid drills at school. Additionally, her best friend has moved away, and her family is having hard economic times. Wendy's fears, however, are soon dealt with by her loving family and a new friend, and she realizes she will be able to deal with the new challenges. "Realistically drawn characters and down-to-earth dialogue let Ransom deliver her message neatly," wrote a reviewer for *Publishers Weekly,* who also felt that contemporary children "will be heartened" by Wendy's ability to deal with problems from another era which still resonate with today's adolescent fears.

In *There's One in Every Family* nine-year-old Millicent takes center stage with her efforts to make her parents love her more than all the other children. However, most of Millicent's strategies to make her the favorite end up backfiring. Yet through it all the young girl is "thoroughly likeable," according to Diane Roback in *Publishers Weekly.* Roback also felt that the "book's pace is as energetic as its heroine," and that middle-grade readers may find tears in their eyes at points in this "old-fashioned family story that genuinely warms the heart."

Ransom also used childhood memories to help create the character of Kobie Roberts, who appears in *Thirteen, Fourteen and Holding,* and *Fifteen at Last.* In her first appearance, Kobie is thirteen and positive that this will be the worst year of her life. She is short, has no figure, and cannot get into the "in" group at her junior high. Things turn around by the end of the book, though, when Kobie makes new friends through her involvement in a school play and earns her own kind of recognition for her art work. New problems arise for Kobie in *Fourteen and Holding* when she finds herself facing high school without her best friend, Gretchen. Getting into trouble with a home-ec teacher and a tough girl, Kobie must face her problems alone and come up with solutions. "Ransom offers an honest and humorous portrayal of the trauma of growing up," maintained Betty Ann Porter in her *School Library Journal* review of *Thirteen.* And a *Publishers Weekly* contributor wrote of *Fourteen and Holding:* "Ransom has a buoyant style; she understands just how complicated school and family life can be."

The complications that can arise between younger and older sisters is the focus of another set of Ransom's novels: *My Sister, the Meanie, My Sister, the Traitor,* and *My Sister, the Creep.* Jackie desperately wishes she could be more like her older, more popular sister, Sharon, following her around and imitating her in an effort to make this wish come true. This only makes Sharon angry, though, and she declares war on Jackie until she herself has a crisis and her little sister comes to her rescue. In *My Sister, the Traitor* Jackie is now thirteen and looking forward to her new, exciting teenage life. When nothing new happens, she finds herself facing a long, boring summer, which gets even worse when Sharon starts dating the same boy Jackie likes. In *My Sister, the Creep,* Sharon is leaving for college, and though Jackie is at first excited to see her sister go, she soon misses her. At the same time, Jackie is trying to fit in as a freshman in high school, and just as she makes friends and has her first date, Sharon returns to make things difficult again.

Ransom "effectively portrays the way each sister's actions grate on the other, even when no provocation is intended," wrote a *Booklist* contributor, adding that *My Sister, the Meanie* "is bound to trigger flashes of recognition for the younger sisters of the world." Andrea Davidson, writing in *Voice of Youth Advocates,* pointed out that "Jackie is an engaging character as she tries so hard to emulate her big sister; and she is instrumental in getting Sharon together with the boy she likes, showing how much she truly loves Sharon." And Rita M. Fontinha stated in her *Kliatt* review of *My Sister, the Creep:* "Full of laughable situations, the book provides fun and a bit of truth."

Another relationship between young girls is the focus of Ransom's *Shooting Star Summer.* The narrator of the story is not looking forward to her cousin Shannon's visit to her farm. She is a tomboy, while Shannon once won a baby contest and arrives with a suitcase full of dresses. The hostility between the two fades when they realize that they actually have a lot in common, and that they can also teach each other a few new things. "Ransom's comfortably accessible narration reads smoothly, with details that make the changed relationship believable," observed Anne Larsen in *Kirkus Reviews.* Cyrisse Jaffee, writing in *School Library Journal,* stated, "In this charming story of friendship, Ransom introduces two seemingly incompatible girls who manage to overcome their differences," adding that *Shooting Star Summer* "is an enormously appealing story."

Changing genres and age groups again, Ransom tells the story of a little girl and her mother's bus ride and morning of errands in her picture book *The Big Green Pocketbook.* At the beginning of the day, the girl's pocketbook is empty, but as the day progresses she fills it up with gifts and mementos from the trip, including a key chain, a bag of gumdrops, a box of new crayons, and used bus tickets. Falling asleep on the way home, the girl leaves her pocketbook on the bus, but the thoughtful driver drops it off on his way back to the station. *The Big Green Pocketbook* is an "engaging picture book," observed Deborah Abbott in *Booklist,* adding that the pictures "enhance the simple and smooth text, and the essence and enthusiasm of childhood glow from each carefully designed page. A solid choice for story hour." A critic for *Publishers Weekly* had similar praise for this picture book, noting that Ransom follows "a likable girl and her mother as they run errands" in this "winsome story with its timeless theme."

Families adjusting to changes in structure are the topic of both *We're Growing Together* and *More Than a Name.* The first finds a young girl and her sister adapting to a new stepfather as well as a new home in the country far away from their friends and everything familiar. *More Than a Name* similarly deals with eight-year-old Cammie, who also has a new stepfather and a new town to cope with, as well as her strong desire to be adopted

by her new father. *Booklist* contributor Ilene Cooper stated in her review of *We're Growing Together:* "Stepchildren will easily understand all the muddle of feelings that come with the entry of a new parent into the household, and this is the story's main attraction." In a review of *More Than a Name,* a *Publishers Weekly* contributor concluded that Ransom "addresses Cammie's recognizable concerns ... with true-to-life characterizations and a dose of gentle humor." *Booklist* critic Kay Weisman likewise felt that "Ransom's strength lies in her attention to Cammie's feelings in this all-too-common situation," and that young readers "will appreciate the story's upbeat tone and a chance to read about a family that works."

Ransom's picture book *When the Whippoorwill Calls* has been widely praised as an empathetic and even-handed treatment of change. In this work, set in the 1930s, young Polly and her family are forced to leave their home in the beautiful Blue Ridge Mountains of Virginia to accommodate the government's creation of Shenandoah National Park. "Instead of simply lamenting a vanished way of life," noted Julie Yates Walton in a review in *Booklist,* "Ransom writes with a full spectrum of emotion, wringing from the story a well-considered metaphor for the mixed blessings of progress." Championed as a "stunning effort" by *School Library Journal* contributor Barbara Chatton, *When the Whippoorwill Calls* was summarized by Ann A. Flowers in *Horn Book* as a "thoughtful and sensitive view of change, good and bad."

Ransom deals with the 1932 Veteran's Bonus March in Washington, D.C., in *Jimmy Crack Corn.* Young Jimmy's father lost his job and soon may lose the farm as well; furthermore, the cow has been sold for taxes and the family eats the last chicken. However, Jimmy's father is a veteran of World War I, and he decides to join other veterans on a march on Washington. Jimmy accompanies his dad and is witness to both the initial hopes that the march inspires, and also the despair that follows when the U.S. Army disperses the marchers. *Booklist* contributor Ellen Mandel felt this book told a moving story of a "caring youngster who longs to be a musician amid the arduous struggle for survival in the 1930s."

Ransom sticks with the 1930s in her *Fire in the Sky,* which recalls the destruction of the *Hindenburg* dirigible in New Jersey. The main character, Stenny, is nine, a bit overweight, and continually teased at school. He wishes he could live the adventures of his favorite radio hero, Jack Armstrong. But his biggest preoccupation is reading everything he can about Germany's dirigible. When he learns that it is going to be landing near his hometown, he bikes to the Naval Air Station and manages to get onto the field, only to see the *Hindenburg* burst into flames, its passengers jumping to the ground on fire. At first his impulse is to run away, but he battles against this fear and makes himself help out, taking survivors to a hangar for safety. "Though a loser at marbles and a liar, Stenny finds his world turns around when he discovers that he's no coward," commented *Booklist*'s Carolyn Phelan, who also found the book to be "involving historical fiction." Peggy Morgan, writing in *School Library Journal,* felt that Ransom "has created a believable, sympathetic character and has skillfully placed him in the pre-World War II era." Morgan called the book "excellent historical fiction for younger readers."

Christmas is the inspiration for a pair of Ransom's picture books: *One Christmas Dawn* and *The Christmas Dolls*. In the former title, it is 1917 and the coldest winter ever recorded in the Appalachian Mountains of Virginia. A young narrator awaits her father's return from the sawmill, where he has gone to find work. Come Christmas morning, she awakes to see the yard blooming with flowers; falling asleep again, the snow is back and so is her father. A blend of folklore and tall tale, the book won praise from critics. *Booklist*'s Cooper thought that Ransom's text "is full of everyday poetry" and that readers "should enjoy the warm feelings that flow over a cold Christmas night." A contributor for *Publishers Weekly* also lauded this book, which "nearly sighs with longing before it begins to tingle in anticipation of poignant reunion." And Jane Marino, reviewing the same title in *School Library Journal,* noted that the "apt turns of phrase and quietly understated story make this a lovely family history for the holidays."

*The Christmas Dolls* features another young girl whose father is away from home for the holidays. To take Claire's mind off her father's absence, her mother decides to fix up broken dolls for poor children. While working on this project, the mother tells Claire of one sad Christmas when she did not get the doll she wanted, and the pair now create a new family tradition in this team effort of repairing broken dolls. Claire also makes a rag doll for her mother, to make up for the one she did not receive when she was a child. "This is a book that could have easily become mushy," wrote Cooper, "but Ransom never lets that happen." Cooper further commented that the relationship between the child and mother are too strong "to be overwhelmed by other sentiments."

American Civil War history is at the heart of two other titles by Ransom, *Children of the Civil War* and *The Promise Quilt*. Employing plentiful illustrations, Ransom helps to illuminate the era in *Children of the Civil War,* a book that focuses on life before, during, and after the Civil War. Children as soldiers, slaves, servants, prisoners, and orphans are featured in this book that combines text and photographs to "bring the period to life," according to Janice Schomberg in *School Library Journal.* A more intimate portrait of the same epoch is offered in *The Promise Quilt,* the story of Addie, whose father promised to send her to school when she got older. But her father went off to war as a guide for General Lee and never returned home. Now Addie, her mother, and her brother have to learn how to survive in the defeated South, and all that she has to remind her of her father is his red flannel shirt. However, when it is time for her to go to school, she ultimately sacrifices this prized shirt so that her mother can complete a quilt to

raffle off to buy supplies for the school. "This realistic tale ... is very touching," noted Anne Knickerbocker in a *School Library Journal* review. "Themes of resiliency, sacrifice, and hard work rewarded are gracefully woven into the narrative."

Ransom has also turned her hand to biography with *Maria von Trapp: Beyond the Sound of Music* and *Mother Teresa.* With *Maria von Trapp,* Ransom presents a portrait of the woman whose life inspired both the Broadway musical and movie *The Sound of Music.* "Clearly written ... the book gives a sense of Maria's forceful personality as well as the events in her life," according to *Booklist*'s Phelan. Ransom's *Mother Teresa* does the same for the woman who devoted her life to working with the poor in India. "Although there are many biographies of Mother Teresa," wrote Jean Gaffney in *School Library Journal,* "this one stands out as an inviting and inspiring beginning reader."

And with *Danger at Sand Cave* and *Rescue on the Outer Banks* Ransom provides two true adventure stories from little-known events in American history. *Danger at Sand Cave* tells of the 1925 attempts to save Floyd Collins, an experienced spelunker, or cave explorer, who became trapped in a Kentucky cavern. For weeks rescue teams tried to reach him with no success. Ransom's account inserts into the historical action a fictional ten-year-old boy, Arly, who thinks his small size will allow him to succeed in saving Collins where others have failed. By the time the rescuers finally reached Collins, however, he was dead. "Ransom effectively conveys Arly's frustration but refrains from turning his foolhardy act into a dramatic rescue and instead sticks with the historical conclusion," commented a reviewer for *Horn Book.* This same critic felt that such realism "shows a respect for those who prefer endings that reflect what really happened rather than what one might wish happened." Nancy A. Gifford, reviewing *Danger at Sand Cave* in *School Library Journal,* felt that this "adventure will appeal to beginning and reluctant readers."

*Rescue on the Outer Banks* tells another true story, this one about the first African American life-saving station on North Carolina's Outer Banks. The time is 1896 and Sam Deal finds these men to be model heroes in their dangerous work. The men in turn let Sam tag along sometimes and take part in their drills, but they also tease him about his age and his horse, Ginger. However, during one rescue both Sam and his horse prove invaluable to these surfmen. "Selfless heroism, personal sacrifice, and courage come together during a rescue," wrote a contributor for *Kirkus Reviews.* "This exciting, fast-paced tale will inspire its young readers."

Ransom's ability to accurately describe the feelings, thoughts, and actions of children both in contemporary and historical situations is closely linked to her vivid memories of her own experiences while growing up. And it is a feeling remembered from these childhood days that brings Ransom the most satisfaction as a writer. "Best of all," she concluded for *SATA,* "I am able to recapture that shivery feeling of anticipation I once had whenever I turned the first page of a new library book. Only now the pages are blank, waiting for me to fill them." Writing on her Web site, Ransom noted, "Through my work, I have traveled back in time, relived my own past (and fixed the awful parts!), and explored every corner of my home state. I wouldn't trade my life with anyone else's!"

## Biographical and Critical Sources

PERIODICALS

*Booklist,* April 15, 1987, p. 1278; February 1, 1989, review of *My Sister, the Meanie,* p. 941; May 15, 1993, pp. 1690, 1692; July, 1993, Deborah Abbott, review of *The Big Green Pocketbook,* pp. 1976-1977; October 1, 1993, Ilene Cooper, review of *We're Growing Together,* p. 354; July, 1994, Ellen Mandel, review of *Jimmy Crack Corn,* pp. 1948-1949; July, 1995, Kay Weisman, review of *More Than a Name,* p. 1880; September 15, 1995, Julie Yates Walton, review of *When the Whippoorwill Calls,* p. 176; October 15, 1996, Ilene Cooper, review of *One Christmas Dawn,* p. 437; May 1, 1997, Carolyn Phelan, review of *Fire in the Sky,* p. 1498; September 1, 1998, Ilene Cooper, review of *The Christmas Dolls,* p. 134; November 1, 1999, Shelley Townsend-Hudson, review of *The Promise Quilt,* p. 540; March 1, 2002, Carolyn Phelan, review of *Maria von Trapp,* pp. 1147-1148.

*Bulletin of the Center for Children's Books,* June, 1994, pp. 331-332.

*Horn Book,* March-April, 1996, Ann A. Flowers, review of *When the Whippoorwill Calls,* pp. 190-191; July-August, 2000, review of *Danger at Sand Cave,* p. 464.

*Horn Book Guide,* spring, 1997, p. 44; spring, 1999, reviews of *The Christmas Dolls,* p. 41, *Children of the Civil War,* p. 150.

*Kirkus Reviews,* October 15, 1991, p. 1348; October 1, 1992, Anne Larsen, review of *Shooting Star Summer,* p. 1264; June 1, 1993, p. 726; February 1, 2002, review of *Rescue on the Outer Banks,* p. 187.

*Kliatt,* September, 1990, Rita M. Fontinha, review of *My Sister, the Creep,* p. 14.

*Publishers Weekly,* July 10, 1987, review of *Fourteen and Holding,* p. 71; December 11, 1987, p. 66; January 4, 1991, Diane Roback, review of *There's One in Every Family,* p. 72; September 27, 1991, review of *Ladies and Jellybeans,* p. 58; May 31, 1993, review of *The Big Green Pocketbook,* p. 53; October 11, 1993, pp. 88-89; July 3, 1995, review of *More Than a Name,* p. 61; September 30, 1996, review of *One Christmas Dawn,* p. 90.

*School Library Journal,* September, 1984, p. 133; September, 1986, p. 149; October, 1987, Betty Ann Porter, review of *Thirteen,* p. 142; November, 1988, pp. 112, 114; February, 1989, p. 82; March, 1990, p. 220; December, 1991, p. 118; February, 1993, Cyrisse Jaffee, review of *Shooting Star Summer,* pp. 77-78; July, 1993, p. 94; June, 1994, p. 134; July, 1995, p. 80; November, 1995, Barbara Chatton, review of *When the Whippoorwill Calls,* pp. 80-81; October, 1996, Jane Marino, review of *One Christmas Dawn,*

p. 40; August, 1997, Peggy Morgan, review of *Fire in the Sky,* p. 139; October, 1998, Mary N. Hopf, review of *The Christmas Dolls,* p. 44; January, 1999, Janice Schomberg, review of *Children of the Civil War,* p. 120; November, 1999, Anne Knickerbocker, review of *The Promise Quilt,* p. 128; August, 2000, Nancy A. Gifford, review of *Danger at Sand Cave,* p. 164; July, 2001, Jean Gaffney, review of *Mother Teresa,* p. 97.

*Voice of Youth Advocates,* April, 1988, p. 29; April, 1989, Andrea Davidson, review of *My Sister, the Meanie,* p. 31; June, 1989, p. 106.

*Wilson Library Bulletin,* December, 1993, pp. 114-115.

OTHER

*Candice Ransom Home Page,* http://www.candiceransom. com/ (August 13, 2002).

*Society of Children's Book Writers and Illustrators* (newsletter), March/April, 1989, Candice F. Ransom, "The Road to Success."

*       *       *

# REES, (George) Leslie (Clarence) 1905-2000

OBITUARY NOTICE—See index for *SATA* sketch: Born December 28, 1905, in Perth, Australia; died August 9, 2000, in Sydney, Australia. Journalist, playwright, and author. Leslie Rees published forty-five books in his career, including twenty-seven for children. Some of his most popular books were the "Digit Dick" series which included *Digit Dick on the Great Barrier Reef, Digit Dick and the Tasmanian Devil,* and *Digit Dick in Black Swan Land.* Digit Dick was a tiny boy "only as big as his mother's toe" and thousands of Australian children loved him. Rees received the Australian Children's Book-of-the-Year Award in 1946 for *The Story of Karrawingi, the Emu.* He was also awarded the Order of Australia in 1981. In 2000, just months before the author died, he was honored in the NSW Premier's Literary Awards for his contribution to Australian theater and writing.

OBITUARIES AND OTHER SOURCES:

PERIODICALS

*Sydney Morning Herald,* (Sydney, Australia) August 14, 2000.

OTHER

*Australian Literature Gateway,* http://www.austlit.edu.au (August 17, 2000).

*       *       *

# RICHARDS, Jean 1940-

## Personal

Born September 9, 1940, in New York, NY; daughter of Hans (a law professor and sociologist) and Eva (an industrial designer) Zeisel; married Brent C. Brolin (an architecture writer); children: Talisman. *Education:* Attended Pembroke College, Yale School of Drama. *Religion:* Unitarian.

## Addresses

*Home*—25 Washington Square North, New York, NY, 10011-9108. *E-mail*—nonsequito@earthlink.net.

## Career

Actress, voice-over artist, author of children's books and children's audiotapes. Has appeared in Broadway and Off-Broadway plays.

## Member

Screen Actors' Guild, American Federation of Television and Radio Artists, Actors Equity.

## Awards, Honors

Notable Social Studies Book for Young People Selection, Children's Book Council/National Council for the Social Studies, 2001, for *The First Olympic Games: A Gruesome Greek Myth with a Happy Ending.*

## Writings

*God's Gift,* illustrated by Norman Gorbaty, Doubleday (New York, NY), 1993.

*The First Olympic Games: A Gruesome Greek Myth with a Happy Ending,* illustrated by Kat Thacker, Millbrook Press (Brookfield, CT), 2000.

*A Fruit Is a Suitcase for Seeds,* illustrated by Anca Hariton, Millbrook Press (Brookfield, CT), 2002.

*How the Elephant Got Its Trunk,* illustrated by Norman Gorbaty, Henry Holt (New York, NY), in press.

Also author of the activities side of audiotapes for fifteen audio books; adapted the *Magic School Bus* series for audiotape.

## Work in Progress

*The Magic Tree in the Garden of Eden,* an expulsion story for young readers; *Jonah and the Two Great Fish,* based on the Old Testament and the Midrash; two science books; a cartoon book on Latin roots of English words for junior and senior high school students.

## Sidelights

An actress and children's book writer, Jean Richards deals with themes from religion to myth to science. She came to writing in a round-about manner. "I have recorded over two hundred children's books for various publishers," Richards told *SATA.* "My writing is a direct outgrowth of these recordings." At the suggestion of a childrens' audiotape producer, Richards first began writing the second side of these tapes, the activities side. "I had not written much before but [the producer] was sure I could do it. I ended up writing over a dozen

*Jean Richards*

activity sides for such books as the "Madeleine" series and *The Story of Ping.* I also performed on them."

This eventually led to a book contract in 1993 for *God's Gift,* based on the second version of the creation story in Genesis. "I was much influenced by Harold Bloom's *The Book of J* in writing *God's Gift,*" Richards told *SATA.* "Bloom thinks that the version I used is the oldest version possibly written by a woman and probably written originally as children's literature." Reviewing the title in *Booklist,* Elizabeth Bush thought that this "charming retelling ... is ideal for the lap-sitter audience." A critic for *Publishers Weekly* found that an "undercurrent of playfulness sweeps through the text as God molds each creature and Man chooses names." One such humorous aside comes in the book as Man decides to name an exquisite little creature "butterdog," but God frowns so Man changes its name to "butterfly."

Richards's next book was a retelling of a Greek myth which is the basis for the Olympic Games. In this story, Pelops becomes chopped meat for a stew at the hands of his father, Tantalus. Enraged by this action, Zeus restores poor Pelops to life, and the young man proceeds to find his own kingdom far from his father. Coming upon the kingdom of Elis, he decides to make a bold wager. He challenges the ruler to a chariot race. If he wins, he marries the daughter of the king and succeeds to the throne. But if he loses, he loses his life. In the end, Pelops wins, takes the hand of Princess Hippodamia, and becomes king of Elis. Myth has it that Pelops later instituted the Olympic Games in honor of this victory and in memory of the fallen king of Elis. *Booklist* contributor John Peters found the book to be a "colorful account" as well as a "vividly told story" which will "sweep children along and give them an interesting perspective on the Olympics." Reviewing the same title in *School Library Journal,* Ann Welton felt that the retelling was "marred on occasion by condescending language," but on the whole thought that the book would be a good vehicle "for introducing young children to the Olympic Games and their history."

Richards is also the author of the children's science book, *A Fruit Is a Suitcase for Seeds,* which provides an illustrated description of how fruit seeds are dispersed. As Richards told *SATA,* "Almost all my writing consists of retellings. I'm not too good at making things up!"

## Biographical and Critical Sources

*BOOKS*

Richards, Jean, *God's Gift,* illustrated by Norman Gorbaty, Doubleday (New York, NY), 1993.

*PERIODICALS*

*Booklist,* October 15, 1993, Elizabeth Bush, review of *God's Gift,* pp. 447-448; October 15, 2000, John Peters, review of *The First Olympic Games,* p. 439.
*Publishers Weekly,* October 18, 1993, review of *God's Gift,* p. 72.
*School Library Journal,* December, 1993, Patricia Dooley, review of *God's Gift,* p. 108; November, 2000, Ann Welton, review of *The First Olympic Games,* p. 130.

\*          \*          \*

## RUBEL, Nicole 1953-

### Personal

Born April 29, 1953, in Miami, FL; daughter of Theodore (an importer) and Janice (an importer; maiden name, Berman) Rubel; married Richard C. Langsen (a family therapist), May 25, 1987. *Education:* Tufts University and Boston Museum School of Fine Arts, B.S. (joint degree), 1975. *Hobbies and other interests:* "My Siamese cat, Corgi dog, two saddlebred horses, and [my] plum farm."

### Addresses

*Home*—Aurora, OR. *Agent*—c/o Author Mail, Harper-Collins, 10 East 53rd St., New York, NY 10022-5299.

### Career

Painter, illustrator, and writer. Designer of toys and greeting cards. *Exhibitions:* Boston Public Library, 1977; Boston Museum of Fine Arts, 1979; Belmont Library, 1979; Brookline Public Library, 1979; American Illustrators Graphic Association Traveling Show, 1979; Master Eagle Gallery, New York, NY, 1981 and 1984; Justin Schiller Gallery, New York, NY, 1981; Key

*Nicole Rubel*

Biscayne Library, 1990; Gresham City Hall, 1995; and Wilsonville Library, 2002.

### Awards, Honors

Children's Books Showcase Award for Outstanding Graphic Design, 1977, for illustrating *Rotten Ralph;* American Book Association (ABA) award and American Institute of Graphic Arts award, both 1979; *American Bookseller*'s Pick of the Lists, 1984, for *Rotten Ralph,* and 1992, for *It Came from the Swamp* and *Grizzly Riddles; A Cowboy Named Ernestine* was an ABA Pick of the List and a Junior Literary Guild selection.

### Writings

*FOR CHILDREN; AND ILLUSTRATOR*

*Bruno Brontosaurus,* Avon, 1983, published as *Pete Apatosaurus,* Bantam (New York, NY), 1991.
*Me and My Kitty,* Macmillan (New York, NY), 1983.
*I Can Get Dressed,* Macmillan (New York, NY), 1984.
*Bernie the Bulldog,* Scholastic (New York, NY), 1984.
*Pirate Jupiter and the Moondogs,* Dial (New York, NY), 1985.
*Uncle Henry and Aunt Henrietta's Honeymoon,* Dial (New York, NY), 1986.
*It Came from the Swamp,* Dial (New York, NY), 1988.
*Goldie,* Harper (New York, NY), 1989.
*Goldie's Nap,* HarperCollins (New York, NY), 1991.
*The Ghost Family Meets Its Match,* Dial (New York, NY), 1992.
*Conga Crocodile,* Houghton (Boston, MA), 1993.
*Cyrano the Bear,* Dial (New York, NY), 1995.
*No School for Penelope Pig,* Troll (Mahwah, NJ), 1997.
*A Cowboy Named Ernestine,* Dial (New York, NY), 2001.
*No More Vegetables,* Farrar, Straus, 2002.
*Grody's Golden Rules,* Harcourt Brace (San Diego, CA), in press.

*"SAM AND VIOLET" SERIES; AND ILLUSTRATOR; FOR CHILDREN*

*Sam and Violet are Twins,* Avon (New York, NY), 1981.

*Sam and Violet Go Camping,* Avon (New York, NY), 1981.

*Sam and Violet's Christmas Story,* Avon (New York, NY), 1981.

*Sam and Violet's Birthday Book,* Avon (New York, NY), 1982.

*Sam and Violet's Get Well Story,* Avon (New York, NY), 1985.

*Sam and Violet's Bedtime Mystery,* Avon (New York, NY), 1985.

*ILLUSTRATOR; FOR CHILDREN*

Jack Gantos, *Sleepy Ronald,* Houghton (Boston, MA), 1976.

Jack Gantos, *Fairweather Friends,* Houghton (Boston, MA), 1977.

Jack Gantos, *Aunt Bernice,* Houghton (Boston, MA), 1978.

*Willy's Raiders,* Parents Magazine Press, 1978.

*The Perfect Pal,* Houghton (Boston, MA), 1979.

*Greedy Greeny,* Doubleday, 1979.

*The Werewolf Family,* Houghton (Boston, MA), 1980.

*Swamp Alligator,* Simon & Schuster, 1980.

Steven Kroll, *Woof! Woof!,* Dial (New York, NY), 1982.

Michaela Muntean, *The House that Bear Built,* Dial (New York, NY), 1984.

Michaela Muntean, *Alligator's Garden,* Dial (New York, NY), 1984.

Michaela Muntean, *Little Lamb Bakes a Cake,* Dial (New York, NY), 1984.

Michaela Muntean, *Monkey's Marching Band,* Dial (New York, NY), 1984.

Patty Wolcott, *This Is Weird,* Scholastic (New York, NY), 1986.

Richard C. Langsen, *When Someone in the Family Drinks Too Much: A Guide for Children,* Dial (New York, NY), 1996.

Marilyn Singer, *The One and Only Me,* HarperFestival (New York, NY), 2000.

*"ROTTEN RALPH" SERIES; ILLUSTRATOR; FOR CHILDREN*

Jack Gantos, *Rotten Ralph,* Houghton (Boston, MA), 1975.

Jack Gantos, *Worse Than Rotten Ralph,* Houghton (Boston, MA), 1979.

Jack Gantos, *Rotten Ralph's Rotten Christmas,* Houghton (Boston, MA), 1984.

Jack Gantos, *Rotten Ralph's Trick or Treat,* Houghton (Boston, MA), 1986.

Jack Gantos, *Rotten Ralph's Show and Tell,* Houghton (Boston, MA), 1989.

Jack Gantos, *Happy Birthday Rotten Ralph,* Houghton (Boston, MA), 1990.

Jack Gantos, *Not So Rotten Ralph,* Houghton (Boston, MA), 1994.

Jack Gantos, *Rotten Ralph's Rotten Romance,* Houghton (Boston, MA), 1997.

Jack Gantos, *Rotten Ralph's Halloween Howl,* HarperFestival (New York, NY), 1998.

Jack Gantos, *Back to School for Rotten Ralph,* HarperCollins (New York, NY), 1998.

Jack Gantos, *The Christmas Spirit Strikes Rotten Ralph,* HarperFestival (New York, NY), 1998.

Jack Gantos, *Rotten Ralph's Thanksgiving Wish,* HarperFestival (New York, NY), 1999.

Jack Gantos, *Wedding Bells for Rotten Ralph,* HarperCollins (New York, NY), 1999.

Jack Gantos, *Rotten Ralph Helps Out,* Farrar, Straus (New York, NY), 2001.

Jack Gantos, *Practice Makes Perfect for Rotten Ralph,* Farrar, Straus (New York, NY), 2002.

*"RIDDLES" SERIES; ILLUSTRATOR; FOR CHILDREN*

Katy Hall and Lisa Eisenberg, *Grizzly Riddles,* Dial (New York, NY), 1989.

Katy Hall and Lisa Eisenberg, *Batty Riddles,* Dial (New York, NY), 1993.

Katy Hall and Lisa Eisenberg, *Bunny Riddles,* Dial (New York, NY), 1997.

Katy Hall and Lisa Eisenberg, *Mummy Riddles,* Dial (New York, NY), 1997.

Katy Hall and Lisa Eisenberg, *Dino Riddles,* Dial (New York, NY), 2002.

*OTHER*

*Getting Married: A Guide for the Bride to Be* (for adults), St. Martin's Press, 1988.

Also contributor of illustrations to periodicals, including *Boston, Instructor, Redbook, Spider,* and *Scholastic Pre-K.*

## Adaptations

*Rotten Ralph* was adapted for audio cassette, 1988, and for television for the Fox Family channel, 1999; *It Came from the Swamp, Pirate Jupiter and the Moondogs,* and *Goldie* were all adapted for CD-ROM, 1995-96.

*Rubel illustrated* **Rotten Ralph,** *a story about a mischievous feline written by Jack Gantos.*

## Sidelights

Nicole Rubel's illustrations feature zany cats, argumentative alligators, overly artful bears, and brazen bull dogs. They have earned her the title of "one of the best primitive illustrators" in children's books, according to a reviewer for *School Library Journal*. Her signature artwork has been inspired by the paintings of Henri Matisse and by the art deco architecture of her hometown, Miami, Florida. Author-illustrator Rubel is best known for her illustrations for the "Rotten Ralph" series, authored by Jack Gantos, which is fifteen titles strong and growing. In other collaborative work, she has created artwork for the "Riddle" series by Katy Hall and Lisa Eisenberg. Working as an author and illustrator, Rubel has additionally created more than a score of self-illustrated picture books, among them the popular "Sam and Violet" books about twin kittens, as well as the role-reversal picture book *A Cowboy Named Ernestine*.

Rubel was born and raised in Florida, and the palette of that sun-drenched state has remained with her in her illustrations for children's books. "My art work has been described as brightly colored and bold," Rubel noted in an autobiographical sketch for *Fifth Book of Junior Authors and Illustrators*. "I must say that growing up in Miami had an everlasting influence on my sense of reality." Being born an identical twin has also affected her chosen career: her "Sam and Violet" books are inspired by her relationship with her sister, Bonnie. As a child, Rubel noted on her Web site, she let her sister speak for her. Finally, through the encouragement of a teacher, Rubel found her own voice, learning to speak and write for herself. A result of this early influence is that finding your true self and learning to express thoughts and feelings have become dominant themes in Rubel's work.

Rubel attended school in Coral Gables, Florida, and started drawing and painting at an early age, in part spurred by the colorful houses across the street from her family home built in the Chinese style. She loved to draw these buildings as well as the vibrant flowering bushes and trees that abound in and around Miami. At age fourteen she stopped drawing for a time and began experimenting with papier-maché monsters, which she painted with bright colors.

Attending art school in Boston, Rubel further experimented with ceramics and silk screen. A series of drawings about goldfish started her on the path to illustrating children's books. The children's author Jack Gantos offered to put one series of her pictures to words, which started the fruitful collaboration on the "Rotten Ralph" books and others. Rubel had what she called in *Fifth Book of Junior Authors and Illustrators* "an awful cat," which was Gantos's inspiration for Ralph the cat. All the books deal with "the exploits of the truly terrible cat belonging to a little girl, Sarah, who has the patience of a saint," according to a *Publishers Weekly* writer.

The series takes Ralph through the hoops of Christmas, birthdays, romance, Halloween, and show and tell, just to mention some of the adventures. From the outset, it was clear that Rubel had captured the essence of the naughty cat in her illustrations. In *Kirkus Reviews* a critic noted that, with the third title in the series, *Rotten Ralph's Rotten Christmas,* "Rubel's antic, naive illustrations keep this open display of sibling rivalry at a delectable, cathartic remove—while the conjunction with Christmas doubles the stakes." A reviewer for *Horn Book* noted that Rubel's "energetic illustrations are a marvel."

In *Rotten Ralph's Trick or Treat* Gantos and Rubel send Sarah and her cat to a Halloween costume party dressed as each other. When Ralph performs as usual—stealing all the candy and pouring the goldfish bowl into the punch—all the party-goers blame Sarah, and the two are asked to leave. Ralph is unrepentant, and it is this very trait that "has great appeal for children," according to a critic for *Publishers Weekly*. Sarah, however, still loves him—what else can you do with a rotten cat?

In the fifth story, *Rotten Ralph's Show and Tell*, Sarah takes Ralph to school for show and tell after he ruins her other plans—breaking the strings on her violin and decorating himself with her stamp collection. At school, Ralph continues his antics by ringing the dismissal bell early. Ellen Fader, writing in *Horn Book,* commented that "Rubel's trademark illustrations, bright and flat in a cartoonlike style, supply the humorous details that make Ralph's unrepentant antics all the more outrageous." Reviewing the book in *Publishers Weekly,* a critic noted that "readers will be cheered by the cat's awful antics," while *Booklist*'s Ilene Cooper concluded that "the wildly colored pictures capture all of the naughty goings-on with sizzle and snap."

Ralph continues to wreck the best-laid plans of Sarah in *Happy Birthday Rotten Ralph,* but for once he shows some remorse as Sarah tricks him with a surprise party. Hanna B. Zeiger noted in *Horn Book* that Rubel's "wildly bright, cartoonlike drawings once again capture Ralph's rotten antics to perfection." *Booklist*'s Stephanie Zvirin particularly commented on Rubel's "busy, brightly colored paintings, done in child-appealing primitive style," which "are a perfect match for the text." A contributor for *Publishers Weekly* observed that as usual the antics of this "fractious feline" are "totally outrageous, and entirely enjoyable." The same reviewer concluded, "Thanks to this talented author and illustrator, Ralph more than lives up to his reputation in his latest captivating caper."

In *Not So Rotten Ralph* the disobedient feline is sent to finishing school, but Sarah is unhappy with his ensuing polite behavior and happy when Ralph once again returns to his mischievous ways. Zvirin noted in *Booklist* that "Rubel's naive artwork, busy with pattern and witty detail, is as good as ever," and a *Publishers Weekly* reviewer commented on Rubel's "electrically colored, eccentrically patterned illustrations."

Valentine's Day provides the venue for a further escapade in *Rotten Ralph's Rotten Romance,* in which antisocial Ralph rubs himself in garbage so as to be left alone at a party that Sarah drags him to. Zvirin remarked in *Booklist* that as with all the other books in the series this one, too, allows children "the vicarious thrill of being unabashedly naughty," and that Rubel's illustrations "invest the obstreperous cat with more than enough personality to make him memorable." In a starred *Publishers Weekly* review, a contributor wrote that in this "Valentine-themed eighth adventure, misbehaving cat Rotten Ralph remains rude and remorseless." The same critic also praise Rubel's artwork: "The wildly colorful illustrations, loaded with comic details, busy with floral motifs and tiny hearts, gleefully convey the sentimentality Ralph despises and his vain attempts to avoid it."

In *Back to School for Rotten Ralph* the mischievous cat is left at home all alone when Sarah starts school. But Ralph has a plan: he will disguise himself and become Sarah's new school friend. However, not all evil plans are fulfilled, and despite Ralph's efforts, Sarah manages to make new friends at school. "Gantos and Rubel have collaborated to create another wickedly funny adventure about a cat so rambunctiously rotten that you've just gotta love him," wrote Michael Cart in a *Booklist* review. "Rubel's illustrations depict a consistently naughty feline," noted *Horn Book*'s Elizabeth S. Watson, "yet manage to make him believable whether worried and abandoned or loved and purring."

Sarah is a flower girl in a wedding in *Wedding Bells for Rotten Ralph,* and the cat just has to get into the act, too. He manages to insinuate himself in the ceremony, spoiling every wedding photo, getting the bride to kiss a mouse instead of the groom, and generally turning what should be a joyous occasion into a nightmare. "Rubel's jam-packed, slyly amusing artwork captures all the devilry," *Booklist*'s Ilene Cooper said. "Bright as the almost Day-Glo watercolors are, kids' eyes will always be drawn to the red cat up to his old tricks."

In *Rotten Ralph Helps Out* Gantos and Rubel have created a chapter book for their rascally feline to romp about in. Sarah is working on a school project on ancient

*Ernestine, a red-headed girl, disguises herself as a cowboy and becomes part of a cattle drive in* **A Cowboy Named Ernestine.** *(Written and illustrated by Rubel.)*

Egypt, and as usual Ralph wants to be included. But he manages to cause disaster wherever he goes. Accompanying her to the library, he constructs a pyramid out of books while Sarah does her research; then he practices drawing hieroglyphics on the walls. Back home the cat floods the bathroom when Sarah is trying to build a model of an Egyptian boat and fills the living room with sand to recreate an oasis. Finally, Ralph comes to the rescue, however, dressing up as a Sphinx to add zest to Sarah's project. A *Horn Book* critic felt that Rubel's illustrations "not only parallel the story but also reflect the underlying frenzy through contrasting colors, busy detail, and diagonal lines." A contributor for *Publishers Weekly* similarly praised the "animated pictures," which feature "ample amusing particulars and reveal the less-than-rotten Ralph with a range of diverting facial expressions."

A second chapter book in the series, *Practice Makes Perfect for Rotten Ralph,* sees the cagey feline learning lessons about honesty. Sarah and Ralph go to the carnival, joined by over-achieving Percy, an orange tabby. This cat has been building his skills to shine at the carnival, practicing the baseball throw as well as darts. Jealousy rears its ugly head with Ralph when Percy wins all the prizes for Sarah. Ralph decides it is his turn to win prizes for Sarah, and so begins to cheat at every chance, winning all manner of toys. But Sarah becomes suspicious and the contrite Ralph returns all the prizes unfairly won. *Booklist* reviewer Gillian Engberg wrote that fans of the series will enjoy this story's "humor, real emotions, and silly cat-inspired wordplay." Engberg further lauded Rubel's "bright, clear illustrations," which "nicely extend all the fun."

Rubel has also teamed up with Katy Hall and Lisa Eisenberg on the "Riddle" series of books, featuring a different animal for each title. Featured animals have been bats, bears, and bunnies, each providing a variety of riddles from the silly to the sophisticated. *Booklist*'s Zvirin, reviewing *Bunny Riddles,* noted that while Rubel's cartoons do not necessarily provide clues to the solution of the riddles, they are a "strong, colorful complement to the goofy conundrums and are loaded with clever details." Hazel Rochman, writing in *Booklist,* felt that Rubel's "bright, detailed illustrations" for *Mummy Riddles* "are as deadpan and silly as the words." And Rubel's 2002 collaboration with the same writing team, *Dino Riddles,* collects silly puzzlers about dinosaurs in an easy-reader format. This is combined with Rubel's "colorful cartoons" to create a "winning title," according to Patricia Manning in a *School Library Journal* review.

Another of Rubel's multi-book collaborative efforts was with Michaela Muntean, for whom Rubel did the illustrations for *The House That Bear Built, Alligator's Garden, Little Lamb Bakes a Cake,* and *Monkey's Marching Band.* Rubel has also teamed up with her family-therapist husband on the illustrations for his *When Someone in the Family Drinks Too Much: A Guide for Children,* which is intended to help children cope with alcoholism in the family setting. *School*

*Rubel uses her imagination to create unique illustrations, like this one of two alligators playing on the beach.*

*Library Journal* critic Marsha McGrath felt the book was "a reassuring approach to a problem that affects so many children in today's society." A reviewer for *Publishers Weekly* called the book a "highly accessible title on a troublesome topic," and noted that "this picture book by a husband-and-wife team could be of inestimable value to children struggling with alcoholism in their families."

Teaming up with Marilyn Singer, Rubel additionally provided artwork for *The One and Only Me,* in which a little girl describes how she is similar to various members of her extended family. Both drawings and rhymes indicate that while parts of her anatomy resemble other family members, still the child is uniquely herself. "The simple, childlike cartoons are brightly colored and have lots of action and changes of scenery," wrote Shanla Brookshire in a *School Library Journal* review.

Rubel also has produced a respected body of work of her own as an author-illustrator. Starting in 1981 with her "Sam and Violet" books about twin cats, she has continued to write and illustrate books that feature real issues for children splashed with a sense of humor and colorful pictures. With the first two titles, *Sam and Violet Are Twins* and *Sam and Violet Go Camping,* Rubel established a style of illustration that was "vibrant and rough-hewn," according to George Shannon in *School Library Journal.* Nancy Palmer, reviewing *Sam and Violet's Birthday Book* in *School Library Journal,* commented on Rubel's "original, attention-holding pictures" with their "wonderfully patterned interiors." Rubel has commented that she was influenced by the work of the painter Henri Matisse, and such influence can be seen especially in the rich ornamentation of her interiors.

More felines are to be found in her *Me and My Kitty,* but with *Bruno Brontosaurus* Rubel began to go further afield for animal inspiration. A takeoff on the ugly duckling theme, this book with its "bright and simple pictures . . . will have high child appeal," according to Lauralyn Levesque in *School Library Journal.* The counting book *Pirate Jupiter and the Moondogs* features a tough bulldog and his crew of moondogs who search the galaxies for treasure. Jean Hammond Zimmerman noted in *School Library Journal* that "Rubel's use of black ink and colored markers is well suited to the text." A critic writing in *Publishers Weekly* remarked that with "trenchant wit and mad cartoony types . . . Rubel has attracted an army of boys and girls who will embrace this blastoff into space."

Crocodiles and alligators inspire several Rubel titles. *Uncle Henry and Aunt Henrietta's Honeymoon* is a bedtime reminiscence about the honeymoon of these two green crocodiles. It is "a humorous romp," according to Denise M. Wilms writing in *Booklist.* Writing in *Kirkus Reviews,* a contributor felt that the book would "tickle funny bones" and that "Rubel's one-of-a-kind illustrations enhance her series of yarns with bold, eye-catching colors throughout." Alfie the alligator is the star of *It Came from the Swamp,* the story of a baseball-playing critter who gets hit by a line drive and subsequently suffers from amnesia. He does not realize he is an alligator and leaves the Everglades to cause havoc in the civilized world of humans. Phillis Wilson commented in *Booklist* that "Rubel's cartoon illustrations are awash with humor and sun-drenched vitality." And with the drum-playing crocodile in *Conga Crocodile,* Rubel "introduces yet another obstreperous fellow—and again displays her wry sense of humor," according to a *Publishers Weekly* reviewer.

Additionally, Rubel has featured a mischievous chick called Goldie in two titles, *Goldie* and *Goldie's Nap,* and a clutch of ghosts in *The Ghost Family Meets Its Match.* In the last-named book, the Ghost family has been successful for a century in scaring people away from their haunted house, but as the title implies, they meet their match with new tenants, the Merry family, who have their own surprise to share. *Horn Book* writer Mary M. Burns, while noting that the "premise of the story is clever, matched by detailed, framed illustrations which expand the tongue-in-cheek humor of the text," also concluded that *The Ghost Family Meets Its Match* was

"a winning answer to requests for 'scary stories that aren't too scary.'" Anna Biagioni noted in *School Library Journal* that the "book is sure to be a favorite." And a reviewer for *Publishers Weekly* drew special attention to Rubel's artwork for this title: "Teeming with the sort of eccentric, eye-catching detail that characterizes Rubel's illustrations for the Rotten Ralph books, depictions of the interior of the haunted house are a paean to the delights of excess."

Rubel puts a new twist on the Cyrano story with *Cyrano the Bear,* in which that brave sheriff does not want to let Roxanne, the town librarian, know he has been writing love poems to her. Denia Hester, reviewing the story in *Booklist,* concluded that the "illustrations, scintillating watercolors punched-up with black-ink outlines, create a handsome setting for this funny tale." A reviewer for *Publishers Weekly* similarly noted that Rubel includes a "pleasing profusion of detail in her art," and that she also "stuffs the narrative with plenty of plot elements."

A feisty cowgirl takes center stage in Rubel's *A Cowboy Named Ernestine.* Mail-order bride Ernestine O'Reilly has come all the way from Ireland to Lizard Lick, Texas, only to discover that her intended husband is a rather rotten human. In fact Ernestine has seen "neater pigs and more courteous donkeys," as Rubel writes in the book. The Irish lass decides that she has not come all this distance to play second fiddle to a boor. Instead, she disguises herself as a man, runs off, and becomes a cattle herder under the name of Ernest T. O'Reilly, trying to earn money to get her back to Ireland. Soon Ernestine discovers she has a real talent for being a cowboy, loves the life, and begins to compete in rodeos. During one such competition, however, her hat falls off, revealing her true identity. No tragedy, though, for this opens the door to true love with her cowboy buddy, Texas Teeth.

Reviewers had high praise for this tall tale. "Rubel's words and pictures work together to bring this Wild West romp to life," wrote *School Library Journal* critic Steven Engelfried, who felt that Rubel's "bold ink-and-marker drawings capture the humor perfectly," brimming with "expressive figures and funny details." Engelfried also had praise for the text: "The colorful language adds to the atmosphere without being overdone." Reviewing the title in *Booklist,* Shelle Rosenfeld lauded this "delightful western tale," which features a "folksy, droll narrative; plenty of action; and an admirably resourceful heroine." Rubel's "signature" artwork also has "whimsy and charm," according to Rosenfeld, including the hidden armadillo that young readers must find on every page. In a starred *Publishers Weekly* review, a contributor also had positive words for Rubel's artwork, noting that she "creates a vibrant landscape with clapboard saloons, cactus and critters galore." The same reviewer concluded that fans of "Annie Oakley and Calamity Jane will root for independent-minded Ernestine in this humdinger of a campfire story."

In her collaborative efforts as well as her self-illustrated titles, Rubel has created a style of artwork that is immediately recognizable. Funny tales are what Rubel excels in: stories that blend off-beat, wry humor with distinctively colorful and richly detailed illustrations. From Rotten Ralph to Ernestine, "Rubel contributes a unique artistic vision to the art of children's books," concluded a critic for *Children's Books and Their Creators.*

## Biographical and Critical Sources

*BOOKS*

Holtze, Sally Holmes, editor, *Fifth Book of Junior Authors and Illustrators,* H. W. Wilson (New York, NY), 1983, pp. 269-270.
Silvey, Anita, editor, *Children's Books and Their Creators,* Houghton (Boston, MA), 1995.

*PERIODICALS*

*Booklist,* May 1, 1986, Denise M. Wilms, review of *Uncle Henry and Aunt Henrietta's Honeymoon,* p. 1317; October 15, 1988, Phillis Wilson, review of *It Came from the Swamp,* p. 414; October 1, 1989, Ilene Cooper, review of *Rotten Ralph's Show and Tell,* p. 348; October 1, 1990, Stephanie Zvirin, review of *Happy Birthday Rotten Ralph,* pp. 338-339; March 1, 1994, Stephanie Zvirin, review of *Not So Rotten Ralph,* p. 1269; June 1, 1995, Denia Hester, review of *Cyrano the Bear,* pp. 1788-1789; November 15, 1996, Stephanie Zvirin, review of *Rotten Ralph's Rotten Romance,* p. 593; November 15, 1996, Stephanie Zvirin, review of *Bunny Riddles,* p. 596; August, 1997, Hazel Rochman, review of *Mummy Riddles,* p. 1909; August, 1998, Michael Cart, review of *Back to School for Rotten Ralph,* p. 2014; June 1, 1999, Ilene Cooper, review of *Wedding Bells for Rotten Ralph,* p. 1841; April 1, 2001, Shelle Rosenfeld, review of *A Cowboy Named Ernestine,* p. 1480; May 1, 2001, Gillian Engberg, review of *Wedding Bells for Rotten Ralph,* p. 1689; March 1, 2002, Gillian Engberg, review of *Practice Makes Perfect for Rotten Ralph,* p. 1136.
*Bulletin of the Center for Children's Books,* May, 1985, p. 127.
*Horn Book,* November-December, 1984, review of *Rotten Ralph's Rotten Christmas,* p. 279; November-December, 1989, Ellen Fader, review of *Rotten Ralph's Show and Tell,* p. 759; January-February, 1991, Hanna B. Zeiger, review of *Happy Birthday Rotten Ralph,* p. 94; January-February, 1993, Mary M. Burns, review of *The Ghost Family Meets Its Match,* pp. 77-78; August, 1994, p. 479; September-October, 1998, Elizabeth S. Watson, review of *Back to School for Rotten Ralph,* p. 598; September-October, 2001, review of *Rotten Ralph Helps Out,* p. 582.
*Kirkus Reviews,* September 1, 1984, review of *Rotten Ralph's Rotten Christmas,* p. J60; February 15, 1986, review of *Uncle Henry and Aunt Henrietta's Honeymoon,* p. 306.
*Publishers Weekly,* May 24, 1985, review of *Pirate Jupiter and the Moondogs,* p. 70; August 22, 1986, review of *Rotten Ralph's Trick or Treat,* p. 95; August 11, 1989, review of *Rotten Ralph's Show and Tell,* pp. 457-458; June 29, 1990, review of *Happy Birthday Rotten Ralph,* pp. 100-101; July 27, 1992, review of *The Ghost Family Meets Its Match,* pp. 61-62; July 5, 1993, review of *Conga Crocodile,* p. 71; January 10, 1994, review of *Not So Rotten Ralph,* pp. 61-62; May 29, 1995, review of *Cyrano the Bear,* p. 84; June 17, 1996, review of *When Someone in the Family Drinks Too Much,* pp. 64-65; November 25, 1996, review of *Rotten Ralph's Rotten Romance,* pp. 75-76; July 26, 1999, review of *Bunny Riddles,* p. 93; January 22, 2001, review of *A Cowboy Named Ernestine,* p. 323; July 2, 2001, review of *Rotten Ralph Helps Out,* p. 76; March 25, 2002, "Beginning Reader Buddies," p. 66.
*School Library Journal,* November, 1981, George Shannon, review of *Sam and Violet Are Twins* and *Sam and Violet Go Camping,* p. 81; May, 1982, Nancy Palmer, review of *Sam and Violet's Birthday Book,* p. 80; February, 1984, Lauralyn Levesque, review of *Bruno Brontosaurus,* pp. 63-64; October, 1985, Jean Hammond Zimmerman, review of *Pirate Jupiter and the Moondogs,* pp. 161-162; January, 1989, review of *It Came from the Swamp,* p. 66; November, 1992, Anna Biagioni, review of *The Ghost Family Meets Its Match,* p. 77; November, 1993, p. 90; April, 1994, p. 102; July, 1995, p. 68; July, 1996, Marsha McGrath, review of *When Someone in the Family Drinks Too Much,* p. 79; November, 1997, Eunice Weech, review of *Mummy Riddles,* p. 107; June, 1999, Jane Marino, review of *Wedding Bells for Rotten Ralph,* pp. 94-95; July, 2000, Shanla Brookshire, review of *The One and Only Me,* p. 87; March, 2001, Steven Engelfried, review of *A Cowboy Named Ernestine,* p. 219; June, 2001, Teresa Bateman, review of *Happy Birthday Rotten Ralph* (audiobook), p. 76; February, 2002, Patricia Manning, review of *Dino Riddles,* p. 120.
*Times Educational Supplement,* March 6, 1987, p. 37.
*Wilson Library Bulletin,* December, 1991, p. 98.

*OTHER*

*Nicole Rubel Web Site,* http://www.nicolerubel.com/ (February 8, 2002).

—*Sketch by J. Sydney Jones*

\*      \*      \*

# RYE, Anthony
# See YOUD, (Christopher) Sam(uel)

# S

## SALTZBERG, Barney 1955-

### Personal

Born April 30, 1955, in Los Angeles, CA; son of Irving and Ruth Saltzberg; married, 1985; wife's name, Susan; children: two. *Education:* Graduated from Sonoma State College, 1977.

### Addresses

*Home*—Los Angeles, CA. *Agent*—c/o Harcourt 525 B St., San Diego, CA 92101.

### Career

Artist, illustrator, children's book author, and singer-songwriter. Performed concerts for children in numerous locations. Songwriter and producer of albums adapted from the Public Broadcasting System (PBS) children's series *Arthur.*

### Member

Society of Children's Book Writers and Illustrators.

### Awards, Honors

Junior Library Guild selection, and Parents' Choice Award, both 2000, and California Young Reader Medal nominee, 2003, all for *The Soccer Mom from Outer Space;* California Young Reader Medal finalist, 1999, for *Mrs. Morgan's Lawns;* Oppenheim Award, for *The Flying Garbanzos.*

### Writings

#### SELF-ILLUSTRATED

*Utter Nonsense,* McGraw-Hill (New York, NY), 1980.
*It Must Have Been the Wind,* Harper & Row (New York, NY), 1982.
*What to Say to Clara,* Atheneum (New York, NY), 1984.
*The Yawn,* Atheneum (New York, NY), 1985.

*Barney Saltzberg*

*Cromwell,* Atheneum (New York, NY), 1986.
*Hi Bird, Bye Bird,* Barron's (New York, NY), 1990.
*What Would You Do with a Bone?,* Barron's (New York, NY), 1990.
*Mrs. Morgan's Lawn,* Hyperion (New York, NY), 1993.
*This Is a Great Place for a Hot Dog Stand,* Hyperion (New York, NY), 1994.

*Where, Oh, Where's My Underwear?,* Hyperion (New York, NY), 1994.

*Show and Tell,* Hyperion (New York, NY), 1994.

*Phoebe and the Spelling Bee,* Hyperion (New York, NY), 1996.

*Backyard Cowboy,* paper engineered by Renée Jablow, Hyperion (New York, NY), 1996.

(With Laura Numeroff) *Two for Stew,* illustrated by Salvatore Murdocca, Simon & Schuster (New York, NY), 1996.

*The Flying Garbanzos,* Crown (New York, NY), 1998.

*Animal Kisses,* Harcourt (San Diego, CA), 2000.

*The Soccer Mom from Outer Space,* Crown (New York, NY), 2000.

*Baby Animal Kisses,* Harcourt (New York, NY), 2000.

*The Problem with Pumpkins: A Hip and Hop Story,* Harcourt (San Diego, CA), 2001.

*Hip, Hip, Hooray Day!: A Hip and Hop Story,* Harcourt (San Diego, CA), 2002.

*Peekaboo Kisses,* Harcourt (San Diego, CA), 2002.

*ILLUSTRATOR*

Lisa Rojany, *Jake and Jenny on the Farm: A Finger Puppet Play Book,* Price Stern Sloan (Los Angeles, CA), 1990.

Wendy Boyd-Smith, *There's No Barking at the Table Cookbook,* Lip Smackers, Inc., 1991.

Lisa Rojany, *Jake and Jenny on the Town: A Finger Puppet Lift-the-Flap Book,* Price Stern Sloan (Los Angeles, CA), 1993.

Lisa A. Marsoli and Stacie Strong, *Bow, Wow, and You on the Farm,* Child's Play of England, 1996.

Judy Sierra, *There's a Zoo in Room 22,* Harcourt (San Diego, CA), 2000.

Amy Ehrlich, *Kazam's Magic,* Candlewick Press (Cambridge, MA), 2001.

Amy Ehrlich, *Bravo, Kazam!,* Candlewick Press (Cambridge, MA), 2002.

Stuart Murphy, *Slugger's Carwash,* HarperCollins (New York, NY), 2002.

*OTHER*

Also creator of two musical recordings, *The Soccer Mom from Outer Space* and *Where, Oh, Where's My Underwear?*

## Work in Progress

*Crazy Hair Day,* for Candlewick Press; illustrating *How Many Elephants Are in the Closet,* written by Selby Beeler, for Candlewick Press.

## Sidelights

Barney Saltzberg is an author and illustrator of children's books. In addition to writing, Saltzberg also composes songs, often performing concerts for children in schools, libraries, and hospitals across the country. Discussing the beginning of his writing career on his Web site, Saltzberg explained that although he dreamt of being a musician early on in his life, a career as a writer did not become a possibility until he took a printmaking class while also studying art at Sonoma State College in California. The assignment he completed for this class

*Saltzberg's pencil-and-watercolor illustrations depict twenty-six class pets, each of whose names start with a different letter of the alphabet. (From* There's a Zoo in Room 22, *written by Judy Sierra.)*

resulted in one of his first children's books, *It Must Have Been the Wind.*

As with *It Must Have Been the Wind,* Saltzberg's subsequent books for children have been both written and illustrated by him. In *What to Say to Clara,* for example, Saltzberg accompanied his text with black-and-white cartoon-like pictures, telling the simple story of a shy boy named Otis and his attempts to gather enough courage to speak to a classmate. "Droll" and "firmly etched" drawings accompany the text of this "larky" story, noted a reviewer in Publishers Weekly. Saltzberg's next work, *The Yawn,* was another simple narrative, although this time he tells the story without words as a young boy begins his day with a huge yawn, passing it on to a dog, who passes it to someone else. Thus, a chain reaction begins, until it even affects the moon. In a review for *School Library Journal,* Deb Andrews praised the simple illustrations of this book, saying that the narrative will "spark discussion among young children" because it relates an experience they are all familiar with.

Another familiar subject, the stereotypical unpleasant and mean neighbor, is the subject of Saltzberg's 1993 offering, *Mrs. Morgan's Lawn.* As the protagonist of this tale contemplates the dreaded task of asking Mrs. Morgan to return his ball from her yard, he imagines a number of other possibilities that would also retrieve the ball for him. Eventually, though, he does venture into the yard to make the request. "The boy's forthright narration rings true" and the author's "naïve ... illustrations are a funny complement to the text" said Elizabeth Bush in *Booklist*. Saltzberg continued to focus on everyday activities and realistic actions in several of his other books, including *Where, Oh Where Is My Underwear?, Show and Tell,* and *Backyard Cowboy*.

A more involved story is told in *This Is a Great Place for a Hot Dog Stand,* a tale of "individual enterprise and ingenuity" according to Jane Marino of the *School Library Journal*. The book tells of hopes and dreams, as Izzy, a factory worker, quits his job to begin a business selling hot dogs. In *Phoebe and the Spelling Bee,* Saltzberg returns to a familiar theme: dealing with fear and unpleasant tasks. Writing in *Booklist*, Stephanie Zvirin remarked that although the spelling list Phoebe is confronted with would be a bit complicated for the book's intended audience, readers "will readily recognize themselves in Phoebe's ... attempts to avoid ... something new and scary." And a reviewer for *Publishers Weekly* praised Saltzberg for providing children with a new tactic to learning words.

A family of circus acrobats named the Garbanzo's take center-stage in *The Flying Garbanzos,* in which the family of five, including a two-year-old baby fly and perform acrobatic tricks even when they are not on stage. "Sure to be a hit," enthused Virginia Golodetz in the *School Library Journal*. A critic for *Publishers Weekly* also remarked favorably upon the book, stating that "fast action and shouted dialogue ensure that the pages turn in a hurry" with two-year-old Beanie ending this "amiable" tale in true Garbanzo style: "a death-defying swan dive into the icing." Outrageous behavior of another sort is the subject of Saltzberg's *The Soccer Mom from Outer Space,* an exaggerated look at an overly enthusiastic soccer mom. Lena's mom's excitement about her daughter's upcoming soccer game leads her dad to tell her the tale of his own mother and her antics during his childhood, and the book eventually ends with the three of them equally eager to attend Lena's first soccer game. Reviewing this book for the *School Library Journal*, Blair Christolon noted that while children would certainly relate to the story, it was also a "particularly good choice for coaches to use for a meeting with new soccer parents."

*Saltzberg wrote and illustrated* **Baby Animal Kisses,** *a touch-and-feel book for young children.*

## Biographical and Critical Sources

*BOOKS*

Ward, Martha E., and others, *Authors of Books for Young People,* Scarecrow Press (Metuchen, NJ), 1990.

*PERIODICALS*

*Booklist,* December 1, 1993, Elizabeth Bush, review of *Mrs. Morgan's Lawn,* p. 701; October 1, 1997, Stephanie Zvirin, review of *Phoebe and the Spelling Bee,* p. 339.
*Horn Book Guide,* spring, 1994, Amy Quigley, review of *Mrs. Morgan's Lawn,* p. 52; spring, 1998, Patricia Riley, review of *Phoebe and the Spelling Bee,* p. 64.
*Publishers Weekly,* December 21, 1984, review of *What to Say to Clara,* p. 88; November 8, 1993, review of *Mrs. Morgan's Lawn,* p. 75; October 13, 1997, review of *Phoebe and the Spelling Bee,* p. 74; September 7, 1998, review of *The Flying Garbanzos,* p. 93.
*School Library Journal,* August, 1982, review of *It Must Have Been the Wind,* p. 105; December, 1984, review of *What to Say to Clara,* p. 76; December, 1985, Deb Andrews, review of *The Yawn,* p. 82; April, 1986, Ronald Van de Voorde, review of *Cromwell,* p. 79; May, 1995, Jane Marino, review of *This Is a Great Place for a Hot Dog Stand,* p. 94; September, 1998, Virginia Golodetz, review of *The Flying Garbanzos,* p. 181; August, 2000, Blair Christolon, review of *The Soccer Mom from Outer Space,* p. 164.

*OTHER*

*Barney Saltzberg's Web Site,* http://www.barneysaltzberg.com (October 2, 2001).

*       *       *

# SCHMIDT, Gary D. 1957-

## Personal

Born April 14, 1957, in Massapequa, NY; son of Robert H. (a bank vice-president) and Jeanne A. (a teacher) Schmidt; married Anne E. Stickney (a writer), December 22, 1979; children: James, Kathleen, Rebecca, David, Margaret, Benjamin. *Education:* Gordon College, B.A., 1979; University of Illinois at Urbana-Champaign, M.A., 1981, Ph.D., 1985. *Religion:* Christian Reformed. *Hobbies and other interests:* Gardening.

## Addresses

*Home*—Alto, MI. *Office*—Department of English, Calvin College, Grand Rapids, MI 49546. *E-mail*—schg@calvin.edu.

## Career

Calvin College, Grand Rapids, MI, professor of English, 1985—, department head, 1991-97.

## Member

Children's Literature Association, Early English Text Society, Phi Kappa Phi, Phi Alpha Chi.

## Awards, Honors

Honorable mention, Book Award Committee, Children's Literature Association, 1993, for *Robert McCloskey;* Best Books for Young Adults citation, American Library Association (ALA), 1997, for *The Sin Eater. Booklist* "10 Best Historical Fiction novels" for *Anson's Way,* 2001.

## Writings

*FOR CHILDREN*

*John Bunyan's Pilgrim's Progress,* illustrated by Barry Moser, Eerdmans (Grand Rapids, MI), 1994.
*Robert Frost,* illustrated by Henri Sorensen, Sterling Publishing (New York, NY), 1994.
*The Sin Eater* (novel), Dutton (New York, NY), 1996.
*The Blessing of the Lord: Stories from the Old and New Testaments,* illustrated by Dennis Nolan, Eerdmans (Grand Rapids, MI), 1997.
*William Bradford: Pilgrim of Answerable Courage,* Eerdmans (Grand Rapids, MI), 1997.
*Anson's Way,* Clarion Books (New York, NY), 1999.
*William Bradford: Plymouth's Faithful Pilgrim,* Eerdmans (Grand Rapids, MI), 1999.
*Saint Ciaran: The Tale of a Saint of Ireland,* illustrated by Todd Doney, Eerdmans (Grand Rapids, MI), 2000.
(Editor, with Frances Schoonmaker Bolin and Brod Bagert) *The Blackbirch Treasury of American Poetry,* Blackbirch Press (Woodbridge, CT), 2001.
*Mara's Stories,* Henry Holt (New York, NY), 2001.
*Straw into Gold,* Clarion Books (New York, NY), 2001.
*The Wonders of Donal O'Donnell: A Folktale of Ireland,* Henry Holt (New York, NY), 2002.
*The Great Stone Face,* illustrated by Bill Farnsworth, Eerdmans (Grand Rapids, MI), 2002.

*FOR ADULTS*

*Supplementary Essays for College Writers,* Prentice-Hall (Englewood Cliffs, NJ), 1988.
(Editor, with Charlotte F. Otten) *The Voice of the Narrator in Children's Literature: Insights from Writers and Critics,* Greenwood Press (Westport, CT), 1989.
*Robert McCloskey,* Twayne (Boston, MA), 1990.
*Hugh Lofting,* Macmillan (New York, NY), 1992.
(Editor, with Donald R. Hettinga) *Sitting at the Feet of the Past: Retelling the North American Folktale for Children,* Greenwood Press (Westport, CT), 1992.
(Editor, with William J. Vande Kopple) *Communities of Discourse: The Rhetoric of Disciplines* (includes instructor's manual), Prentice-Hall (Englewood Cliffs, NJ), 1993.
*Katherine Paterson,* Macmillan (New York, NY), 1994.
*The Iconography of the Mouth of Hell: Eighth-Century Britain to the Fifteenth Century,* Susquehanna University Press (Cranbury, NJ), 1995.
*Robert Lawson,* Macmillan (New York, NY), 1997.

*With only seven days to solve a riddle or lose his life, Tousle seeks the answer from the banished queen whose son was stolen by Rumpelstiltskin. (Cover illustration by Cliff Nielsen.)*

(With Carol Winters) *Edging the Boundaries of Children's Literature,* Allyn & Bacon (Boston, MA), 2001.

Contributor to books, including *Text and Matter: New Critical Perspectives of the Pearl Poet,* edited by Robert J. Blanch, Miriam Miller, and Julian Wasserman, Whitston (Troy, NY), 1991. Contributor of articles, essays, stories, poems, and reviews to journals, including *Christian Home and School, Lion and the Unicorn, Studies in American Humor, Christian Educators Journal,* and *Martha's KidLit Newsletter.* Guest editor, *Children's Literature Association Quarterly,* 1989.

## Work in Progress

A biography of Hannah Adams.

## Sidelights

Gary D. Schmidt has blended a career as professor of English with one that involves writing both for children and adults. His fiction and nonfiction children's books span genres from young adult and middle grade novels to picture books and deal with topics from biography to

suicide. His novels include *The Sin Eater, Anson's Way,* and *Straw into Gold,* while in other books, including *The Blessing of the Lord: Stories from the Old and New Testaments, William Bradford: Plymouth's Faithful Pilgrim,* and *Saint Ciaran: The Tale of a Saint of Ireland,* Schmidt mixes religious themes with biographical tales and retellings.

Schmidt's first books were for adults, but after writing a few biographies of children's writers, including *Robert McCloskey* and *Katherine Paterson,* he turned his hand to his own children's books. Ilene Cooper, reviewing Schmidt's biography of Paterson in *Booklist,* commented that he does "an excellent job of chronicling" the life of this two-time Newbery Award winner. Schmidt once told *SATA:* "My first two children's books, the retelling of *Pilgrim's Progress* and *The Sin Eater,* both came out of my own past. *Pilgrim's Progress* had been with me some fifteen years before I finally turned to a retelling. It seemed to me that there were strong reasons why children would have turned this into a child's story back in the seventeenth and eighteenth centuries, and I was not convinced that those reasons no longer pertained in the late twentieth century. I wrote the retelling thinking of my own early responses to the book, cutting out the parts that bored and that struck discordant notes."

Schmidt's retelling of *Pilgrim's Progress* "is much more accessible than the original version," according to *School Library Journal* contributor Kate Hegarty Bouman, voicing a common response to the work. Bouman noted that Schmidt's "mix of both historical periods and ethnic groups is a fascinating way to extend the text spatially and temporally." A reviewer for *Publishers Weekly* similarly praised Schmidt's "masterly rendition" as "a treasure sure to delight young and old."

Schmidt's first young adult novel was *The Sin Eater.* "For *The Sin Eater,* I reached back into my own family's past and that of my wife," Schmidt told *SATA.* "The house is not the same as, but is like a real house in Brunswick, Maine. Though the action of the novel itself is not based on real events, the responses of the characters mirror responses that I have had in my past to not dissimilar events and people. The places around the farmhouse are all real, though drawn from sites in upper New York state, the Catskill Mountains, the White Mountains of New Hampshire, and Cape Cod."

In *The Sin Eater,* middle-schooler Cole and his father move in with Cole's maternal grandparents in rural New Hampshire after Cole's mother dies of cancer. Cole delights in their new surroundings and in the village lore and tales of ancestry told him by his grandparents and other locals. Cole's father, however, remains grief-stricken and ultimately commits suicide. "A work laden with atmosphere and meaning, this is a promising debut from an author who captures with admirable accuracy both the dark and light of life," asserted a *Kirkus Reviews* critic. A *Publishers Weekly* reviewer also found Schmidt's *Sin Eater* an "engrossing first novel," adding that the plot forms a "point of departure for a profound and lyrical meditation on life and the importance of shared history."

*The Blessing of the Lord: Stories from the Old and New Testaments* includes retellings from "unusual perspectives," as Shelley Townsend-Hudson commented in *Booklist.* Schmidt retells the stories of Jonah, Deborah, Barak, Peter, and others, with a twist that gives the "often tired old tales ... new life," according to Townsend-Hudson. Maeve Visser Knoth, writing in *Horn Book Guide,* felt that Schmidt emphasized "the humanity of the characters," while a *Publishers Weekly* reviewer praised the "dramatic spin" Schmidt gave to these tales.

Further religious and spiritual matters are served up in *William Bradford: Plymouth's Faithful Pilgrim* and *Saint Ciaran: The Tale of a Saint of Ireland.* The former biography, intended for older readers, looks at the guiding light of the Plymouth Colony, painting "a warm and cohesive picture of William Bradford's role in that colony's foundation and growth," as a critic for *Kirkus Reviews* observed. Bradford, an orphan from early childhood, embraced Puritan ideals as a teenager and ultimately led a group of Separatists on a perilous mission to found a colony in the New World. Schmidt uses Bradford's own writings as well as contemporary journals and prints to take the reader back into the religious beliefs of those early colonists. "The author clearly presents Bradford's religious views and shows how those beliefs affected his life and actions and those of the Pilgrims," wrote Elaine Fort Weischedel in a *School Library Journal* review.

Schmidt's *Saint Ciaran* is a picture book intended for younger readers. "In mouth-filling cadences of Gaelic ... Schmidt tells the story of the sixth-century Irish saint," noted GraceAnne A. DeCandido in *Booklist.* Growing up a spiritual child, Ciaran went to Rome and discovered religion in the city's churches. Sent back to Ireland by St. Patrick, he founded a religious community that attracted members from all over the island. DeCandido felt that this was a "beautiful picture book for older children," and Kathleen Kelly MacMillan, writing in *School Library Journal,* similarly thought the book was a "gently moving tribute to a lesser-known saint."

"Teaching children's literature as I do, I have the opportunity to read many of the extraordinary children's books published each year," Schmidt continued to *SATA.* "But teaching also means that I need to balance each day between my family, my writing, and my students. This, especially when the care of a hundred-fifty-year-old farm is thrown into the balance, becomes a delicate act. It means that I can spend one to three hours a day on my writing, but that's all. Afterwards, there are other worlds to turn to.

"Working at a college also means that I combine several levels of writing. Having finished one novel and begun work on another, I also want to try my hand at picture books. At the same time, I work on books that are slightly more arcane: a study of the medieval image of the mouth of hell and a biography of an eighteenth-century female historian. For me, these two very different kinds of writing (both creative, but one more scholarly than the other) help keep each project exciting rather than burdensome, even though there are the days when neither seems to have much energy."

Schmidt demonstrates the variety of his prose styles in two further books, *Anson's Way* and *Straw into Gold.* Again using Ireland for a setting, this time in the eighteenth century, Schmidt features a young Anson Granville Staplyton who follows his family calling and joins the Staffordshire military, the Fencible. Dreaming of glory, he is sent to Ireland as a mere drummer to help keep the peace. When he sees fellow soldiers persecuting the locals, he begins to have mixed loyalties. He meets an Irish hedge master, a person who illegally teaches the Irish their forbidden language and culture, and he soon befriends some of the Irish rebels. Ultimately, Anson is forced to choose between his comrades in arms and his new Irish friends. This book "realistically portrays not only the tragedies of war but also the battle between heart and mind of a young soldier," as *Booklist* writer Shelle Rosenfeld remarked. Janice M. Del Negro, reviewing the title in *Bulletin of the Center for Children's Books,* also praised this "complex action/adventure novel" with its "shifting moral center." "Replete with drama and action," wrote Hilary Crew in *Voice of Youth Advocates,* "Schmidt's story presents a side of Irish history that is frequently marginalized in textbooks."

In his middle grade novel *Straw into Gold,* Schmidt spins a new twist in the old Rumpelstiltskin tale, extending it to see what could have happened. In Schmidt's rendering, young Tousle leaves his forest cottage with his magical father, Da, to travel to the city and view the king's procession. He becomes separated from his father and then surprises himself by calling out for mercy for some rebels facing execution. One other voice raised against the execution is that of the queen herself. The king will spare the lives only if Tousle and a blind young rebel, Innes, are able solve the riddle the king sets for them: "What fills a hand fuller than a skein of gold?" "So begins a suspenseful quest that adds surprising twists and turns to the traditional fairy tale," wrote *Booklist* critic Frances Bradburn. *School Library Journal* reviewer Ginny Gustin was also beguiled by the tale, calling it a "fantasy-flavored quest."

"In thinking about my own work in children's literature, it seems to me that I am interested in showing the beatific and terrible complexities of our lives." Schmidt concluded for *SATA.* "I have had one reader tell me that *The Sin Eater* was sadder and funnier than he thought it would be. It seems to me that our lives are just that: often sadder and funnier than we ever thought they would be. They are also more beatific than we have any reason to expect, and my hope is to show that in the context of a world that is often dark."

## Biographical and Critical Sources

*PERIODICALS*

*Booklist,* April 1, 1990, p. 1563; May 1, 1994, Ilene Cooper, review of *Katherine Paterson,* p. 1611; November 1, 1994, p. 1611; December 1, 1994, Hazel Rochman, review of *Robert Frost,* p. 669; November 1, 1996, Ilene Cooper, review of *The Sin Eater,* p. 491; November 1, 1997, Shelley Townsend-Hudson, review of *The Blessing of the Lord,* p. 469; April 1, 1999, Shelle Rosenfeld, review of *Anson's Way,* p. 1428; April 1, 2000, GraceAnne A. DeCandido, review of *Saint Ciaran,* p. 1459; August, 2001, Frances Bradburn, review of *Straw into Gold,* p. 2108.

*Bulletin of the Center for Children's Books,* May, 1994, p. 306; November, 1996, p. 114; May, 1999, Janice M. Del Negro, review of *Anson's Way,* pp. 327-328.

*Horn Book,* July-August, 1990, p. 476.

*Horn Book Guide,* spring, 1997, p. 84; spring, 1998, Maeve Visser Knoth, review of *The Blessing of the Lord,* p. 96; fall, 1998, Tanya Auger, review of *William Bradford,* p. 416.

*Kirkus Reviews,* September 1, 1996, review of *The Sin Eater,* p. 1328; June 1, 1998, review of *William Bradford,* p. 816.

*New York Times Book Review,* November 13, 1994, p. 30.

*Publishers Weekly,* December 19, 1994, review of *John Bunyan's Pilgrim's Progress,* pp. 54-55; October 14, 1996, review of *The Sin Eater,* p. 84; August 25, 1997, review of *The Blessing of the Lord,* p. 66; March 1, 1999, review of *Anson's Way,* p. 70; April 10, 2000, review of *Saint Ciaran,* p. 95.

*School Library Journal,* December, 1994, Kate Hegarty Bouman, review of *Pilgrim's Progress,* p. 130; February, 1995, p. 104; October, 1997, Patricia Pearl Dole, review of *The Blessing of the Lord,* p. 154; April, 1999, Starr E. Smith, review of *Anson's Way,* p. 12; June, 1999, Elaine Fort Weischedel, review of *William Bradford,* p. 153; August, 2000, Kathleen Kelly MacMillan, review of *Saint Ciaran,* p. 175; August, 2001, Ginny Gustin, review of *Straw into Gold,* p. 188.

*Voice of Youth Advocates,* August, 1994, p. 176; June, 1998, Kathleen Beck, review of *The Sin Eater,* p. 103; August, 1999, Hilary Crew, review of *Anson's Way,* pp. 185-186.

\*          \*          \*

# SCHUR, Maxine Rose 1948-

## Personal

Born October 21, 1948, in San Francisco, CA married; children: Aaron, Ethan. *Education:* University of California—Berkeley, B.A. (dramatic arts), 1971; Stanford University, M.L.A., 1999. *Hobbies and other interests:* Reading, traveling, visiting art museums.

## Addresses

*Agent*—c/o Dial Books for Young Readers, 345 Hudson St., New York, NY 10014. *E-mail*—mschur@ promethod.com.

## Career

New Zealand National Film Unit, Wellington, New Zealand, film editor, 1974-75; actress in television program *Close to Home,* New Zealand Broadcasting Corp. and Downstage Theater; freelance writer, 1977—; Addison-Wesley Publishing Co., staff writer, 1978-80; Wordwright Inc., cofounder and educational software designer, 1981-84; Hewlett-Packard, Corporate Communications Manager, 1988-1990; Software Publishing Co., marketing project manager, 1990-92. Currently marketing communications consultant, copywriter, travel essayist, and children's and adult book author.

## Member

Society of Children's Book Writers and Illustrators, PEN, Authors Guild, Society of American Travel Writers, Business Marketing Association.

## Awards, Honors

Work-in-Progress Grant, Society of Children's Book Writers and Illustrators, 1981, and Louis B. Dessauer Award, 1994, both for *The Circlemaker;* nominee, National Jewish Book Award, 1987, for *Hannah Szenes: A Song of Light;* Parents' Choice Award, 1994, for *Day of Delight: A Jewish Sabbath in Ethiopia;* Lowell Thomas Award, Society of American Travel Writers, 1995, for "Hitchhiking the Caribbean"; Sydney Taylor Award, Association of Jewish Libraries, 1997, and Sugarman Family Award, Washington, D.C. Jewish Community, 1997, both for *When I Left My Village;* National Jewish Book Award finalist, 1997, Notable Book, American Social Studies Council, 1998, Outstanding Book for a Global Society, International Reading Association, 1998, and Hoosier Award finalist, 1999, all for *Sacred Shadows;* Best Book List, *Smithsonian,* 1999, Sydney Taylor Award, Top One Hundred Titles, New York Public Library, 2000, and Best Book List, *California Reader,* all 2000, all for *The Peddler's Gift.*

## Writings

*Weka Won't Learn,* illustrated by Clare Bowes, Viking/Sevenseas (Wellington, New Zealand), 1977.

*The Witch at the Wellington Library,* illustrated by Clare Bowes, Viking/Sevenseas (Wellington, New Zealand), 1978.

*Shnook the Peddler,* illustrated by Dale Redpath, Dillon Press (Minneapolis, MN), 1985, published as *The Peddler's Gift,* illustrated by Kimberly Bulcken Root, Dial (New York, NY), 1999.

*Hannah Szenes: A Song of Light,* illustrated by Donna Ruff, Jewish Publication Society of America (Philadelphia, PA), 1986, paperback, 2000.

*Samantha's Surprise: A Christmas Story* (see also below), illustrated by Nancy Niles and R. Grace, Pleasant Co. (Middleton, WI), 1986.

*The Reading Woman: A Journal,* Pomegranate Art Books (Rohnert Park, CA), 1991.

*The Circlemaker,* Dial (New York, NY), 1994.

*Day of Delight: A Jewish Sabbath in Ethiopia,* illustrated by J. Brian Pinkney, Dial (New York, NY), 1994.

*The Marvelous Maze* (picture book), illustrated by Robin DeWitt and Patricia DeWitt-Grush, Stemmer House (Owings Mills, MD), 1995.

*When I Left My Village,* illustrated by J. Brian Pinkney, Dial (New York, NY), 1996.

*Enchanted Islands: Voices and Visions from the Caribbean: A Journal,* Pomegranate Art Books (Rohnert Park, CA), 1996.

*Sacred Shadows,* Dial (New York, NY), 1997.

*Heart Notes* (journal), Menus and Music (Emeryville, CA), in press.

Contributor of articles and reviews to periodicals, including *Australia/New Zealand Bookworld, Carribean Travel and Life, Christian Science Monitor, Escape Magazine, Los Angeles Times, Insight Guides, Salon.com,* and *San Francisco Examiner.*

## Adaptations

A sound recording of *Samantha's Surprise: A Christmas Story* was produced by Pleasant Co., 1986; a sound recording of *Day of Delight,* read by Gregory Hines, was produced by The Jewish Community Library of Los Angeles Public Radio Series, 2002; *The Peddler's Gift* was read by Gregory Hines for National Public Radio.

## Sidelights

An author of both picture books and historical novels, Maxine Rose Schur has set her writing against such diverse backgrounds as mid-nineteenth-century Russia, the rural highlands of Ethiopia, and prewar Poland. Many of her books feature Jewish characters whose lives, placed against these diverse backgrounds, illuminate the Jewish past and add to the understanding and compassion of contemporary readers. Among Schur's award-winning works for young readers are *The Circlemaker* and *Day of Delight,* both published in 1994, *Sacred Shadows,* published in 1997, *Day of Delight*'s sequel, *When I Left My Village,* and the 1999 title *The Peddler's Gift.*

As a child, Schur had what she later termed the "good fortune" to contract rheumatic fever, which required a long period of rest as she recovered. During this time she learned to read and to enjoy books, with no television to distract her. Her favorite books were those that transported her to far-off places or back in time: *Black Beauty, Heidi, Little Women, Little Lord Fauntleroy,* and *Anne of Green Gables,* among others. These books strongly influenced Schur's career as a writer in the decades to come: she still enjoys writing books set in different historical periods.

Despite her early love of books, Schur did not plan to be a writer. Graduating from high school in the mid-1960s, she majored in drama and received a degree in dramatic arts from the University of California-Berkeley. Soon after graduation, she married and set out with her husband on a trip around the world for a year and a half, traveling by bus, train, car, donkey, truck, and tramp steamer during an adventure that took them to over forty countries. In 1972 the Schurs began a five-year stopover in Wellington, New Zealand, where Schur became a documentary and feature film editor, children's book critic, and actress. While living in New Zealand, she found that her thoughts were "haunted by exotic scenes, unforgettable people, and incredible anecdotes, 'traveler's tales,'" as she once recalled. Schur began to write, first about the adventures she and her husband had in southern Turkey. These autobiographical writings were made into story books illustrated by the Caldecott Award-winning illustrator Victor Ambrus. "These first small beginnings got me hooked on writing as a means of remembering and communicating," Schur revealed. "I've been hooked ever since. Much of my writing is still drawing inspiration from that journey [around the world] ... but much also takes its inspiration from the journeys I made in distance ... and time in my own mind."

Returning with her husband to the United States in 1977, Schur was unsure about what direction her life should take. Now a mother with a small child at home, she quickly realized that writing was a more practical occupation than acting, so she began taking on freelance writing assignments. A year later Schur was hired as an in-house writer for Addison-Wesley Publishing Company. "I didn't know such dream jobs existed," she recalled of the position. "Each day I'd come to work and brainstorm with a wonderful group of crazy, creative types and then go into my office to write original poems, stories, riddles, and articles. It was not only bliss, but a great training that really honed my writing skills."

In 1981 Schur and a partner founded Wordwright, a company that created educational software for young people. During this "exciting time," the author recalled. "we worked with several of the pioneering companies in computer games, and we learned a tremendous amount about not only computer design but marketing children's products." Schur later began work as a marketing communications manager for the high-tech industry. For several years she balanced her growing responsibilities with her writing projects, still managing to find time to work on several children's book projects, including *Shnook the Peddler* and *Hannah Szenes.* Finally, after three of her books were sold to Dial in quick succession—*The Circlemaker, Day of Delight,* and *When I Left My Village*—Schur was able to return to her writing full-time.

Characteristic of Schur's work is *Hannah Szenes: A Song of Light,* a biography of the World War II resistance fighter and poet who was executed for treason in 1944 at the age of twenty-three. Nominated for the National Jewish Book Award, the book is based on the diaries of Szenes, whose idealism prompted her to parachute into war-torn Hungary to aid resistance fighters during the Nazi takeover of Europe. In her 1997 book *Sacred Shadows,* Schur describes the life of a German Jew living in Poland between the two world wars. Reviewing that novel in *Booklist,* Hazel Rochman noted that Schur "combines one person's coming-of-age story with a strong sense of the time." Rochman concluded that the account in *Sacred Shadows* of what it was like to grow up Jewish during this time is "most compelling." A critic for *Kirkus Reviews* also found much to like in Schur's novel, concluding: "The novel offers readers a moving glimpse of how public opinion set the stage for genocide."

In *The Circlemaker,* readers are introduced to twelve-year-old Mendel, a Russian Jew living in the Ukraine who disguises his Jewish heritage and flees from the Russian soldiers who have come to his town to conscript children for service in the czar's army. The year is 1852, and Mendel, along with fellow runaway Dovid, must make it to the Hungarian border without being caught. *The Circlemaker* is not only a story of a boy taking on the moral responsibilities of adulthood but "an exciting story of terror and disguise, of leaving home and outwitting the enemy," according to Rochman, writing in *Booklist.* A *Publishers Weekly* commentator, who gave the book a starred reveiw, called *The Circlemaker* an "atmospheric and suspenseful" work that "maintains an edge-of-the-seat tension until the very last words." A critic for *Kirkus Reviews* wrote, "The genuinely evoked setting and the plucky boy's narrow escapes compel attention." In *Booklist,* a reviewer commented that the book "combines fast-paced adventure with a compelling sense of history." Susan Faust, writing for the *San Francisco Examiner,* called it a "gripping children's novel" that is "taut and tender ... pages seem to turn themselves."

Two books that reveal a less familiar Jewish world are Schur's award-winning *Day of Delight: A Jewish Sabbath in Ethiopia* and *When I Left My Village.* Both books focus on black African Jews who inherited Jewish traditions many centuries ago while living in the remote Gondar province of Ethiopia. Their culture was so isolated from the rest of the world that many Beta Israel (Ethiopian Jews) did not even realize that other Jews existed in the world. Unfortunately, the famine that plagued their country in the 1980s forced many of the Beta Israel to leave for the Sudan and Israel, and many of the old ways were lost. In *Day of Delight,* Schur records these traditions, including the weekly preparations for what the Beta Israel call the "Day of Delight," the Sabbath. Described from the point of view of a ten-year-old boy named Menelik, the story is "an economical evocation of an entire way of life," according to a reviewer for *Publishers Weekly,* who called the book "fascinating." A reviewer for *School Library Journal* called this book "a gem," and *Horn Book* contributor Hanna Zeiger wrote that *Day of Delight* is "simply and tenderly told, a beautifully crafted book." *Day of Delight* won the 1994 parent's choice award, the Smithsonian

Best Book of the Year citation, and was a finalist for the Sydney Taylor Award.

The exodus of Menelik's family to Israel in the face of famine and civil war is brought to life in *When I Left My Village,* a 1996 book that Maria Salvadore described in *Horn Book* as "provocative and emotional ... a riveting family story." A reviewer for *Publishers Weekly* noted that the book featured "writing with pathos deepened by memorable imagery. A trenchant sequel." A contributor to *Kirkus Reviews* noted, "With great artistry, Schur weaves history, adventure, and family drama into a polished narrative." *When I Left My Village* was awarded the 1997 Sydney Taylor Award by the Association of Jewish Libraries for the most outstanding contribution to Jewish children's literature.

With *The Peddler's Gift,* Schur presents another aspect of Jewish culture in a new version of a wise fool story set in a shtetl. Everyone believes Shimon the peddler is a simpleton. One night young Leibush steals a dreidel from him, but racked with guilt, he tracks Shimon down alone in the synagogue to return the stolen item. There Leibush discovers Shimon's secret. Far from being the fool that everyone takes him for, Shimon is, in the words of *Booklist*'s Rochman, "wise, strong, and kind." A reviewer for *School Library Journal* explained, "This gentle story is written with a fine folkloric tone that evokes both the richness and simplicity of a time long past." A contributor for *Publishers Weekly* praised the book's "poignantly handled themes about forgiveness" and further applauded Schur's "colorful delivery and scene-setting," which "give her message a fresh impact." Kathleen Burke of the *Smithsonian Magazine* wrote, "This nuanced portrait of shtetl life opens a window onto a lost world." In the *Atlantic Journal and Constitution,* Julie Bookman praised the book as "A season standout!" and Faust of the *San Francisco Examiner* noted, "Schur writes with poetic grace ... with color and depth, making a painful incident poignant and underscoring some of life's elusive lessons." *The Peddler's Gift* earned the Sydney Taylor Award, making Schur the only author to win this prestigious award twice.

Schur divides her time between her travel writing, children's books, teaching at conferences, and consulting work. She enjoys talking to her readers—especially her young readers—at bookstores, libraries, conferences, and schools. She travels the world as a travel writer and also still likes to "noodle around" with game ideas and designs for gift products—she's developed calendars, bookmarks, and journals. "I have a busy, diverse, satisfying life right now," Schur once commented, "with just enough time to read."

## Biographical and Critical Sources

*PERIODICALS*

*Atlantic Journal and Constitution,* December 4, 1999, Julie Bookman, review of *The Peddler's Gift.*
*Booklist,* January 15, 1994, Hazel Rochman, review of *The Circlemaker,* p. 919; October 1, 1994, Stephanie Zvirin, review of *Day of Delight: A Jewish Sabbath in*

*Ethiopia,* p. 334; February 15, 1996, Stephanie Zvirin, review of *When I Left My Village,* p. 1023; September 15, 1997, Hazel Rochman, review of *Sacred Shadows,* p. 224; October 1, 1999, Hazel Rochman, review of *The Peddler's Gift,* p. 375.

*Bulletin of the Center for Children's Books,* October, 1986, Betsy Hearne, review of *Hannah Szenes: A Song of Light,* p. 36.

*Children's Literature,* July 23, 1988, Jan Lieberman, review of *Sacred Shadows.*

*Contra Costa Times,* October 15, 1997, Judith Rose, review of *Sacred Shadows.*

*Horn Book,* November-December, 1994, Hanna B. Zeiger, review of *Day of Delight,* p. 747; May-June, 1996, Maria B. Salvadore, review of *When I Left My Village,* p. 333.

*Kemper County Messenger,* December 21, 1995, Brook Sledge, review of *The Marvelous Maze.*

*Kirkus Reviews,* January 1, 1994, review of *The Circlemaker;* December 15, 1995, Grace A. De Candido, review of *When I Left My Village;* October 15, 1997, review of *Sacred Shadows,* p. 1588.

*Publishers Weekly,* December 6, 1993, review of *The Circlemaker,* p. 73; September 5, 1994, review of *Day of Delight,* p. 110; January 8, 1996, review of *When I Left My Village,* p. 70; August 11, 1997, review of *Sacred Shadows,* p. 403; September 27, 1999, review of *The Peddler's Gift,* p. 52.

*San Francisco Examiner,* December 12, 1993, Susan Faust, review of *The Circlemaker;* November 28, 1999, Susan Faust, review of *The Peddler's Gift.*

*School Library Journal,* February, 1994, Ann Welton, review of *The Circlemaker,* p. 104; October, 1994, Loretta Kreider, review of *Day of Delight;* March, 1996, Susan Scheps, review of *When I Left My Village,* p. 198; December, 1997, Ellen Fader, review of *Sacred Shadows,* p. 131; October, 1999, Teri Markson, review of *The Peddler's Gift,* p. 72.

*Smithsonian Magazine,* November, 1999, Kathleen Burke, review of *The Peddler's Gift.*

*Spalding University Library Journal,* August, 1996, review of *The Marvelous Maze.*

OTHER

*Author Maxine Rose Schur,* http://www.maxineroseschur.com/ (October 19, 2001).

\*       \*       \*

---

## *Autobiography Feature*

# Maxine  Rose  Schur

I always think that I had the good fortune to have grown up in a happy, secure family in San Francisco. My father was an electrical engineer for the Southern Pacific Railroad. My mother was a housewife. She was a German Jew who grew up in Poland and immigrated to the United States in 1933. They met at a dance and married in 1938. They bought a small house in the foggy Sunset District of San Francisco, near the ocean. In 1940 my brother, Irvin, was born, and in 1948 I came into the world.

I also believe I was fortunate to have gotten rheumatic fever as a child. I was four years old when I became ill, and for a year I could not walk. I couldn't play with other children and we didn't have a television then, so I was motivated to learn to read to keep from being bored. I spent long hours poring over the Dick and Jane readers that we used in the fifties. Of course now they're looked upon as unrealistic and monotonous, but to me they were fascinating. My imagination filled in the repetitive, dull lines. I added all sorts of funny anecdotes and secrets to the characters so that Dick and Jane were far more interesting in my head than they were on the page! That's pretty much what I've been doing ever since. Making things up.

At the age of four I fell in love with books, and the first one I became smitten with was *Heidi.* My version had black-and-white photos of Switzerland and the actors that appeared in the 1952 movie, *Heidi,* which I think is still the best. I made my mother read it to me and as soon as she finished, I made her begin again. Over the years I fell in love with lots of books, in particular *Alice in Wonderland, The Wheel on the School, Little Women* and all the other books by Louisa May Alcott. I didn't want to read about kids whose lives were like mine. I sure didn't want to read about kids in T-shirts! No, I loved the "Anne of Green Gables" series and had a passion for historical books such as *Little Lord Fauntleroy, Caddie Woodlawn, The Silver Sword,* and *The Secret Garden.* I also had a great passion for biography, especially biographies of ballet dancers such as Anna Pavlova and legendary actresses such as Katherine Cornell. At that time too, my elementary school took in dozens of blind students. At lunchtime I used to help the younger children who were blind. I read a lot of books about the world of the blind and even started teaching myself braille.

My great love was reading and it was also the love of my father. I think that much of my passion for literature, certainly an appreciation for the beauty of the *sound* of words, came from him. My father was an electrical engineer who had taught himself literature. He particularly liked Dickens and Shakespeare. I was no more than seven when he taught me to recite whole passages of Longfellow's "Evangeline." I had only a vague idea what the story was about but I delighted in the poem's powerful descriptive expressions such as "hemlocks, Bearded with moss, and in garlands green" and "the deep-voiced neighboring ocean."

My father had little chance to travel as he had to work hard during the Depression. He was, however, an enthusiastic armchair traveler. Early on, he introduced me to the old 1930s books of Richard Halliburton and so vicariously I traveled to exotic lands with archaic names: Siam, Malaya, Belgian Congo, TransJordan. I would pore over the black-and-white photographs of those books and yearn to travel myself. From my mother, I was given a love of music. Each day when I arrived home from school, I found our house perfumed with music. My mother often played her classical music records, so from an early age I was familiar with melodies by Strauss, Chopin, Beethoven, Mozart, and Verdi. Looking back now, I think my childhood was quite enriched. From an early age, I was taken to operas, ballets, and plays. We visited the art museums and attended concerts in Golden Gate Park and Sigmund Stern Grove. Growing up in San Francisco, every Saturday morning I was taken to mandolin lessons in the heart of bohemian North Beach. In the mid-1950s, they still had live theater in Chinatown. Once my father took me to a play there. The actors were dressed in beautiful costumes and spoke in Chinese. My father and I sat on rough benches and were the only non-Chinese in the small audience. I still remember the thrill of this little experience. He also took me to the Turnabout Theatre. In this theater, all the children watched a puppet show, and when it was over, they turned their seats about to face the opposite direction where there was another stage and then, they watched a play! I learned from my father to always be open to something new ... to the unknown.

We also traveled as much as my parents' budget would allow. In my early childhood this meant camping up at Yosemite. Later, because my father worked for the Southern Pacific Railroad, it meant traveling by train to Vancouver, Salt Lake City, Los Angeles, San Diego, and other western destinations. This may not seem exotic now, but in those days, before mass tourism, it was full of romance. We ate in the dining car and slept in a little bedroom on the train. I remember the wonder of waking up around midnight at one of the stops and, from my bed, seeing a great arched neon sign "Reno, the Biggest Little City in the World," and then falling back to sleep as the train speeded east.

Perhaps because of my early exposure to the theater, by the time I entered high school, I was determined to be an actress. I loved drama for I loved the very thought of "becoming" someone else and entering an imagined world. I joined the San Francisco Children's Opera, a theater group founded by Austrian-Jewish refugees. They wrote all their own musicals and directed a children's group to perform them. We sang and acted with gusto, producing a different musical every couple of months. Once a year we put on a performance at the San Francisco Opera House,

*Maxine Rose Schur*

and it was a great thrill to just stand on that enormous stage and look up into the vast house. I went to rehearsals twice a week after school. I took drama in high school too and got top grades in it. I acted in the term play and danced in the senior show, *West Side Story*. In my senior year, the theater was of utmost importance to me. At this time, in 1965, a new repertory company was founded in San Francisco, The American Conservatory Theater. I went to all their performances with a student discount card, often attending several plays a month. I was so in love with the theater that I deliberately missed an Honors English final exam to go to a play. Here's what happened: I was an Honors English student and never skipped a class in my life. My English teacher told me that if I didn't show up for the final exam, he would give me a grade of "F" on it. I was in the California Scholarship Federation and so very ambitious about school, but I had a dilemma. Eva Le Gallienne, the great French actress, was appearing in Euripides's *The Trojan Women* in San Francisco for one performance only. It would be this acting legend's last performance, and I knew I couldn't miss it. I went to see Eva Le Gallienne and never regretted my decision. In 1966 I entered San Francisco State University as a drama major.

I found majoring in drama both wonderful and frightening. It was wonderful because San Francisco State was at that time one of the finest places in the country to study professionally for the theater. I loved my classes and soon saw that the history of theater encompassed almost everything a person needed to know. It taught me world history, literary history, art history, religion, and psychology, public speaking, and poise. But studying there was also frightening because it was highly competitive. Auditions were grueling, sometimes lasting two weeks and with five hundred other people. The standards were high. Each year you had a private conference with your advisor and at this conference you were told whether the faculty deemed it worth your while to continue. Luckily, I was encouraged as I was quite good in acting as well as dancing. In fact, because of my dancing skill in doing the Charleston, I was the only undergraduate ever to be allowed into a graduate show. The show was the musical *The Boyfriend* by Sandy Wilson, and I got into it because of my dancing ability after two weeks of grueling auditions.

In 1968 my liberal arts studies fueled my passion for travel; I wanted to see the world for myself. In January of that year, I decided to go to college only part time, and I worked as a file clerk part time at a saddle-making company to save the money to go to Israel in the summer. I planned to stay with my aunt (my mother's sister) in Tel Aviv and travel around the country. For six weeks I lived in Israel, a tiny nation still hopeful from their victory in the Six-Day War. My journey to Israel proved fascinating and just fed my itch for travel. From Israel, I flew by myself to Athens, Greece. I was nineteen and this was the first time I was completely on my own. I arranged travel around the Peloponnesian peninsula with a group of six students and a guide, a girl my own age! As a drama student, I particularly related to Greece where drama as we know it was born. One balmy evening I took myself to the Theater of Herodus Atticus in Athens to see a production of *Hecuba*. I basked

*At age two*

in my adventurous new freedom. That single week exploring ancient theaters and temples remains one of my dearest memories.

In the fall of 1968, San Francisco State exploded into antiwar and free-speech riots. Campus life was chaos. A bomb was planted and blew up in our drama department. Crockery flew in the cafeteria when fights broke out between all kinds of activist and political student groups. Students shouted on bullhorns and used loudspeakers mounted on pickup trucks. I had to weave through crowds and picket lines just to get to class. Once I saw the strangest sight: the U.S. cavalry in their dark blue uniforms galloping across our campus lawn! At that time I was working as a helper and reader for several blind students. I loved this job because I got to use my drama training in recording their textbooks on tape. I loved the students I worked with; they became my friends. I began to study braille again and thought seriously that if acting didn't turn out, I could become a braille teacher.

I experienced the hippie world firsthand. I was really in love with the music of that era. Each weekend I went to the Avalon Ballroom or the Fillmore Auditorium or Winterland. For three dollars I could see The Grateful Dead, Jefferson Airplane, Quicksilver Messenger Service, Janis Joplin, The Doors, John Mayall, Jimi Hendricks, and a host of other wonderful musicians. I didn't know of course that I was witnessing legends at the time. All I knew was that I loved this original, powerful music. In the autumn of 1968, I attended a football game with a boyfriend at the University of California at Berkeley. I had never been on this campus before and its size and beauty impressed me deeply. At that time Berkeley was, in many ways, the heart of the hippie movement and of the antiwar movement. The streets and campus were alive with speakers, dancers, bongo drum players, and of course thousands of students. I was twenty years old and had one year of college left to go. I decided to transfer to "Cal." I moved into a small apartment with two girlfriends and got involved in the drama department.

One of my reasons for leaving San Francisco State was to get away from the riots, but when I entered U. C., the riots in Berkeley made San Francisco State look like child's play. Often when I walked to class, I could hear the drone of the police helicopters overhead. I had to be always sure to have a damp washcloth wrapped up in my purse in case they started the tear gas again. There were antiwar riots on Telegraph Avenue and riots to save People's Park. One day, as I was hurrying to a Shakespeare class, I passed two odd things: a giant slingshot about twenty feet high that the students had set up and an army truck upside down and on fire. I had become so immune to the chaos of college life, I barely blinked at either of these bizarre, frightening things.

It was in Berkeley that I met the man I was to marry: Stephen. He was not a student but working at the Lawrence Radiation Laboratory as a computer operator. When I graduated we got married and by that time Berkeley had become even more chaotic. I wanted to leave. I wanted to see the world, to travel to Paris, London, and Rome. My husband had already seen Europe. In fact he had lived in France for more than two years, attending the Sorbonne and teaching. He and I struck a deal. We would travel to Europe but then we would venture overland through Asia and Australia. We would come to New Zealand and settle there

*The author in September, 1971*

as he felt there would be lots of opportunity and he liked the idea that New Zealand was an underpopulated place. I had no knowledge of New Zealand as I barely knew where it was but I agreed.

In January of 1971, we bought an old Opel Rekord for a hundred dollars and said goodbye to our families. We drove down through Arizona to Mexico then down to Guatemala and Honduras. Our journey took about three months. We went leisurely and we went deep. I loved every minute. When we came to Honduras, we sold our car and hitchhiked on a tramp steamer all around the Caribbean. We were signed on as crew and no one, not even the captain, had any idea where the ship was to go next! For a month we sailed from island to island on this rusty old boat with a rope ladder. Once the crew held a mutiny and threw all the crockery out the porthole! Once the captain gambled away the crew's pay and once a former cook came aboard and threatened to poison us all! The ship stopped at Aruba, Curacao, Trinidad, and Puerto Rico. This "honeymoon cruise" was so unusual and so funny that years later I wrote about it. My travel essay, "Hitchhiking the Caribbean," was awarded the 1995 Lowell Thomas Award for excellence in

travel journalism by the Society of American Travel Writers.

From Puerto Rico, we flew to New York City and then a week later to London. We toured England and Wales then traveled to Germany where we bought a Volkswagen van and went to Paris. There by the banks of the Seine in the heart of the city, we camped. This odd experience I wrote about in another essay, "My Idea of Paris" which was published in numerous publications including a travel anthology, *Real-Life Tales of Adventure and Romance,* published in 2000 by Random House.

From Paris we traveled around Western Europe and at last came to Switzerland where we met up with some friends from Berkeley who were employed by a German entrepreneur in a new laser company. They were all living near the town of Monthey in the French-speaking canton of Valais. The moment we crossed the border into Switzerland, I was smitten. All my romantic childhood memories of *Heidi* combined to make me yearn to live there. To experience the *Heidi* life firsthand. Then my husband, who spoke excellent French, was invited to work for the laser company as well, as a kind of bilingual liaison. I was thrilled. The other Americans lived in apartments in the town, but we rented a traditional chalet high in the Alps in the tiny hamlet of Troistorrents. I loved living in this small traditional community. I made friends with my landlady and improved my college French. To this day, my idyllic "Heidi" life in Switzerland has stayed with me as the dearest of memories. It is an experience I wrote about years later in an essay called simply "Troistorrents" that was published in the *San Francisco Examiner.*

In winter of 1971, we left Switzerland in our van with no heater and drove all the way to Pakistan. It was a rough, sometimes dangerous journey, but the rewards were great. We went over the St. Bernard Pass in winter, across the Alps down to foggy Venice, down through sunny Yugoslavia, and east to Bulgaria. Then, as soon as we crossed the border from Bulgaria into Turkey, it seemed as if the world had turned magical. We fell in love with Turkey and lingered in every town. Because the road east, from Turkey to Iran, was closed due to snow, we decided to stay several weeks on the southern Mediterranean coast until the road was clear. In a café in the town of Silifke we met a poor Turkish fisherman who spoke broken English. He invited us to stay in his small dung and straw home with his family. For two months we lived the traditional life of Turkish villagers. This was a beautiful experience that in some way changed my life. It remains one of my most cherished memories. The family sewed traditional Turkish clothes for me: baggy cotton flowery pants and a white headscarf rimmed with green bead flowers. I wore these clothes, and we traveled with them to the high Caucasus mountains to visit their relatives. We celebrated holidays together and went off on all kinds of adventures. From Turkey we traveled through snow-covered Iran and then crossed into Afghanistan. We traveled extensively throughout Afghanistan, and it was much like having entered a time machine and finding ourselves in a medieval world. These countries impressed me deeply. I was especially in love with Afghanistan. I found beauty, poetry, and poignancy there in a land little known and understood.

In Pakistan we sold our van and traveled by public transport throughout Northern India and Nepal. In India we journeyed by train, third class. Once we slept in the luggage rack! Traveling on the trains then was difficult. There was no air conditioning so we had to keep the windows wide open in the sweltering heat. The problem was that the trains were steam trains and the smoke and soot flew in the windows, dirtying our clothes. Then we flew to Burma and then on to Thailand, Malaysia, and Singapore where we boarded a boat sailing to Perth, Australia. In Australia we hitchhiked across the whole country, all the way to Sydney. I loved traveling across Australia this way. Each morning we would eat breakfast in a trucker café. We would eat a big steak, fries, and eggs and wash it down with what the Aussies called "white coffee," that's coffee with milk. At night, traveling through the Nullarbor desert was enchanting. Kangaroos would jump about on the road that was a thousand miles long and seemed to lead nowhere. After a month living in a sad little flat in the Chippendale neighborhood of Sydney, we boarded an immigrant ship, the *S. S. Ellinis,* that took us to our final destination: New Zealand.

At first I did not like New Zealand at all. After living in San Francisco and Berkeley, New Zealand seemed provincial. Few New Zealanders at that time had ever left New Zealand, and so I felt as if my head was bursting with romantic and unique images of many lands, yet I had no one except Stephen to share them with. I also sensed that the long journey I had just taken had changed me in some deep, irrevocable way, but I wasn't yet sure *how* it had changed me. I felt out of place.

However, slowly, I began to fit in. We settled in the capital, Wellington, where I made friends. I got involved in amateur theater and acted in several plays, even taking the lead role in a musical melodrama. But I was still yearning to tell someone about the wondrous things I had seen. I took low-paying jobs, because the truth was I had little job experience. In one of my jobs, I sat at a table all day with six other women in a factory and added numbers up on a calculator. It was grueling, and the irony was that I was pretty poor in math. If I made a mistake, I'd have to start all over again. In Wellington I took a job with a greengrocer selling vegetables. I actually enjoyed this job, lowly as it was, because I learned interesting names for fruits and vegetables like kumara and silverbeet and greengage. And of course I learned to say "toe-mot-toe." In 1973 I took a job as an assistant film editor with Pacific Film Company. One day at our teatime, my friend Mona Williams, the film projectionist from Guyana, read some short stories for children she had written about growing up in that country. The stories were wonderful, full of color and interest. Her beautiful stories gave me the idea that perhaps I could *write* my travel memories rather than tell them. A few weeks later on a borrowed typewriter, I began to write down my memories of living in a small fishing cooperative on the Turkish coast. These memories I wrote simply for children and sent them. I sent them to Mona's editor at the New Zealand School Journals, which are published by the Department of Education. The editor not only loved them, she asked for more.

That's how I became a writer.

Those first Turkish tales were illustrated by the celebrated British children's book illustrator Victor Ambrus who based his drawings on photos from our trip. I also began to write short stories for children based on incidents

*Maxine and Stephen arriving in New Zealand, 1972*

of my childhood growing up in San Francisco. These stories were also published in the New Zealand School Journals. I wrote about my ancient Hebrew teacher, how he fell asleep as soon as he began teaching. I wrote how my friend Freda and I once tried on wedding dresses at Macy's when we were thirteen, and I wrote about an eccentric cousin who sang operetta late at night on the cable cars. Soon I was thought of as a writer. I wrote poems and stories for Radio New Zealand and for the BBC television program, "Playschool." I also at this time became a children's book critic, writing reviews for both *The New Zealand Listener* and *Australia and New Zealand Book World.* I loved reviewing because it made me think hard about what made a good children's book. Also I got to interview well-known writers such as New Zealand's great children's book author Margaret Mahy and also Theodore Geisel, better known as Dr. Seuss.

New Zealand gave me the opportunity to blossom in many ways. I wrote short stories that were published in the country's literary journal, *Landfall,* and I wrote my first two children's books there, *Weka Won't Learn,* a small picture book that describes the curious habits of New Zealand's flightless birds, and *The Witch at the Wellington Library,* about an artistic witch who lives in a broom closet of the public library and paints beautiful, but spooky pictures.

During the years I was writing, I was also working as a film editor. In 1974 I took a job working for the New Zealand National Film Unit. I edited both documentary and feature films. At this time, too, I was also appearing on television as an actress. First in the situation comedy *Buck House* and then on the soap opera, *Close to Home.* While working on *Close to Home* I became pregnant. I was very happy because the director simply wrote my pregnancy into the television script so I could continue being in the show. My life was going great. I was doing everything I loved: working in film, writing for children, and acting professionally.

Then a terrifying accident happened.

One weekend when I was five months pregnant, Stephen and I flew in a small plane that was piloted by my friend's boyfriend. Our plan was to fly from Wellington to Rotorua. We flew over the mountains in the fog. The four-seater Cessna bounced in the clouds. Up and down we went, unable to see a thing. Because of the poor weather, we decided to land in Hamilton and continue to Roturua the next day. The next day proved sunny and we were hopeful as we took off. But twenty seconds later, the engine stopped (we found out later that the fuel line was clogged by a piece of rust), and the plane, not high enough yet to glide, fell toward the earth. The quick thinking of the pilot saved our lives. Heading straight down toward a field, he decided not to put the wheels down. If he had they would have tangled in a fence. Instead, we cleared the fence by a few feet and belly-flopped on wet grass then skidded a long way before stopping. The plane was smashed, but as if by a

*Acting in professional theatre company, "Downstage" in Wellington, New Zealand, 1975*

miracle, we all survived. I was the most hurt. A crushed vertebrae and a subsequent six weeks in Hamilton Hospital ended my soap opera career.

After my son, Aaron, was born, I tried out for the professional theater. I auditioned to be a member of Wellington's repertory company Downstage Theater, and I was one of three accepted. But I decided that being in a traveling theater company would be too difficult with a young child. Instead, I tried out for a play at Downstage, *Happy Birthday Wanda June,* by Kurt Vonnegut. I got the lead part. This became my first professional theater job. It worked in well with my life, because I could take care of our baby during the day and work in the evenings. I was very happy.

I was also writing more and more. I wrote stories from my childhood in San Francisco, and I tried my hand at folk tales. Sometimes Aaron would try to take the paper from my hand or eat it! I came up with a solution. I sat in his playpen and wrote, keeping an eye on him while he played outside of it.

In 1977 we moved back to the United States. We rented an apartment in San Francisco near the foggy ocean, and now after being away for seven years away, I found myself in my own country yet didn't know what I could do or be. I felt estranged and knew that I would have to start anew my life in my own hometown.

One day I visited the Jewish Community Library in San Francisco and came across a diary written by a Hungarian girl named Hannah Szenes. She had started the diary when she was thirteen and it was ended before her execution by the Arrow Cross, the Hungarian Nazis at the age of twenty-three. I was fascinated by the story of the courageous young woman who was a poet and also a paratrooper for the British Air Force. I was determined to write her story. In the meantime I had taken freelance jobs in San Francisco as a creative writer. I wrote for large publishing companies such as Scholastic, Houghton Mifflin and Harcourt Brace Jovanovich. In 1978 I took a dream job. It was a full-time, two-year creative writing contract for Addison-Wesley Publishing Company. It was on this job that I met other wonderful writers who remain my dear friends to this day. And it was on this job that I really honed my writing skills by having to write on demand and to limited vocabulary lists. I wrote everything: poetry, riddles, short stories, essays, and games. Once I was asked to produce a funny poem about soybeans—in an hour.

In 1980, my second son, Ethan, was born. Soon after his birth, I began working as a copywriter for the burgeoning high-tech companies and that year founded a copywriting company, Wordwright Inc., with three other writers from Addison-Wesley. A year later, one of the writers and I turned the company into an educational software design firm. As consultants and designers, we became part of the booming children's software industry. With our experience and skill in writing for children, we easily created original, imaginative games, designed all the graphics, and even wrote the package copy! Our clients included Tomy Toys, Atari, Activision, and the Children's Television Workshop. We were on a roll; seeing our own creations sold at Macy's and other stores was very exciting. By 1984 the educational software market took a dive and by this time Ethan was four years old and I was looking to do something full time at home. I wrote short stories for adults and an original Russian-Jewish folktale, *Shnook the Peddler,* that was published by Dillon Press. Also, I returned to the idea of a book for young people about the life of Hannah Szenes. For two years I researched her tragic but inspirational story. I interviewed her classmates, neighbors, fellow paratroopers, teachers, friends, mother, and brother. I discovered an idealistic and romantic girl of great intelligence who found herself caught in an evil web of deceit and treachery when Hungary allied themselves with the German Nazis in the late 1920s. In 1986 my book *Hannah Szenes: A Song of Light* appeared and became a National Jewish Book Award finalist. More important to me though was what Hannah's brother wrote me in a letter. "You are the only writer," he said, "who has captured the spirit of Hannah."

In 1988 I took a full-time job as a corporate communications manager at Hewlett-Packard Company. My job was challenging and enjoyable for I could be very creative. I wrote articles, developed and gave workshops, wrote for and managed a magazine, and led a team that developed a book on writing for HP worldwide. However, as much as I loved my job, I never learned to love the corporate politics.

One day while driving home from work, it suddenly occurred to me that I had seen quite a lot of fine art images of women reading a book. Over the next year, I collected more than a hundred of these images and created a proposal for a journal or diary that women could write in. The journal would be enhanced by twenty-five or so of these images as well as quotations by famous women about their relationship to books and to reading. I licensed my idea to Pomegranate Publications. In 1991 the *Reading Woman* journal appeared. It is still in print and now, more than ten years later, I've also created *Reading Woman* boxed note cards, postcard books, and every year a new *Reading Woman Calendar.* Also, around this time I began to go to an annual Haitian art exhibit at the Alliance Française in San Francisco. I fell in love with Haitian Art and when I visited The Dominican Republic in 1992, I saw a completely different Caribbean art and was privileged to meet many of that country's great artists and art critics. I soon became curious about what art from all the other Caribbean islands was like, and my curiosity grew into a great love for Caribbean art. In 1994, I created another journal for Pomegranate, *Enchanted Islands: Voices and Visions from the Caribbean: A Journal.* This journal, too, became a labor of love as through the research, I met artists, gallery owners, and museum curators throughout the Caribbean. Like *Reading Woman,* for this product I developed a calendar and boxed note cards as well.

In 1990 I took a job as a marketing project manager for another high-tech company, Software Publishing Corporation. In this job I could use a lot of my creativity, conceiving ideas for trade show themes, producing videos, writing ad copy and PR and white papers, and giving classes on how to develop and manage a newsletter. At this time I had written three books and sold them all to Penguin Putnam, for Dial, their juvenile hardback division. Selling all my books in one day to a "big New York publisher" was a dream come true. They were bought by no less than the president of the company herself, the publisher, Phyllis Fogelman. The first book, *Day of Delight,* was a picture book about the traditional life of the Beta Israel, the black Jews who live in the high tabletop mountains of Gondar province in Ethiopia. Through the eyes of a village boy, the book reveals one Sabbath day as observed by the villagers. The second book, *When I Left My Village,* is its sequel. Now the boy, a few years older, must escape with his family to Sudan. They escape persecution and famine and find themselves in a dusty refugee camp before they are miraculously airlifted to their new life in Israel. The third book is a middle-grade historical novel called *The Circlemaker.* It tells the adventurous story of a twelve-year-old Jewish boy who must escape from his village in the Ukraine across the Austro-Hungarian border and then on to America. The boy is escaping a twenty-five-year conscription in the Czar's army, for the story takes place in the 1850s during the thirty-year Cantonist period when all Jewish boys from the age of twelve to eighteen were conscripted for this twenty-five-year service in the eastern provinces or "cantons" of Siberia.

All three books have won awards.

*The Circlemaker* took me thirteen years to write because I rewrote so many times, at last throwing away everything but the first chapter, starting all over again. While I worked on it, I won the Society of Children's Book Writers and Illustrators Work in Progress Grant. The encouragement of this wonderful award and my persistence paid off. *The Circlemaker* became a 1994 American Booksellers "Pick of the Lists" and a Mark Twain Award nominee. It won the 1994 Louis B. Dessauer award as well.

In 1992 I had left full-time work and became a marketing communications consultant. Working independently for our company, Productive Methods Inc., gave me

*Maxine Rose Schur accepting the 1995 Lowell Thomas Award for Adventure Travel Writing, presented by Governor Brereton Jones at the Governor's Mansion in Frankfurt, Kentucky, May 1995*

*"Sometimes travel writing is not too hard!," the Bahamas, 1995*

the flexibility to do more writing. From 1992 I consulted to several of the major companies in Silicon Valley including Intel, Adaptec, and HP. And yes, I have had more time for the creative juices to flow. In 1995 my original fairy tale, *The Marvelous Maze,* was published by Stemmer House. This romantic story of a spoiled, lonely prince and the plain but clever girl that wins his heart, was inspired by a 1986 trip to Hampton Court when a friend and I got lost in the castle's intricate garden maze. *The Kemper County Messenger* described it as a "Wonderful story... a diamond jewel among picture books" and the Book Review Center of Spalding University wrote, "Maxine Rose Schur wraps a powerful message within a charming allegory."

Some time in 1992, a year after my beloved father died, I began a story that I believe I've been writing all my life. *Sacred Shadows* is a young adult book that is loosely based on anecdotes my mother told me about her life growing up in a small town in Poland between the two world wars. I also took much information from my aunts who grew up there as well. I had heard these stories all my life. *Sacred Shadows* is a love story set against the anti-Semitic milieu of pre-Holocaust Europe. The book became a National Jewish Book Award Finalist and a 1998 Notable Book in the Field of Social Studies as well as a 1998 Notable Book for a Global Society by the International Reading Association. *The Horn Book* called *Sacred Shadows,* "exquisitely rendered." *The Contra Costa Times* said it was "A moving story, exquisitely told ... a novel with the ring of authenticity as well as artistry." *Children's Literature* wrote that "The magic of this book lies in the

remarkable writing style of the author whose depiction of time and place is so vivid that you walk the streets and recognize the people."

Nineteen ninety-seven was a very exciting year for me. I flew to Washington D.C. to accept the Sugarman Family Award. I had the great privilege to meet Joan Sugarman herself. Ms. Sugarman invited me to be the guest speaker in the Baker—Nord Humanities Center at Case Western Reserve University. That winter I flew to Cleveland and delivered a lecture that combined both my loves. My lecture was about how I use theater techniques in my fiction writing for young people. I went to Cleveland again that year to give a lecture at the American Jewish Library Association's annual conference, and it was there in Cleveland where I was awarded my first Sydney Taylor Award.

In 1999 my publisher, Dial, had bought the rights to and published a new version of *Shnook the Peddler,* now renamed *The Peddler's Gift.* With new color illustrations by Kimberly Root, the wistful story of a boy who steals a toy from a foolish peddler only to discover he's not so foolish after all, took on a new life. The book won me my second Sydney Taylor Award, a Bay Area Book Reviewer's Nomination, an IRA Notable Book for a Global Society, and a 1999 Smithsonian Notable Book of the Century. The reviews for *The Peddler's Gift* were glowing, and it was wonderful to see this small, simple story of kindness so appreciated.

All the while I was writing children's books, I was still haunted by the long trip I had taken many years before.

*The author with Iban Chief, Stamang Longhouse in Sarawak Borneo, 1996*

One day at my parents house in 1980, I had bemoaned the fact that I had not kept a journal on that wondrous journey. "Oh, but you did," my father had replied quietly. "No, I countered. I didn't write about it at all!" He said nothing but he stood up and went to a drawer of the sideboard in the dining room. He pulled out about forty letters, each one at least six pages. These were the letters I had sent home from that journey. "This," he said, "is your journal." That year when the Soviets invaded Afghanistan, I realized that most Americans knew nothing about Afghanistan, and many had no idea where it was. I wanted to do my part in bringing Afghanistan to the attention of the public. In that year I wrote "A Memory of Heart," an essay that described my stay in this unique city. In that essay I put in all the conversations with Afghans, all the sights, sounds, and smells that I remembered. The essay was published in *San Francisco Magazine* and later in the *San Francisco Examiner,* accompanied by photos I had taken. Years later in 1989, I wrote about the unusual North African Jewish wedding of my brother-in-law that I had attended in Marseilles, France. This essay, "Journey into Marriage" was also published in the *San Francisco Examiner*. The response from readers was heartfelt, and I began to think that maybe I could be a travel writer. Soon I was writing essays about Turkey, Nepal, Mexico, Switzerland, and France, all published in the travel section of the *San Francisco Examiner.* And when people asked me why I am writing about a trip so long ago, my answer was simple: "Only now do I understand it."

Travel writing became my second love. In 1995 an essay I had written about our experience on a tramp steamer drifting about the Caribbean was awarded the Lowell Thomas Award by the Society of American Travel Writers. I was surprised and greatly honored. This award became a turning point for me, because I flew to Lexington, Kentucky, where I accepted the award at a banquet with the governor and his wife at the governor's mansion. On this trip, I met dozens of other travel writers and began to think of myself as one of them. Because the award I had won was in the category of "Adventure Travel Writing," I was invited that year to the International Adventure Travel Conference in Nassau, Bahamas. I fell in love with the Bahamas and the Bahamian people. I flew to Eleuthera and saw how truly beautiful these islands are. I wrote a travel article about Eleuthera and its wonderful people. The following year I went to Malaysia with a group of American travel journalists. In Sarawak I stayed in a longhouse in the rainforest with the Dayak tribe, the former "headhunters" of Borneo. My essay, which included an interview with the tribal chief, was published on *Salon.com* and won for me my second Lowell Thomas Award. Later in 1996 I flew to Vienna and Prague. I wrote a feature article about the extraordinary Austrian artist, architect, and philosopher Friedenreich Hundertwasser, whom I had first met at his exhibit in New Zealand. The article was published in the *Los Angeles Times* and picked up by publications around the world.

By 1997 I was traveling more and more and publishing travel articles and essays for a wide variety of newspapers, travel magazines, and in-flight magazines. I wrote about my love for the ancient ruined city of Petra in Jordan, the famed Copacabana Hotel in Rio, and my nearby city neighbor: San Jose, California. My new role as a travel journalist filled my life with some unforgettable adventures from piranha fishing in Brazil's Amazon rainforest, to bathing in hidden hot springs in Baja California, to snorkeling alongside giant sea turtles in Kauai.

In February of 1997 I was invited to return to the Dominican Republic where I had visited in 1992. I had fallen in love with Dominican art on that first trip and now spent two glorious weeks with the top artists of this small nation. One of the highlights of my visit was to experience Carnival in the mountain top village of La Vega. Here each year a good part of the town dresses up as devils with extraordinary papier-maché masks. They parade to the wild Dominican merengue music and every now and then step out of the parade to whack a spectator's bottom at random with a sand-filled balloon! The festivity for Carnival in La Vega is odd and ribald. I wrote an article about it for several newspapers as well as for the magazine, *Caribbean Travel & Life.*

Later that year I visited South Africa and Zimbabwe to visit three luxury safari lodges. The result was an article, "Elegance with Elephants," about a remarkable experience at a watering hole near Matetsi, thirty miles from Victoria Falls, in which our little Landover became surrounded at dusk by hundreds of elephants . . . some of them threatening us. A surreal, unforgettable vision.

In the next few years, I returned to the Bahamas again and again because I love it so. I love the aqua sea, the pink-sand beaches, the friendliness of the people, the fabulous artists there, and not least of all: Junkanoo. Junkanoo is a celebration with a great parade at Christmas time that is unique to the Bahamas. As in New Orleans at Mardi Gras, groups compete with each other to create the most spectacular float and costumes and choreographed dances. They work in top secrecy in "shacks" until their gargantuan, spectacular creations make a grand appearance at the Junkanoo parade. The drum music of Junkanoo has its roots in West Africa, from which the Bahamian population came as slaves two hundred years ago. When you hear Junkanoo music, you *have* to dance. The last time I visited Nassau, I fulfilled a dream of mine: to be the first non-Bahamian to get inside the shacks and witness the feverish and clandestine preparation for Junkanoo. The result was the article "Time for the Soul to Go Home."

Researching Junkanoo certainly was a most exciting experience. Afterward I flew to Andros, the largest island in the Bahamas and the most still unexplored land in the Western Hemisphere. In Andros I traveled to the very north to the tiny community of Red Bays. Red Bays is a unique community that few people know about. The people of Red Bays are of mixed ancestry. They descend from African slaves brought there in the early nineteenth century and from Seminole Indians who escaped from Florida to the Bahamas during the Indian wars. Today the people of Red Bays have retained both African and Native American lore. Their basket weaving is distinctly Seminole, and I had the privilege to interview and write about the matriarch of the community who has taught nearly everyone in Red Bays how to make watertight baskets that are woven with the colorful locally made batik.

In 1999 I received a master of liberal arts degree from Stanford University. I had begun to study there in 1993 when I had decided that there were so many things in the world I still wanted to learn. I applied and was accepted to the Stanford University's Master of Liberal Arts program. This is a fabulous program geared to working adults, so all the classes are in the evening. I worked on my masters for five years and the experience was a highlight of my life. I soon saw how all my classes, no matter how seemingly different, connected. I studied Darwin and Dante. I studied French history and physics and Egyptian archaeology and nineteenth-century English literature, eighteenth-century European philosophy, Irish poetry, and a host of other enthralling subjects. All the courses made me see the world differently and greatly enhanced my travel. For a year, much of my writing skill went into my thesis which was on the little-known French Baroque artist, George de la Tour. After writing the thesis I had to give a colloquium on this artist before the faculty and the other MLA students. A funny thing happened. Giving that presentation made me yearn for being in front of an audience again. I really enjoyed the whole experience. So in 1999 I began to do more teaching. I developed and gave workshops and lectures on writing for children as well as travel writing. I taught at writing conferences and gave workshops at universities and lectures and readings throughout the San Francisco Bay Area. I love helping other writers realize their writing goals and in particular, helping them find their own voice.

In 1999 I received a phone call from *Caribbean Travel & Life*. They wanted me to do a monthly column and write feature articles that would introduce to their readers the arts and culture of the Caribbean region. I signed a contract with them and so began another labor of love. To this day, I write for the magazine. The job allows me to explore the many islands of the Caribbean and learn more about its varied cultures and little-known but vibrant artists.

Of course, all the time that I've been writing for children and writing travel pieces, I have continued to work in the high-tech industry. As a marketing communications consultant and copywriter, I use all my experience and skill as a creative writer but apply it to the needs of the corporate world. I consult on corporate identity, positioning messaging, and write everything from annual reports to ads. The funny thing is that I have found my experience as a children's writer to be extremely helpful in copywriting when the goal is to get complex ideas across simply and with creativity and enhanced by images, as in a picture book.

Sometimes wearing three or more writing hats isn't easy. I need to be extremely disciplined with my time and juggle several projects in a day. The problem is that I'm greedy; I just don't want to give up any of my vocations!

Recently I have created three new books. The first one is a lovely hardback journal that you can write in as in a diary. It's called *Heart Notes*. My idea was to create a beautiful book that is full of soulful excerpts from famous women's diaries. Also included would be intriguing images of women by contemporary American and international

*"Me in oasis of Gabes, Tunisia"*

artists. The gift book packaged with a CD of solo music by members of the San Francisco symphony is published by Menus and Music.

Also, I have completed a book that is in essence a collection of my travel essays about my eighteen-month honeymoon many years ago. This travel narrative, *A Thirst for Faraway Things,* arose out of a need to at last document an extraordinary experience to several places in the world whose culture has since drastically changed or even vanished. In this book, which begins in Berkeley, California, and ends soon after our arrival in New Zealand, I try to show the rewards for the independent traveler, the one who goes off the path to meet the people of a strange land— human to human.

Lastly, I've always been fascinated by the biblical story of Ruth. Perhaps because my mother's name is Ruth, and when I was a child there was in our house, a beautifully illustrated book of this moving, ancient story. I wanted to make the story relevant to young people today, and I wanted to emphasize the strength of the two women, Naomi and Ruth.

What especially interests me now is the plight of cultures around the world that are threatened by mass tourism, war, and globalization. After I returned from Borneo, for example, I did some research at Stanford and learned that the fascinating, traditional way of life of the Dayak tribes is not expected to survive another twenty years. Where, I wondered, will we be able to witness the heart-stopping magic of an ancient shaman dancing or learn the healing properties of rainforest plants? Recently I took a course at Stanford on how to create your own television program. So that's what I'm working on now: a show for public broadcasting that discovers and showcases fascinating, inspirational people and what they do.

Today I still consult, write, teach, and dream. I especially *dream.* I have a pile of books in my head yet to be written! I want to write a book about the Loire Valley of France, and I want to write more about Mexico. I want to write a science fiction screenplay of an idea I have had for years. I want to write a novel that takes place in Renaissance Venice, and I want to sell an electronic toy idea I have. Also, because I'm an unrepentant Francophile, I still take French lessons (this is my fifth decade of lessons!) and dream of one day living part of the year in Paris and the French countryside.

When I teach or talk to students in class visits, I'm always asked, "Where do you write?" I write in an old garden shed in the backyard that we converted to an office. It's nice and spacious with a big curved desk, an electric heater, and a closet. The walls are painted blue like the

Caribbean and there's a big plum-velvet club chair. Photographs are everywhere: pictures of my family and of travels past. Sometimes my office gets really messy, because when I write I seem to throw papers every which way. Once a month I run around like a demon cleaning it all up. There are windows all around, and I can hear squirrels jumping on the porch and doves in their nest in the tree outside. It's my home away from home. Most important, it's the place I can be most me.

When I'm not writing, I'm thinking about writing. I also am reading, having lunch with friends, talking with my two grown sons, being with my mother, hiking and going to all manner of music concerts with my husband, visiting museums, seeing foreign films, cleaning my house, and dreaming about some yet-to-see travel destination.

I think if I were going to tell someone some important hints about writing, one thing I would say is "Don't be afraid of failure!" As much as I've accomplished, as many books and articles and stories I've had published, I've also had lots of my work not succeed. I have in my files to this day several book manuscripts that I think are great yet have never sold. Perhaps they're not that great or perhaps their time has not yet come. I'm not discouraged, though, because I know from experience that if you keep trying to perfect your craft, you will succeed. I've been sending out one of my stories for more than twenty years! Well, that may seem crazy to some, but I have a lot of faith in it so I'm not daunted even after two decades. After all, for five years, I submitted my manuscript *Day of Delight* to publishers. Yes, that little story went out and was read at sixty publishing houses. I received only rejections. Then one afternoon, on coming home from work, I found three messages on my answering machine—all from New York City. They were messages from the children's book editors at the three top publishing houses in the country. They each wanted to buy my story! So after five years and sixty rejections, I was sitting in the cat seat. How and why did this happen? I will never know. It's a mysterious, sometimes chaotic business, and that's why I never give up and I don't take failure personally. I take it at worst as a temporary setback and at best as a message or a challenge.

Another important thing I would say is, "Write not to make money," because chances are more than likely that you won't make much. Write because you cannot *not* write, because you desperately and passionately have a story that you just have to tell someone. If you do this, you will never be disappointed or hurt by the fickleness and seeming unfairness of the publishing world. No, you will be happy doing exactly what *you* want. Exactly what you were meant to do.

# SILVEY, Diane F. 1946-

## Personal

Born 1946, in Vancouver, British Columbia, Canada; married; children: Joe R., one daughter. *Education:* Earned degree from the Native Indian Teacher Education Program at the University of British Columbia.

## Addresses

*Office*—c/o Author Mail, Raincoast Books, 9050 Shaughnessy St., Vancouver, British Columbia, Canada V6P 6E5.

## Career

Greater Victoria School District, Victoria, Canada, First Nations Education Division, teacher for seventeen years.

## Awards, Honors

Woman of Distinction Award in Education, Training, and Development, 2000.

## Writings

*Little Bear's Spirit Quest,* illustrated by son, Joe Silvey, First Nations Education Division, Greater Victoria School District #61 (Victoria, British Columbia, Canada), 1995.

*Brittney Diana Reading Series* (includes seven student workbooks, two teacher's guides, and twenty-four readers), illustrated by Joe Silvey, First Nations Education Division, Greater Victoria School District #61 (Victoria, British Columbia, Canada), 1995.

*Whale Girl,* illustrated by Joe Silvey, First Nations Education Division, Greater Victoria School District #61 (Victoria, British Columbia, Canada), 1996.

*Spirit Quest,* illustrated by Joe Silvey, Beach Holme Publishers (Vancouver, British Columbia, Canada), 1997.

*Tidepools & Book Report,* illustrated by Joe Silvey, First Nations Education Division, Greater Victoria School District #61 (Victoria, British Columbia, Canada), 1997.

*Brittney Diana First Nations Cultural Series,* illustrated by Joe Silvey, First Nations Education Division, Greater Victoria School District #61 (Victoria, British Columbia, Canada), 1997.

*From Time Immemorial: The First People of the Pacific Northwest Coast,* illustrated by Joe Silvey, Pacific Edge Publishers (Gabriola, Canada), 1999.

(With Diana Mumford) *From Time Immemorial: The First People of the Pacific Northwest Coast* (teacher's guide), illustrated by Joe Silvey, Pacific Edge Publishers (Gabriola, Canada), 1999.

*Raven's Flight,* Raincoast Books (Vancouver, British Columbia, Canada), 2001.

Also author of *Brittney Diana Reading Series and the Sight, Sound and Spell Key Program* (teacher's guide), illustrated by Joe Silvey, First Nations Education Division, Greater Victoria School District #61 (Victoria, British Columbia, Canada).

## Sidelights

Canadian author and teacher Diane F. Silvey has written several books for young readers as well as numerous educational materials focusing on the First Nations people of the Pacific Coast. Being a descendant of the Coast Salish people, she frequently includes in her books themes relating to the original inhabitants of North America. Teaming up with her illustrator son, Joe, Silvey created the 1997 *Spirit Quest,* a tale for children about a set of twins who must join together on a journey to reclaim a special box containing the sacred spirits of their culture. Following the advice and guidance of their grandfather, Kaya and Tala travel across the Earth and through the underworld and heavens in order to find the stolen box, bring hope to their people, and restore ideas such as honesty and gentleness. Reviewing the work in

*Coast Salish Indian twins Kaya and Tala encounter creatures both real and spiritual as they travel through the British Columbian wilderness in search of a sacred box symbolizing the spirit of their people. (From Diane F. Silvey's* Spirit Quest, *illustrated by Joe Silvey.)*

*Canadian Children's Literature,* critic Marie Mendenhall found that the mother and son team "use their Coast Salish background to create a rich redemption legend in *Spirit Quest.*"

In 2001, Silvey published *Raven's Flight,* a young adult novel about a fifteen-year-old girl named Raven who lives in a small Canadian town. After her older sister decides to move to Vancouver to stay with a cousin, Raven looks forward to the letters her sister sends home. However, when the letters stop and no one hears from Marcie, Raven decides to travel to the costal city to find out what happened to her sister. Discovering that her sister had been lying about her situation in Vancouver and living in the seedy, rundown slums instead of the clean apartment she wrote about in her letters home, Raven is further horrified to learn that Marcie became a drug addict involved with a man known for his trafficking in both drugs and humans. With the help of a homeless boy and woman, Raven quickly learns about life on the streets and struggles to find her missing sister. "Silvey gives face and soul to some memorable characters," wrote *CM: Canadian Materials* reviewer Cora Lee. Remarking that the book tells the rest of the story omitted in newspaper reports and the evening television news, Lee claimed that *Raven's Flight* "has drawn much-needed attention to the plight of people desperately in need. She has also armed young people with the awareness they need against drugs, alcohol and the promise of an easy answer to the problems at home." Writing in *School Library Journal,* Cathy Coffman similarly found that "all of the horrors of the drug culture are clearly brought home in this story."

## Biographical and Critical Sources

### PERIODICALS

*Canadian Children's Literature,* winter, 1999, Marie Mendenhall, review of *Spirit Quest,* p. 94.
*CM: Canadian Materials,* April 27, 2001, Cora Lee, review of *Raven's Flight.*

*School Library Journal,* December, 2001, Cathy Coffman, review of *Raven's Flight,* p. 146.

### OTHER

*Island Treasures,* http://www.swiftly.com/ (February 27, 2002), "Get to Know Diane & Joe Silvey."
*Raincoast Kids,* http://www.raincoast.com (January 17, 2002), "About the Author: Diane Silvey."*

\*          \*          \*

# SLOBODKINA, Esphyr 1908-2002

*OBITUARY NOTICE*—See index for *SATA* sketch: Born September 22, 1908, in Cheliabinsk, Siberia; died July 21, 2002, at her home in Glen Head, NY. Abstract artist, author, and illustrator. Esphyr Slobodkina emigrated to the United States in 1928 from Siberia. Slobodkina was an abstract artist who worked in paintings and sculptures. Her work can be seen in the Whitney Museum of American Art and the Philadelphia Museum of Art. She was also a founding member of the American Abstract Artists. Slobodkina started writing and illustrating children's books during the Depression to make extra money. Her most well-known book, *Caps for Sale,* was first published in 1938 and continues to sell steadily. *Caps for Sale* tells the story of a cap salesman who is pestered by a group of playful monkeys. They take his caps up into the trees. Slobodkina wrote and illustrated a number of other children's book, including *The Wonderful Feast* (1955), *The Long Island Ducklings* (1961), and *Circus Elephant* (reissued as *Circus Caps for Sale* in 2002).

## OBITUARIES AND OTHER SOURCES:

### PERIODICALS

*Concord Monitor,* July 28, 2002.
*Dallas Morning News* (Dallas, TX), July 28.
*Publishers Weekly,* August 12, 2002, p. 151.

# T

## TAYLOR, Mildred D. 1943-

### Personal

Born September 13, 1943, in Jackson, MS; daughter of Wilbert Lee and Deletha Marie (Davis) Taylor; married Errol Zea-Daly, August, 1972 (divorced, 1975). *Education:* University of Toledo, B.Ed., 1965; University of Colorado, M.A., 1969.

### Addresses

*Home*—Boulder, CO. *Agent*—c/o Dell Books, 2 Park Avenue, New York, NY 10017.

### Career

Writer. United States Peace Corps, English and history teacher in Tuba City, AZ, 1965, and in Yirgalem, Ethiopia, 1965-67, recruiter, 1967-68, instructor in Maine, 1968; University of Colorado, study skills coordinator, 1969-71; proofreader and editor in Los Angeles, CA, 1971-73.

### Awards, Honors

First prize in African-American category, Council on Interracial Books for Children, 1973, and outstanding book of the year citation, *New York Times,* 1975, both for *Song of the Trees;* American Library Association Notable Book citation, 1976, National Book Award finalist, *Boston Globe-Horn Book* Honor Book citation, and Newbery Medal, all 1977, and Buxtehuder Bulle Award, 1985, all for *Roll of Thunder, Hear My Cry;* outstanding book of the year citation, *New York Times,* 1981, Jane Addams honor, 1982, American Book Award nomination, 1982, and Coretta Scott King Award, 1982, all for *Let the Circle be Unbroken;* Coretta Scott King Award, 1988, for *The Friendship; New York Times* notable book citation, 1987, and Christopher Award, 1988, both for *The Gold Cadillac;* Coretta Scott King Book Award, 1990, for *The Road to Memphis,* and 2002, for *The Land;* Christopher Award, 1991, for *Mississippi*

*Bridge;* Alan Award for Significant Contribution to Adult Literature; National council of Teachers of English, 1997; Jason Award, 1997, for *The Well: David's Story;* Scott O'Dell Historical Fiction Award, 2002, for *The Land.*

### Writings

*Song of the Trees,* illustrated by Jerry Pinkney, Dial, 1975.
*Roll of Thunder, Hear My Cry,* Dial, 1976, reprinted (25th anniversary edition), Phyllis Fogelman Books (New York, NY), 2001.
*Let the Circle Be Unbroken,* Dial, 1981.
*The Friendship,* illustrated by Max Ginsburg, Dial, 1987.
*The Gold Cadillac,* illustrated by Michael Hays, Dial, 1987.
*The Road to Memphis,* Dial, 1990.
*Mississippi Bridge,* illustrated by Max Ginsburg, Dial, 1990.
*The Well: David's Story,* Dial (New York, NY), 1995.
*The Land,* Phyllis Fogelman Books (New York, NY), 2001.

### Adaptations

*Roll of Thunder, Hear My Cry* was recorded by Newbery Awards Records in 1978, and as a three-part television miniseries of the same title by American Broadcasting Corporation (ABC), 1978; *Let the Circle Be Unbroken* was made into an audio book by Recorded Books, Incorporated, 1998; *Roll of Thunder, Hear My Cry,* and *The Land* were made into audio books by Listening Library, both 2001.

### Sidelights

With her writings, award-winning author Mildred D. Taylor shares pride in her racial heritage and provides historical fiction about life for black Americans. As a child, Taylor was regaled with stories of proud, dignified ancestors, but she received a different version of history from white, mainstream America. Believing that school history texts diminished the contributions of blacks and glossed over the injustices to which they had been subjected, Taylor vowed to write stories offering a truer

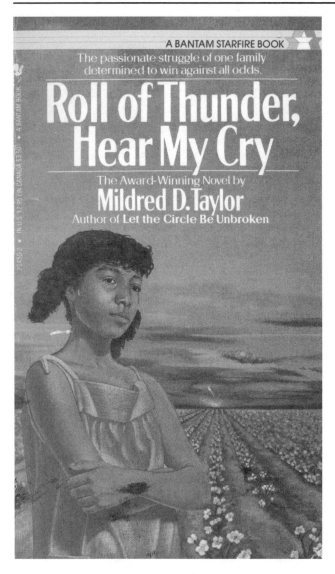

*Nine-year-old Cassie is at first bewildered by and then hardened toward the racism in the rural South of the 1930s. (Cover illustration by Sal Baracca.)*

vision of black families and their racial struggles. Taylor draws upon family narratives, using a first-person voice that mirrors her relatives' rendition of such tales, and she has been praised for the authentic ring of her characters' ordeals. Taylor invented the chronicle of the Logan family, and her series of books follows the group's activities and experiences throughout the mid-twentieth century. Taylor uses this period because she wishes to emphasize how this generation's reactions to segregation helped to pave the way for the reforms of the civil rights movement and an improvement of interracial relations in the United States.

Taylor brings a unique vantage point to her fiction. Born in 1943, she was part of a transitional generation that witnessed both blatant discrimination against black Americans and the legislative reform to amend historical transgressions. Taylor also experienced the differing racial climates of the North and South. Although born in Jackson, Mississippi, Taylor moved north with her

family when she was only three months old. In an essay for *Something about the Author Autobiography Series* (*SAAS*), she recounted that her father, infuriated by repeated racial incidents, decided to leave the South in the mid-1940s because "he refused to allow my older sister, Wilma, and me to live our lives as he had to live his, in a segregated, racist society that allowed little or no opportunity to blacks." Although racism was persistent throughout the country, the North was perceived as an area offering greater freedom and job opportunities. Despite their relocation, the family did not abandon their Southern roots; they made an annual trek to visit relatives.

Reminiscing about such trips in her Newbery Award acceptance speech, printed in *Horn Book*, Taylor remarked, "As a small child, I loved the South.... In my early years, the trip was a marvelous adventure; a twenty hour picnic that took us into another time, another world." At that time Taylor did not understand that the nature of these trips was a direct result of the racist policies of the South; the family packed food because they were not allowed in Southern restaurants and hotels, and they travelled back roads out of fear of harassment from bigoted police officers. Yet Taylor soon realized that she was expected to act—and was treated—differently in the South merely because of the color of her skin. She continued, "one summer I suddenly felt a climbing nausea as we crossed the Ohio River into Kentucky" because of the blatant discrimination in the South and the fear it inspired. Despite the uneasiness these vacations involved, Taylor's father insisted that his daughters be aware of these injustices commonly invoked in the United States. His reasoning, as she explained in her essay for *Something about the Author Autobiography Series (SAAS),* was "that without understanding the loss of liberty in the south, we couldn't appreciate the liberty of the North."

Yet, for the author, the South also held pleasant memories as the home of her ancestors. In an article for *Horn Book* she remarked, "I also remember the other South—the South of family and community, the South filled with warmth and love—and how it opened to me a sense of history and filled me with pride." This vision of the South was passed down in an oral tradition; when Taylor's extended family gathered, relatives would recreate the family's history with stories acted out on porches and around bonfires. Her father was a noted storyteller, engaging family members with fascinating tales of colorful, proud ancestors who retained dignity even when faced with the inhumanity and degradation of slavery. In an article for *Books for Schools and Libraries,* Taylor disclosed the effect such tales had on her: "I began to imagine myself as a storyteller.... But I was a shy and quiet child, so I turned to creating stories for myself instead, carving elaborate daydreams in my mind."

When the author was ten years old, her family moved into a newly integrated Ohio town, and she was the only black child in her class. This was a scene repeated throughout her formative years, and Taylor felt burdened by the realization that her actions would be judged—by whites unfamiliar with blacks—as representative of her entire race. In school, when the subject was history, Taylor was uncomfortable because her understanding of black heritage contrasted sharply with that presented in textbooks. In *Horn Book,* she commented that such publications contained only a "lackluster history of Black people . . . a history of a docile, subservient people happy with their fate who did little or nothing to shatter the chains that bound them, both before and after slavery." Knowing this to be false, Taylor tried to think of ways to repudiate the information in those books. In her *SAAS* essay she recalled, "I remember once trying to explain those [family] stories in class, about the way things really were. . . . Most of the students thought I was making the stories up. Some even laughed at me. I couldn't explain things to them. Even the teacher seemed not to believe me. They all believed what was in the history book."

The bias of such accounts had a motivating effect on Taylor. In *Horn Book* she explained, "By the time I entered high school, I had a driving compulsion to paint a truer picture of Black people. I wanted to show the endurance of the Black World, with strong fathers and concerned mothers; I wanted to show happy, loved children. . . . I wanted to show a Black family united in love and pride, of which the reader would like to be a part."

However, it was not until 1973 that Taylor wrote her first book. Spurred on by a contest deadline, she produced the manuscript for *Song of the Trees* in only four days. Three months later she received a telegram naming her the winner in the African-American category of the Council on Interracial Books for Children contest. *Song of the Trees* introduced the Logan clan: Big Ma, Papa, Mama, Uncle Hammer, Stacey, Christopher-John, Cassie, and Little Man. This book, based on an actual incident, is told through the voice of the Logan daughter, Cassie. Jobs are scarce in 1930s Mississippi because of the Depression, and Cassie's father is away in Louisiana trying to earn enough money to pay the taxes on the family's land. In his absence, white men threaten to cut down tree's on the Logan's property. However Papa returns in time to take a stand against the white men. Ruby Martin, in a *Journal of Reading* review, praised *Song of the Trees* as "so beautifully told, the prose rings poetry."

Taylor's next book, *Roll of Thunder, Hear My Cry,* which earned the prestigious Newbery medal in 1977, continues the story of the Logan family and the author "creates a remarkable family portrait," according to David A. Wright in *Dictionary of Literary Biography.* Using a limited time frame, the book examines the family's life and demonstrates how discrimination is an everyday occurrence. Stacey, Christopher-John, Cassie, and Little Man all attend school, suffering humiliations such as being splashed by the school bus that only picks up white children and receiving school texts in poor condition only because the white school no longer had need for them. Mama loses her teaching job because she

defies school district officials by including a discussion of slavery in a history lesson even though it is not in the book. After a horrifying racial incident in which several black men are set on fire, the Logans help orchestrate a boycott of a crooked white merchant's store, a suspected ringleader in the burnings. This act sets off a series of events, including the threat of foreclosure on the Logan's land, the near lynching of the Logan children's classmate, and a suspicious fire.

Stuart Hannabuss, writing in *Junior Bookshelf,* commented that *Roll of Thunder, Hear My Cry* is "full of episodes of emotional power." Noting the effect of such scenes, David Rees, in his work *The Marble in the Water: Essays on Contemporary Writers of Fiction for Children and Young Adults,* remarked that "it's impossible not to feel anger and a sense of burning in reading this book." And *Interracial Books for Children Bulletin* contributor Emily R. Moore concluded, "*Roll of Thunder, Hear My Cry* deserves to become a classic in children's literature."

In the next addition to the Logan chronicle, *Let the Circle be Unbroken,* "Taylor's recurrent theme of family unity has its strongest appearance," according to Wright. Cassie recounts the hardships of the Depression for both white and black sharecroppers and shows how sometimes people of the same economic status work together regardless of race. Yet, the author also presents more situations of racial struggle. The Logan children's classmate is unfairly convicted for his part in a robbery that took place in *Roll of Thunder, Hear My Cry.* Cassie helps an elderly black woman memorize the state constitution so that she can register to vote, but nonetheless the woman is refused this basic civil right. *New York Times Book Review* contributor June Jordan praised the book for its "dramatic tension and virtuoso characterization." In a review of *Let the Circle be Unbroken* for the *Christian Science Monitor,* Christine McDonnell observed, "Though many of Cassie and Stacey's experiences happen because they are black, their growing pains and self-discovery are universal." McDonnell added, "The Logans' story will strengthen and satisfy all who read it."

*The Friendship,* written in 1987, presents a racial confrontation between two men in 1930s Mississippi. Tom Bee, a black man, had saved the life of John Wallace, a white storekeeper, when the two were young men. In gratitude, John insisted that the two would always remain friends, evidenced by their using first names to address each other. However, years later, John reneges on this promise and shoots Tom for addressing him by his first name in public—an act considered insubordination because blacks were supposed to refer to white men or women as mister and misses. Frances Bradburn, writing in *Wilson Library Bulletin* stated, "This is a story that children will experience rather than simply read. . . . The humiliation, the injustice, but above all the quiet determination, courage, and pride of Mr. Tom Bee will speak to all children."

Taylor's next work, *The Gold Cadillac,* is set in the 1950s and chronicles a black family's car trip to the South to visit relatives. Much like the family vacations of Taylor's youth, the family is confronted with "whites only" signs and suffer harassment from white police officers who are both jealous and suspicious of the family's car and the prosperity it represents. Such incidents help the two young sisters appreciate the greater freedom and opportunity they enjoy in their Ohio hometown.

In the fourth book of the Logan saga, *The Road to Memphis,* Cassie is a high school senior dreaming of becoming a lawyer. She attends school in Jackson, Mississippi, and is for the first time without the protection of her parents and grandmother. Her brother Stacey and a friend are also in Jackson working in factories. There the trio face more racial incidents and also must contend with the outbreak of World War II. After Stacey's friend is forced to flee the city because he defended himself against a white attack. even though he realized he would be punished, Cassie grapples with her decision to pursue a career in the white-controlled legal system.

Another of Taylor's works, *Mississippi Bridge,* is told from the point of view of Jeremy Simms, a white character who has been presented in the Logan books. In these works Jeremy was distinguished from the racist townsfolk in that he continually made offers of friendship to the Logan children. *Mississippi Bridge* chronicles another racist incident in which, during stormy weather, black bus passengers are forced to get off of the bus to make room for white riders. This story concludes in an incident that some critics perceived as judgment for the white's discriminatory actions.

*The Well: David's Story,* which Taylor published in 1995, revisits the Logan family, this time focusing on ten-year-old David Logan (father of Cassie in *Roll of Thunder, Hear My Cry)* and his family, who share their well water with both black and white neighbors in Mississippi in the early 1900s. Despite their kindness, the Logans are still treated with disrespect by the white neighbors. A reviewer writing for *Publishers Weekly* noted, "Taylor, obviously in tune with these fully developed characters, creates for them an intense and compelling situation and skillfully delivers powerful messages about racism and moral fortitude." Taylor's next book, *The Land,* also a prequel to *Roll of Thunder, Hear My Cry,* deals with Paul-Edward Logan, Cassie's grandfather, during the period right after the Civil War. Writing in *Publishers Weekly,* a reviewer said, "Like any good historian, Taylor extracts truth from past events without sugarcoating issues." Noting that Taylor's tone "is more uplifting than bitter," the reviewer added, "Rather than dismissing hypocrisies, she digs beneath the surface of Paul-Edward's friends and foes, showing how their values have been shaped by the social norms." A reviewer for *Horn Book* noted Taylor's masterful use of the realities of racism "to frame a powerful coming-of-age story of a bewildered boy becoming a man beholden to no one." Finally, Hazel Rochman, writing

for *Booklist,* pointed out, "The novel will make a great discussion book in American history classes dealing with black history; pioneer life; and the Reconstruction period, about which little has been written for this age group."

With each of her books, Taylor has provided a glimpse into the history of black Americans. Even though her characters face repeated racial indignities, they show courage and resourcefulness in overcoming their problems. Taylor has earned esteem and recognition for her writing, but she gives her father credit for much of her success. Both the stories he told and the example he set in fighting against discrimination helped her form the basis of her books. The author accepted her Newbery medal for *Roll of Thunder, Hear My Cry* on behalf of her father and remarked that "without his teachings, without his words, my words would not have been." Taylor added in *Horn Book* that she hopes her books about the Logan family "will one day be instrumental in teaching children of all colors the tremendous influence that Cassie's generation ... had in bringing about the great Civil Rights movement of the fifties and sixties." In her acceptance speech for the 1997 Alan Award, Taylor also pointed out, "In the writing of my books I have tried to present not only a history of my family, but the effects of racism, not only to the victims of racism but also to racists themselves." Taylor has said that she still has a final book to write about the Logans and will be returning to Cassie's voice to tell the story.

## Biographical and Critical Sources

*BOOKS*

*Beacham's Guide to Literature for Young Adults,* Beacham Publishing (Osprey, FL), Volume 3, 1990, pp. 1135-1143, Volume 8, 1994, pp. 3890-3897.
*Children's Literature Review,* Volume 9, Gale (Detroit, MI), 1985.
*Contemporary Black Biography,* Volume 26, Gale (Detroit, MI), 2000.
*Contemporary Literary Criticism,* Volume 21, Gale (Detroit, MI), 1982.
Crowe, Chris, *Presenting Mildred D. Taylor,* Twayne (New York, NY), 1999.
*Dictionary of Literary Biography,* Volume 52: *American Writers for Children since 1960: Fiction,* Gale (Detroit, MI), 1986, pp. 365-367.
Rees, David, *The Marble in the Water: Essays on Contemporary Writers of Fiction for Children and Young Adults,* "The Color of Skin: Mildred Taylor," pp. 108-109.
*Something about the Author Autobiography Series,* Volume 5, Gale (Detroit, MI), 1988, pp. 267-286.

*PERIODICALS*

*Alan Review,* Spring, 1995, Barbara T. Bontempo, "Exploring Prejudice in Young Adult Literature through Drama and Role Play;" Spring, 1998, Mildred D. Taylor, "Acceptance Speech for the 1997 Alan Award."
*Booklist,* December 1, 1990, p. 740; May 15, 1997, Karen Harris, review of *The Road to Memphis,* p. 1596;

August, 2001, Hazel Rochman, review of *The Land,* p. 2108.

*Books for Schools and Libraries,* 1985, Mildred D. Taylor, autobiographical article.

*Christian Science Monitor,* October 14, 1981, Christine McDonnell, "Powerful Lesson of Family Love," pp. B1, B11.

*Horn Book,* August, 1977, Mildred D. Taylor, Newbery Award Acceptance Speech, pp. 401-409.

*Horn Book Magazine,* September, 2001, review of *The Land,* p. 596

*Interracial Books for Children Bulletin,* volume 7, 1976, Emily R. Moore, "The Bookshelf: *Roll of Thunder, Hear My Cry,*" p. 18.

*Journal of Reading,* February, 1977, Ruby Martin, "Books for Young People," pp. 432-435.

*Junior Bookshelf,* October, 1982, Stuart Hannabuss, "Beyond the Formula: Part II," p. 175.

*New York Times Book Review,* November 15, 1981, June Jordan, "Mississippi in the Thirties," pp. 55, 58; May 20, 1990.

*Publishers Weekly,* April 13, 1990, review of *The Road to Memphis,* p. 67; July 17, 1990, review of *Mississippi Bridge,* p. 234; January 2, 1995, review of *The Well: David's Story,* p. 77; August 13, 2001, review of *The Land,* p. 313; October 22, 2001, Jennifer M. Brown, "Stories Behind the Book," p. 24.

*School Library Journal,* Bruce Anne Shook, review of *The Land,* p. 190.

*Times Literary Supplement,* March 26, 1982.

*Wilson Library Bulletin,* March, 1988, Frances Bradburn, "Middle Readers' Right to Read," p. 42.*

# W

## WALKER, Sally M(acArt) 1954-
### (Sally Fleming)

### Personal

Born October 16, 1954, in East Orange, NJ; daughter of Donald (an insurance agent) and Cleo (an accounting clerk; maiden name, Crooks) MacArt; married James Walker (an igneous petrologist), August, 1974; children: one daughter, one son. *Education:* Upsala College, B.A., 1975. *Hobbies and other interests:* Hiking, reading, cooking, gardening.

### Addresses

*Home*—DeKalb, IL. *Agent*—c/o Author Mail, Lerner Publishing Group, 241 First Ave. N, Minneapolis, MN 55401. *E-mail*—sallymacwalker@hotmail.com.

### Career

Author and literature consultant. Junction Book Store, DeKalb, IL, children's book buyer, 1988-94; Anderson's Bookshops, Naperville, IL, children's book specialist, 1994—. Children's literature consultant, 1988—; Northern Illinois University, adjunct instructor, 1992-93. Presenter at reading conferences.

### Member

International Reading Association, Society of Children's Book Writers and Illustrators.

### Awards, Honors

Outstanding Science Trade Book designation, National Science Teachers' Association/Children's Book Council, 1997, for *Earthquakes,* and 2002, for *Fireflies;* Children's Choice Award, International Reading Association, 2001, for *Mary Anning, Fossil Hunter.*

### Writings

*NONFICTION; FOR CHILDREN*

*Born near the Earth's Surface: Sedimentary Rocks,* Enslow (Hillside, NJ), 1991.
*Fireflies* ("Early Bird Nature" series), Lerner (Minneapolis, MN), 2001.
*Mary Anning: Fossil Hunter,* illustrated by Phyllis V. Saroff, Carolrhoda (Minneapolis, MN), 2001.
(Under pseudonym Sally Fleming) *Ferocious Fangs,* North Word Press, 2001.
(Under pseudonym Sally Fleming) *Fantastic Flyers,* North Word Press, 2001.
(Under pseudonym Sally Fleming) *Rapid Runners,* North Word Press, 2002.
*Fossil Fish Found Alive: Discovering the Coelacanth,* Carolrhoda (Minneapolis, MN), 2002.
*Life in an Estuary* ("Ecosystems in Action" series), Lerner (Minneapolis, MN), 2002.
*Jackie Robinson* (biography), illustrations by Rodney S. Pate, Carolrhoda (Minneapolis, MN), 2003.

*"EARTH WATCH" SERIES*

*Glaciers: Ice on the Move,* Carolrhoda (Minneapolis, MN), 1990.
*Water Up, Water Down: The Hydrologic Cycle,* Carolrhoda (Minneapolis, MN), 1992.
*Volcanoes: Earth's Inner Fire,* Carolrhoda (Minneapolis, MN), 1994.
*Earthquakes,* Carolrhoda (Minneapolis, MN), 1996.

*"NATURE WATCH" SERIES*

*Rhinos,* photographs by Gerry Ellis, Carolrhoda (Minneapolis, MN), 1996.
*Dolphins,* Carolrhoda (Minneapolis, MN), 1998.
*Hippos,* photographs by Gerry Ellis, Carolrhoda (Minneapolis, MN), 1998.
*Manatees,* Carolrhoda (Minneapolis, MN), 1999.
*Sea Horses,* Carolrhoda (Minneapolis, MN), 1999.
*Rays,* Carolrhoda (Minneapolis, MN), 2003.

*Readers can learn all about dolphins and how scientists study them in Sally M. Walker's* **Dolphins.** *(Photograph by David B. Fleetham/Visuals Unlimited.)*

*"EARLY BIRD PHYSICS" SERIES*

(With Roseann Feldman) *Work,* Lerner (Minneapolis, MN), 2002.

(With Roseann Feldman) *Inclined Planes and Wedges,* photographs by Andy King, Lerner (Minneapolis, MN), 2002.

(With Roseann Feldman) *Levers,* photographs by Andy King, Lerner (Minneapolis, MN), 2002.

(With Roseann Feldman) *Pulleys,* photographs by Andy King, Lerner (Minneapolis, MN), 2002.

(With Roseann Feldman) *Screws,* photographs by Andy King, Lerner (Minneapolis, MN), 2002.

(With Roseann Feldman) *Wheels and Axles,* photographs by Andy King, Lerner (Minneapolis, MN), 2002.

*OTHER*

*Opossum at Sycamore Road,* illustrated by Joel Snyder, Soundprints (Norwalk, CT), 1997.

*Seahorse Reef: A Story of the South Pacific,* illustrated by Steven James Petruccio, Soundprints (Norwalk, CT), 1997.

*The Eighteen-Penny Goose* (historical fiction), illustrated by Ellen Beier, HarperCollins (New York, NY), 1998.

(Compiler, with Sandy Whiteley and Kim Summers) *The Teacher's Calendar, 1999-2000,* Contemporary Books (Lincolnwood, IL), 1999.

## Work in Progress

*Bessie Coleman,* a biography, expected in 2003.

## Sidelights

Sally M. Walker is the author of a number of nonfiction books for young people brimming with questions about nature and the out-of-doors. Titles such as *Glaciers: Ice on the Move* and *Water Up, Water Down: The Hydrologic Cycle* attest to the author's personal interest in physical science, while in the books *Hippos, Fireflies,* and *Dolphins* the life cycle and habits of creatures inhabiting land, sea, and sky are discussed. In addition to her nonfiction works, Walker has also delved into fiction, with *The Eighteen-Penny Goose,* and has written biographies of African-American baseball great Jackie Robinson and noted nineteenth-century British paleontologist Mary Anning.

After Walker graduated from high school, she enrolled at Upsala College to study for her B.A. in physical science. As she told *SATA:* "I first thought about becoming an author when I was a child. At the time, I was worried that the world might run out of horse stories and mysteries. My love of the outdoors led me into the field of geology. Those pursuits melded perfectly with another love: history. In college I took many archeology courses. So when I wasn't looking at rocks I was usually digging in the dirt. Maybe that's why I enjoy gardening now."

As a nonfiction author, Walker has contributed books to several series, among them the "Early Bird Physics" series, with coauthor Roseann Feldman, and the "Nature Watch" and "Earth Watch" series, both published by Carolrhoda. *Rhinos, Hippos, Manatees,* and *Sea Horses,* all part of the "Nature Watch" series, contain information about the diet, behavior, life cycle, predators, and habitat of these creatures, and they also provide a sense of the creature's future on a planet threatened by a variety of ecological ills. Dramatic photographs, an index, and a glossary containing key terms all add to the books' usefulness to students. Walker explains in *Hippos* that new DNA evidence has shown that the hippopotamus is a relative of the dolphin and whale rather than the horse or pig—"hippopotamus" means "river horse"—and in *Sea Horses* she reveals an intricate ritual greeting shared by courting sea horses. In *Rhinos* readers learn that all but five of one hundred different species of the ancient animal have been made extinct, due in part to hunting the creature for its horn. In a review of *Manatees* for *Booklist,* Ellen Mandell praised "Walker's intriguing writing style" and her "lucid, comprehensible explanation" of the physiological mysteries of these sea creatures. Praising *Rhinos,* Susan Oliver noted in *School Library Journal* that the "text is not only appropriately simple, but also rich with information and descriptions that bring the facts to life." In *Appraisal,* Harry Levine called *Hippos* "a concise and thoughtful treatment of an endangered animal species whose habitat, the author points out, is in need of protection."

Walker told *SATA:* "The most rewarding research project I have undertaken recently is solving the mystery of the 'missing pennies' that are mentioned in my book *The Eighteen-Penny Goose.* That search is a story in itself." *The Eighteen-Penny Goose* takes place during the Revolutionary War, when an advance by hostile British troops forces Letty Wright and her family to abandon their home. Worried that her pet goose Solomon might be hurt, the young girl leaves a note asking that he be treated well. When she and her family return, she finds her pet alive, but all the rest of the family's geese are gone and the homestead is a mess. However, the soldiers have been somewhat considerate: in addition to not putting Letty's goose in the cooking pot, they have put around his neck a bag containing a penny for

each goose they did have for dinner. Noting that "Walker maintains the inherent suspense of the story throughout," a *Kirkus Reviews* contributor found the conclusion of *The Eighteen-Penny Goose* "rewarding" and the watercolor illustrations by Ellen Beier "realistic." Reviewing the book for *Horn Book,* Maeve Visser Knoth added that the book is one of a "handful of other successful historical easy readers ... which hold real substance and interest for young readers."

*Born near the Earth's Surface: Sedimentary Rocks* was one of the first books by Walker to focus on Earth science. Written as part of a four-book series titled "Earth's Processes," the book covers such things as sinkholes, mudrocks, and erosion and shows how such formations and phenomena provide clues to the earth's history. Noting that "everything you always wanted to know about glaciers ... is covered in this book," an *Appraisal* reviewer explained that Walker's *Glaciers: Ice on the Move* informs readers about the formation, location, and movement of glaciers and discusses the way that ice has molded the face of the Earth over time. *Earthquakes,* which presents explanations of how earthquakes occur and what to do when one occurs, is a book that *School Library Journal* contributor Eunice Weech hailed as useful for report-writing, "yet readable and visually appealing to browsers." Delving deep into the Earth's core, *Volcanos: Earth's Inner Fire* performs an equally important service to young students through its discussion of lava, pyroclastics, magma, plate tectonics, and the location of volcanoes around the planet; the "succinct and intelligible information contained in this book will be an asset" to students, according to an *Appraisal* reviewer.

Walker also told *SATA:* "My husband, Jim, is a geologist. He and his colleagues have provided wonderful support (and pictures!) for my many earth science books. My two children—now grown—are my 'reality touchstones,' who remind me that there is a world outside of children's literature. Our two cats let me know when it's time to stop writing and make dinner.

"One of the reasons I write is to learn more about the many subjects that interest me," Walker revealed. "I have so many questions! Writing nonfiction is the perfect solution: I combine the joy of doing research with the satisfaction of finding answers to my questions. The fun afterward is sharing the 'story' of the information I have discovered." Walker's conclusions, based on her years of work as both an author and a children's literary consultant: "There can never be too many children's books. Let's make sure all children are able to read them."

## Biographical and Critical Sources

*PERIODICALS*

*Appraisal,* autumn, 1990, John D. Stackpole, review of *Glaciers: Ice on the Move,* p. 38; autumn, 1991, Elizabeth C. Schwarzman, review of *Born near the Earth's Surface,* pp. 59-60; winter, 1993, review of *Water Up, Water Down: The Hydrologic Cycle,* pp. 54-55; spring, 1995, review of *Volcanoes: Earth's Inner Fire,* pp. 57-58; winter, 1999, Harry Levine, review of *Hippos,* p. 40; autumn, 1999, Thomas Thomasi, review of *Dolphins,* p. 52.

*Booklist,* January 15, 1993, Carolyn Phelan, review of *Water Up, Water Down,* p. 905; December 1, 1996, Julie Corsaro, review of *Rhinos,* p. 660; February 1, 1998, Hazel Rochman, review of *The Eighteen-Penny Goose,* p. 928; May 1, 1998, Stephanie Zvirin, review of *Hippos,* p. 1518; May 1, 1999, Carolyn Phelan, review of *Sea Horses,* p. 1592; September 1, 1999, Carolyn Phelan, review of *Dolphins,* p. 130; December 15, 1999, Ellen Mandel, review of *Manatees,* p. 779; September 15, 2001, Catherine Andronik, review of *Seahorse Reef: A Story of the South Pacific,* p. 220.

*Book Report,* November-December, 1991, Anne Marie Lilly, review of *Born near the Earth's Surface,* p. 60.

*Bulletin of the American Meteorological Society,* Lawrence E. Greenleaf, review of *Water Up, Water Down,* p. 872.

*Bulletin of the Center for Children's Books,* September, 1990, review of *Glaciers,* p. 18.

*Childhood Education,* spring, 1993, Joan M. Hildebrand, review of *Water Up, Water Down,* p. 176.

*Horn Book,* May, 1998, Maeve Visser Knoth, review of *The Eighteen-Penny Goose,* p. 350.

*Kirkus Reviews,* December 1, 1997, review of *The Eighteen-Penny Goose,* p. 1781.

*School Library Journal,* August, 1990, Roseanne Cerny, review of *Glaciers,* p. 161; December, 1992, Carolyn Angus, review of *Water Up, Water Down,* p. 132; June, 1996, Eunice Weech, review of *Earthquakes,* p. 1996; December, 1996, Susan Oliver, review of *Rhinos,* p. 134; March, 1998, Sharon R. Pearce, review of *The Eighteen-Penny Goose,* p. 189; April, 1998, Michele Snyder, review of *Hippos,* p. 126; November, 1999, Karey Wehner, review of *Sea Horses,* p. 150.

*Science Books and Films,* March, 1993, Doris M. Ellis, review of *Water Up, Water Down,* p. 50; June, 1996, Eugene C. Robertson, review of *Earthquakes,* pp. 143-144; July, 2001, Karey Wehner, review of *Fireflies,* p. 100.

*Voice of Youth Advocates,* October, 1991, June Muldner, review of *Born near the Earth's Core,* pp. 253-254.*

\*     \*     \*

# WARREN, Jackie M. 1953-

## Personal

Born September 20, 1953, in Burlington, IA; daughter of Robert W. (a pilot) and Phyllis (Boughton) Sharar; married Dennis Kennedy (divorced); married Mathew C. Warren (an attorney), September 3, 1983; children: (first marriage) Alisha M., Denette A. *Education:* Attended Western Illinois University, 1986-91; University of Kansas, degree in fine arts, 1994. *Hobbies and other interests:* Flying, gardening.

## Addresses

*Home*—12205 Knox, Overland Park, KS 66213. *E-mail*—jw4art@aol.com.

## Career

Artistic Solutions, Overland Park, KS, owner, 1996—. Kansas City Artists Coalition, director of marketing, 1999—, and member of board of directors; Overland Park Chamber of Commerce, chairperson of Diplomats; Kansas City Chamber of Commerce, member.

## Member

Phi Kappa Phi.

## Awards, Honors

Purchase Award, Springfield Museum, 1997.

## Writings

*Marni's Mirror,* Unity School of Christianity, 2000.

Also author of *My Time Called Life,* privately printed, 1996.

## Sidelights

Jackie M. Warren told *SATA:* "Whether it be painting, writing, or music, the whole purpose is communication. We spend our lives trying to communicate feelings, attitudes, desires, and countless moments in our lives. That is the driving force behind my art. I attempt to communicate in a fashion that can be understood, so ideas can be conveyed and dialogue can begin. Without connection to others, our lives here on this earth would be, oh, so dull!"

\*     \*     \*

# WEBB, Sophie 1958-

## Personal

Born November 30, 1958, in New Haven, CT; daughter of Dwight W. and Nancy M. (an artist) Webb. *Education:* Boston University, B.A.

## Addresses

*Home and office*—P.O. Box 683, Bolinas, CA 94924. *E-mail*—swebb@prbo.org.

## Career

Ornithological illustrator and contract biologist. Research Associate, Point Reyes Bird Observatory.

## Member

Guild of Natural Science Illustrators, American Birding Association, Wilson Ornithological Society.

## Awards, Honors

Children's Book Award, Robert F. Sibert Honor Award, National Parenting Publication Award, Parent's Choice Honor Award, International Reading Association, 2001, for *My Season with Penguins: An Antarctic Journal.*

## Writings

(With Steven N. G. Howell, and illustrator) *A Guide to the Birds of Mexico and Northern Central America,* Oxford University Press (New York, NY), 1994.
(And illustrator) *My Season with Penguins: An Antarctic Journal,* Houghton Mifflin (Boston, MA), 2000.
(Contributor of illustrations) *Birds of Venezuela,* Princeton University Press (Princeton, NJ), in press.

Illustrator of *Birds of Mexico City* and *Monterey Breeding Bird Atlas.*

## Work in Progress

Children's book about studying seabirds; research vessels for Houghton Mifflin; plates for illustrating *A Guide to the Birds of Peru,* for Princeton University Press (Princeton, NJ); illustrations for *Napa Solano County Breeding Birds Atlas.*

*Sophie Webb gives a first-hand account of her two months living with Adèlie penguins in the Antarctic in her self-illustrated journal* **My Season with Penguins.**

## Sidelights

Sophie Webb told *SATA:* "When I was a kid I was always fascinated by animals, and I loved to draw. I spent most of my summers on Cape Cod wandering on the beaches, going to an Audubon nature camp, and riding horses. When I went to college, I started in art school but, after a couple years, changed my major to biology. It was a good decision.

"After graduation I began to travel. First I headed to the West to work on a project in New Mexico, then it was on to California for an internship at Point Reyes Bird Observatory. The Bay area became my home base from which I traveled and worked on a myriad of projects to study birds. All the while I was sketching and keeping journals of my experiences. In 1986 I teamed up with Steve Howell, and we spent the next nine years traveling in Mexico and working on *A Guide to the Birds of Mexico and Northern Central America.*

"I continued to work on various other projects and, in 1995, I was asked if I would like to work on a project in the Antarctic, studying penguins. Little did I realize how much it would change my life. I fell in love with the place and the Adélie penguins. While there I continued my drawing, painting, and writing, and thus *My Season with Penguins: An Antarctic Journal* was conceived. My hope is through the book (and hopefully my next one) that I can give a sense of what it is like to be a field biologist, and what sorts of questions scientists are asking and the potential importance they have in understanding and monitoring the natural world. Although, on a less serious note, I suppose I mostly would like to impart some of the joy, fun, and wonder there is in watching birds and being able to catch a glimpse of their lives."

## Biographical and Critical Sources

*PERIODICALS*

*Auk,* October, 1996, A. Townsend Peterson and Adolfo G. Navarro-Siguenza, review of *A Guide to the Birds of Mexico and Northern Central America,* p. 975.
*Horn Book,* November, 2000, Danielle J. Ford, review of *My Season with Penguins: An Antarctic Journal,* p. 774.
*Nature Canada,* autumn, 1996, Jack Seigel, review of *A Guide to the Birds of Mexico and Northern Central America,* p. 49.
*Publishers Weekly,* August 7, 2000, review of *My Season with Penguins,* p. 96.
*Reading Today,* June, 2001, "IRA Names Award-Winning Children's Books," p. 17.
*School Library Journal,* December, 2000, Ellen Heath, review of *My Season with Penguins,* p. 166.

# WEGMAN, William (George) 1943-

## Personal

Born December 2, 1943, in Longmeadow, MA. *Education:* Massachusetts College of Art, B.F.A., 1965; University of Illinois—Champaign-Urbana, M.F.A., 1967.

## Addresses

*Home and office*—239 West 18th St., New York, NY 10011. *E-mail*—wegman@infohouse.com.

## Career

Artist, photographer, painter, illustrator, and author. Associate professor at University of Wisconsin—Madison, 1968-70, and at California State University—Long Beach, 1970; also was an instructor at University of Wisconsin—Wausau. Since 1971 has exhibited solo shows of photographs, videos, drawings, and paintings in numerous cities throughout the United States and Europe, including Boston, MA, Boulder, CO, Chicago, IL, Cleveland, OH, Genoa, Italy, Hanover, Germany, Houston, TX, London, England, Los Angeles, CA, Miami, FL, Milan, Italy, Naples, Italy, New York, NY, Paris, France, San Francisco, CA, Scottsdale, AZ, and Washington, DC; since 1969 has exhibited work in group exhibitions, including venues in the Netherlands and Australia; work held in permanent collections at the Brooklyn Museum, Museum of Modern Art (New York, NY), Whitney Museum of American Art, Chrysler Museum, Museum of Modern Art (Paris, France), Los Angeles County Museum of Art, International Museum of Photography (Rochester, NY), Honolulu Academy of Arts, Australian National Gallery, San Francisco Museum of Modern Art, Kunsthaus (Zurich, Switzerland), and the Walker Art Center (Minneapolis, MN); since 1997 has exhibited work at film and video festivals in numerous cities throughout the United States and Europe, including Chicago, IL, New York, NY, Berkeley, CA, Dallas, TX, Tulsa, OK, and Milan, Italy.

## Awards, Honors

Guggenheim fellowships, 1975, 1986; National Endowment of the Arts grants, 1975-76, 1982; Creative Artists Public Service Award, 1979; New York Foundation for the Arts honor, 1987.

## Writings

*Man's Best Friend: Photographs and Drawings,* introduction by Laurence Wieder, Abrams (New York, NY), 1982.

*Everyday Problems* (drawings), Brightwaters (New York, NY), 1984.

*Nineteen Dollars & Eighty-four Cents,* CEPA Gallery, 1984.

*The History of Travel: The Catalogue of an Exhibition of Paintings by William Wegman,* Taft Museum/Butler Institute of American Art, 1990.

*William Wegman*

*William Wegman: Paintings, Drawings, Photographs, Videotapes,* edited by Martin Kunz, Abrams (New York, NY), 1990.

*William Wegman Photographic Works, 1969-1976,* Fonds Regional d'Art Contemporain (Limousin, France), 1991, Distributed Art Publishers, 1992.

(With Carole Kismaric and Marvin Heiferman) *Cinderella,* Hyperion (New York, NY), 1993.

*Little Red Riding Hood,* Hyperion (New York, NY), 1993.

*ABC,* Hyperion (New York, NY), 1994.

*123,* Hyperion (New York, NY), 1995.

*Triangle, Circle, Square,* Hyperion (New York, NY), 1995.

*William Wegman's Mother Goose,* Hyperion (New York, NY), 1996.

*William Wegman's Farm Days,* Hyperion (New York, NY), 1997.

*Puppies,* Hyperion (New York, NY), 1997.

*My Town,* Hyperion (New York, NY), 1998.

*What Do You Do?,* Hyperion (New York, NY), 1999.

*William Wegman's Pups,* Hyperion (New York, NY), 1999.

*Fay,* Hyperion (New York, NY), 1999.

(With Ingrid Sischy) *William Wegman: Fashion Photographs,* Abrams (New York, NY), 1999.

*Surprise Party,* Hyperion (New York, NY), 2000.

(Photographer) Clement C. More, *The Night before Christmas,* Hyperion (New York, NY), 2000.

*Wegmanology,* Hyperion (New York, NY), 2001.

*Chip Wants a Dog,* Hyperion (New York, NY), 2002.

Also creator of more than seventeen videos, among them some featuring himself, including *Deodorant* and *Rage & Depression,* and several videos featuring Wegman's first dog, Man Ray, including *Spelling Lesson, Smoking,* and *New & Used Car Salesman;* also creator of video segments for *Sesame Street,* 1989, and 1992-99, as well as film and video works for *Saturday Night Live, Tonight Show, Late Night with David Letterman,* and Nickelodeon. Director/creator of advertising works, including work for the 2000 Honda Odyssey minivan and for Colorado State's Animal Cancer Center's "Paws for a Cause." Creator of films, including *Dog Baseball,* 1986, and *The Hardly Boys in Hardly Gold,* 1995. Contributor to magazines, including *Avalanche.* Photos are also featured in other formats, including postcards, calendars, note cards, and address books.

## Sidelights

Following the flip of a coin, William Wegman bought a grey Weimaraner, taking the only male from a litter of seven because, as he recalled in an interview with Michael Gross for *New York,* it looked to him "strange and distant." He did not actually want a dog, but had decided that, if he did own one, he would name it Bauhaus, a pun on the minimalist German school of design popular during the 1920s. Unfortunately, the puppy did not really suit the name, resembling instead a "little old grey man." Pondering his dilemma, the artist watched, he explained in his Gross interview, as a "shaft of light like a ray blasted down," bathing the dog with an eerie brilliance. He related to Gross, "It was as if the God of Art were telling the dog, 'Your name is Man Ray'"—an appropriately ironic form of homage to the American artist Man Ray (1890-1976) whose deft innovations as a filmmaker and photographer would influence Wegman's own innovative work in video and photography.

Wegman's photographs and videos of Man Ray (the dog), made between 1970 and 1982, won critical praise for their irony, deadpan humor, pathos, and clever commentaries on art and innocence. Wegman and Man Ray also became popular with television viewers, including the audiences of *Saturday Night Live, Tonight Show,* and *Late Night with David Letterman,* who greeted Wegman's curious, sensitive videos with enthusiasm.

In 1982 Man Ray died of cancer, after which Wegman presumed that his work with Weimaraners was finished. However, several years later, Fay Ray entered his life. Since 1986, Wegman's work with Fay Ray (who, in 1995, also died of cancer) and her descendants—children Crooky, Chundo, and Batty, and grandson (via Batty) Chip—has continued to both move and amuse audiences, such as in Wegman's parodies of the classic children's books, *Cinderella* and *Little Red Riding Hood,* and in his alphabet book, *ABC.* In addition to his photographs and videos of dogs, Wegman has produced conceptual and altered (cut-up or drawn-on) photographs, minimalist line drawings, and, since 1986, paintings. However, the extraordinary popularity and artistic success of his partnership with Man Ray and Fay Ray have tended to overshadow his other artistic accomplishments.

Wegman was born in 1943 and grew up in a small town in western Massachusetts, where, as a precocious toddler, he started drawing and painting in watercolors. In 1949, Wegman contracted Rocky Mountain spotted fever, a life-threatening disease of extreme rarity east of the Rockies. He recovered completely and became, he asserted in his *New York* interview, "a good, normal kid." However, as Wegman grew into his teen years, his endless curiosity about all kinds of activity made it hard for him to fit in completely with any one crowd: the car kids did not trust him because he played sports, and the athletes did not trust him because he toyed with cars. By the time he entered high school, Wegman had become a typical loner: a guy with many skills and interests but few friends. And, he recalls, he felt a little bit lost.

Direction entered Wegman's life in his senior year, when his art teacher recognized his gifts for drawing and painting and encouraged his desire to be an artist. "She saved my life in a way," he recounted to Gross, "because I would not have known what to do with myself." Wegman enrolled at the Massachusetts College of Art where, by his third year, he had become well known as "Willy Wegman the artist." While forming passionate interests in philosophy, music, and literature, he embraced rebellious or anti-art movements, like Dada and Surrealism. Their playful and idiosyncratic elements, as well as their mocking and socially satirical qualities, would both find new expression in Wegman's later, more mature work.

Receiving his bachelor of fine arts degree in 1965, Wegman enrolled in graduate school at the University of Illinois—Champaign-Urbana, where he married an undergraduate art student, Gayle Schneider. He also developed an interest in electrical engineering which, as he related in *New York,* he saw as a means of aligning himself with the "forefront of thinking—information theory." He had come to regard working in traditional mediums, such as painting and sculpture, as a retreat into the past, a "cop out."

Wegman earned his master of fine arts degree in 1967. Moving to Wisconsin that year, where he would have jobs teaching art at the University of Wisconsin's Wausau campus and, later, in Waukesha, he developed a personal philosophy of never working "over his head." He found he worked best in a relaxed, amiable style and by focusing on what actually moved him, rather than on what he had been instructed ought to move him. For Wegman, artistry grew naturally out of his perceptions of the everyday world. Instead of alluding to lofty notions about art in order to push people around, he preferred to engage and delight people by having them look at unexceptional things in a new way.

The art world at the end of the 1960s was radicalized, reflecting the turmoil and seemingly irreconcilable conflicts that were shaking American society. As the decade passed through its final convulsive years, Wegman gravitated toward the new anti-art movement of conceptual art (or mind art), which de-emphasized the art object to concentrate on the idea or concept behind it.

Arguing that creating paintings and sculptures merely served to flatter the affluent classes, the conceptualists sought instead to invent original and unexpected presentations.

Wegman adapted the conceptualist creed by working with surprisingly ordinary materials, such as cellophane, rubber, and household utensils. His choices intended to challenge complacent and hierarchical assumptions about what could constitute art. Departing from the mainstream of conceptualism, however, Wegman infused his work with a strong element of humor, which tended to mask his intellectual ambitions. One piece he fashioned during this period wryly commented upon the consumerist approach to art, using inflatable rubber. While fixing up his home, Wegman attached a sculpture of his to the heating vent so that whenever the heat came up, the inflatable artwork would slowly expand and, at the same time, snake upstairs. Eventually, as the house became warm, it also became filled with Wegman's giant balloon.

In another work, Wegman made eloquent use of Styrofoam by floating rows of Styrofoam commas down the Milwaukee River. Drifting into the medium of sound, he also composed a concerto for one hundred car horns. Sometimes Wegman used a camera to record or document his work, or included photographs within the work itself. It was not until 1969, however, commencing with "Cotto," a black and white photograph of the artist's hand, that he would come to consider a photograph as actual art in itself.

Wegman assumed the position of artist-in-residence at Wisconsin's Madison campus in 1969, where he added elements of performance art and process art to his now solid conceptual base. He attached a felt-tip marker to a plank of Styrofoam and stuck it in a pail of liquid solvent. As the plank dissolved, the marker left a wavy line on his studio wall. The finished "drawing," the wavy line, merely represented the completed process, or one haphazard effect of the process. No aesthetic object, in the accepted sense, its chief value was informational or documentary. The process itself, with its odd life caught and shaped by the flow of time and to a certain extent subject to the random intrusions of its surroundings, was the thing of paramount interest.

It was during this period that Wegman began to make black-out video sketches which would become, according to Gross, "classics" of the genre. On a bare set, dressed simply, usually in jeans and a t-shirt, Wegman would face the camera and talk. In *Deodorant* he demonstrates a new underarm spray that he feels is an excellent product, although one has to spray it on for a couple of minutes for it to really work. While Wegman talks monotonously about how functional it is, he seems to be untroubled that he is smothering his armpit under waves of billowing foam. In *Rage & Depression* he pretends to be a guy who has had to undergo shock therapy because he was always so angry at everyone. He explains that when the doctors put the electrodes on his chest he started to giggle and that silly, giggly, expres-

sion became forever frozen on his face. He tells us he is still miserable, but now, with his unchanging smile, everyone assumes he is happy—which makes everything worse. In these sketches Wegman portrays, according to Sanford Schwartz in the *New York Review of Books,* a "somewhat unfocused, fallible and physically inept character," a reinvention of the Modernist persona. The popularity of Wegman's videos attests to the universality of this comic figure, as well as the egalitarian ideals that underlie it.

Holly Solomon, who later became one of Wegman's dealers, maintained in her interview with Amy Hempel for the *New York Times Magazine,* that "Video before Wegman was Andy Warhol recording a man sleeping for twenty-four hours. It was art about art. Billy [Wegman] felt a real responsibility to engage an audience, and not just art people." And art critic Bruce Boice remarked that Wegman's videotapes suggest the funniest television show he has ever seen.

In 1970, Wegman moved to California to teach at a state college in Long Beach. There he came into contact with other conceptual artists, including Ed Ruscha, John Baldessari, Allen Ruppersberg, and Bruce Nauman, and entered an idyllic chapter of his life. He would fish, swim, and play on the beach with his new artist friends and the dog his wife had urged him to buy, Man Ray. Having been uninterested in owning a dog, Wegman originally had not thought of using him in his work. But Man Ray would not sit submissively by; he would howl when leashed in a corner, and gambol bothersomely onto the set in front of the camera when he was freed. By training the camera on him one day, Wegman discovered that, on video, Man Ray looked "absolutely gorgeous." At the same time he discovered that Man Ray liked the work. So, while it had been nearly impossible to work around Man Ray, it became increasingly appealing for Wegman to work with him.

The videos with Man Ray, made primarily between 1970 and 1977, evince droll parody, elaborating upon themes of Wegman's earlier work. In *Smoking,* the artist tries unsuccessfully to persuade the dog to smoke a cigarette; in *New & Used Car Salesman,* the duo spoof low-budget television commercials. *Milk/Floor* has Wegman crawling away from the camera, spitting a line of milk as he goes, disappearing around a corner. A moment later, Man Ray turns the corner, lapping up the trail of milk until his black nose runs smack into the camera lens. In *Spelling Lesson,* Wegman pretends to correct May Ray's spelling test, much to the dog's confusion; he pedantically points out that Ray has spelled the word "beach, the place" when what was called for was the word "beech, the tree."

Schwartz observed that, having established his video persona, Wegman discovered in Man Ray a natural balance, a creature "of undiluted sinewy muscle … [who] was keener, leaner and sexier than his owner." Man Ray's discomfort in *Spelling Lesson* palpably conveys the dog's creatural vitality and displaced strength. Having surprised himself, Wegman found that his early videos of Man Ray astonished others as well. Art audiences, having grown used to Wegman's cool, ironic, and disembodied work, did not expect to see a great big animal suddenly lunge around the corner.

But Wegman's California period was far from perfect. Aside from some gallery interest in Europe and the support of fellow artist, Ed Ruscha, collectors largely ignored him. While intellectually engaging, conceptual art, without its stock of beautiful or exotic art objects, was difficult to collect. After his teaching job ended, Wegman and his wife lived on food stamps and the money Wegman took in through odd jobs.

In late 1972 the Wegmans left California for New York, where Wegman signed with the Sonnabend Gallery, earning a monthly stipend of five hundred dollars. He augmented his video performances with small drawings that would evolve over the next few years from scant, minimalist sketches to parodies of contemporary attitudes about sex, mass media, class, and art. In one of his drawings, a prisoner smugly asserts that even though he is a convicted felon, he will smoke only his brand of cigarettes. In another, Wegman has depicted eleven blocks of university buildings, the largest of which is labeled Administration, and the smallest, Art. Another drawing presents a romantic couple in classical Roman costumes embracing in a typically Hollywood clinch; Wegman's caption, "I love you Elizopatra," facetiously alludes to the conceptual elevation of a film star, Elizabeth Taylor, into the legendary Cleopatra, and to the parallel reduction of the legendary Cleopatra into a banal, celluloid cliché.

Some critics felt his drawings to be stylistically similar to *New Yorker* cartoons. About the later drawings, Martin Kunz wrote in his introduction to *William Wegman: Paintings, Drawings, Photographs, Videotapes,* "Wegman's references to the topics of sex, beautiful women, the hackneyed themes of the entertainment media and of society in general, are aligned with the central motif of his work, the transferral of the most banal, least artistically incriminated pictorial material to the domain of art without making noticeable changes."

At this time, influential collectors such as Holly Solomon started buying his work, and international celebrities such as Mick Jagger and Andy Warhol began to attend his openings. Still a shy, small-town boy at heart, with a penchant for the whimsical and the ordinary, Wegman was unprepared for this caliber of attention. Instead of meeting success head-on and enjoying it, Wegman told Gross that he simply "freaked out and kind of hid." He became involved with alcohol and drugs as he began to feel increasingly isolated; work became nearly impossible. Wegman recalled in his *New York* interview: "I'd go into my video room and come out screaming."

Although Wegman acknowledged that his life gained some stability when he married Laurie Jewell, a graphic designer, and moved into his third New York studio, on Thames Street near the Battery, his dependence on

alcohol and drugs continued to destroy him. Becoming, in his own words, "a demon," Wegman was nevertheless heartbroken when a fire ravaged the building on Thames Street, consuming many of his oldest negatives, including the early pictures of Man Ray. Feeling himself mentally unable to produce art, Wegman experienced increasingly difficult financial times when Sonnabend chose to cut off his monthly stipend. With the offer of a teaching position in hand, Wegman fled alone to California late that year. California had changed considerably since the early 1970s, and Wegman failed miserably to recapture the serenity for which he longed. He returned to New York City immediately when Holly Solomon, a friend since 1975, offered to sign him up for her New York gallery.

In 1979, Wegman began showing at Solomon and accepted Polaroid's invitation to use its new large-format camera, producing his first work in color since 1966. The Polaroids Wegman would produce over the next several years entailed a significant change from his previous photography. In addition to their larger size, (twenty by twenty-four inches), Wegman's Polaroid photography demonstrates a marked degree of technical mastery and artistic control. Large-format Polaroid photography also required trust and cooperation: Wegman learned to rely upon the expertise of skilled technicians who light the sets and run the camera, and who charged one thousand dollars a day—a costly procedure compounded by the thirty dollars the artist pays for each exposure. (Wegman estimated that he shoots about sixty frames a day, of which only five will be usable.) And Wegman had to balance the competing claims of conceptualism with the glamour of the medium, its rich, gorgeous colors and striking visual appeal.

Although he had to considerably alter his method of working, he found one constant: Man Ray remained his primary model. In 1982, Wegman published his Polaroids of Man Ray under the doubly punning title, *Man's Best Friend,* cited by Schwartz as the "most original book of photographs since Robert Frank's *The Americans* [1959]." Some of the most effective photographs from this collection include "Brooke," a parody of jeans advertisements in general, and the adolescent model Brooke Shields in particular, in which Man Ray seems to be wearing a droopy pair of jeans over his behind and fixing the camera with a 'come hither' stare; "Frog," in which Man Ray has been given a pair of fake bulging eyes and a pair of flippers for his back feet, and appears to be communicating happily with a plastic frog on a plastic lily pad placed before him; and "Dusted," in which Man Ray sits patiently, his body as articulate as a Rodin sculpture, as flour pours down over him and covers him.

Schwartz declared "Dusted" to be the "single most powerful image in *Man's Best Friend,*" in which Wegman expresses "the attachment he and Ray had for each other," the force that inspired Wegman "in one cycle after another, to release more of his talent." Schwartz concluded his praise for "Dusted" by observing that the book also conveys Wegman's somber awareness of Man Ray's imminent death, invoking "the moment that Man Ray has died and is being taken up into the light." At the same time, "Dusted" also recalls the moment, a decade earlier, when the young California puppy found his rightful name.

The year *Man's Best Friend* appeared, Wegman entered a rehabilitation clinic. Having determined once and for all to rid himself of his substance addiction, Wegman sought professional help and emerged, as he told Gross, "liberated, healthy, spiritually awakened." Six months later Man Ray died. At the time of his death, Man Ray, Wegman's companion and model for almost twelve years, had become so widely known and loved that the *Village Voice,* parodying *Time* magazine, ran a full-cover photo of him as "Man of the Year."

After the passing of Man Ray, a hard-fought victory over drugs and alcohol, and a second divorce, Wegman recalled in his *New York* interview that he was ready to "leave my life and really start over." He described the following period of his life as a kind of "renaissance," during which he began to meet people again. Along with his social desirability, his stature as an artist increased with the success of *Man's Best Friend,* and the following year his first retrospective was mounted at the Walker Art Center in Minneapolis. No longer able to photograph Man Ray, he began drawing again and taking photographs of props, drawings, and people. The photographs he took of his girlfriend, Eve Darcy, lampooned the current fitness craze, comically probing its narcissism and self-importance. Despite the artist's productivity, Wegman's public experienced a gap in the artist's work. "Everyone kept looking for the dog pictures, and they weren't getting them," he explained to Gross.

In 1986, four years after Man Ray died, Wegman acquired another Weimaraner puppy named Cinnamon

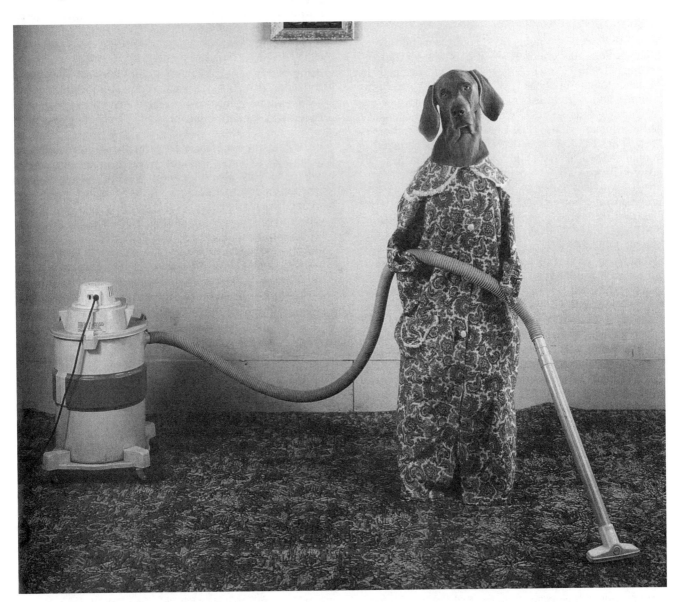

*A host of expressive weimaraners are showcased in* **Wegmanology,** *written and photographed by Wegman.*

Girl. He renamed her Fay Ray, in part a tribute to her predecessor and, within a year, he began using her as a new model. Comparing Man Ray with Fay Ray, Wegman related in his interview with Hempel that "[Man] Ray was more of an equal. He had a sense of gamesmanship: if you do this to me, I can do this to *you*. Fay does things because I want her to."

Among Wegman's most unexpected uses of Fay were the children's books he wrote and illustrated for Hyperion, the publisher owned by the Walt Disney Company. The books were grouped under a series title, "Fay's Fairy Tales." For his first children's publication, issued in early 1993, Wegman retold the classic fairy tale *Cinderella,* using seventeen Weimaraners. His casting decisions reveal the acuteness of his eye as well as his relish of visual imagination. He told Gross: "I play with the specific character of the dogs. From below, Fay looks like Joan Crawford. She looks guilty. Fay can't be Cinderella. Batty can be Cinderella.... She's totally trusting and innocent. There's something eternally, everlastingly cute about her."

Some reviewers thought his "adult sensibility" too sophisticated for children. While Kate McClelland, writing in the *School Library Journal,* deemed his "urbane, tongue-in-cheek text" appropriate to the illustrations and welcomed the "unique portraiture" of "elaborately dressed dogs" with "mournful countenances and . . . human hands," Lee Lorenz declared in the *New York Times Book Review* that *Cinderella* is betrayed by implausibility. "Every child wants to know 'why?' and just too many why's are left hanging here."

Wegman followed with *Little Red Riding Hood,* which was received more positively by critics. A *Publishers Weekly* reviewer pointed out instances of sublime irony, in which illustrations comically undermine the traditional text, such as when the wolf dissembles as grandmother. Since the image of dog-as-wolf-as-grandmother is exactly identical to that of dog-as-grandmother, the sequence beginning "what big ears you have!" produces tongue-in-cheek silliness instead of the customary thrill of foreboding. Rather than framing the act of discovery as a fearful and potentially disastrous experience, Wegman has pedagogically chosen to present it as a means of overcoming fright and finding pleasure.

Throughout the 1990s and into the twenty-first century, Wegman has continued to publish books suitable for younger readers, creating various stories with his dogs. *Surprise Party* finds delivery-"boy"/birthday-dog Chip absent from the party that is secretly organized by small-town Crooky, Batty, and Chundo. A retro environment is presented by "props and settings" that a *Publishers Weekly* reviewer positively recognized as effectively upstaging "the deadpan storytelling" with its "no-holds-barred campiness." But according to the *Publishers Weekly* reviewer, the story's full enjoyment is lost for kids because they do not have "a sort of jaded sensibility or a taste for nostalgia." Linda M. Kenton's *School Library Journal* assessment stated that "older children" may take pleasure in the surface appearance of the work.

However, Kenton commented on "Wegman's standard dressed-up dogs" and the stories' "flat and predictable" text.

Wegman's photographic work with Weimaraner dogs continued in 1999 with *Fay,* a "memoir" of Fay Ray, and with *William Wegman: Fashion Photographs,* a collection derived from Wegman's after-hours pick-through of a Saks Fifth Avenue store. In a *Women's Wear Daily* interview with Wegman that described *Fashion Photographs* as "a whimsical walk through the topography of fashion," Holly Haber quoted Wegman commenting on his creative intent. "'I don't have a sarcastic bone in my body,'" Wegman told Haber, adding: "'I have ironic or humorous ones, but I don't intend to skewer anyone. If something looks like a parody, it is just something that happens along the way—It's not an impulse.'" Wegman was quoted in *Scholastic Art,* "'I never want to make fun of any creature, human or animal.'" It is, in fact, an "innocent, friendly, compassionate" amusement that *Booklist*'s Ray Olson found in *Fashion Photographs,* a "lovely, large complement to Wegman's new traveling exhibition." *Fay,* commended a *Publishers Weekly* reviewer, is "almost always funny" and expresses affection without being overly serious "or falling into jargon." Wegman's collection of images "attracts the reader's attention; the deadpan intelligence of the text holds it," continued the *Publishers Weekly* contributor.

In 1990, using the money he earned from the sale of his Polaroids, Wegman bought a large house in Maine where he was able to continue work on his newest artistic enterprise: painting. Although he had once spurned traditional forms of expression, in 1986, at age forty-three, Wegman decided to start over as a painter. Of his turnabout decision, Angela Westwater, one of his dealers, remarked to Gross: "At this point, New York has lots of artists in mid-career repeating themselves ad infinitum. It is such a testimony to Bill that he's able to push himself into new work—and invest mediums he's used before with new energy and insight."

His first small, exploratory, paintings, done on birch bark, are colorful, textured versions of his cartoonish drawings, and brushy, abstract paintings traceable to the influence of Wegman's college friend, Neil Jenney. After 1990, with larger studio space available, Wegman attempted larger and more involved canvasses. His bravado was immediately apparent in his thorough rejection of the prevailing orthodoxy, the neo-expressionism popularized by such dynamic contemporaries as Julian Schnabel and David Salle.

Employing a style he has whimsically deprecated as "sophomore surrealism," Wegman covers his paintings in a thin, mottled wash of acrylic, creating a surface texture that uses warmth, coolness, and density to evoke the works of J. M. Turner and Raoul Dufy. Upon this, he uses small brushes and oil paint to daub on simple, childlike figures like planes, ships, cowboys, Greek temples, and water sprinklers, culled from generic sources such as elementary readers and illustrated encyclopedias. What emerges has been defined as a stream-of-conscious, nationalistic tapestry, reminiscent of the optimism and innocence of the Eisenhower era—the period of Wegman's boyhood—but enlarged to epic scope and infused with wide-eyed wonder.

Wegman's career has thus far been characterized by independence, prankish yet graceful irony, sensitivity to the process of making art, an extraordinary range of emotional color ranging from cool detachment to poignant tenderness, and a complete investment in art's ability to communicate. Of this last characteristic of Wegman's work, Peter MacGill, his Polaroid dealer, told Gross: "His videos are on *Sesame Street,* he's shown in the best galleries in the world, he's in the collection of virtually every museum, some of the most important critics cherish his work, and so does my four-year-old. It's amazing to see his breadth of appeal without compromise."

## Biographical and Critical Sources

*BOOKS*

Kunz, Martin, editor, *William Wegman: Paintings, Drawings, Photographs, Videotapes,* Abrams (New York, NY), 1990.

*PERIODICALS*

*Advertising Age,* February 14, 2000, p. 76.
*ADWEEK Western Advertising News,* October 16, 2000, David Lipin, "Man's Best Friend," p. 7.
*ARTnews,* January, 1990, pp. 150-155.
*Booklist,* December 1, 1998, Kathleen Squires, review of *My Town,* p. 673; September 15, 1999, Ray Olson, review of *Fay,* p. 207; April 15, 2000, Ray Olson, review of *Fashion Photographs,* p. 1513.
*Entertainment Weekly,* February 23, 1996, Kristen Baldwin, "Dressed to the Canines," p. 108; October 10, 1997, Alexandra Jacobs, review of *William Wegman's Puppies,* p. 86.
*Library Journal,* June 1, 1999, Michael Rogers, review of *Man's Best Friend,* p. 188.
*Life,* May, 1997, "Almanac," p. 40.
*Los Angeles Times Book Review,* November 25, 1990, p. 3.
*Modern Maturity,* May-June, 1999, Lori Erickson, "Pet Project," p. 19A.
*New York,* March 30, 1992, interview with Michael Gross, pp. 44-50.
*New York Review of Books,* August 18, 1983, Sanford Schwartz, pp. 44-45.
*New York Times,* October 6, 1999, Stuart Elliott, "William Wegman's Dogs Take the Plunge into TV Commercials for the Honda Odyssey Minivan," p. C11.
*New York Times Book Review,* May 16, 1993, Lee Lorenz, p. 22.
*New York Times Magazine,* November 29, 1987, pp. 40-44; December 25, 1988, pp. 18-19; August 17, 1997, Amy Hempel, review of *William Wegman's Puppies,* p. 38.
*People Weekly,* September 9, 1991, pp. 105-108; November 17, 1997, Michael A. Lipton, "Puppy Love," p. 248.
*Publishers Weekly,* October 4, 1993, p. 77; July 22, 1996, review of *William Wegman's Mother Goose,* p. 240;

April 14, 1997, review of *William Wegman's Farm Days,* p. 73; September 22, 1997, review of *William Wegman's Puppies,* p. 79; October 26, 1998, review of *My Town,* p. 64; September 13, 1999, review of *Fay,* p. 73; April 3, 2000, review of *Surprise Party,* p. 79; September 25, 2000, Elizabeth Devereaux, review of *The Night before Christmas,* p. 67.
*Scholastic Art,* March, 2000, p. 10.
*School Arts,* December, 1996, Gaye Leigh Green, "Performance Art Criticism," p. 22.
*School Library Journal,* April, 1993, Kate McClelland, p. 138; October, 1996, Harriett Fargnoli, review of *William Wegman's Mother Goose,* p. 119; July, 1997, Patricia Manning, review of *William Wegman's Farm Days,* p. 78; July, 2000, Linda M. Kenton, review of *Surprise Party,* p. 112.
*Time,* March 23, 1992, pp. 74-75; May 3, 1993, p. 81.
*Time of Kids,* February 16, 1996, "Nothin' but Hound Dogs," p. 8.
*W,* November, 1999, "Dogging Fashion," p. 74.
*Women's Wear Daily,* June 7, 2000, Holly Haber, "Puttin' on the Dog; Saks Turns William Wegman and His Canines Loose for a Spree," p. 10S.

*OTHER*

*William Wegman's Web Site,* http://www.wegmanworld. com/ (March 2, 2001).*

\*        \*        \*

# WELLING, Peter J. 1947-

## Personal

Born August 6, 1947, in South Bend, IN; son of Gerard "Dutch" and Margaret (Springer) Welling; married Darlene Warnock (a development and leasing manager), June 19, 1987; children: P. Shawn, Justin M., Michael D., Andrew G. *Ethnicity:* "Dutch." *Education:* Indiana University—South Bend, B.A., 1977. *Religion:* Christian.

## Addresses

*Home*—8051 Cardinal Cove E., Indianapolis, IN 46256. *E-mail*—aldertag@home.com.

## Career

Writer and illustrator. *Military service:* U.S. Air Force, 1966-72; became staff sergeant.

## Member

Society of Children's Book Writers and Illustrators, Veterans of Foreign Wars.

## Writings

*AUTHOR AND ILLUSTRATOR*

*Andrew McGroundhog and His Shady Shadow,* Pelican Publishing, 2001.

*Shawn O'Hisser: The Last Snake in Ireland,* Pelican Publishing, 2002.

## Sidelights

Peter J. Welling told *SATA:* "I've been a storyteller for most of my life. Now I am putting my tales on paper. My wife, sons, and their families strongly urged me to write and have continued to support my efforts.

"As an illustrator as well as author, I create my tales thusly. I pick a subject, say Groundhog Day. Mentally I create the character, then I create a story about him. I try to pick subjects that have not been done *ad nauseum*. Unless I come up with something truly fresh, you won't see a Christmas story from me. I try to challenge my young readers and give them a laugh at the same time. My goal is to make the stories interesting enough that parents won't groan if their child asks 'read this one to me.' I insert humor that parents will get, but probably not the child. I put historical items or references to songs in the pictures. In *Andrew McGroundhog and His Shady Shadow* a signpost gives directions to 'the high road' and 'the low road.' Parents will probably start humming the tune. The kids will enjoy it, too."

## Biographical and Critical Sources

*OTHER*

*Peter J. Welling Web Site,* http://www.peterjwelling.com/ (March 2, 2002).*

\*     \*     \*

## WESTON, Carol 1956-

## Personal

Born September 11, 1956, in New York, NY; daughter of William (a producer and writer for television) and Marybeth (an editor and writer) Weston; married Rob Ackerman (a playwright), August 28, 1980; children: Elizabeth, Emme. *Education:* Yale University, B.A. (French/Spanish comparative literature; summa cum laude), 1978; Middlebury College, M.A. (Spanish), 1979.

## Addresses

*Home*—New York, NY. *Agent*—Laura Peterson, Curtis Brown, 10 Astor Place, 3rd Floor, New York, NY 10003.

## Career

Author. Advice columnist for *Girls' Life* magazine; appeared on numerous television programs, including *Today Show, Oprah,* and *View.*

## Member

American Society of Journalists and Authors, Society of Children's Book Writers and Illustrators.

## Awards, Honors

*Girltalk: All the Stuff Your Sister Never Told You* and *For Girls Only: Wise Words, Good Advice* were both selected as Best Books for the Teen Age by the New York Public Library.

## Writings

*Girltalk: All the Stuff Your Sister Never Told You,* Harper & Row (New York, NY), 1985, third edition, Harper-Collins (New York, NY), 1997.

*How to Honeymoon: A Romantic and Practical Guide for Newlyweds,* Harper & Row (New York, NY), 1986.

*Girltalk about Guys: Real Questions, Real Answers,* Harper & Row (New York, NY), 1987.

*From Here to Maternity: Confessions of a First-Time Mother,* Little, Brown (Boston, MA), 1991.

*For Girls Only: Wise Words, Good Advice,* HarperCollins (New York, NY), 1998.

*Private and Personal: Questions and Answers for Girls Only,* HarperCollins (New York, NY), 2000.

*The Diary of Melanie Martin; or, How I Survived Matt the Brat, Michelangelo, and the Leaning Tower of Pizza,* Knopf (New York, NY), 2000.

*Melanie Martin Goes Dutch: The Private Diary of My Almost Bummer Summer with Cecily, Matt the Brat, and Vincent van Go Go Go,* Knopf (New York, NY), 2002.

*Carol Weston*

Contributor to periodicals, including *Seventeen, Glamour, New York Times, Cosmopolitan, Chicago Tribune, Ladies' Home Journal, Essence, Parenting, Bride's, Redbook, Family Circle,* and *McCall's.* Author of "Dear Carol" (advice column), *Girls' Life,* 1994—.

Weston's books have been translated into many languages, including Chinese, Russian, Polish, and Italian.

## Work in Progress

*For Teens Only: Quotes, Notes, and Practical Wisdom,* publication due in 2003; *Melanie Martin Speaks Spanish.*

## Sidelights

An expert on the trials and tribulations of being a girl, Carol Weston has been doling out advice to young readers for years in her column for *Girls' Life* and other magazines. In her first book of advice for young girls, *Girltalk: All the Stuff Your Sister Never Told You,* Weston covers a wide variety of subjects, from acne and friendships, to job plans and applying to college. All in all, the book is "a collection of sensible advice and practical information" according to Judith Janes in *Library Journal.* A *Publishers Weekly* contributor noted that, in addition to being a well-planned book, *Girltalk* is effective because "Weston takes on the voice of an understanding, good-natured older sister" as she addresses the concerns of interest to teenage girls. *Voice of Youth Advocates* critic Susan A. Hopkins also noted the popularity of *Girltalk,* pointing out that Weston's light-hearted, humorous tone combines with practical advice to create a "wonderful book."

Positive reviews and feedback from readers prompted Weston to pen a second advice book for teens: *Girltalk about Guys: Real Questions, Real Answers.* In this book, Weston addresses relationship issues, crushes, and break-ups. The book was praised by a *Kirkus Reviews* critic for its "depth and authentic feeling." Similarly, a contributor wrote in *Publishers Weekly* that the questions and answers Weston includes in the book are "satisfying in their fullness and genuine sound."

*For Girls Only: Wise Words, Good Advice* is a departure from Weston's previous books for girls in that it contains a collection of inspirational thoughts focused on broad subjects, including family, friendships, and love. Weston quotes from a wide variety of sources, including Aesop, Susan B. Anthony, Madonna, and Oprah Winfrey, in this "source of inspiration and guidance" wrote Carrie Eldridge in *Voice of Youth Advocates.* Weston's other advice books for girls include *Private and Personal: Questions and Answers for Girls Only,* a collection of letters from her fans and her responses to them. "My book *For Teens Only* will be a further departure," the author told *SATA,* "because it addresses guys as well as girls."

In addition to books offering advice, Weston also penned a book of fiction, *The Diary of Melanie Martin;*

*While vacationing in Italy, Melanie discovers how much her family means to her. (Cover illustration by Marci Roth.)*

*or, How I Survived Matt the Brat, Michelangelo, and the Leaning Tower of Pizza,* in 2000. The first of a series, the novel traces the adventures of fourth-grader Melanie Martin as she and her family travel in Italy. Drawing a parallel between the no-nonsense and unaffected style of writing Weston used in her nonfiction works and her first foray into fiction, a *Booklist* reviewer praised the author for creating a "smooth, authentic-sounding journey" in Melanie's first adventure. A *Publishers Weekly* critic also lauded Weston's ability to realistically portray her young heroine, following Melanie through Italy and tracking her adventures in "quirky rhymes and handwritten jottings that reflect her moods." Her second novel, *Melanie Martin Goes Dutch,* takes place in the Netherlands.

"When I was in grade school and middle school, I wrote all the time," Weston told *SATA.* "I filled dozens of diaries with ordinary words about myself, about whether my crush said 'hi' and what I had for lunch and how much I earned babysitting. I wrote and wrote and wrote. I found my voice and lost my fear of the blank page.

"In college I majored in French and Spanish comparative literature and reveled in the extraordinary words of

Molière and Márquez, Sartre and Fuentes. I also wrote my first published essay. In fact, I remember buying a magazine with my byline, clutching it to my chest, and crossing Silliman courtyard at Yale. A professor asked, 'Aren't you a little old to be reading *Seventeen*?' And I proudly showed him that I wasn't reading it—I was writing for it.

"My first book, *Girltalk: All the Stuff Your Sister Never Told You* has been in print ever since 1985. My other advice books include *For Girls Only* and *Private and Personal*, and I've been writing a 'Dear Carol' personal advice column for *Girls' Life* since the magazine's first issue in 1994.

"I love the privilege of being a self-employed author and advice-giver for girls. But in my heart, I knew that I had set out to be a novelist. Why couldn't I find the courage to write fiction? Finally I gave myself some advice: How about writing a novel for girls?

"Out poured *The Diary of Melanie Martin; or, How I Survived Matt the Brat, Michelangelo, and the Leaning Tower of Pizza*. It's my seventh book, but first novel, and it's the story of a Manhattan fourth-grader who goes to Italy with her art teacher mom, history buff dad, and little brother Matt the Brat. I'm so glad that girls—and boys—have liked Melanie's adventures; I'm planning to 'escort' Melanie to other countries as well: Holland and Spain are next. Stay Tuned!"

Madrid, Spain is where Weston and her husband, playwright Rob Ackerman, met; they now live in Manhattan with their two daughters, Elizabeth and Emme, "as well as our bunny, mouse, and fish," Weston was quick to add. "My daughters inspire me often, and when one of them says or does something funny, the other sometimes says, 'Mom, write that down!' and tells me just how I can use it in an episode of a future Melanie novel. They also like when we travel as a family. My advice to young writers: Keep writing! My advice to young readers: Come visit me at carolweston.com."

## Biographical and Critical Sources

*PERIODICALS*

*Booklist*, May 1, 2000, GraceAnne A. DeCandido, review of *The Diary of Melanie Martin; or, How I Survived Matt the Brat, Michelangelo, and the Leaning Tower of Pizza*, p. 1671.
*Kirkus Reviews*, March 15, 1988, review of *Girltalk about Guys: Real Questions, Real Answers*, p. 461.
*Library Journal*, July, 1985, Judith Janes, review of *Girltalk: All the Stuff Your Sister Never Told You*, p. 79;
*Publishers Weekly*, May 24, 1985, review of *Girltalk*, p. 67; January 29, 1988, review of *Girltalk about Guys*, p. 432; May 8, 2000, review of *The Diary of Melanie Martin*, p. 221.
*School Library Journal*, July, 1998, review of *For Girls Only: Wise Words, Good Advice*, p. 112.

*Voice of Youth Advocates*, April, 1986, Susan A. Hopkins, review of *Girltalk*, p. 55; August, 1998, Carrie Eldridge, review of *For Girls Only*, p. 228.

*OTHER*

*Carol Weston Web Site*, http://carolweston.com (February 22, 2002).
*Melanie Martin Web Site*, http://www.melaniemartin.com (February 22, 2002).

\* \* \*

# WHITMAN, Sylvia (Choate) 1961-

## Personal

Born March 15, 1961, in New York, NY; daughter of Alexander Harvey (a retired ship broker) and Sylvia (Choate) Whitman; married Mohamed Ben Jemaa (a chef and teacher's aide), June 2, 1985. *Education:* Harvard University, B.A., 1984; University of Texas—Austin, M.A. (American studies), 1989; University of Virginia, M.F.A. (creative writing), 1997. *Hobbies and other interests:* Travel, photography, squash.

## Addresses

*Home*—515 Christor Pl., Orlando, FL 32803. *E-mail*—sylviawhitman@post.harvard.edu.

## Career

Freelance writer and editor, 1985—. *Miami Herald*, Fort Lauderdale, FL, intern reporter, summer, 1984; Phillips Junior College, Marrero, LA, part-time English instructor, 1985; Berlitz Language School, New Orleans, LA, part-time English as a second language instructor, 1985; University of Texas—Austin, teaching assistant, 1988-89; *Orlando Sentinel*, Orlando, FL, part-time copy editor on the international/national desk, 1989-93; Vassar College, Poughkeepsie, NY, public relations coordinator, 1993-95; *Daily Progress*, Charlottesville, VA, part-time copy, photo, and layout editor, 1995-96; Rollins College, Winter Park, FL, learning specialist, 1997-98, writing center coordinator, 1998—.

## Member

Society of Children's Book Writers and Illustrators.

## Awards, Honors

First place, *Redbook Young Writers' Fiction Contest*, 1985; Feature Award, Educational Press Association of America, 1988; National Journalism Award, Epilepsy Foundation of America, 1992; Notable Children's Trade Book in the Field of Social Studies selection, National Council for the Social Studies/Children's Book Council Joint Committee, and Association of Children's Librarians of Northern California Distinguished Book selection, 1993, both for *"V" Is for Victory: The American Home Front during World War II;* New York Public Library "Books for the Teen Age" citation, 1995, for *Uncle Sam*

*Sylvia Whitman*

*Wants You: Military Men and Women of World War II;* Thomas Balch Short Story Prize, University of Virginia, 1996 and 1997; Best Children's Book of the Year Selection, Bank Street College, 2001, for *What's Cooking? The History of American Food.*

## Writings

*Hernando de Soto and the Explorers of the American South,* Chelsea House (New York, NY), 1991.

*"V" Is for Victory: The American Home Front during World War II,* Lerner (Minneapolis, MN), 1993.

*Uncle Sam Wants You: Military Men and Women of World War II,* Lerner (Minneapolis, MN), 1993.

*This Land Is Your Land: The American Conservation Movement,* Lerner (Minneapolis, MN), 1994.

*Get Up and Go!: The History of American Road Travel,* Lerner (Minneapolis, MN), 1996.

*Children of the Frontier,* Carolrhoda Books (Minneapolis, MN), 1998.

*Immigrant Children,* Carolrhoda Books (Minneapolis, MN), 2000.

*Children of the World War II Home Front,* Carolrhoda Books (Minneapolis, MN), 2001.

*What's Cooking? The History of American Food,* Lerner (Minneapolis, MN), 2001.

Also contributor of fiction and nonfiction to periodicals, including *Cobblestone, Faces, Redbook, Boston Globe Magazine, Creative Ideas for Living, France Today, Harvard Magazine, Ladies Home Journal, Los Angeles Times, McCall's, Miami Herald, Orlando Magazine, Reader's Digest, Student Writer, Seventeen, Writer,* and *Jack and Jill.* Contributing editor, *National Culinary Review.* Contributor to books, including *The Writer's Handbook 1994,* The Writer, Inc.; *Texas Women Writers: A Tradition of Their Own,* Texas A & M Press, 1997; *The Writer's Handbook 1998,* The Writer, Inc.; and *Like a Second Mother: Nannies and Housekeepers in the Lives of Wealthy Children,* Trio Press, 1999.

## Work in Progress

*Empires of Gold: The Great Trading Kingdoms of Early Africa,* for Core Knowledge. *Caterpillar Dreams In Color.* *"Marhaba" Means "Welcome."*

## Sidelights

Children's book writer Sylvia Whitman is known for her works of nonfiction, which incorporate a broad view of American history while relating a smaller history focused on one specific topic, such as food or transportation. In her book *Get Up and Go!: The History of*

*American Road Travel,* Whitman uses the "engaging context" of transportation, as a critic from *Voice of Youth Advocates* phrased it, to create a focused, fascinating history of the United States. Beginning with simple Native American foot trails and detailing the various developments in transportation, from horse and coach to automobile, the author shows how each development made an impact on the growth of the nation. Throughout her work, Whitman also includes "interesting stories," noted *Booklist* critic Susan DeRonne, about individuals who made a name for themselves in the world of transportation, such as Alice Ramsey, the first woman to drive across the United States. *School Library Journal* reviewer Shirley Wilton also remarked favorably on the "fascinating insights [that] emerge" in Whitman's account.

Critics offered similar positive reviews for Whitman's *What's Cooking? The History of American Food.* Here, rather that discussing the variety of food consumed in the United States, the author instead covers "how food reflects and influences culture," according to *Booklist* contributor Heather Hepler. Whitman shares with readers how advances in technology affected the food Americans eat, as well as how historical events, like the Great Depression and World War II, inspired people to make the most of limited and rationed food. In a *School Library Journal* review, Joyce Adams found that "in its broad look at the American diet, this clearly written volume also offers a concise overview of American history."

Whitman once told *SATA:* "As the caboose in a family with five children, I was always watching grown-up goings-on or listening to conversations not intended for my ears. One of my sisters dubbed me 'the little reporter.' For about twenty years I've kept a journal. So it's fitting that although I have always loved reading novels and stories, I made my way into print through nonfiction. My first published article described my

*Whitman discusses the history of American road travel from walking to superhighways in her book* **Get Up and Go!** *(Photograph from the Library of Congress.)*

experience volunteering with Mother Teresa's Missionaries of Charity in Calcutta. Lots of less exotic freelance pieces have followed, for both adults and children. Nepotism helped me land my first book assignment: Chelsea House asked one of my history professors to write the introduction to a series about explorers and to recommend some graduate-student writers.

"My other books grew out of proposals. Fortunately, my letters crossed the desk of a kindred spirit at Lerner, an editor with an interest in history as everyday experience. Although politicians and intellectuals get most of the press, average folks also shape the fate of a nation as they implement policies or embrace ideas. For my books on World War II—the first in Lerner's people's history series—I interviewed a number of veterans of the military front and the home front, including my parents.

"It's ironic that I'm writing history after so studiously avoiding it all the way through high school. How boring, I used to think. Growing up on the eve of multiculturalism, I resented that stuffy white men got all the starring roles in the pageant. My academic work in folklore and American studies, however, gave history a richer and more relevant texture. I'd love for kids to share that view."

## Biographical and Critical Sources

*PERIODICALS*

*Booklist,* February 15, 1993, p. 1057; May 1, 1993, p. 1587; December 15, 1994, April Judge, review of *This Land Is Your Land: The American Conservation Movement,* p. 751; October 15, 1996, Susan DeRonne, review of *Get Up and Go!: The History of American Road Travel,* p. 419; August, 2001, Heather Hepler, review of *What's Cooking? The History of American Food,* p. 2105.
*Book Report,* May, 1994, p. 28.
*Childhood Education,* summer, 1993, p. 247.
*Horn Book Guide,* fall, 1991, p. 326; spring, 1993, p. 151; fall, 1993, p. 384, spring, 1997, review of *Get Up and Go!,* p. 176.
*Kirkus Reviews,* December 1, 1992, p. 1512.
*Library Talk,* May, 1993, p. 45.
*School Library Journal,* March, 1993, p. 233; June, 1993, p. 141; December, 1994, Eva Elizabeth Von Ancken, review of *This Land Is Your Land,* p. 129; October, 1996, Shirley Wilton, review of *Get Up and Go!,* p. 161; July, 2000, Patricia Mahoney Brown, review of *Immigrant Children,* p. 95; July, 2001, Joyce Adams, review of *What's Cooking?,* p. 133; July, 2001, Barbara Buckley, review of *Children of the World War II Home Front,* p. 101.
*Social Education,* April, 1993, p. 204.
*Voice of Youth Advocates,* August, 1997, review of *Get Up and Go!,* p. 167.

# WILHELM, Hans 1945-

## Personal

Born September 21, 1945, in Bremen, West Germany (now Germany); immigrated to the United States; son of Heinrich (a bank executive) and Hanna (a homemaker; maiden name, Jurgens) Plate. *Education:* Attended business and art schools in Bremen, West Germany.

## Addresses

*Home and office*—P.O. Box 109, Westport, CT 06881.

## Career

Writer, illustrator, and lecturer, 1977—. HAG, Bremen, West Germany (now Germany), commercial apprenticeship, 1963-65; VOLKS, Johannesburg, South Africa, office manager, 1965-67; BASF, Johannesburg, South Africa, marketing manager, 1967-77; actor, artist, and telephone counselor, Johannesburg, South Africa, 1967-77.

## Member

Authors Guild, Society of Children's Book Writers and Illustrators.

## Awards, Honors

Best Book of the Year, *Eltern* magazine, 1983, for *The Trapp Family Book;* Best Children's Books of the Year citation, *Time* magazine, 1983, for *Tales from the Land under My Table;* Parents' Choice Award, 1985, for *Blackberry Ink;* Children's Book Award, International Reading Association, 1986, for *A New Home, a New Friend;* Children's Books of the Year list, Child Study Association, 1986, for *Blackberry Ink,* and 1987 for *The Funniest Knock-Knock Book Ever!* and *Let's Be Friends Again!;* Gold Medallion Book Award, Christian Publishers Association, 1988, for *What Does God Do?;* Book Can Develop Empathy Award, 1990, for *I'll Always Love You.*

## Writings

*FOR CHILDREN; SELF-ILLUSTRATED*

*The Trapp Family Book,* Heinemann (London, England), 1983.
*Tales from the Land under My Table,* Random House (New York, NY), 1983.
*I'll Always Love You!,* Crown (New York, NY), 1985.
*Our Christmas 1985,* Grolier (Danbury, CT), 1985.
*Bunny Trouble,* Scholastic (New York, NY), 1985.
*A New Home, a New Friend,* Random House (New York, NY), 1985.
*Don't Give up, Josephine!,* Random House (New York, NY), 1985.
*Totally Bored Boris,* Random House (New York, NY), 1986.
*Not Another Day like This!,* Grolier (Danbury, CT), 1986.
*Let's Be Friends Again!,* Crown (New York, NY), 1986.

*Hans Wilhelm*

*Waldo and the Desert Island Adventure,* Random House (New York, NY), 1986.

*Mother Goose 1986,* Sterling Publishers (New York, NY), 1986.

*Waldo 1986 für jung und alt,* Heye (Unterhaching, Germany), 1986.

*Waldo 1986 mit Liebe,* Heye (Unterhaching, Germany), 1986.

*Waldo 1986 Freundschaft,* Heye (Unterhaching, Germany), 1986.

*What Does God Do?,* Sween Publishing (Ft. Worth, TX), 1986.

*Pirates Ahoy!,* Parents Press (New York, NY), 1987.

*Mother Goose 1987,* Sterling Publishers (New York, NY), 1987.

*Waldo 1987 für jung und alt,* Heye (Unterhaching, Germany), 1987.

*Waldo 1987 mit Liebe,* Heye (Unterhaching, Germany), 1987.

*Waldo 1987 Freundschaft,* Heye (Unterhaching, Germany), 1987.

*Waldo und sein toller Trick,* Otto Maier, 1987.

*Oh, What a Mess,* Crown (New York, NY), 1988.

*Tyrone the Horrible,* Scholastic (New York, NY), 1988.

*Waldo and the Christmas Surprise,* Random House (New York, NY), 1988.

*Waldo, Tell Me about Guardian Angels,* C. R. Gibson (Norwalk, CT), 1988.

*Waldo, Tell Me about Me,* C. R. Gibson (Norwalk, CT), 1988.

*Waldo, Tell Me about God,* C. R. Gibson (Norwalk, CT), 1988.

*Waldo, Tell Me about Christ,* C. R. Gibson (Norwalk, CT), 1988.

*Waldo und der Riese Plansch,* Carlsen (Hamburg, Germany), 1988.

*Waldo und die Bootsfahrt,* Carlsen (Hamburg, Germany), 1988.

*Waldo und das Orchester,* Carlsen (Hamburg, Germany), 1988.

*Waldo und das Waldfest,* Carlsen (Hamburg, Germany), 1988.

*Waldo, eins, zwei, drei,* Carlsen (Hamburg, Germany), 1988.

*Waldo im Zoo,* Carlsen (Hamburg, Germany), 1988.

*Waldo, guten Morgen,* Carlsen (Hamburg, Germany), 1988.

*Waldo, alle meine Farben,* Carlsen (Hamburg, Germany), 1988.

*Freunde gibt es überall,* Carlsen (Hamburg, Germany), 1988.

*Friends Are Forever,* Grolier (Danbury, CT), 1988.

*I Wouldn't Tell a Lie,* Grolier (Danbury, CT), 1988.

*Never Lonely Again,* Grolier (Danbury, CT), 1988.

*Waldo 1988 Datebook,* Heye (Unterhaching, Germany), 1988.

*Waldo 1988 mit Liebe,* Heye (Unterhaching, Germany), 1988.

*Waldo 1988 Freundschaft,* Heye (Unterhaching, Germany), 1988.

*Der Mond muss weg!* Carlsen (Hamburg, Germany), 1989.

*More Bunny Trouble,* Scholastic (New York, NY), 1989.

*Mother Goose on the Loose,* Sterling Publishers (New York, NY), 1989.

*Waldo, Tell Me about Christmas,* C. R. Gibson (Norwalk, CT), 1989.

*Schnitzel's First Christmas,* Simon & Schuster (New York, NY), 1989.

*Waldo 1989 Datebook,* Heye (Unterhaching, Germany), 1989.

*Waldo 1989 mit Liebe,* Heye (Unterhaching, Germany), 1989.

*Waldo 1989 Freundschaft,* Heye (Unterhaching, Germany), 1989.

*Waldo 1990 Datebook,* Heye (Unterhaching, Germany), 1990.

*A Cool Kid like Me,* Crown (New York, NY), 1990.

*Waldo hilft dem Oberförster,* Carlsen (Hamburg, Germany), 1990.

*Waldo und das müde Sandmännchen,* Carlsen (Hamburg, Germany), 1990.

*Waldo und die Geburtstagshose,* Carlsen (Hamburg, Germany), 1990.

*Waldo und die Marzipankartoffel,* Carlsen (Hamburg, Germany), 1990.

*Waldo und Wilma, die Wüstenmaus,* Carlsen (Hamburg, Germany), 1990.

*Waldo 1991 Datebook,* Heye (Unterhaching, Germany), 1991.

*Eine neue Weihnachtsgeschichte,* Carlsen (Hamburg, Germany), 1991.

*Schnitzel Is Lost!,* Simon & Schuster (New York, NY), 1991.

*Tyrone, the Double Dirty Rotten Cheater,* Scholastic (New York, NY), 1991.

*Waldo with Friends 1992,* Te Neues (Kempen, Germany), 1992.

*Waldo 1992,* Te Neues (Kempen, Germany), 1992.

*The Bremen Town Musicians,* Scholastic (New York, NY), 1992.

*Susi auf der Kirchturmspitze,* Carlsen (Hamburg, Germany), 1992.

*Toeff-Toeff, der kleine Trecker,* Carlsen (Hamburg, Germany), 1992.

*Waldo with Friends 1993,* Te Neues (Kempen, Germany), 1993.

*Waldo 1993,* Te Neues (Kempen, Germany), 1993.

*The Boy Who Wasn't There,* Scholastic (New York, NY), 1993.

*Eine Hamstergeschichte,* Carlsen (Hamburg, Germany), 1993.

*Ein Dino hat's schwer!,* Carlsen (Hamburg, Germany), 1993.

*Waldo und das schönste Weihnachtsgeschenk,* Carlsen (Hamburg, Germany), 1993.

*Waldo und die Hasenlümmel,* Carlsen (Hamburg, Germany), 1993.

*Waldo, Tell Me about Dying,* C. R. Gibson (Norwalk, CT), 1993.

*Waldo with Friends 1994,* Te Neues (Kempen, Germany), 1994.

*Waldo 1994,* Te Neues (Kempen, Germany), 1994.

*Bad, Bad Bunny Trouble,* Scholastic (New York, NY), 1994.

*Waldo with Friends 1995,* Te Neues (Kempen, Germany), 1995.

*Waldo 1995,* Te Neues (Kempen, Germany), 1995.

*The Big Boasting Battle,* Scholastic (New York, NY), 1995.

*I Hate My Bow!,* Scholastic (New York, NY), 1995.

*Tyrone and the Swamp Gang!,* Scholastic (New York, NY), 1995.

*Freude,* Carlsen (Hamburg, Germany), 1995.

*Leben,* Carlsen (Hamburg, Germany), 1995.

*Trost,* Carlsen (Hamburg, Germany), 1995.

*Freundschaft,* Carlsen (Hamburg, Germany), 1995.

*The Royal Raven,* Scholastic (New York, NY), 1996.

*Waldo 1997 Datebook,* Te Neues (Kempen, Germany), 1997.

*Waldo-Bella 1997,* Te Neues (Kempen, Germany), 1997.

*Don't Cut My Hair!,* Scholastic (New York, NY), 1997.

***After the death of his dog, a young boy is comforted by remembering that he had told her "I'll always love you" every night.***
*(From* I'll Always Love You!, *written and illustrated by Hans Wilhelm.)*

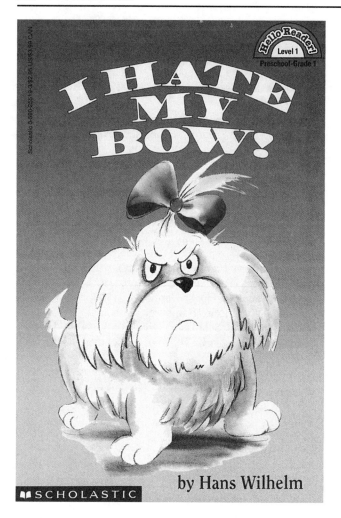

*A little dog is mad that other dogs won't play with him because of his bright orange bow.* (Cover illustration by Wilhelm.)

*I Am Lost!,* Scholastic (New York, NY), 1997.
*Waldo 1998,* Te Neues (Kempen, Germany), 1998.
*Waldo!,* Heine, 1998.
*Glück im Unglück,* Gabriel, 1999.
*I Lost My Tooth!,* Scholastic (New York, NY), 1999.
*I Love Colors!,* Scholastic (New York, NY), 2000.
*It's Too Windy!,* Scholastic (New York, NY), 2000.
*Waldo, Tell Me about Praying,* Regina Press, 2001.
*I Love My Shadow!,* Scholastic (New York, NY), 2002.
*I'm Not Scared!,* Scholastic (New York, NY), 2002.
*I Can Help!,* Scholastic (New York, NY), 2003.

*FOR CHILDREN; ILLUSTRATOR*

Yoshihiko Funazaki, *King Raven,* Yugakusha, 1983.
Pat Boone, *Pat Boone's Favorite Bible Stories,* Random House (New York, NY), 1984.
William Furstenberg, *Stone Soup,* Weekly Reader Family Books, 1984.
Eve Merriam, *Blackberry Ink,* Morrow (New York, NY), 1985.
Joseph Rosenbloom, *The Funniest Riddle Book Ever!,* Sterling Publishers (New York, NY), 1985.
Joseph Rosenbloom, *The Funniest Joke Book Ever!,* Sterling Publishers (New York, NY), 1986.

David L. Harrison, *Wake up, Sun!,* Random House (New York, NY), 1986.
Joseph Rosenbloom, *The Funniest Knock-Knock Book Ever!,* Sterling Publishers (New York, NY), 1987.
Joseph Rosenbloom, *The Funniest Dinosaur Book Ever!,* Sterling Publishers (New York, NY), 1987.
Emily Little, *David and the Giant,* Random House (New York, NY), 1987.
Jane Gerver, *Piggy's Wig,* Random House (New York, NY), 1989.
Joseph Rosenbloom, *The Funniest Haunted House Book Ever!,* Sterling Publishers (New York, NY), 1989.
Kathryn Cristaldi, *Little Squirrel's Christmas Ride,* Random House (New York, NY), 1989.
Cheyette Lewison, *Buzzzz—Said the Bee,* Scholastic (New York, NY), 1992.
Jean Marzollo, *Halloween Cats,* Scholastic (New York, NY), 1992.
Jean Marzollo, *I'm Tyrannosaurus!,* Scholastic (New York, NY), 1993.
James Preller, *Hiccups for Elephant,* Scholastic (New York, NY), 1994.
Eve Merriam, *Higgle Wiggle,* Morrow (New York, NY), 1994.
Grace Maccarone, *Oink! Moo! How Do You Do?,* Scholastic (New York, NY), 1994.
Nurit Karlin, *Ten Little Bunnies,* Simon & Schuster (New York, NY), 1994.
Steve Metzger, *Dinofours—It's Time for School,* Scholastic (New York, NY), 1996.
Steve Metzger, *Dinofours—I'm Not Your Friend!,* Scholastic (New York, NY), 1996.
Steve Metzger, *Dinofours—I'm Super Dino!,* Scholastic (New York, NY), 1996.
Jean Marzollo, *Valentine Cats,* Scholastic (New York, NY), 1996.
Steve Metzger, *Dinofours—It's Class Trip Day!,* Scholastic (New York, NY), 1997.
Steve Metzger, *Dinofours—It's Time-out Time!,* Scholastic (New York, NY), 1997.
Steve Metzger, *Dinofours—It's Fire Drill Day!,* Scholastic (New York, NY), 1997.
Steve Metzger, *Dinofours—Where's Mommy?,* Scholastic (New York, NY), 1997.
Jean Marzollo, *Christmas Cats,* Scholastic (New York, NY), 1997.
Steve Metzger, *Dinofours—It's Apple Picking Day!,* Scholastic (New York, NY), 1998.
Steve Metzger, *Dinofours—I'm the Boss!,* Scholastic (New York, NY), 1998.
Steve Metzger, *Dinofours—It's Beach Day!,* Scholastic (New York, NY), 1998.
Steve Metzger, *Dinofours—It's Snowing!,* Scholastic (New York, NY), 1999.
Steve Metzger, *Dinofours—It's Halloween!,* Scholastic (New York, NY), 1999.
Steve Metzger, *Dinofours—I'm the Winner!,* Scholastic (New York, NY), 1999.
Jean Marzollo, *Thanksgiving Cats,* Scholastic (New York, NY), 1999.
Steve Metzger, *Dinofours—My Seeds Won't Grow!,* Scholastic (New York, NY), 2000.

Steve Metzger, *Dinofours—Let Me Play!,* Scholastic (New York, NY), 2000.

Steve Metzger, *Dinofours—It's Fall!,* Scholastic (New York, NY), 2000.

Steve Metzger, *Dinofours—I'm so Grumpy!,* Scholastic (New York, NY), 2000.

Steve Metzger, *Dinofours—It's Valentine's Day!,* Scholastic (New York, NY), 2001.

Steve Metzger, *Dinofours—We Love Bugs!,* Scholastic (New York, NY), 2001.

Steve Metzger, *Dinofours—It's Pumpkin Day!,* Scholastic (New York, NY), 2001.

Steve Metzger, *Dinofours—It's Thanksgiving Day!,* Scholastic (New York, NY), 2001.

Steve Metzger, *Dinofours—Puppet Play!,* Scholastic (New York, NY), 2001.

Carol Pugliano-Martin, *The Lamb Who Loved to Laugh,* Scholastic (New York, NY), 2001.

Maria Fleming, *Copy Cats,* Scholastic (New York, NY), 2001.

Steve Metzger, *Dinofours—It's Rest Time!,* Scholastic (New York, NY), 2001.

Steve Metzger, *Dinofours—Cubby Buddies!,* Scholastic (New York, NY), 2001.

Steve Metzger, *Dinofours—Where Is Mrs. Dee?,* Scholastic (New York, NY), 2001.

Steve Metzger, *Dinofours—It's My Birthday!,* Scholastic (New York, NY), 2001.

Steve Metzger, *Dinofours—Let's Go Sledding!,* Scholastic (New York, NY), 2002.

Steve Metzger, *Dinofours—Rain, Rain, Go Away!,* Scholastic (New York, NY), 2002.

Steve Metzger, *Dinofours—It's Class Picture Day!,* Scholastic (New York, NY), 2002.

Steve Metzger, *Dinofours—The Holiday Show!,* Scholastic (New York, NY), 2002.

Steve Metzger, *Dinofours—I'm Sorry! I'm Sorry!,* Scholastic (New York, NY), 2002.

Steve Metzger, *Dinofours—We Love Mud!,* Scholastic (New York, NY), 2002.

Steve Metzger, *Dinofours—It's Gym Time!,* Scholastic (New York, NY), 2002.

Steve Metzger, *Dinofours—The Restaurant Game,* Scholastic (New York, NY), 2002.

Steve Metzger, *Dinofours—That's My Dino!,* Scholastic (New York, NY), 2002.

Steve Metzger, *Dinofours—Let's Pretend!,* Scholastic (New York, NY), 2002.

Steve Metzger, *Dinofours—The Class Next Door!,* Scholastic (New York, NY), 2002.

Wilhelm's books have been translated into Japanese, Spanish, Swedish, German, Norwegian, Turkish, Greek, Danish, Flemish, Korean, Dutch, Indonesian, Finnish, Chinese, French, and several other languages.

*OTHER*

*The Chinese Horoscope,* Avon (New York, NY), 1980.
*Fun Signs,* Simon & Schuster (New York, NY), 1981.

## Adaptations

*Tales from the Land under My Table* was adapted for a Braille book, Random House, 1983; *Bunny Trouble* was adapted for a read-along audiocassette, Scholastic, 1985; *Mother Goose on the Loose* was adapted for a television program, Cablevision, 1987; *The Trapp Family Book* was made into an animated television series, as have many of the "Waldo" stories and *The Three Robbers.*

## Sidelights

The author-illustrator of over one hundred and fifty picture books, Hans Wilhelm is best known for his shaggy dog, Waldo, and the myriad adventures the cuddly canine has experienced, both between the covers of books and on television shows adapted by Wilhelm. Illustrating for other writers, Wilhelm has also won kudos for his artwork for the many titles in Steve Metzger's "Dinofour" series. Praised for dealing with subjects such as death and loss, which most picture books shy away from, Wilhelm combines the light, whimsical touch of his realistic water colors with simple text full of plot surprises. The world of Wilhelm is populated by irascible pups, intelligent pigs, felicitous felines, peculiar bunnies, and the occasional human boy and girl. "In the making of books," Wilhelm told Elizabeth H. O'Neil in the *Westport News,* "the important issue is the authenticity and honesty of the artist. Children's books are a very revealing form of art. ... Giving and sharing hope, joy, and confidence with others are the main reasons I create books. I have no illusions that my books will change the world or greatly influence the minds of future generations. If I can only bring a little light into the darkness and fears in the lives of children and adults alike, I am a very happy person."

Wilhelm's own life has mostly been filled with such light. As he recalled in an essay for *Something about the Author Autobiography Series* (*SAAS*), he spent a fairly charmed childhood in a country house just outside of Bremen, Germany. Born in 1945, not long after the end of World War II, Wilhelm managed to avoid the privations of the post-war world suffered by most of his fellow Germans. His father returned from a prisoner-of-war camp and resumed his life as a prosperous banker, while his beloved grandmother "Oma" became one of two "fairy godmothers," as he described them in *SAAS.* The other was an aunt who owned a printing shop and provided Wilhelm with plentiful supplies of paper, an item otherwise difficult to come by at the time. She encouraged the artistic leanings of her young nephew. "I could draw to my heart's content," Wilhelm noted in *SAAS.* "This was one area in which I could experience total power and I had no restrictions. Here I could express my emotions, my dreams, my hopes, fears, and fantasies. Nobody could tell me how my pictures should look because nobody saw them as I did."

Another early influence on Wilhelm was the adventures of Mickey Mouse, a "literary" venue not much appreciated by his parents. "They thought that anything with speech-balloons could not have any redeeming value for their tender, highly impressionable child." Later, Wilhelm fell under the spell of the "Prince Valiant" comics, written and drawn by Harold R. Foster. "What stories, what pictures!," Wilhelm enthused in his *SAAS* essay. "Even today I still feel these adventures were some of the best written, paced, and illustrated stories of our time. Thank you, Harold R. Foster! Thank you, Walt Disney! I learned more about good storytelling from you than from any other source."

Wilhelm did well at school and "actually enjoyed [it]," as he confessed in *SAAS*. "In those days it was still okay to get good marks. You were not ridiculed as a nerd. On the contrary, you were actually liked, as long as you allowed others to copy from you." His artistic talent also came in handy: "Very often, when we were asked to write a report on our vacation or some similar boring subject, I simply drew it. By using very few words I substantially reduced the likelihood of spelling mistakes." Growing up on a large suburban estate with siblings far removed in age, Wilhelm had a lot of time to practice his art, even producing illustrated books as a teen and attempting to get them published. Form rejection letters, however, met such youthful attempts.

When it came time to determine his way in life, Wilhelm had a difficult choice to make. His father recommended he train for business; Wilhelm's heart, however, lay with art. But art is not an easy profession in which to make a living. Accustomed to the good life, Wilhelm "chickened out" as he noted in *SAAS*, and went for business. Attending business classes at the university, he prepared for a career in sales, but also took art classes at night. After a commercial apprenticeship in Bremen, he was ready to branch out, if not professionally, at least geographically. Attracted to the sun, he decided to move to South Africa, where he worked in sales for the next dozen years, while pursuing more artistic avenues in his free time. As part of a cabaret team he enjoyed a life in the theater, and as a help-line counselor he tried to reach out to others in crisis. However, his time in South Africa came to a close after the country's increasingly repressive government struck out at apartheid protestors.

By the time he left South Africa, Wilhelm realized that he had to try his hand at making a living from art. His employer, BASF, was willing to transfer him back to Germany, but as he noted in *SAAS*, "I could not imagine myself returning to a country of gray skies and short summers. What were my options?" Consulting an atlas, he found several beautiful alternative places where he could live. Finally he decided to take the plunge, sold his little farm and all the antiques he had collected over the years in South Africa, and left the country just as he had arrived, with one suitcase in hand, and bound for adventure. For the next several years he traveled around the world, from Australia to Indonesia, Singapore, Thailand, Malaysia, the Philippines, Papua New Guinea, Fiji, Tonga, Tahiti, the United States, Mexico, Spain, and finally England.

Wilhelm's book career began in England almost by chance. Increasingly involved in spiritual matters and in astrology, Wilhelm illustrated a birthday card for a friend with the Chinese symbol of the Year of the Horse. "I drew several whimsical cartoons that made fun of the various characteristics of anybody born" in that year, as he reported in *SAAS*, and the card was so well received at the friend's birthday party that Wilhelm was encouraged to create an entire book with similar cartoons for all the signs of the Chinese zodiac. Finishing the project, he queried a number of publishers and soon had a contract with Pan Books in London, where his first book was successfully published in 1980. Taking this book to New York, he soon won a contract from Avon Books for U.S. publication.

"Knowing today how extremely difficult it is to enter the publishing world, I am still amazed at my initial success," Wilhelm wrote in *SAAS*. "Partly it was a question of timing. . . . And it also helped me that I was very ignorant about the publishing field—otherwise I would probably not have been so gutsy and bold." This New York business trip soon turned into another move for the peripatetic Wilhelm, and he settled in Connecticut, first in Fairfield, then in Westport, and finally in Weston, where he still lives.

Another astrology book, *Fun Signs,* followed, and thereafter Wilhelm focused on children's books. His first picture book was *Tales from the Land under My Table,* which was selected as one of the best children's books of 1983 by *Time* magazine. With his career now off and running, the pragmatic Wilhelm set out to learn all he could about writing and illustrating for children. Contacting many of those whose work he prized, he became friends with many of the best contemporary writers and illustrators, including Maurice Sendak. In 1985 he published one of his best-loved titles, *I'll Always Love You,* a book inspired by the death of Wilhelm's beloved dog Elfie. After working and reworking the manuscript about loss with his editor Janet Schulman of Random House, Wilhelm finally had to take the book elsewhere because the publisher's sales department felt that a book about death would be counter to their image in the book market. In the event, Wilhelm's friend Sendak helped him place it at Crown where it was successfully published. "In the best tradition of books that help children deal with the death of a pet," wrote a contributor in *Language Arts,* "[*I'll Always Love You*] focuses on the good times, yet doesn't ignore the grief." "This book was my first real breakthrough in the children's book market—in America as well as abroad," Wilhelm noted in *SAAS*.

That same year Wilhelm introduced the dog character that has been definitive for his career. In *A New Home, a New Friend,* the author deals with what he sees as a chronic problem in his adopted country. Looking at the typical childhood in America, he discovered that half the children lose one of their parents—usually the father— through divorce. Additionally, he found out that the average length of home ownership is only seven years. "With little opportunity for young people to form lasting, trusting relationships, I don't think it is very surprising that psychiatry or drugs are so popular in this country," Wilhelm noted in his *SAAS* entry. To address this issue, he has the little boy Michael in *A New Home, a New Friend* discover a new friend who is part father, part grandfather, and part best friend. All these attributes are wrapped up in the lovable form of Waldo, a "shaggy and huggable dog," according to Wilhelm. "When Waldo came into my life I soon realized that he was a very unusual dog with great strength, humor, and charm," the author noted to O'Neil.

An instant success, the "Waldo" books soon began appearing around the world, appealing to those for whom some primary relationship was missing as well as anyone who enjoyed a good story and entertaining illustrations. From the initial title, the "Waldo" books have grown to include over fifty titles dealing with friendship, love, the age gap, religion, culture, and even death. "Waldo" calendars and television shows are part of this cottage industry revolving around Wilhelm's nurturing canine.

Other helpful mutts make appearances in many of Wilhelm's titles. In the "Schnitzel" books, a rambunctious puppy takes center stage. Reviewing *Schnitzel Is Lost!*, *Booklist* contributor Julie Corsaro paid special attention to the "autumn-hued wash-and-crayon paint-ings [that] portray the mayhem in the European town from the little lost dog's perspective." Corsaro also felt that this "[b]reezy and affectionate" tale "should appeal" to a wide readership. Another dog shows up in *Don't Cut My Hair!*, a "charming story," according to Suzanne Hawley in *School Library Journal*, about a little white dog called Noodles, who does not like the idea of getting shorn and is afraid that he will look silly once his hair is cut. After the cut, he hides from his friends at first, but then puts on sunglasses and a hat to look cool, winning the envy of other little pups. "Few words and expressive watercolors will assure the popularity of this amusing early reader," concluded Hawley. Noodles saves the baby of the family in *It's Too Windy!*, by wrapping its leash around a lamppost and halting a runaway stroller. Reviewing this title, *Booklist* reviewer Carolyn Phelan praised Wilhelm's "cartoon-like ink drawings, brightened with watercolor washes [which] tell the tale with great verve and humor."

Wilhelm turns to the world of dinosaurs not only in the Metzger series, but also in his own books about the self-willed Tyrannosaurus Rex, Tyrone. The miserable Tyrone, a rather naughty dinosaur whom kids "love to hate," according to a reviewer for *Publishers Weekly*, makes his debut in *Tyrone the Horrible*. In *Tyrone, the*

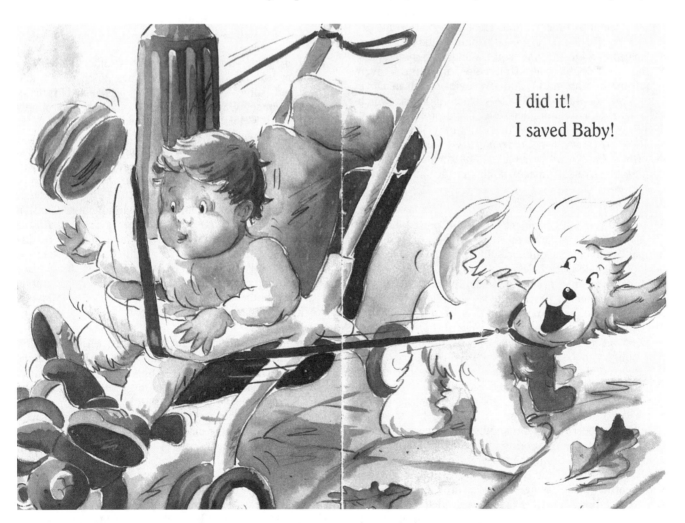

I did it!

I saved Baby!

*A faithful dog stops Baby's stroller from rolling away in Wilhelm's self-illustrated* **It's Too Windy!**

*Double Dirty Rotten Cheater,* big, bad Tyrone the dinosaur wins all the games at Swamp Island. The only problem is that he has won by cheating. The mild-mannered Boland and his other dinosaur pals become increasingly disgusted with tag-along Tyrone. Finally, however, Tyrone cheats himself in his attempts to win the treasure hunt. "As usual," wrote a contributor to *Publishers Weekly,* "Wilhelm knows what will tickle the funny bones of young readers; they will snicker at Tyrone's dreadful behavior, shifty eyes and caustic tongue." Nancy A. Gifford, writing in *School Library Journal,* praised *Tyrone, the Double Dirty Rotten Cheater* for its "Large, colorful illustrations of dinosaurs" that she maintained "are sure to attract young readers, even though the creatures are given all-too-human personalities."

From dinosaurs, Wilhelm takes to the air with *The Royal Raven,* the story of Crawford the Raven who does not like his ordinary appearance. Crawford feels special inside, but just cannot understand why he looks so boring on the outside. Consulting a woman known for her special powers, he has her give him some special flash in the form of glorious and colorful feathers. However his new exotic look soon lands him in a cage, a pet to the royal family. Crawford must lose his glorious new plumage to regain his freedom and determines that being special is not such a great thing after all. A contributor for *Publishers Weekly* praised the artwork as a "sparkling, kid-thrilling sight," and also noted that Wilhelm's "double-page watercolor art glitters even where there is no gold." *Booklist* reviewer Susan Dove Lempke also praised Wilhelm's watercolor art, which she deemed "as winning and ever," and prophesied that *The Royal Raven* is a book "that will rarely be left on the shelf." A reviewer for *Children's Book Review Service* described *The Royal Raven* as an "outstanding book for gaining positive self-image—a classic for the home and classroom."

More positive self-image messages are presented in *A Cool Kid like Me,* one of the few Wilhelm titles with a human protagonist. Cool and with-it on the outside, the hero of this tale nonetheless feels all the usual fears and frustrations of any kid on the inside. Finally an obliging grandmother and a peaceful teddy bear teach the boy that he does not have to be tough to be cool. Clare Kelly, reviewing the picture book in *School Librarian,* remarked that it would "connect with many children who feel obliged to be 'tough' despite their tender years." Another youthful human protagonist is served up in Wilhelm's three-chapter ghost story, *The Boy Who Wasn't There.* A mysterious, ghostly boy meets lonely Sarah on a New England beach and tells her she will soon meet a best friend. On another occasion, this same boy tells Sarah she must bring all her favorite toys to the house of Angela. Going there, Sarah sees the picture of the boy-messenger: it is Angela's brother lost at sea two years earlier while trying to save a drowning child. A contributor for *Publishers Weekly* called Wilhelm's ghost story "quietly dramatic" and a "beguiling choice for beginning readers." Susan Hepler of *School Library*

*Wilhelm illustrated this tale about the perfect sledding day for a group of dinosaur friends.*

*Journal* praised Wilhelm's "dramatic watercolor landscapes and bold use of color."

Illustrating the work for numerous other authors in addition to his own, Wilhelm has also retold and reworked some classic children's stories. Originally from Bremen, Germany, Wilhelm has created a new edition of the classic story *The Bremen Town Musicians,* which deals with four animals no longer wanted by their masters. They set out to become musicians in the town of Bremen, but en route they are set upon by a den of thieves. "An insouciant text and vibrant full-color illustrations make this retelling of the Grimm Brothers' classic a rollicking performance," commented Carolyn Noah in a *School Library Journal* review. A *Kirkus Reviews* contributor felt that Wilhelm's retelling of this tale "has unusual panache," while a reviewer for *Publishers Weekly* noted that Wilhelm's "trademark lighthearted, somewhat cartoony watercolors ... imbue ... this blithe retelling with a timeless, fairy-tale setting."

Wilhelm is a tireless worker at his craft, each new book going through several re-workings and revisions before he is satisfied with it. The time from conception to publication can last up to two to three years, so he works on several projects at the same time, creating a steady stream of both books and television adaptations. "I take great care with all the characters I draw," Wilhelm noted in *SAAS.* "They must 'speak' to me. Every movement, the turn of the head, the expression of eyes, etc., are all carefully planned." A morning person, he gets most of his work down before noon, but is also adept—because of his business background—with the corporate end of the work, as well. In addition to his writing and illustrating, Wilhelm also maintains a busy lecture series, touring schools not only in the United States, but also in Europe, Asia, and Africa.

Wilhelm rejects the notion that he writes only for children. "I make books for everyone who likes to hear or read a good story," he concluded in *SAAS*. "We all carry in us that 'inner child' who wants to believe in truth, honesty, values, and a good ending. This inner child is still living, even in those who try to act cool and avoid showing any emotions. Deep down this inner child craves nourishment, warmth, and a sense of security. And through all ages and cultures no tool has satisfied these needs more than the telling of a story. I regard all the ancient fairy tales—and lots of new ones—as food for our souls."

## Biographical and Critical Sources

*BOOKS*

Wilhelm, Hans, essay in *Something about the Author Autobiography Series,* Volume 21, Gale (Detroit, MI), 1997.

*PERIODICALS*

*Booklist,* November 1, 1991, Julie Corsaro, review of *Schnitzel Is Lost!,* p. 534; April 15, 1992, pp. 1533-1534; April 1, 1994, p. 1457; March 15, 1996, Susan Dove Lempke, review of *The Royal Raven,* p. 1269; July, 2000, Carolyn Phelan, review of *It's Too Windy!,* p. 2046.
*Books for Keeps,* May, 1991, p. 29; November, 1991, p. 8; July, 1992, p. 9; September, 1992, p. 24.
*Children's Book Review Service,* March, 1996, review of *The Royal Raven,* p. 90.
*Horn Book,* September-October, 1988, pp. 658-659.
*Kirkus Reviews,* April 1, 1992, review of *The Bremen Town Musicians,* p. 474; December 1, 1993, p. 1532.
*Language Arts,* January, 1986, review of *I'll Always Love You.*
*Los Angeles Times Book Review,* July 27, 1980; December 15, 1985.
*New York Times Book Review,* December 11, 1983.
*Publishers Weekly,* May 13, 1988, p. 273; August 26, 1988, p. 88; December 9, 1988; June 8, 1990, p. 52; January 4, 1991, review of *Tyrone, the Double Dirty Rotten Cheater,* p. 71; October 25, 1991, p. 70; February 3, 1992, review of *The Bremen Town Musicians,* p. 80; November 8, 1993, review of *The Boy Who Wasn't There,* p. 76; January 24, 1994, p. 54; March 7, 1994, pp. 71-72; August 8, 1994, p. 426; March 25, 1996, review of *The Royal Raven,* pp. 82-83; September 27, 1999, p. 50.
*Resource Links,* April, 2001, p. 46.
*School Librarian,* November, 1991, Clare Kelly, review of *A Cool Kid like Me,* p. 143.
*School Library Journal,* July, 1991, Nancy A. Gifford, review of *Tyrone, the Double Dirty Rotten Cheater,* p. 65; October, 1991, p. 106; April, 1992, Carolyn Noah, review of *The Bremen Town Musicians,* pp. 105-106; March, 1994, Susan Hepler, review of *The Boy Who Wasn't There,* p. 212; May, 1994, p. 109; January, 1995, p. 89; July, 1996, p. 75;

August, 1998, Suzanne Hawley, review of *Don't Cut My Hair!,* p. 147; September, 1999, p. 209.
*Time,* December 19, 1983.
*Westport News,* August 5, 1987, Elizabeth O'Neil, "Snoopy, Move Over. Waldo Is Here."

*OTHER*

*Hans Wilhelm, Author/Illustrator,* http://www.hanswilhelm. com (December 7, 2001).

—*Sketch by J. Sydney Jones*

\*        \*        \*

# WILLIAMS, Sophy 1965-

## Personal

Born October 23, 1965, in Surrey, England; married Mark Robertson (an illustrator), June, 1990; children: Oscar, Leo. *Education:* Foundation in Arts Central School of Art (London, England), B.A. (with honors; graphic design); attended Kingston Polytechnic.

## Addresses

*Home*—24 Frome Road, Bradford-on-Avon, Wiltshire, England BA15 2EA.

## Career

Freelance illustrator and author.

## Awards, Honors

Young Illustrators Award, *Readers Digest,* 1988; Mother Goose Award, 1990, for *When Grandma Came.*

## Writings

(And illustrator) *Nana's Garden,* Hutchinson (London, England), 1993, Viking (New York, NY), 1994.

*ILLUSTRATOR*

Jill Paton Walsh, *When Grandma Came,* Viking (New York, NY), 1992.
Michael Rosen, *Moving,* Viking (New York, NY), 1993.
Robert Westall, *The Witness,* Dutton (New York, NY), 1994.
Peter Elbling, *Aria,* Viking (New York, NY), 1994.
Belinda Hollyer, *Stories from the Classical Ballet,* Viking (New York, NY), 1995.
Richard Edwards, *You're Safe Now, Waterdog,* Viking (New York, NY), 1996.
Paul and Emma Rogers, *Cat's Kittens,* Viking (New York, NY), 1996.
Aneve Turnball, *The Sleeping Beauty,* MacDonald (London, England), 1997.
Robert Nye, *Lord Fox and Other Spine Chilling Tales,* Orion (London, England), 1997.
Geraldine McCaughrean, *The Orchard Book of Starry Tales,* Orchard (London, England), 1998, published as

*Starry Tales,* Margaret K. McElderry Books (New York, NY), 2001.

Adrian Mitchell, *My Cat Mrs. Christmas,* Orion (London, England), 1998.

Fiona Waters, *Cat in the Dark, and Other Cat Poems,* Francis Lincoln (London, England), 1999.

Martin Waddell, *The Orchard Book of Ghostly Stories,* Orchard (London, England), 2000.

Toby Forward, *Once upon an Everyday,* Transworld, 2000.

Wendy McCormick, *The Night You Were Born,* Peachtree (Atlanta, GA), 2000.

## Work in Progress

Illustrating *The Oxford Treasury of Fairy Tales,* by Geraldine McCaughrean.

## Sidelights

Sophy Williams is an author and illustrator whose work has enhanced the stories of several other authors of children's picture books, among them Robert Westall, Jill Paton Walsh, and Robert Nye. Praised for her softly colored, gentle renderings, Williams has also created her own picture book, complete with text. Called a "quiet, understated story, beautifully told" by a *Junior Bookshelf* reviewer, *Nana's Garden* benefitted from its author's sure touch with pastels. Published in England in 1993, *Nana's Garden* quickly made its way across the Atlantic, much to the excitement of picture-book aficionados in the United States.

*Nana's Garden* is the story of a young boy named Thomas who is left alone in a deserted garden, saddened that his "Nana" is too elderly to play with him. A newfound, if somewhat mysterious, friend named Rose, the discovery of a toy bunny, and the exploration of many out-of-the-way places keep Thomas amused within his grandmother's fragrant, much-loved garden. Praising the work for its depiction of a child engaging in imaginative play outside the home, Mary Harris Veeder added in *Booklist* that the story of *Nana's Garden* is "nicely evoked in the pictures."

Born in Surrey, England, in 1965, Williams recalled her childhood as a happy one, most of it spent in Berkshire, England, but, as she told *SATA,* "with periods living in Singapore, the United Arab Emirates, where we had no television, and Hong Kong. I was always reading stories (Joan Aiken being one of my favorite children's authors), and drawing or painting, and when I wasn't training for gymnastic competitions, I used to make scrapbooks and illustrate the (awful) poems that I had written. My bedroom carpet was ruined by glue and paint."

Williams met her husband, fellow children's book author and illustrator Mark Robertson, in 1986, while both were attending Kingston Polytechnic. "He and I both work in separate studios in our house.... We both find it useful having someone around to offer advice although I'm not always very good at following it." Her first illustration project was for Jill Paton Walsh's *When*

*Jamie's aunt tells him about the night he entered the world while they await the birth of his sister. (From* The Night You Were Born, *written by Wendy McCormick and illustrated by Sophy Williams.)*

*Grandma Came,* published in 1992. Praising Williams' artistic contribution as "the book's greatest strength," *School Library Journal* contributor Jody McCoy added that Walsh's story of a young girl and her granddaughter are successfully "captured in rich, warm colors."

Other works illustrated by Williams include Michael Rosen's *Moving,* wherein "Williams's soft, striking pastel drawings capture the mysterious quality ... of Rosen's evocative poem," according to *Booklist* contributor Julie Corsaro. Her "softly colored" renderings for Richard Edwards's *You're Safe Now, Waterdog* "complement the story perfectly," in the opinion of *Booklist* reviewer Shelley Tonwsend-Hudson, who went on to note the illustrations' "rich texture" and "tactile quality." In her pastel illustrations for Wendy McCormick's *The Night You Were Born,* Williams' ability to create artwork "glow[ing] with soothing tones" enhances McCormick's sensitive portrayal of a boy awaiting the arrival of a new member of the family, according to a *Publishers Weekly* critic. And, in the words of *School Library Journal* contributor Shirley Wilton, the artwork she contributed to Peter Elbling's 1994 picture book titled *Aria* is "worth a leisurely inspection and lingering appreciation."

Williams explained to *SATA* that her illustrations are "are all done in chalk pastel and pastel pencil. I love layering colours (a trick I borrowed from Degas) and inventing colour combinations—soft subtle ones and vibrant bright ones. I'm happiest drawing animals, especially groups of animals. I'm sure that spending some of my childhood in Asia has influenced the sort of landscapes that appeal to me—empty deserts for example—but the frosty breath and hazy horizons of the English countryside have provided lots of inspiration."

Williams and her husband live in Wiltshire, England, with sons Oscar and Leo, "who of course love books," their mother is quick to note, adding: "We also have two black cats!"

## Biographical and Critical Sources

*PERIODICALS*

*Booklist,* November 1, 1992, Stephanie Zvirin, review of *When Grandma Came,* p. 523; December 15, 1993, Julie Corsaro, review of *Moving,* p. 766; June 1, 1994, Mary Harris Veeder, review of *Nana's Garden,* p. 1846; November 15, 1994, Hazel Rochman, review of *Aria,* p. 611; February 15, 1997, Shelley Townsend-Hudson, review of *Cat's Kittens,* p. 1029; July, 1997, Shelley Townsend-Hudson, review of *You're Safe Now, Waterdog,* p. 1821.

*Horn Book,* November-December, 1994, Ann A. Flowers, review of *The Witness,* p. 715; March-April, 1996, Mary M. Burns, review of *Stories from the Classical Ballet,* p. 225.

*Junior Bookshelf,* April, 1994, review of *Nana's Garden,* pp. 51-52.

*Publishers Weekly,* September 19, 1994, review of *The Witness,* p. 27; September 26, 1994, review of *Aria,* p. 69; October 9, 2000, review of *The Night You Were Born,* p. 86.

*School Library Journal,* March, 1993, Jody McCoy, review of *When Grandma Came,* p. 187; March, 1994, Carolyn Noah, review of *Moving,* p. 208; October, 1994, Jane Marino, review of *The Witness,* p. 45; January, 1995, Shirley Wilton, review of *Aria,* pp. 84-85; July, 1997, Susan M. Moore, review of *You're Safe Now, Waterdog,* p. 67; December, 2000, Martha Topol, review of *The Night You Were Born,* p. 114.\*

\*      \*      \*

# WINCHESTER, Stanley
## See YOUD, (Christopher) Sam(uel)

# Y

## YOUD, (Christopher) Sam(uel) 1922- (John Christopher, Hilary Ford, William Godfrey, Peter Graaf, Peter Nichols, Anthony Rye, Stanley Winchester)

### Personal

Born April 16, 1922, in Knowsley, Lancashire, England; married Joyce Fairbairn, October 23, 1946 (marriage ended); married Jessica Valerie Ball, December 24, 1980 (died, 2001); children: (first marriage) Nicholas, Rose, Elizabeth, Sheila, Margret. *Education:* Attended Peter Symonds School, Winchester, England. *Politics:* Tory Radical.

### Addresses

*Home*—One Whitefriars, Rye, East Sussex TN31 7LE, England; and c/o Society of Authors, 84 Drayton Gardens, London SW10 9SB, England.

### Career

Freelance writer, 1946-48; worked in and eventually headed the Industrial Diamond Information Bureau of the Diamond Corporation, 1949-58; full-time writer, 1958—. *Military service:* British Army, Royal Signals, 1941-46.

### Awards, Honors

Rockefeller Foundation grant, 1946-48; International Fantasy Award runner-up, 1957, for *The Death of Grass;* American Library Association Notable Book award, c. 1967, for *The White Mountains; Guardian* Award runner-up, 1969, and George G. Stone Center for Children's Books Recognition of Merit Award, 1977, both for *The Tripods Trilogy;* Christopher Award, 1970, and *Guardian* Award for children's fiction, 1971, both for *The Guardians;* German Children's Book Prize, 1976, for *Die Wächter* (German translation of *The*

*Sam Youd*

*Guardians*); Parents' Choice Award from Parents' Choice Foundation, 1983, for *New Found Land.*

### Writings

*UNDER PSEUDONYM JOHN CHRISTOPHER; FOR CHILDREN*

*The Tripods Trilogy,* Macmillan (New York, NY), Book 1: *The White Mountains,* illustrated by John Raynes, 1967, Book 2: *The City of Gold and Lead,* 1967, Book 3: *The Pool of Fire,* 1968, all published in 2nd edition, Collier (New York, NY), 1988.
*The Lotus Caves,* Macmillan (New York, NY), 1969.

*The Guardians,* Macmillan (New York, NY), 1970, reprinted, Collier Books (New York, NY), 1992.

*The Sword Trilogy,* Macmillan (New York, NY), Book 1: *The Prince in Waiting,* 1970, Book 2: *Beyond the Burning Lands,* 1971, Book 3: *The Sword of the Spirits,* 1972, all published in 2nd edition, Collier (New York, NY), 1989.

*In the Beginning* (structural readers edition; also see below), illustrated by Clyde Pearson, Longmans, Green (London, England), 1972.

*Dom and Va* (expanded from *In the Beginning*), Macmillan (New York, NY), 1973.

*Wild Jack,* Macmillan (New York, NY), 1974.

*Empty World,* Hamish Hamilton (London, England), 1977, Dutton (New York, NY), 1978.

*The Fireball Trilogy,* Dutton (New York, NY), Book 1: *Fireball,* 1981, Book 2: *New Found Land,* 1983, Book 3: *Dragon Dance,* 1986.

*When the Tripods Came,* Viking (London, England), 1988, Dutton (New York, NY), 1988.

*A Dusk of Demons,* Hamish Hamilton (London, England), 1993, Macmillan (New York, NY), 1994.

*UNDER PSEUDONYM JOHN CHRISTOPHER; FOR ADULTS*

*The Twenty-second Century* (short stories), Grayson, 1954, Lancer, 1962.

*The Year of the Comet,* M. Joseph, 1955, published as *Planet in Peril,* Avon (New York, NY), 1959.

*No Blade of Grass,* Simon & Schuster (New York, NY), 1956, published as *The Death of Grass,* M. Joseph (London, England), 1956.

*The Caves of Night,* Eyre & Spottiswoode, 1958, Simon & Schuster (New York, NY), 1959.

*A Scent of White Poppies,* Eyre & Spottiswoode, 1959, Simon & Schuster (New York, NY), 1959.

*Daughter Fair,* M. Joseph, 1959.

*The Sapphire Conference,* M. Joseph, 1959.

*The White Voyage,* Simon & Schuster (New York, NY), 1960, published as *The Long Voyage,* Eyre & Spottiswoode (London, England), 1960.

*The Long Winter,* Simon & Schuster (New York, NY), 1962, published as *The World in Winter,* Eyre & Spottiswoode (London, England), 1962.

*Sweeney's Island,* Simon & Schuster (New York, NY), 1964, published as *Cloud on Silver,* Hodder & Stoughton (London, England), 1964.

*The Possessors,* 1965, Simon & Schuster (New York, NY), 1965.

*A Wrinkle in the Skin,* Hodder & Stoughton (London, England), 1965, published as *The Ragged Edge,* Simon & Schuster (New York, NY), 1966.

*The Little People,* Simon & Schuster (New York, NY), 1967.

*Patchwork of Death,* Robert Hale, 1967.

*Pendulum,* Simon & Schuster (New York, NY), 1968.

*Bad Dream,* Spectrum, 2001.

*UNDER PSEUDONYM HILARY FORD*

*Felix Walking* (novel), Simon & Schuster (New York, NY), 1958.

*Felix Running* (novel), Eyre & Spottiswoode (London, England), 1959.

*Having escaped the City of Gold and Lead, Will sets off to stop the Masters from destroying Earth in the chilling third book of the "Tripods" trilogy.*

*Bella on the Roof* (novel), Longmans, Green (London, England), 1965.

*A Figure in Grey* (juvenile), World's Work, 1973.

*Sarnia* (novel), Doubleday (New York, NY), 1974.

*Castle Malindine* (novel), Hamish Hamilton (London, England), 1975, Harper (New York, NY), 1976.

*A Bride for Bedivere* (novel), Hamish Hamilton (London, England), 1976, Harper (New York, NY), 1977.

*UNDER PSEUDONYM PETER GRAAF*

*Give the Devil His Due,* Mill, 1957, published in England as *Dust and the Curious Boy,* M. Joseph, 1957.

*Daughter Fair,* Ives Washburn, 1958.

*The Sapphire Conference,* Ives Washburn, 1959.

*The Gull's Kiss,* P. Davies, 1962.

*UNDER PSEUDONYM STANLEY WINCHESTER*

*The Practice,* Putnam, 1967, W. H. Allen, 1967.

*Men With Knives,* Putnam, 1968, published as *A Man with a Knife,* W. H. Allen, 1968.

*The Helpers,* Putnam, 1970, W. H. Allen, 1970.
*Ten Per Cent of Your Life,* W. H. Allen, 1973.

ADULT NOVELS

*The Winter Swan,* Dobson, 1949.
*Babel Itself,* Cassell (London, England), 1951.
*Brave Conquerors,* Cassell (London, England), 1952.
*Crown and Anchor,* Cassell (London, England), 1953.
*A Palace of Strangers,* Cassell (London, England), 1954.
*The Opportunist,* Harper (New York, NY), 1955, published
    as *Holly Ash,* Cassell (London, England), 1955.
*The Choice,* Simon & Schuster (New York, NY), 1961,
    published as *The Burning Bird,* Longmans, Green
    (London, England), 1964.
*Messages of Love,* Simon & Schuster (New York, NY),
    1961.
*The Summers at Accorn,* Longmans, Green (London,
    England), 1963.

OTHER

(Under pseudonym William Godfrey) *Malleson at Mel-
    bourne,* Museum Press, 1956.
(Under pseudonym William Godfrey) *The Friendly Game,*
    M. Joseph, 1957.

*Ben and his stepsister search for their families after
Demons set fire to their home. (Cover illustration by
Rebecca Guay.)*

(Under pseudonym Anthony Rye) *Giant's Arrow* (novel),
    Gollancz, 1956, published under name Samuel Youd,
    Simon & Schuster (New York, NY), 1960.
(Under pseudonym Peter Nichols) *Patchwork of Death*
    (novel), Holt (New York, NY), 1965.

Contributor to various anthologies and of articles and
short stories to periodicals, including *Astounding Stories, Esquire, Cricket, Playboy, Ellery Queen, New
Worlds, Fantasy and Science Fiction, Galaxy,* and
*Encounter.*

## Adaptations

*No Blade of Grass* was made into a film produced and
directed by Cornell Wilde, c. 1970; *The Tripods Trilogy*
was made into two television series produced by Richard
Bates and broadcast by the British Broadcasting Corp.
and the Public Broadcasting Service, and was also
puchased for film by Disney in 2001; *The Caves of
Night* has been made into a film by Wilde; *The
Guardians* (a six-part serial) and *Empty World* (a ninety
minute teleplay) have been adapted for German television. Many of Youd's books have been published in
Braille and as talking books.

## Sidelights

An author of novels for both children and adults under
several pseudonyms, Sam Youd has been most highly
acclaimed for the science fiction novels he has written
under the pseudonym John Christopher. Among these
are three trilogies for children, the "Tripods Trilogy,"
the "Sword Trilogy," and the "Fireball Trilogy," the
award-winning *The Guardians,* and a book for adults,
*No Blade of Grass,* which was runner-up for the
International Fantasy Award behind J. R. R. Tolkien's
*The Lord of the Rings.* Although many of his books are
set in the future, Youd told *Children's Literature in
Education* interviewer John Gough, "I don't now like
being classified as a science fiction writer because I
regard science fiction as having strayed from extrapola-
tion into error: there seems to me no credible means of
exploring beyond the solar system; and the solar system,
of course, we now know to be barren and uninteresting."
The author's books instead reveal an interest in the past,
the future societies he portrays often resembling those of
medieval times; he is also more concerned with characterization than with speculations about the future.

"I have been involved with writing since my early teens,
in the thirties," Youd wrote in his *Something about the
Author Autobiography* (SAAS) entry. "Prior to [World
War II], I published an amateur magazine (*The Fantast*)
and wrote pieces—verse, articles, fiction—for it and
similar magazines. In the first winter of the war I had my
first short story published professionally, in *Lilliput,* and
wrote part of a novel, fairly heavily derived from the
fiction of Aldous Huxley which I then intensely admired." He later submitted his unfinished novel for
consideration for the Atlantic Awards in Literature,
funded by the Rockefeller Foundation, hoping to win a
grant worth 250 pounds. But the award committee asked

Youd if he could submit something that he had written more recently; so the author sent them the first chapters of what would later become *The Winter Swan* and won the grant.

From that point on, Youd considered himself a professional writer. Finding a steady job to support himself, he began writing short stories for science fiction magazines like *Galaxy* and *Astounding*. He wrote his science fiction stories under a pseudonym so that he could associate his real name with his other novels. With the 1950s came the "Golden Age of Science Fiction," an opportune time for Youd to come out with his story collection, *The Twenty-second Century*. This book later led to the novel *The Year of the Comet,* which was based on some of the ideas in his short stories.

By this time Youd had become a father. His growing family, he realized, could not be adequately supported by a job that he said in *SAAS* was "poorly paid and had no prospects." So the author "began to write with increasing urgency, working in the evenings and through weekends." He wrote everything from science fiction to comedies to thrillers to mainstream novels, "using a different pen name for each genre, regarding it as only fair that a reader should know what he might reasonably expect under a particular label." His first great success came with the publication of *No Blade of Grass,* which was later bought for movie production by Metro-Goldwyn-Mayer. From then until the late 1960s, Youd wrote science fiction and mainstream novels. "This was the point at which another publisher suggested I try my hand at writing for children. What he wanted was science fiction, on which the small reputation I possessed was founded. But during the preceding years I had tired of this ... : the past interested me more. I wondered if it might be possible to blend his requirement with my inclination."

Youd came up with the idea of writing about a future world in which society had become as primitive as that of the Middle Ages after some great calamity. The calamity he chose for the "Tripods Trilogy," which includes *The White Mountains, The City of Gold and Lead, The Pool of Fire,* and a more recent prequel, *When the Tripods Came,* was the staple science fiction idea of an alien invasion in which the aliens take control of the human race by controlling people's minds. To keep humans even more firmly under their control, the aliens impose on their subjects a feudal system modelled after medieval Europe. In Youd's other trilogies—the "Sword Trilogy," which includes *The Prince in Waiting, Beyond the Burning Lands,* and *The Sword of the Spirits,* and the "Fireball Trilogy," which includes *Fireball, New Found Land,* and *Dragon Dance*—the author uses similar settings that resemble the past. Natural disasters cause society to regress into the Dark Ages in the "Sword Trilogy," while in the "Fireball Trilogy" Youd uses the device of a parallel reality to take his characters to a world where the Roman Empire rules Europe, Aztecs have extended their rule into North America, and China is ruled by warlords and a form of magic.

A recurring theme in several of Youd's novels is, as John Rowe Townsend put it in his *A Sense of Story: Essays on Contemporary Writers for Children,* "the question of freedom and authority: painful freedom and comfortable submission to authority." In the "Tripods Trilogy," for example, while people are made servants of the aliens, "it is a happy servitude," according to Hugh Crago and Maureen Crago in *Children's Book Review.* "The struggle for freedom succeeds, but the new world government breaks down in its own inner conflicts." Similarly, the alien plant that takes control of a moon colony in *The Lotus Caves* and the aliens in *The Guardians*—who take over the Earth with a form of surgical mind control similar to that in the "Tripods Trilogy"—also offer an easy, subservient way of life. Yet Youd's characters struggle to win their freedom even if it means loss of security. About this theme Youd told Gough that "freedom of thought is perhaps the greatest good, and needs to be fought for and sacrificed for. I suppose it's something of a reverse of the conventional Eden story: the apple which tempts my characters is one that will remove the knowledge of good and evil. As to free will versus determinism, ... I have an instinctive belief in free will probably because I feel that a life excluding that belief would not be worth living."

Some critics of Youd's writing have become frustrated with his science fiction stories because they do not emphasize science and technology very much. The author recalled in his *SAAS* essay how the television adaptation of his "Tripods Trilogy" was criticized by respected science fiction writer Brian Aldiss: "He was scathing of what he termed 'backwards looking science fiction,' and especially scathing about the Tripods themselves. 'They don't even,' he observed with crushing contempt, 'have infra-red....' (This, incidentally, is an interesting example of the way in which science fiction's preoccupation with technology builds in obsolescence: infra-red vision is an accepted part of the scene today, but was not when I wrote the books in the sixties.)" Youd agrees that speculating about advanced technology is not one of his main considerations. "I am more concerned with what happens inside the individual than what happens to society as a whole," he states.

In 1994 the young adult novel *A Dusk of Demons* was published. It revisits the post-catastrophe setting, with an Earth population reduced to mere millions by an epidemic of drug overdoses, causing a collapse of the infrastructure that feeds people and death of billions by famine. The hero Ben lives in a world where the surviving cultures oppose one another. The first is anti-machine; the second secretly preserves technology to make a better world. Ben plays a key role in the machine culture's conflict over whether to leave the anti-machinists in a "demon"-ruled state of only locally vicious superstition, or to jump-start an advanced civilization by freeing the people of the "Demons" (which are holographic projections) and letting the whole of the population have the benefits and the dangers of technology again. Ben's machine-technology confederates are in the ascendancy as the story ends, and he, with girlfriend Paddy, has a big job to do.

The few additional pieces published by Christopher in the 1980s and 1990s are exclusively for young adults. The course seems a happy one. In terms of narrative art, Christopher's stories for young readers are, he believes, equal to his finest achievement.

Over the years, Youd has published more than fifty adult and children's books. The popular writer was once paid tribute on the 1960s television *Star Trek* first season episode "Tomorrow Is Yesterday" by naming the Air Force pilot that is beamed up to the *Enterprise* John Christopher. (Naming characters after famous SF writers was an early tradition of the series.) Of his stories for the young, Youd said in Townsend's book: "What I have learned is that writing for children is at least as exacting and concentration-demanding as writing for adults. But one can add another word: stimulating. It is the form of writing which I can now least imagine giving up."

# Biographical and Critical Sources

*BOOKS*

Amis, Kingsley, *New Maps of Hell: A Survey of Science Fiction,* Harcourt, 1960.

Arbuthnot, May Hill, and Zena Sutherland, *Children and Books,* 4th edition, Scott, Foresman, 1972, p. 260.

*Children's Literature Review,* Volume 2, Gale (Detroit, MI), 1976.

Crouch, Marcus, *The Nesbit Tradition: The Children's Novel in England, 1945-1970,* Benn, 1972, pp. 51-52.

*Dictionary of Literary Biography,* Volume 255: *British Fantasy and Science Fiction Writers, 1918-1960,* Gale (Detroit, MI), 2002.

Fisher, Margery, *Who's Who in Children's Books: A Treasury of the Familiar Characters of Childhood,* Holt, 1975, pp. 306, 309.

Moskowitz, Samuel, *Seekers of Tomorrow: Masters of Modern Science Fiction,* World Publishing, 1966.

*Something about the Author Autobiography Series,* Volume 6, Gale (Detroit, MI), 1988, pp. 297-312.

*St. James Guide to Science Fiction Writers,* 4th edition, St. James Press (Detroit, MI), 1996.

*St. James Guide to Young Adult Writers,* 2nd edition, St. James Press (Detroit, MI), 1999.

Townsend, John Rowe, *A Sense of Story: Essays on Contemporary Writers for Children,* Lippincott, 1971, pp. 48-55.

Townsend, John Rowe, *Written for Children: An Outline of English-Language Children's Literature,* Lippincott, 1974, pp. 215-216.

*PERIODICALS*

*Books and Bookmen,* February, 1965.

*Books for Keeps,* July, 1981, pp. 14-15.

*Bulletin of the Center for Children's Books,* December, 1967, p. 57; February, 1972, p. 88; July-August, 1973, p. 168; May, 1986.

*Chicago Tribune,* July 1, 1962.

*Children's Book Review,* February, 1971, pp. 18-19; June, 1971, Hugh Crago and Maureen Crago, "John Christopher: An Assessment with Reservations," pp. 77-79; September, 1971, pp. 122-123; September, 1972, p. 113; December, 1973, pp. 176-177, winter, 1974-75, p. 150.

*Children's Literature in Education,* summer, 1984, John Gough (interview with John Christopher, pseudonym for Samuel Youd), pp. 93-102.

*Christian Science Monitor,* November 7, 1968.

*Fantastic Universe,* June, 1958.

*Horn Book,* December, 1969, pp. 673, 675; December, 1971, p. 619; August, 1974, p. 375.

*Interzone,* March, 2001, Paul Brazier, "A Celebration of John Christopher."

*Junior Bookshelf,* February, 1968, p. 59; February, 1971, pp. 51-52; December, 1973, p. 402; February, 1975, p. 58.

*Kirkus Reviews,* March 15, 1973, p. 324; August 1, 1974, pp. 803-804.

*Publishers Weekly,* October 24, 1994, Paul Nathan, "Keeping an Author Happy," p. 18.

*Saturday Evening Post,* April 27, 1957.

*School Librarian,* June, 1971, p. 155.

*School Library Journal,* September, 1968, p. 131.

*Signal,* January, 1971, pp. 18-23.

*Space Voyager,* June-July, 1984, pp. 52-54.

*Times* (London), May 25, 1967.

*Times Literary Supplement,* April 16, 1970, p. 417; December 11, 1970, p. 1460; July 2, 1971, p. 767.

*Writer,* June, 1966; November, 1968.

# Cumulative Indexes

# Illustrations Index

(In the following index, the number of the *volume* in which an illustrator's work appears is given *before* the colon, and the *page number* on which it appears is given *after* the colon. For example, a drawing by Adams, Adrienne appears in Volume 2 on page 6, another drawing by her appears in Volume 3 on page 80, another drawing in Volume 8 on page 1, and so on and so on....)

## YABC

Index references to *YABC* refer to listings appearing in the two-volume *Yesterday's Authors of Books for Children,* also published by The Gale Group. *YABC* covers prominent authors and illustrators who died prior to 1960.

## A

Aas, Ulf *5:* 174
Abbé, S. van *See* van Abbé, S.
Abel, Raymond *6:* 122; *7:* 195; *12:* 3; *21:* 86; *25:* 119
Abelliera, Aldo *71:* 120
Abolafia, Yossi *60:* 2; *93:* 163
Abrahams, Hilary *26:* 205; *29:* 24-25; *53:* 61
Abrams, Kathie *36:* 170
Abrams, Lester *49:* 26
Accorsi, William *11:* 198
Acs, Laszlo *14:* 156; *42:* 22
Adams, Adrienne *2:* 6; *3:* 80; *8:* 1; *15:* 107; *16:* 180; *20:* 65; *22:* 134-135; *33:* 75; *36:* 103, 112; *39:* 74; *86:* 54; *90:* 2, 3
Adams, Connie J. *129:* 68
Adams, John Wolcott *17:* 162
Adams, Lynn *96:* 44
Adams, Norman *55:* 82
Adams, Pam *112:* 1, 2
Adams, Sarah *98:* 126
Adamson, George *30:* 23, 24; *69:* 64
Addams, Charles *55:* 5
Ade, Rene *76:* 198
Adinolfi, JoAnn *115:* 42
Adkins, Alta *22:* 250
Adkins, Jan *8:* 3; *69:* 4
Adler, Peggy *22:* 6; *29:* 31
Adler, Ruth *29:* 29
Adragna, Robert *47:* 145
Agard, Nadema *18:* 1
Agee, Jon *116:* 8, 9, 10
Agre, Patricia *47:* 195
Ahl, Anna Maria *32:* 24
Ahlberg, Allan *68:* 6-7, 9
Ahlberg, Janet *68:* 6-7, 9
Aicher-Scholl, Inge *63:* 127
Aichinger, Helga *4:* 5, 45
Aitken, Amy *31:* 34
Akaba, Suekichi *46:* 23; *53:* 127
Akasaka, Miyoshi *YABC 2:* 261
Akino, Fuku *6:* 144
Alain *40:* 41
Alajalov *2:* 226
Alborough, Jez *86:* 1, 2, 3
Albrecht, Jan *37:* 176
Albright, Donn *1:* 91
Alcala, Alfredo *91:* 128
Alcorn, John *3:* 159; *7:* 165; *31:* 22; *44:* 127; *46:* 23, 170
Alcorn, Stephen *110:* 4; *125:* 106; *128:* 172
Alcott, May *100:* 3
Alda, Arlene *44:* 24
Alden, Albert *11:* 103
Aldridge, Andy *27:* 131
Aldridge, George *105:* 125
Alex, Ben *45:* 25, 26
Alexander, Ellen *91:* 3
Alexander, Lloyd *49:* 34
Alexander, Martha *3:* 206; *11:* 103; *13:* 109; *25:* 100; *36:* 131; *70:* 6, 7

Alexander, Paul *85:* 57; *90:* 9
Alexeieff, Alexander *14:* 6; *26:* 199
Alfano, Wayne *80:* 69
Aliki *See* Brandenberg, Aliki
Allamand, Pascale *12:* 9
Allan, Judith *38:* 166
Alland, Alexandra *16:* 255
Allen, Gertrude *9:* 6
Allen, Graham *31:* 145
Allen, Jonathan B. *131:* 3, 4
Allen, Pamela *50:* 25, 26-27, 28; *81:* 9, 10; *123:* 4-5
Allen, Rowena *47:* 75
Allen, Thomas B. *81:* 101; *82:* 248; *89:* 37; *104:* 9
Allen, Tom *85:* 176
Allender, David *73:* 223
Alley, R. W. *80:* 183; *95:* 187
Allison, Linda *43:* 27
Allon, Jeffrey *119:* 174
Allport, Mike *71:* 55
Almquist, Don *11:* 8; *12:* 128; *17:* 46; *22:* 110
Aloise, Frank *5:* 38; *10:* 133; *30:* 92
Althea *See* Braithwaite, Althea
Altschuler, Franz *11:* 185; *23:* 141; *40:* 48; *45:* 29; *57:* 181
Alvin, John *117:* 5
Ambrus, Victor G. *1:* 6-7, 194; *3:* 69; *5:* 15; *6:* 44; *7:* 36; *8:* 210; *12:* 227; *14:* 213; *15:* 213; *22:* 209; *24:* 36; *28:* 179; *30:* 178; *32:* 44, 46; *38:* 143; *41:* 25, 26, 27, 28, 29, 30, 31, 32; *42:* 87; *44:* 190; *55:* 172; *62:* 30, 144, 145, 148; *86:* 99, 100, 101; *87:* 66, 137; *89:* 162; *134:* 160
Ames, Lee J. *3:* 12; *9:* 130; *10:* 69; *17:* 214; *22:* 124
Amon, Aline *9:* 9
Amoss, Berthe *5:* 5
Amundsen, Dick *7:* 77
Amundsen, Richard E. *5:* 10; *24:* 122
Ancona, George *12:* 11; *55:* 144
Andersen, Bethanne *116:* 167
Anderson, Alasdair *18:* 122
Anderson, Brad *33:* 28
Anderson, C. W. *11:* 10
Anderson, Carl *7:* 4
Anderson, Catherine Corley *72:* 2
Anderson, Cecil *127:* 152
Anderson, David Lee *118:* 176
Anderson, Doug *40:* 111
Anderson, Erica *23:* 65
Anderson, Laurie *12:* 153, 155
Anderson, Lena *99:* 26
Anderson, Susan *90:* 12
Anderson, Wayne *23:* 119; *41:* 239; *56:* 7; *62:* 26
Andreasen, Daniel *86:* 157; *87:* 104; *103:* 201, 202
Andrew, Ian *111:* 37; *116:* 12
Andrew, John *22:* 4
Andrews, Benny *14:* 251; *31:* 24; *57:* 6, 7
Anelay, Henry *57:* 173
Angel, Marie *47:* 22
Angelo, Valenti *14:* 8; *18:* 100; *20:* 232; *32:* 70

Anglund, Joan Walsh *2:* 7, 250-251; *37:* 198, 199, 200
Anholt, Catherine *74:* 8; *131:* 7
Anno, Mitsumasa *5:* 7; *38:* 25, 26-27, 28, 29, 30, 31, 32; *77:* 3, 4
Antal, Andrew *1:* 124; *30:* 145
Apostolou, Christy Hale *See* Hale, Christy
Apple, Margot *33:* 25; *35:* 206; *46:* 81; *53:* 8; *61:* 109; *64:* 21, 22, 24, 25, 27; *71:* 176; *77:* 53; *82:* 245; *92:* 39; *94:* 180; *96:* 107
Appleyard, Dev *2:* 192
Aragonés, Sergio *48:* 23, 24, 25, 26, 27
Araneus *40:* 29
Arbo, Cris *103:* 4
Archambault, Matthew *85:* 173
Archer, Janet *16:* 69
Ardizzone, Edward *1:* 11, 12; *2:* 105; *3:* 258; *4:* 78; *7:* 79; *10:* 100; *15:* 232; *20:* 69, 178; *23:* 223; *24:* 125; *28:* 25, 26, 27, 28, 29, 30, 31, 33, 34, 35, 36, 37; *31:* 192, 193; *34:* 215, 217; *60:* 173; *64:* 145; *87:* 176; *YABC 2:* 25
Arenella, Roy *14:* 9
Argent, Kerry *103:* 56
Armer, Austin *13:* 3
Armer, Laura Adams *13:* 3
Armer, Sidney *13:* 3
Armitage, David *47:* 23; *99:* 5
Armitage, Eileen *4:* 16
Armstrong, George *10:* 6; *21:* 72
Armstrong, Shelagh *102:* 114
Arno, Enrico *1:* 217; *2:* 22, 210; *4:* 9; *5:* 43; *6:* 52; *29:* 217, 219; *33:* 152; *35:* 99; *43:* 31, 32, 33; *45:* 212, 213, 214; *72:* 72; *74:* 166; *100:* 169
Arnold, Emily *76:* 7, 9, 10
Arnold, Katya *115:* 11
Arnold, Tedd *116:* 14; *133:* 152
Arnosky, Jim *22:* 20; *70:* 9, 10, 11; *118:* 3, 5
Arnsteen, Katy Keck *105:* 97; *116:* 145
Arrowood, Clinton *12:* 193; *19:* 11; *65:* 210
Artell, Mike *89:* 8
Arting, Fred J. *41:* 63
Artzybasheff, Boris *13:* 143; *14:* 15; *40:* 152, 155
Aruego, Ariane *6:* 4
Aruego, Jose *4:* 140; *6:* 4; *7:* 64; *33:* 195; *35:* 208; *68:* 16, 17; *75:* 46; *93:* 91, 92; *94:* 197; *109:* 65, 67; *125:* 2, 3, 4, 5; *127:* 188
Asare, Meshack *86:* 9
Ascensios, Natalie *105:* 139
Asch, Frank *5:* 9; *66:* 2, 4, 6, 7, 9, 10; *102:* 18, 19, 21
Ashby, Gail *11:* 135
Ashby, Gwynneth *44:* 26
Ashley, C. W. *19:* 197
Ashmead, Hal *8:* 70
Aska, Warabe *56:* 10
Assel, Steven *44:* 153; *77:* 22, 97
Astrop, John *32:* 56
Atene, Ann *12:* 18
Atherton, Lisa *38:* 198
Atkinson, Allen *60:* 5

Illustrations Index

# Author Index

The following index gives the number of the volume in which an author's biographical sketch, Autobiography Feature, Brief Entry, or Obituary appears.

This index includes references to all entries in the following series, which are also published by The Gale Group.

**YABC**—*Yesterday's Authors of Books for Children: Facts and Pictures about Authors and Illustrators of Books for Young People from Early Times to 1960*

**CLR**—*Children's Literature Review: Excerpts from Reviews, Criticism, and Commentary on Books for Children*

**SAAS**—*Something about the Author Autobiography Series*

**Author Index**